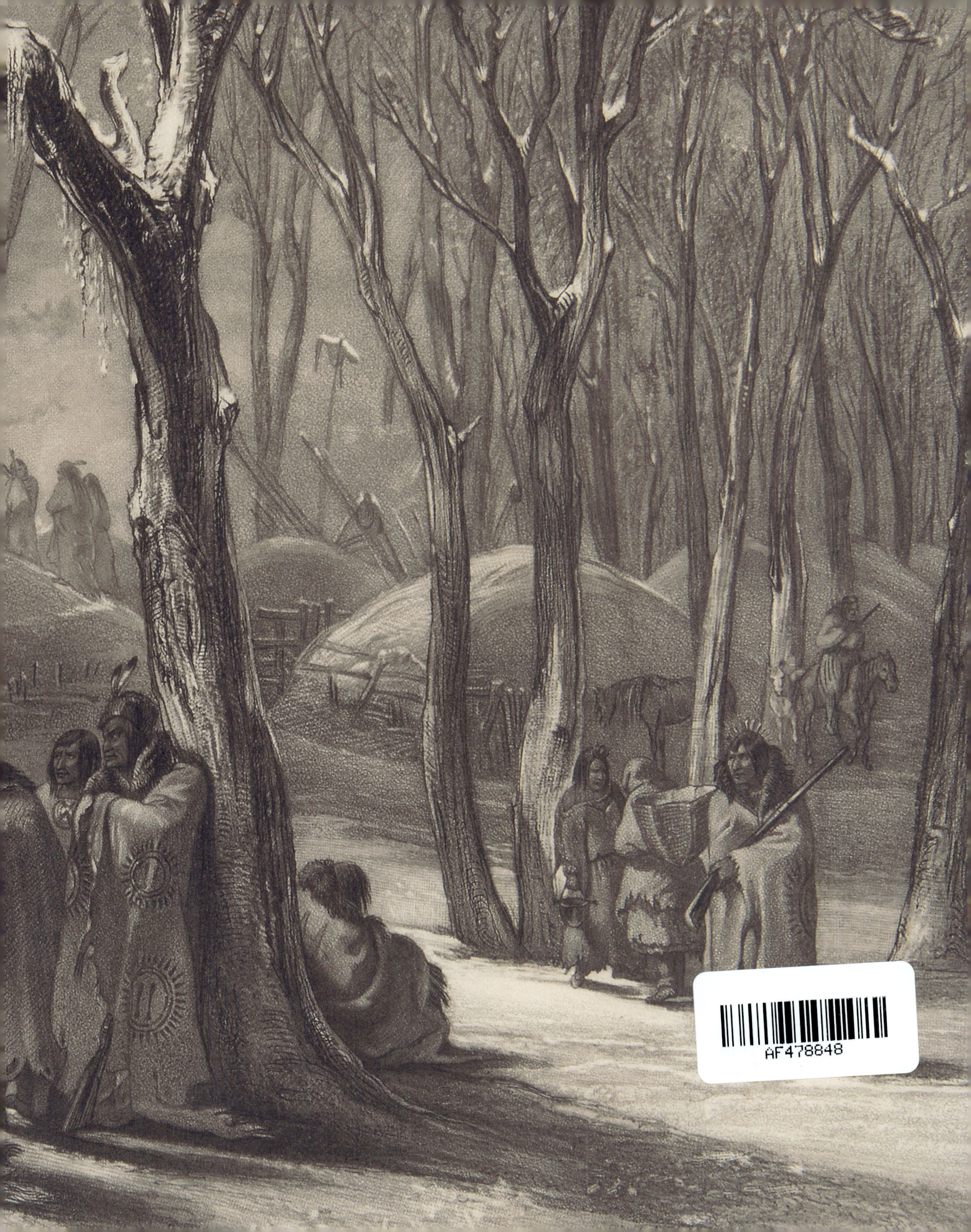

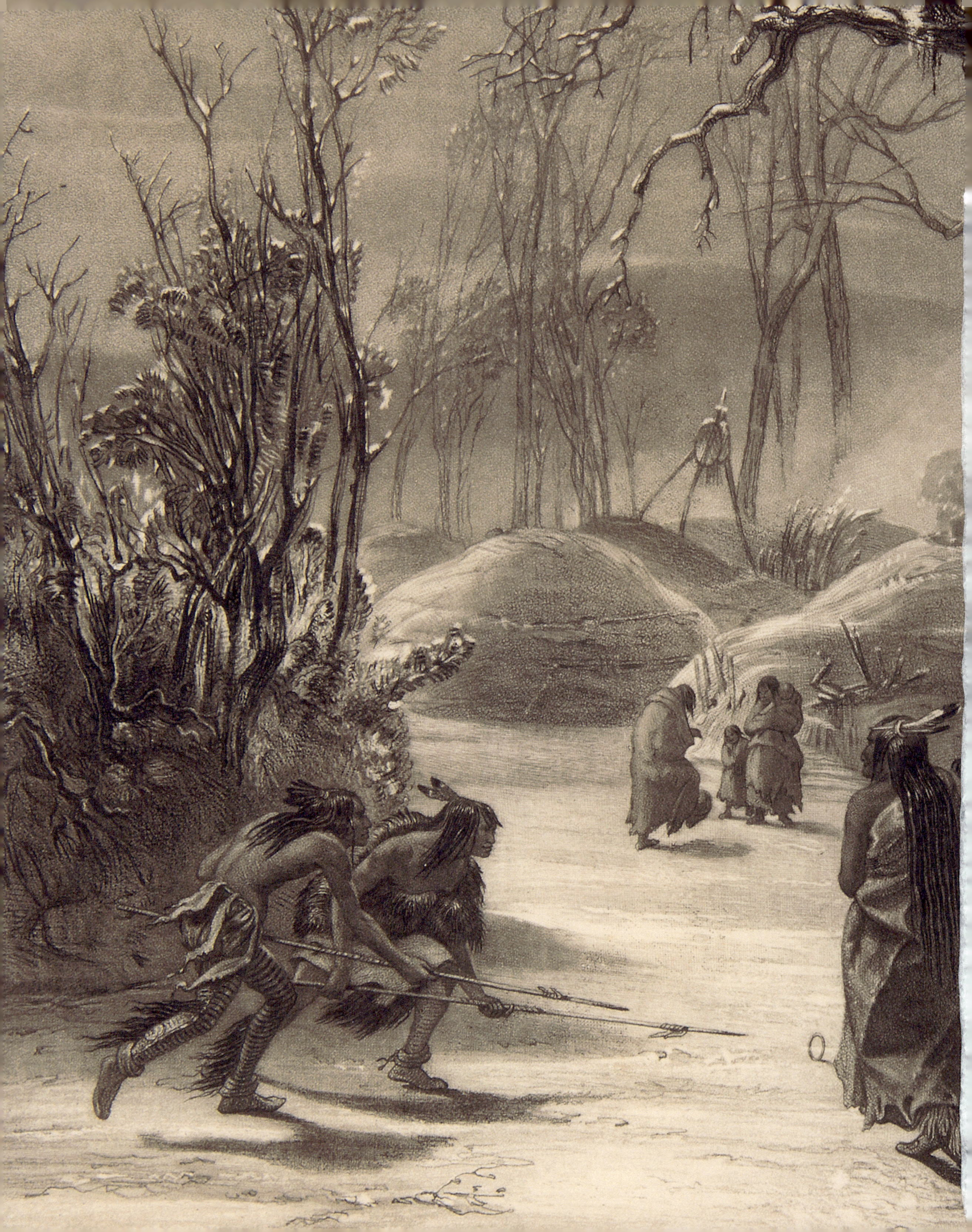

ART OF THE AMERICAN WEST

THE HAUB FAMILY COLLECTION AT TACOMA ART MUSEUM

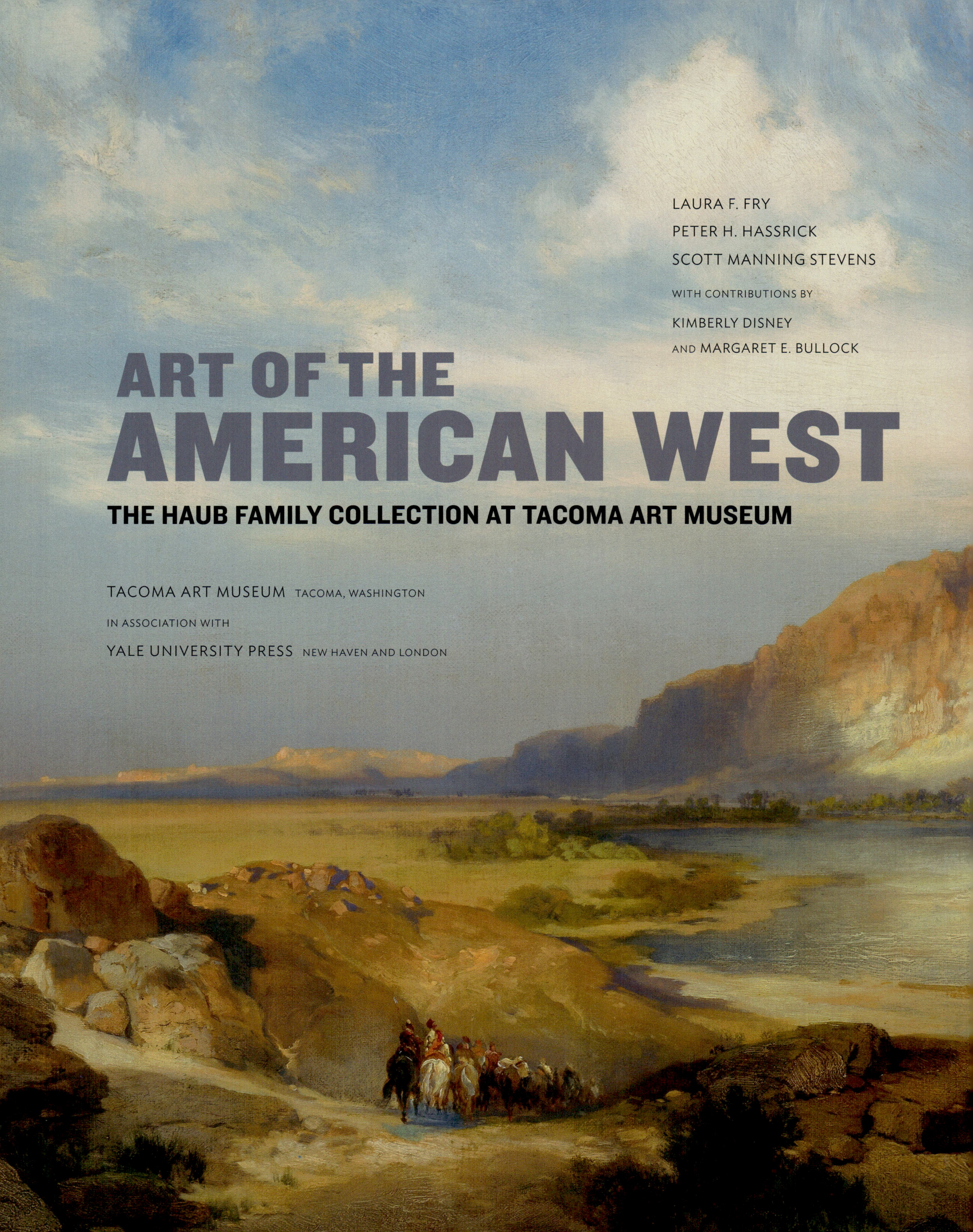

ART OF THE AMERICAN WEST

THE HAUB FAMILY COLLECTION AT TACOMA ART MUSEUM

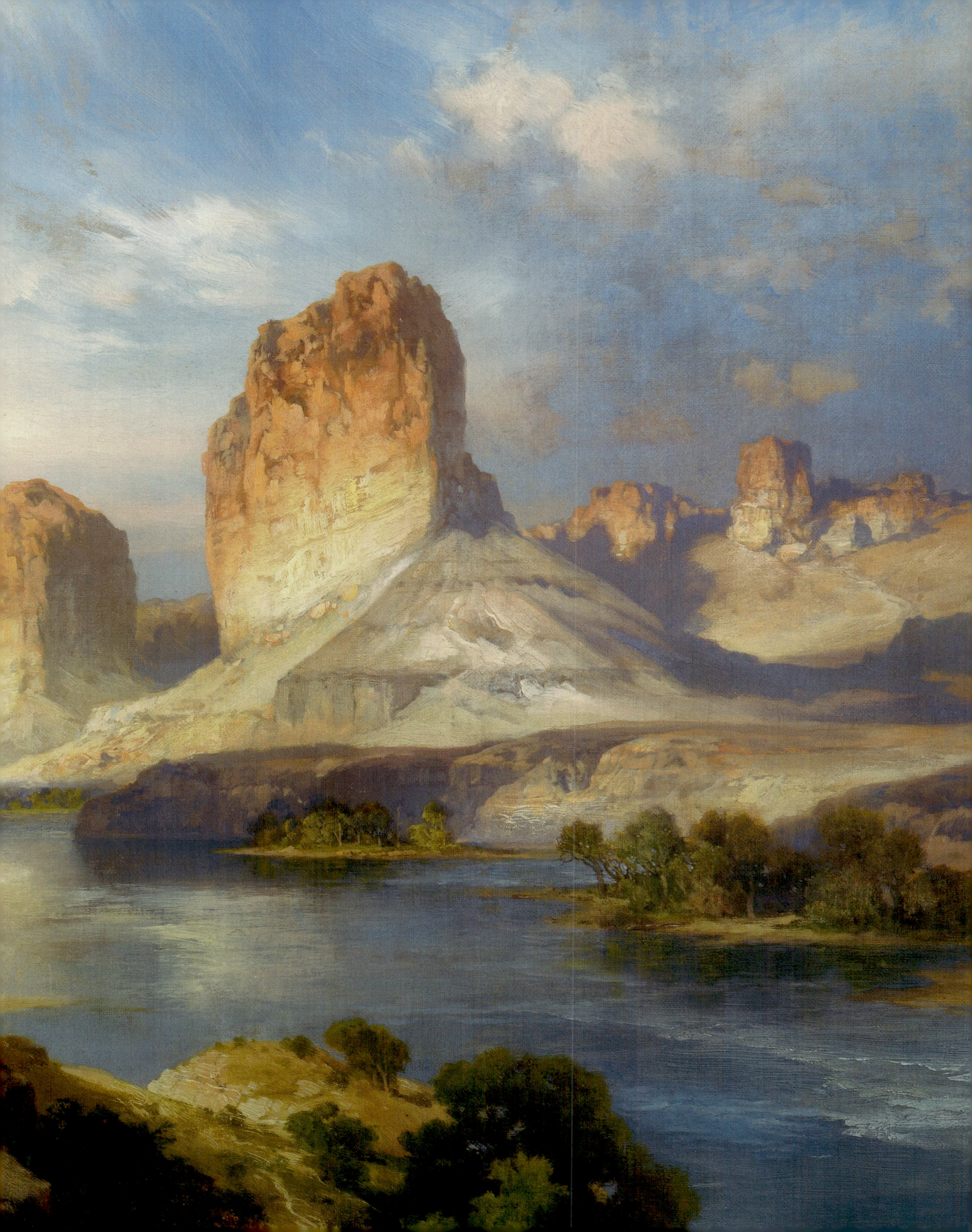

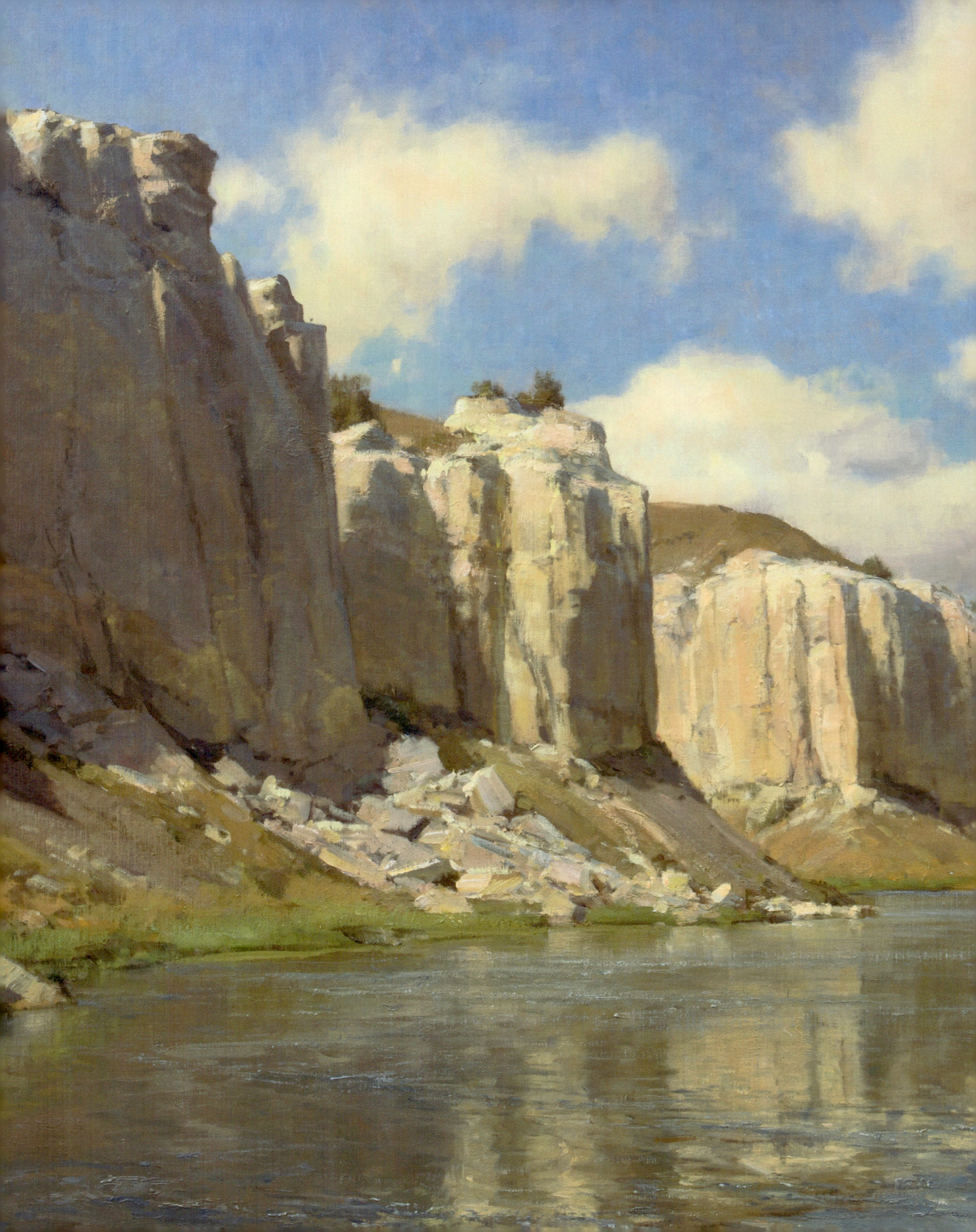

CONTENTS

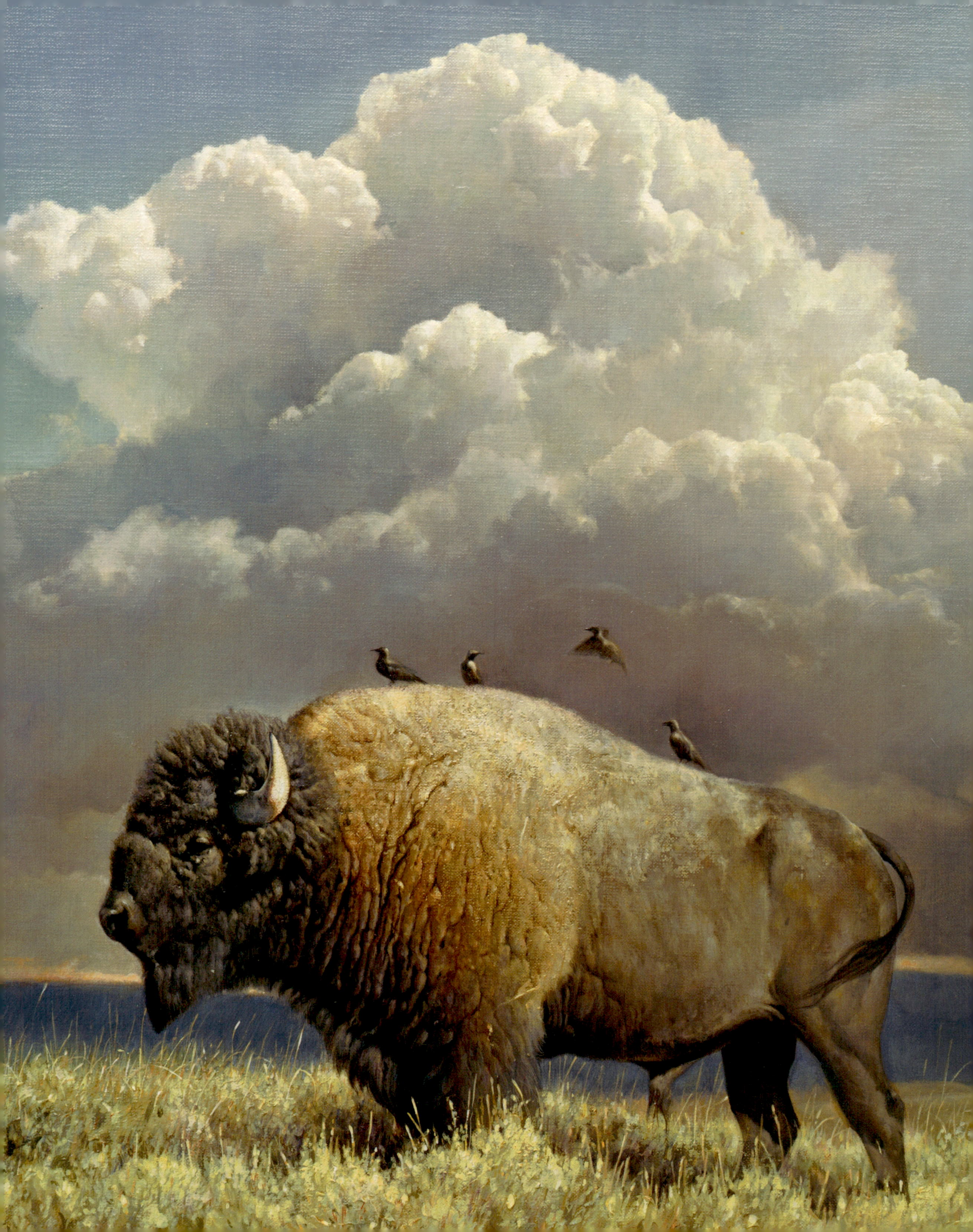

STEPHANIE A. STEBICH

DIRECTOR'S FOREWORD

How did the Tacoma Art Museum become home to the Haub Family's spectacular collection of western American art, assembled over 30 years by Helga and Erivan Haub? The answer involves both coincidence and fate. In fall 2011 the museum was raising funds to redesign its plaza and lobby spaces, and I approached the Haubs' representative, Tacoma attorney John Barline, about a possible contribution. He offered an entirely unexpected proposal instead. Would the Tacoma Art Museum be interested in the donation of the Haub collection of western American art?

In the late 1950s Helga and Erivan first came to the Pacific Northwest as newlyweds to visit friends Annelise and Warder Stoaks, who introduced them to the natural beauty of the region. Soon thereafter the Haubs chose to have their three sons, Karl-Erivan or "Charlie," George, and Christian, enter the world in Tacoma, the "City of Destiny," to carry dual citizenship. They established a home here and returned regularly for summer vacations.

In the mid 1980s Helga and Erivan purchased a ranch in Wyoming and their collecting began. In the summer of 2011 the family decided to explore gifting the collection to Tacoma, where their American experience started. I recall our first exciting conversation and their expansive vision for the collection. We also delighted in the coincidence of my birth city, Mülheim an der Ruhr, being the headquarters for their family business, the Tengelmann Group.

The museum's Trustees embraced the Haubs' proposal to donate their collection, underwrite new galleries, and provide critical endowment funds. This dovetailed with the plaza redesign underway with the superb team from Olson Kundig Architects of Seattle. Tom Kundig's Northwest aesthetic and elegant horizontal design of the new wing recall both the Puyallup Indian longhouse and a boxcar, the latter referencing Tacoma's importance as a western rail terminus.

With the expertise of Director Emeritus and Senior Scholar of the Buffalo Bill Center of the West Peter H. Hassrick, and newly appointed Haub Curator of Western American Art Laura F. Fry, the collection was shaped into a gift of artworks spanning more than 200 years of American history. Tapped by Helga and Erivan, youngest son Christian and his wife Liliane joyfully took on the project. Art dealers Christine Mollring and Gerald Peters, longtime advisers to the Haubs, offered generous counsel and facilitated additional gifts to the museum.

We are immensely grateful to Helga and Erivan Haub and their entire family for placing their cherished collection at the Tacoma Art Museum. We acknowledge the pivotal role played by Christian and Liliane, as well as John Barline, in helping us plan the new expansion. The museum is proud to present this publication featuring new scholarship by Laura Fry, Peter Hassrick, and Scott Manning Stevens, Director of the Native American Studies Program at Syracuse University and member of the Akwesasne Mohawk nation.

In finding a home here, the Haub Family Collection establishes the only major museum collection of western American art in the Pacific Northwest, offering a new dimension of artistic discovery to Tacoma, the State of Washington, and beyond.

Detail of Nancy Glazier, *Birds of a Feather*, circa 1983 (page 233).

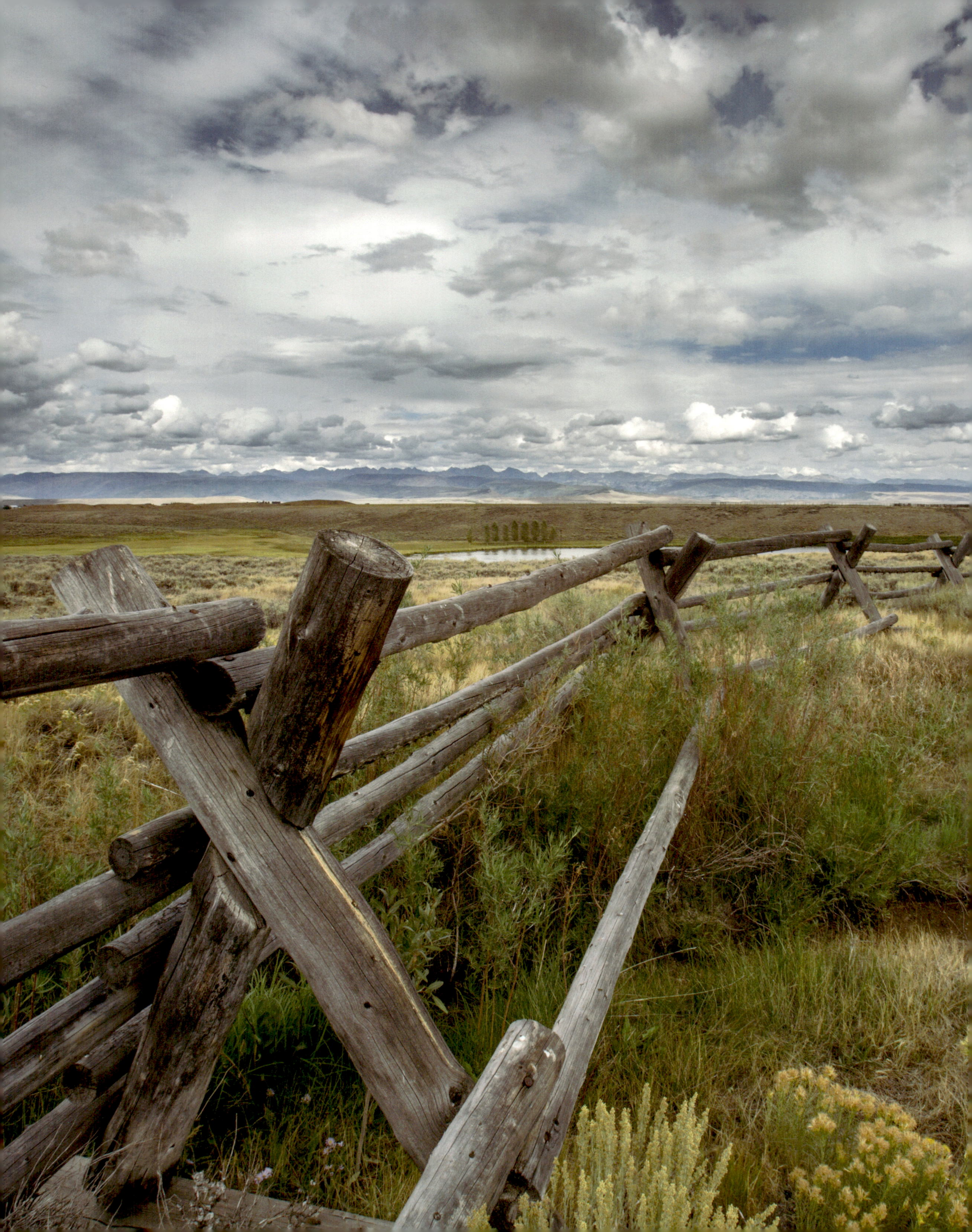

FALLING IN LOVE WITH THE AMERICAN WEST

When we first visited Washington State together more than 50 years ago, we were amazed by the natural beauty of the region. In our native Germany we were both raised in the countryside, and have always loved nature and wildlife. In 1958, we traveled to Tacoma on our honeymoon to visit friends on nearby Fox Island. The tall trees around Puget Sound reminded us of the Black Forest in Germany, and we loved the views of expansive waters and distant mountain peaks. Our enchantment with Tacoma resulted in our decision to have our three sons born here and find a home for us to visit regularly. Soon our family began spending summers near Tacoma on the shores of Puget Sound.

Years later, in the summer of 1982, we were invited to visit friends at their Wyoming ranch. After hearing descriptions of a place with wide-open rangeland, abundant wildlife, and real working cowboys, we were intrigued. As children we had read of the American West in the books of Karl May, a popular German author who wrote thrilling tales of the American frontier—although he never traveled to the West himself. The chance to visit this region sounded irresistible. Upon landing in Jackson, we were overwhelmed by the great sight of the towering Teton Mountains. After several days of riding along mountain trails we found ourselves entranced by the sense of adventure and openness. Within a few months of that first visit to Wyoming, we acquired a ranch at the base of the Wind River Mountains—in time to celebrate Helga's 50th birthday in grand western style two years later.

Not long after purchasing the ranch in Wyoming, Erivan happened across a striking painting at Trailside Galleries in Jackson: *Birds of a Feather* by Nancy Glazier (page 233). The painting's brilliant blue sky above a proud group of bison perfectly captured the feel of our Wyoming surroundings. Although we did not realize it at the time, acquiring this painting in 1984 would be the start of our wonderful adventure with the art of the American West. We soon became dear friends with Christine and Ted Mollring, the owners of Trailside Galleries. With Christine's guidance, we studied the artists of the West and began building a collection. In addition to Christine's assistance, Gerald Peters has been an immense help in providing advice and locating historic paintings and sculptures for the collection.

To select artwork, we have been guided by our love of nature and our interest in western history. As a rule, we avoid images that depict violence and conflict. Rather, we collect artworks that celebrate the people and cultures of the West. Along the way we have discovered fascinating stories of individual artists, and have been fortunate enough to meet several of the artists represented in our collection. From the shores of Puget Sound to the sagebrush of Wyoming, we have found inspiration, adventure, and peace in the landscapes of the western United States. It is our hope that this collection at Tacoma Art Museum will continue to inspire others in the years to come.

View from the Haub Family ranch, Wyoming.

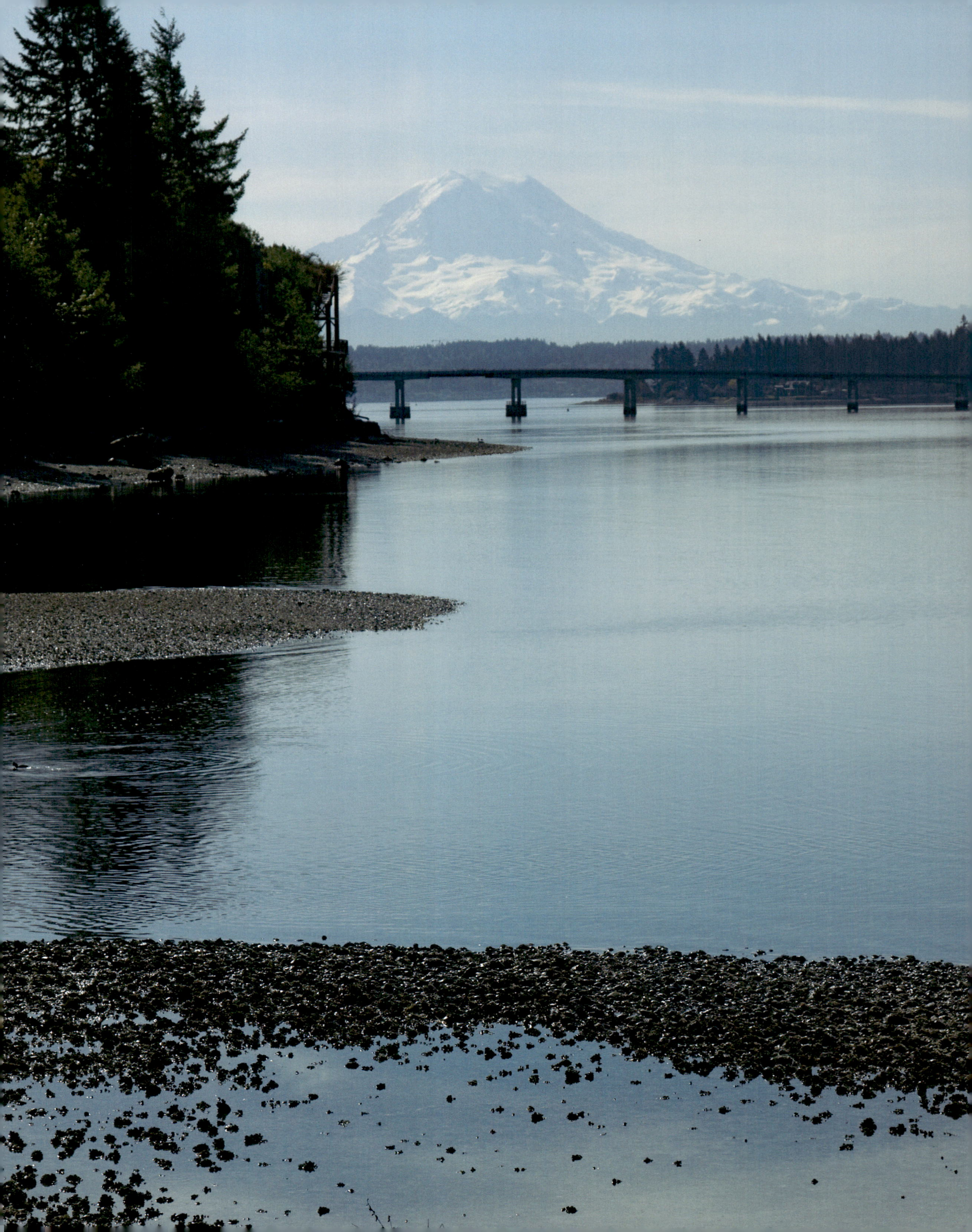

WESTERN ART FOR THE PACIFIC NORTHWEST

Each time we visited our parents, we explored the house to see the latest additions to their collection of western American art. My father encouraged our sense of discovery, and would never tell us where to look! As the collection grew, we also became involved in the process of scouting for new artworks. We both vividly remember seeing the painting *Conjuring Back the Buffalo* by Frederic Remington (page 92) for the first time in a New York City gallery. The lone figure against a blue sky was awe-inspiring, and captured a deeper meaning of mourning for a lost era. Over the years, we were fascinated to learn the stories contained in these artworks.

In three decades the collection grew by leaps and bounds, including artworks spanning 200 years of history. We realized our parents had assembled something incredible—and keeping the collection together would be a great way to honor their legacy. We gathered as a family at our ranch in Wyoming in the summer of 2011 and agreed that the collection should come to a place where our family had a heritage. Before long, Tacoma, Washington, became a clear choice for the Haub Family Collection.

For the three Haub sons, the Puget Sound region represented freedom and adventure. For nearly 20 years we spent our summers near Tacoma, sailing on the Sound, fishing in the Methow Valley, and hiking on the Olympic Peninsula. As teenagers we piled into a car and took off to explore the beaches and cliffs along the Pacific Coast. We were fascinated by the history of local Native American cultures in Washington State, and we loved the stunning beauty of the mountains and the water. Later, we brought our own children to vacation in the Tacoma area. For our family, Washington was the first place in the American West that we came to know and love. By placing the Haub Family Collection in Tacoma, we hope to honor our connection to this place. In addition, we feel that placing the collection in the Pacific Northwest will bring a unique perspective to this artwork.

While the Puget Sound region might be more famous for its salmon than its cowboys, Washington remains an integral part of the western United States. By making this collection available to the public, we hope to expose more people to the art of the American West. We hope visitors will take the opportunity to learn about these artists and explore how art and history are connected. In the years to come, we look forward to continuing work with the Tacoma Art Museum to build this collection and find new opportunities for western American art.

In conclusion, we would like to extend a heartfelt thanks to our parents, for assembling a great collection and for donating their artwork to the people of Tacoma. We are excited to see the new discoveries that the future holds for the art of the West.

View from the Haub Family home, Washington.

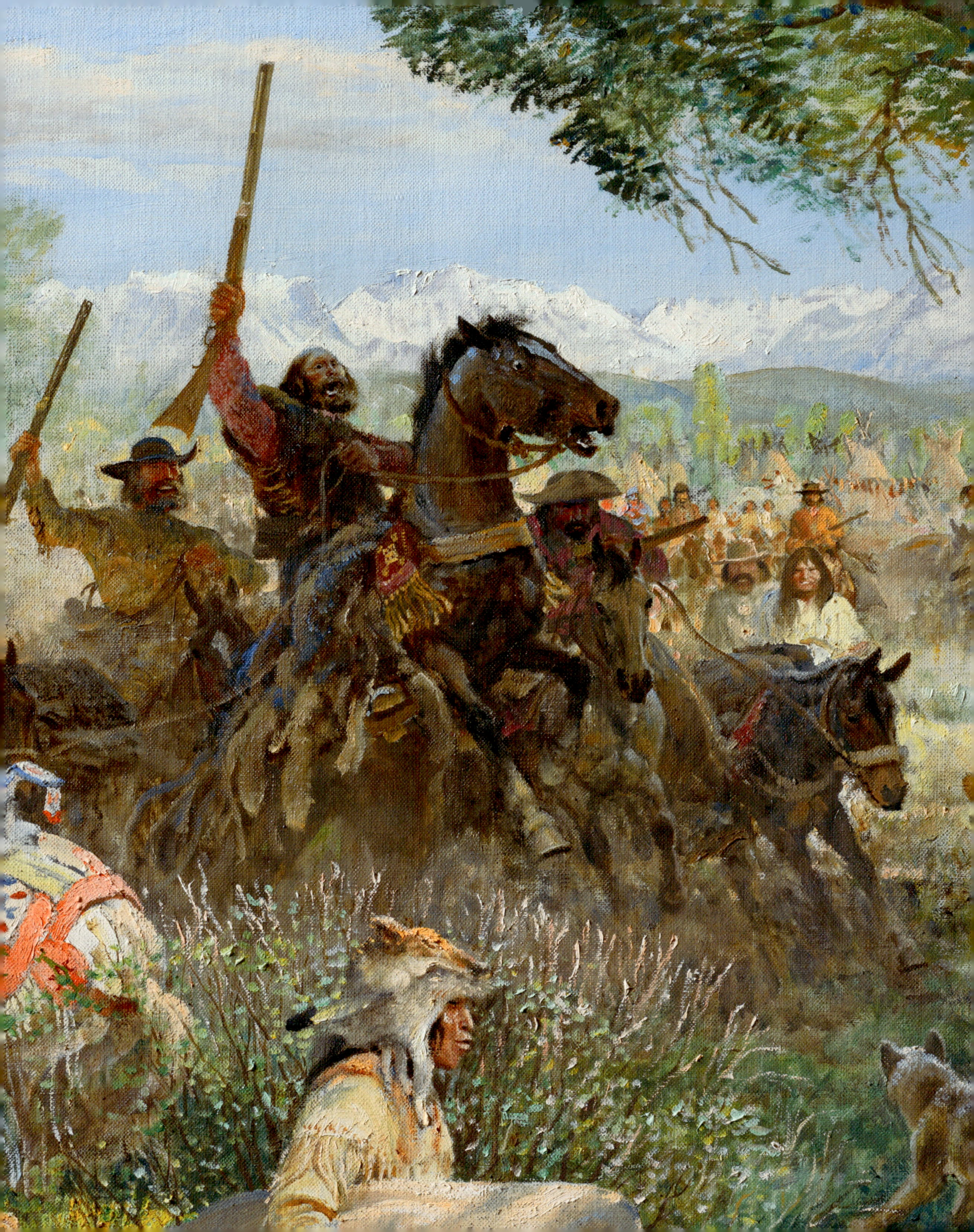

CHRISTINE MOLLRING

BUILDING THE HAUB COLLECTION

For the past three decades, it has been incredibly exciting to participate in the growth and appreciation of art of the American West. From a burgeoning market, to new publications and scholarship, to museum expansions and new institutions, western art has come into its own. As the owner of Trailside Galleries in Jackson, Wyoming, and Scottsdale, Arizona, it was my pleasure to meet many artists and collectors who were also inspired by the West—and my husband Ted and I are especially fortunate to have met Erivan and Helga Haub 30 years ago.

We soon discovered that we had much in common, including a love of nature, art, history, and travel. Soon, Ted and I looked forward to the arrival of the Haubs from Germany every summer. Over the years we traveled extensively with Erivan and Helga, visiting art museums, galleries, artists, art auctions, and historic sites. Though I have helped guide the Haubs through their journey as western art collectors, they both have an excellent eye and, most important, have always purchased what they love.

As Erivan and Helga carefully built their collection, they have been guided by their overall interests and values. For example, they deliberately avoided images of violence. In addition, protecting the environment has been an important part of Erivan Haub's business practices with the Tengelmann Group since the 1970s. It is no surprise that their love of nature has influenced their art collection, which includes many wonderful landscapes and images of wildlife, especially buffalo. They presently nurture a herd of over 400 buffalo on their ranch in Wyoming, which is also a part of their conservation efforts.

Erivan and Helga have long been interested in history, and I was thrilled to introduce them to artist John Clymer and his wife Doris. John specialized in painting historical scenes of the West, and Doris assisted him in researching the past. Together they traveled to historic sites every summer. After Erivan and Helga learned of the wonderful history of the mountain men who traversed Wyoming in the early 19th century, they began collecting images of these iconic figures. In 1987 the Haubs commissioned John Clymer to paint a scene of the Green River Rendezvous, depicting a variety of mountain men, fur trappers, and Native Americans who gathered to trade once a year on the Green River in Wyoming in the 1830s. John was delighted to paint this commission for them and the resulting piece *Late Arrivals—Green River Rendezvous* (page 194) was one of his most ambitious works and the last major historical painting completed before his death in 1989.

Over the past 15 years, Gerald Peters has been an immense help to me and the Haubs, giving freely of his advice and helping us locate important historical pieces for their collection. I feel very privileged that Erivan and Helga entrusted me to help build this outstanding collection of western American art and I am so proud that it will form a lasting public legacy as part of the Tacoma Art Museum.

Detail of John Clymer, *Late Arrivals—Green River Rendezvous*, 1988 (page 194).

ESSAYS AND SELECTED WORKS FROM THE COLLECTION

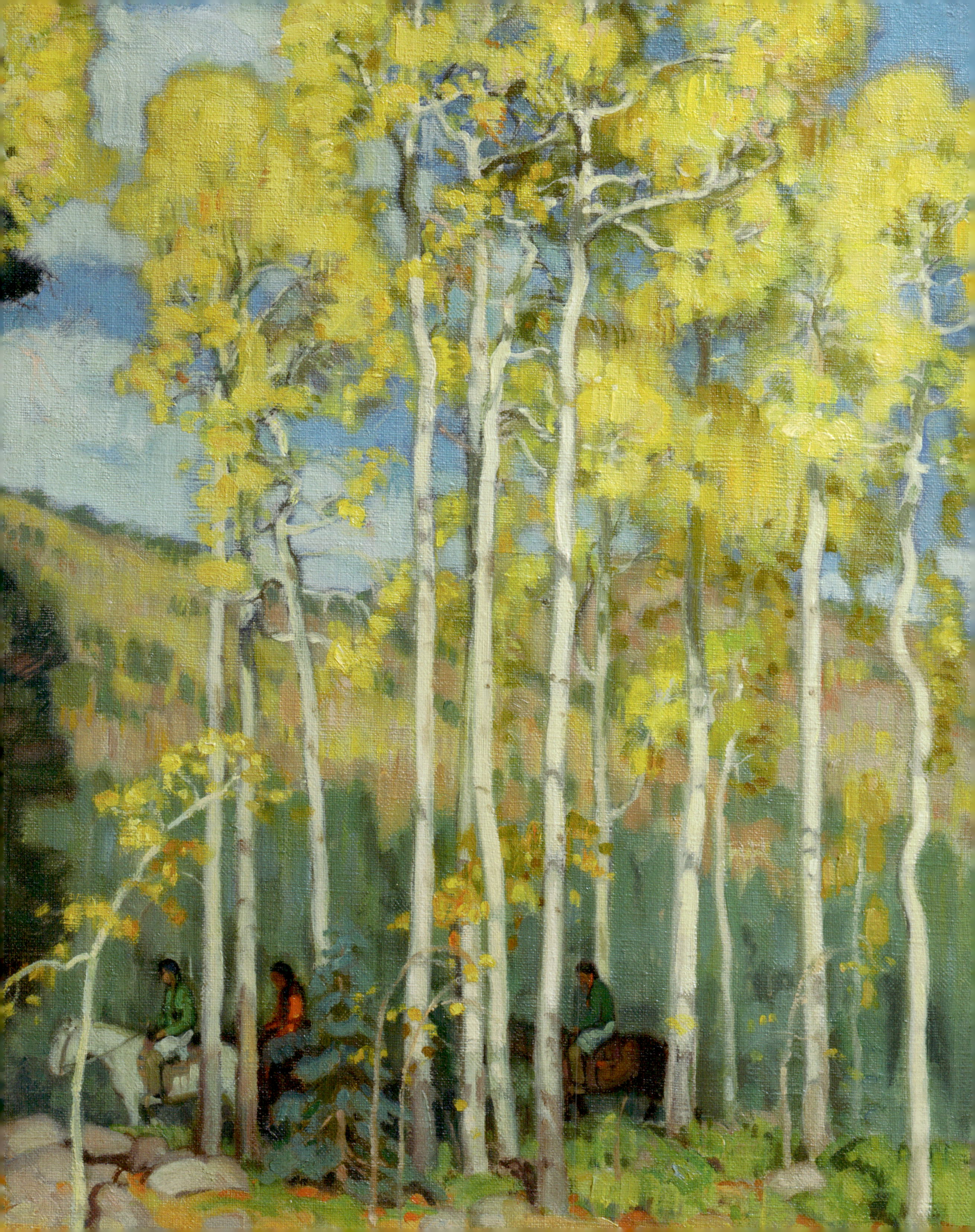

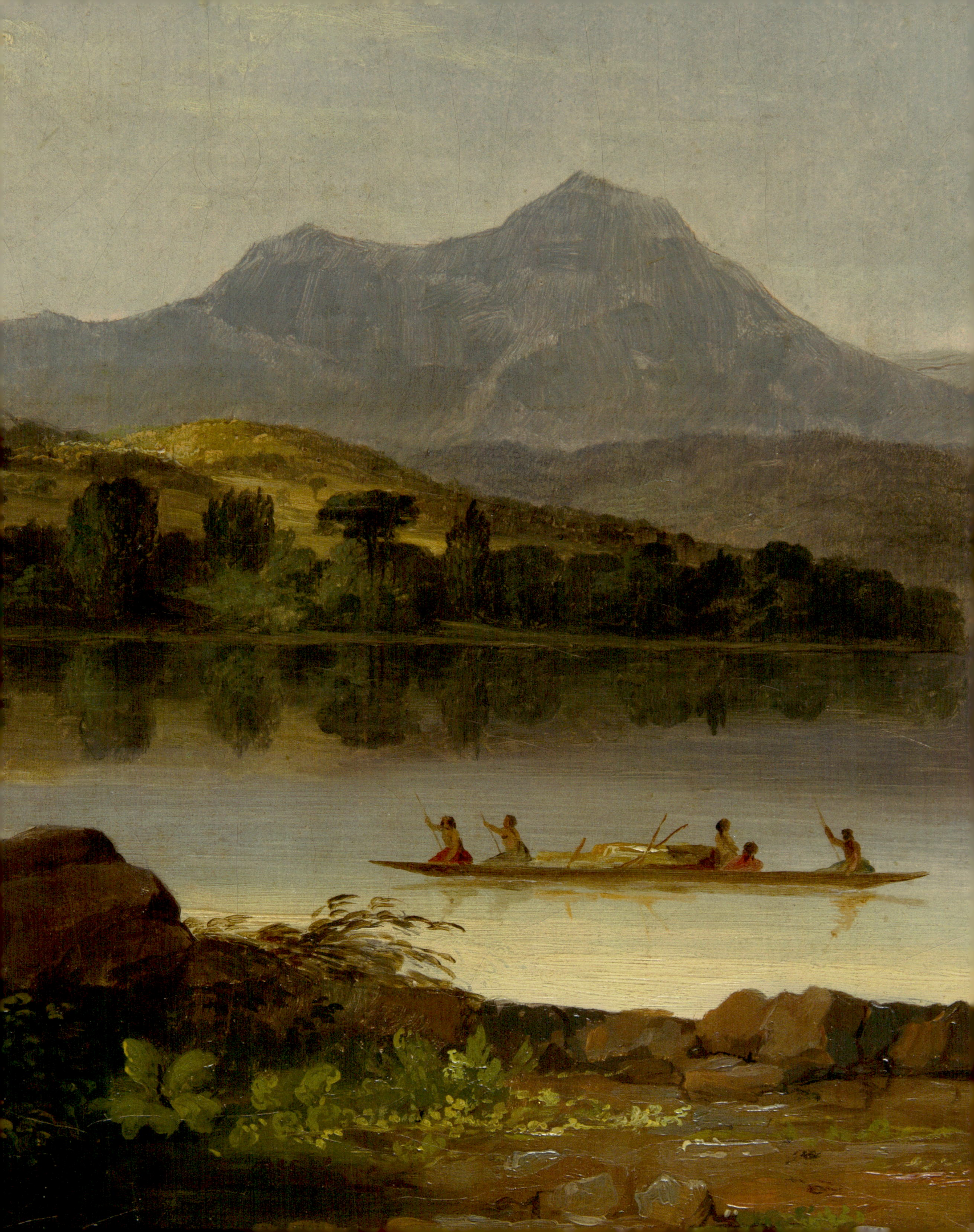

PETER H. HASSRICK

WEST BY NORTHWEST
TREASURES FROM THE HAUB FAMILY COLLECTION COME HOME

The story of western art museums in America is by now a fairly old one, dating back over six decades to the efforts of a passionate Oklahoma oilman, Thomas Gilcrease. In 1949, he established in Tulsa the Thomas Gilcrease Institute of American History and Art with a mission to collect art that would champion the aesthetic genius of some of the nation's most talented, creative forces and document the western saga, or what he called the "Great Adventure of America."[1] Today, known as the Gilcrease Museum, it houses the largest and most comprehensive collection of western American art in existence.

The Gilcrease Museum, however, is not alone in its charge to preserve, interpret, and promote western American art. There are now well over a dozen museums that devote their attention to the subject. The most recent institution to join those ranks is the Tacoma Art Museum, with the celebrated Haub Family Collection and a new wing to house and present it. The western art museums are dotted around the country. Some are found as far east as New York State and Georgia, though most are situated in the Rocky Mountain West and the Southwest. For unknown reasons, though, none until now have been located in the Northwest. Tacoma is currently the newest and loneliest outpost for this cultural prize. Its closest fellow institution is east by nearly 1,000 miles in Cody, Wyoming, at the Buffalo Bill Center of the West, which contains the famed Whitney Western Art Museum as one of its five interrelated museums.

Yet as distant as that connection may seem, the Cody museum at the foot of the northern Rockies and the Tacoma Art Museum nudged up against the Pacific Ocean embrace a region that has long shared a unity of history. In between these two museums is an area that was known by the mid-19th century as Oregon Territory. As defined in 1848 by the pathfinder John C. Frémont, it was bordered on the north by the 49th parallel and to the south by the 42nd (figure 1). It contained such grand features as the Rocky Mountains and the Cascades as well as such wonders as Yellowstone and the vast drainage of the mighty Columbia River. The area's history is rich in myths and real human chronicles both Native and European American. Over the last century and a half, this area, which might aptly be called the Far Northwest, has attracted countless Anglo artists. It is these artists, whose works now fill the galleries of the Whitney Western Art Museum and the Tacoma Art Museum, who preserved and molded those myths and chronicles into aesthetic narratives that fascinate and instruct modern audiences about how and why the West mattered in our national history. The Haub family, which has made the Tacoma Art Museum the northwestern center for western American art, would agree with Thomas Gilcrease that this art is not only representative of the nation's finest artistic talents but also documents the "Great Adventure of America" as it unfolded in the Far Northwest.

Throughout the 19th century, artists who ventured into the Far Northwest came with a wide variety of incentives and styles. It was this diversity of motivation and the individual artistic approaches that made for such a rich store of

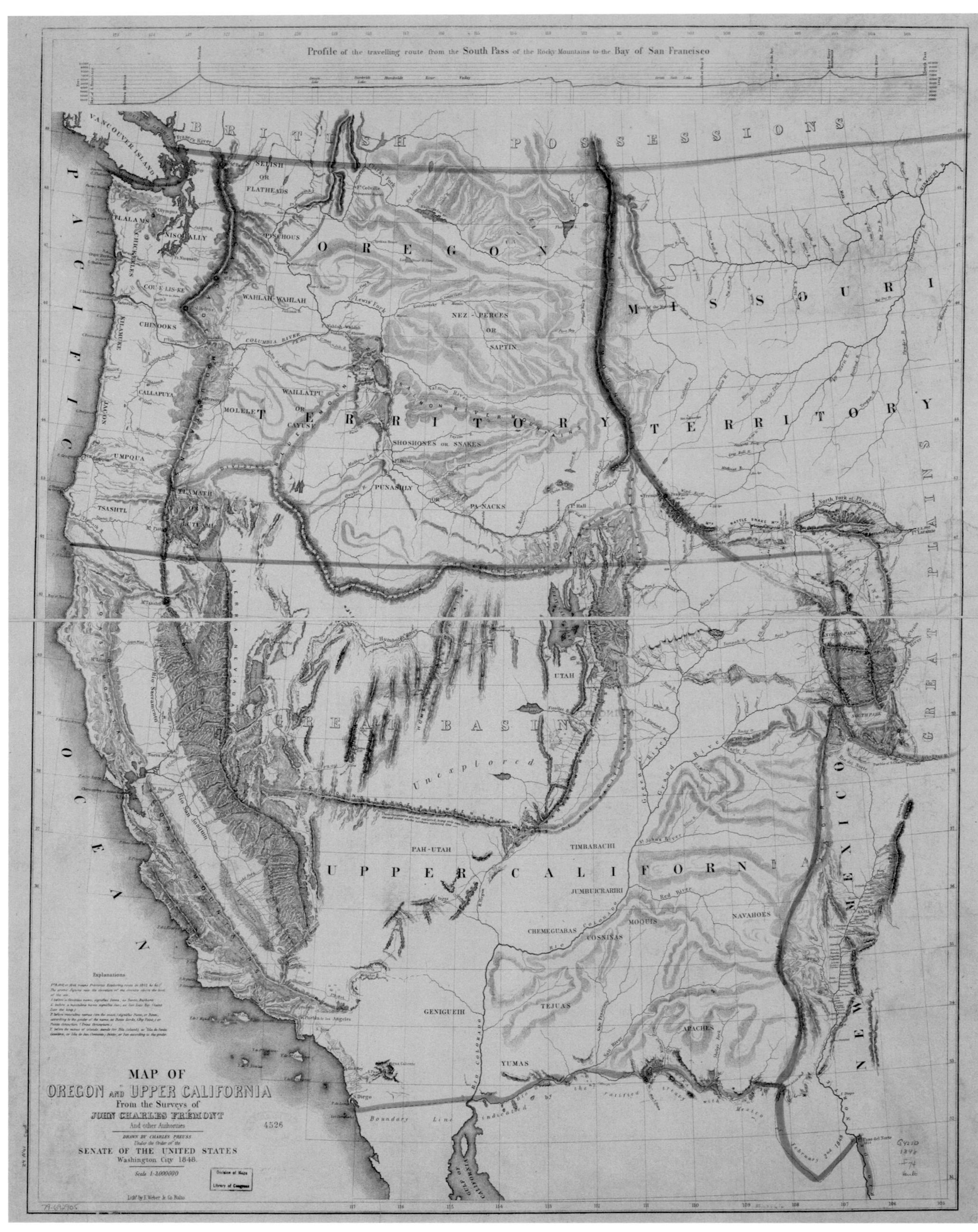

FIGURE 1 Map of Oregon and Upper California from the surveys of John Charles Frémont and other authorities, 1848. Published by The Senate. Library of Congress Geography and Map Division, Washington, DC, 79692905.

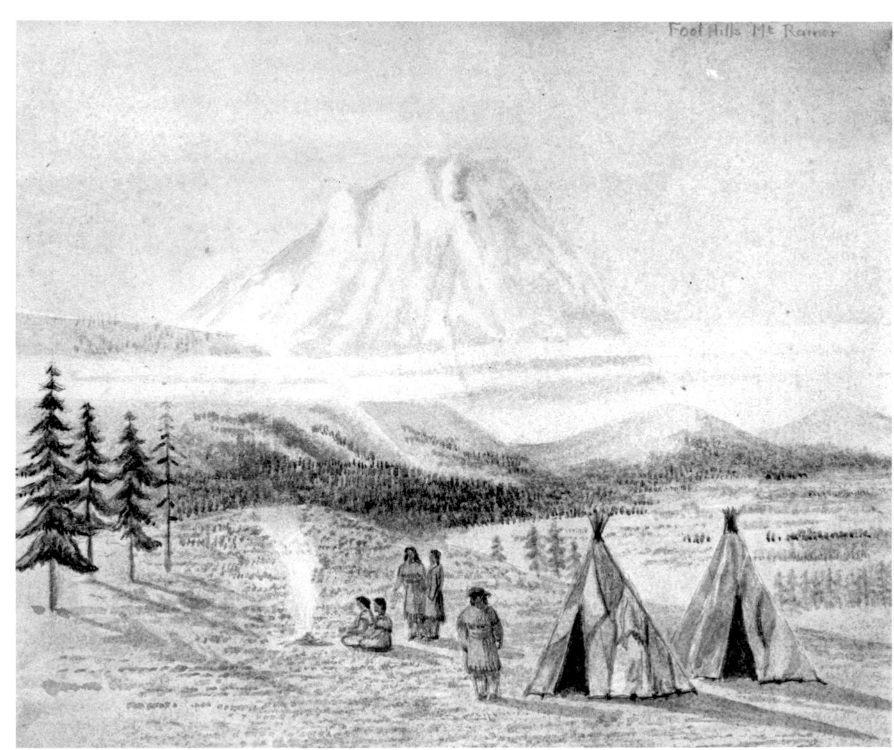

creative responses to the area. Some were documentary artists who came in the service of science, some were pure romantics who fancied an exotic experience, some were grand manner landscape painters who exulted in the splendor of mountain scenery, and yet others were pictorial historians who preserved the narrative of the West. They each had their agendas, and they each deserve to be celebrated for their artistic accomplishment as well as their insightful perceptions of the scene.

Probably the first painter to venture into the area was Joseph Drayton (1795–1856), a Philadelphia artist who arrived at the mouth of the Columbia River in 1841 with the United States Exploring Expedition, the first official government scientific tour to the Northwest. He produced perhaps the first watercolor view of Mount Rainier and of the lower Willamette Valley (figure 2). Working under an arrogant martinet of a boss, Lieutenant Charles Wilkes, Drayton labored to document scenes from life that would illustrate his commander's published journals and inform Congress and the American people about what wonders lay to the west on the expansive North American continent.

At the eastern edge of the Far Northwest a few years earlier, a painter from Baltimore secured the position of expeditionary artist for a gentleman's outing to the Wind River Mountains south of the Yellowstone region. In the company of Scottish nobleman Captain William Drummond Stewart, artist Alfred Jacob Miller (1810–1874) documented the whimsies of his adventuresome host at the 1837 mountain man rendezvous. His depictions of Indians encountered along the way (page 44) are romantic reprises of exotic life well beyond the farthest boundaries of the United States at that time.

Miller's contemporary, John Mix Stanley (1814–1872), traveled far more widely than to the Rockies. He was interested in assembling a gallery of Indian portraits and scenes, and by 1855 had amassed a collection of over 150 paintings that was placed on long-term display in the Smithsonian Institution in Washington, DC. Stanley had by that date visited the Far Northwest twice, once in 1847 and again in 1853. He was especially enamored of the Indians along the Columbia River and painted *Scene on the Columbia River* (1852; page 55) as a memento of his first visit. Created in the

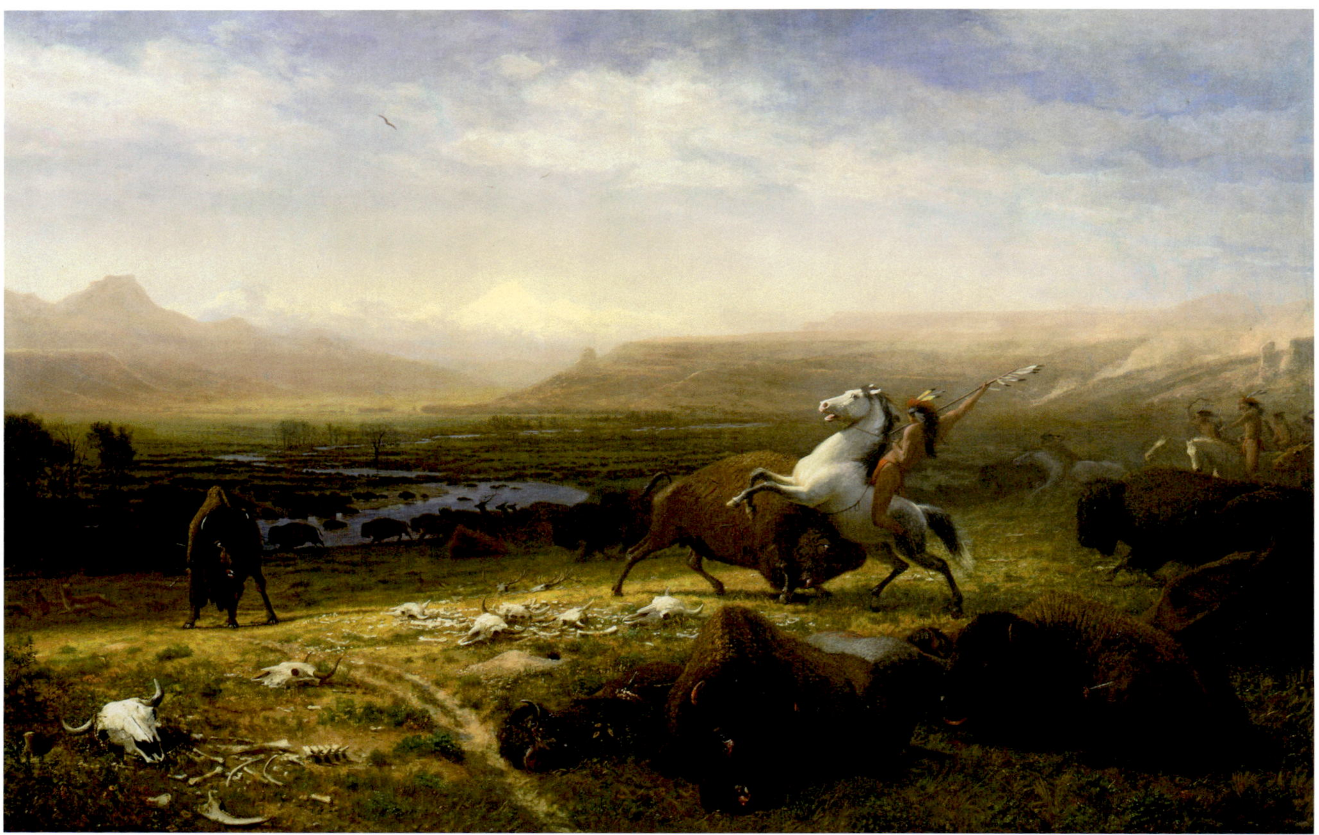

FIGURE 3 Albert Bierstadt, *The Last of the Buffalo*, circa 1888. Oil on canvas, 60¼ × 96½ inches.
Buffalo Bill Center of the West, Gertrude Vanderbilt Whitney Trust Fund Purchase, 2.60.

manner of the Hudson River school artists of his generation, this work entwines the lyrical beauty of wilderness nature and the quietude of a divine blessing.

Several artists of the time endeavored to assemble Indian Galleries like Stanley's. George Catlin (1796–1872) is perhaps the most famous. His gallery numbered over 600 works at its height, around 1840. He fruitlessly sought Congressional support for his dream of seeing his collection purchased by the US government; foiled in this hope, he took his collection to Europe. It eventually found its way home to America, but not before Catlin had gone bankrupt and was forced to sell it to a private collector at a pitiably low price.

Catlin and Stanley both sought government patronage. Beyond that, though, their motivations and aesthetic impulses were quite different. Catlin was driven by a quasi-scientific impulse that followed the dictates of the German scientist Alexander von Humboldt. The Indian was, in Catlin's mind, something to be catalogued as a way of understanding the scientific and divine order of the natural world.

Stanley had no such objective. He was driven by entrepreneurial zeal and regarded his Indian Gallery as a means of making money. Catlin, in service to his cause, worked in a hasty manner that caused many of his works to look unfinished. Stanley was technically a more accomplished painter whose pictures, while sometimes loosely constructed in figural depictions, are polished and highly sophisticated oil paintings. His portraits were enthusiastically sought after and were, whether of Indian or of Anglo subjects, said to be consummate likenesses.

The painter Charles Bird King (1785–1862) had earlier attempted the same thing. His 1826 portrait of Wanata, head chief of the Yankton Sioux (page 31), shows his skill as a portraitist and the chief's powerful presence as an influential member of his tribe. When visited by the western explorer Major Stephen H. Long in 1835, Wanata struck a pose in his impressive white buffalo robe and owl feather headdress that caused Long to proclaim, "We have never seen a nobler face, or a more impressive character, than that of 'Wanata' as he stood that afternoon."[2] King amassed a collection of about 90 such portraits by 1837 that he called his National Indian Portrait Gallery. This portrait was painted separately for a patron and fortunately survives today. The King gallery was totally destroyed, along with almost all of the Stanley Indian Gallery, in a disastrous fire that consumed much of the old Smithsonian building in 1865.

Another artist of this period, William Ranney (1813–1857), explored the West not with his physical presence but through his imagination. Ranney had visited Texas in his youth, but never got far enough north and west to see the Rocky Mountains that formed the backdrop of many of his later western scenes. In invented works such as *The Trappers* of 1856 (page 50), this New Jersey genre and history painter searched for an American experience beyond that of almost all Americans, one that played out in the Rockies. Like Miller, he was infatuated with the mountain man as an archetype of the American quest for adventure, its embrace of independent, entrepreneurial fervor, and its belief in man's potential perfectibility in nature. His pictorial commentary was at once patriotic and quixotic.

In 1859, just three years after Ranney painted *The Trappers*, a New York landscape painter named Albert Bierstadt (1830–1902) traveled to the same Wind River Mountains as Miller had 22 years earlier. He returned to his eastern studio to produce grand manner landscapes of the scenery that were peopled with Shoshoni Indians and their camps. His painting *Departure of an Indian War Party* (1865; page 67) is an early example of his work stemming from that trip. It presents the Indians passing beneath the arbor of giant cottonwood trees with the snow-capped crests of the Wind River Mountains' granite peaks behind. United in this composition are the primary elements of Bierstadt's vision, natural man and unspoiled nature, fixed in a tableau of unity, grace, and splendor.

The Green River has its source in the Wind River Mountains. By 1871 the transcontinental railroad crossed the West, and one of its stops for water was at the Green River. It was here that Bierstadt's major rival, Thomas Moran (1837–1926), sketched the dramatic cliffs that would become, next to Yellowstone, his favorite subject. Moran, unlike Bierstadt

in his early years, was not especially interested in Indians as themes in art. Moran used them merely as exotic staffage in his large canvases. In his *Green River, Wyoming* of 1907 (page 72), a troop of Indians rides away from the viewer and into the valley below. They toss up a small cloud of dust that, like them, is incidental to the sublime grandeur of the resplendent monoliths that loom above them. Glorious nature for Moran was best when left pristine with no human intrusion, even Indians, to mitigate its wonder.

In 1889 Bierstadt exhibited a monumental historical allegory devoted to the cause of saving the desperately depleted numbers of bison and acknowledging that with the loss of their food source the Indians were doomed to suffer profound loss as well. This painting was titled *The Last of the Buffalo* (figure 3).[3] It was hugely popular, though it suffered from considerable critical disparagement. The scene was set in Yellowstone National Park's Lamar Valley. Bierstadt was a charter member of the world's first conservation organization, the Boone and Crockett Club. The first matter of business when the club was initially formed in 1888 was to press for federal legislation to protect the remnant herd of bison in the park, numbering at that time fewer than 500 animals. The painting was created in part to support that effort.

Younger artists were drawn to the picture, or at least to its theme. A 28-year-old painter, Frederic Remington (1861–1909), had recently returned from a trip to southern Alberta when Bierstadt's painting started attracting notice. He had studied among the Blackfeet Indians and took the opportunity to make a statement similar to Bierstadt's in his 1889 painting *Conjuring Back the Buffalo* (page 92). Remington was not a grand manner painter like Bierstadt but was compelled to relate the story of the Indians' reliance on the bison and the tragic consequences of their near extinction on Native cultures. The painting showed artifacts such as the leggings and moccasins he had purchased in Alberta (now in the Remington Studio Collection in Cody's Buffalo Bill Center of the West; figure 4). It was later illustrated in *Century Magazine*, so many Americans saw his powerful testimonial.

At the same time that the easterners Remington and Bierstadt were proclaiming their resolve to assure the survival of the Indian and the bison, a western painter and

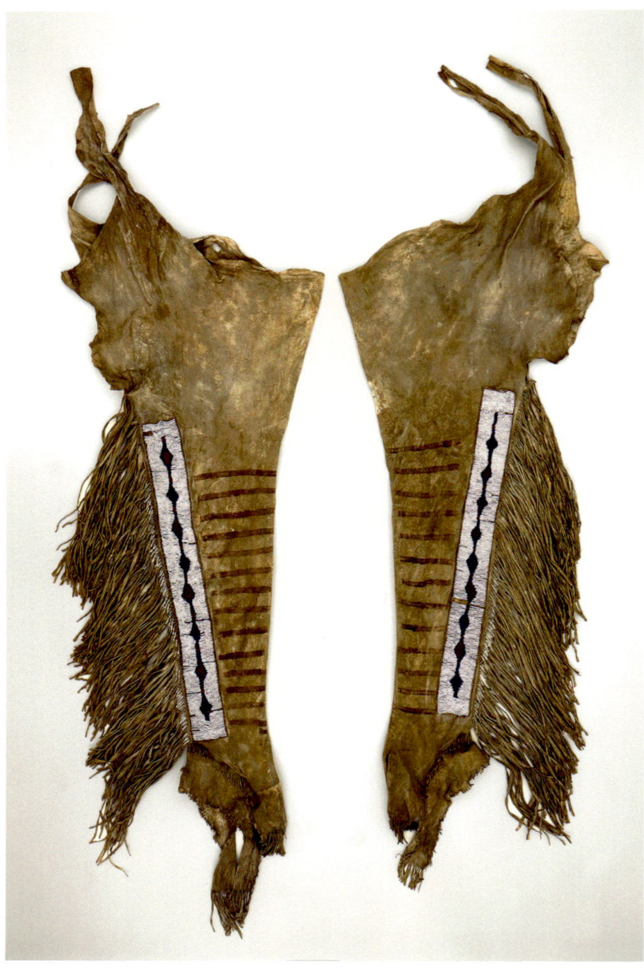

sculptor was emerging on the national scene. His name was Charles Russell (1864–1926), and he had earned the popular moniker "the cowboy artist" with such paintings as his 1890 oil *Rider of the Rough String* (figure 5). Bierstadt and Remington lived in New York and came west from time to time to gather inspiration and subjects. Russell's birthplace was St. Louis, but as early as 1880 he had begun to call Montana his home. Later works like his 1906 watercolor *Indian Canoe Party* (figure 6) positioned him not only as an astute painter of Native people of the Northwest but as one of the most devoted and sympathetic recorders of their cultural legacy. The warrior in the bow of the canoe stands as a symbol of Native oneness with nature and valor in the face of uncertainty.

Russell viewed the Indians of the Northern Plains as the true Americans, as did his Colorado-raised contemporary the sculptor Alexander Phimister Proctor (1860–1950). Proctor's early equestrian bronze of a Blackfeet chief, *Indian Warrior* (figure 7), shares Russell's portrayal of one who to them was an undeniable national hero—an indomitable paragon of strong-willed masculine strength. Graceful in form, noble in countenance, and resolute in focus, this was the quintessential beau ideal of the Indian as celebrated at his most exalted historical moment. It was also, sadly, something of a salve for the national conscience, given the way

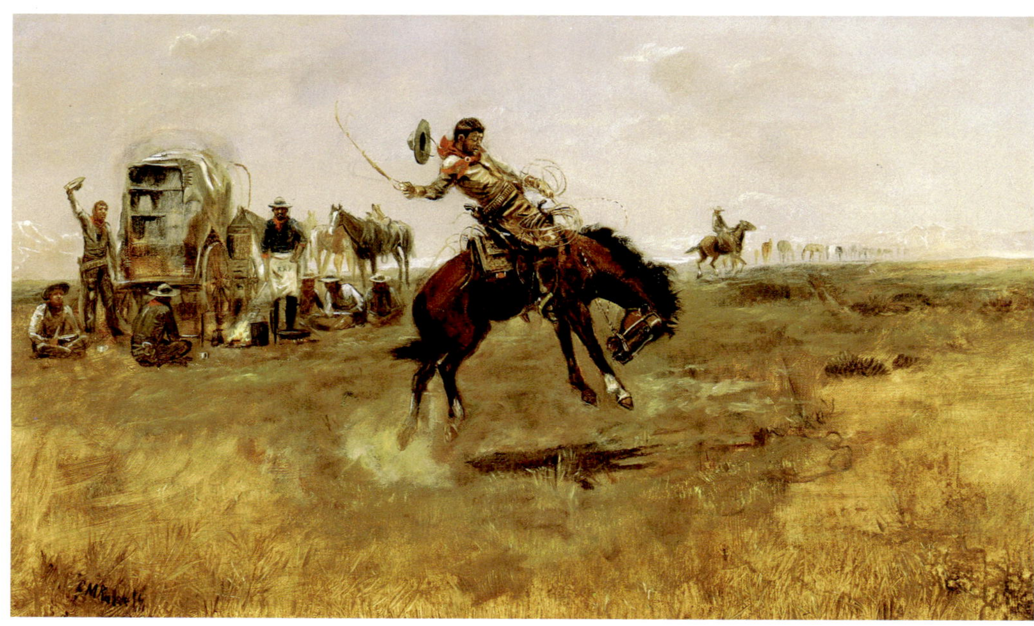

FIGURE 5 Charles M. Russell, *Rider of the Rough String*, 1890. Oil on canvas, 14 × 24 inches. Tacoma Art Museum, Haub Family Collection, Promised gift of Erivan and Helga Haub.

HASSRICK

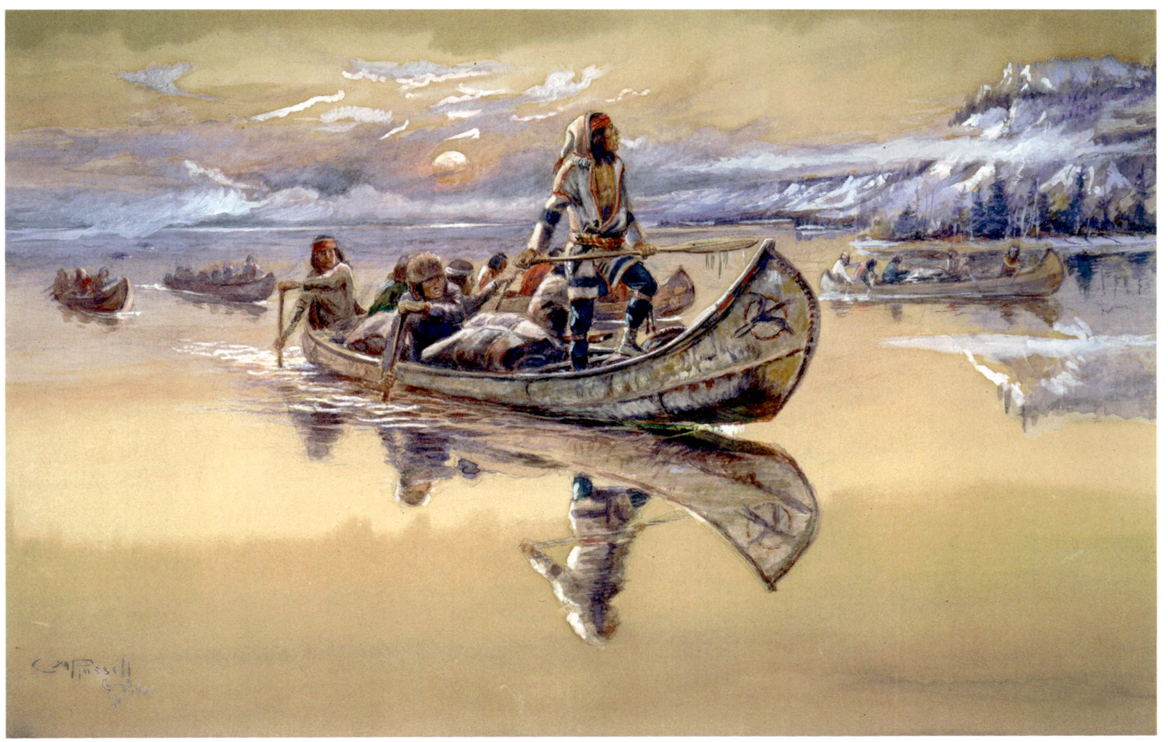

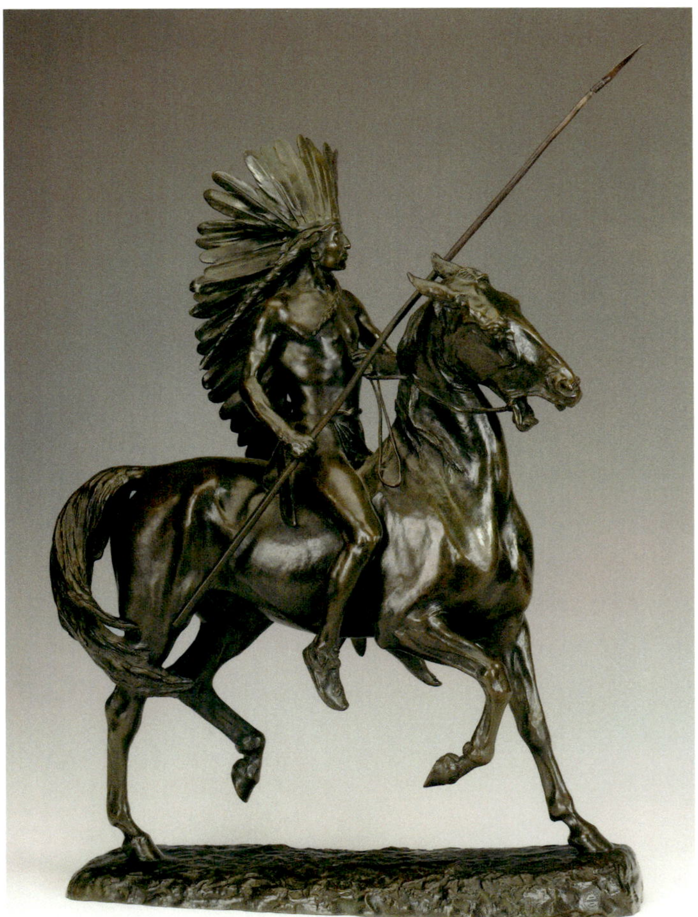

in which the US government and most American people actually treated Indians at the end of the 19th century. Consider the pose of *Signal of Peace* by Cyrus Dallin (1861–1944; page 91), completed just eight years before, in which a similarly attired and mounted chief welcomes newcomers to the West with his spear raised as a sign of peace—a peaceful welcome, Dallin implies, that was bitterly betrayed.

For many, the means of escaping the realities of the late 19th-century Far Northwest was to avoid depictions of Anglo progress and Native subjugation and to concentrate on the universally appealing allure of nature's grandeur. The national parks, especially Yellowstone, provided that outlet. John Fery (1859–1934), an Austrian-born and Munich-trained painter, came to the United States in 1886. He was soon hired by the Northern Pacific Railway to record the beauties of Glacier National Park. In 1914 he spent a summer

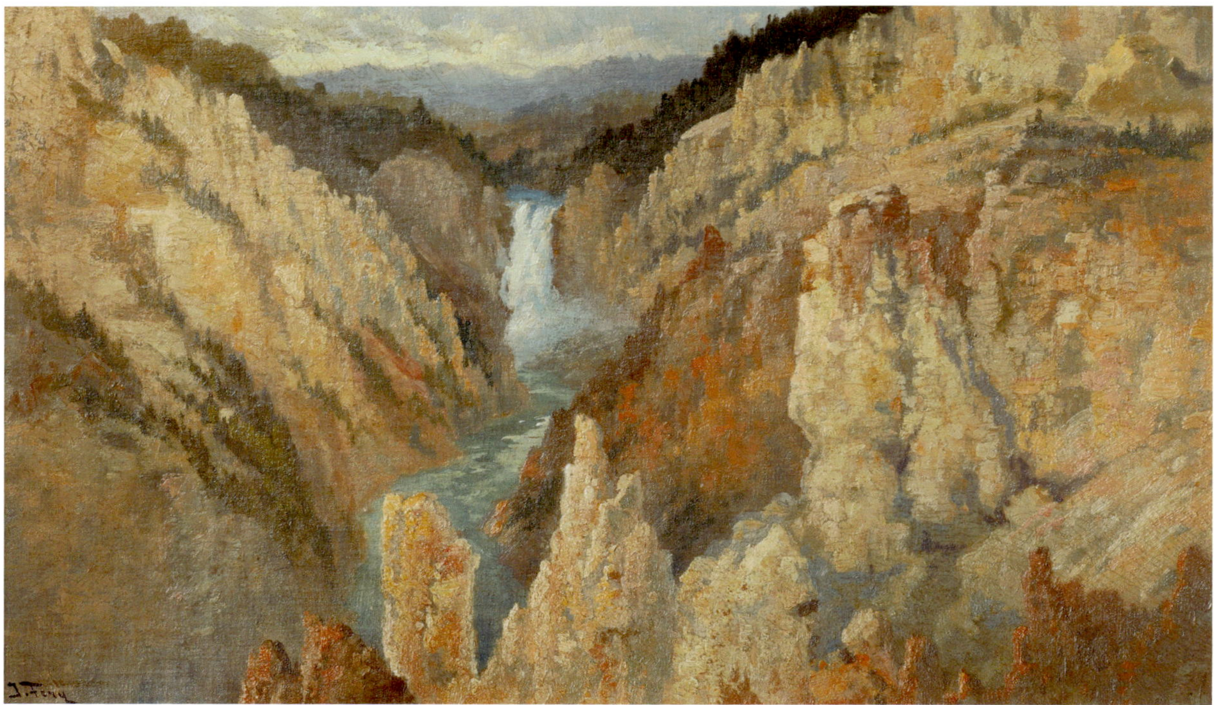

FIGURE 8 John Fery, *Lower Yellowstone Falls*, 1914. Oil on canvas on board, 14 × 24 inches.
Tacoma Art Museum, Haub Family Collection, Promised gift of Erivan and Helga Haub.

in Yellowstone embracing the glories of the park's landscape wonders in spirited oils. Recorded without people, scenes like *Lower Yellowstone Falls* (figure 8) promoted a western experience that was at once magnificent and inviting. The park had been set aside for public enjoyment and artists like Fery presented such pleasures as an enduring life experience.

By the second decade of the 20th century, the Far Northwest had lessened as a subject for painters and sculptors of national distinction and increasingly became the muse for regional artists. At the same time the Southwest, especially New Mexico, rose in prominence. The Haub Family Collection is especially strong in the work of the painters from Taos and Santa Fe.

The railroads had much to do with popularizing the American Southwest in these years. The artists of Taos in particular nurtured a relationship with the Santa Fe Railway after 1910 and, in concert with the promotions department of the company, endeavored to create an exotic yet accessible image of the Pueblo Indians that would—rather unlike that of the Northern Plains people at the time (noble and warlike or beaten down and disheartened)—make them

come alive in a nonthreatening, inviting way. This contrast between depictions of the Native worlds of the Northwest and the Southwest was dramatic.

The six painters who formed the Taos Society of Artists in 1915 shared many perceptions. They followed the dicta of the great promoter of the Southwest Charles Lummis, who had proclaimed in 1908 that New Mexico was an artists' paradise.[4] They delighted in the location of the little adobe village nestled in the shadow of Taos Mountain, its local color, its people and their complex history. The Native people and Hispanics fascinated them and inspired their art. The artists mutually dreamed of creating there a new national art, one that was purely American in theme and aesthetic force. Yet, presented with the same models and Native ways, they diverged significantly in their interpretations. About half strove to depict New Mexican life as it was, while the other half sought to impose historical antecedents on the models they used.

The first of the group to visit Taos was Joseph Henry Sharp (1859–1953) in 1893. Despite the fact that he often painted the current scene, many of his images historicize the Indian, as in *Taos Indians in the Sunlight* (page 87). The

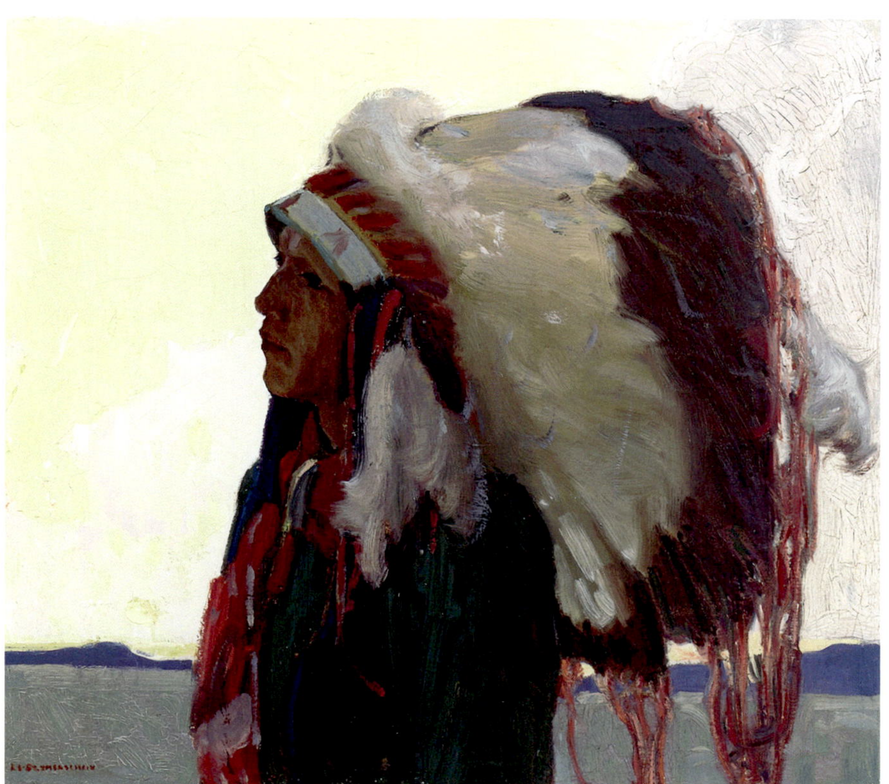

FIGURE 9 Ernest L. Blumenschein, *Taos Indian Chief*, circa 1915. Oil on canvas, 14½ × 16½ inches. Tacoma Art Museum, Haub Family Collection, Promised gift of Erivan and Helga Haub.

painting exudes a sense of reverie and peace. The quiescence and interiority of the figures graces them with a mantle of romantic idealism that is at once safe and accessible yet removed and evanescent. Sharp's masterful Beaux-Arts style and musing thematic approach were shared equally by his compatriot E. Irving Couse (1866–1936), who first came to Taos in 1902. *Music of the Waters* (page 116) was one of Couse's most celebrated early works.[5] It reveals another proclivity of many of the Taos painters, that of viewing the Indians as inextricably intertwined with nature and inherently gifted as craftspeople and artists. Such an approach was popular with the public and with the railroad that brought people to New Mexico as tourists.

Ernest Blumenschein (1874–1960) and Bert Phillips (1868–1956), both fresh from studies abroad at the Académie Julian in Paris, traveled to Taos in 1898. Phillips married the local doctor's sister and stayed. Blumenschein, who made his living as an illustrator, returned to his home in New York. Their initial approach to the Taos scene was essentially the same. Both glorified the Indian as a historical figure, as in Blumenschein's *Taos Indian Chief* (figure 9) and Phillips's *Portrait of a Chief* (circa 1925; page 124). Blumenschein

gradually moved toward more modern art expressions and focused on contemporary Indian life as well.

An artist from St. Louis, Oscar Berninghaus (1874–1952), seemed to embrace the wonder of present-day Pueblo life and people from the start. He arrived in 1899, just a year after Blumenschein and Phillips. His clearly articulated, everyday figures surrounded by magnificently vibrant atmosphere, as seen in *Taos Rabbit Hunt* (circa 1935; page 141) expressed Berninghaus's commitment to simple but celebratory works.

The last founding member of the Taos Society of Artists to arrive was Herbert Dunton (1878–1936). A student of Blumenschein's at the Art Students League in New York, Dunton first came to paint in Taos in 1912 at his mentor's behest. Initially inspired to produce pictures of the bygone Indian similar to the early works of Blumenschein and Phillips, he subsequently fell under the spell of a Taos latecomer, E. Martin Hennings (1886–1956), who practiced a form of the art nouveau decorative style. Dunton's *Summer Silhouette* (circa 1930; page 155) evinces the curvilinear grace and elegant fluidity of that European school.

Hennings, who first came to Taos in 1917, was one of the town's most accomplished artists. Having studied in

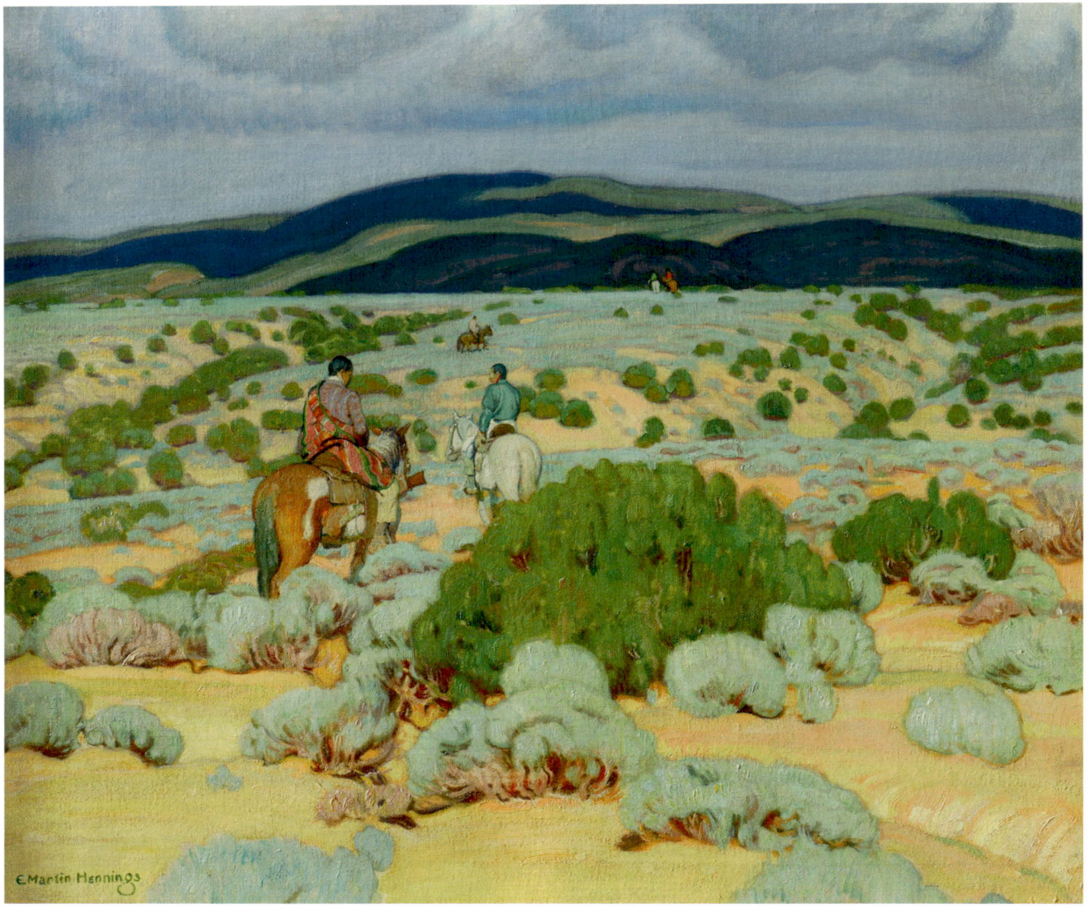

FIGURE 10 E. Martin Hennings, *Rabbit Hunt, Taos*, circa 1930. Oil on canvas, 25 × 30 inches.
Tacoma Art Museum, Haub Family Collection, Promised gift of Erivan and Helga Haub.

Munich as well as in Chicago, he lent an elegant stylishness to his renditions of the New Mexico landscape and its inhabitants. His decorative, almost ornamental scenes of Indian riders in the sage-covered hills near Taos, like *Rabbit Hunt, Taos* (figure 10), invited enthusiastic patronage and critical acclaim. He and his friend Walter Ufer (1876–1936), another Chicago-reared and Munich-trained painter who settled in Taos, took the everyday life of the Hispanics and Pueblo Indians as a subject and shaped it into wondrous compositions and powerfully crafted evocations of an exotic land and fascinating culture. Ufer once claimed that the Taos artists would someday be a pivotal force in American art.[6] He secured his contention with such boldly experimental post-impressionist canvases as *Evening Rays* (circa 1923; page 146). Hennings, with his adaptations of the Jugendstil model (the German equivalent of the French art nouveau)

and Ufer, with his pointillist skies and rayonist structural interpretations, fashioned a counterpoint to the other Taos painters with their basic reliance on the traditional French Beaux-Arts methods.

The Taos Society of Artists only lasted 11 years. A battle of egos and a difference of opinion about whether modern trends in art should be included in their pictorial vocabulary were two causes of the breakup. Many modern artists, crafting their styles after the latest trends from Europe's ateliers, had found their way to Taos in those years, including the cubist painter John Marin (1870–1953), the post-impressionist B. J. O. Nordfeldt (1878–1955), and the abstractionist Raymond Jonson (1891–1982). One painter who showed up in the late 1920s, Georgia O'Keeffe (1887–1986), was just as modern as the others but resolutely determined to avoid European influence in order to remain creatively untainted and purely American. Her elegant, ethereal arrangements of nature's wonders from the New Mexico desert, such as *Piñons with Cedar* from 1956 (page 169), maintain a simplicity and purity that is indeed unspoiled by the myriad isms swirling through the art world on the East Coast and as deep into the continent as northern New Mexico. She alone combined most of the motives and the compelling sense of quest that had driven artists west since the 1830s. She was entrepreneurial, adventuresome, and unabashedly fascinated with and devoted to preserving a West that would help define America with its people, its landscape, and its history. It has been these qualities that, in the final analysis, have defined much of the creative pictorial work that is today known as western American art. It is Tacoma's great glory to now feature such treasures for the public's enrichment.

1 Letter from the Gilcrease Museum's third director, James T. Forrest, to the author, quoted in Peter H. Hassrick, "Western Art Museums: A Question of Style or Content," *Montana: The Magazine of Western History* 42 (Summer 1992), 30.

2 Long is quoted in James D. Horan, *The McKenney-Hall Portrait Gallery of American Indians* (New York: Crown, 1972), 144.

3 A second version, slightly larger, is in the collection of the Corcoran Gallery of Art, Washington, DC.

4 Charles Lummis, "The Artists' Paradise," *Out West* 29 (September 1908), 191.

5 Virginia Couse Leavitt, *Eanger Irving Couse: Image Maker for America* (Albuquerque: The Albuquerque Museum, 1991), 152.

6 Walter Ufer, "The Santa Fe–Taos Art Colony," *El Palacio* (August 1916), 75.

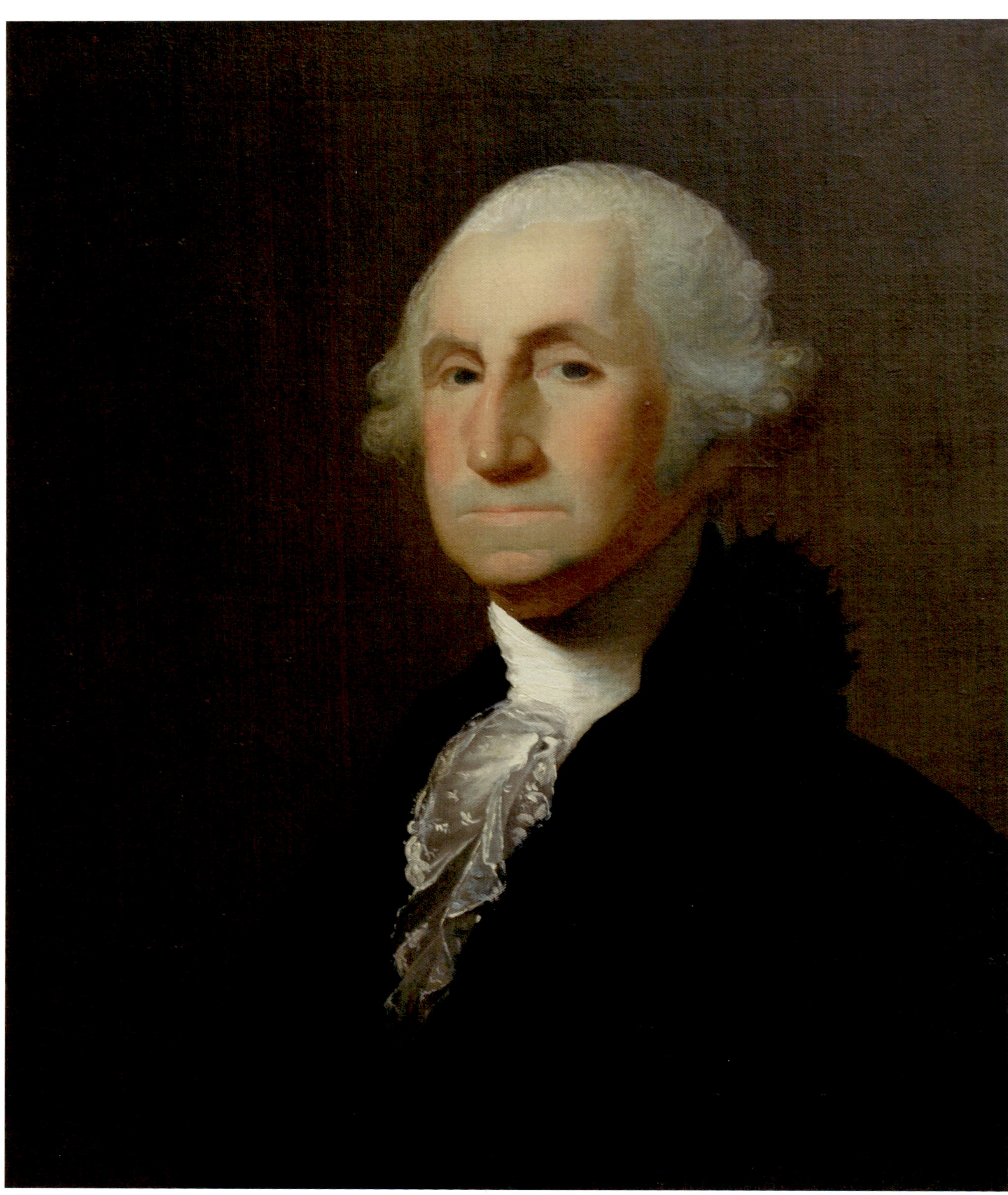

GILBERT STUART (1755–1828)

Portrait of George Washington

circa 1797
Oil on canvas
28⅛ × 24³⁄₁₆ inches

Before the ink was dry on the Declaration of Independence, Americans began crafting an origin myth to define the new nation. Recognizing George Washington's significance as the first president of the new country, artist Gilbert Stuart painted him from life in 1795 and 1796. Based on his three life portraits, Stuart created at least a hundred copies, selling them briskly on both sides of the Atlantic and cementing Washington's central role in the stories of America's founding. This particular portrait was once owned by Washington's nephew George Steptoe Washington.

Raised in Colonial Virginia, the nation's first president reminds us that the western expansion of the United States started in the East—even before the country's founding. A century after Stuart's portrait was completed, author Owen Wister emphasized the gradual movement from the eastern colonies to the American West in his 1902 novel *The Virginian*, starring an iconic Wyoming cowboy who hailed from the green hills of Washington's home state. From Washington's time to the present, the concept of "West" is ever changing and moving.

Wanata (The Charger), Grand Chief of the Sioux

1826
Oil on canvas
39 × 27¼ inches

Charles Bird King never had a chance to meet Wanata, a revered Native American leader from present-day Minnesota. Nor did he ever travel to the American West. Like the vast majority of Americans in the early 19th century, King lived along the eastern seaboard, where he worked as a portrait painter in the nation's capital. Then, in 1821, a major commission changed his career. Thomas L. McKenney, then Superintendent of Indian Trade, hired King to paint portraits of Native American delegates visiting Washington, DC. Over the next 15 years King created an Indian Gallery of nearly a hundred portraits, most of them painted from life. But the famous Yankton Sioux leader Wanata never came to his studio. King had only a rough field sketch by artist James Otto Lewis to use as a guide.

To transform the stiff figure from Lewis's drawing into an elegant painting, King recalled the stately British portraits he had seen while living in London. King's full-length image shows Wanata like an English nobleman, a dignified individual in his finest clothing against a landscape of rolling hills and a patch of blue sky. By using a European portraiture style, King introduced Wanata as a worthy, independent leader to his Euro-American audience in the eastern United States.

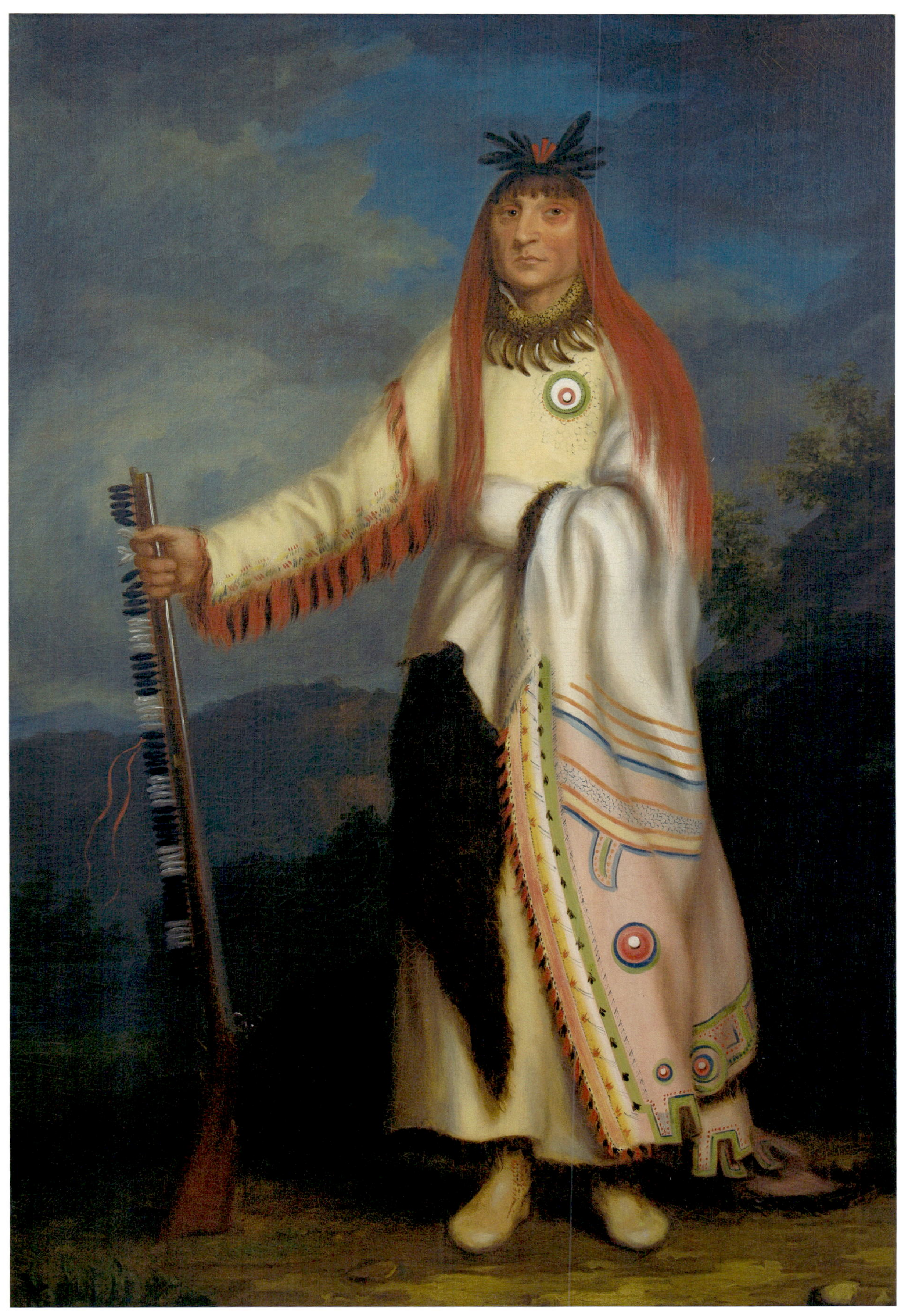

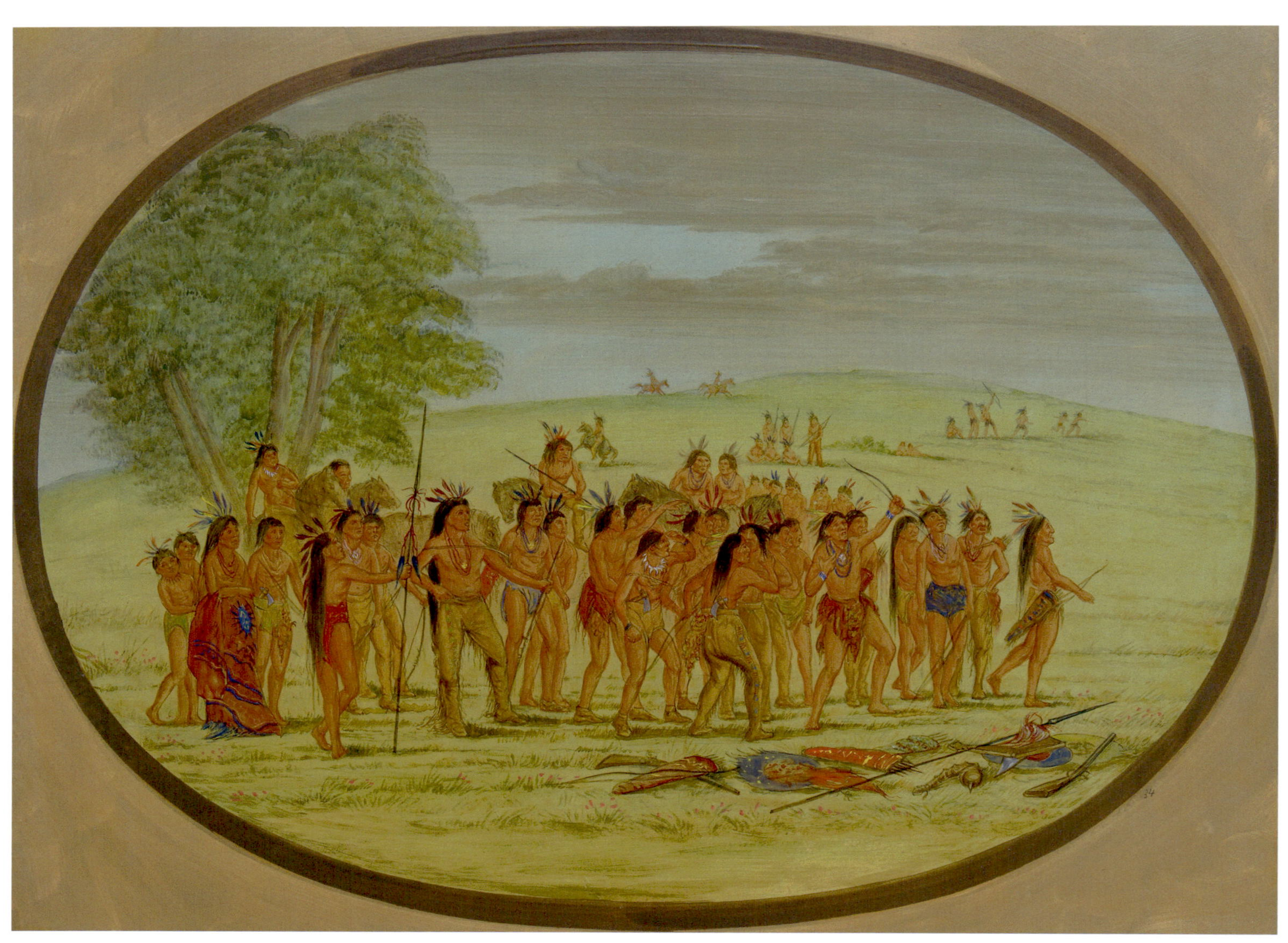

Archery of the Mandan

1855–65
Oil on board
15¼ × 22 inches

Surrounded by eager observers, a warrior smoothly raises his bow, string stretched taut. The Mandan "Game of the Arrow" has begun. Artist George Catlin first witnessed and sketched this archery contest in the early 1830s, at a Mandan village along the Missouri River in present-day North Dakota. The game, he wrote, "is something like that of an Archery Club in the civilized world, but for a different mode of shooting. . . . The strife in this game was to decide who could discharge from his bow the greatest number of arrows before his first one should fall to the ground." Captivated by the spirited competition, Catlin remarked, "I never beheld a more classic and beautiful group, nor a more graceful and gentlemanly rivalry."* Based on recollections from his travels, Catlin composed this painting of Mandan people gathering on a green plain, keenly watching the elegant skill and strength of the "Game of the Arrow."

*George Catlin, *Catlin's North American Indian Portfolio: Hunting Scenes and Amusements of the Rocky Mountains and Prairies of America, From Drawings and Notes of the Author Made During Eight Years' Travel Amongst Forty-Eight of the Wildest and Most Remote Tribes of Savages in North America* (London: Geo. Catlin, 1844), 18.

Naw-Kaw

circa 1832
Oil on canvas
30¼ × 25¼ inches

In 1828, the elderly Winnebago (Ho-Chunk) leader Naw-Kaw journeyed from his home in present-day Wisconsin to Washington, DC. He came with a delegation from his tribe to speak on behalf of his people, meeting with President John Quincy Adams and captivating the public. Thomas L. McKenney, head of the new Bureau of Indian Affairs, remembered Naw-Kaw was "a man of large stature and fine presence. He was six feet tall, and well made." McKenney soon commissioned a portrait of the chief by artist Charles Bird King, and later commissioned this copy by Henry Inman. Naw-Kaw's portrait "affords ample evidence of his taste," McKenney wrote, "the three medals, presented to him at different times . . . are worn with as much pride and as much propriety as the orders of nobility which decorate the nobles of Europe."*

*Thomas L. McKenney and James Hall, *History of the Indian Tribes of North America, With Biographical Sketches and Anecdotes of the Principal Chiefs, Embellished with One Hundred Portraits from the Indian Gallery in the War Department at Washington* (Philadelphia: D. Rice, 1872), 320.

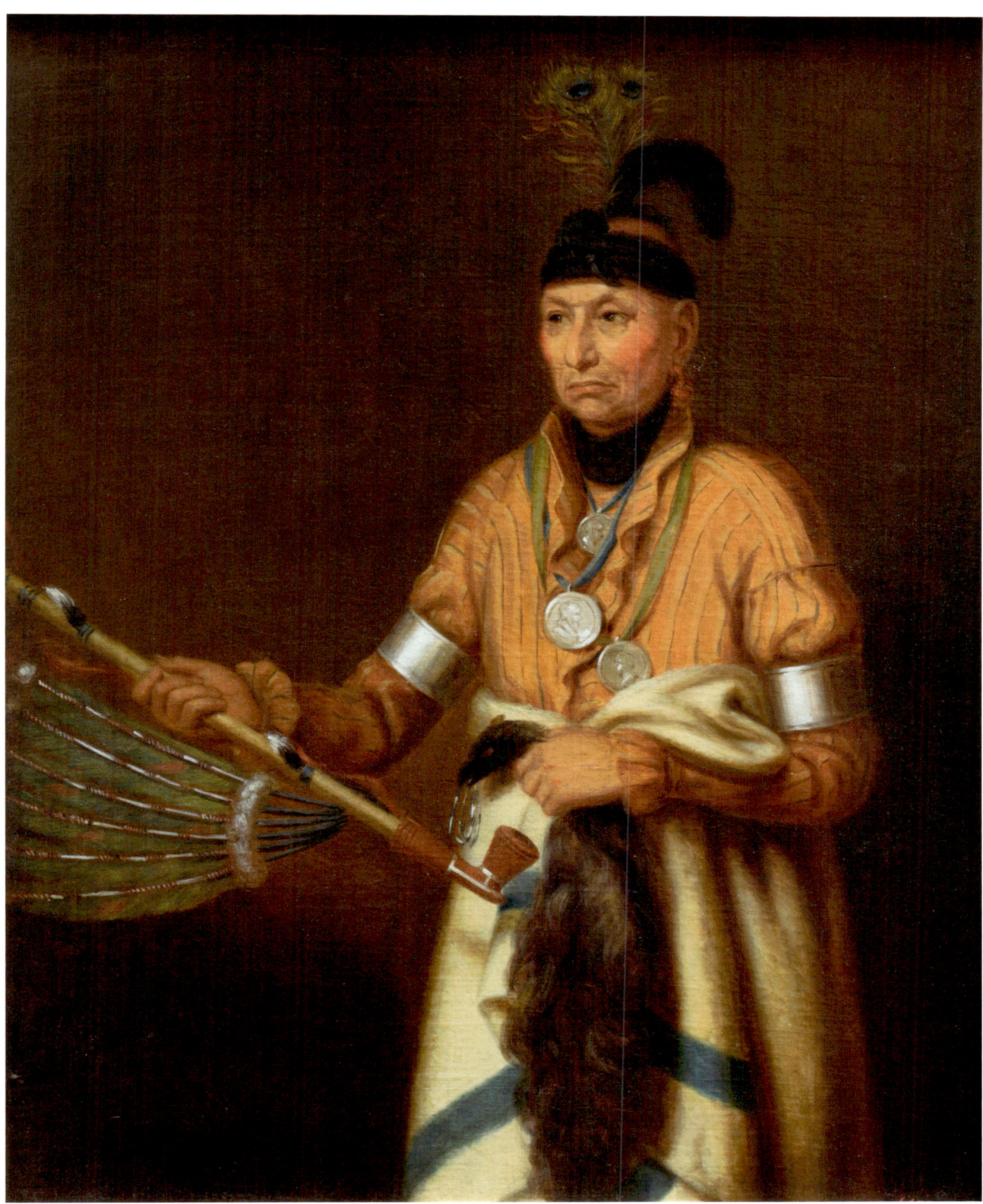

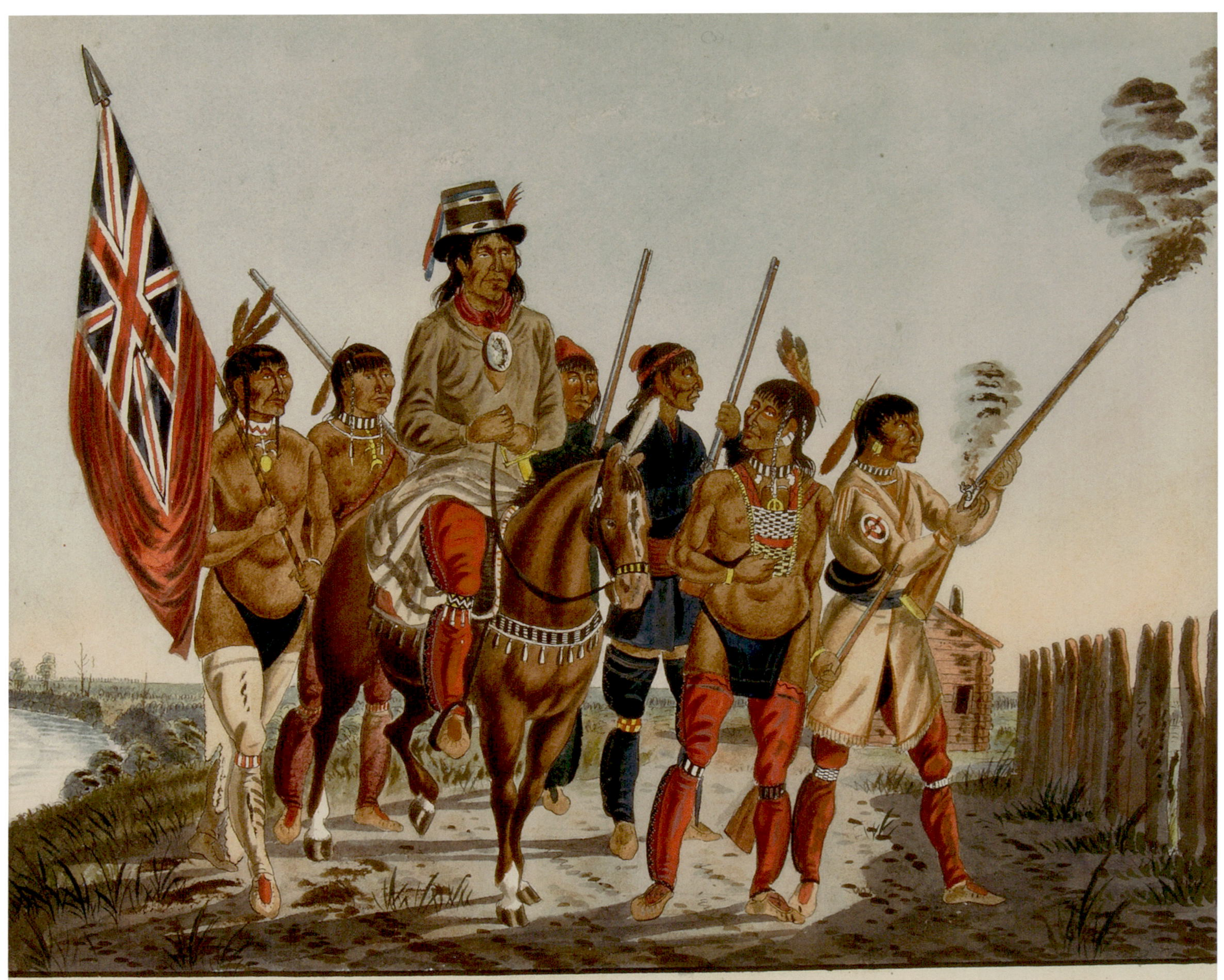

The Indian Chief, Black Robe, from Portage de Prairie, approaching the Colony House, upon a visit to the Governor.

The Indian Chief, Black Robe, from Portage de Prairie, approaching the Colony House, upon a visit to the Governor

circa 1823
Watercolor on paper
8 × 9½ inches

The War of 1812 represented more than simply a fight between the United States and Britain: Native American groups also became strategic allies for both the Americans and British. To hold the territory around Fort McKay in Prairie du Chien (in present-day Wisconsin), British fort commander Andrew H. Bulger sought alliances with Native Americans in the Great Lakes region. But despite his efforts the region was returned to United States' control at the war's end in 1815. Years later, when Bulger met Peter Rindisbacher at the Red River Colony in Canada, he commissioned a series of watercolor paintings depicting the Native Americans who had assisted him at Fort McKay during the war. The artist was just 17 years old, and this was his first major commission. With a direct narrative style, Rindisbacher here shows a delegation of Native Americans coming to meet Bulger at Fort McKay, firing a salute into the air and carrying the Hudson's Bay Company flag as a symbol of their alliance.

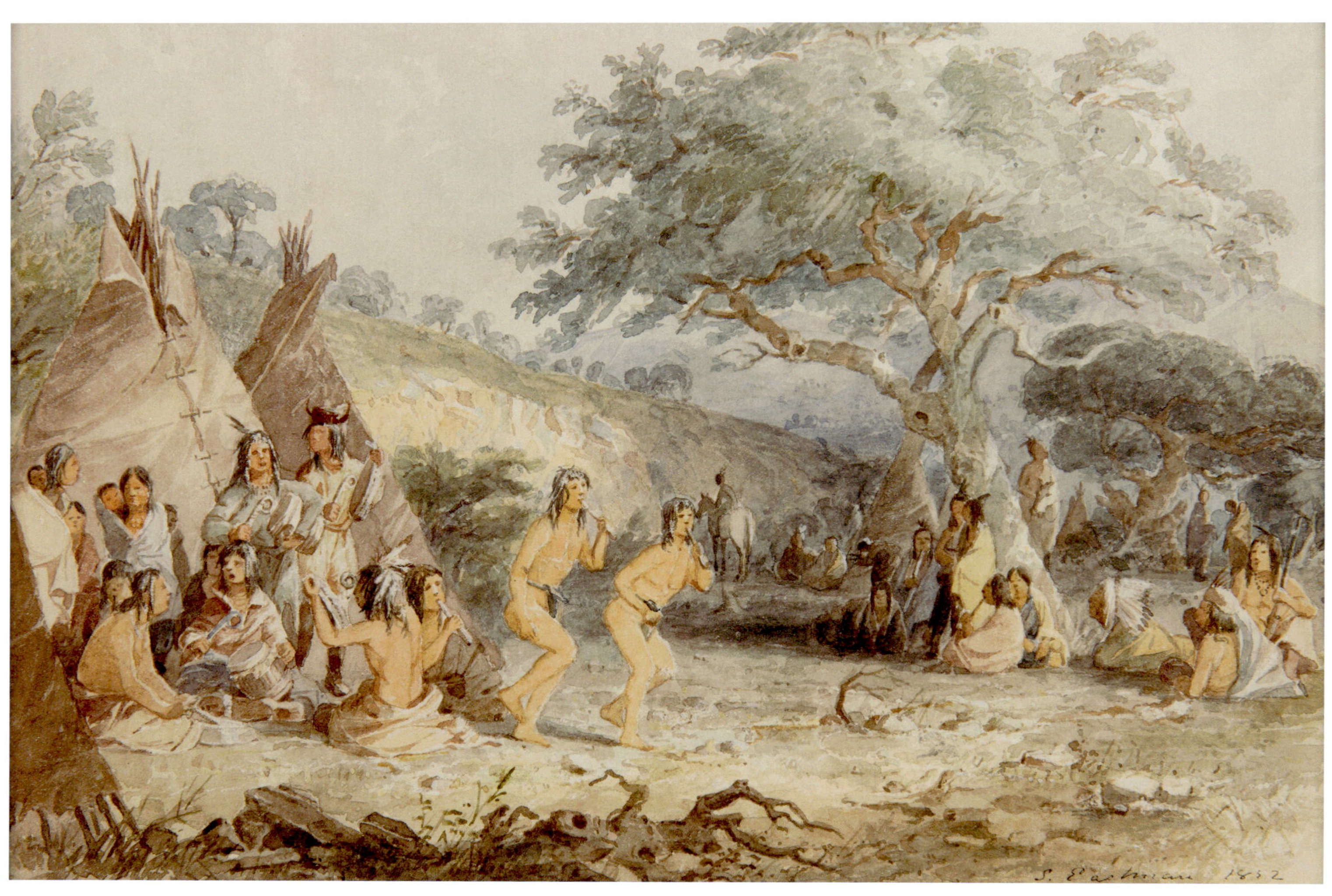

SETH EASTMAN (1808–1875)

Worship of the Sun—Dakota Indian Dancers

1852
Watercolor on paper
6 × 9 inches

A "soldier-artist," Seth Eastman developed a love for drawing and art while studying for a military career at West Point. When the army sent him to the northern outpost of Fort Snelling, at the site of present-day Minneapolis, he seized the opportunity to study and visually record the local Dakota Sioux and Ojibwe people. Unlike other artists who depicted the American West in the early 19th century, Eastman's military assignments allowed him to live in the West for years at a time in the 1830s and 1840s. He learned the Sioux language and avidly studied and painted intimate details of daily life, gradually building up an immense portfolio of images.

An illustration for Henry Rowe Schoolcraft's six-volume publication *Information Respecting the History, Conditions, and Prospects of the Indian Tribes of the United States*,* this watercolor shows Eastman's ability to capture a specific ceremonial event amid the everyday bustle of life in a Dakota community.

*Henry Rowe Schoolcraft, *Information Respecting the History, Conditions, and Prospects of the Indian Tribes of the United States; Collected and Prepared Under the Direction of the Bureau of Indian Affairs, per Act of Congress of March 3, 1847, Part III* (Philadelphia: Lippincott, Grambo, 1853), 227, plate 27.

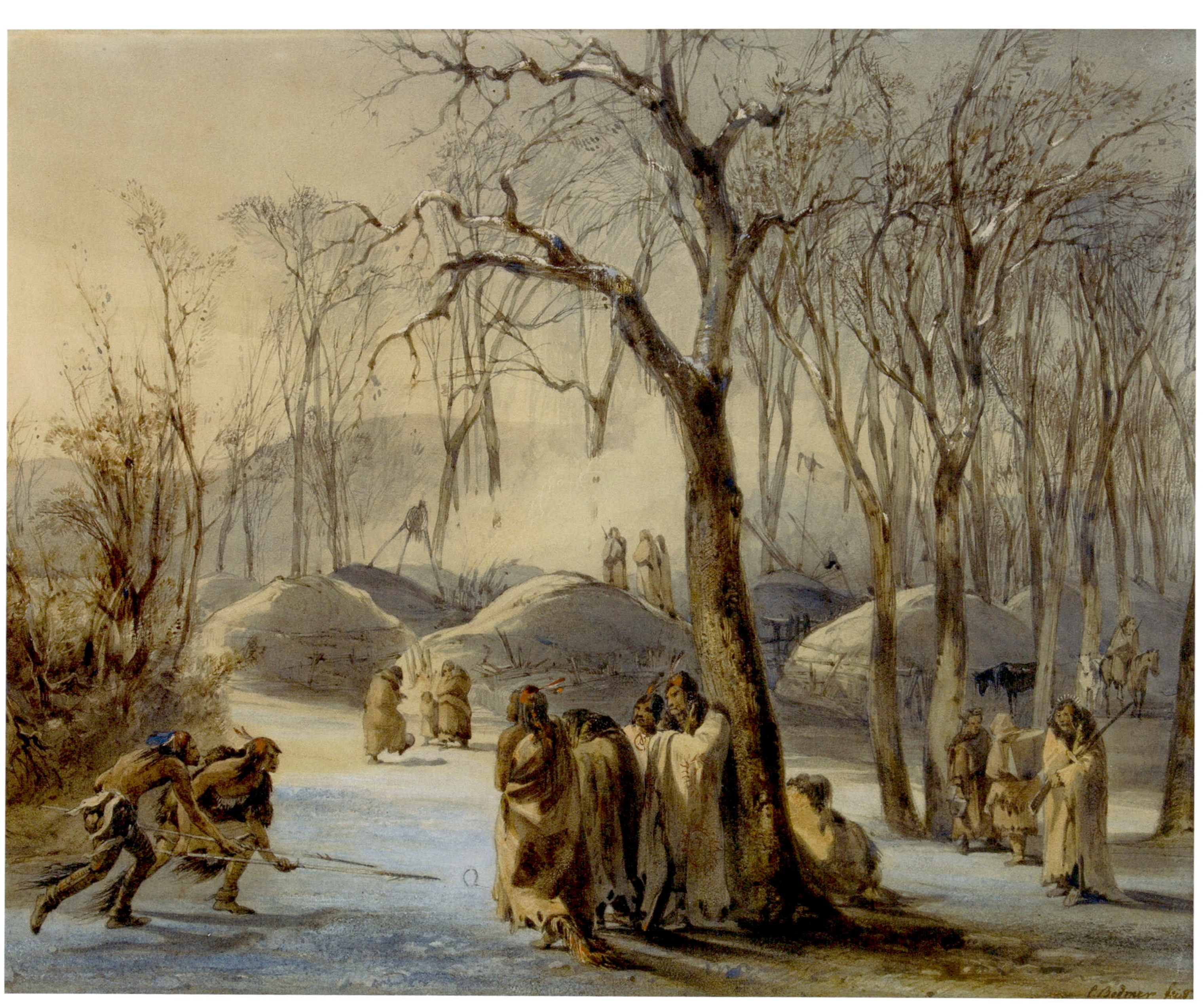

Winter Village of the Minatarres

circa 1834
Watercolor on paper
10⅜ × 13¼ inches

The cold was extreme. Snow covered the ground in patches—where the howling wind had not blown it away. The young Swiss artist Karl Bodmer struggled to work in the frigid winter of 1833–34, when he lived in the villages of the Minatarres (Hidatsa) and Mandan in present-day North Dakota. On one occasion, his employer Prince Maximilian of Wied recounted, "the mercury was again 20 degrees below zero, and it was too cold in our room to paint, for colors and pencils were frozen . . . and had to be thawed in hot water."*

Bodmer painted outdoors when he could. In this watercolor, the people of a Hidatsa village huddle under heavy bison robes while smoke from the domed earth lodges rises through the trees. But the Hidatsa did not allow the bitter temperatures to dampen their spirits. Two men in the foreground defy the cold by casting aside their heavy robes, darting about to play a game with spears and a small hoop, embracing the winter.

*Maximilian, Prince of Wied, *Travels in the Interior of North America,* translated from the German by H. Evans Lloyd (London: Ackermann, 1843), 58.

Portrait of Maungwudaus

circa 1851
Oil on canvas
30 × 25 inches

Maungwudaus was no stranger to sitting for a portrait. Raised near Toronto, Canada, he was educated by Methodist missionaries and was fluent in spoken and written English. When he began a public career as a performer, dance troupe leader, and speaker, he embraced the new medium of photography and posed for numerous daguerreotypes dressed in his full regalia (page 175). From 1845 to 1848 Maungwudaus led his troupe to Europe. For a time they partnered with artist George Catlin, staging performances alongside his Indian Gallery—while Catlin made sketches of Maungwudaus and members of the troupe. By the time Paul Kane had the chance to paint Maungwudaus in the early 1850s, numerous images of the Ojibwe performer already existed. Kane created two versions of Maungwudaus's portrait, both based on stately European portraiture with a classic triangular composition (the other is in the collection of the Royal Ontario Museum in Toronto, Canada). With Kane's paintings added to the existing images of Maungwudaus, the Ojibwe performer and speaker became one of the most widely depicted Native Americans of his day.

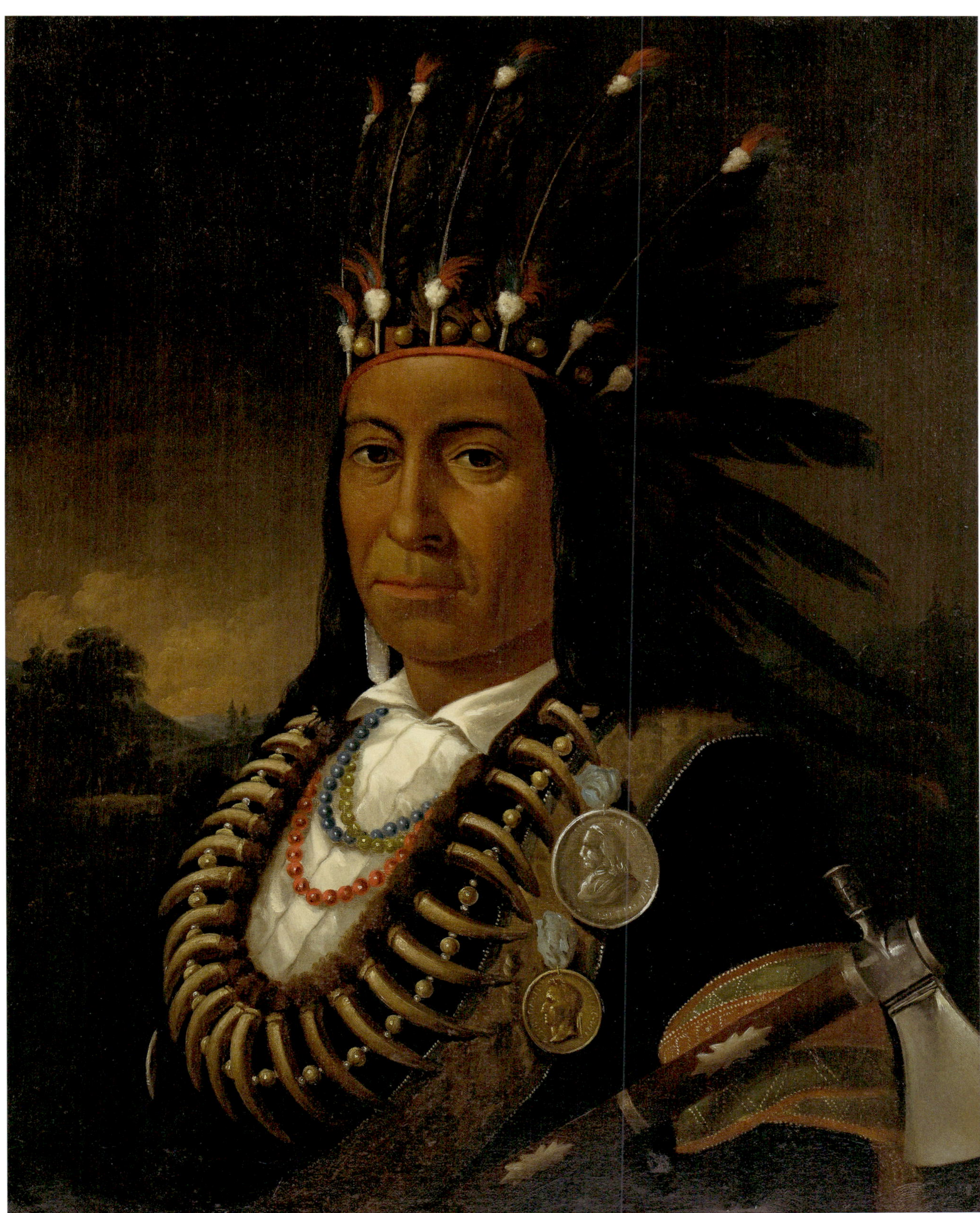

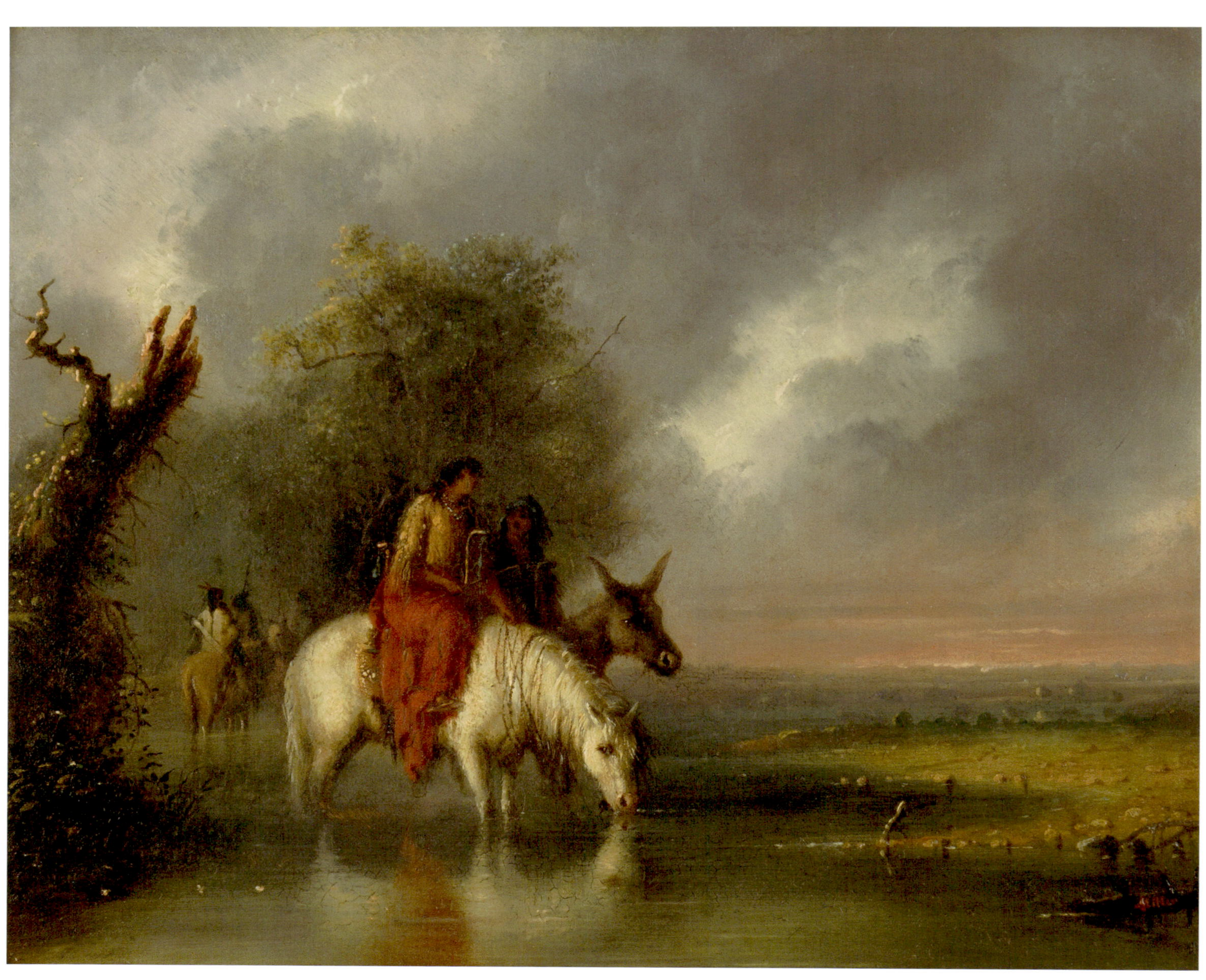

Scene on the Big Sandy River

circa 1860
Oil on paper mounted on board
9¼ × 12 inches

This painting, explained artist Alfred Jacob Miller, "may be said to represent a small slice of an Indian paradise—Indian women, horses, a stream of water, shade trees, and the broad prairie to the right."* Miller's image of the white horse and rider reflected in the still water shows a balance between the Native American woman and her land. Rather than acknowledging the changes caused by burgeoning travel and immigration in the Great Plains, in Miller's imagination the West remained an exotic, unchanging place with harmony between humans and nature. Enamored of the peaceful scene of plenty, Miller returned to this subject multiple times; his watercolor versions can be found in the Museum of Fine Arts, Boston, and at the Walters Art Museum in Baltimore.

*Marvin C. Ross, *The West of Alfred Jacob Miller (1837): from the Notes and Water Colors in the Walters Art Gallery, with an Account of the Artist* (Norman: University of Oklahoma Press, 1951), 20.

The Meeting of Tecumseh and William Henry Harrison at Vincennes

1851
Oil on canvas
33⅜ × 43⅜ inches

How does a new nation record its past? By memorializing scenes from American history in his paintings, Junius Brutus Stearns sought to connect the young United States to the prestige of ancient Rome. Early in his career the artist revealed his love of classical history by changing his name to "Junius Brutus"—probably referencing Marcus Junius Brutus, who tried to save the Roman Republic by leading the assassination of dictator Julius Caesar in 44 BC.

In this painting Stearns depicts the Shawnee leader Tecumseh like a Roman statesman, his right hand raised and his figure draped in a stately cloak, similar to the statue of Augustus of Prima Porta in the Vatican Museums. Stearns made Tecumseh the dominant person in the composition, and his powerful stance in the center of the canvas immediately draws the viewer's eye. In creating this fanciful image some 40 years after the Shawnee leader's confrontation with General William Henry Harrison in 1810, Stearns presented the scene of an American conflict between two epic leaders in the same light as the legendary events of ancient Rome.

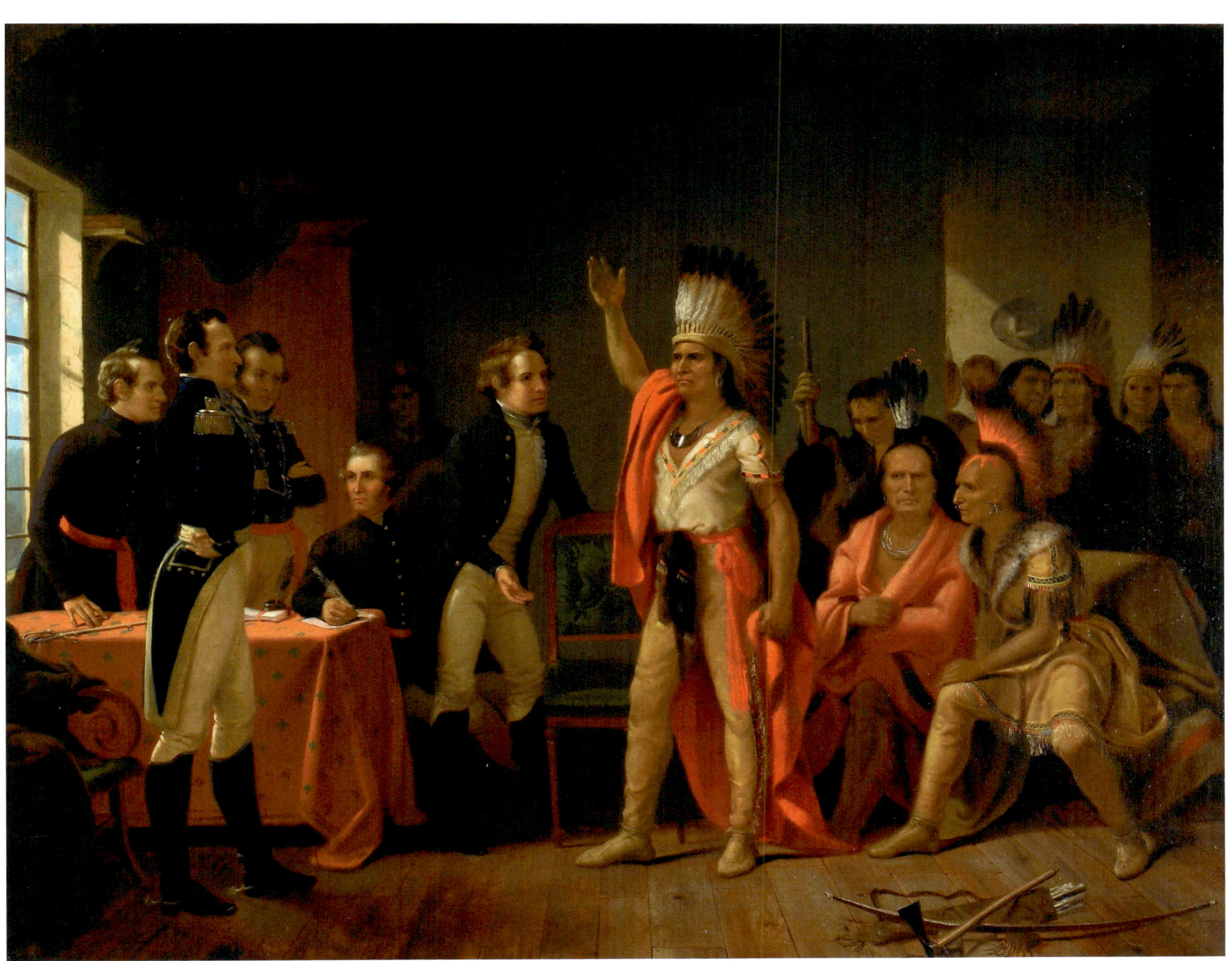

Fur Traders Descending the Missouri

circa 1845
Oil on panel
4 × 6½ inches

Called "half alligator, half horse," the boatmen of the Ohio and Mississippi valleys became American folk heroes in the 1820s and 1830s. Popular serials, novels, and newspaper humorists delighted the public with romantic stories of the rough-and-tumble boatmen of the western rivers. Raised on the lower Missouri River, artist George Caleb Bingham contributed to the myth of the American boatmen with his luminous paintings of flatboats and fur traders along the Mississippi and Missouri rivers. This oil sketch is related to his painting *Fur Traders Descending the Missouri*, in the collection of the Metropolitan Museum of Art. The scene of relaxed figures on a calm river presents the West as a peaceful land of possibility—with a hint of nostalgia. By the time Bingham completed the painting in 1845, steamboats were on the rise and the era of the western boatmen was already fading into the past.

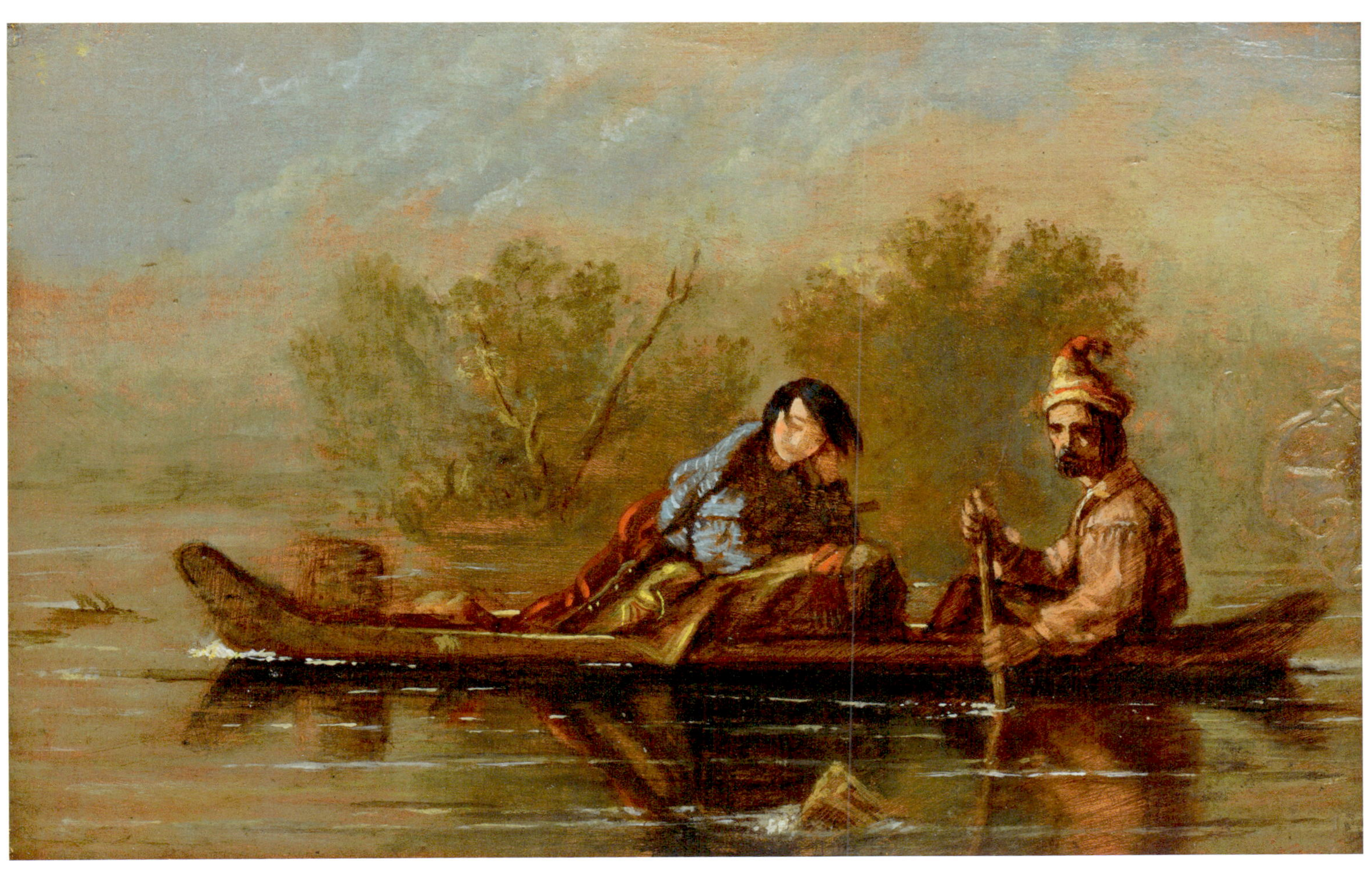

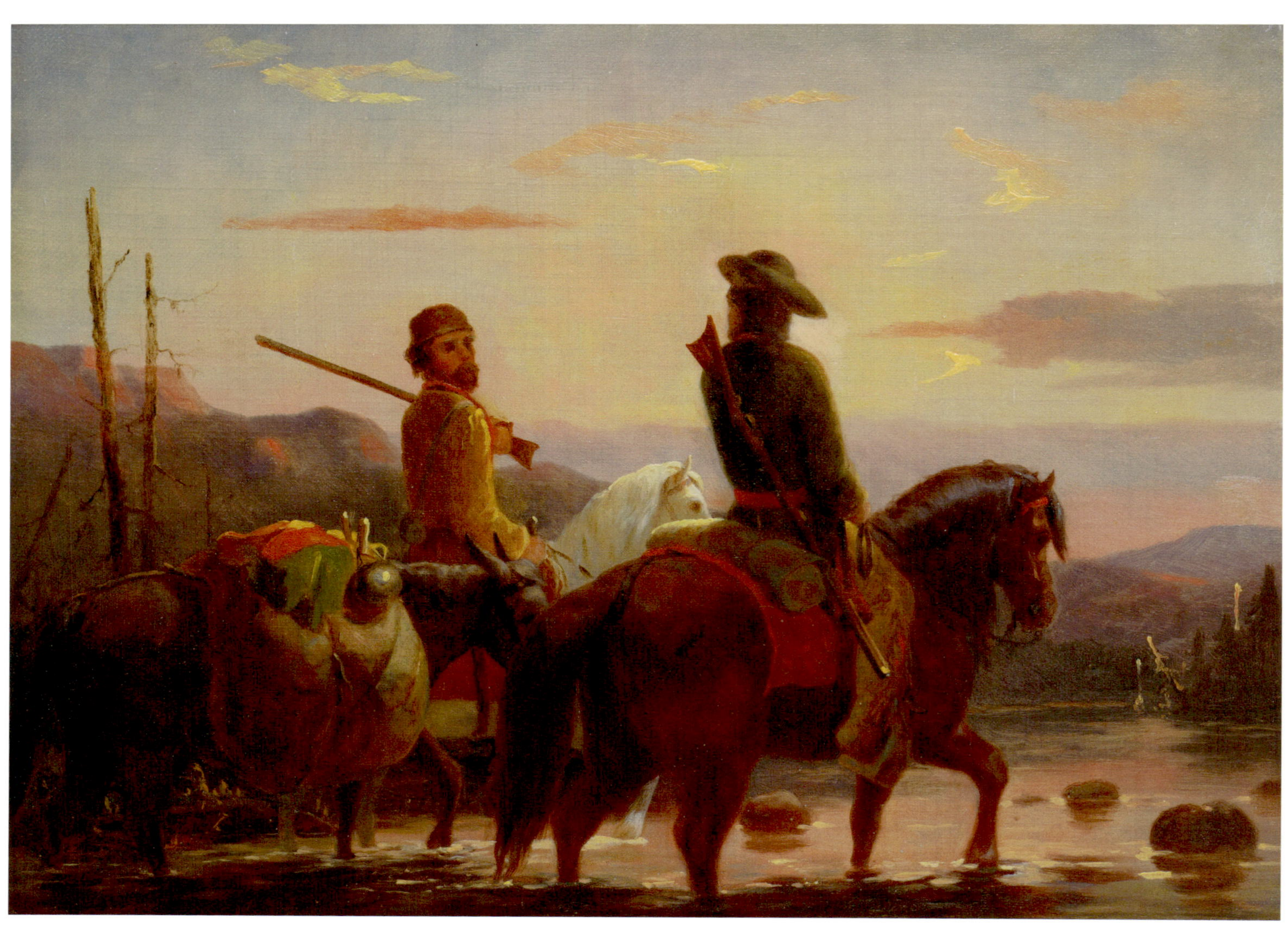

The Trappers

circa 1856
Oil on canvas
8¾ × 12 inches

From his studio in New Jersey, artist William Ranney pre-sented the rugged mountain men of the West as a symbol of an ideal America. Without visiting the Rocky Mountains or seeing these trappers and fur traders at work, Ranney imagined the mountain men as hardy individuals in perfect accord with their environment. In this study, two wilderness hunters ride along the shallow edge of a calm mountain lake, leading their pack mule. The ethereal glowing sky forms a halo around the riders, like a blessing from the land itself. They glance at one another but do not speak, preserving the soft stillness of the tranquil scene. Not long before the Civil War, in an era of profound discord across the United States, Ranney's mountain men symbolized brotherly friend-ship in harmony with nature—the very thing a torn nation needed most.

Canonicus and the Governor of Plymouth

1841
Oil on canvas
28¾ × 35¾ inches

In 1841 artist Albertus del Orient Browere imagined a time two centuries earlier, when the Narragansett chief Canonicus first encountered British settlers in present-day Massachusetts. He was inspired by the description in an 1832 *Indian Biography*: "Early in 1622, their threats of hostility were so open . . . Canonicus sent a herald to Plymouth, who left a bundle of arrows enclosed in a rattle-snake's skin— the customary challenge to war. The Governor dispatched a messenger in return, bearing the same skin stuffed with gunpowder and bullets."* Browere focused this painting on the first part of the challenge: A man in a black tunic approaches the elegantly dressed governor and his Native American allies, raising the symbol of impending war in his clenched fist. While the governor's ally to the right cowers at the gesture, the governor himself remains composed— confident that his heavier firepower will halt the threat of conflict. Browere's painting contains the message that Native American resistance to new Anglo settlers would ultimately prove futile—a haunting message for his own time, in the era of the Indian Removal Act and the gradual rise of immigration into the West.

*B. B. Thatcher, *Indian Biography, or, An historical account of those individuals who have been distinguished among the North American natives as orators, warriors, statesmen, and other remarkable characters*, vol. 1 (New York: J. & J. Harper, 1832), 180-81.

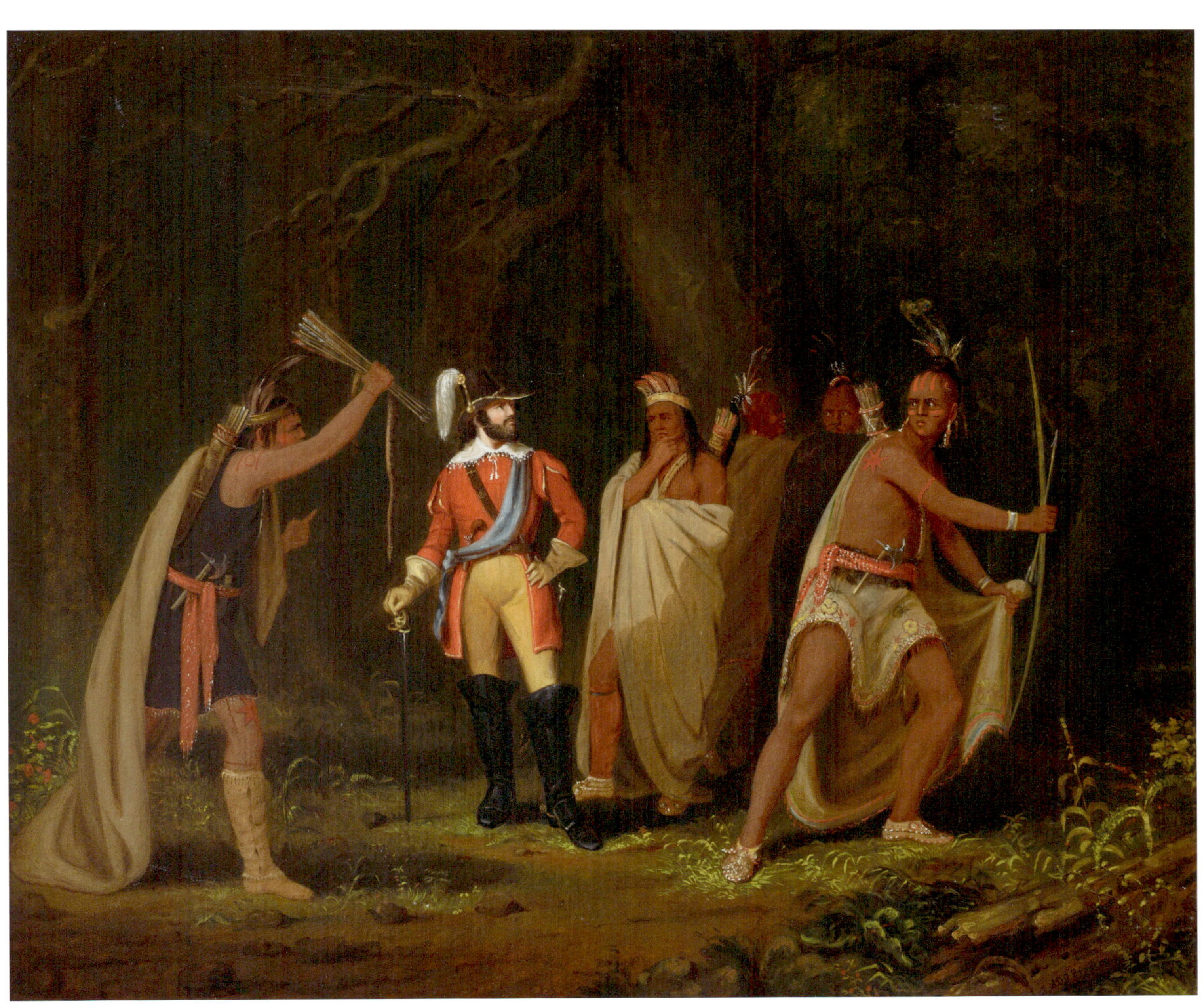

Scene on the Columbia River

1852
Oil on canvas
17⅛ × 21⅛ inches

An adventurer at heart, John Mix Stanley journeyed through vast areas of the American West in search of new subjects to paint. Following his goal of creating his own Indian Gallery in the manner of George Catlin or Charles Bird King, in 1847 Stanley became one of the first Anglo American artists to travel through the Pacific Northwest. Recalling the grand landscapes of the Hudson River school painters in the eastern United States, Stanley suffused this lush landscape along the Columbia River with a soft light, creating a peaceful scene of nature's splendor.

In 1853 Stanley again returned to the northwestern region with the Pacific Railroad Survey led by Isaac Stevens, the new governor of Washington Territory. In an arduous journey up the Missouri River and down the Columbia, the group mapped a railroad route from St. Paul, Minnesota, to Puget Sound. As the official artist on the team, Stanley made copious sketches to illustrate Stevens's report of the expedition. Stanley's illustrations of the Northwest show a bountiful, intriguing landscape, an inviting destination for the new railroad passengers who would eagerly travel west in the late 19th century. Stevens's report—with Stanley's illustrations—would later serve to determine the route for the Northern Pacific Railway, with a western terminus in Tacoma, Washington.

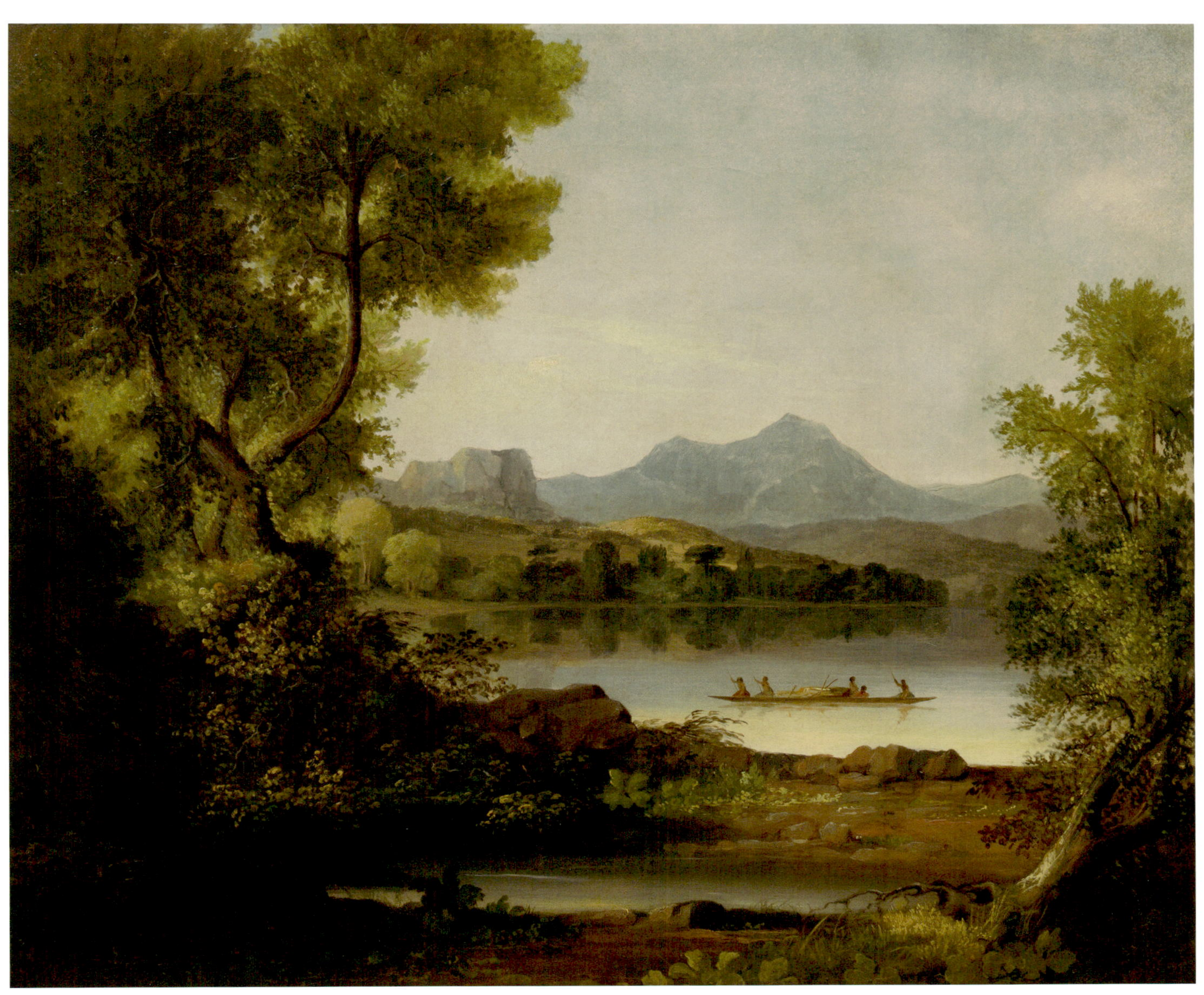

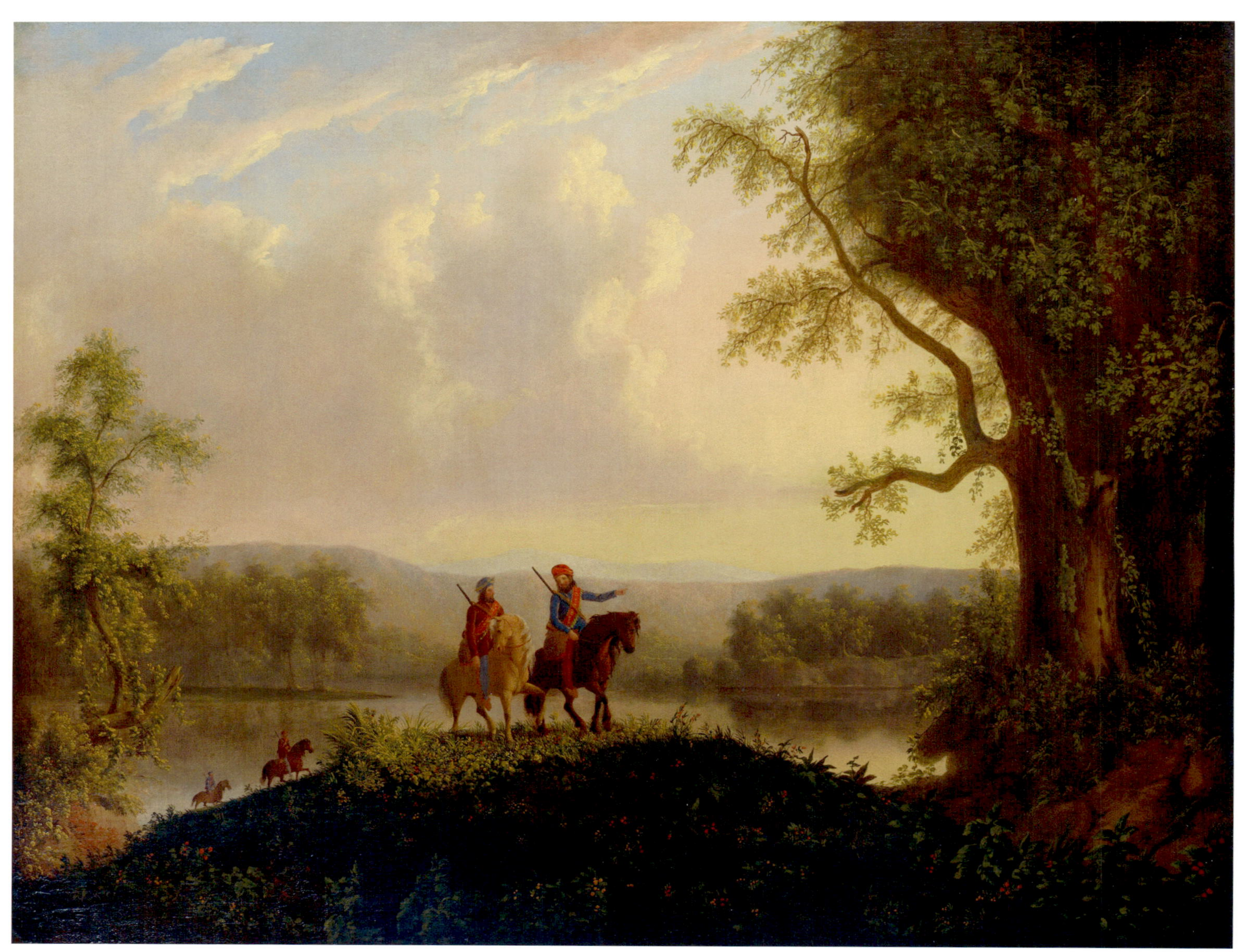

The Lewis and Clark Expedition

circa 1850
Oil on canvas
36½ × 48 inches

Almost 50 years after Meriwether Lewis and William Clark completed their seminal transcontinental journey, stories of their expedition from St. Louis to the Pacific Coast were embedded in the mythic history of the United States. In the 1850s, artist Thomas Mickell Burnham portrayed a scene of Lewis and Clark traveling along a calm river in a verdant landscape, mounted on spirited horses and dressed in vivid, swashbuckling colors, courageously leading their men toward the dark primeval wilderness of the West. In reality, Burnham's painting resembles the hardwood forests of his native New England far more closely than the arid plains and rugged mountains along Lewis and Clark's journey. And rather than an empty wilderness, the Corps of Discovery encountered lands already inhabited by a myriad of Native American cultures. His fictionalized portrayal made the American West an open, plentiful Eden, a symbol of peace and opportunity in the bounty of nature.

Dragoons Crossing River

circa 1844
Oil on canvas
12¼ × 18 inches

Prairie grasses extend in every direction, brown and dusty in the dry heat of late summer. A cacophony of barking dogs, splashing horses, whip cracks, and wagon wheels breaks the calm of the shallow stream. The United States dragoons, mounted infantrymen, do not hesitate to plunge across the muddy waters on their expedition into present-day Nebraska. Despite the dust and the looming gray skies, artist Charles Deas relished the chance to travel with Major Clifton Wharton's expedition of dragoons from Fort Leavenworth. Here he was able to observe the Great Plains directly and could experience the dust in the air and the splattered mud from the stream firsthand. As a result, although both images of the West were painted at nearly the same time, *Dragoons Crossing River* looks nothing like Thomas Mickell Burnham's *The Lewis and Clark Expedition* (page 56). Stripping away romantic notions of the West as a bountiful Eden, Deas instead focused on the raw strength and determination of the soldiers themselves as they travel through an inhospitable land.

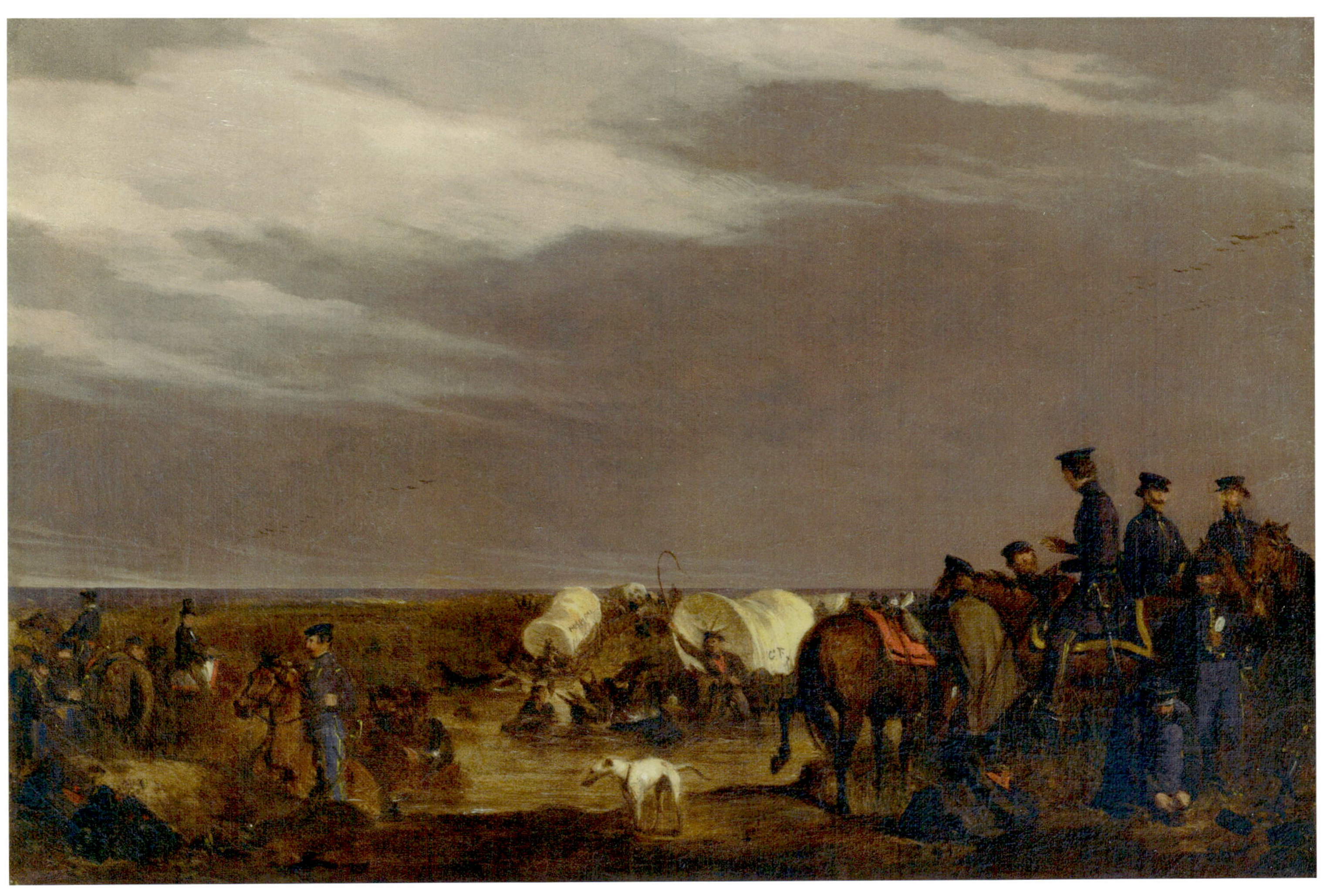

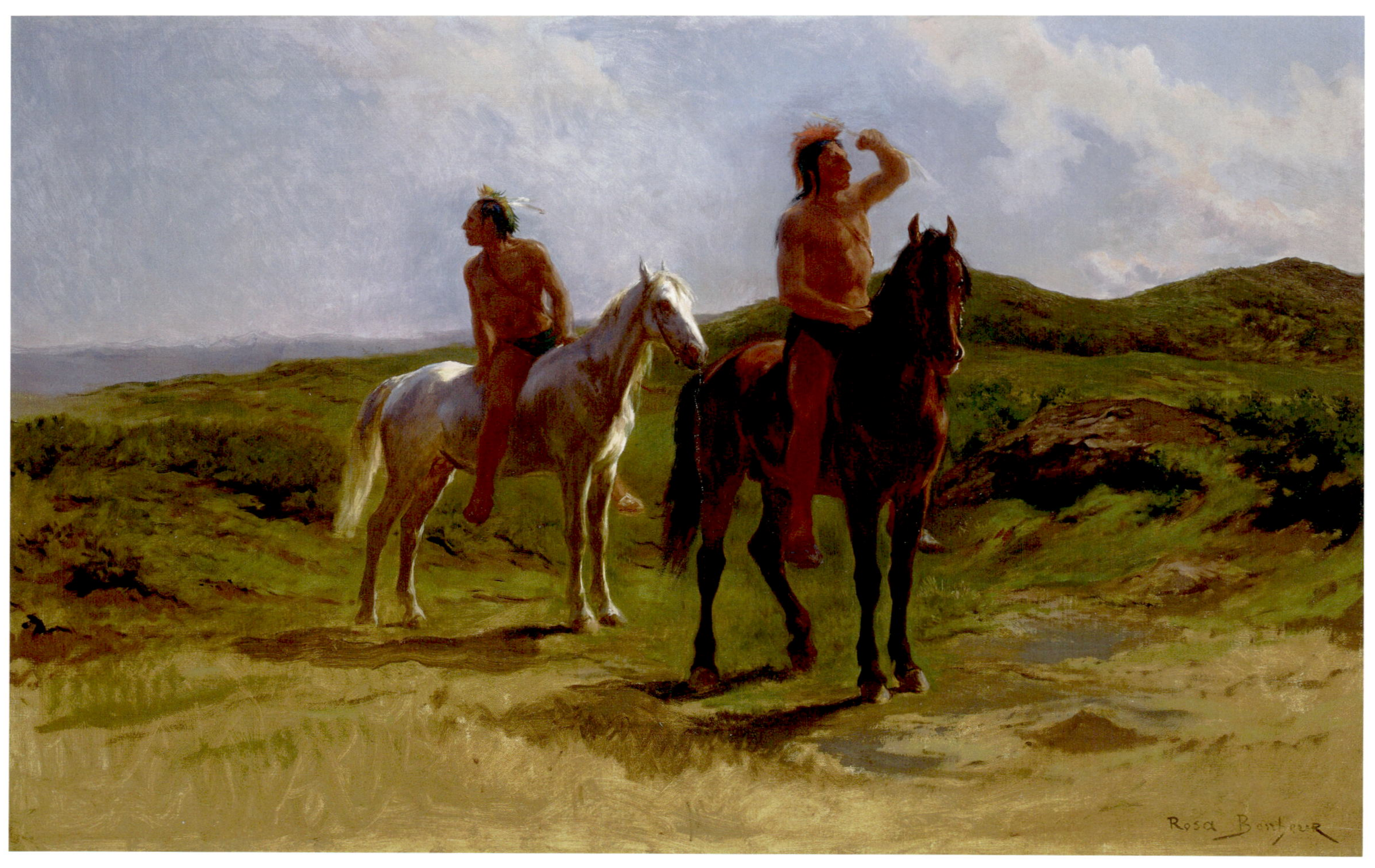

Rocky Bear and Chief Red Shirt

1889
Oil on canvas
25 × 39¾ inches

Rosa Bonheur's lifelong companion Nathalie Micas died in 1889, leaving the successful French artist grieving and alone. To lift her spirits, she visited one of the strangest spectacles in Paris—the encampment of Buffalo Bill's Wild West. William F. "Buffalo Bill" Cody had brought his outdoor exhibition of Native Americans, buffalo, sharpshooters, and cowboys overseas to perform at the 1889 Paris Exposition Universelle and quickly became a top attraction at the fair. On her first visit Bonheur met Lakota cast members Rocky Bear and Red Shirt and marveled at the tipis, campfires, and buffalo grazing on the Wild West grounds. She returned often to sketch the Lakota performers, becoming something of an artist-in-residence. "Observing them at close range really refreshed my sad old mind," Bonheur recalled. "I watched everything they did, and talked as best I could with the warriors."* Here Bonheur captures an impression of Rocky Bear and Red Shirt against a pastoral landscape, perfectly at ease on their horses as they gaze in opposite directions—perhaps a metaphor for glancing back into the past and peering forward into the future.

*Anna Klumpke, *Rosa Bonheur: The Artist's (Auto)biography* (Ann Arbor: University of Michigan Press, 1997), 24, 193.

Study for Cayambe

circa 1857
Oil on paper mounted on board
3½ × 5½ inches

Frederic Edwin Church began his life as an artist by studying in the picturesque hills of Catskill, New York. Like fellow artists Albert Bierstadt and Thomas Moran, Church brought the ideas of the Hudson River school—celebrating the sublime beauty of the untamed wilderness—to far-flung regions of the Americas. Around the same time Bierstadt first traveled west to the Rocky Mountains, Church ventured south to the Andes. On a trip to Ecuador in 1857 Church concentrated on the changing light at Cayambe, a volcano on the Equator's line rising nearly 20,000 feet into the atmosphere. Both magnificent and daunting, the snow-covered peak perfectly represented the vast wilderness of the Americas. Church may have used this small oil study as a preparatory sketch for a larger *Cayambe* painting, four feet across, now in the New-York Historical Society.

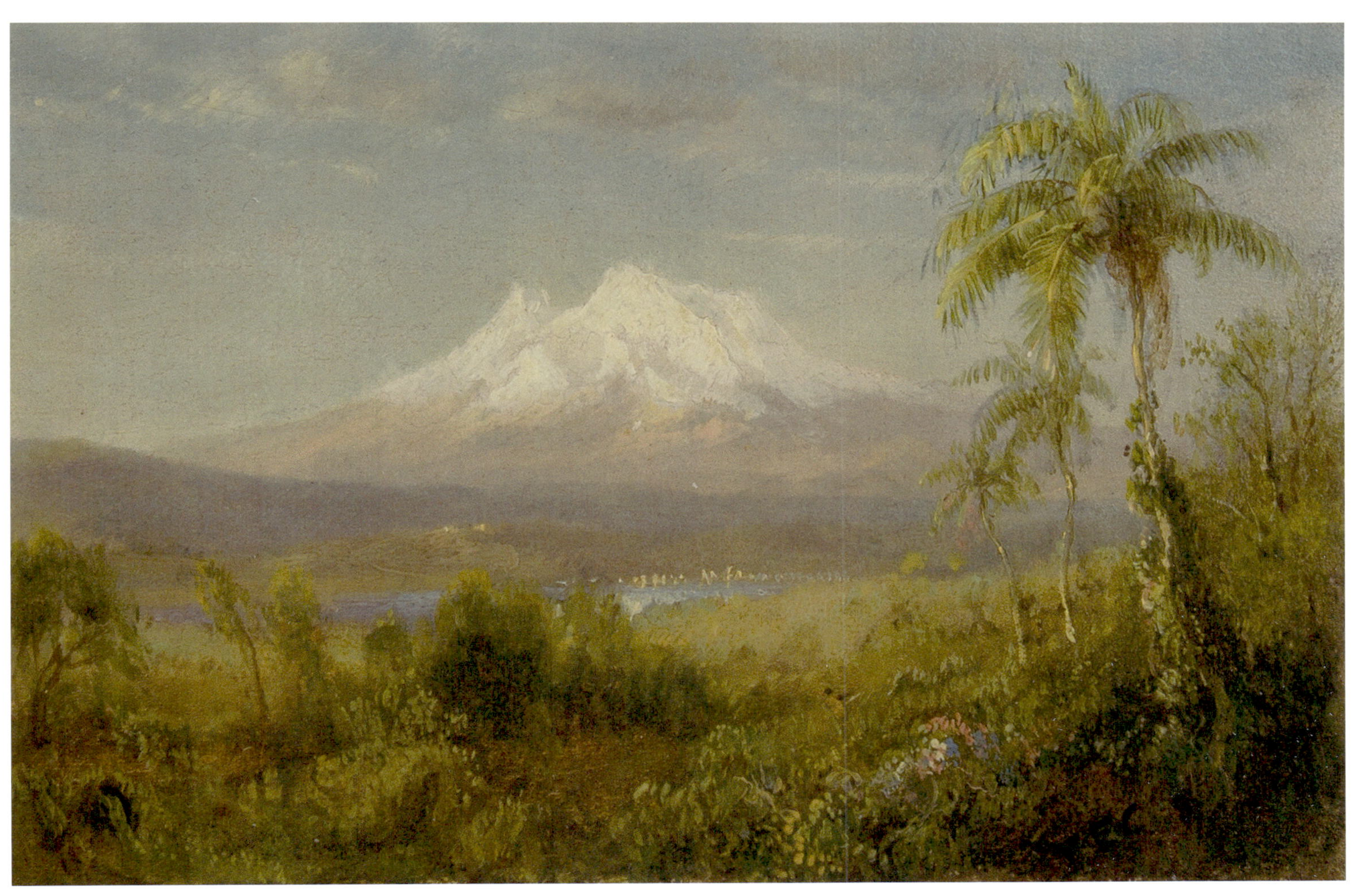

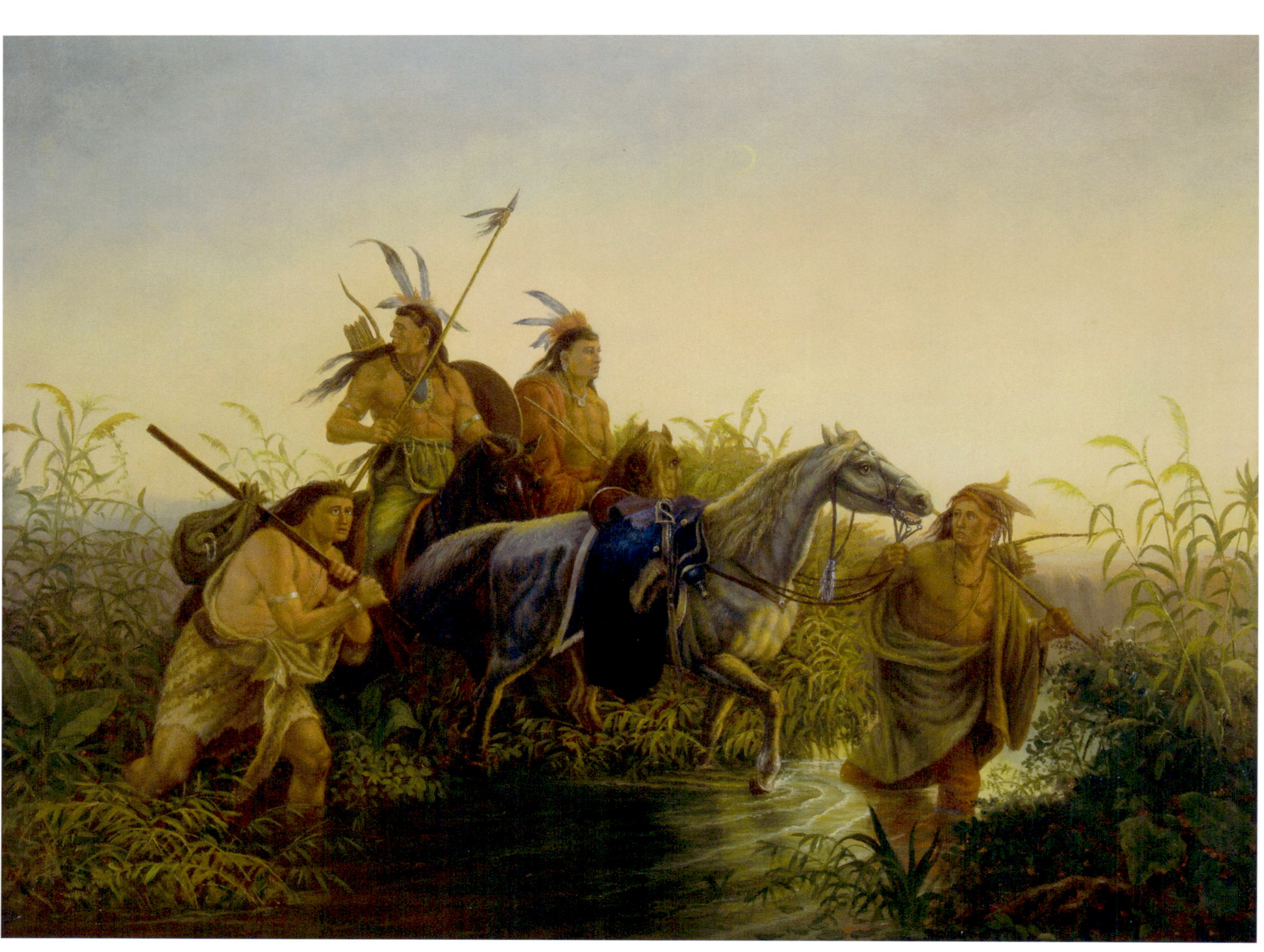

Captive Charger

1854
Oil on paper mounted on board
12⅞ × 17¾ inches

Four men dash through the tall grasses, two glancing nervously over their shoulders for pursuers as they lead their prize—a stolen cavalry horse—across a shallow stream to hide their trail. Smitten with stories of the American frontier, Carl Wimar painted this image of Native Americans on the prairie while living on the other side of the world in Düsseldorf, Germany. The young artist, a German immigrant to St. Louis, had returned to his native country to study painting under Emanuel Leutze. In the imagined scene of *Captive Charger*, Wimar constructs the message that Native American attempts to thwart the Anglo settlers—represented by the proud horse—will ultimately fail. While these men have accomplished the small victory of winning a horse, the setting sun and waning moon in the background symbolized, for 19th century audiences, the approach of an inevitable defeat.

Departure of an Indian War Party

1865
Oil on board
17¼ × 24¼ inches

From his first journey west of the Mississippi in 1859, Albert Bierstadt became famous for his immense, operatic paintings of the Rocky Mountains, rendered in crisp detail with dramatic light washing across craggy peaks. Many of his grand paintings, influenced by his studies in Düsseldorf, Germany, focus almost entirely on lofty mountaintops, deeply carved valleys, and towering waterfalls—the largest, most prominent features of the land. But in *Departure of an Indian War Party* Bierstadt shifted his focus to the people who lived in the midst of the landscapes he loved. In this smaller, more intimate scene, horses splash through a shallow stream with a faithful dog bounding ahead. The men on horseback converse with one another under the shade of a cottonwood tree. A village humming with activity emerges from the mist behind them, below soaring mountain peaks in the far background. The calm scene appears to be an ideal image of humans in harmony with nature—but the title foreshadows an impending conflict, adding an underlying tension to the painting.

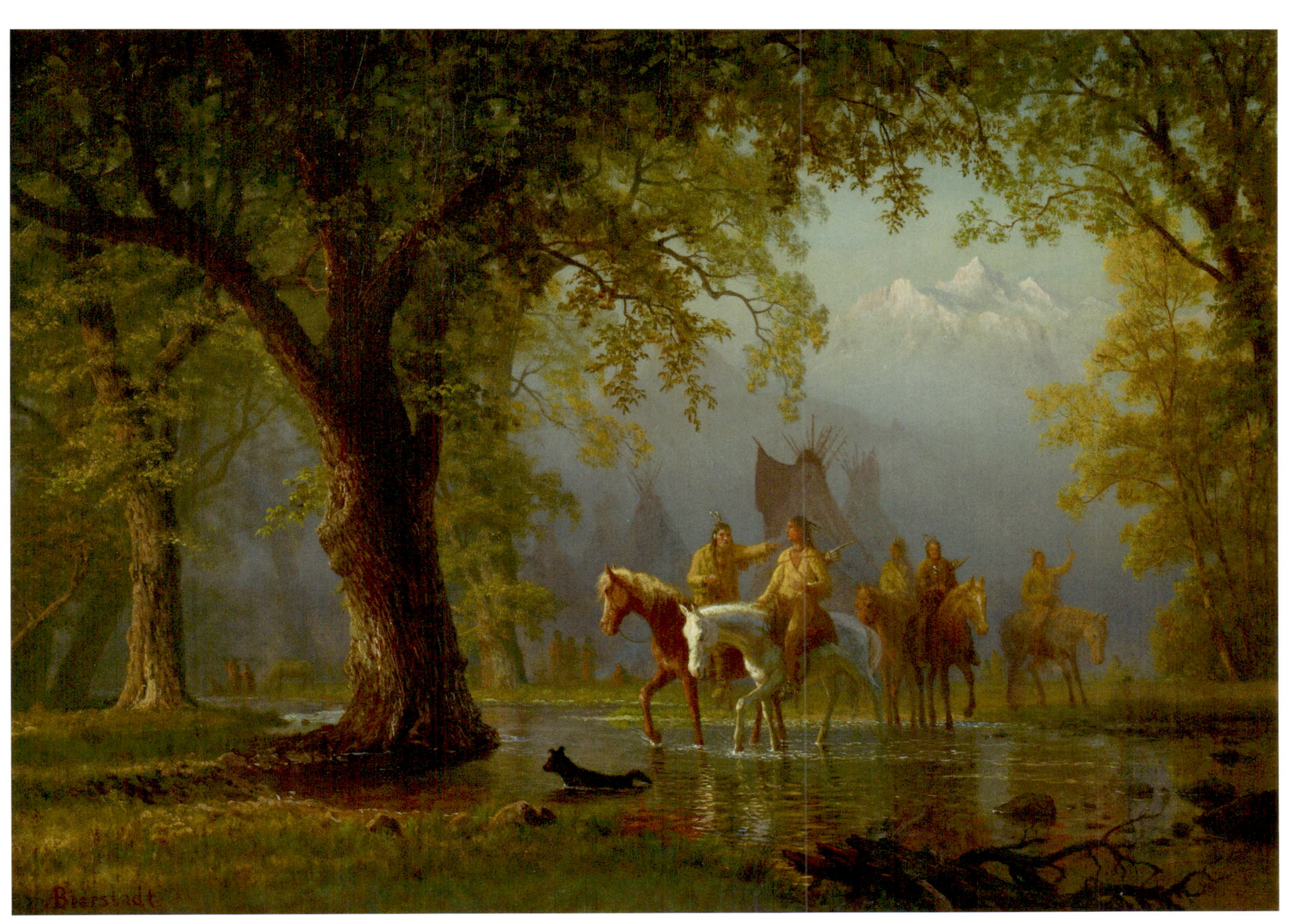

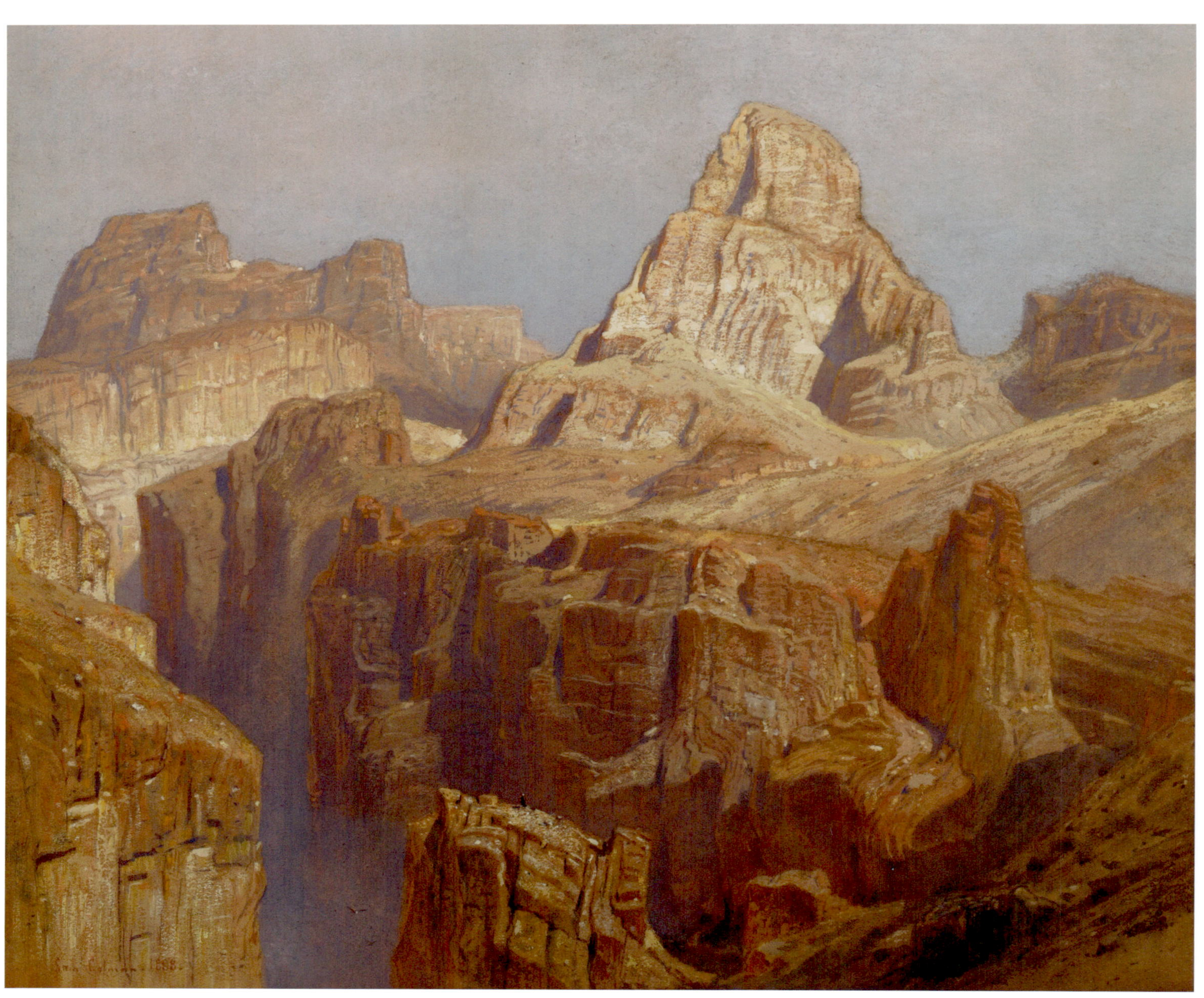

The Grand Canyon

1888
Pastel and watercolor on board
17 × 21 inches

With deft handling of line and form, Samuel Colman renders one cleft of the colossal Grand Canyon with soft tones and geometric precision. Like his fellow artist Thomas Moran, Colman found watercolor to be an ideal medium for the hues of the American West. By depicting mountains and rock features in chalky pastel over washes of watercolor, he created unique, tactile surfaces that convey the rough textures and smooth planes of the western landscape. A constant traveler, Colman made multiple trips to the Grand Canyon in the 1880s. Following the example of Asher B. Durand, Colman brought influences from Hudson River school landscape painting to the towering natural features of the American West. In this image, the only living creatures are two tiny birds in the foreground, providing a sense of scale for the tall rock uplifts around them. By focusing purely on the unique forms of the canyon's spires and cliff bands Colman manages to convey the vast, unearthly feel of this place.

FREDERICK BILLING (1835–1914)

THOMAS MORAN (1837–1926)

PETER MORAN (1841–1914)

Falls of the Grand Canyon of the Yellowstone River

circa 1894
Oil on canvas
28 × 24 inches

In 1894 Frederick Billing had the chance of a lifetime—to explore Yellowstone with painter Thomas Moran, one of the artists responsible for making the remarkable area famous. In 1872, it was Moran's watercolors that helped convince Congress to preserve the Yellowstone region as the first national park in the United States. A businessman who lived and traveled in the West, Billing eagerly sought opportunities to paint the American landscape when he could. After befriending Thomas and his brother Peter Moran and touring Yellowstone's most famous sights with them, Billing was delighted when the Morans offered to contribute to his painting of the lower falls of the Yellowstone River. Thomas painted a large, gnarled tree in the left foreground, balancing the painting's composition between the tree and the cascading waterfall in the background. Peter, who preferred animal subjects, painted a proud stag in the foreground as a lone observer of the scene. When the painting was finished, all three artists initialed the canvas in the lower right corner, recording their collaboration and friendship.

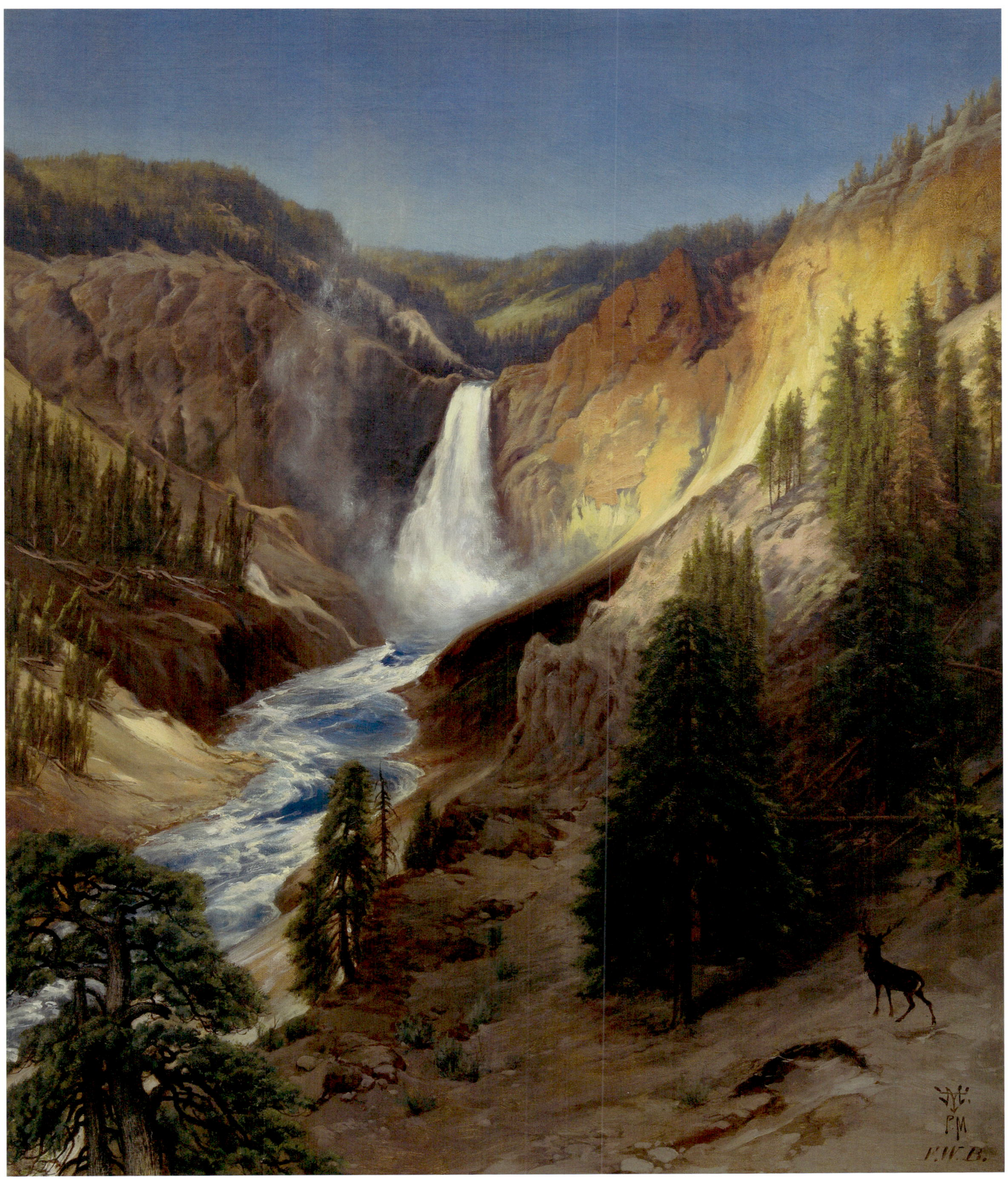

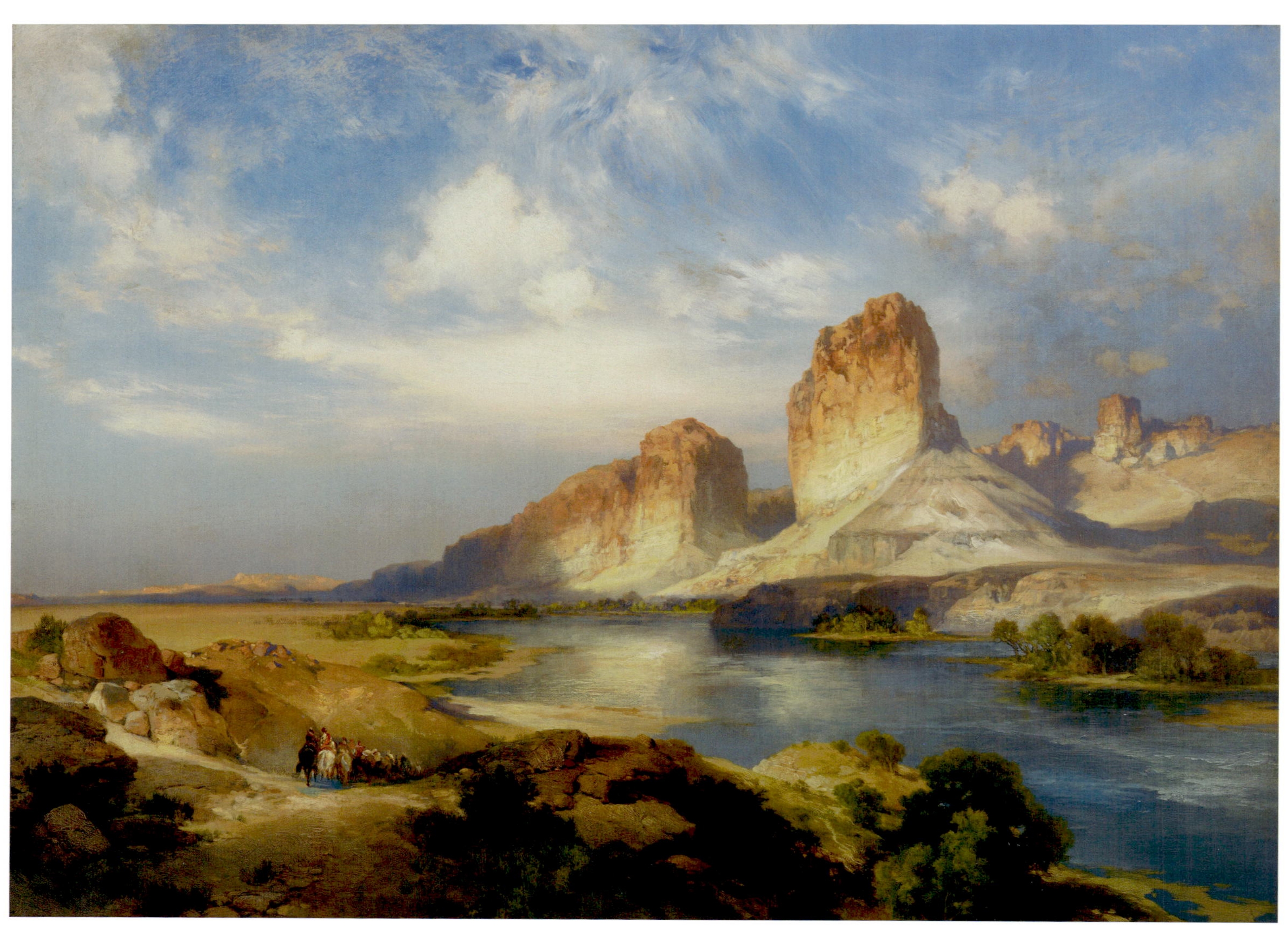

Green River, Wyoming

1907
Oil on canvas
20 × 28½ inches

When Thomas Moran stepped off the train in Green River, Wyoming, he did not notice the rail cars or the newly constructed buildings clustered around the railroad junction. Instead, it was the golden sandstone cliffs against a deep blue sky that held him riveted. He dashed off a quick pencil drawing with dabs of watercolor, capturing the towering rock formations in loose flowing colors—his first landscape sketch in the American West. From the time he first visited Green River in 1871 to the end of his career, the golden cliffs remained one of Moran's favorite subjects. As his career evolved, so did his approach to the sandstone spires. Moran's earliest paintings of Green River are bathed in a luminous glow, with smudged shadows and soft light. In this later painting the focus is sharper, with crisp contours defining the rock faces and wispy cirrus clouds. The sheer cliffs and calm river resonate in bright jewel-like tones, and a tiny party of riders on horseback emphasizes the grand scale of the landscape features. Moran chose not to include the town and rail lines running through the river valley, creating instead a pristine, idealized image of the land in the West.

Group of Buffalo on the Plains

1883
Oil on canvas
22 × 30⅛ inches

As a teenager in the 1850s, John Howland witnessed end-less herds of buffalo when he visited the plains of Nebraska Territory—a sight he never forgot. In 1873 Howland settled in Denver, becoming one of the first Anglo professional artists to reside west of the Mississippi River. In addition to work-ing as a painter, Howland helped promote the cultural life of the growing city by founding the Denver Arts Club in 1886. While he gained recognition for his portraits and landscape paintings, Howland found himself drawn to the plight of the buffalo. By the time he painted *Group of Buffalo on the Plains* in 1883, the thundering herds he had seen in his youth were almost demolished. The setting sun behind this group indi-cates that their time in the West is coming to a close. Two of the animals stare directly toward the viewer, seeming to demand recognition of their importance in the West—and their peril.

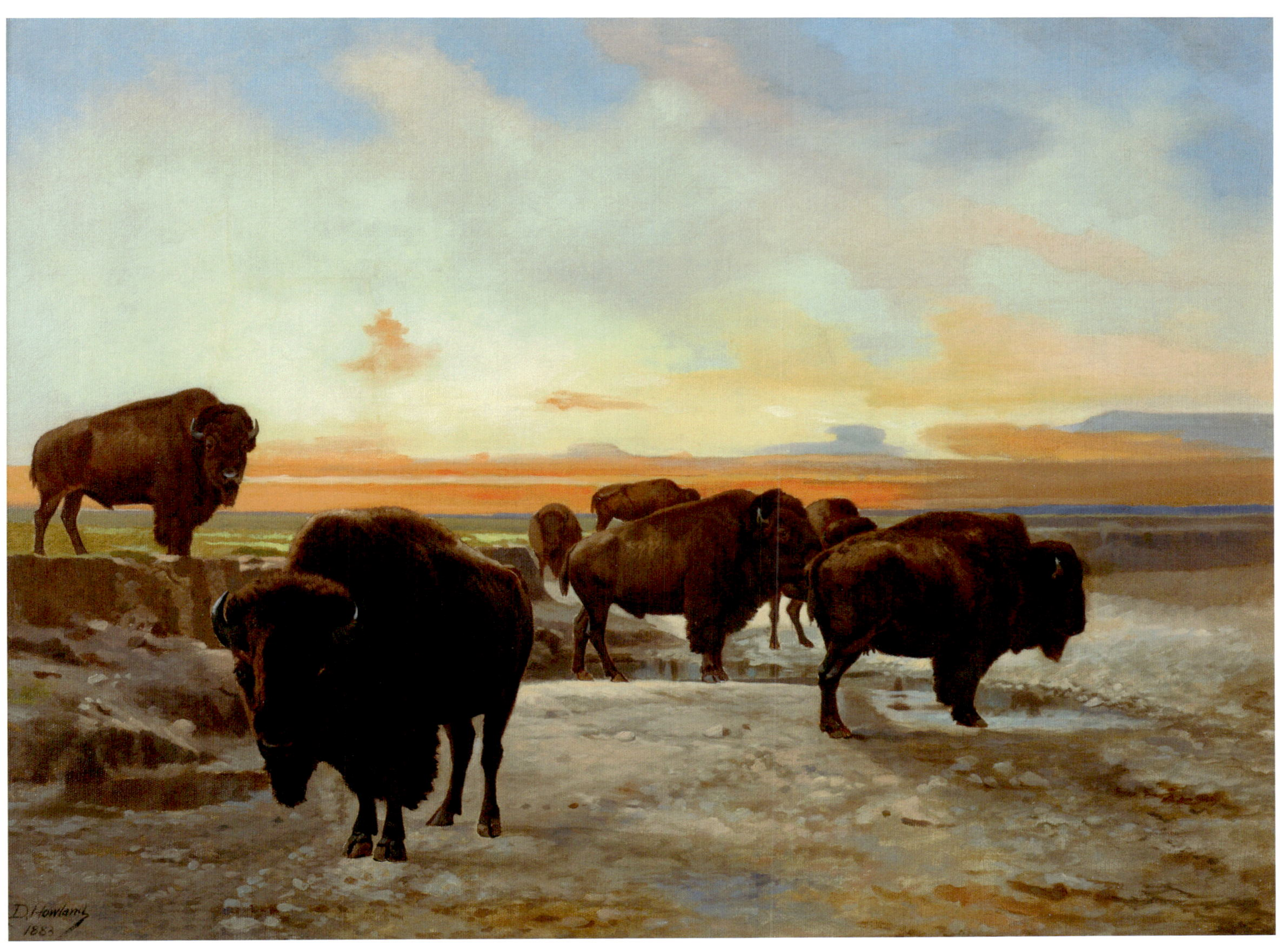

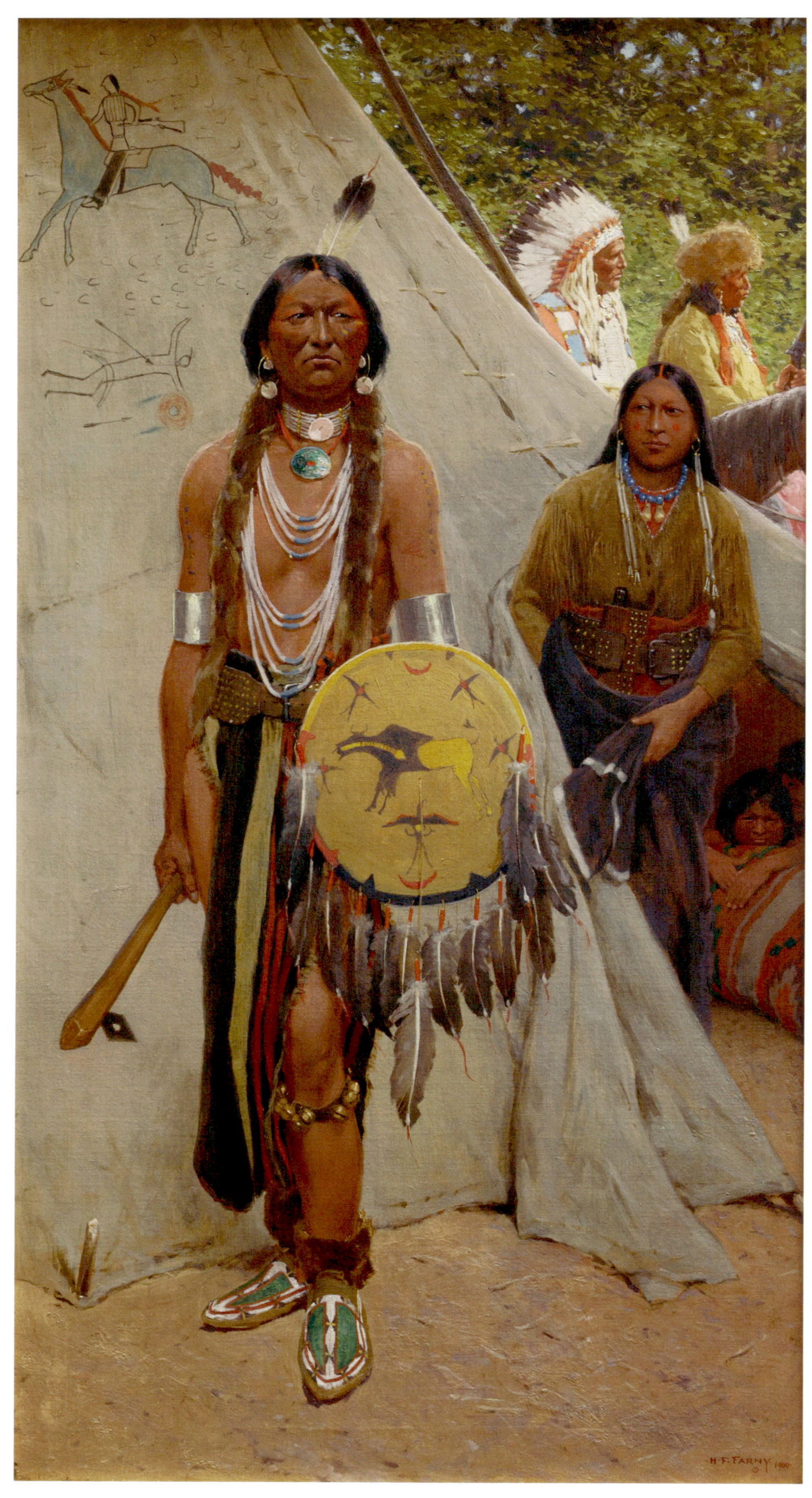

Indians

1900
Oil on canvas
40⅛ × 22 inches

Tension runs through a calm moment between two people. Rather than portraying the height of an action-filled event, artist Henry Farny frequently painted quiet, everyday scenes that contain subtle clues to a larger story. Here, a man of the Great Plains stands erect and resolute before his home, his wife behind him. Farny renders him in exquisite detail, adorned with a studded belt, polished metal armbands, elaborately beaded moccasins, brass bells, and cascading rows of shell necklaces. Yet in spite of the man's ornate regalia and quiet stance, his expression looks grim and he grips a wooden club with a sharp metal point in his right hand. In the background two men ride past, showing that people are moving and gathering. A painting on the side of the tipi shows one warrior charging on horseback and another falling wounded, foreshadowing a coming battle.

Farny's sympathetic views toward Native Americans were shaped by his western travels in the 1880s, when he observed appalling conditions on newly established reservations. As a result, rather than portraying a Plains warrior as a faceless, violent menace, in this painting Farny shows a man who simply seeks to protect those he loves—a feeling with which we can all identify.

Shoshonie Scout, 1877–78

1901
Oil on canvas
25 × 19 inches

When Edgar S. Paxson left his home near Buffalo, New York, and moved to Montana in 1877, he embraced a thoroughly western persona. Like William F. "Buffalo Bill" Cody, he wore his hair long and sported a full mustache and pointed goatee in the style of a frontier scout. He adopted the pseudonym "Pistol Grip" for articles he wrote in the hunting journal *American Field.* A self-taught artist, he began by painting signs and theatrical backdrops and gradually shifted to easel painting. To find subjects to paint, he gathered information about past events on the Great Plains by interviewing both Native Americans and US Army veterans. In addition to his magnum opus—a six by nine foot painting depicting the height of action in the Battle of the Little Bighorn—he also painted numerous portraits of Native Americans in Montana. This portrait of a dignified Shoshone scout in the 1870s shows Paxson's interest in the individual characters who shaped the American West in the late 19th century.

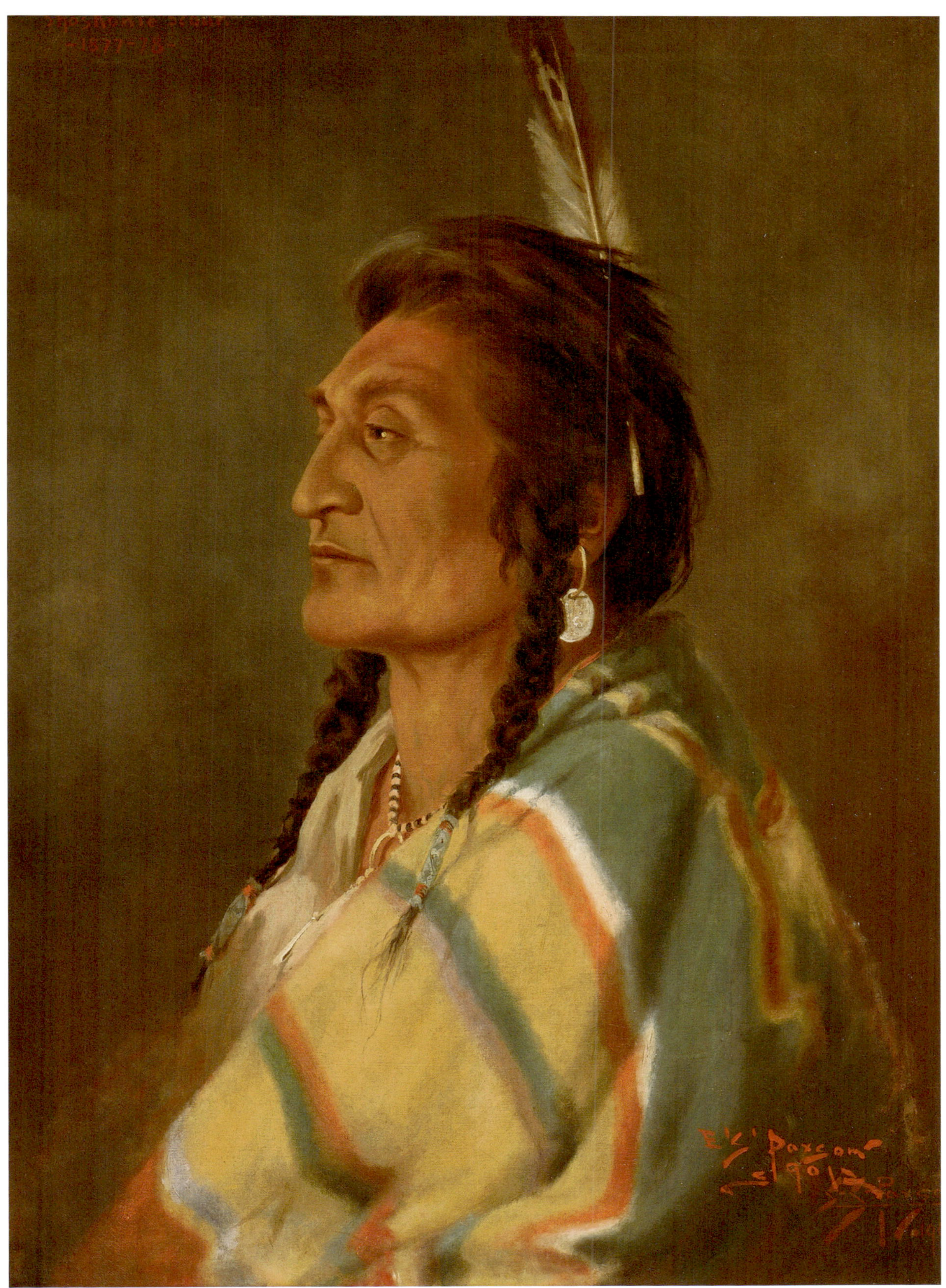

After the Drive

date unknown
Oil on canvas
24⅛ × 36⅛ inches

Thundering hooves pound the dry desert earth as the dust-caked riders shout, urging their spirited horses into a gallop, free at last from the endless days of driving slow-moving cattle forward. Herman Hansen's *After the Drive* shows an ideal image of hearty cattlemen riding into town for a celebration after the hard work is finished.

Hansen was born in Germany and moved to the United States as a young man. After studying at the Art Institute of Chicago, he embraced a life-long interest in the American West by permanently relocating to San Francisco in 1882. From his California home, Hansen observed a gradual change in the perception of western cattlemen. Thanks to performers and writers such as Buffalo Bill and Theodore Roosevelt, cowboys were elevated from unruly, shiftless degenerates to dashing American folk heroes by the end of the 19th century. Although barbed wire, railroad tracks, and roads had forever changed the vast open range cattle industry by the time Hansen painted *After the Drive,* he presented the cowboy as a new American archetype, a fitting metaphor for an exuberant young nation galloping forward into the modern era.

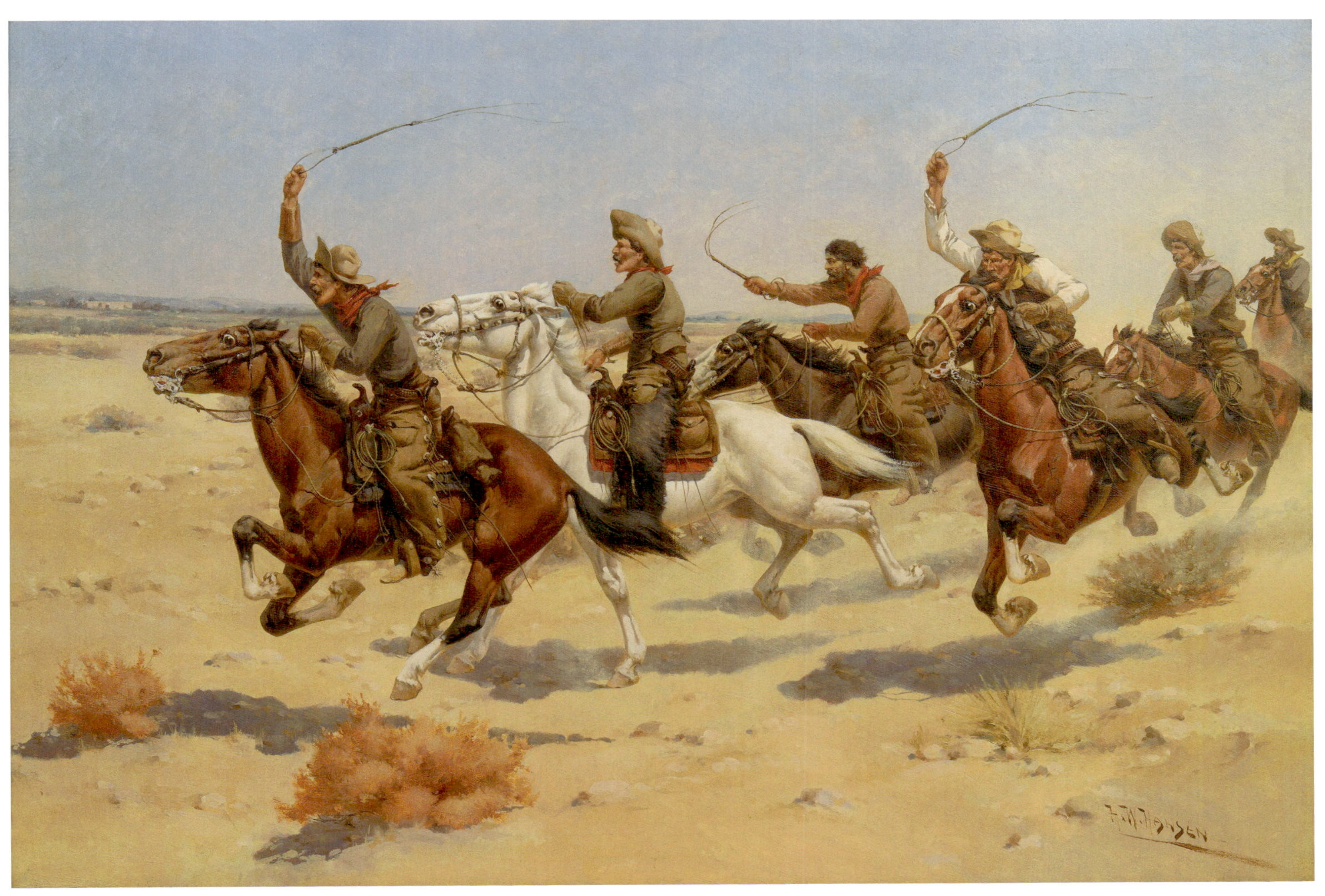

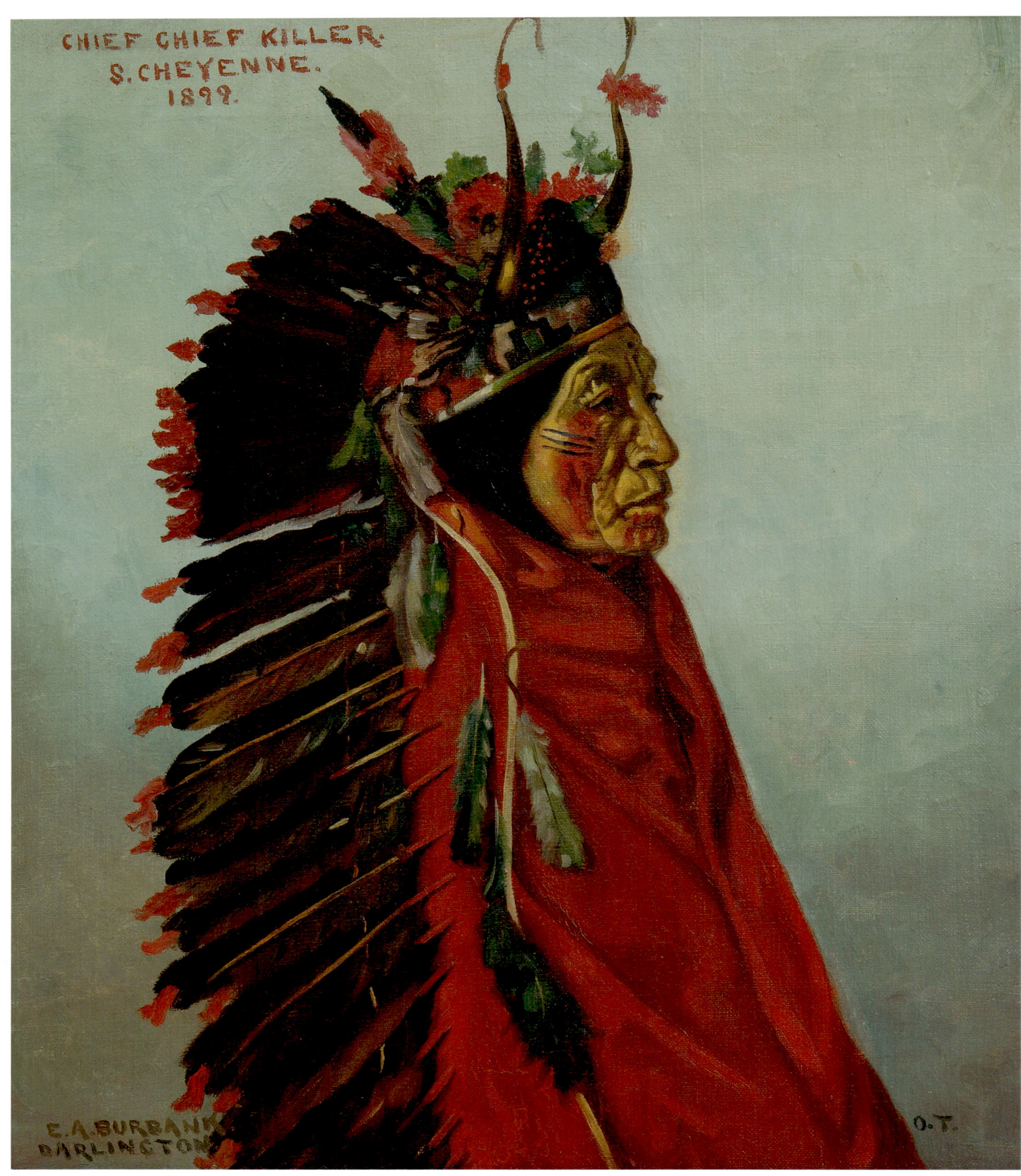
CHIEF CHIEF KILLER.
S. CHEYENNE.
1899.
E.A. BURBANK
DARLINGTON
O.T.

Chief Chief Killer, S. Cheyenne

1899
Oil on canvas
15 ⅞ × 13 ⅞ inches

Elbridge Ayer Burbank first traveled west in 1897 after his uncle Edward E. Ayer—the first president of the Field Museum of Natural History in Chicago—commissioned him to create portraits of prominent Native American leaders in the West. The commission changed Burbank's career. Thrilled with the work, he journeyed far and wide seeking new subjects. By the end of his career Burbank had created more than 1,200 portraits of Native Americans, depicting leaders and ordinary individuals in oil, watercolor, and conté crayon. Two years after beginning his commission in the West, Burbank painted this polished portrait of Chief Chief Killer in Darlington, Oklahoma. The crimson-cloaked figure seems to leap off its subtly shaded green background. With careful consideration of color and precise rendering of the chief's face and detailed split-horn bonnet, Burbank created a proud image of the Southern Cheyenne leader.

Taos Indian Man

circa 1920
Oil on canvas
24 × 20 inches

One of the "Duveneck Boys," Julius Rolshoven studied art with a group of boisterous expatriate youths in Germany and Italy under American painter Frank Duveneck. Duveneck's paintings of expressive individuals rendered in a free, spontaneous style would remain an important influence on Rolshoven's work throughout his career. Traveling to far-flung locations, from Venice to Paris to Tunisia, Rolshoven constantly sought new characters to paint. When the onset of World War I sent him back to the United States, he paid a visit to his friend Irving Couse in northern New Mexico —and found a remarkable source of inspiration in the cultures of the Southwest. In *Taos Indian Man*, he renders a proud Native American gentleman in vivid hues with loose brushstrokes, using the expressive style he had developed during his European studies. Carefully posed in Rolshoven's studio, the figure with draped blanket and large earthenware jars recalls his images of Tunisia—blending influences from overseas with the patterns, colors, and textures of the American Southwest.

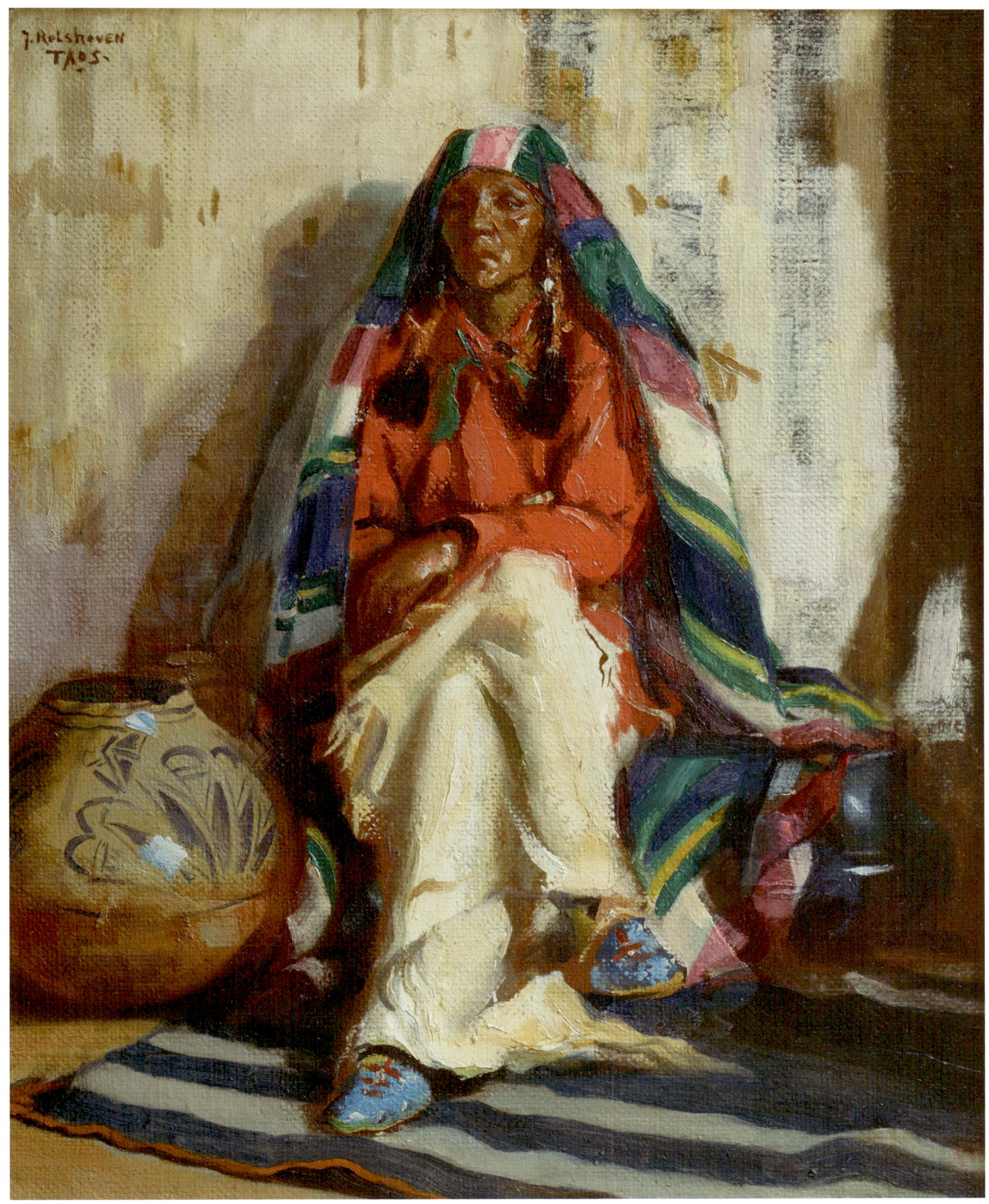
J. Kulshoven
TAOS.

JOSEPH HENRY SHARP (1859–1953)

Taos Indians in the Sunlight

circa 1920
Oil on canvas
18 × 24 inches

When Joseph Henry Sharp first visited New Mexico in 1883, he found a very different place from the Great Plains region portrayed by Frederic Remington and dramatized by Buffalo Bill's Wild West. The rolling hills, calm sunlight, and historic roots of the Southwest represented a location distinct from that of the action-packed scenes of buffalo hunts and cowboys often depicted in popular media. The Taos Pueblo architecture and the surrounding high desert landscapes captivated Sharp, and he eagerly encouraged other artists to visit the area. By 1908 he had purchased a home in Taos, and after 1910 it became his primary residence.

Rather than representing an elaborate vision of the past, *Taos Indians in the Sunlight* shows a dirt road in Sharp's own day, with local residents resting against an adobe wall in the golden afternoon sun. Rendered in a loose painting style with quick dabs of color, the image shows the calm beauty of northern New Mexico. By depicting a scene with no overt signs of industrialization, Sharp portrays Taos as a place frozen in time, removed from the hurry and noise of modern society.

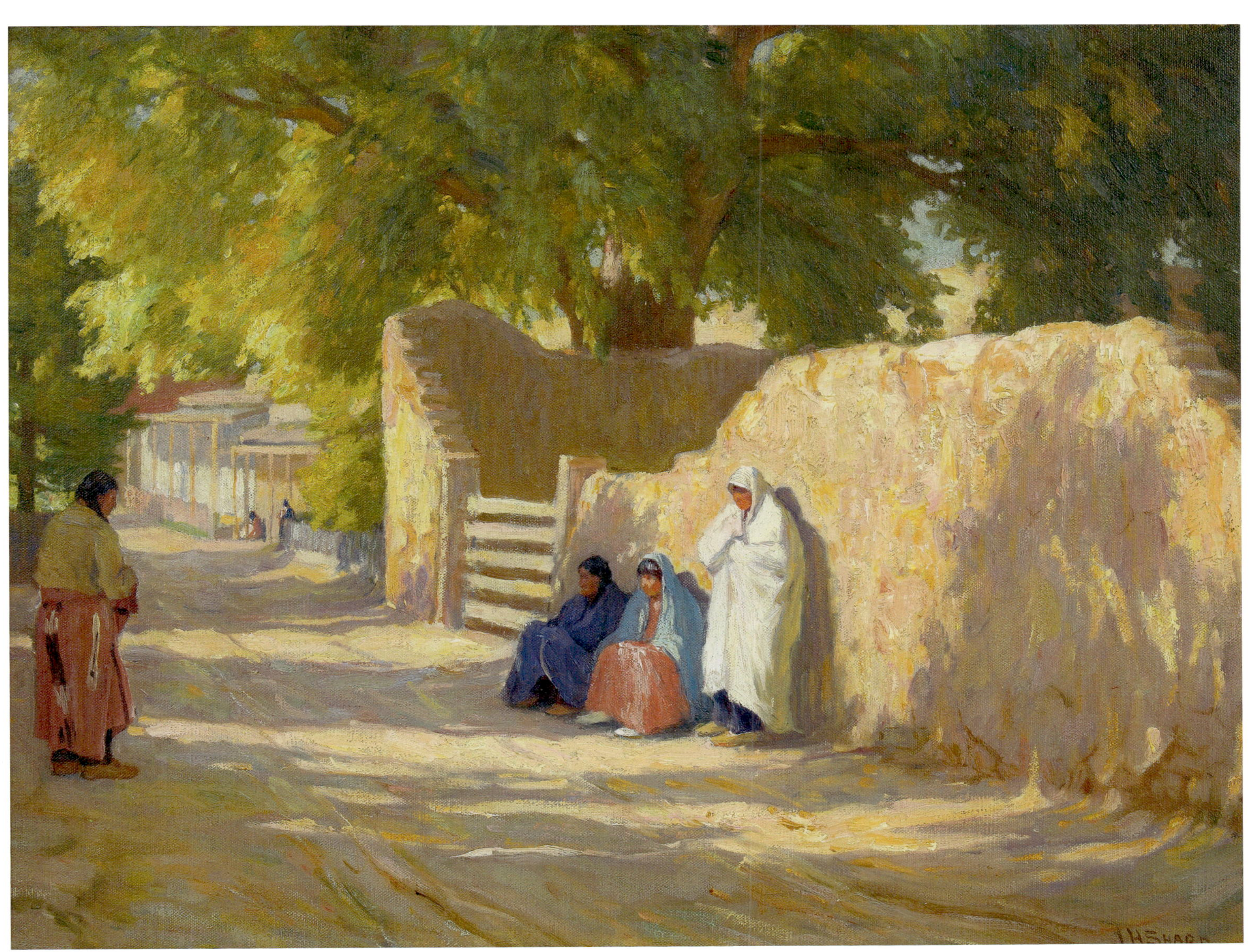

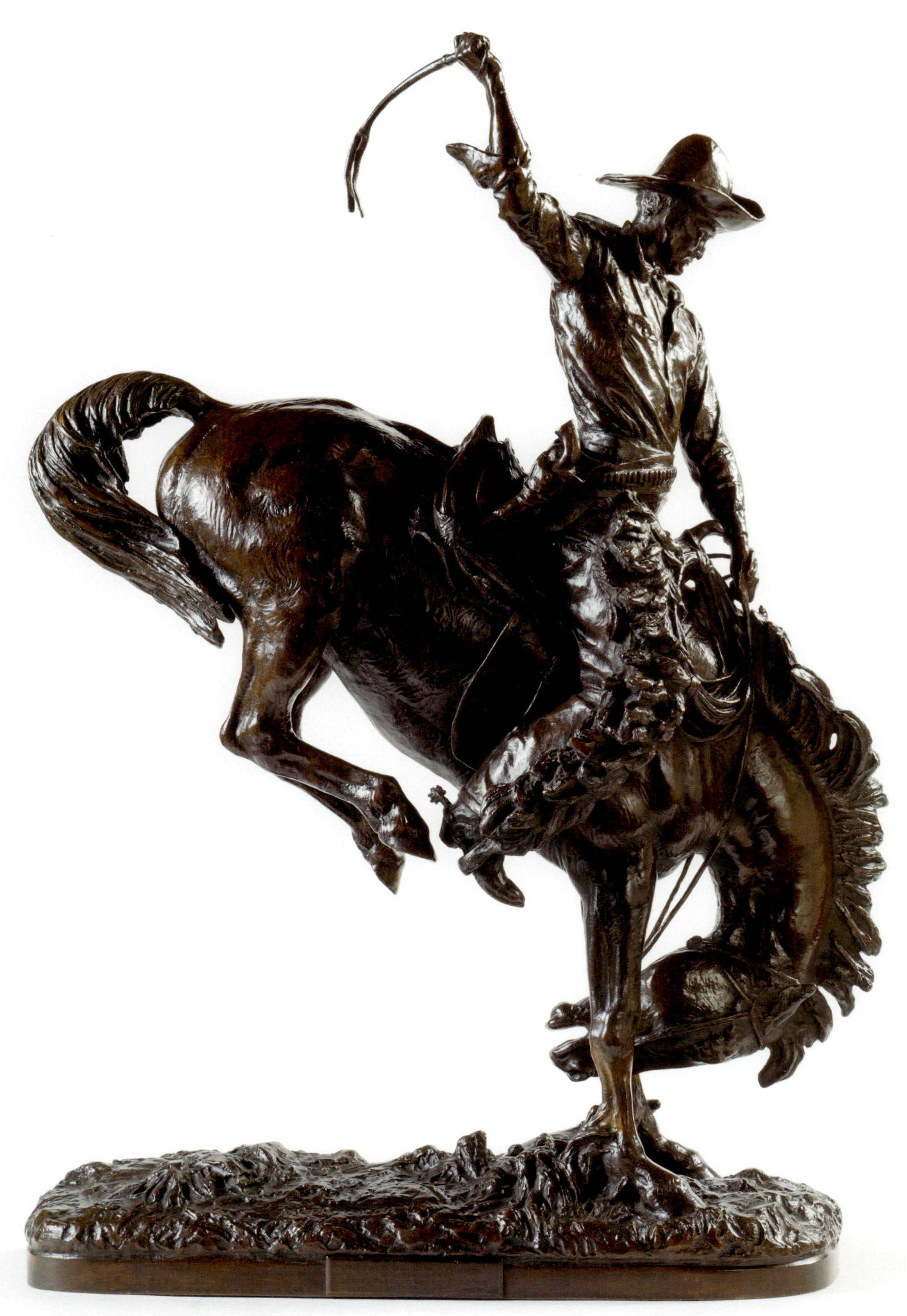

Buckaroo

1915
Bronze
28⅜ × 20½ × 8 inches

"When you want to get a figure of a cowboy on a bucking horse," explained sculptor Alexander Phimister Proctor, "you get a cowboy and put him on the horse and then let them buck past the door of your studio."* On his first visit to the rodeo at the Pendleton Round-Up in Oregon in 1914, Proctor was captivated by the wild, magnificent bucking horses. He selected a local rodeo star, Bill "Slim" Ridings, to model for him, and observed the rider and plunging horse as he sculpted in clay. Proctor's resulting sculpture caught the rough, earth-shaking motion of a bucking bronco in graceful, fluid curves flowing from the horse's bowed neck to its arched tail. Proctor titled the work *Buckaroo*, a term referring to cowboys of the Northwest and Great Basin regions—and thought to be an Anglicization of the Spanish word *vaquero*.

*"Cowboys Live in Clay Under Skillful Hands of A. Phimister Proctor," *Portland Evening Telegram*, July 24, 1915, quoted in Peter H. Hassrick, *Wildlife and Western Heroes: Alexander Phimister Proctor, Sculptor* (Fort Worth, TX: Amon Carter Museum, 2003), 171.

Signal of Peace

1890
Bronze
10½ × 9 × 2¾ inches

Not long after Cyrus Dallin arrived in Paris to study sculpture, the American artist from Utah was confronted by an astonishing sight. Buffalo Bill's Wild West opened in Paris in the spring of 1889, with Native Americans, cowboys, marksmen, and William F. Cody himself performing scenes from the American frontier in the shadow of the newly constructed Eiffel Tower. Watching the Lakota cast members evoked Dallin's memories of the Ute and Paiute peoples he had seen in Utah as a boy. As French artist Rosa Bonheur sketched Native Americans in the Wild West camp (page 60), Dallin was inspired to begin modeling *Signal of Peace*, an equestrian sculpture loosely based on the Lakota performers in Paris.

By portraying a Native American leader with his spear pointing upward in a sign of peace, Dallin suggested the sense of trust and openness Native Americans brought to their first meetings with Anglo travelers in their land. Sympathetic to the grave injustices dealt to Native peoples in the West, Dallin made *Signal of Peace* the first of four equestrian sculptures representing the history and plight of Native Americans in his day.

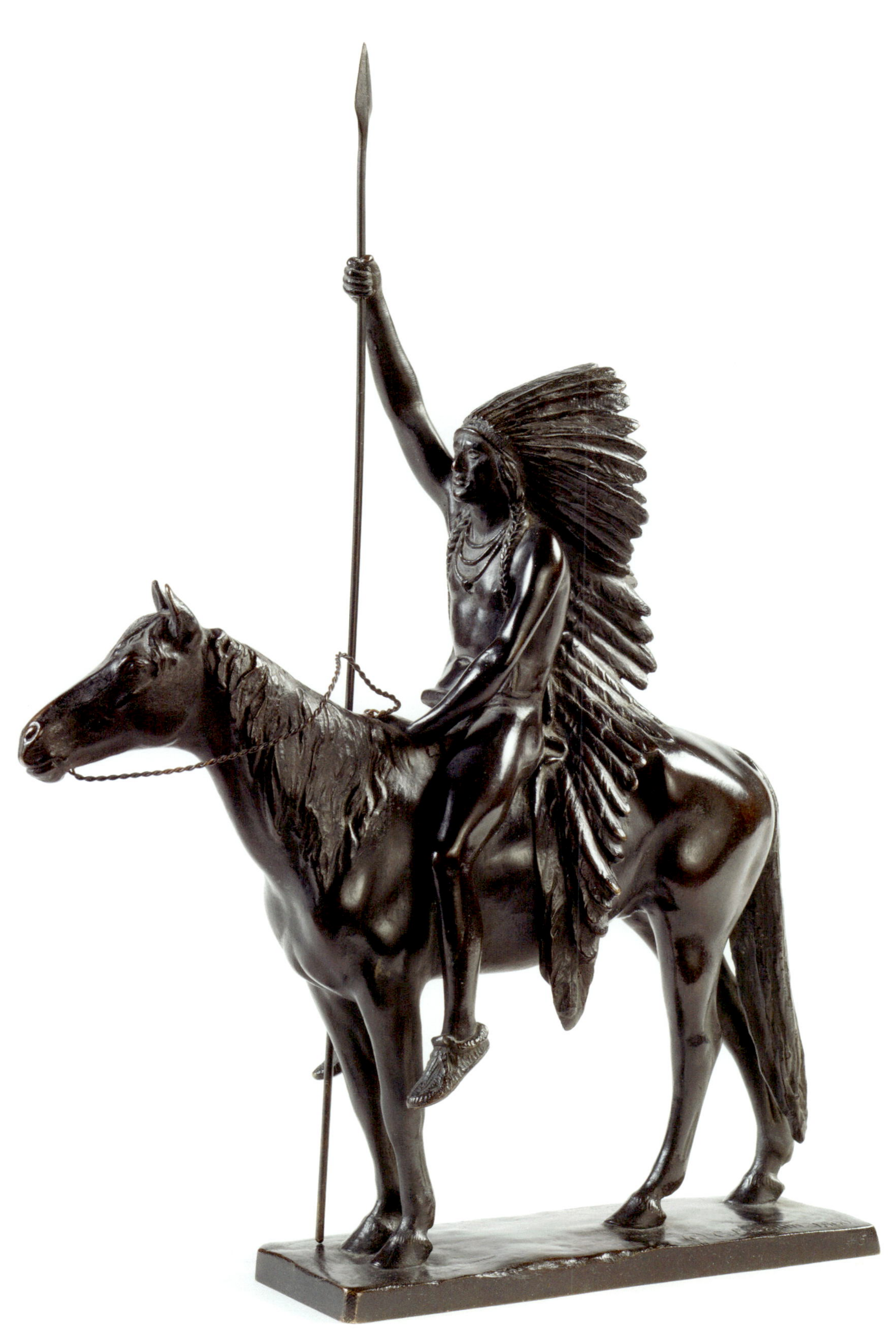

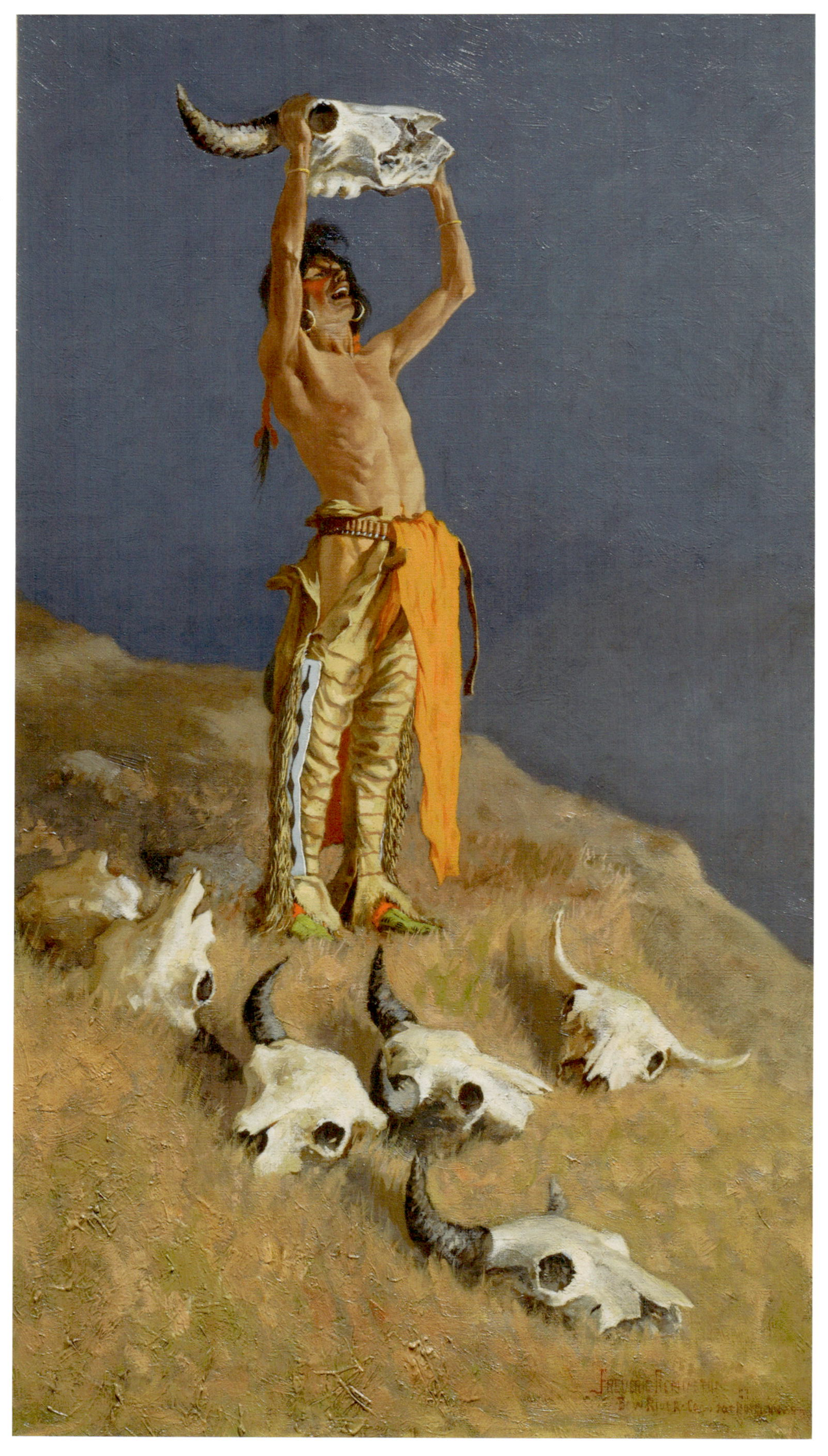

Conjuring Back the Buffalo

circa 1889
Oil on canvas
35 × 20 inches

After completing *Conjuring Back the Buffalo* in his New York studio, Frederic Remington recorded the location of the scene on a corner of the finished painting: "Bow River–Can. Far North West." While Remington's most famous paintings of burly cowboys and Native Americans evoke images of the Dakotas, the artist also made multiple trips to Canada and the Pacific Northwest. In 1887, he traveled to Canada on a commission as an artist correspondent for *Harper's* magazine. There, he observed members of the Blackfoot Confederacy along the Bow River near Calgary, and collected several Blackfoot items including a pair of beaded, fringed leggings (page 22). But on this trip through Alberta it was impossible for Remington to ignore the worn trails and grisly bones of the vanished bison herds that had so recently covered the northern plains in countless numbers. After he returned to New York, Remington used the Blackfoot leggings and his memories of the journey as guides for *Conjuring Back the Buffalo*. This image of the "Far North West" expresses Remington's lament for the heedless destruction of the bison, and contains the idea—common in his time—that Native Americans were doomed to follow their fate.

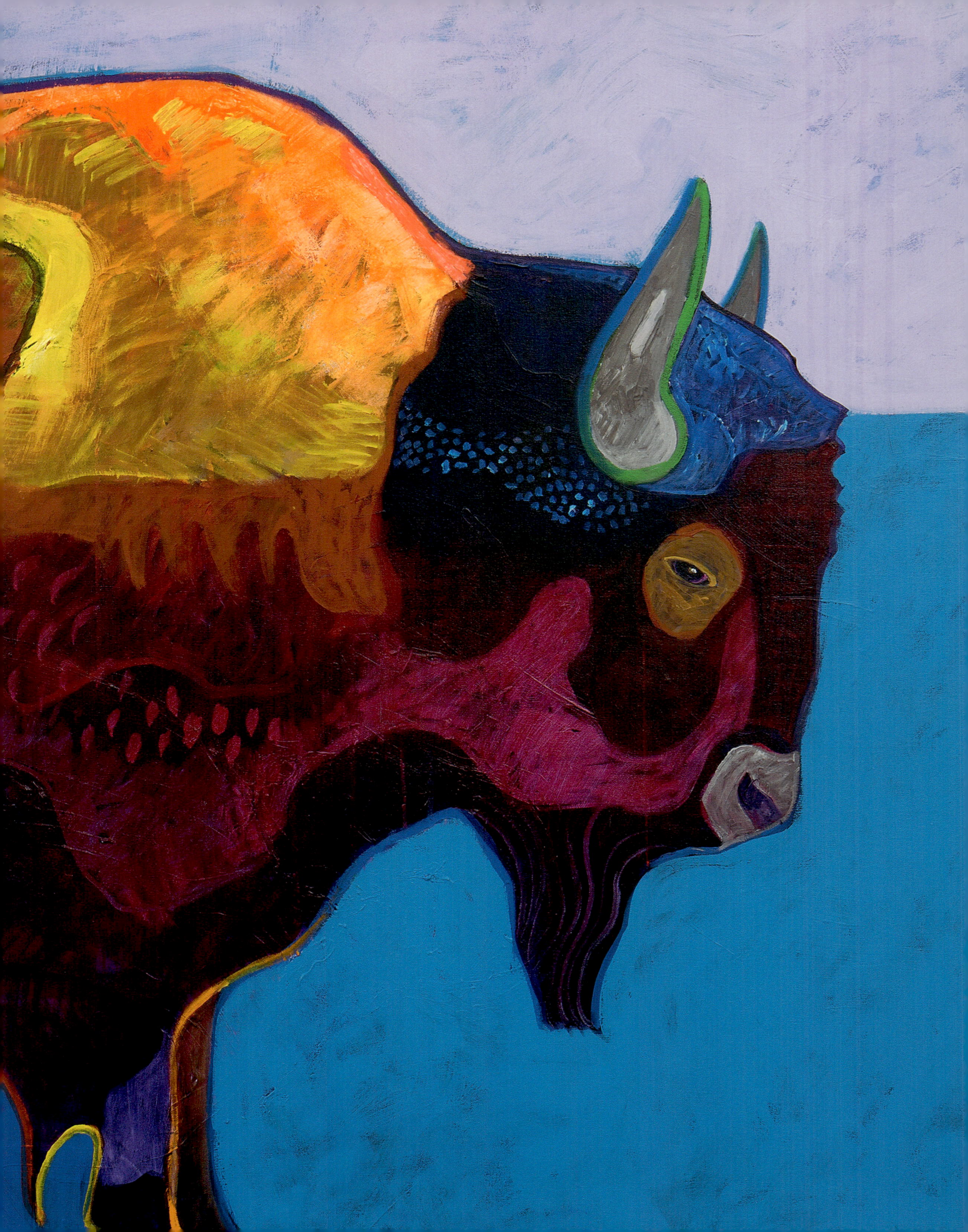

SCOTT MANNING STEVENS

NATIVE AMERICAN ARTISTS LOOKING BACK

When considering the development of Native American arts we are often reminded that for most Native American societies the notion of a designated category of fine arts is a foreign one. Europeans had developed distinctions between the fine arts and applied arts over the course of the Renaissance and early modern periods, but these were not universal categories. Most of the visual culture of the Americas was in service of enhancing either everyday objects or those reserved for sacred practices with the artistic and aesthetic traditions of a particular people. Eventually distinctive styles emerged across different regions and historical periods that we have come to associate with the art of the American Southwest or Inuit art or the art of the Great Plains.

Among the most recognizable visual traditions within Native American cultures is that of the peoples of the Northwest Coast (figure 1). Part of the legacy of this aesthetic tradition can be seen as marking our sense of place through our associations with these patterns and images. The totem pole has become an iconic marker of the Northwest and can be seen as giving the specificity of place that marks a painting such as *Thunderbird Wings* by Carl Hall (figure 2). We have an almost instantaneous recognition of the region and the traditions of its indigenous peoples through such visual cues. Even in the commercial world we see the appropriation of these traditions to emphasize regional specificity—such as in the logo of the Seattle Seahawks (figure 3). The artistic traditions of the Northwest are arguably among the most cohesive among Native Americans today, but this is not to say that, like all art, these traditions have not evolved with the introduction of new materials and technologies. Likewise, Native artists of the Northwest are aware of the longstanding and complex tradition of the representation of Native Americans in the visual arts by non-Native artists. Much of the American tradition of representing Native Americans has been done at the expense of an accurate depiction of Indigenous life. All Native artists must look back, back to their own traditions, and also look back in the sense of returning the gaze of the non-Natives who have long depicted their cultures.

WHEN THE WEST IS EAST

The Haub Family Collection makes it possible to see the traditions of the Northwest within the contexts of Native American history on a much broader scale than was possible in the museum's collection before, just as it brings together two aspects of the American West that have too long been separated from one another—those aspects being the Northwest and the Old West. It is a curiosity of American history that the Northwest (i.e., Oregon and Washington) has remained distinct from our generalized notions of the American West—be that the "Wild West" or the "Old West." Somehow the iconic West could accommodate regions as different as the Northern Plains and the Southwest and even California, but the Northwest remained apart. The West was that region well east of the Cascades, where it became the realm of cowboy and Indian lore, of buffalo hunts, cattle drives, and covered wagons. The Northwest with its dense

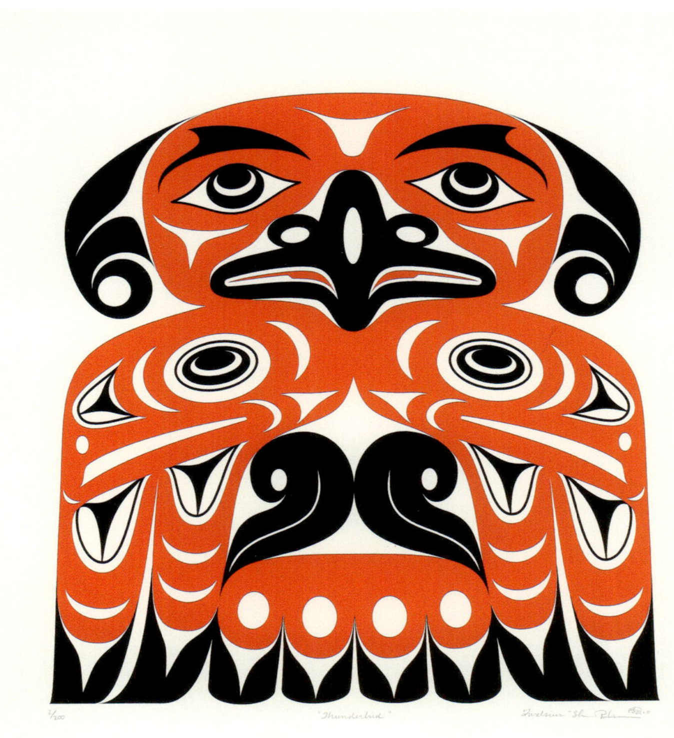

FIGURE 1 Shaun Peterson (Qwalsius), born 1975. Tribal Affiliation: Puyallup. *Thunderbird*, 2010. Inkjet print, no. 2 from an edition of 200, 15 × 13 inches. Tacoma Art Museum, Gift of the artist, 2010.10.

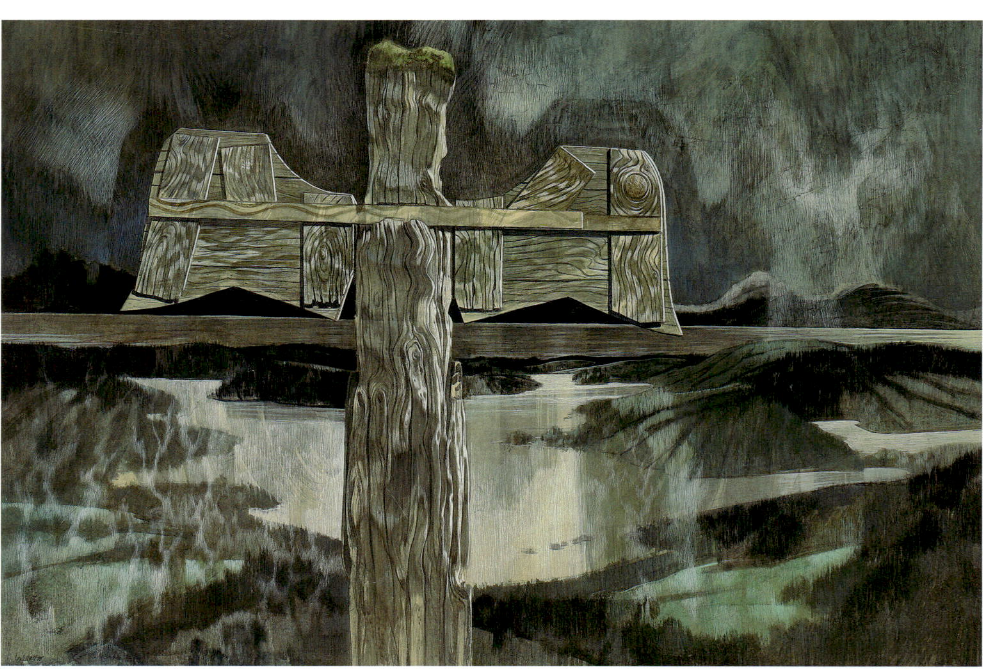

FIGURE 2 Carl Hall (1921–1996), *Thunderbird Wings (Alert Bay Cormorant)*, 1975. Gouache and tissue paper on illustration board, 35½ × 54½ inches. Tacoma Art Museum, Gift of the Carl Hall Family through Bill Rhoades, 2012.3.

forests, fur trappers, and coastal fisheries has been treated as a distinct region for obvious reasons. Even our childhood schoolbooks made it clear that Oregon Territory was different from the West of Geronimo, Kit Carson, and Annie Oakley. But this division is misleading, and the works from the Haub Family Collection help us see beyond regionalism to a larger notion of the West in the cultural life of Americans and Native Americans alike. We can see these works as linking the Puget Sound with the Palouse region by bringing the various American Wests together. A key aspect of those Wests is the presence of Native Americans within those regions, and this is richly represented in the Haub Family Collection as well.

DEPICTING THE AMERICAN INDIAN

The history of Native Americans within American art is a long and complex one. From the early Colonial period onward there have been paintings depicting the first inhabitants of this continent. In the 18th century, while Native nations such as the Iroquois and the Cherokee commanded considerable military strength, we often find portraits of diplomatic delegations or of specific chiefs and headmen. But following independence and several victories over Native alliances, such as Tecumseh's, Americans began to see

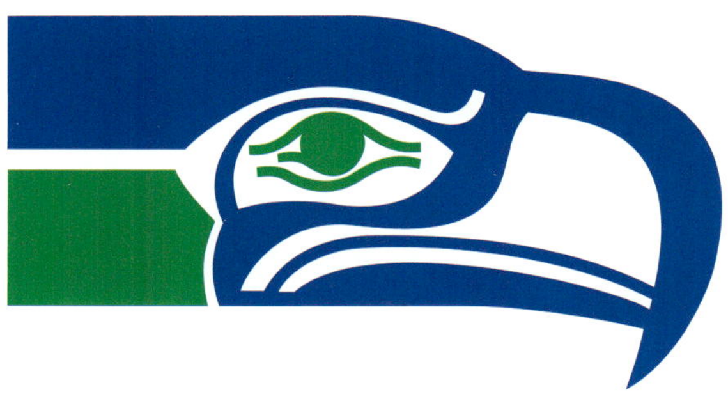

 Seattle Seahawks logo in use from 1976 to 2001. Courtesy of the Seattle Seahawks.

force and dispossession, rather than diplomacy, as the most effective means of achieving their quest for more land. The American Indian became both a romanticized figure of a disappearing past in the beginning years of the 19th century and a symbol of conflict over the land as settlers flooded westward in ever greater numbers. The notions of Manifest Destiny and the American Frontier became intertwined, and with them the lives of countless Native American communities. During the period of the Early Republic, the Frontier was just over the Appalachian Mountains in the Ohio Country and the Old Northwest (Michigan, Wisconsin, and Minnesota), but within several decades those regions too would be securely in the hands of the settler government and US presidents, such as Andrew Jackson and Martin Van Buren, would carry out a ruthless policy of Indian removal. For the first time it became possible to imagine an America without Native Americans. We were to be marginalized, dispossessed, or killed off as part of something resembling a notion of historical inevitability. In effect that is what Manifest Destiny was—an assertion of an unstoppable course of history.

In *The Meeting of Tecumseh and William Henry Harrison at Vincennes* by Junius Brutus Stearns (1810–1885) from 1851 (page 47) we have an example of a painter celebrating what was considered an appropriately and wholly American heroic scene: Two worthy opponents confront one another in a tableau representing Tecumseh's noble but doomed cause and Harrison's stalwart command. The Battle of Tippecanoe had been fought some 40 years before this imagined confrontation was painted, but that victory was widely recognized as the beginning of American ascendency in the Trans-Appalachian West. Tecumseh's depiction here

is telling. With no known images of him from life to draw on, he is a composite Indian chief, a stereotype meant to convey the defiant Shawnee leader. Stearns depicts him in a Plains-style war bonnet—arguably the single most recognized ethnic marker for all Native Americans regardless of region, historical period, or tradition. The artist is already engaged in "westernizing" the American past and its Native people.

Only after the specter of a united intertribal alliance under a leader such as Tecumseh passed could Euro-Americans feel more secure in their presumptions about the disappearance of the Indians. This was made policy when Jackson enacted his scheme of Indian Removal in the 1830s. The so-called Indian plays of the 1820s and 1830s were a popular means of dramatically representing on stage the much-anticipated demise of the American Indian. John Augustus Stone's *Metamora, or the Last of the Wampanoags* was typical of such Indian plays and was widely performed and just as widely imitated.[1] We begin to see examples of what Renato Rosaldo has called "imperialist nostalgia" or "people mourning the passing or transformation of what they have caused to be transformed" and the emergence of the figure that literary scholar Gordon Sayre has described as "the Indian chief as tragic hero." This was especially true for frequently eulogized figures such as Tecumseh and Black Hawk.[2] There was a sense that the only real Indians were those tragically doomed to go down fighting, whereas the communities that survived and attempted to subsist on reservation lands were somehow not the authentic representatives of their more noble, if more "savage," forebears. This notion of the "vanishing Red Man" would become an unfortunately durable stereotype of its own. Depictions of Native America took on a certain urgency as it appeared our societies would eventually die out.

There are excellent examples in the Haub Family Collection to illustrate this period of depicting Native peoples and their leaders from throughout North America, and not just the West. But it might be argued that even in the days in which they were painted, these images were part of the "West of the imagination," to borrow William H. Goetzmann's useful phrase.[3] Portraits of leaders such as the Seminole leader Holato Mico or the Ho-Chunk leader Naw-Kaw

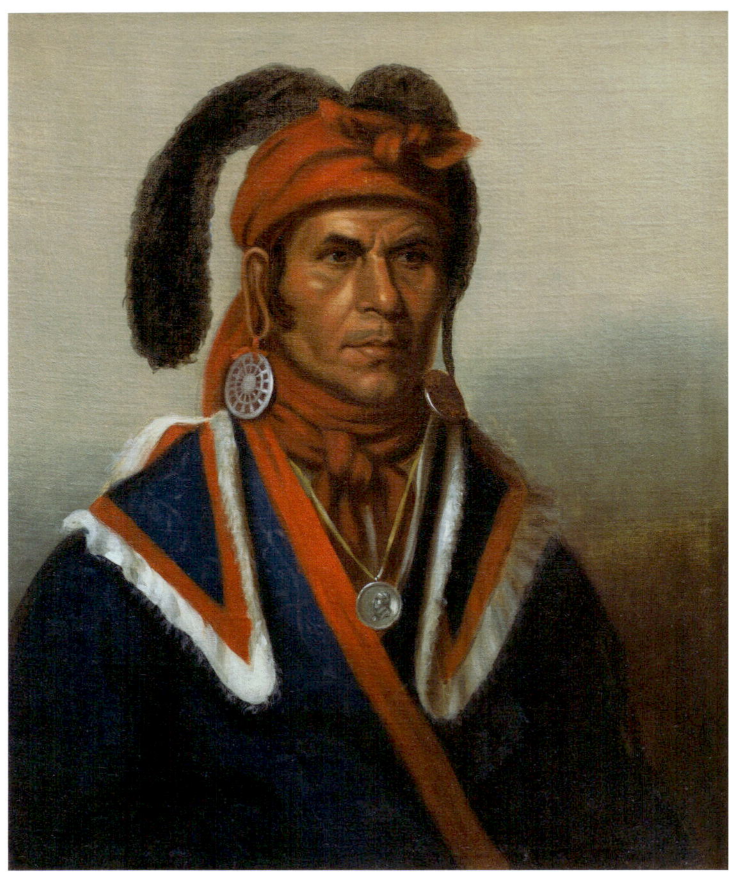

by Henry Inman (1801–1846) were painted at the beginning of the removal period of the 1830s and represent communities as distant as Florida and Wisconsin, respectively (figure 4 and page 35). These portraits depict leaders determined to resist removal, even though they were often only able to delay their displacement. One of the best-known artists of Native American life, George Catlin (1796–1872), was explicit about his sense that artists like himself were needed to save Native history from obscurity. We could even argue that artists led the way in what has come to be called salvage ethnology.[4] Though their motivations were more romantic and nationalistic than those of the professional ethnologists who followed, their inclination to collect and preserve the fast-disappearing traces of an ancient way of life is evident in the writings of artists such as Catlin: "I have flown to their rescue—not of their lives or their race (for they are 'doomed' and must perish), but to the rescue of their looks and their

modes, at which the acquisitive world may hurl their poison and every besom of destruction, and trample them down and crush them to death; yet, phoenix-like, they rise from the 'stain on a painter's palette,' and live again upon canvass [*sic*], and stand forth for centuries yet to come, the living monuments of a noble race."[5] This passage captures a sense of how so many artists saw their role in recording Native American life.

Native life was being recorded in the works of artists such as Charles Bird King (1785–1862), Karl Bodmer (1809–1893), and Seth Eastman (1808–1875). Each spent considerable time with Native Americans and should not be dismissed as merely partaking in a form of nostalgia—even if some element of that exists in their works. King was one of the most prolific and important painters of Native American diplomatic portraits, which he painted for over 20 years in his Washington, DC studio (1826; page 31). Because of his work we have a visual record of the various Native leaders who traveled to the Capitol as members of delegations throughout the early 19th century. Bodmer prided himself on the documentary accuracy of his images, which remain invaluable resources for scholars studying the Native nations of the upper Missouri River (circa 1834; page 40). And Eastman, a West Point graduate and trained draftsman and illustrator for the army, left a tremendous body of work depicting Dakota and Ojibwe life in the Minnesota Territory as well as illustrations of communities in the American Southwest (1852; page 38). These early artists of Native peoples and their traditions were deeply invested in portraying what they actually saw as opposed to the merely exotic or sensational. Later genre painters tended to favor narrative drama over ethnological accuracy, whereas the above-mentioned painters provided a treasured record for the descendants of the peoples they depicted.

CREATING THE OLD WEST

Whatever accuracy of depiction we may praise in the works of a few of the artists of Native American life, accuracy was not necessarily the rule. If the West was to stand for something above and beyond the facts on the ground, that image would be created by visual artists, authors, and poets. Then as now, most people learned about Indians through popular sources such as news accounts, fiction, popular illustrations, and paintings. Art itself was of course a commercial venture, and those who were successful in it were just as likely to produce the images that they knew would sell as they were to attempt to capture the details and nuances of Native life. Catlin and King were both men who promoted their Indian galleries and, at times and with varying levels of success, sought either private or government patronage. As printed books became more readily available, so did the dispersal of what would become the iconography of the American Indian. Figures like the artist James Otto Lewis (1799–1858) and the former Superintendent of Indian Trade Thomas McKenney were both responsible for the publication of highly influential collections of lithographs depicting Native Americans of many different Native nations (figure 5). Lewis used his own drawings as the source of his portfolio, while McKenney drew mostly on the work of King and, to a lesser extent, George Cooke (1793–1849).[6] These works became a standard resource for later artists and illustrators who did not work with Native people firsthand. Though largely documentary in intent, the images could be applied in any number of ways in completely ahistorical fashion.

Other painters of Native Americans were primarily concerned to place them as a feature of the West as the US frontier pressed into their homelands. While the early landscape painters of the Hudson River school, such as Thomas Cole (1801–1848) and Sanford Gifford (1823–1880), placed Indians in their landscapes as signals that these were American landscapes and not those of the European romantic painters, a new generation of American painters such as Alfred Jacob Miller (1810–1874) and Carl Wimar (1828–1862) had firsthand experience of life in the Trans-Mississippi West. Both were interested in atmosphere and narrative drama as much as they were in documenting actual Native American life. Their images contributed greatly to the creation of the genre of western art in the American tradition. Another peer of that generation of American artists of the West was John Mix Stanley (1814–1872). Stanley painted both landscapes of the West, which he had encountered

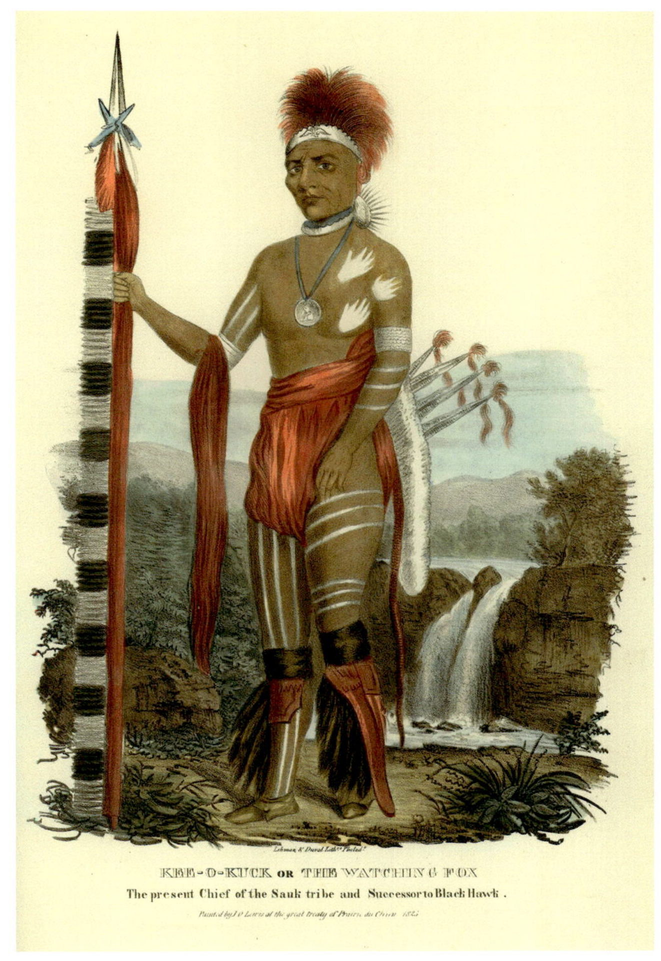

FIGURE 5 James Otto Lewis, *Kee-o-kuck or the Watching Fox, the Present Chief of the Sauk tribe and Successor to Black Hawk.* Hand-colored lithograph from the *Aboriginal Portfolio,* circa 1835. Wisconsin Historical Society, WHS-26781.

on various expeditions following the US–Mexican War, and of the Natives who lived there. He also created a variety of historical tableaux using often anachronistic or culturally inaccurate depictions of events and local customs. The two paintings by Stanley from the Haub Family Collection are fine illustrations of this. His depiction of the Columbia River landscape (1852; page 55) is the result of his travels through the Northwest, while the sentimental image of a young Indian boy, titled *Young Chief* and soon reproduced as *Young Chief Uncas* (figure 6), raises the issue of ethnological accuracy. The name Uncas was most likely associated with the character out of James Fenimore Cooper's *The Last of the Mohicans,* and not the Mohegan leader from 17th-century Connecticut. Either way, the boy wears Plains-style clothing

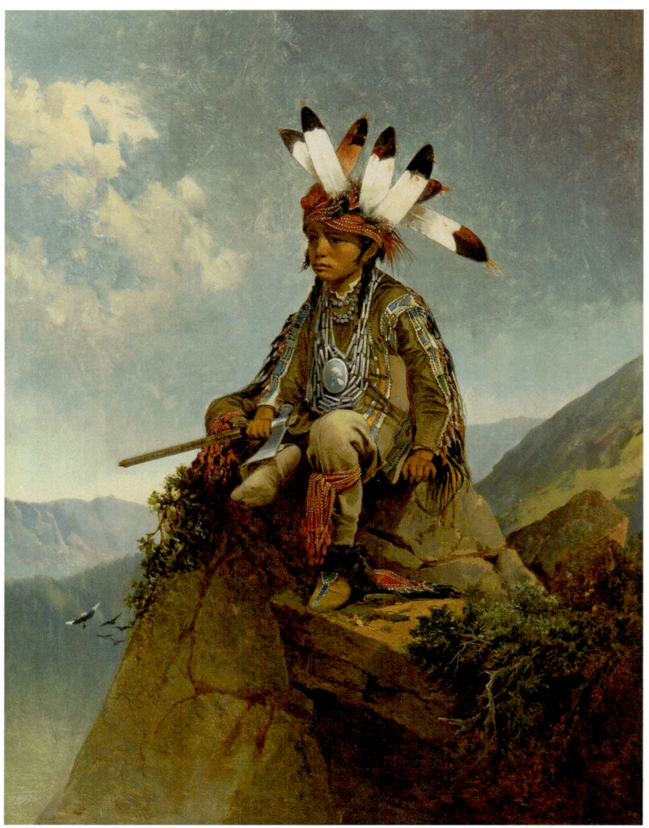

FIGURE 6   John Mix Stanley, *Young Chief*, 1868. Oil on canvas, 20 × 16 inches. Tacoma Art Museum, Haub Family Collection, Promised gift of Erivan and Helga Haub.

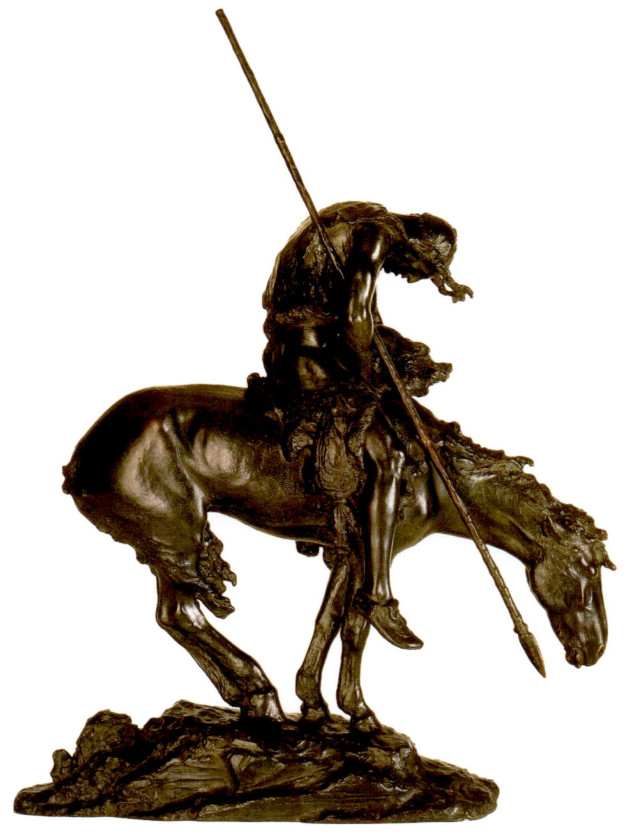

FIGURE 7   James Earle Fraser, *End of the Trail*, circa 1918–23. Bronze, 33¾ × 26 × 8 inches. Buffalo Bill Center of the West, Clara Peck Purchase Fund, 112.67.

and a peace medal (most unlikely on a child) and appears in a landscape more typical of the Rockies than the Eastern seaboard of New England.[7] Such depictions would become the norm as the 19th century drew on.

One inescapable reality of the 19th-century American West was the Indian Wars that followed hard in the wake of the US Civil War. From the 1870s until 1890 there were almost constant military campaigns against Native nations from the Great Plains to the Southwest. The figures of Sitting Bull, Geronimo, and Chief Joseph became icons of Native American resistance to US attempts to restrict their people to reservation lands and curtail their traditional sovereignty. As these wars drew to their conclusions it seemed to many Euro-Americans that their predictions of an Indian-free America were coming true. It also became clear to others that the storied Frontier was closing and with it a chapter in American history. To artists such as Frederic Remington (1861–1909) and Charles Russell (1864–1926), the waning of

the Old West was a bittersweet development for the United States. Their art, perhaps more than that of any other American artists, created a lasting image of the American West that has remained the model for western art to this day.

For Remington, there is always the weight of nostalgia hanging in the air—a sort of impending loss of that which he valued most, the open land that served as the proving ground of his romantic value system—a place where men were tested by the elements and each other. Battle remained more of a face-to-face experience than modern warfare would prove to be, and the soldier could play the hero in this dramatic struggle between savagery and civilization. The paradox being that when civilization won, the end of that struggle would immediately be mourned. Likewise, Remington's depictions of Native Americans follow the same declension narrative that we have seen in other depictions of Indian life. There have been paintings with titles such as *Last of Their Race*, by John Mix Stanley (1857),

STEVENS

that echo Cooper's *Last of the Mohicans* with their same pre-dictions of disappearance or extinction. Remington's highly evocative *Conjuring Back the Buffalo* (circa 1889; page 92) is a superlative example of this celebratory nostalgia. The message is clear: No depth of traditional beliefs in age-old ceremony will turn the tide of history for the doomed American Indian. Such images of what we might call cultural defeat became standard in the depiction of the Native peoples and, even more problematically, they often were internalized by Native viewers as well. Most of us can call to mind the sculpture *End of the Trail* by James Earle Fraser (1876–1953) and all that it implies (figure 7). Works like Russell's *When the Plains Were His* (1906; page 109) implicitly refer to the conquest of Indian lands even while casting a nostalgic eye toward the past. Such depictions made up a stock of images to be viewed by Natives and non-Natives alike. No contemporary Native American artists could be free of this visual legacy any more than they could ignore the bitter histories of their peoples.

THE WEST GOES VIRAL

Around the same time that Remington and Russell were creating their enduring images of the Old West, figures like Buffalo Bill Cody were creating their version of the Wild West for public consumption on an international level. After a turn on stage playing himself, famed western military scout William F. Cody founded Buffalo Bill's Wild West in 1883 (figure 8). American audiences had been acquainted with a melodramatic version of the West since the advent of the dime novel in the 1860s. Many of these stories focused on the western adventures of such figures as Kit Carson and Wild Bill Hickok. Their portrayal of American Indians followed the usual stereotypes while creating a few of their own. Indians were essentially foils for the heroic American characters who were celebrated in these stories. But it was Buffalo Bill's shows that popularized the imagery of the Plains Indians. The impressive war bonnets and Native horse gear made them perfect for the circus-like spectacle of the Wild West shows. Often, mock battles were staged complete with burning settler cabins and covered wagons.

Cody famously employed Native Americans in his shows, including such figures as Sitting Bull. This not only added to the claims of authenticity but created a singular image of the American Indian in the public's imagination. To be a real Indian was to be a Plains Indian. Just as Remington had preferred the Blackfoot as his representative Indian, Cody looked to the Northern Plains horse cultures and the almost legendary figure of the Sioux warrior to bring drama to his productions. The fact that his Wild West show traveled to both the eastern United States and beyond to Europe meant that the Plains Indians of his theatrical extravaganzas would come to represent all Indians to white audiences at home and abroad. Their presence alongside such venues as the World's Columbian Exposition in Chicago in 1893 also exposed millions of visitors to this memorable version of

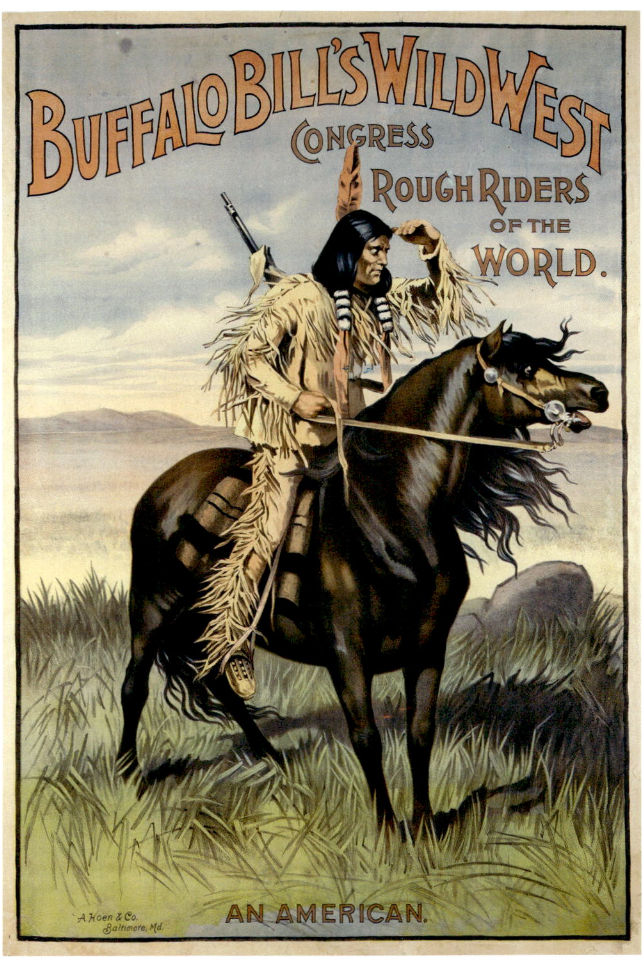

FIGURE 8 Poster from Buffalo Bill's Wild West titled "An American." Printed by A. Hoen & Co., Baltimore, circa 1893. Buffalo Bill Center of the West, Gift of The Coe Foundation, 1.69.51.

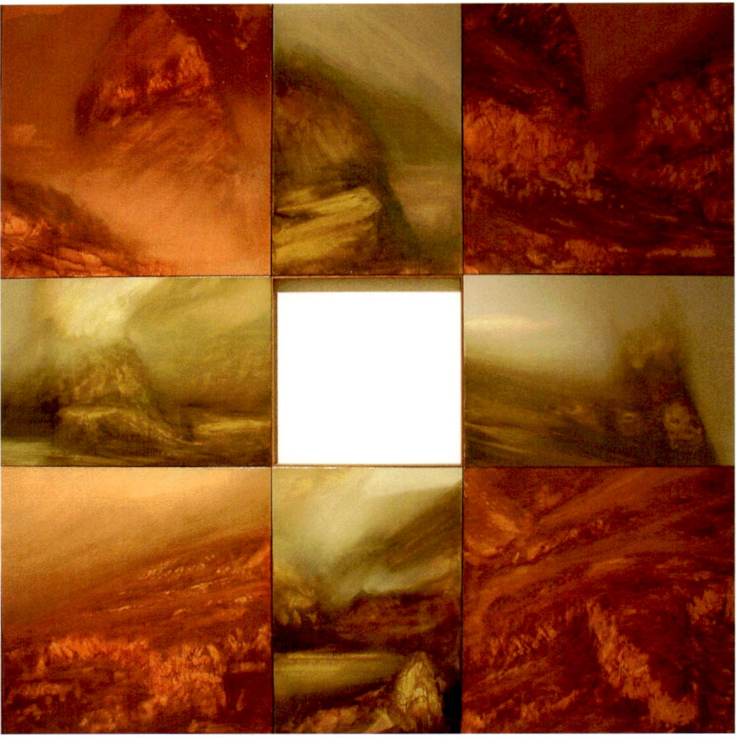

FIGURE 9 James Lavadour, *Release the Sun*, 1990–91. Oil on linen, 83 × 83 inches. Tacoma Art Museum, Gift of Rebecca and Alexander C. Stewart, 2000.43.11.

the American West and Native American culture. Soon all Indians were expected to look like Plains Indians regardless of geography or tradition. This was also one of the darkest periods in Native American history—a nadir in terms of population and living conditions. When Native leaders in the so-called Progressive Era (1890s–1920s) wished to advocate for Native rights, they were often expected to conform to white notions of Indianness. More often than not this meant wearing Plains Indian regalia and especially the war bonnet or "Indian headdress." This usually coincides with what is referred to as Pan-Indianism during the early 20th century.[8] I recall photographs of leaders from the Iroquois communities in upstate New York and southern Ontario wearing Plains garb at a protest in the 1920s. As unlikely as this should be, it was quite common. If a group wished to be recognized as Indians they would have to dress the part.

If art, the popular press, and mass entertainment were not enough, the westernized image of the American Indian would, in today's terms, "go viral" with the advent of movie culture. From the early days of the film industry on, the Western has been a staple of the movies. Edwin Porter's 1903 *The Great Train Robbery* is credited with launching the genre, and it was assumed that stories set in the Old West would include Indians. Porter made his *A Brush Between Cowboys and Indians* in 1904. Film historians have noted the impact of the various Wild West shows such as Cody's on the depiction of Indians in film,[9] but more interesting is the ubiquity of the westernized Indian from that point onward. One has to imagine the many Native Americans across the United States who sat in movie theaters taking in these images over and over again. Even if we rooted for the Indians, we were also aware of their differences from contemporary Native life. Yet somehow these were meant to be the authentic Indians, a kind of idealized image against which we would always be compared and found wanting. No American Indian artist could escape this image—one reinscribed in every printed reproduction of a scene from Remington or Russell. The majority population believed it knew what a real Indian looked like, just as it knew what genuine Indian art must be. Both were concepts tied to the past and usually from one region. The notion that Native American visual culture would adapt to new materials and new social conditions was not a popular one. The "authentic Indian" must be preserved in amber, as it were. Artistic expression in this formulation is meant to be identical with that of the past—innovation and authenticity are still often treated as mutually exclusive concepts. For Native American visual artists, this has remained a quandary, especially for those individuals hoping to make a livelihood from their art. The art market is always unpredictable, but for Native artists there exists the added pressure of the authenticity issue.

The notion of the individual American Indian artist is itself relatively recent. It was only at the beginning of the 20th century that we began to have individual artists signing their work. In the past, such traditional forms of visual culture as weaving, pottery, carving, and jewelry were treated as though they were anonymous activities. To be sure, talented artists were known by their work within their own communities, but they were rarely known to non-Indian collectors. Artists

STEVENS

such as the Hopi-Tewa potter Nampeyo (1859–1942) or the Haida carver Charles Edenshaw (1839–1920) were among the first Native artists to be recognized by name for their talents. But they worked largely within traditional idioms. Many American Indian artists encountered nontraditional arts in a rudimentary way at the various residential schools to which Indian children were sent during the late 19th and early 20th centuries. These young people would know both the trauma of such education and alienation from the traditional arts of their home communities. It is no surprise that when more recent generations of Native Americans turned to art as a means of self-expression it was unlikely to reflect a pristine artistic tradition anchored in the distant past.

As the 19th century progressed and with it American self-confidence, we begin to see the development of an American idiom in art; not just in subject matter, which had always been an important distinction between American art and that of Europe, but in a willingness to experiment with style and form. Europe would remain a dominant influence for decades to come, but increasingly we see a turn to regionalism in the early 20th century. The Santa Fe and Taos schools would loom large in the Southwest, just as northeastern artists would begin to celebrate the modern urban scene of the Jazz Age. With the Great Depression came the Works Progress Administration (WPA) and its support of various regional artistic initiatives under the direction of the Federal Art Project. This was particularly important to a number of Native American artists because for the first time major public art projects, such as murals in federal offices, were awarded to Native artists. Artists such as Julius Twohy (1902–1986), a member of the Ute Tribe, created works that combined traditional themes with modern styles and techniques. He is one of the artists of this period whose work is already part of the Tacoma Art Museum's permanent collection. The founding of the Indian Arts and Crafts Board in 1935 by the Department of the Interior also helped promote and market American Indian arts, with the intent of raising their visibility and helping Native artists gain a place in the art market. It also meant that an increasing number of American Indian youth could look to the arts as a possible career.

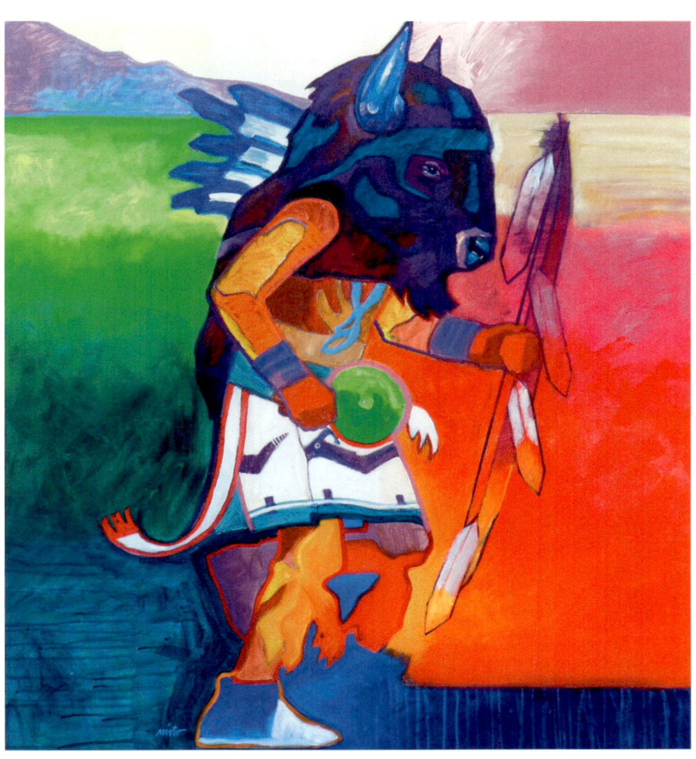

FIGURE 10   John Nieto, *Buffalo Dance*, 2007. Acrylic on canvas, 44 × 40 inches. Tacoma Art Museum, Haub Family Collection, Promised gift of Erivan and Helga Haub.

The post World War II period in the United States was one of anti-Communist anxiety and of social pressures that would lead to the Civil Rights Movement. American Indians were also deeply impacted in this period by such federal policies as the disastrous Termination and Relocation policies that began in 1953 and lasted until 1966. These laws, which unilaterally terminated a reservation's status as Indian land and encouraged the relocation of tribal members to selected urban centers, were meant to encourage the assimilation of Indians into American society and to remove the authority of the Bureau of Indian Affairs. But the result was that the status of 109 reservations was terminated and thousands of Indians were relocated to urban areas during a period of increasing unrest in American cities. Not surprisingly, Native people affected by these policies soon joined in the movement for increased civil rights. The late 1960s saw the takeover of Alcatraz as a part of a national protest and the rise of the Red Power movement in the early 1970s with such organizations as the American Indian Movement (AIM). This upsurge in activism and Native pride affected the arts as well. Native artists increasingly turned to themes of the environment, reconnecting with and reinvigorating their own visual traditions and exploring new media for their culturally focused art.

The work of James Lavadour (born 1951), a member of the Walla Walla Tribe who grew up and lives on the Umatilla Indian Reservation in eastern Oregon, is instructive when we consider the evolution of American Indian art. His work grows out of a dual heritage of abstract 20th-century art and a profound personal connection to the lands of his people. Lavadour credits the landscape as his inspiration, which finds expression in his passionate abstraction and use of vibrant color (figure 9). For many Native Americans it is this connection to our homelands and our relationship to earth that binds us to some of the most deeply held traditional values of our communities. Similarly, we see how Hispanic and Apache painter John Nieto (born 1936) connects the traditional imagery of western art, such as the bison or a traditional Native ceremonial dancer (figure 10), with the vibrant colors we would normally associate with French fauvist painters such as Henri Matisse (1869–1954). This dramatic combination is testimony to the cosmopolitan influences experienced by many Native artists during the post-war period as an increasing number of American Indians attended college and art schools—often as a result of the GI Bill.

One significant development in this same period was the founding of the Institute of American Indian Arts (IAIA) in Santa Fe in 1962. This school brought Native artists together and explored new techniques in the fine arts along with traditional arts. Such important figures in the American Indian arts as Fritz Scholder (1937–2005), Linda Lomahaftewa (born 1947), and Allan Houser (1914–1994) taught at this school and continue to influence the works of students there today. Among the new generation of artists represented in the Tacoma Art Museum's collections who have come from IAIA there is Crow painter Kevin Red Star (born 1943), whose works explore ancient symbols and imagery drawn from his community and its traditions but are now rendered in oil paints on canvas and placed in dialogue with a contemporary painterly tradition (circa 1980; page 225). The formal

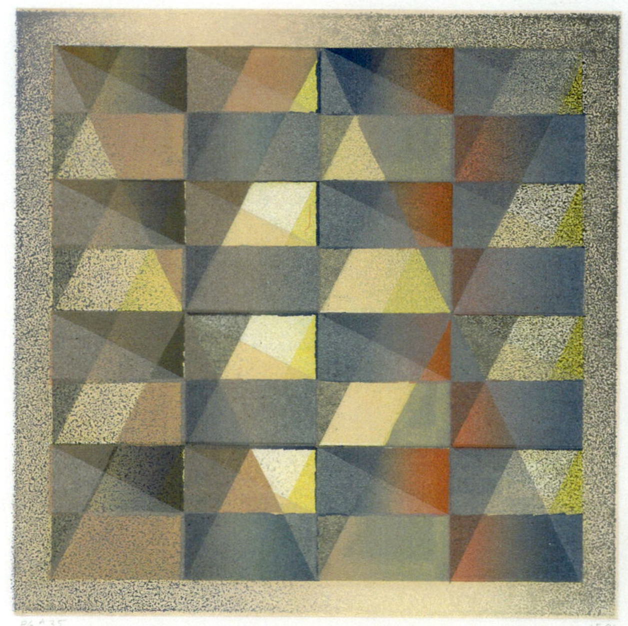

FIGURE 11 Joe Feddersen, *Plateau Geometric #35*, 1996. Monotype, 11⅞ × 11⅞ inches. Tacoma Art Museum, Gift of the artist, 1997.1.2.

training of a new generation of artists at art schools and universities has encouraged individual artists to explore new techniques and adapt other artistic traditions. We can see this in the work of Colville/Okanagan printmaker Joe Feddersen (born 1953), who, while a student at the University of Washington, began to experiment with the printing styles of the famed Japanese printmaker Utagawa Hiroshige (1797–1858). Later, Feddersen's work began to adapt the traditional geometric patterns of his own people in a more abstract and self-consciously modern idiom (figure 11). These surprising juxtapositions demonstrate how liberating such cross-cultural encounters may be while allowing the artists to continue working within their own visual traditions.

The Haub Family Collection makes possible a better understanding of the full trajectory of Native Americans in Euro-American art and art by Native Americans in the post-conquest era. We see the romanticized and mythic past mixed with the artistic legacies of the diverse Native nations that make up modern America. The American West looms large in the world's imaginings about the United States, and Tacoma's collections can help us make sense of this legacy for ourselves. Regional traditions remain strong in many of our communities and the artists who draw on them continue to expand their range. In the works of Marvin Oliver (born 1946) of Quinault/Isleta-Pueblo heritage and the Tlingit artist Preston Singletary (born 1963), we see the highly recognizable traditions of Northwest Coast–style visual arts live on, but now created in glass—a non-Indigenous art form borrowed and transformed for Indigenous art (figure 12). Likewise, Wiyot artist Rick Bartow's (born 1946) use of abstraction in combination with traditional materials such as copper, dried grass, and cedar, and in the traditional form of a mask are examples of how traditions are adapted and made new by contemporary Native artists. The Tacoma Art Museum provides us a wonderful opportunity to explore these traditions and changes within the art of the American West as well as within Native American art.

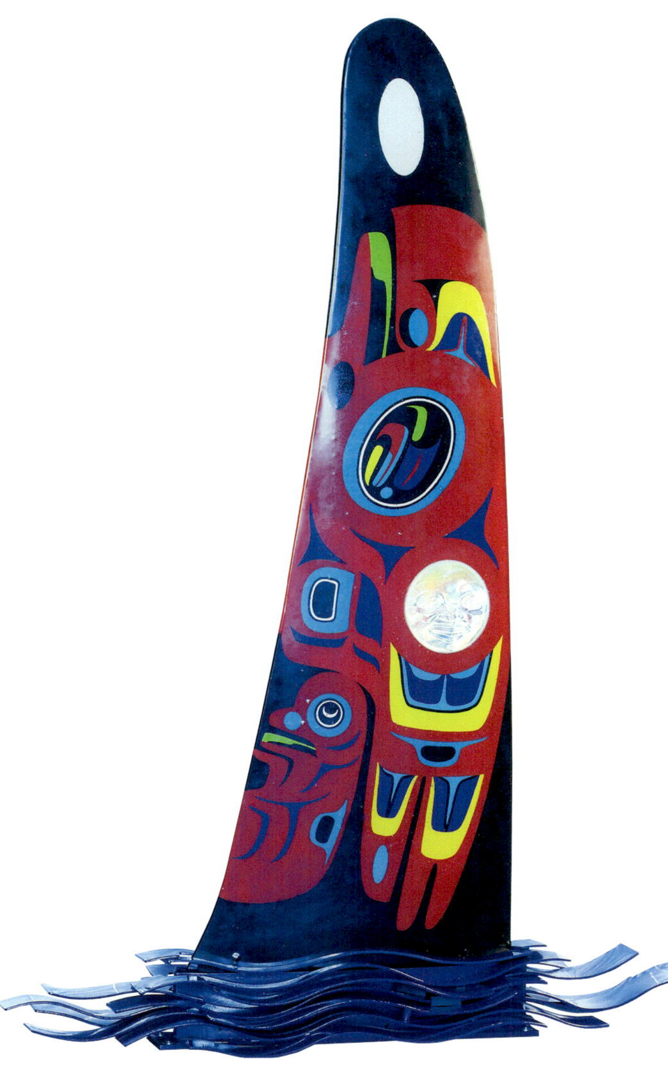

FIGURE 12 Marvin Oliver, *Orca*, 2002. Watercut, fused, and polished glass with cast glass inlay and steel base, 90 × 64 × 22 inches. Tacoma Art Museum, Gift of Norma and Leonard Klorfine, 2009.14.

1 See Scott C. Martin, "Interpreting *Metamora*: Nationalism, Theater, and Jacksonian Indian Policy," in *Journal of the Early Republic* 19, no. 1 (Spring 1999), 73–100, and Werner Sollors, *Beyond Ethnicity: Consent and Descent in American Culture* (Oxford: Oxford University Press, 1986), 102–30.

2 See Renato Rosaldo, "Imperialist Nostalgia," *Representations* 26, Special Issue: Memory and Counter-Memory (Spring 1989), 107–22 and Gordon Sayre, *The Indian Chief as Tragic Hero: Native Resistance and the Literatures of America, from Moctezuma to Tecumseh* (Chapel Hill: University of North Carolina Press, 2005).

3 William H. and William N. Goetzmann, *The West of the Imagination* (New York: Norton, 1986), ix–xiii.

4 Steven Conn, *History's Shadow: Native Americans and Historical Consciousness in the Nineteenth Century* (Chicago: University of Chicago Press, 2004), 76.

5 George Catlin, *Letters and Notes on the Manners, Customs and Conditions of the North American Indians Written During Eight Years of Travel Amongst the Wildest Tribes of North America* (London: H. Bond, 1866), vol. 1, 17.

6 James D. Horan, *The McKenney-Hall Portrait Gallery of American Indians* (New York: Crown Publishers, 1972), 196.

7 We in fact know that Stanley used a photograph taken by Joel Whitney of a Santee Sioux boy named Little Bird Hunter in 1862. Whitney took the photograph in his studio in St. Paul, Minnesota. See George P. Tomko's "The Source of John Mix Stanley's: Young Chief Uncas," *American Art Journal* 10, no. 1 (May 1978), 113-14.

8 Stephen Cornell, *The Return of the Native: American Indian Political Resurgence* (New York: Oxford University Press, 1988), 126–27.

9 Joy S. Kasson, "Life-like, Vivid, and Thrilling Pictures: Buffalo Bill's Wild West and Early Cinema," in *Buffalo Bill's Wild West: Celebrity, Memory, and Popular History* (New York: Hill & Wang, 2000), 161–219.

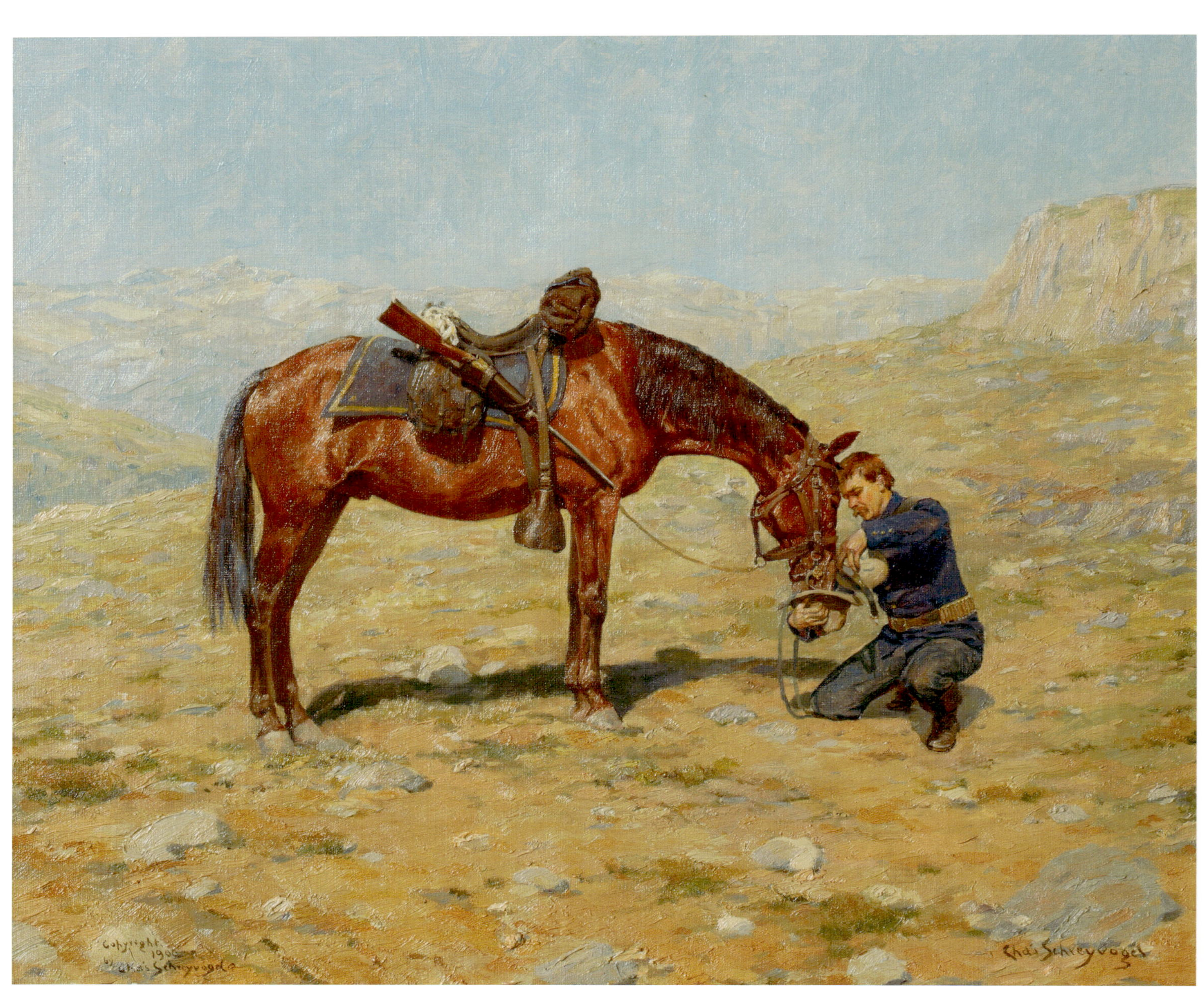

The Last Drop

1900
Oil on canvas
16 × 20 inches

The harsh sunlight radiates from bare dust and rock, with no relief from the beating rays visible in any direction. His decision made, the cavalry soldier dismounts with his near-empty canteen in hand. He sweeps off his campaign hat and pours the last drops of precious water for his horse, a faithful companion to the end. In 1900, a decade after the last conflicts on the Great Plains had ended, Charles Schreyvogel's quiet image of a compassionate cavalryman in the face of certain demise captivated viewers. Rather than battling an opposing army, this soldier and his mount fight against the overwhelming forces of nature itself. To best capture the details of the scene, Schreyvogel created a clay model of the figures to use as a guide. After the painting was completed, Schreyvogel cast the model of the horse and rider in bronze (page 177). More than 150 authorized casts were issued of the bronze sculpture *The Last Drop*, making it one of the most popular bronze statuettes of a western subject ever created.

When the Plains Were His

1906
Oil on canvas
15¼ × 15¼ inches

"Like all things that happen that's worth while," Charles Russell once wrote, "it's a long time ago."* As his career progressed, Russell witnessed increasingly drastic changes in the open spaces of the West. From his earliest days living in Montana as a young man in the 1880s to the end of his life in 1926, Russell saw the region change from a place of open range cattle herds to a land of automobiles, telephones, and boomtowns. His artwork gradually transitioned with the times, from depicting current scenes of life around him to portraying imagined historical events that privileged the past. In the painting *When the Plains Were His,* Russell portrays an idealized image of Native Americans traveling freely on an open plain. But the image also refers to conquest and defeat. A dog running with the travelers stops to examine a bison skull—a symbol foreshadowing future hardship for Native peoples. Rejecting the strangeness of modernity and the realities of the present, Russell preferred to depict a golden past.

*Charles M. Russell, *Trails Plowed Under: Stories of the Old West* (Lincoln: University of Nebraska Press, 1996. First printing 1927), 15.

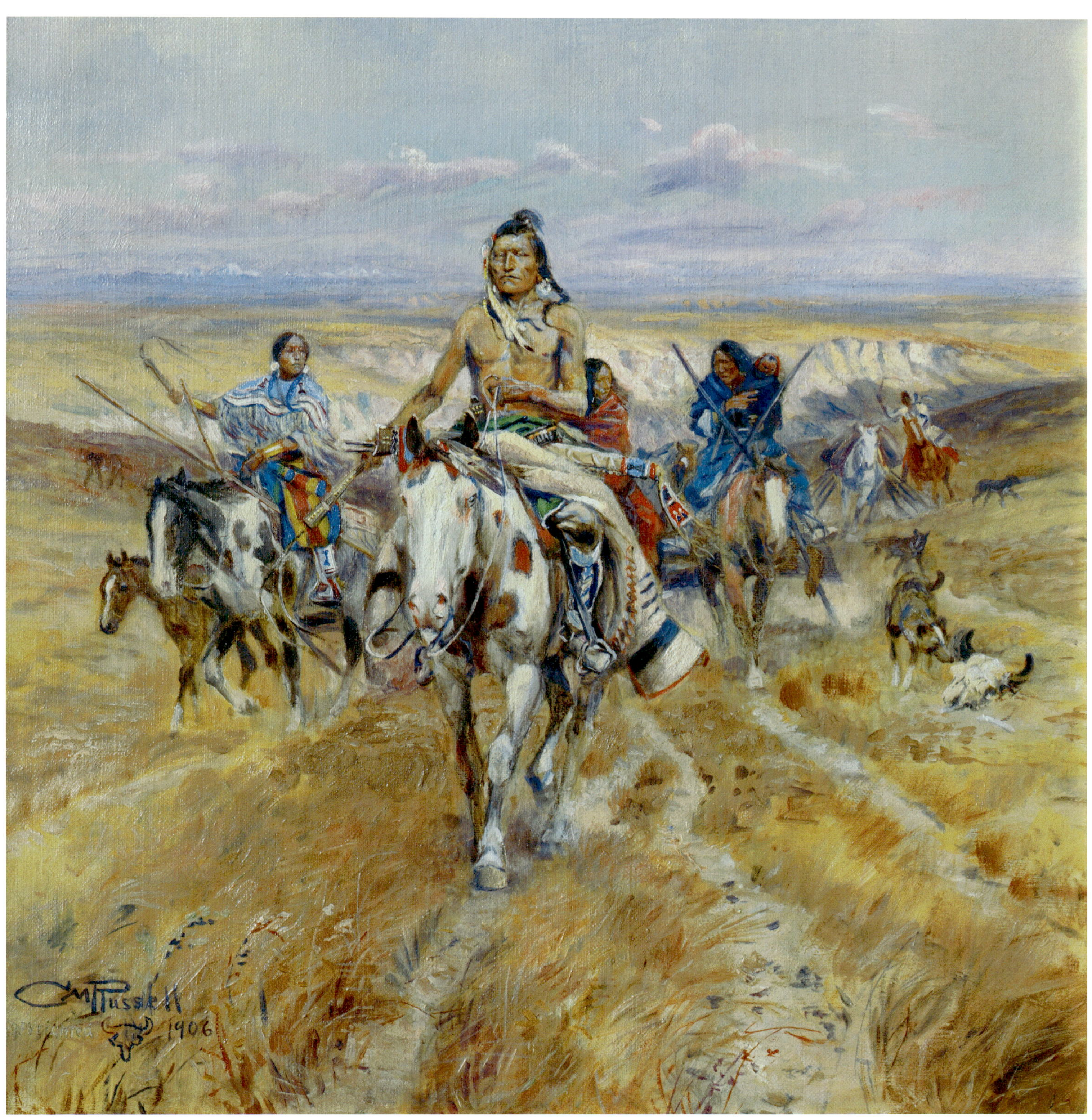

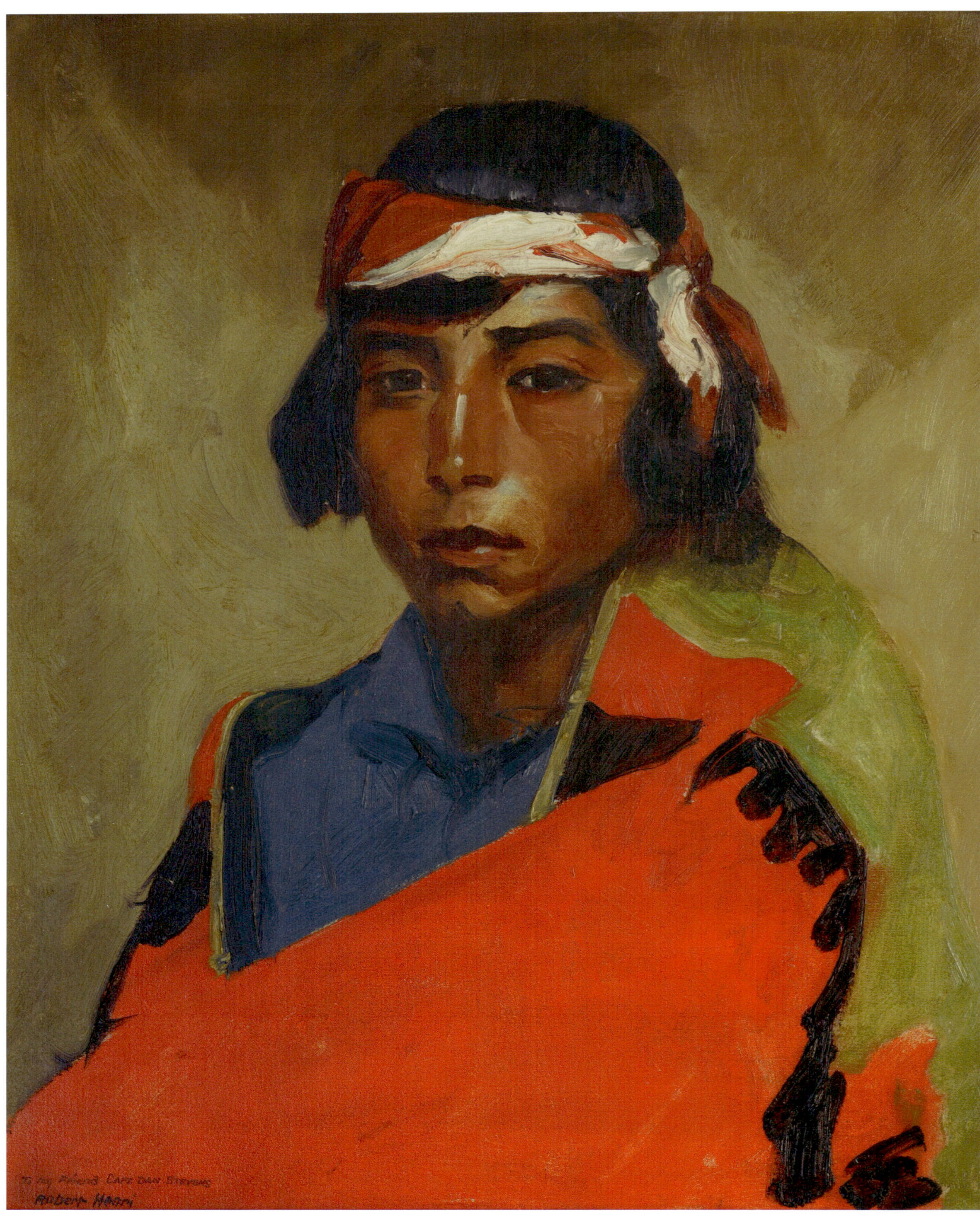
To my friend Capt. Dan Stevens
Robert Henri

Young Buck of the Tesuque Pueblo

1916
Oil on canvas
24 × 20 inches

An influential painter and instructor in New York in the early 20th century, Robert Henri rejected the conservative attitude embodied by the powerful National Academy of Design. Rather than portraying the idealized figures and beautiful landscapes celebrated by the Academy, Henri and a group of fellow artists, who later became known as the Ashcan School, found inspiration in the gritty urban core of New York City. A participant in the Armory Show of 1913, where European modernism was introduced to the United States, Henri hovered between realism and a new modern approach in his art.

When Henri first traveled to New Mexico in 1916 the local residents fascinated him. This portrait of a young man from the Tesuque Pueblo, just north of Santa Fe, shows a distinct individual in a blue collared shirt with a blanket around his shoulders. The solid, bold red flattens the sense of depth in the image, rendering the young man in a modern style—a contemporary figure, not simply a representation of the past.

GRACE HUDSON (1865–1937)

He Loves You (The Song of the Lark)

1914
Oil on canvas
28½ × 22½ inches

"No other artist today is so popular with the picture-loving public of San Francisco," remarked one magazine in 1897. "A canvas from her brush is sold before it leaves the easel."* By the end of the 19th century, artist Grace Hudson had become famous for her poignant paintings of the Pomo people. Born in Potter Valley, California, Hudson was among the first Anglo artists to be raised in the western United States. After studying at the California School of Design (now the Art Institute) in San Francisco, she established a studio in Ukiah in 1889 and focused her efforts on painting the nearby Pomo. In *He Loves You (The Song of the Lark)*, a young Pomo woman lost in a daydream stands before a softly rendered landscape, listening to a singing lark perched on an elaborate basket—basketry being a famous skill among the Pomo people.

While many images of the American West in the early 20th century portrayed a masculine, action-packed world, Hudson's paintings revealed a very different side of life. Her serene depictions of Pomo women and children demonstrate that the West was a far more nuanced, varied place than the images frequently presented in popular media.

*Ninetta Eames, "The California Indian on Canvas," *Frank Leslie's Popular Monthly* 43 (April 1897), 380.

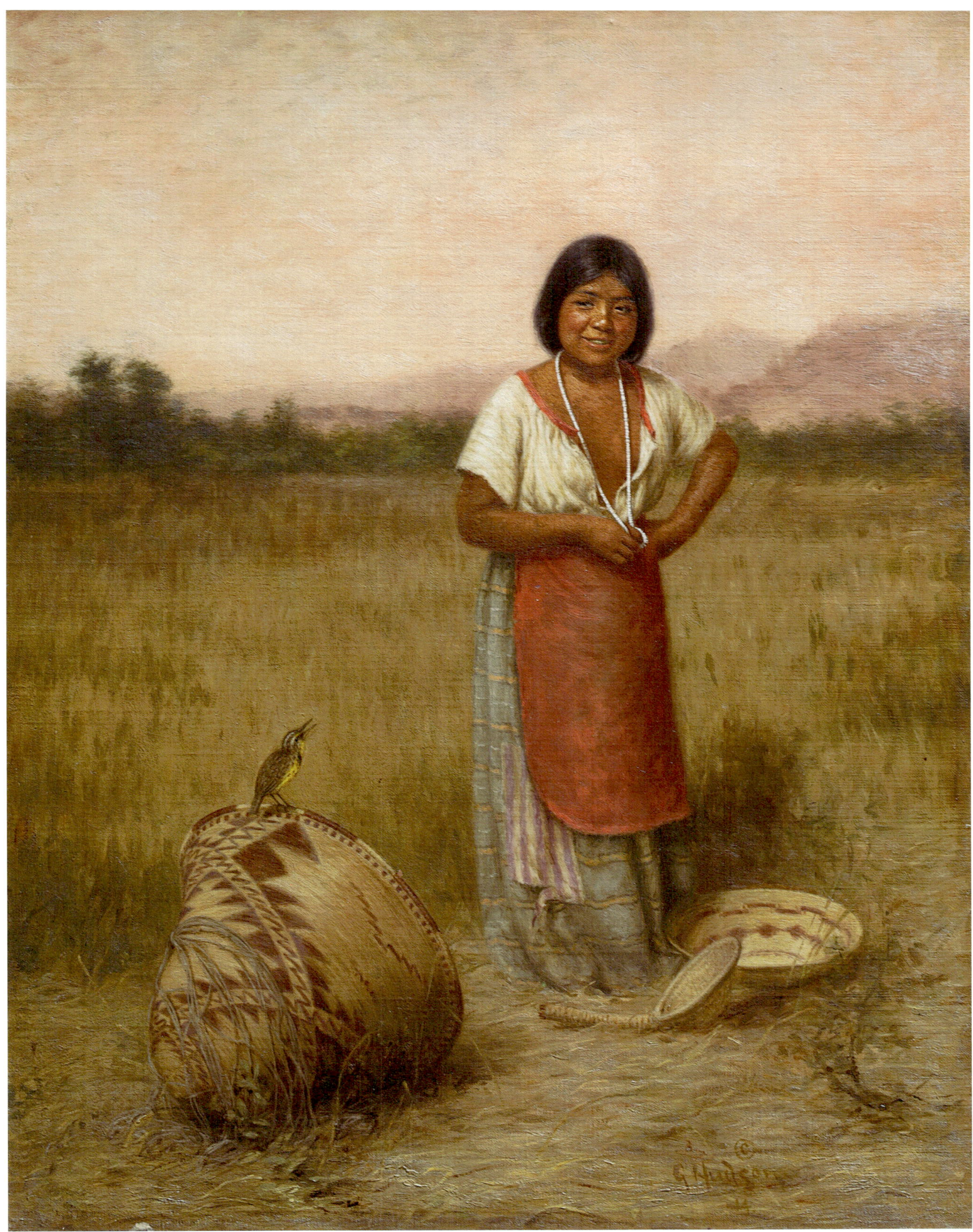

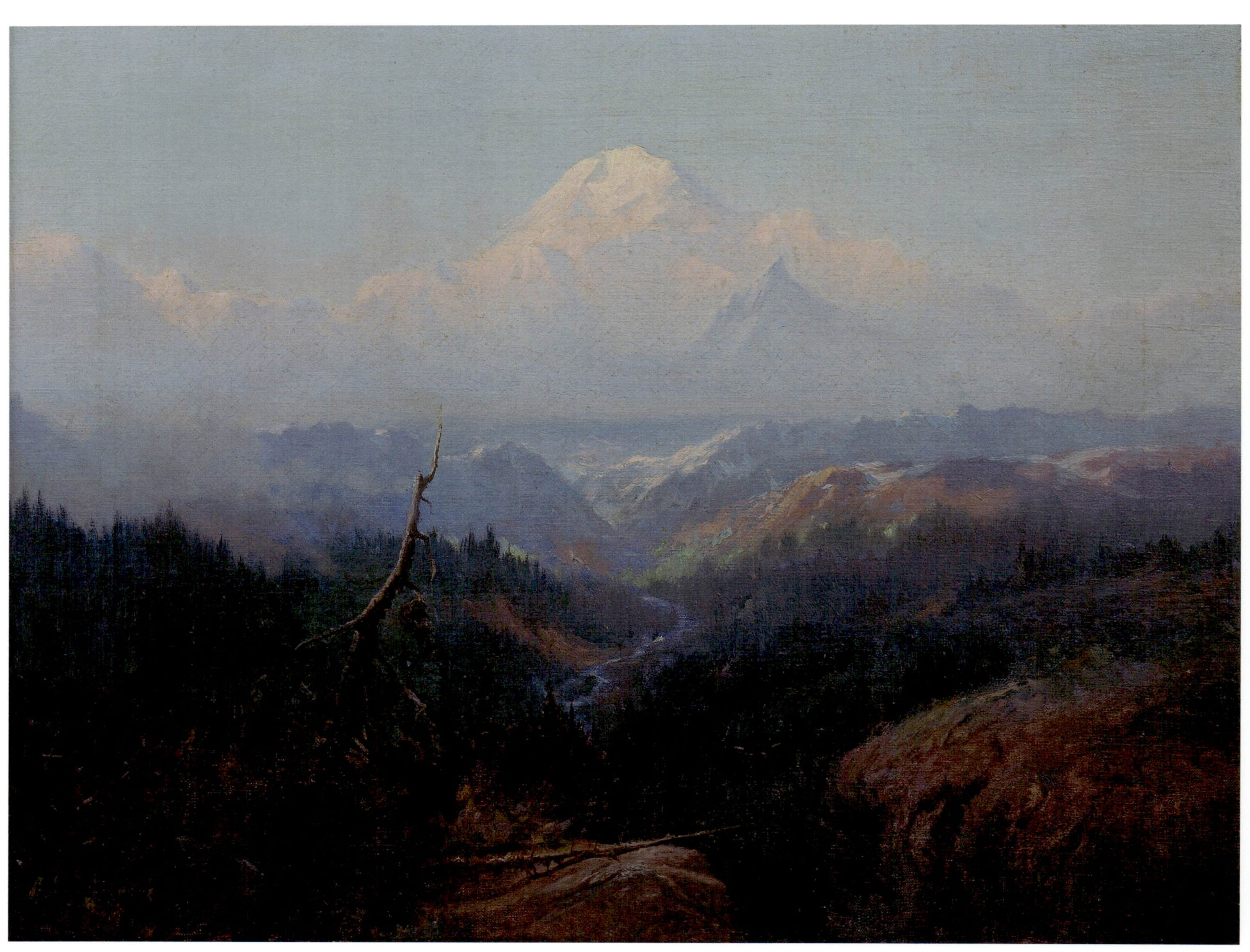

Mount McKinley

1919
Oil on canvas
15 × 20 inches

When artist Sydney Laurence arrived in Alaska in 1904 to search for gold, he found a raw and rugged land of extremes. "Talk of your cold! through the parka's fold it stabbed like a driven nail," wrote poet Robert Service, describing the nearby Yukon.* Not finding success in his mining venture, Laurence continued to paint. The clear light, looming peaks, and overwhelming natural forces in the far north fascinated him. Through the course of his career he painted dozens of images of Mt. McKinley (now also known by its Native American name, Denali), finding an endless source of inspiration in the over 20,000-foot-tall peak. In this painting the mountain seems to float above the foreground, shimmering in the atmosphere. The color palette of pale blue, gray, and deep green conveys the cold feel of the air, while the dark, shadowed rendering of the foreground implies that this place is a mysterious, untrodden land.

*Robert W. Service, *The Spell of the Yukon and Other Verses* (New York: Barse & Hopkins, 1907), 50.

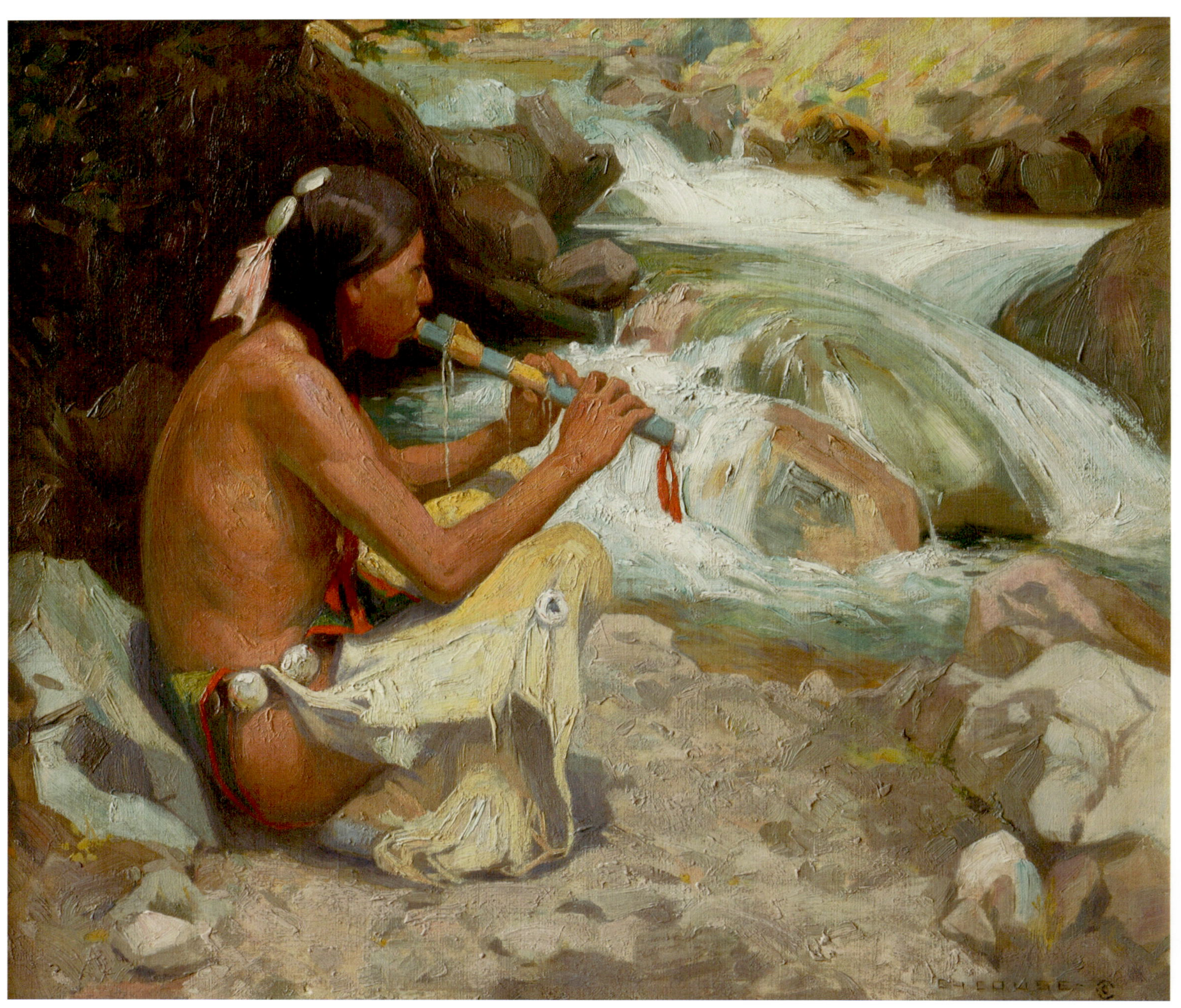

Music of the Waters

1911
Oil on canvas
20 × 24 inches

A flute player crouches next to a tumbling stream, the sound of the waters mingling with his soft notes, an ideal blend of the arts and the natural world. Irving Couse's painting of a calm musician in tune with nature represents a romanticized image of life in Taos, New Mexico. In a nod to classical mythology, the flute player with his buckskin leggings suggests the Greek god Pan, who presided over wild fields and wooded areas while playing rustic melodies on his pipes. By combining references to ancient Greece with Taos imagery, Couse presents the Southwest as a new Arcadia—an unspoiled, harmonious wilderness. Today, Robert Mirabal of the Taos Pueblo, an award-winning flute maker and musician, finds that Couse's paintings continue to resonate in the 21st century. "I'm partial to Couse," writes Mirabal. "To see these works of art, even though very romantic, it is still a world that I know and live, and yes it is very romantic."*

*Robert Mirabal, "Frozen Water in the Horse Troughs & Old Masters," *Robert Mirabal: Music and Myth* (website and blog), May 30, 2012, http://www.mirabalnativeflutes.com/frozen-water-in-the-horse -troughs-old-masters.

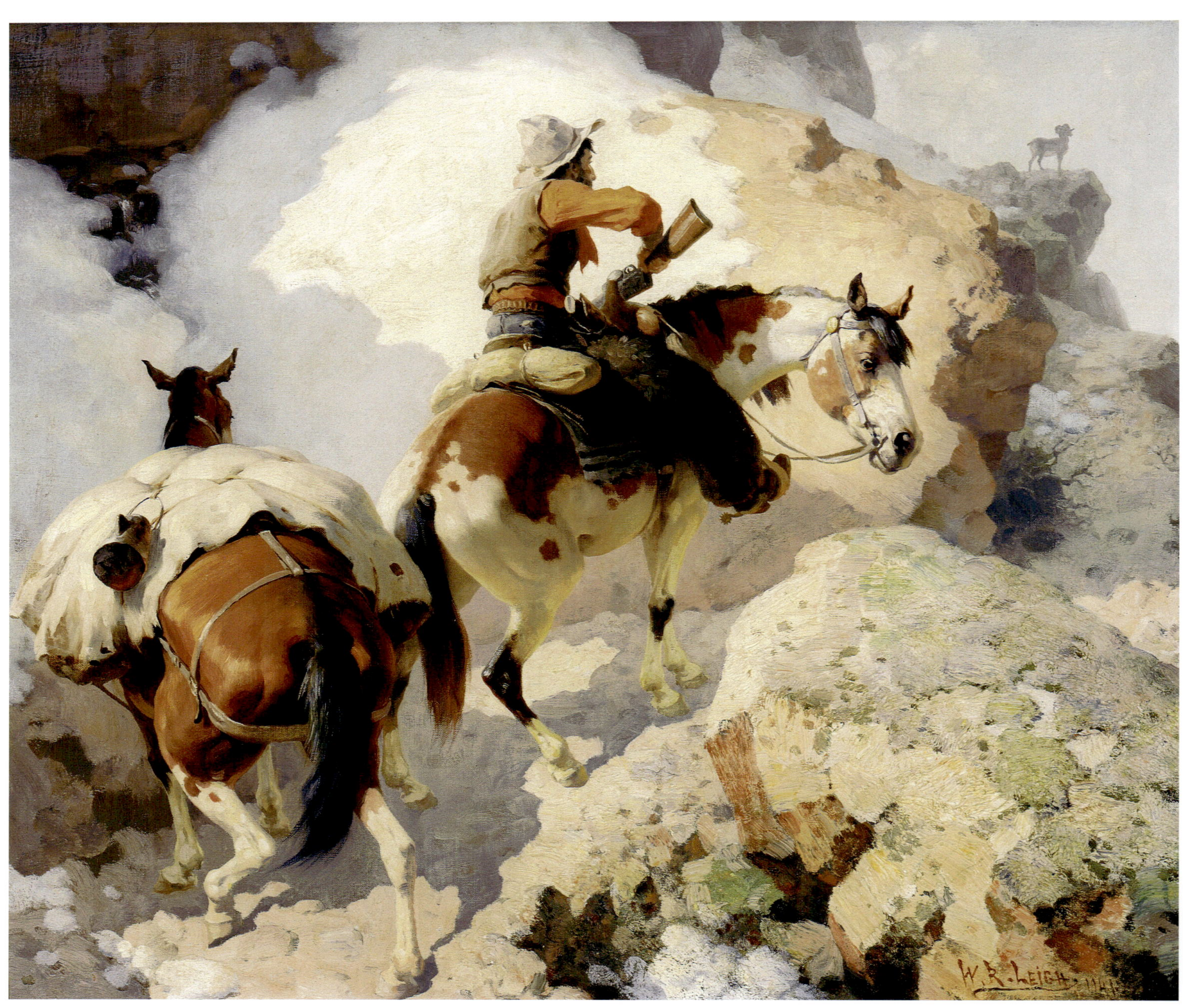

Wyoming Sheep Hunter

1941
Oil on canvas
24 × 29 inches

Across a field of jagged boulders the pursuer spies his prey perched on the edge of a rocky precipice. In a characteristic painting, William R. Leigh captures the tense moment of a hunter drawing his rifle. After Leigh's first visit to Arizona in 1906, the New York painter and illustrator made a career focusing on subjects from the western United States. Traveling for inspiration from Wyoming to New Mexico, Leigh was drawn to nostalgic stories of legendary action and adventure. His paintings typically portray a wild place in sharp contrast to his New York home—making them all the more appealing to his East Coast audience. In this image, sure-footed horses bulge with muscle as the hunter calmly lifts his trusty firearm, unafraid of riding through steep, treacherous terrain in search of his target. The diagonal composition—drawing the viewer's eye from the horse in the lower left to the distant bighorn sheep in the top right—adds a sense of motion. By portraying a lone hunter on a rocky mountainside, Leigh reinforces the myth that the West was solely a land of rugged masculine individuals single-handedly conquering the wilderness.

A Chief of the Multnomah Tribe

modeled 1907; cast 1912–14
Bronze
31½ × 13 × 12 inches

In a wooded corner of Washington Park in Portland, Oregon, you can still see a bronze monument of two Native American men atop a boulder overlooking the Columbia River Gorge. The monument, *Coming of the White Man,* was created by sculptor Hermon Atkins MacNeil and installed in 1904 in anticipation of Portland's 1905 Lewis and Clark Exposition. MacNeil portrayed an imagined historical moment when two members of the Multnomah Tribe, a band of Chinook people who lived near Portland, first saw Anglo explorers approaching from the east. The chief stands stern, with his arms crossed over his chest, wary of the newcomers. MacNeil based the figure on an 1890 account of a legendary Chief Multnomah: "His dark, grandly impassive face, with its imposing regularity of feature, showed a penetration that read everything, a reserve that revealed nothing. . . . The glance that flashed out from this reserved and resolute face—sharp, searching, and imperious—may complete the portrait of Multnomah."* After installing the life-size sculpture, MacNeil created this smaller scale cast of the chief, a lone figure standing dignified and defiant.

*Frederic Homer Balch, *The Bridge of the Gods: A Romance of Indian Oregon* (Chicago: A. C. McClurg, 1890), 58–59.

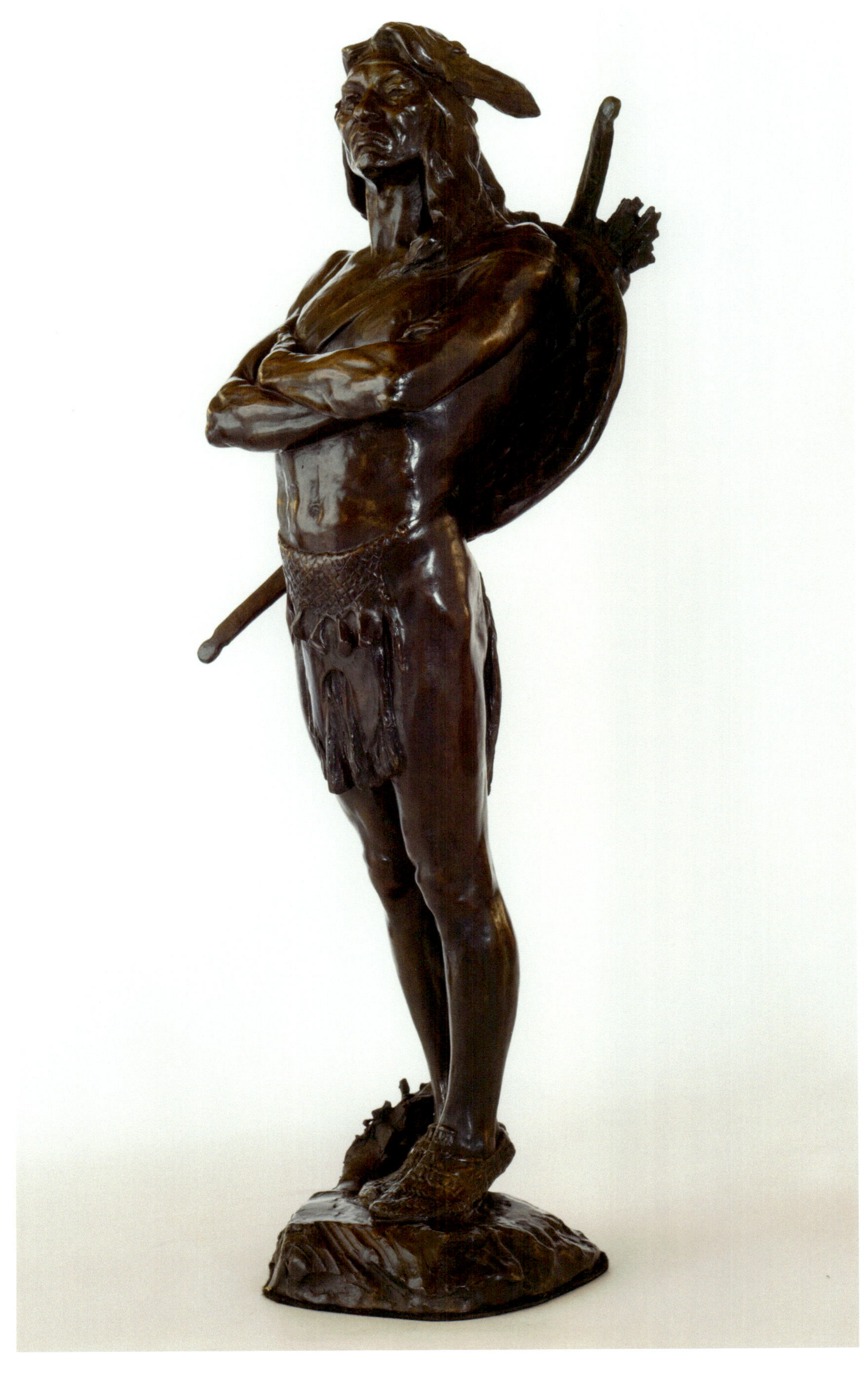

Portrait of Star Road

circa 1930
Oil on canvas
37 × 31¾ inches

Star Road began modeling for Taos painters long before Catharine Critcher first arrived in New Mexico in the 1920s. Although his everyday clothing consisted of jeans and a button-down shirt (sometimes paired with a ten-gallon hat), he was frequently painted or photographed in an elaborate costume. The tension between his actual appearance and his painted, historicized image mirrored his active participation in debates among people of the Taos Pueblo over tradition and assimilation. Star Road advocated for modernization on his own terms. He wore elements of modern dress and he openly used peyote, a mild hallucinogen—although both the traditional elders of the pueblo and the Catholic Church opposed the practice.

To paint this well-known figure in the Taos community, Critcher eschewed an invented costume. Instead, she depicted Star Road in his usual collared shirt with a simple white blanket around his shoulders, a drum and striped blanket forming abstract patterns behind him. He looks up and to the right, as if engaged in a conversation. With Star Road's portrait, Critcher portrayed a person of 20th-century New Mexico forging his own path between the old ways and the new.

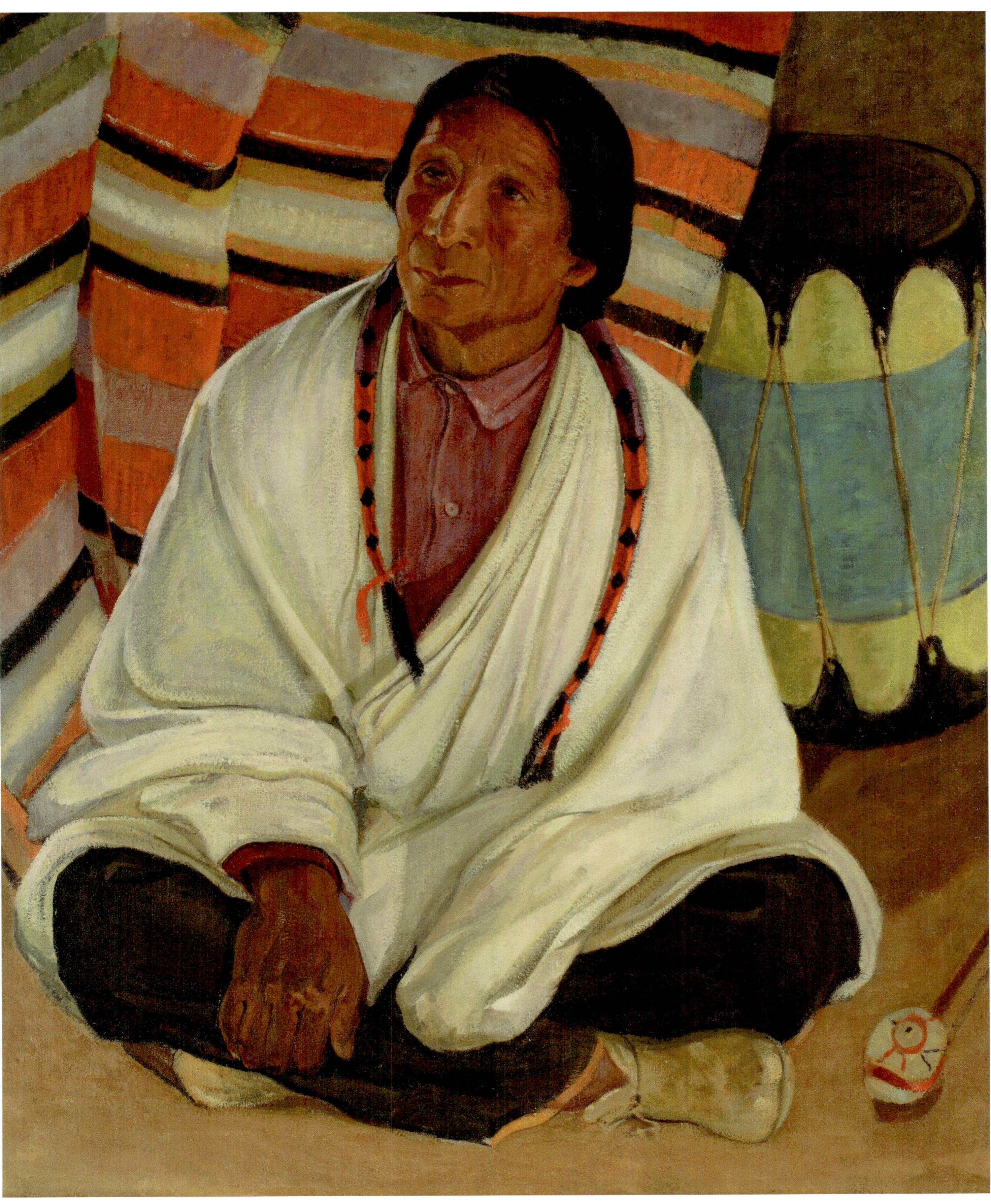

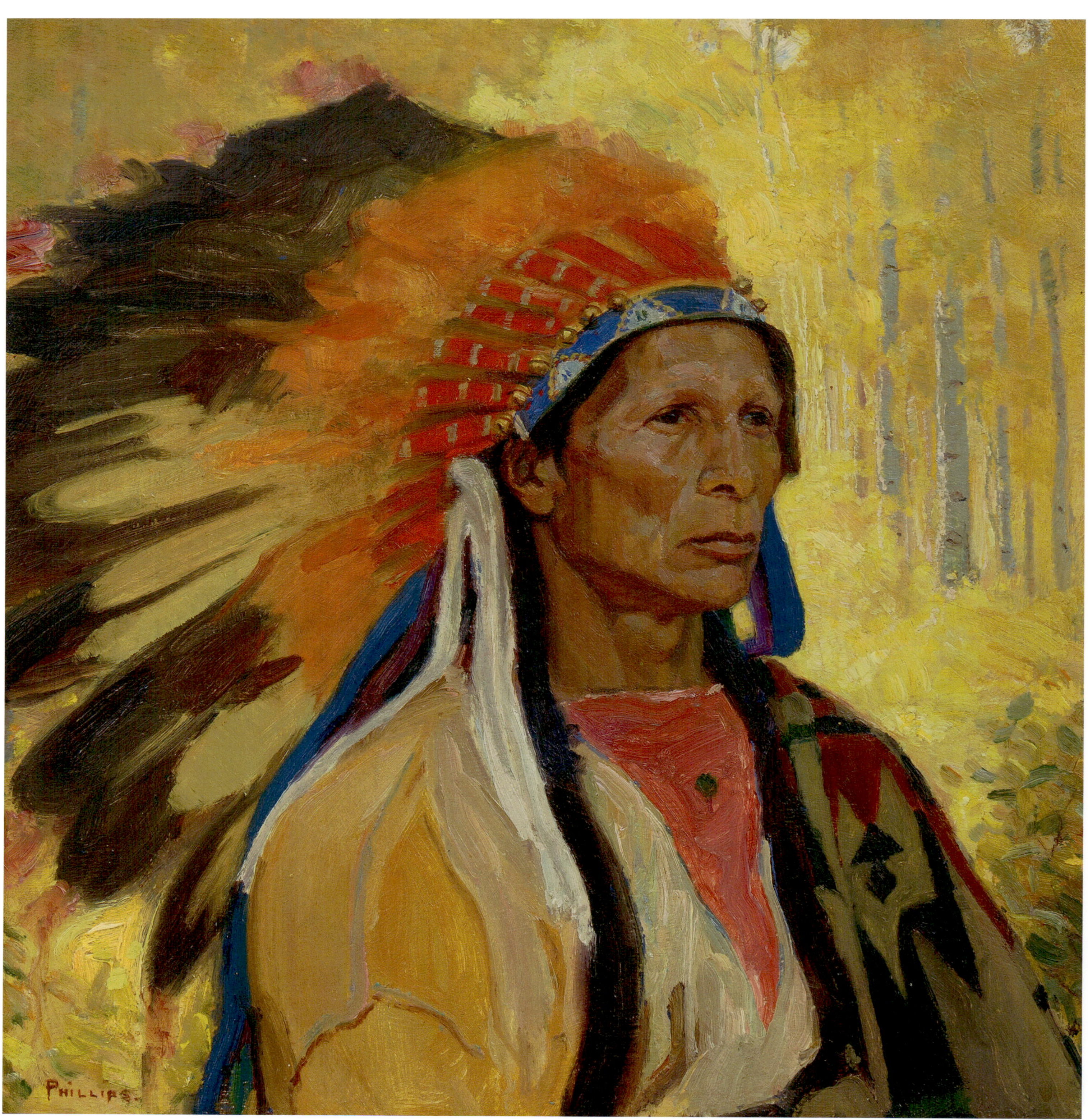

PHILLIPS.

Portrait of a Chief

circa 1925
Oil on board
14 × 14 inches

As an art student at the Académie Julian in Paris in 1895, Bert Phillips eagerly listened to vivid tales of colorful desert scenery half a world away in New Mexico. His fellow student, artist Joseph Henry Sharp, had visited the Southwest and described the region as a perfect subject for American artists. In 1898 Phillips joined Ernest Blumenschein, another friend from the Académie Julian, and together they set out for New Mexico. When a broken wagon wheel sent them to the small mountain town of Taos for assistance, they found an ideal location to inspire an artist's brush. After remaining a few months Blumenschein returned to New York—but Phillips was there to stay. Soon other artists began joining him for summers in Taos, and in 1915 six painters formed the Taos Society of Artists, assuring Taos's status as a center for arts in the West.

In this portrait, a strip of bright blue frames the chief's face, contrasting with the warm hues of ochre and crimson in his clothing and the golden aspen foliage loosely rendered in the background. Rather than portraying traditional Taos regalia, Phillips posed his model in a vibrant feather headdress from the Great Plains—one of the most universally recognized symbols of Native America.

Hopi Indian Pueblo, NM

date unknown
Oil on board
9¾ × 12 inches

Born Ira Diamond Gerald Cassidy in Covington, Kentucky, Cassidy first studied painting across the Ohio River at the Art Academy of Cincinnati under Frank Duveneck—another Covington native. Duveneck's free, slashing brushwork would remain a lasting influence on Cassidy's work. When he later settled in Santa Fe, Cassidy avidly traveled the Southwest region in search of new subjects. In this loosely rendered work, Cassidy gives viewers a sense of wandering through the pueblo architecture by framing the scene in a wide doorway. Repeated colors of vermilion and blue move the viewer's eye around the composition. The portable size of this painting and the quick, energetic brushstrokes indicate that Cassidy may have created the image on site, conveying the immediate feel of the sun on the adobe walls with a bright blue sky overhead.

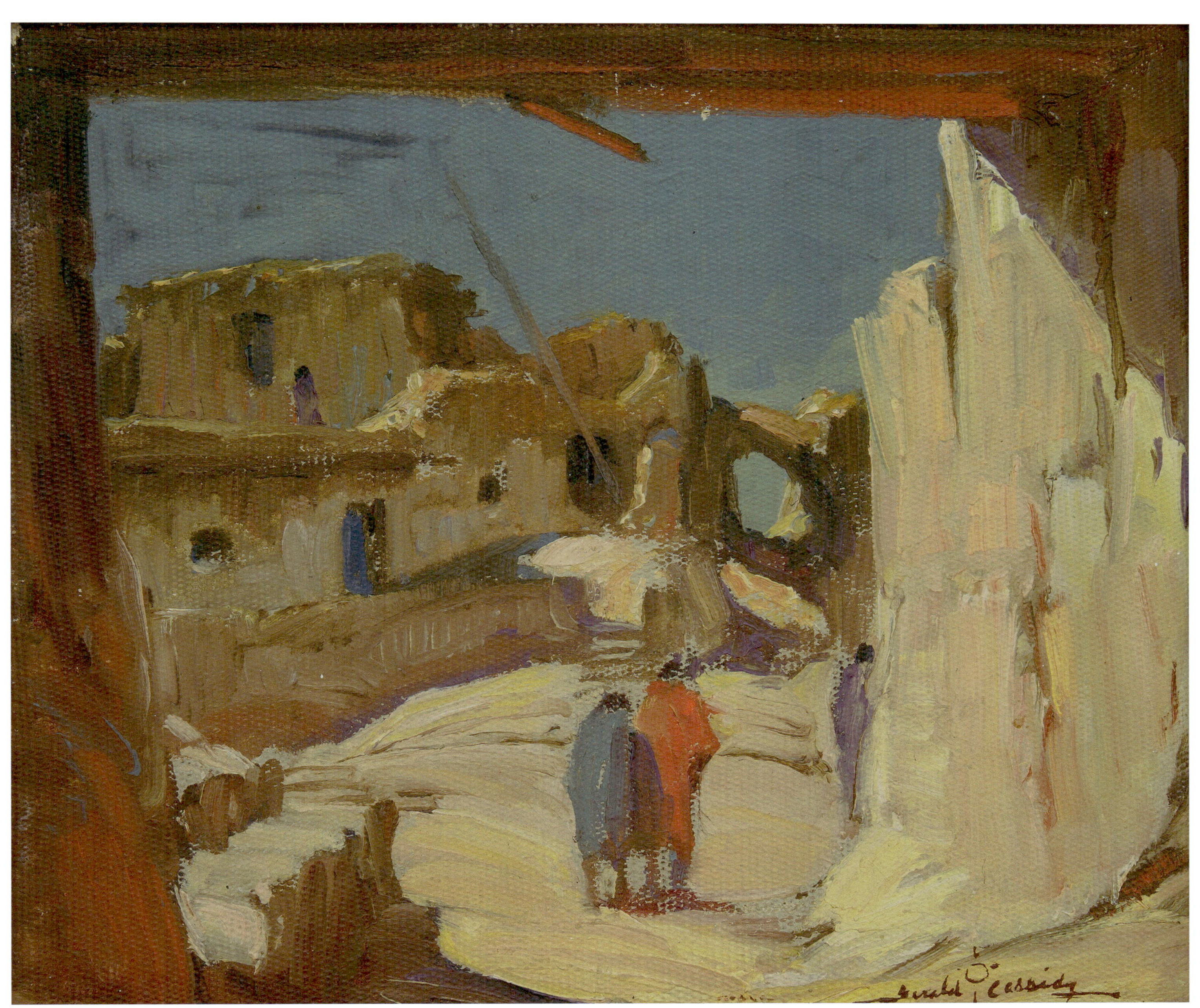

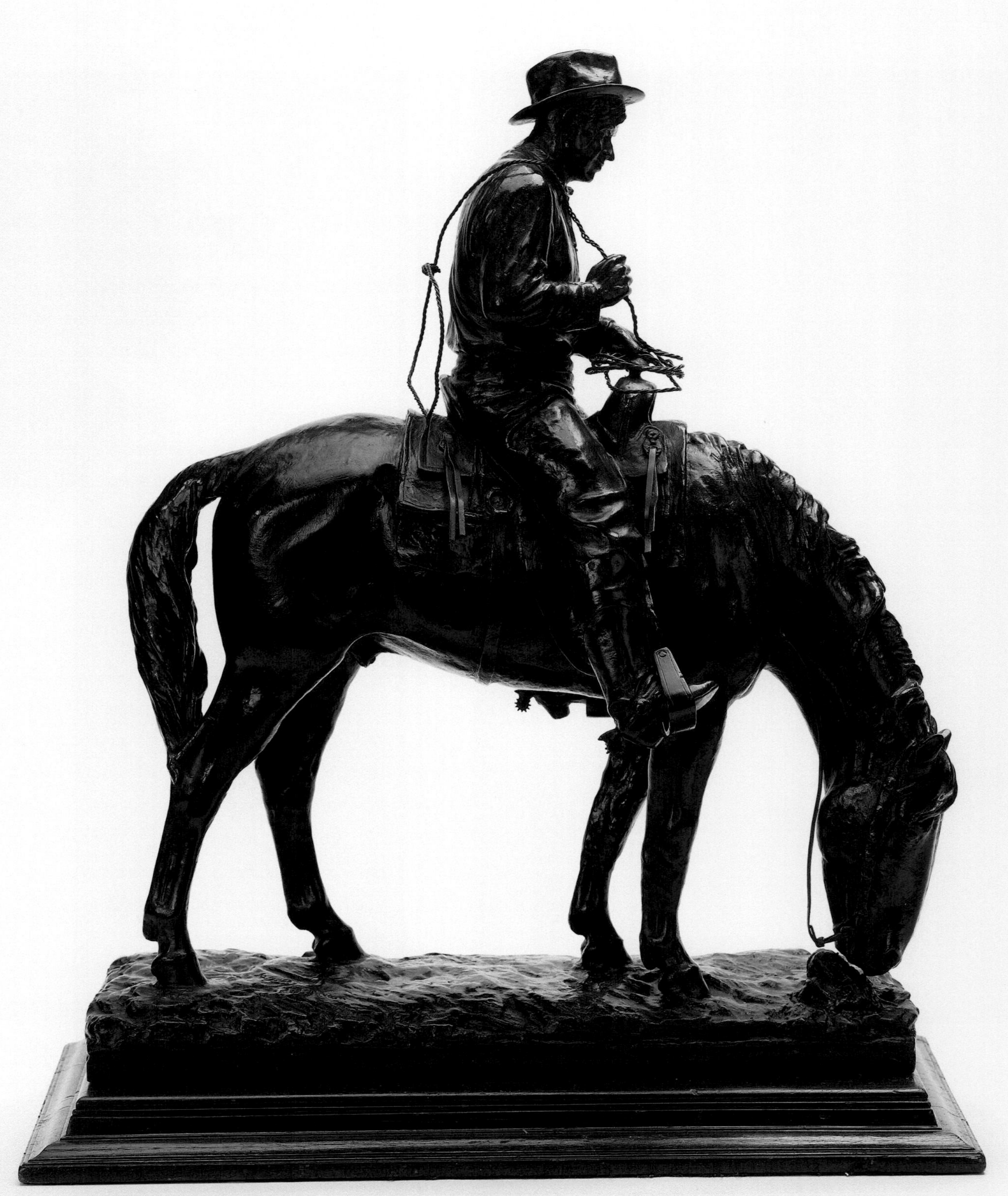

SALLY JAMES FARNHAM (1869–1943)

Will Rogers on Horseback

circa 1938
Bronze
21½ × 17½ × 5½ inches

"I never met a man I didn't like."* This line defined the charismatic western film star Will Rogers, who became the highest paid and most popular Hollywood actor in the early 1930s. After his untimely death shocked the nation in 1935, artist Sally Farnham created *Will Rogers on Horseback* to enter in a competition for a monument to the famous western performer.

When she started sculpting in 1901, Farnham received encouragement and instruction from Frederic Remington, an old family friend. In a strange crosscurrent of popular entertainment and art, Remington's action-packed sculptures of cowboys and Native Americans had influenced many a scene in early American film—and now Farnham, Remington's protégé, took a famous figure from Hollywood cinema and sculpted him in bronze. Farnham did not simply represent the actor in a familiar cowboy pose. Rather, she portrays him in a calm mood astride his favorite roping horse, Dopey, with reins slack, allowing the horse to graze. The grazing horse forms a metaphor for Rogers's support for hunger relief efforts during the Great Depression, showing his genuine care and sympathy for his fellow citizens.

*One of his most famous and most quoted remarks, this phrase was first recorded by Will Rogers in his article "On Leon Trotsky," *Saturday Evening Post*, November 6, 1926.

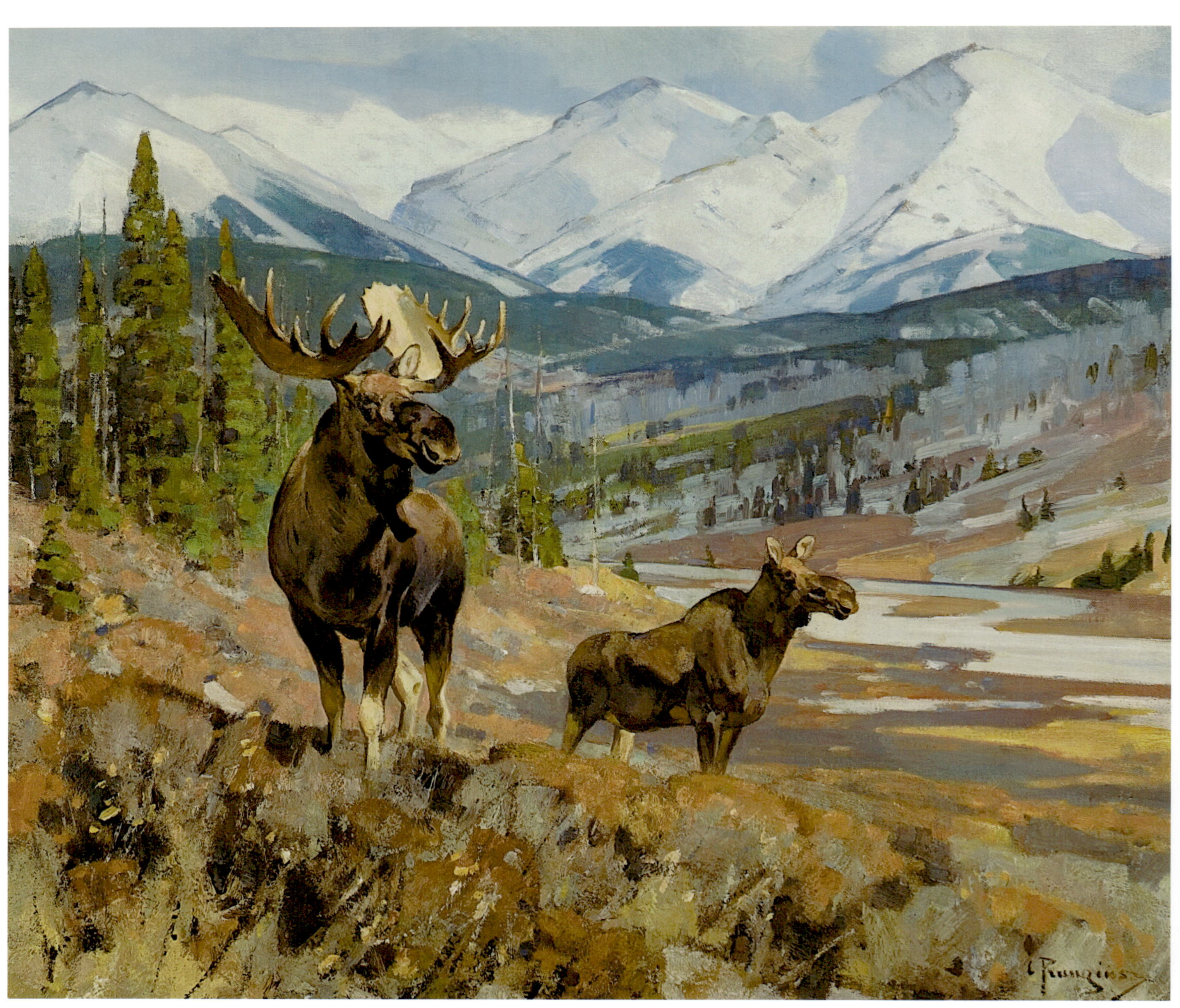

On the Ram River

1938
Oil on canvas
25 × 30 inches

Along the Ram River, with the Canadian Rockies rising in the distance, artist Carl Rungius frequently watched for moose roaming the landscape. Captivated by his first visit to the Rocky Mountains, the German artist had relocated to North America in 1896, spending summers in Wyoming and Canada and winters in New York. Both an avid hunter and conservationist, Rungius was a member of the Boone and Crockett Club, a big game conservation organization founded by Theodore Roosevelt that encouraged protection of wildlife in conjunction with limited, ethical hunting. Influenced by the early 20th-century paintings of Paul Cézanne, Rungius frequently used planes of color and quick brushstrokes to construct a scene. His paintings combine his experiences camping and hunting in the Rocky Mountains with Cézanne's post-impressionist style—an approach that captured the beauty of basic forms and colors in the landscape. By celebrating North America's wildlife and open spaces in his work, Rungius prompted viewers to appreciate the incalculable value of unspoiled wilderness.

Autumn (Smoky Hill River, Kansas)

1944
Oil on canvas mounted on panel
20 × 24 inches

Far from the dramatic peaks of the Rocky Mountains, Birger Sandzén found inspiration in the rolling plains and tranquil rivers of central Kansas. As a young man, he had traveled from his home in Sweden to Paris to study with French symbolist painter Edmond François Aman-Jean. After relocating from Europe to Lindsborg, Kansas, in 1894, Sandzén became a professor at Bethany College, where he remained until his retirement in 1945. While he traveled widely through the American West, teaching for a short while in Colorado and exhibiting his work in New Mexico with the Taos Society of Artists, the changing seasons of the Kansas landscape remained one of his favorite subjects. In this painting, Sandzén renders a Kansas riverbank in his characteristic impasto brushstrokes, building dense foliage with thick daubs of paint in bold colors. Sandzén revealed the understated beauty of the Great Plains landscape in his unique, expressive style.

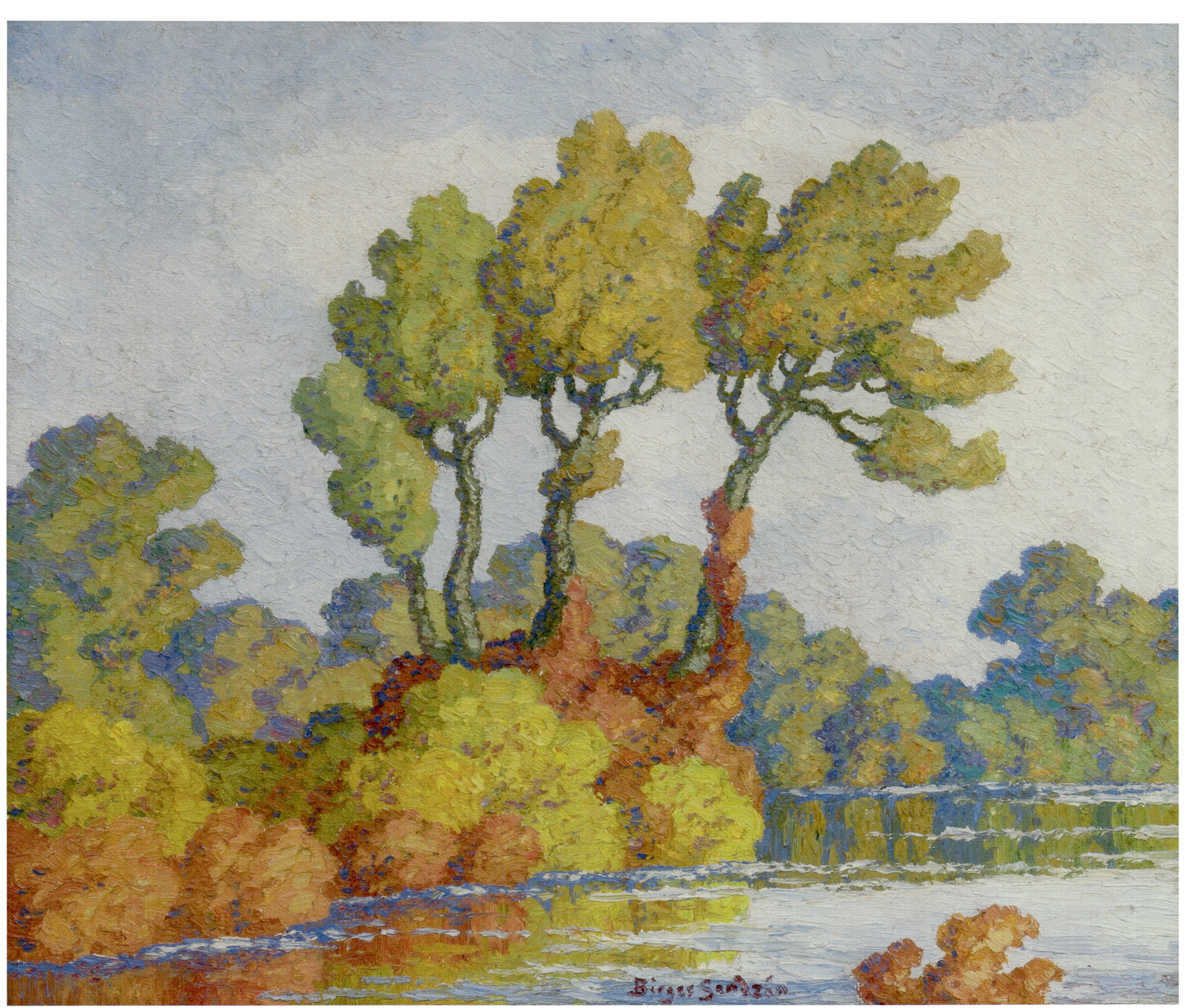
Birger Sandzén

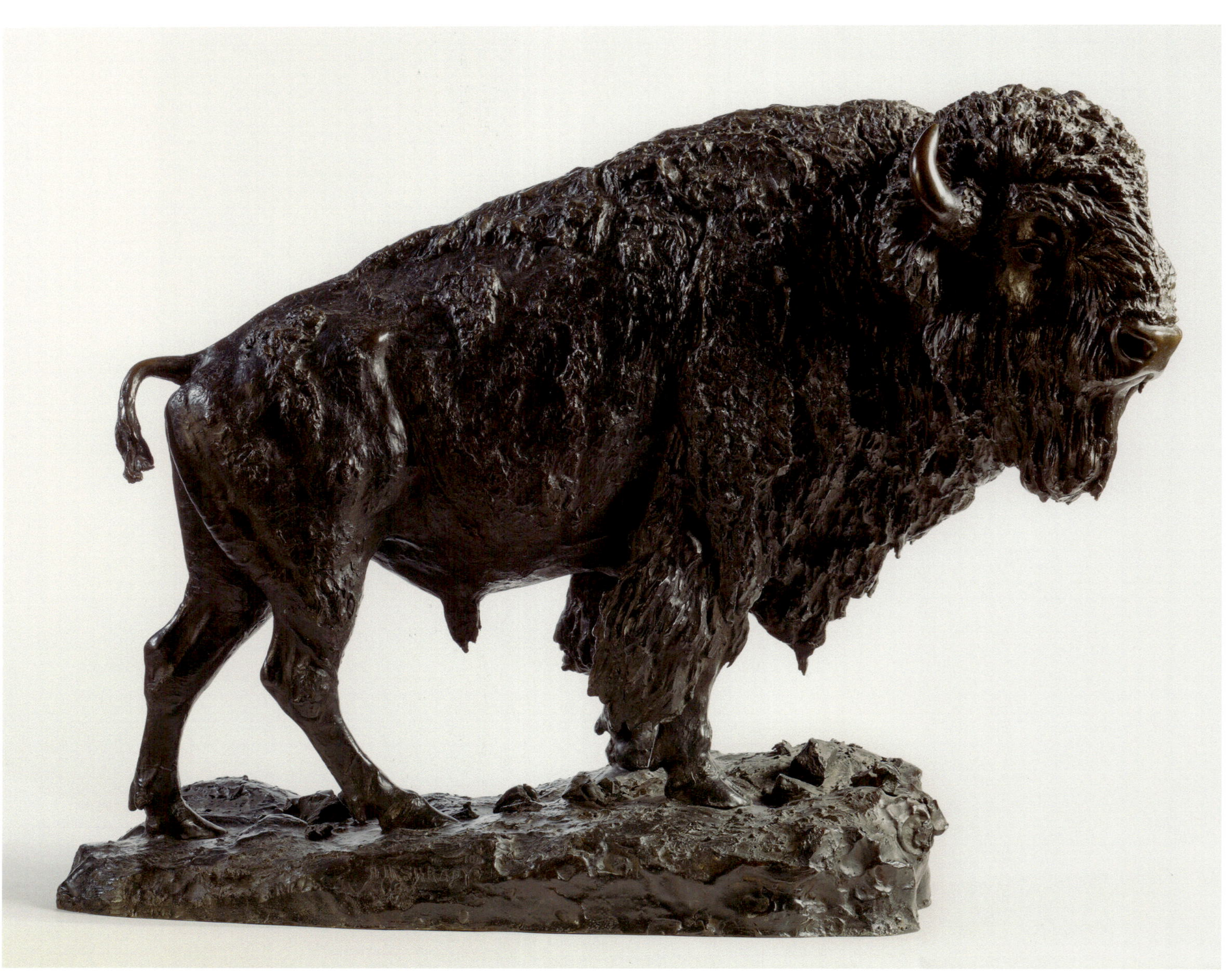

HENRY MERWIN SHRADY (1871–1922)

Elk Buffalo (The Monarch of the Plains)

circa 1900
Bronze
22½ × 24 × 13 inches

Henry Shrady never saw the majestic American bison (commonly called buffalo) roaming free in the wild. Rather, the self-taught New York artist was inspired by his undergraduate classes in biology at Columbia University and his observations of live bison at the Bronx Zoo. To create this sculpture—one of his first works in bronze—he used lost-wax casting, a method newly available in the United States around 1900. Unlike earlier casting processes, the lost-wax method allowed artists to make small adjustments to individual wax models before each piece was cast in bronze, resulting in unique sculptures with small variations. The lost-wax process could capture subtle details with sharp precision, allowing Shrady to create the varied textures of a bison's thick, furry coat in a bronze surface. Portraying a proud, unconquered animal of the West, Shrady's sculpture represents an astonishing technical feat as one of the earliest lost-wax bronze castings in the United States.

Headin' Up the Range

circa 1915
Oil on canvas
30 × 20 inches

"Quite a guy, mostly stubborn as hell," recalled a friend of artist Edward Borein.* A headstrong young man who grew up in San Leandro, California, Borein's early interest in drawing was not enough to keep him engaged at the California School of Design (now the San Francisco Art Institute). After one month he fled the classroom and found employment as a vaquero. From 1894 to 1899 he worked in the centuries-old Spanish cowboy tradition on ranches in southern California and Mexico, becoming fluent in Spanish and constantly making sketches. As he later moved back and forth across the country, from Oakland to New York to Santa Barbara, memories of the working vaqueros in California and Mexico continued to influence his artwork.

In New York Borein received advice from American impressionist painter Childe Hassam, and may have seen Frederic Remington's late impressionist-style paintings of the western landscape. In a nod to impressionism, Borein renders this Mexican vaquero in quick dabs of color; he emerges from a haze of dust and bright desert light as a figment of memory.

*Walter H. Fieberling, quoted in Harold G. Davidson, *Edward Borein, Cowboy Artist: The Life and Works of John Edward Borein 1872–1945* (Garden City, NY: Doubleday, 1974), 43.

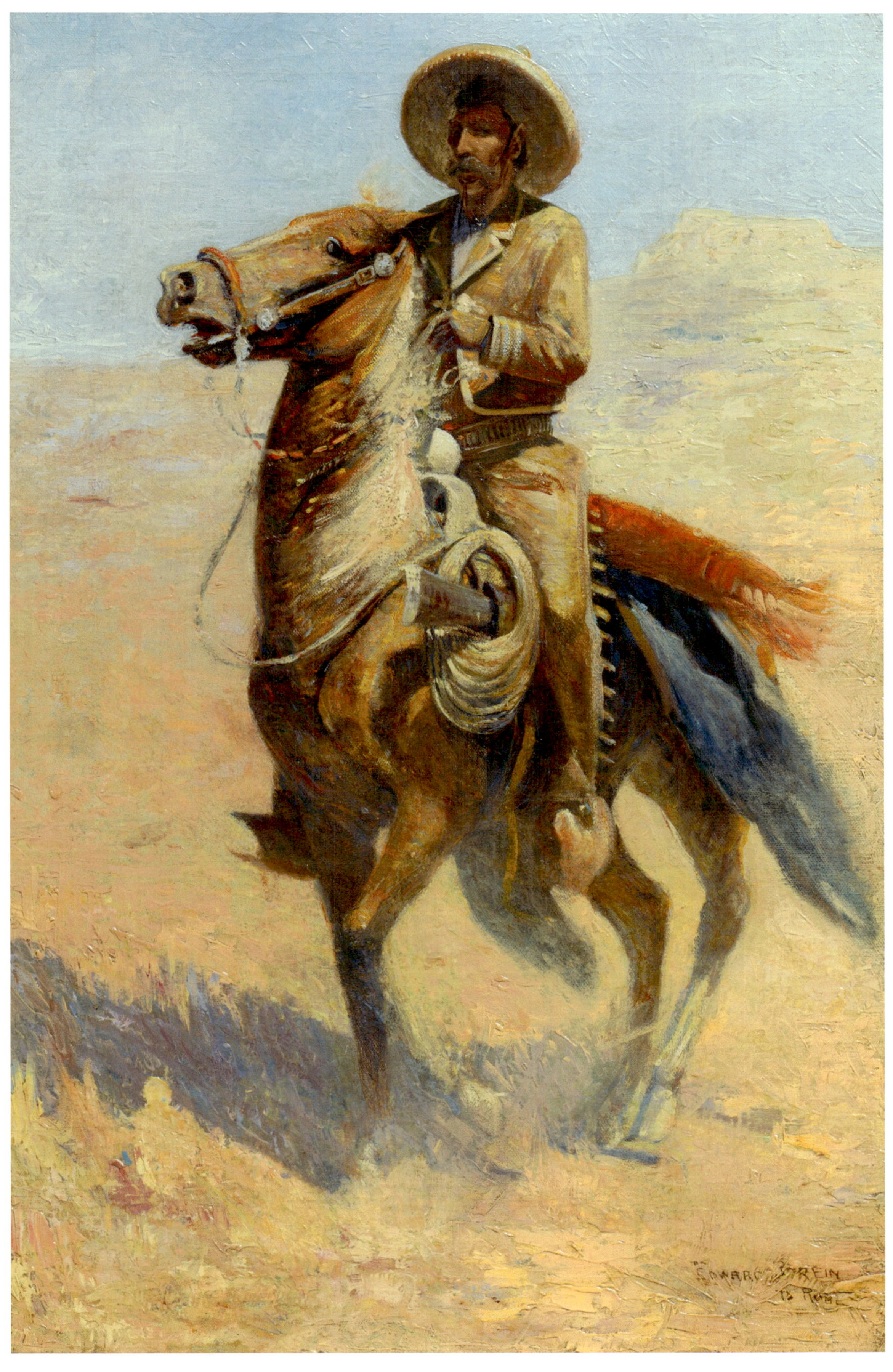

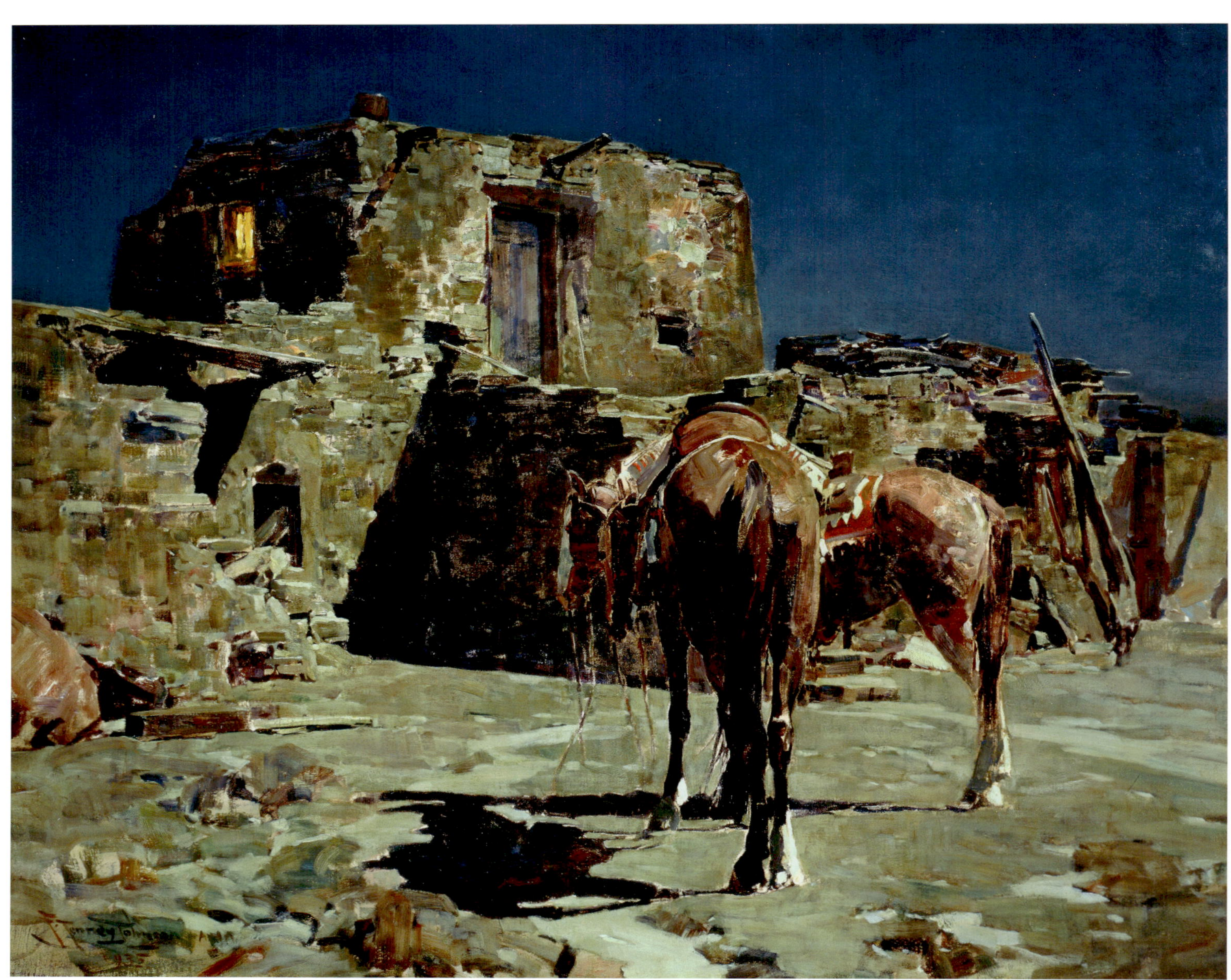

Casa de Indios

1935
Oil on canvas
36¼ × 46⅛ inches

Frank Tenney Johnson loved the shifting shades of nighttime in the arid West—dark turquoise and olive gray awash in muted, pearly light. As an aspiring young artist he traveled to New York in 1902 to study under William Merritt Chase and Robert Henri. When an illustration assignment from *Field and Stream* magazine sent him to Colorado and New Mexico for the first time, Johnson was hooked. He eventually established homes in Alhambra, California, and Cody, Wyoming, bringing the loose painting style and vivid application of color he learned in New York to subjects in the West. In this southwestern night scene, he applies quick, broad brushstrokes to show a drab adobe structure transformed by a wash of silver moonlight. The pinpoint of golden light illuminating a window and the saddled horses hitched outside contain hints of an unknown narrative unfolding in the desert night.

OSCAR E. BERNINGHAUS (1874–1952)

Taos Rabbit Hunt

circa 1935
Oil on canvas
30¼ × 34 inches

All the magical colors of New Mexico are on display in this everyday scene, from the rider's bright crimson shirt and glowing white horse to the rainbow hues in the fields and rolling mountains behind him. Although Oscar Berninghaus had little formal training in art, his background in illustration and his attention to detail allowed him to find beauty in the ordinary life of Taos in the early 20th century. Here, a bareheaded man rides an old, scrawny horse with a freshly killed rabbit lashed to the back of his saddle. Rather than a fanciful historic costume, he wears his usual clothing—a red shirt with a simple white blanket across his lap. The rider rests his bow on his shoulder as his horse ambles home. By showing the colorful splendor of a quiet, unremarkable moment, Berninghaus reveals the visual power that made Taos a mecca for artists.

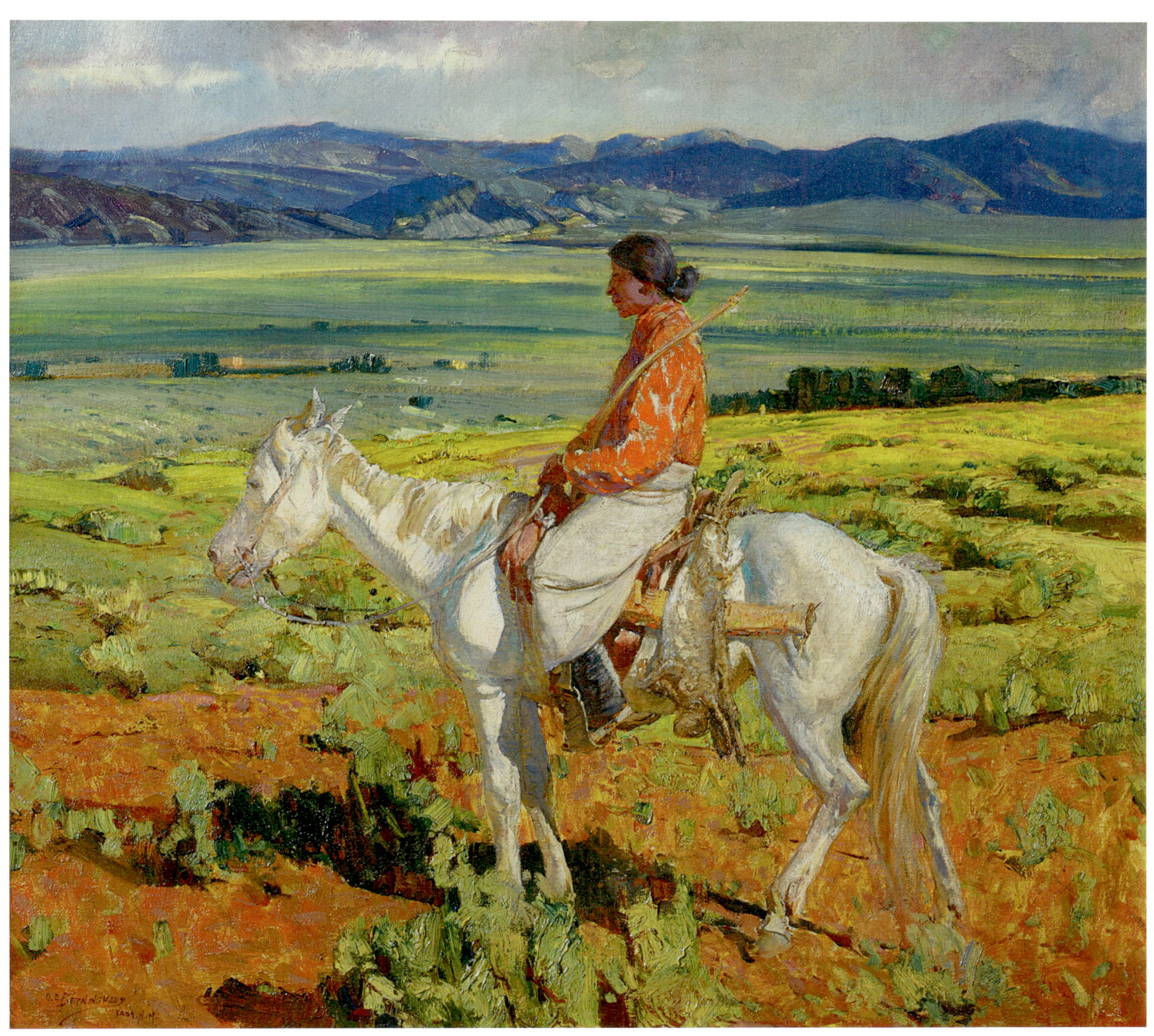

On Pueblo Road

circa 1930
Oil on canvas
16 × 20¼ inches

A founding member of the Taos Society of Artists, Ernest Blumenschein was inspired by the patterns and rhythms of the Southwest landscape. His painting *On Pueblo Road* shows a group of people wrapped in colorful cloaks and shawls, walking and riding along a broad unpaved road in the shade of an adobe wall. But the painting also forms a study of strong abstract triangular forms: the span of road, the trees on both sides, and the mountains in the background form triangles that converge in the center of the canvas. Smaller triangles are repeated in the crags of the mountain face and in the shapes formed by two groups of people as they move toward and away from the viewer. Even the cloaks on the backs of the people form repeated triangles, making the individuals integral to the larger pattern of the scene. For Blumenschein, the Taos region provided ample opportunities for blending representation and abstraction in his painting.

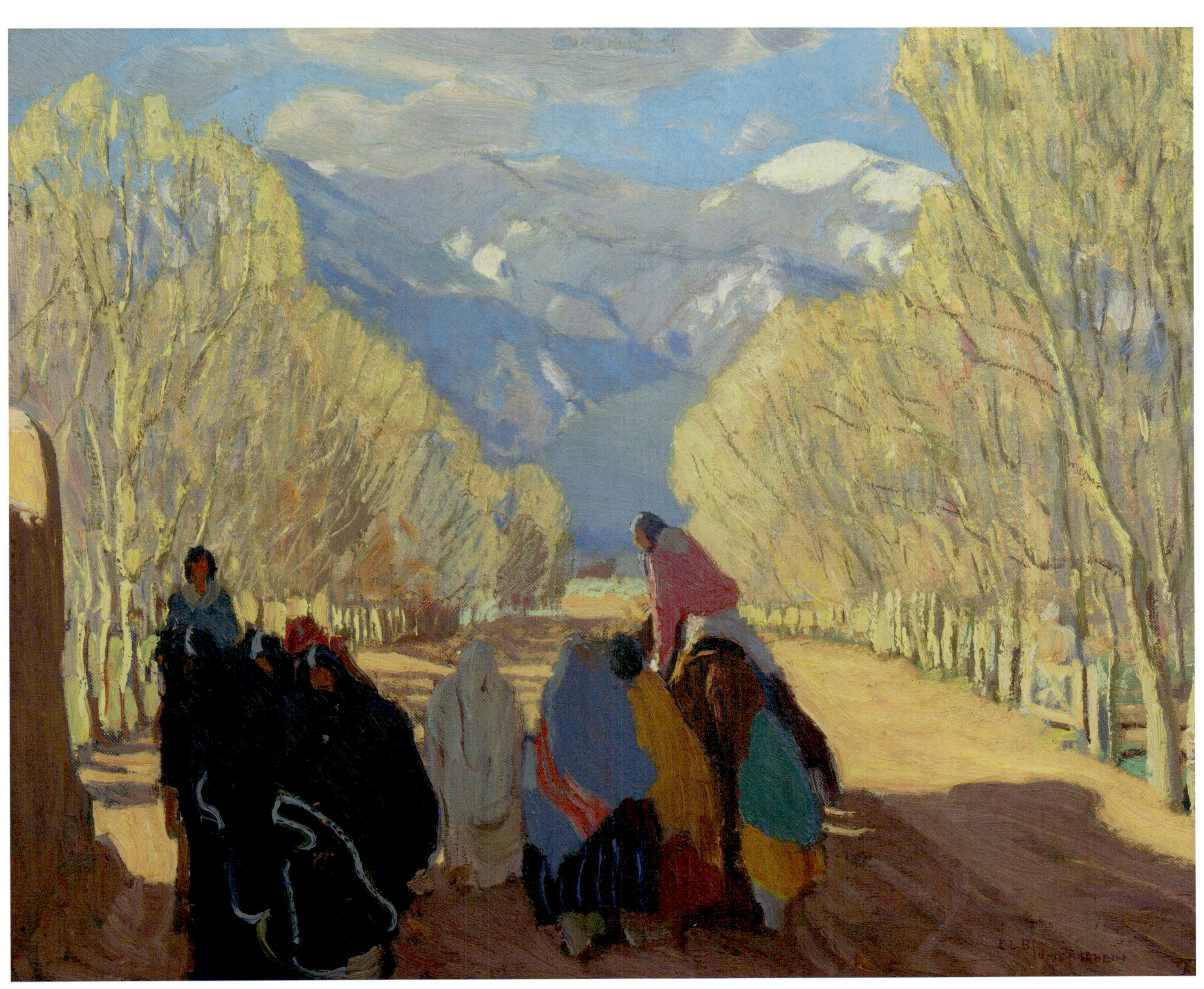

A Desert Valley

1922
Oil on board
22 × 22 inches

In bands of burnt orange and deep blue, brilliant yellow and muted violet, the Panamint Mountains in Death Valley contain a dazzling array of colors for an artist's palette. Maynard Dixon, born and raised in the semi-arid San Joaquin Valley in California, endured the punishing heat of Death Valley for a chance to experience the vivid hues radiating from the sheer rock walls. An active member of San Francisco's burgeoning art scene in the early 20th century, and the husband of photographer Dorothea Lange, Dixon kept abreast of the latest developments in American art. In *A Desert Valley* he reduces the landscape to horizontal stripes and undulating fields of color strumming across a canvas, creating a simplified modern image of the California wilderness.

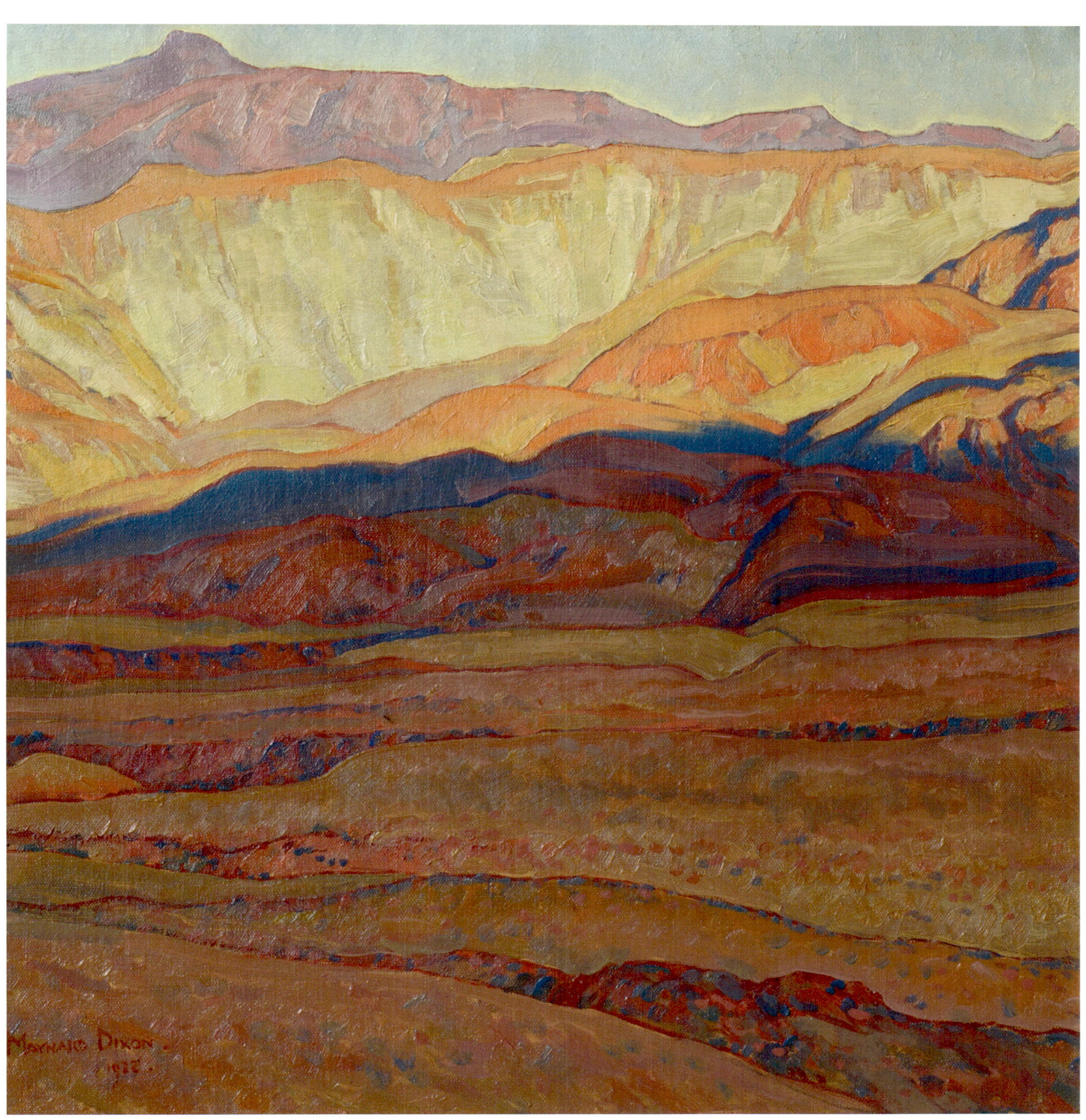

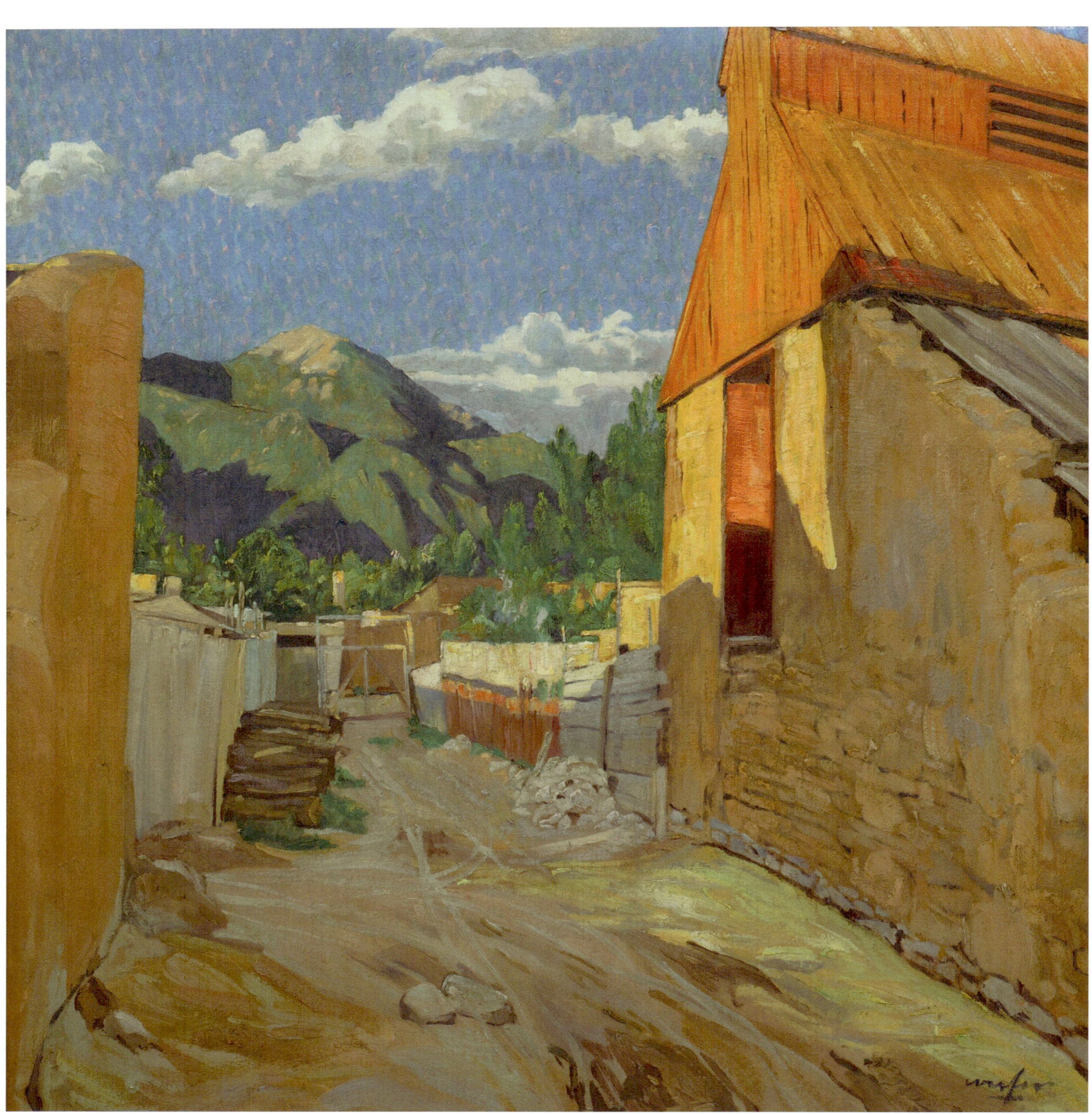

Evening Rays

circa 1923
Oil on canvas
25 × 25 inches

Even a dusty alley in a small mountain town can provide inspiration for a glowing, light-filled painting. Artist Walter Ufer found subjects to paint in the untidiness of everyday life, and took exception to the highly romanticized portrayals of a timeless New Mexico by several of his colleagues in the Taos Society of Artists. Born in Kentucky to German immigrant parents, Ufer studied in Chicago and Germany before his first visit to Taos in 1914. A political radical, he was a member of the Industrial Workers of the World (IWW) and a supporter of Leon Trotsky. In this painting, Ufer captures the amber sunlight in quick post-impressionist brushstrokes, bathing a building in brilliant orange and gold, turning the distant hills a vibrant green. By celebrating the beauty of weathered back alleys in his vivid canvases, Ufer found all places equal in art.

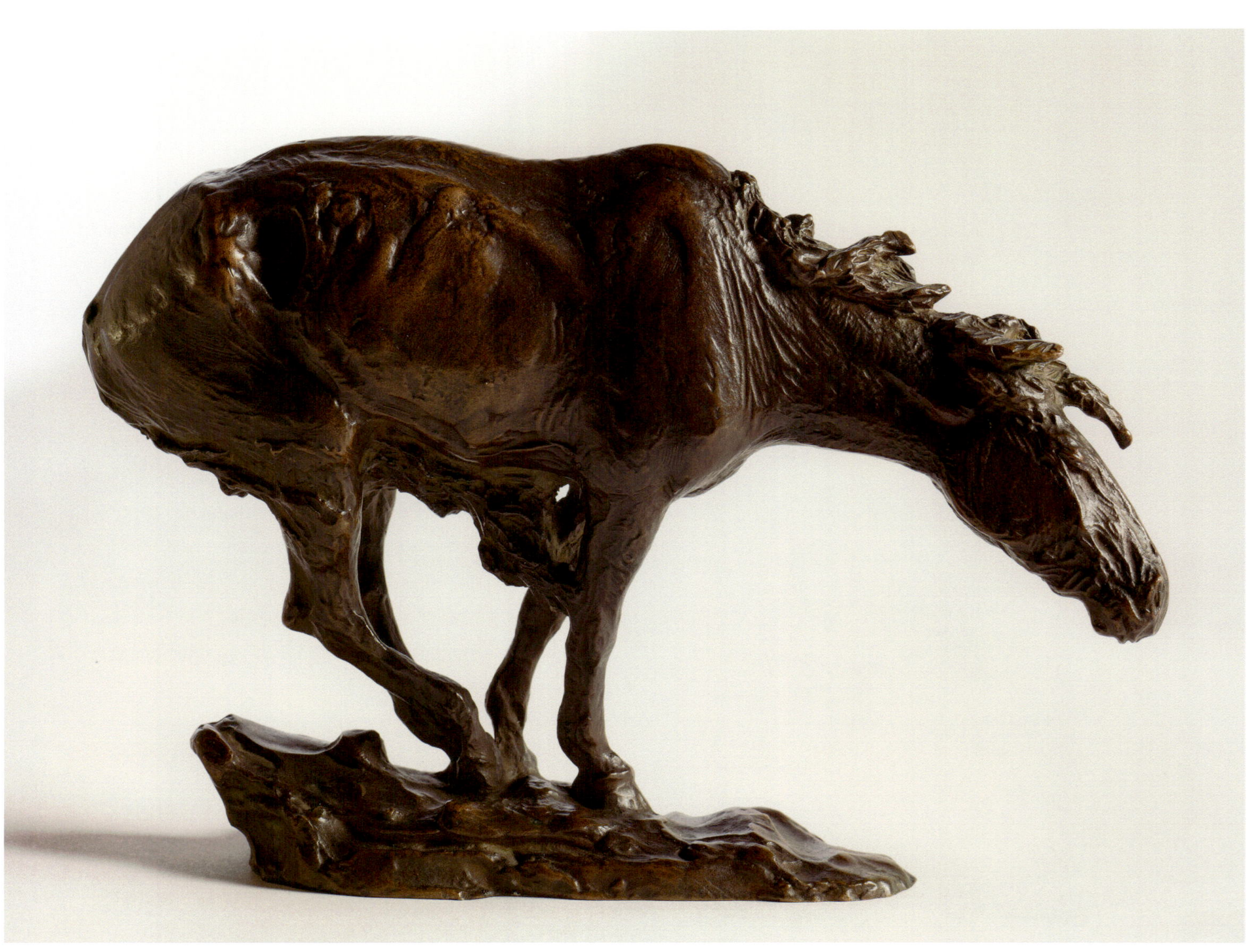

JAMES EARLE FRASER (1876–1953)

In the Wind (Windswept)

circa 1915
Bronze
4⅞ × 7½ × 2 inches

A horse huddles with head lowered, bones showing through its gaunt frame, as the wind whips through its mane and tail. This small, intimate sculpture of a single animal carries a distinct narrative of stoic endurance in the face of powerful natural forces. Artist James Earle Fraser grew up on a ranch in Dakota Territory—a region with harsh winters, scalding summers, and the omnipresent threat of tornadoes. This sculpture, conceived many years later when he lived and worked on the East Coast, reflects Fraser's childhood memories of weather extremes in the Dakotas. It relates to his most famous work, *End of the Trail* (page 100), which portrays a Native American man hunched with his back to the wind, astride a mount in the same stance as this little horse. Both *In the Wind (Windswept)* and *End of the Trail* reveal Fraser's concern, common at the time, that the 19th-century West of Native Americans and horses would be buffeted and overcome by the winds of change in the 20th century.

Driving the Herd

1908
Oil on canvas
20 × 15 inches

When 15-year-old Olaf Carl Seltzer first arrived in Great Falls, Montana, the town on the front range of the Rockies looked nothing like his childhood home in Denmark. While the community was expanding into a modern place with automobiles and electric streetlights, the region proudly maintained its cowboy roots. The aspiring young painter was thrilled to meet artist Charles Russell in 1897—perhaps the town's most prominent resident. Russell and Seltzer developed a lifelong friendship, and Russell happily offered guidance to the younger artist.

Seltzer found inspiration for his artwork by fervently following the work of his mentor. Russell's celebration of cowboy culture and his stories of observing Native Americans on the Great Plains captivated the younger artist. Although he worked for nearly 30 years as a mechanic for the Great Northern Railway, Seltzer found little interest in portraying a modern West of machines and growing industry. In *Driving the Herd,* Seltzer places a cowboy against a glowing pink sunset on a beautiful evening—idealizing the rough, onerous work of guiding a herd. The powerful cattle charging through sagebrush dominate the composition, reinforcing the enduring strength of the cowboy myth in the American West.

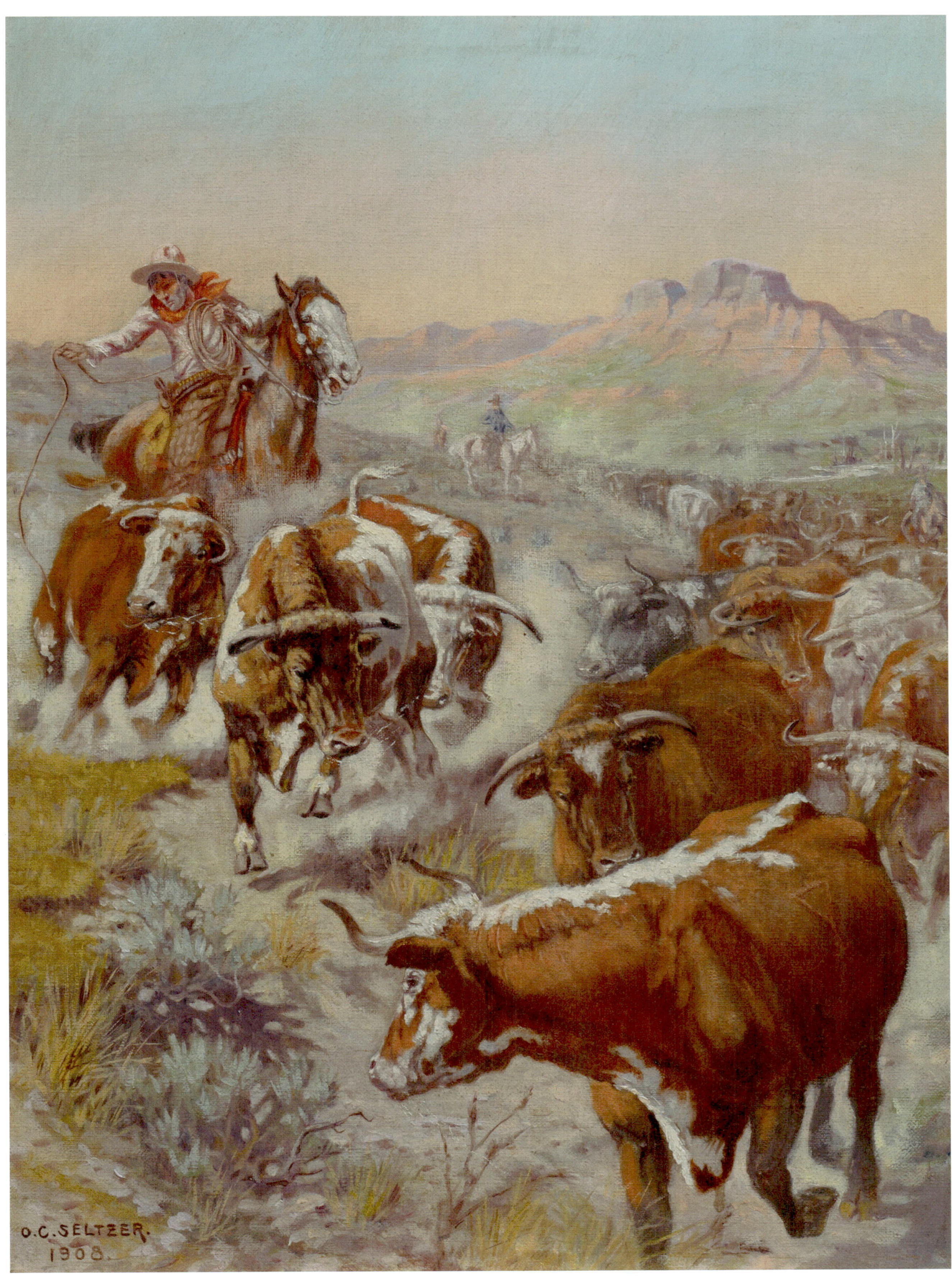

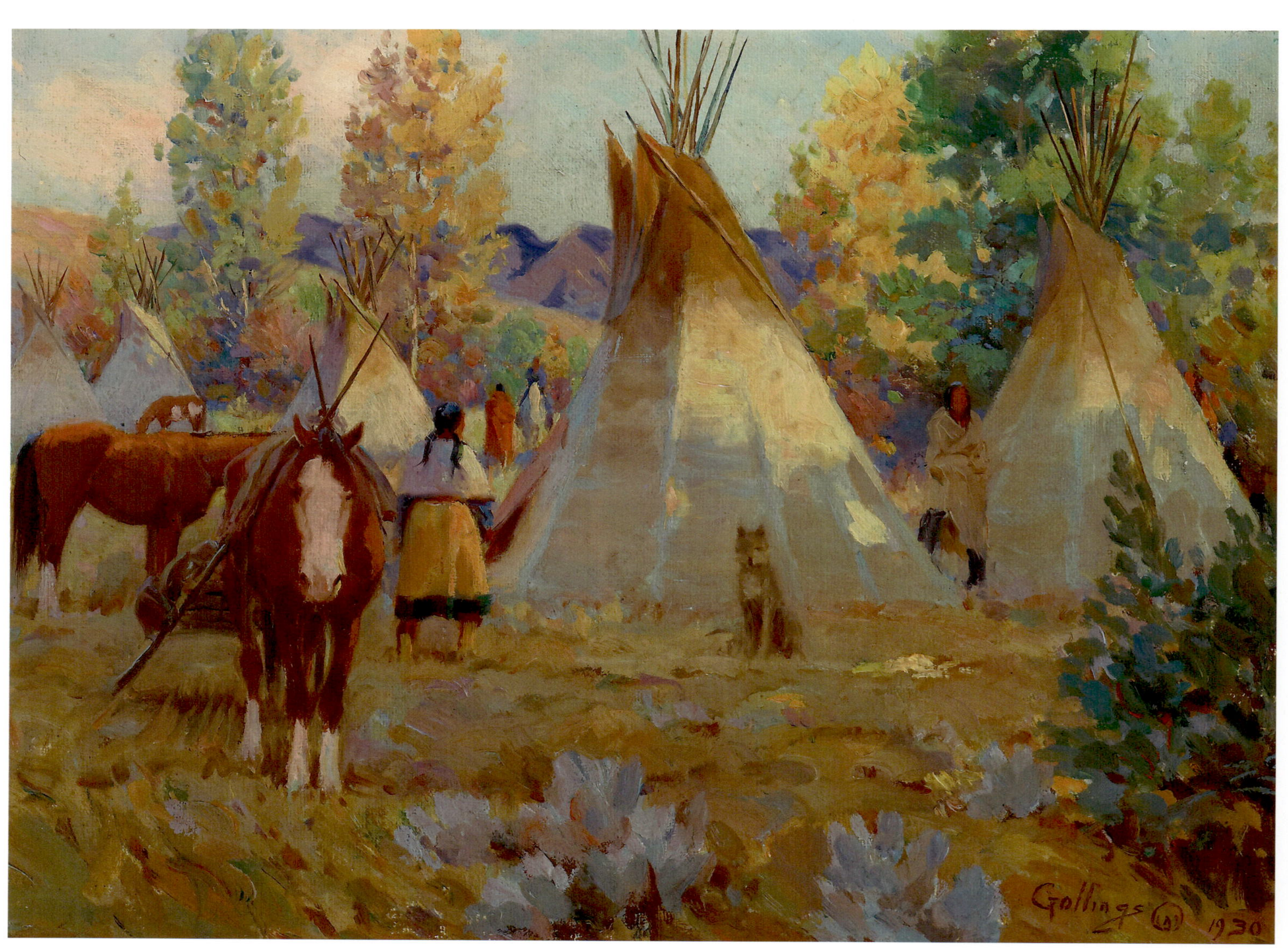

Fall Indian Camp

1930
Oil on canvas
10 × 14 inches

Distant lavender peaks and rustling autumn leaves of yellow and green-gold form a backdrop for chestnut horses and warm cream-colored tipis. In a tranquil scene suffused with color, William Gollings portrays an idealized image of an earlier time. He may have seen the white canvas tipi camps of the Crow Nation while visiting his friend Joseph Henry Sharp in Crow Agency, Montana—just north of his home in Sheridan, Wyoming. Sharp's light-filled paintings of Montana in the early 20th century proved to be a lasting influence on Gollings's work. In this scene of a Crow gathering, Gollings removed any reference to the modern world, preferring to imagine the American West of the past.

Summer Silhouette

circa 1930
Oil on canvas
14 × 14 inches

Dancing lines and luminous emerald colors shine like a Tiffany stained-glass window in *Summer Silhouette* by cowboy-turned-artist William Herbert "Buck" Dunton. As a young man Dunton left his Maine home for the plains of Montana, where he worked odd jobs in the 1890s as a ranch hand. Returning to New York in 1903, he studied art under Ernest Blumenschein, who convinced Dunton to move to Taos. In New Mexico, Dunton's initial focus on cowboys and ranch scenes gradually shifted with the guidance of fellow Taos Society member E. Martin Hennings. As a student in Munich, Hennings had been captivated by the new *Jugendstil* design—the German version of art nouveau—featuring repeated shapes with crisp contours and sinuous curves (page 166). With Hennings's influence, Dunton found the ornate lines of art nouveau design perfectly suited for the intricate patterns of the southwestern landscape. In the curving rhythms of *Summer Silhouette*, he created a decorative, modern image of nature's splendor.

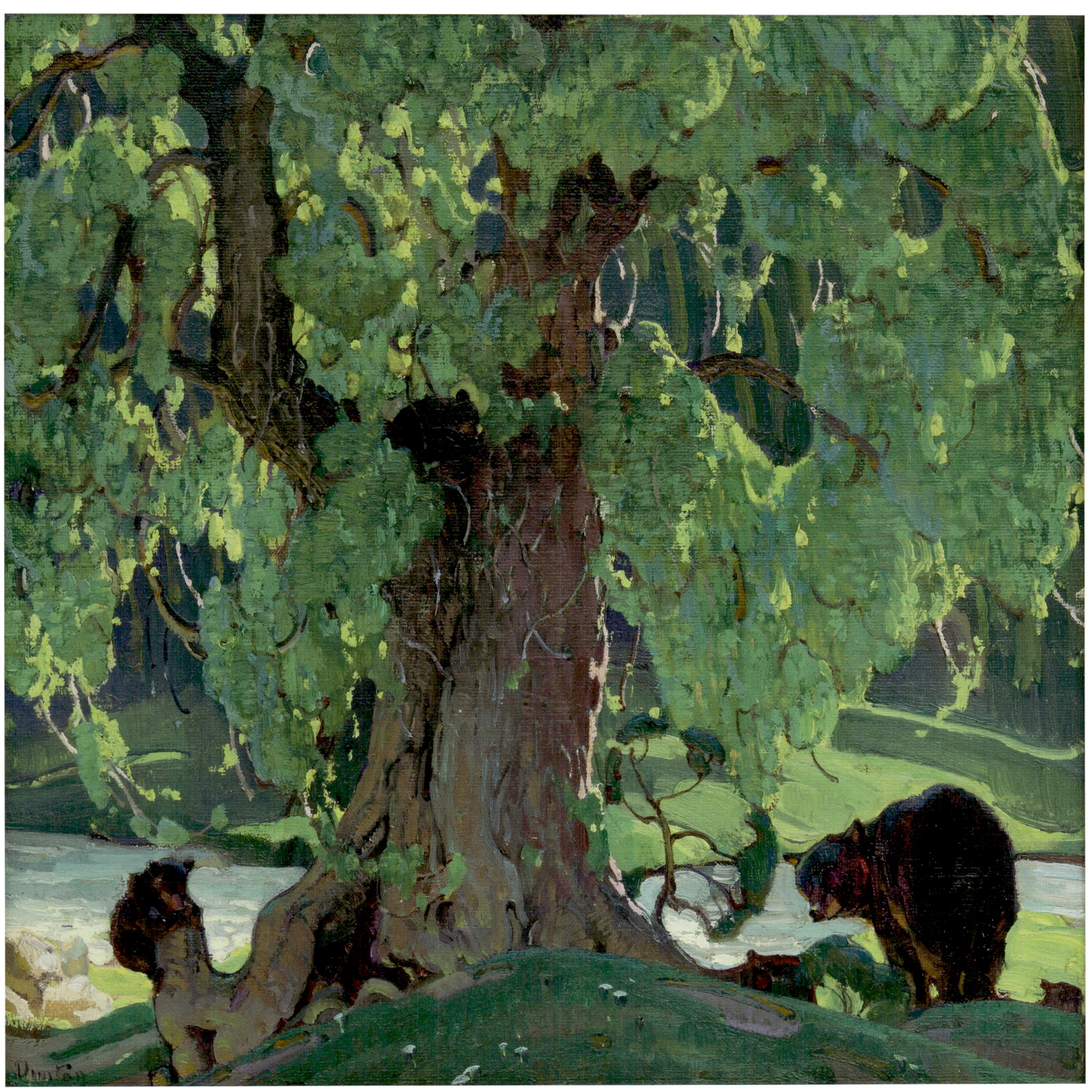

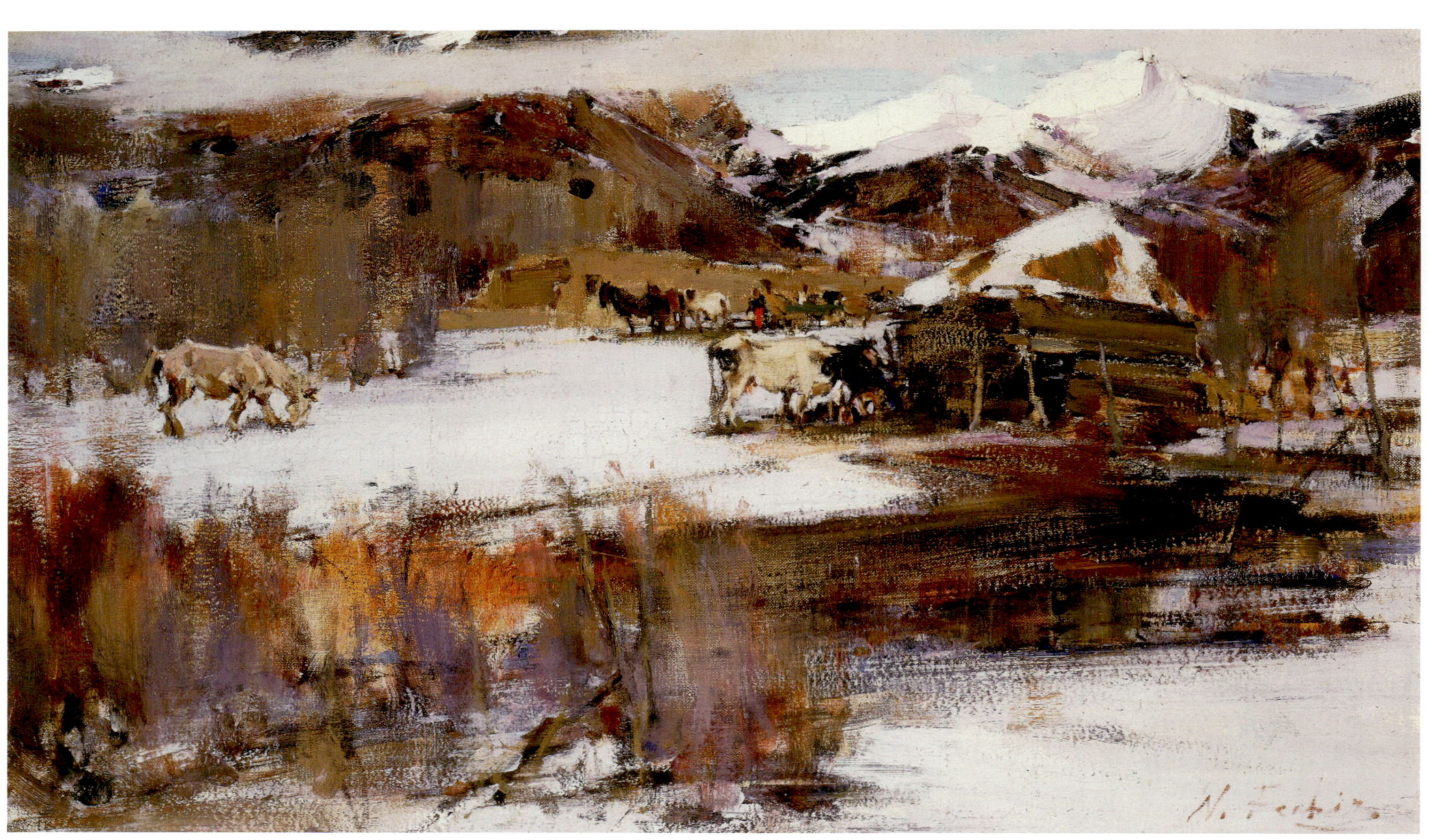

The First Snow

circa 1930
Oil on canvas
18¼ × 31¼ inches

The first snowfall in mid-autumn created stark planes of dark umber and white in the northern New Mexico landscape. Enchanted by the sight of a familiar scene reduced to basic shapes, Nicolai Fechin braved the frigid air to paint *The First Snow*.

The snows of New Mexico may have seemed familiar to Fechin, who moved from central Russia to the United States in 1923. A global artist, he had exhibited paintings in St. Petersburg, Munich, Pittsburgh, and New York—and became acquainted with modernist artists such as Arshile Gorky and David Burliuk. When Fechin moved to Taos in 1927 he brought his own style of painting, using thick layers of paint to create scenes that hover between abstraction and reality. In this painting, the abstracted composition contains a line of willowy brush in the foreground, a horse pawing the snow to graze, a cow next to a ramshackle shed, and a bare hint of a wagon team in the background—all against snow-covered mountain peaks. Rendered with thick brushstrokes and swift dabs of a palette knife, Fechin lends a sense of energy and motion to the calm stillness of a snowy day.

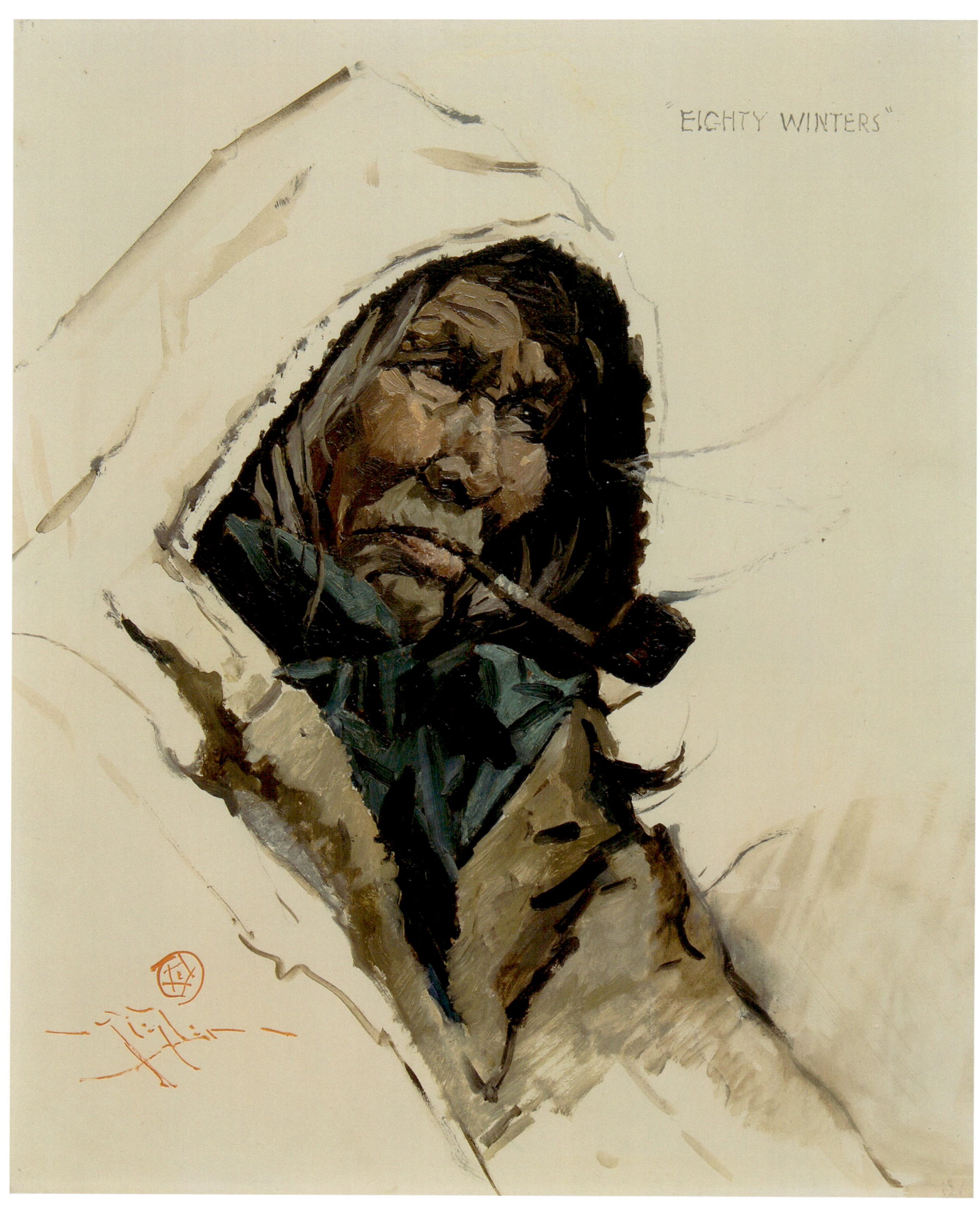
"EIGHTY WINTERS"

Eighty Winters

date unknown
Oil on board
12 × 10 inches

In this portrait of a Native Alaskan, artist Eustace Paul Ziegler conveys the harshness of the frozen northern climate. Deep-set eyes look out from beneath a thick hood, and a warm muffler is pulled up to the chin. Without background or context, the weathered face framed simply by the dark hood lining tells a story of endurance in rough extremes.

Ziegler first moved to Alaska in 1909 to manage an Episcopal Mission in Cordova, and began painting the people of Alaska in his spare time—miners, fishermen, railroad workers, and Native Alaskans. His paintings began to sell, and after being ordained he continued to pursue an art career. In 1924 he moved to Seattle, where he remained for the rest of his life. An active promoter of the arts, Ziegler taught classes and became the first president of the Puget Sound Group of Northwest Painters, still an active organization today. He continued to return to Alaska in the summers, drawn to the rugged beauty of the far north.

Autumn Dawn

1915
Oil on canvas
34 × 46 inches

For the silent men have seen
That Plem-Salia-Kwi walks not alone.
Through all his paths She follows him—his Woman,
*   his Mate—*
Sharing his blanket.
She has no other garment, her breast is bare,
She has given all to him she follows;
So comes he with plenty!

Therefore the silent men, the Hunters and Providers of Life,
Greet Plem-Salia-Kwi, the Harvest-Bringer, their
*   Blood-Brother the Mated One.**

Artist N. C. Wyeth was smitten with the poem *Plem-Salia-Kwi (Autumn Dawn)* by Canadian-born writer Constance Lindsay Skinner. Her imagery of a Native American mythical personification of Dawn and Plenty inspired his painting *Autumn Dawn*. The man, Autumn Dawn himself, symbolizes abundance in nature with his loaded net and the basket of fish to the right. The woman suggests a fertile Madonna figure with her blue cloak, bare breast, and swaddled infant. With heavy Christian overtones and no particular tribal affiliation, Wyeth presents these figures not as specific individuals but rather as an allegory for the wealth of abundance in the natural world.

*From *Plem-Salia-Kwi (Autumn Dawn)* by Constance Lindsay Skinner, in George William Cronyn, ed., *The Path on the Rainbow: An Anthology of Songs and Chants from the Indians of North America* (New York: Boni and Liveright, 1918), 243.

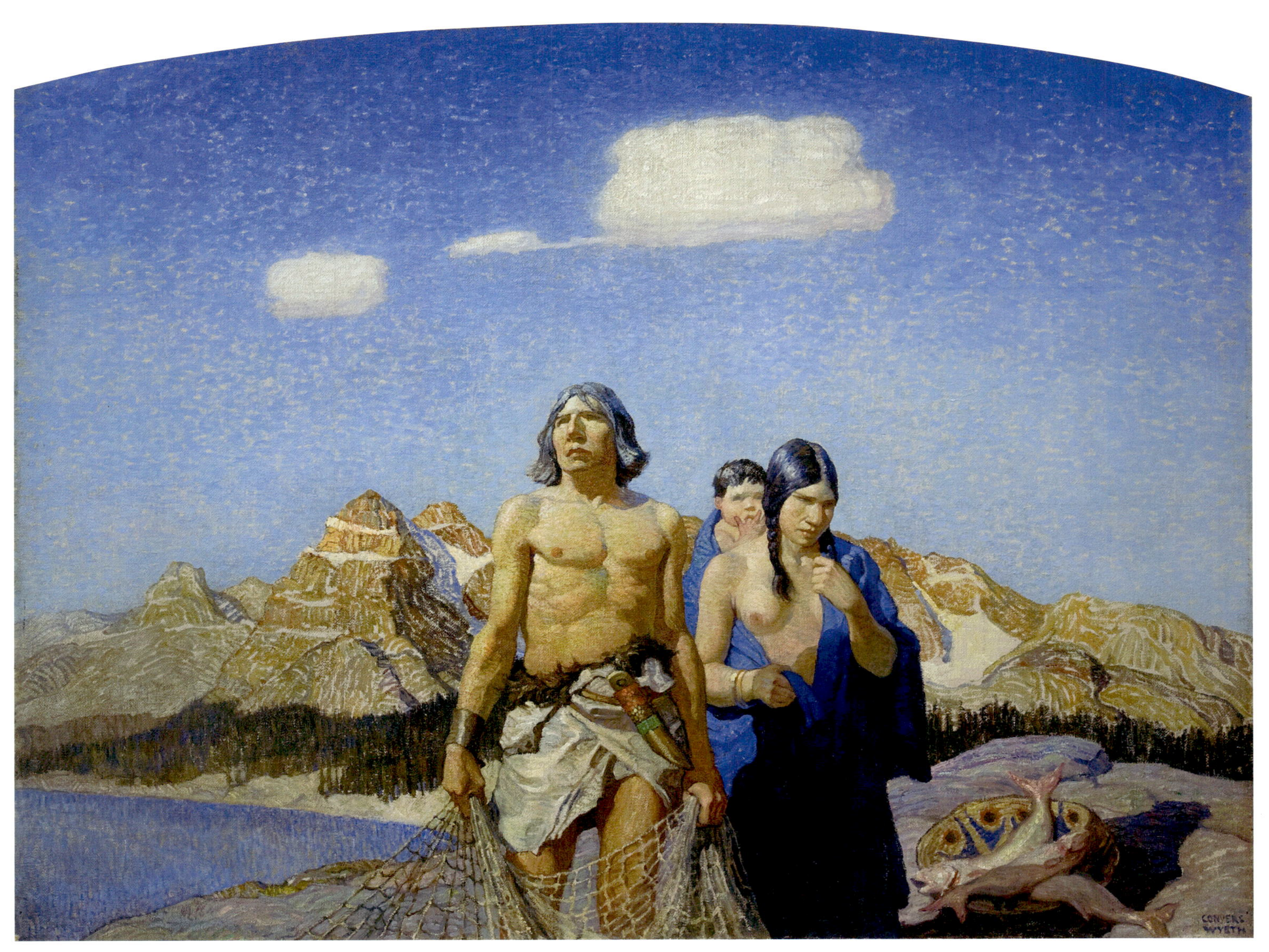

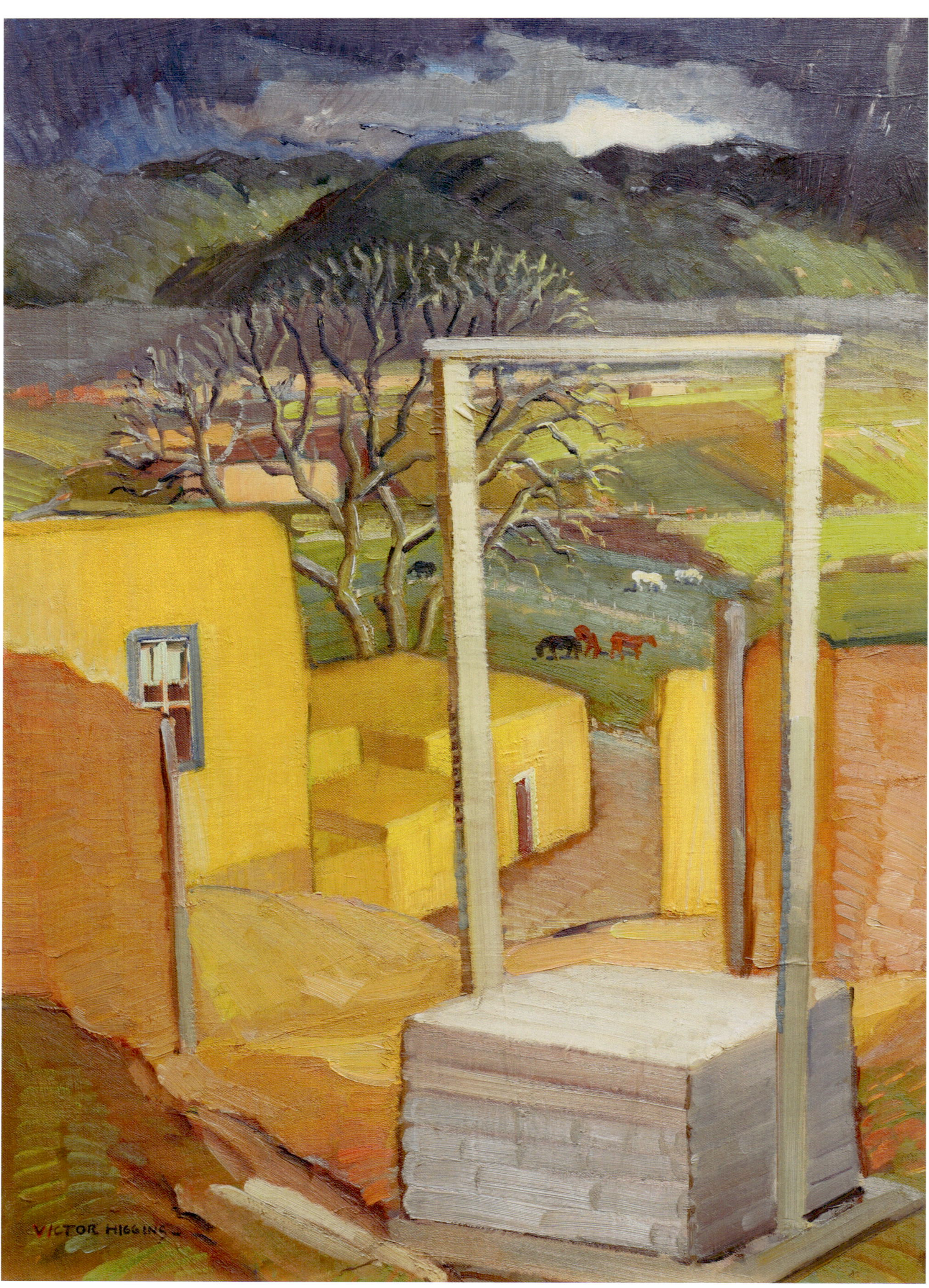

VICTOR HIGGINS

Spanish Well

circa 1935
Oil on canvas
27 × 19¾ inches

When Victor Higgins observed the square adobe buildings, rectangular farm plots, and mountain ridges of Taos, he found tumbling geometric shapes that were perfect for a modern painting. Higgins was familiar with the new styles of art sweeping Europe and the United States in the 1910s. He had studied in New York under Robert Henri, met Walter Ufer and E. Martin Hennings during a year of further studies in Munich, and had then viewed the latest European modernist art at the Armory Show when the exhibition traveled to Chicago in 1913. In *Spanish Well*, the tall, rectangular form of the well in the foreground seems to act as a doorway inviting the viewer into the scene. Higgins repeated the right angles of the well in the varied rectangles and cubes of the golden adobe pueblo—an architecture style readymade for a spare, simplified rendering. Regular geometric shapes continue into the triangular foothills in the background, broken only by a sprawling tree in the middle of the composition. By depicting a Taos landscape in a cubist-inspired style, Higgins brought a place seemingly untouched by time—with wells and horses and centuries-old architecture—into the cutting edge of the 20th century.

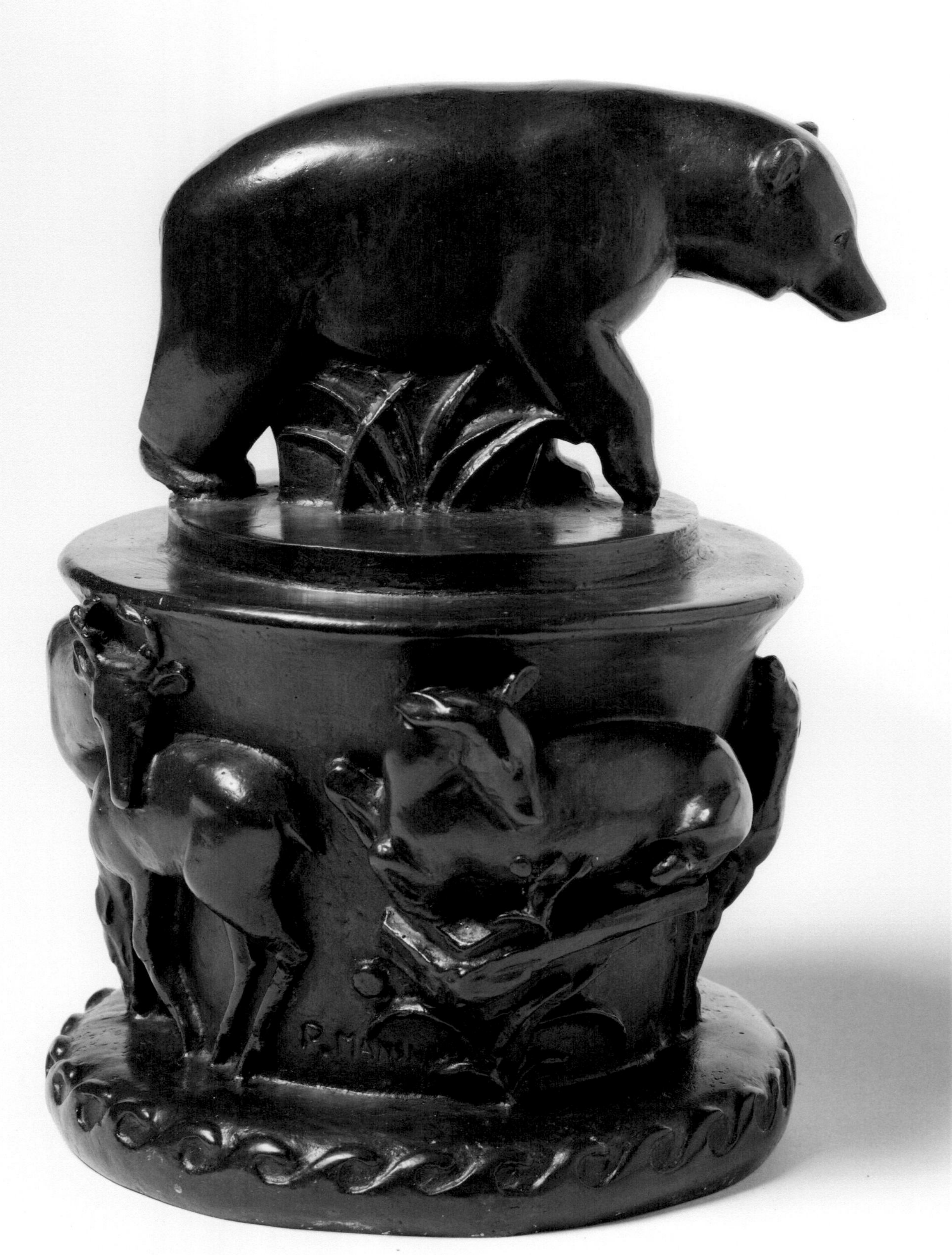

PAUL MANSHIP (1885–1966)

Model for Alfred E. Smith Memorial Flagpole Base

circa 1946
Bronze
9 × 7 × 6 inches

Today, a group of deer and a striding bear invite families to the playground at the Governor Alfred E. Smith Park in Lower Manhattan. An influential figure in the region, Smith was the first Irish Catholic governor of New York in the 1920s, and championed new municipal developments in affordable housing and open park spaces in New York City. After Smith's passing in 1944, artist Paul Manship was commissioned to create a memorial flagpole base for a new park established in honor of the governor. In his fluid art deco style, based on the simplified forms of Archaic Greek and ancient Assyrian sculpture, Manship modeled a pedestal comprised of American wildlife. The whitetail deer and black bear—animals that once roamed from the Atlantic to the Pacific—symbolize Governor Smith's support for conservation. Manship added a beaver and an owl to the final flagpole base, assembling a host of wild creatures in the middle of the city to welcome neighborhood visitors.

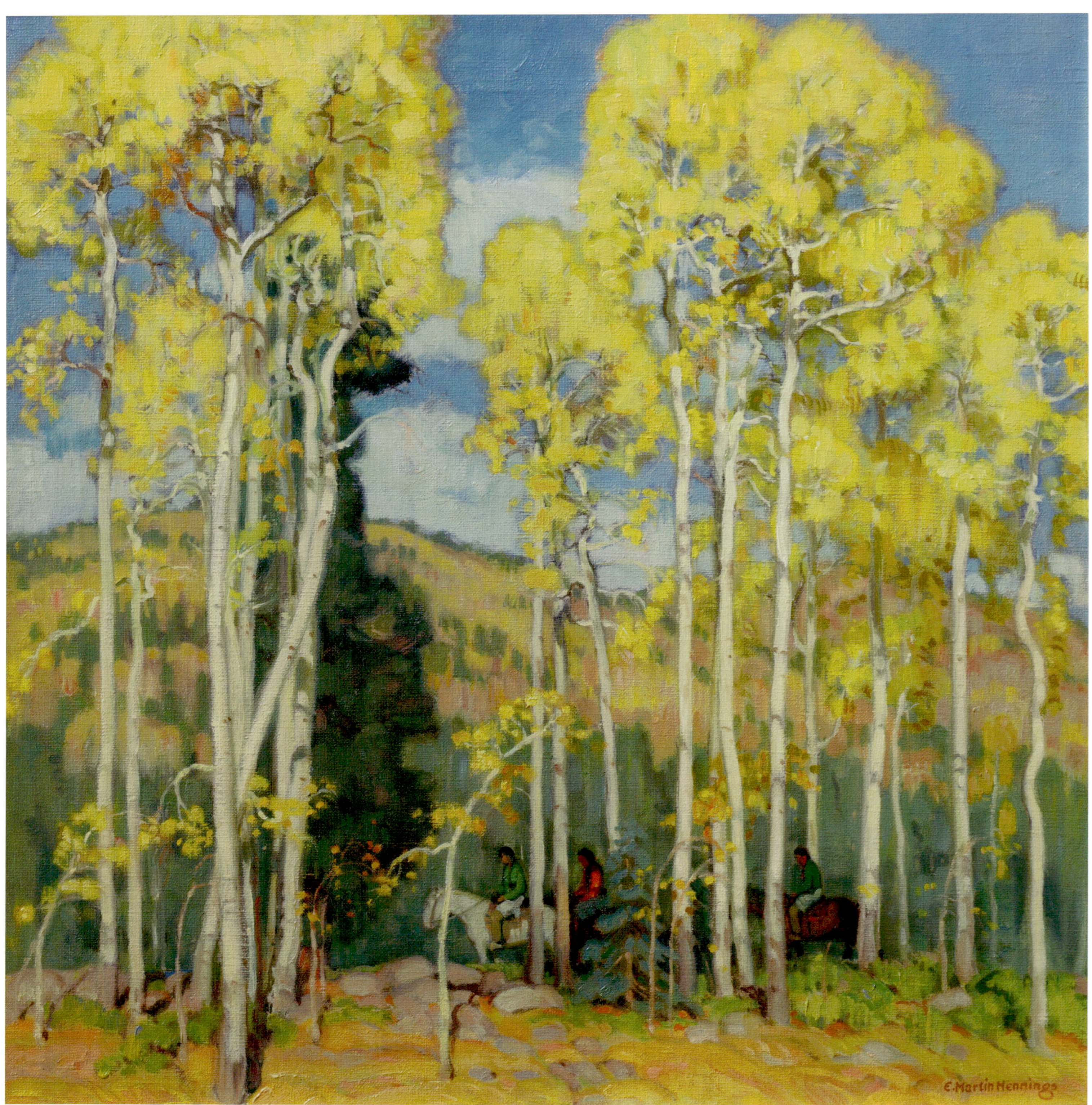

E.Martin Hennings

Towering Aspens

circa 1940
Oil on canvas
20 × 20 inches

Moving between stately white columns and beneath a canopy of shimmering gold, three riders wander through a land graced with beauty. The quaking aspens of autumn in the hills of northern New Mexico burst with color, creating expressive patterns of curved yellow-gold shapes against deep blue. For artist E. Martin Hennings, the forms of the southwestern landscape called to mind European art nouveau or "new art" design, which featured repeated sinuous curves and strong contours and was used in architecture, graphics, and decorative arts in the early 20th century.

Born to German immigrant parents and raised in Chicago, Hennings studied at the Academy of Fine Arts in Munich when German art nouveau design (called *Jugendstil* or "youth style") reached its height of popularity. He later moved to Taos and began painting the people and landscapes of northern New Mexico. By bringing elements of art nouveau design to the landscapes of the Southwest, Hennings blended European influences with American forms to create a unique style of painting.

Piñons with Cedar

1956
Oil on canvas
30 × 26 inches

Throughout the 20th century, artists found new possibilities in the landscapes of the western United States. Traveling through New Mexico for the first time in 1917, Georgia O'Keeffe found herself fascinated by the light and colors of the Southwest. After frequent visits, in 1940 she bought a house on the grounds of Ghost Ranch, near Santa Fe, spending most summers there until she relocated permanently to the region in 1949. She used the landscape, architecture, and objects around her as inspiration, creating crisp, modern compositions influenced by the forms and light found in the Southwest. In *Piñons with Cedar*, O'Keeffe examines the lines and colors found in the New Mexico desert. With soft brushstrokes she smudges the tree limbs into the background, flattening the sense of depth in the painting and focusing the viewer's attention on the repeated curves and twists of the branches. Depicting a verdant cedar shrub emerging from the base of a desiccated piñon, O'Keeffe creates a narrative of the cycles of life and renewal in the western landscape.

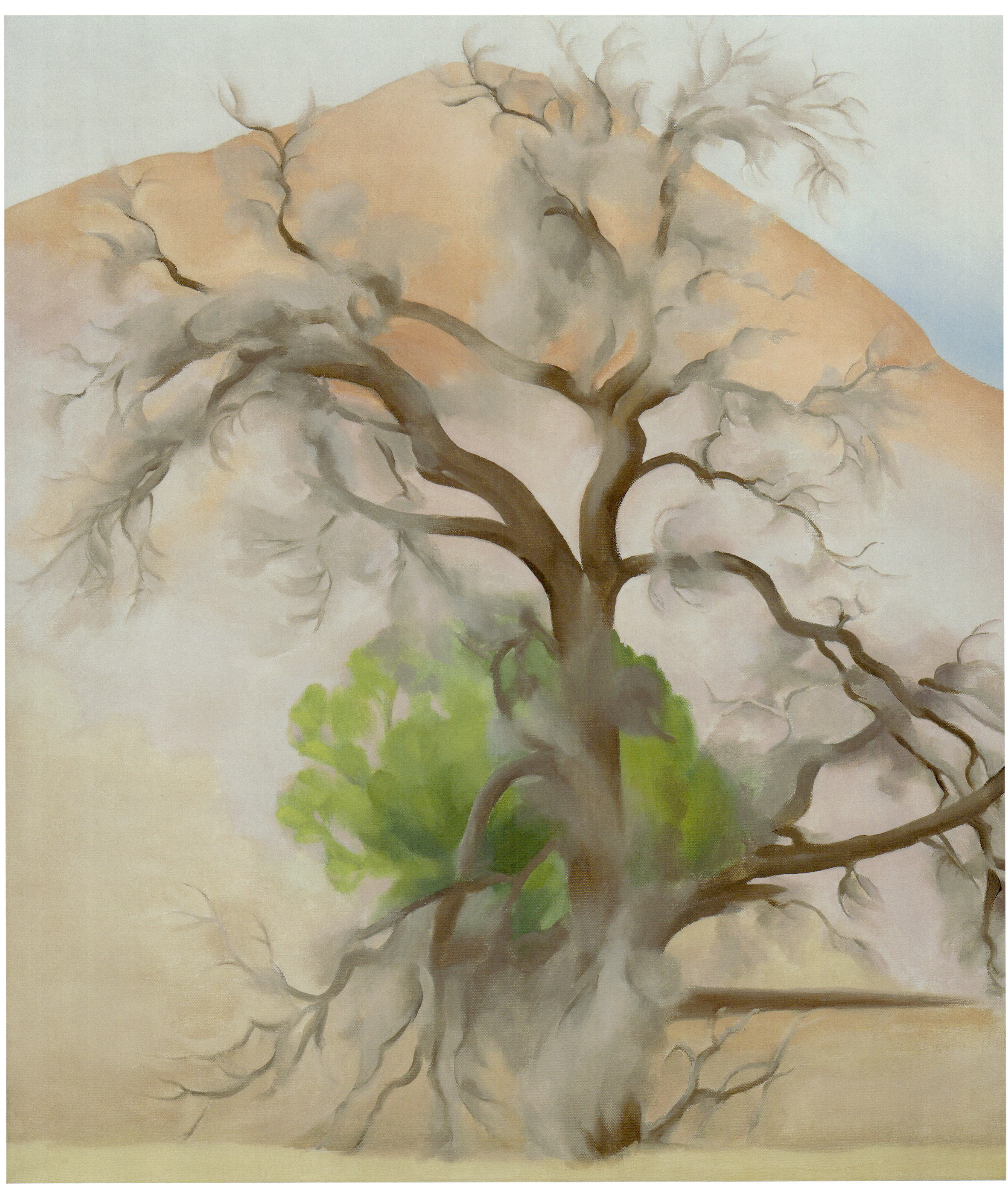

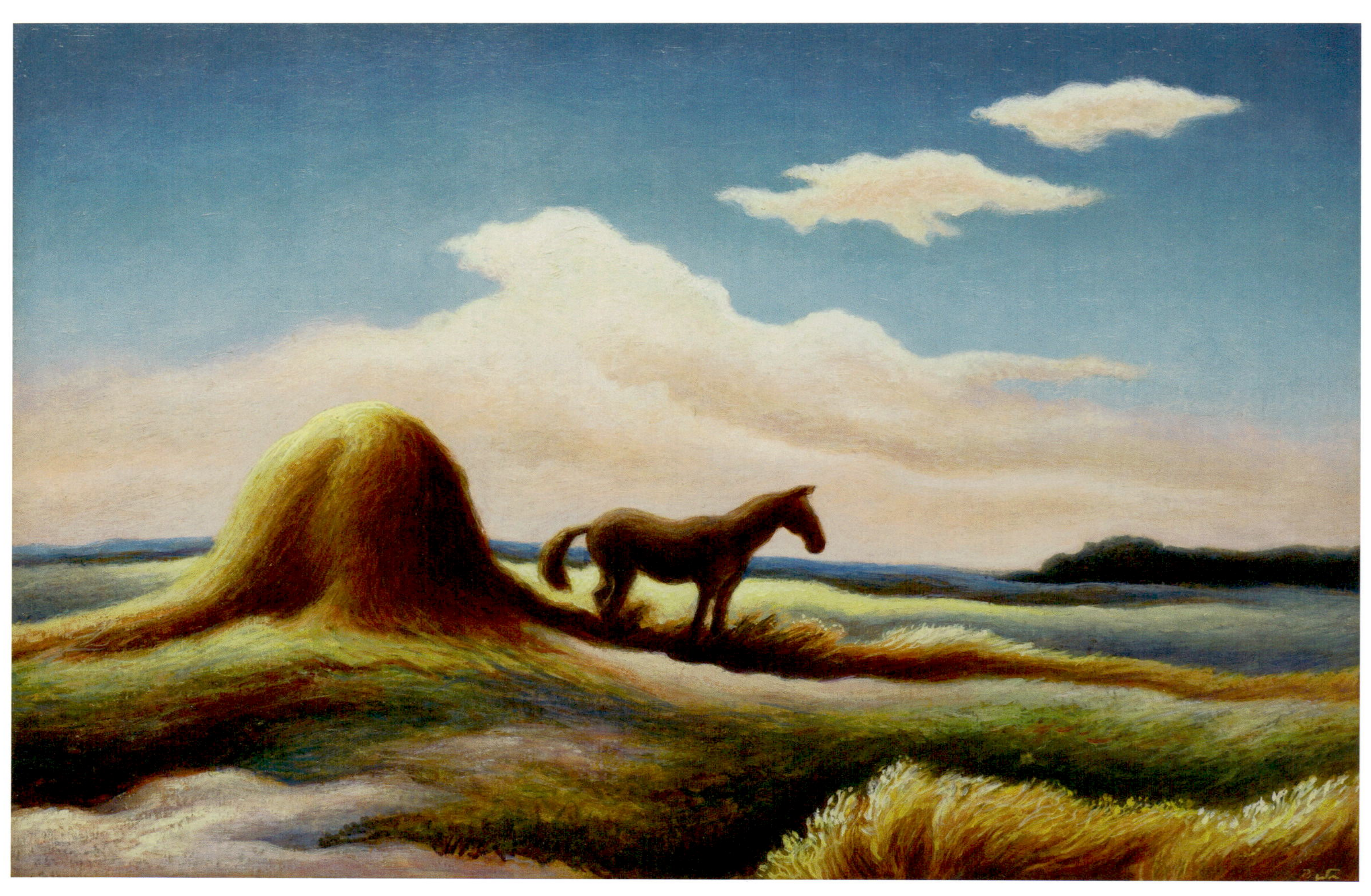

The Lonely Horse

circa 1940
Oil on Masonite
16 × 25 inches

A son of the Ozarks, Thomas Hart Benton grew up in the hills of southwestern Missouri near the former haunts of Wild Bill Hickok and Jesse James. But the lands he observed in the 20th century no longer resembled the region of gunfighters and outlaws described in western legend. "The West, like all other parts of our country, is in a rapid state of change," he wrote in 1937. "A great number of people in the West . . . cling to the bucking, shooting, yelling glamour of the past."* Rather than re-creating a past era, Benton sympathized with the present-day hardships of the small farmers and workers in the West during the Great Depression. Refusing to follow new styles of modernist, abstract art, Benton painted scenes of everyday people that both celebrated and skewered American folklore and myth. *The Lonely Horse* portrays the rolling farmlands that had replaced the cowboys and cattle herds of the 19th century—a place that represents both abundance and isolation. Perhaps Benton saw himself as the lone horse, separated from others in a vast landscape, resolutely following his own path in American art.

*Thomas Hart Benton, *An Artist in America* (New York: R. M. McBride, 1937), 240.

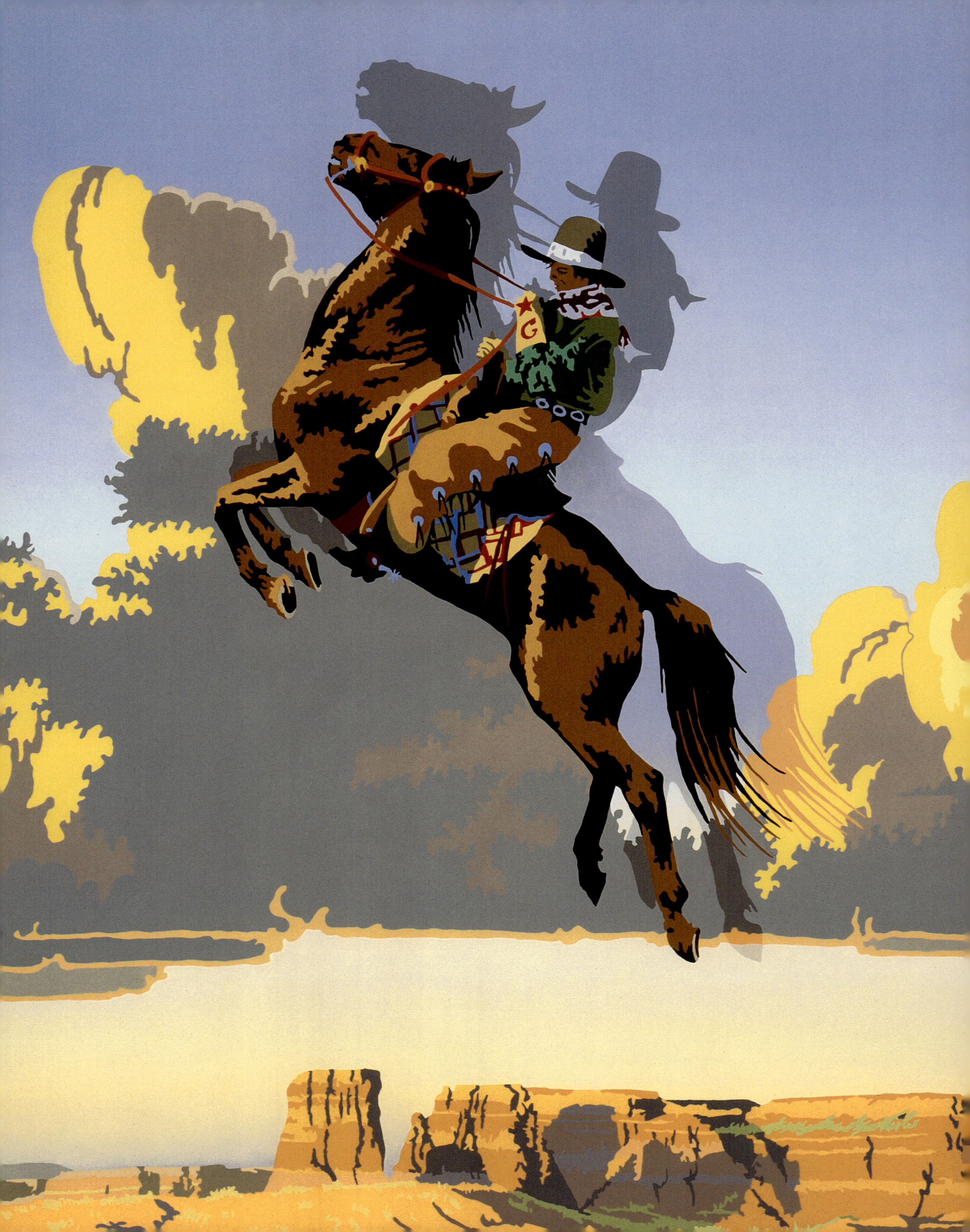

LAURA F. FRY

ART OF THE WEST FOR THE 21ST CENTURY

Dry wind whistled through bare grasses and gnarled sagebrush, buffeting ridges and broad plains. On a lonely stretch of land near the vast stillness of the Great Salt Lake, a large and raucous throng gathered on May 10, 1869, around a commemorative golden spike. For over 20 years the United States had harbored ambitions to complete a transcontinental railroad—an unbroken line connecting the Pacific Ocean to the established railway networks in the East. On that historic day, rail lines built eastward from Sacramento and westward from Council Bluffs, Iowa, finally met at a remote spot in Utah Territory. To mark the event, an iron hammer was wired to the transcontinental telegraph. As the crowd assembled around the last tie, the blows that drove the final spike home were transmitted by telegraph line across the nation. Life in the American West would never be the same.

The completion of a railway across the American continent—soon repeated in multiple routes to the Pacific—was seen as an example of the triumph of industry over wilderness. For artists, the railroad in the West marked a turning point. The railroads funded many artists and distributed their images to entice passengers to ride new lines into the western United States. But even in the 19th century, some observers considered this concept of "progress" a double-edged sword. "We do not ride on the railroad; it rides upon us," declared Henry David Thoreau in 1854.[1] While artists celebrated new access to remote regions, they also created images lamenting the environmental destruction and irrevocable changes that occurred in the railroad's wake as new waves of settlers moved west.

Now, nearly 150 years after the first transcontinental railroad revolutionized travel, we find ourselves in a similar era of change. The exponential increase in communication technology today mirrors the sudden growth in transportation in the 19th century. Today, as it did then, the vast public land in the American West continues to provide an escape, a pause from the ever-increasing hurry and busyness of daily life. As it has for over two centuries, this place continues to inspire artists. The Haub Family Collection, which contains seminal works by American, Native American, European, and Asian artists, demonstrates the enduring global relevance of the art of the American West and illuminates how our culture today has been influenced by threads of the past.

EXPLORING A DISTINCT AMERICAN IDENTITY: THE INDIAN GALLERIES OF HENRY INMAN AND PAUL KANE

In 1830 the established artist Henry Inman (1801–1846) was approached with a most unusual request. Could he paint copies of an entire collection of more than 100 Native American portraits?

Today photographic reproductions are ubiquitous and can be sent across the world in the blink of an eye. But before the advent of photography the first director of the Bureau of Indian Affairs, Thomas L. McKenney, faced a significant logistical challenge. He wished to reproduce the Indian Gallery of portraits by Charles Bird King (1785–1862) as lithographic prints, but the paintings were in Washington, DC,

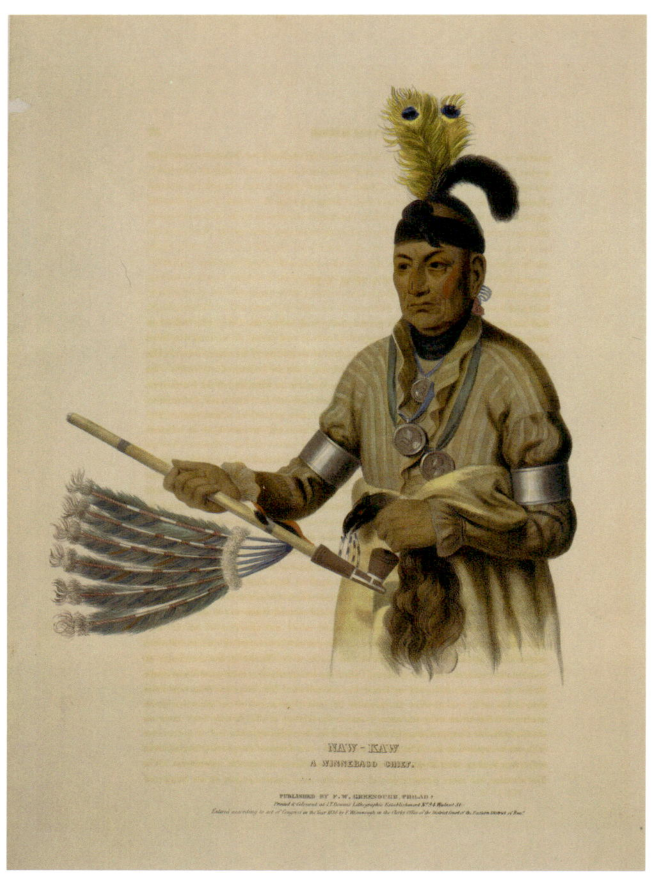

FIGURE 1 *Naw-Kaw, a Winnebago chief.* Hand-colored lithograph from Thomas McKenney and James Hall, *History of the Indian Tribes of North America*, Published by F. W. Greenough, Philadelphia, circa 1836. Library of Congress Prints and Photographs Division, Washington, DC.

and his lithographer worked in Philadelphia. Inman provided the solution by copying King's portraits to serve as guides for the lithographer. He lent his own sensibility to the paintings, rendering figures with crisp edges and increased definition, thus making the images easier for lithographers to reproduce.[2] In 1844, after numerous setbacks, McKenney and writer James Hall completed the final segment of *History of the Indian Tribes of North America*, a monumental three-volume compilation of lithographic portraits created from Inman's paintings (figure 1).

Inman's portrait *Naw-Kaw* depicts a well-known Ho-Chunk chief, his high status conveyed by the elaborate pipe in his right hand and the peace medals—gifts from Washington leaders—around his neck (circa 1832; page 35). "He is an aged Chief, being now ninety-four years old, hale,

strong, firm in muscle and limb," reported the *Saturday Evening Post* in 1828.[3] Naw-Kaw's clothing, a striped shirt paired with feather ornaments, demonstrates a blend of Anglo and indigenous cultures, fitting regalia for a chief who advocated for peace between his people and encroaching settlers. When Inman painted this portrait in the early 1830s, he could not have imagined how significant it would become. The sweeping fire in the Smithsonian Institution that destroyed nearly all of Charles Bird King's original portraits in 1865 made Inman's copies the best existing record of the nation's first Indian Gallery.

Canadian artist Paul Kane (1810–1871) abruptly changed the course of his career following a visit to England in 1843. After studying Renaissance artwork in Italy, Kane traveled to London—and stumbled across the Indian Gallery paintings of George Catlin (1796–1872) on display in the grand Egyptian Hall. Unlike Henry Inman, who lived and worked in the eastern United States, Catlin had journeyed across the American West in the 1830s to find artistic inspiration among Native American cultures. Catlin's gallery left Kane transfixed. By the time he returned to Toronto, Kane was determined to travel to the Frontier and create his own gallery of indigenous Canadians. Between 1845 and 1848 he headed west with the help of the Hudson's Bay Company, traveling from the Great Lakes to the Columbia River Valley and up the Pacific Coast to Vancouver Island. Back in Toronto, he exhibited his sketches as "Kane's Indian Gallery" to much acclaim.[4] His reputation as a painter of Native Americans assured, he continued to seek new subjects. When the Ojibwe performer Maungwudaus visited Toronto in 1851 to speak on the "Manners and Customs" of his people, Kane seized the opportunity to paint him in full regalia (page 43).[5]

A well-known figure, Maungwudaus had been educated by Methodist missionaries in Canada and was fluent in spoken and written English (he alternately used the English name George Henry). With his language skills and an innate entrepreneurial flair, Maungwudaus organized a traveling troupe of Ojibwe performers. From 1845 to 1848 his troupe toured Europe, where for a time he partnered with George Catlin, staging performances alongside Catlin's Indian Gallery. On his return to the United States, a reporter observed of him: "Maungwudaus is a well-educated and highly intelligent man, and no one can fail to be deeply interested by the exhibition and his remarks."[6] When Maungwudaus brought his troupe to Toronto in 1851, he met the artist Paul Kane. Kane's portrait differs slightly from numerous daguerreotype images taken around the same time, suggesting that Kane painted Maungwudaus from life (figure 2).[7]

Like Maungwudaus himself, who participated in both Anglo and Ojibwe cultures, Paul Kane blended influences from Europe and Native America in his portrait. Taking a cue from the Italian Renaissance portraits he had studied at the Uffizi Gallery in Florence, Kane placed Maungwudaus in a traditional triangular composition, with a distant pastoral landscape in the background. Maungwudaus wears a crisp collared shirt under his Ojibwe snakeskin shoulder strap, bear claw necklace, and feather headdress. While George Catlin and many other 19th-century artists depicted Native Americans as a "vanishing race" doomed to disappear, Kane's polished portrait of Maungwudaus seems to present an alternate view—that Native Americans could succeed in a new era, blending cultures without losing their identity.

The first Indian Gallery of Charles Bird King and Henry Inman would inspire successive generations of artists, including Paul Kane, to create Native American portraits. This enduring idea of capturing the details of indigenous individuals in art gave the United States and Canada a method for defining themselves distinct from Europe. The Indian Galleries provided their Anglo audiences in the 19th century with a window to another culture, paradoxically making Native Americans accessible *and* removed—visible yet apart from everyday American life.

EASTERNERS AT THE FRONTIER'S END: FREDERIC REMINGTON AND CHARLES SCHREYVOGEL

When the young Frederic Remington (1861–1909) started traveling through the American West, there was something missing: The thundering bison herds of legend were gone. After the sudden death of his father, the New York native

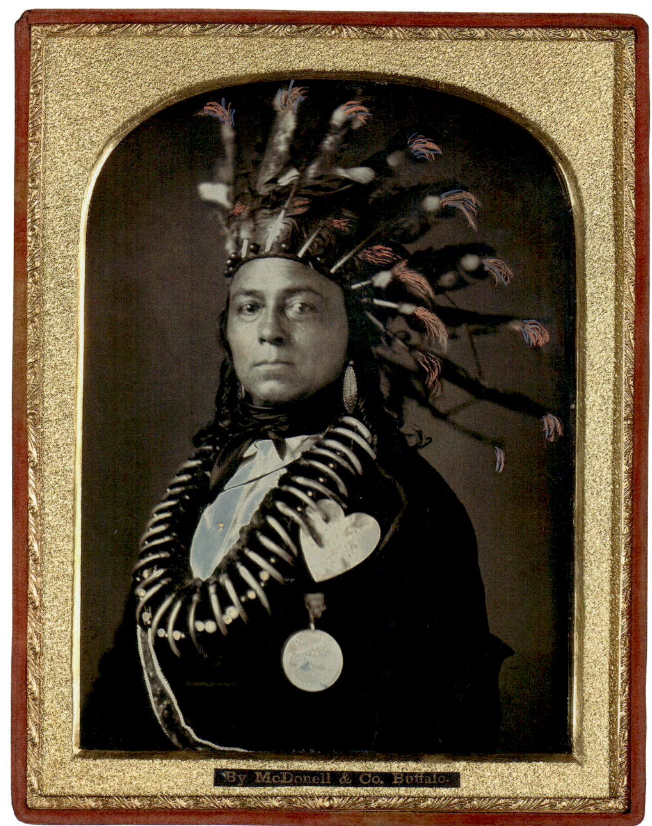

FIGURE 2 Donald McDonnell, *Indian Chief Maungwudaus, Upper Canada*, circa 1850–51. Daguerreotype, half plate. 4¾ × 3⅝ inches. The Nelson-Atkins Museum of Art, Kansas City, Missouri. Gift of Hallmark Cards, Inc., 2005.27.20.

abandoned his art classes at Yale and traveled west for the first time in 1881. His rough early sketches launched his career as an illustrator of the West, and Remington's search for new material led him from New Mexico to Wyoming to British Columbia—but the American bison were nowhere to be seen.[8] "It is within the recollection of all of us," one reporter noted in 1885, "that the buffalo were so numerous on the plains of the West that one could travel for days and never be out of sight of them during the hours of daylight. They have passed away."[9] By the mid-1880s, the power-ful bison that symbolized the western United States had reached the brink of extinction (figure 3). When Remington visited the Blackfoot nation in southern Canada in 1887, the only remnants of the vast herds were bleached bones covering the northern plains.

Struck by the grim sight of endless bison bones, Remington painted his early masterpiece *Conjuring Back the Buffalo*

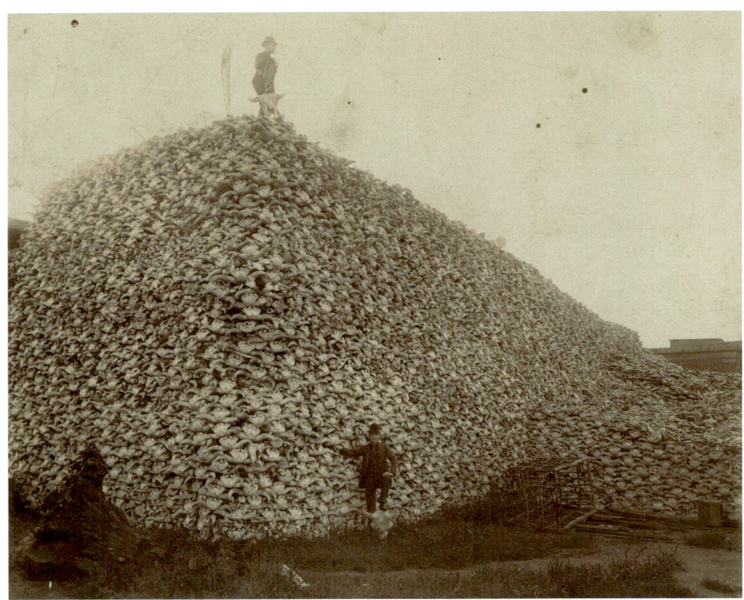

 Photograph of buffalo skulls waiting to be ground for fertilizer, circa 1875. Burton Historical Collection, Detroit Public Library.

around 1889, after returning to New York (page 92). The anguished cry of the central figure likely echoes Remington's own reaction upon seeing evidence of the wanton destruction firsthand. Rather than portraying a verdant West with abundant wildlife, Remington depicted a harsh scene of dry grass and skulls. The Blackfoot man in the center, standing in the sunlight with his arms raised above his head, silhouetted against a brilliant blue, recalls a medieval saint calling out in prayer. By referencing centuries of Christian iconography, Remington portrayed the bison as a sacred symbol of the American West—rendering the scene of a vanishing icon all the more tragic. When the painting was later used to illustrate the *Century Magazine* article "The Great Plains of Canada" in 1892, it perfectly illuminated the author's tone: "It is not long since this noble animal was the monarch of these lonely plains . . . in favorite localities, where they once fed in countless droves, their bones and horns lie scattered on every hand, bleaching and slowly decomposing in the drying wind."[10]

Remington's painting certainly offers a haunting view of environmental destruction and the permanence of extinction—but the image contains another layer of meaning. Remington, like many Anglo Americans in his day,

believed that the destruction of the bison would also bring an end to Native American cultures on the western plains. Thus the painting depicts the end of the bison, the end of Native American cultures, and indeed Remington's view of the end of the Old West itself.

A son of German immigrant parents raised in New York City, Charles Schreyvogel (1861–1912) was captivated by his first visit to Buffalo Bill's Wild West in 1893. Seeing the performance reinforced his life-long interest in stories of the Frontier, and later that year he traveled from his home in Hoboken, New Jersey, to the western plains for the first time. The West in 1893, however, was not the place that had been frozen in time by Buffalo Bill's performances. Schreyvogel seems to have had little interest in exploring the present western culture of growing urban centers. Rather, he sought cavalry veterans who could describe their memories of the conflicts of the 1860s and 1870s.[11] These stories of the past became the primary inspiration for his artwork.

In 1900, just as his action-packed paintings attracted national attention for the first time, Schreyvogel conveyed a calmer, more somber emotion in *The Last Drop* (page 106). Here a cavalryman offers his trusty horse the last sip of water from his Stetson. The implication that both horse and rider face imminent death is emphasized by the desolate landscape, rendered in a hazy mirage of loose brushstrokes. Schreyvogel was so pleased with the painting that he cast the figures in bronze three years later (figure 4). No wonder—the painting speaks directly to Schreyvogel's love of the past and his trepidation about the future.

As Schreyvogel began to travel through the West in the 1890s, rapid changes were happening in the East. At the turn of the 20th century, as the earliest skyscrapers reshaped the New York City skyline, perhaps the greatest changes to daily life came in the form of transportation: expanding rail systems and new automobiles. The crucial role of the horse—portrayed so vividly in Schreyvogel's cavalry paintings—was coming to a swift end. Many who loved horses denied it. "As to the automobile, it is doomed to a short life—it is nothing but a fad, same as the bicycle was. For this reason, I am going to anchor my faith to the horse," said William F. "Buffalo

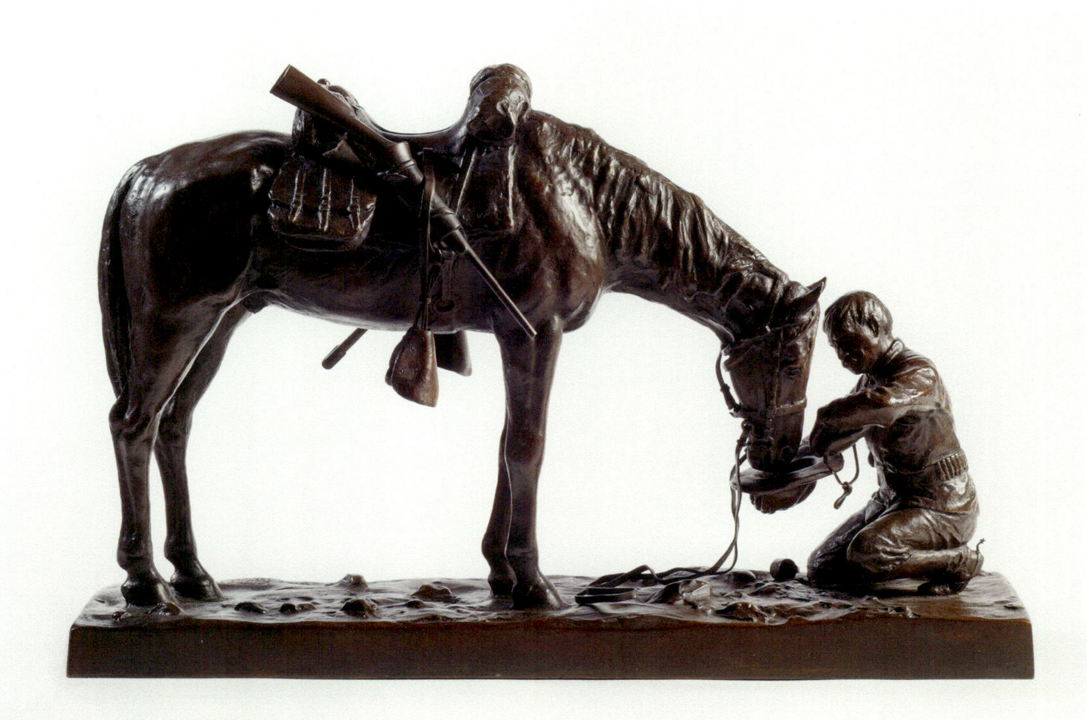

FIGURE 4 Charles Schrey-vogel, *The Last Drop*, 1903. Bronze, 11⅝ × 18¾ × 5¼ inches. Tacoma Art Museum, Haub Family Collection, Promised gift of Erivan and Helga Haub.

Bill" Cody himself in 1900.[12] But others saw the writing on the wall. In 1903 even General Nelson A. Miles, famous horseman and cavalry leader, urged the army to replace its beloved horses with modern motor vehicles.[13] While *The Last Drop* depicts a single rider and steed doomed to die of thirst, the piece also acts as a larger metaphor for the end of the era of the horse, already quickly receding in the dust of the latest automobiles.

Frederic Remington and Charles Schreyvogel, both born in 1861, grew up in the era following the Civil War amid newspaper and dime novel accounts of an old, wild Frontier. Dubious of increasingly crowded cities and growing industries in the East, these artists rejected the idea of a new, modern West, unable to reconcile themselves with the idea of an evolving place. Much of their artwork—depicting either current first-hand observations or an imagined past—contains a sense of loss. But these images also acted as a call to action. For example, as a result of growing awareness of the bison's plight in the late 19th century, in 1901 Congress provided funding to restore and protect a thriving bison population in Yellowstone National Park—where the animals can be found by the thousands today.[14]

THE MUSE IN THE WASTELAND: MAYNARD DIXON, GEORGIA O'KEEFFE, AND THE WESTERN DESERT

Maynard Dixon (1875–1946) was no stranger to the desert valleys of the American West. A westerner by birth, Dixon was born and grew up in the semi-arid San Joaquin Valley near Fresno, California. In 1900, the successful young illustrator followed the advice of his mentor Charles F. Lummis and traveled to Arizona and New Mexico for the first time—in his words, going "East to see the West."[15] An accomplished writer and newspaper editor, Lummis encouraged his readers to embrace the distinct landscapes and blend of cultures found throughout the Southwest. But Lummis provided no such recommendation for the "American Sahara" region near Death Valley. "The most fatally famous part of the Great American Desert is Death Valley, in California," he wrote in 1891, "The valley is walled on each side by savage and appalling cliffs which rise thousands of feet in apparently sheer walls. Not even a bird flies across the hideous waste—nature is absolutely lifeless there."[16]

Yet by the late 1910s, rail lines and roads had reached even the most forbidding regions of eastern California, making the area easily accessible to travelers for the first time. In 1919 and again in 1921, Dixon made his way from his San Francisco home to the Inyo and Panamint mountains surrounding Death Valley. The isolated desert landscapes provided personal and artistic renewal as Dixon grappled with new, radical ideas entering American art.[17] He had seen the "ultra-modern" abstract paintings by European artists at the 1915 Panama-Pacific International Exposition in San Francisco.[18] Both intrigued and skeptical, Dixon urged his fellow artists to maintain their American cultural identity rather than slavishly repeating European formulas.[19] But when Dixon visited the peaks rising above Death Valley, he found an ideal modern subject in the desolate land of harsh extremes—a landscape of the American West reduced to the most fundamental abstract elements and shapes.

Inspired by the sparse forms and golden light, Dixon painted *A Desert Valley* in 1922 on his return to his San Francisco studio (page 145). Rather than creating a precise, photographic image of Telescope Peak in Death Valley, Dixon continued what nature had already begun, further simplifying the shapes of the landscape, clearly delineating geometric planes, and amplifying the crisp colors of the morning light. Much like the sheer valley wall, the painting contains only a minimal sense of depth, with bold hues creating a rhythmic pattern across the canvas surface. This painting—wholly of the American West and strikingly modern—shows Dixon's ability to straddle traditional and modernist art, blending the Old West with the new. Thirty years after his mentor Charles Lummis declared Death Valley to be an appalling wasteland, Dixon's painting presented the place in an entirely different light, celebrating the exuberant beauty of the land and creating an enduring image of the new West.

While Maynard Dixon faced a changing art world in San Francisco, a young painter from Sun Prairie, Wisconsin, burst upon the modernist New York City art scene. When Georgia O'Keeffe (1887–1986) opened her first solo exhibition in New York in 1917, her abstract paintings based on observations of nature attracted immediate attention. But the fiercely independent O'Keeffe felt more at ease outside the city, away from the crowds, surrounded by the landscapes

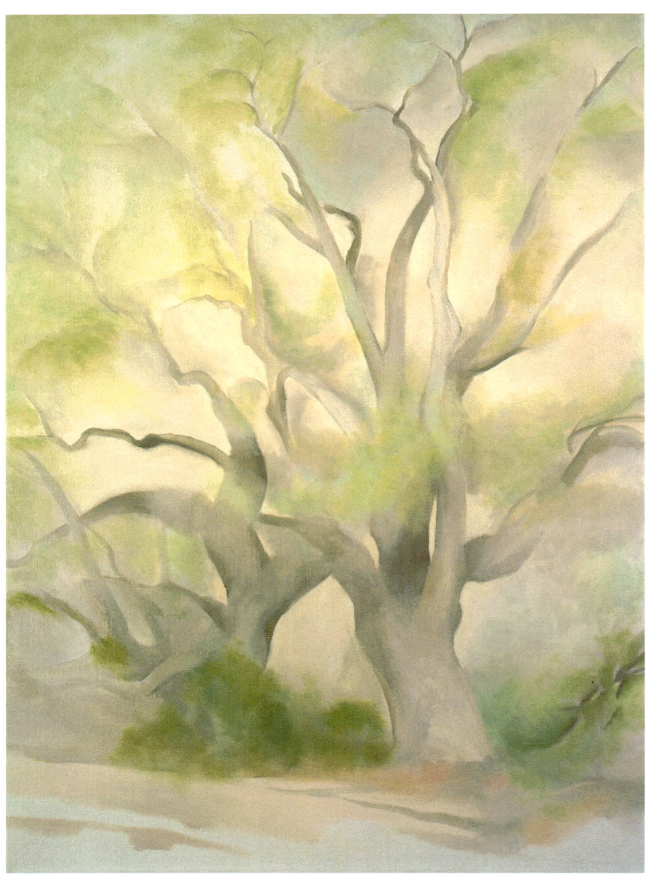

FIGURE 5 Georgia O'Keeffe, *Green Tree*, 1953. Oil on canvas, 41½ × 30⅜ inches. Georgia O'Keeffe Museum, Gift of The Georgia O'Keeffe Foundation, 2006.05.246.

and natural forms that inspired much of her painting. "I wish people were all trees and I think I could enjoy them then," she said in 1921, in the midst of her early success.[20] In the natural world O'Keeffe found symbols for personal thoughts and emotions. As early as the 1920s, she began to depict individual trees as distinct arboreal "portraits."[21] From the tall maple trees reaching toward the heavens in upstate New York, to the twisted, desiccated cedars barely clinging to life in the desert Southwest, trees in O'Keeffe's work form metaphors for human experiences.

In O'Keeffe's search for inspiration in nature, no location swept her away like northern New Mexico. In the summer of 1917 she traveled through Santa Fe for the first time—and was entranced with the brilliant skies and stark landscapes of the region. She later remarked, "From then on I was always on my way back."[22] Starting in 1929, O'Keeffe began spending most of her summers in New Mexico—driving a Model A

Ford alone through the rugged hills and finding new places and forms to portray on her canvases. She strove to convey the power of New Mexico to her New York audience. "All the earth colors of the painter's palette are out there in the many miles of bad lands," she declared, "those hills—our waste land—I think it our most beautiful country."[23] In 1949, after settling the estate of her husband Alfred Stieglitz (1864–1946), O'Keeffe made a permanent move to New Mexico. The basic elements of the place—light, land, architecture, bones, trees, flowers, shrubs—became sources for her paintings.

In the first part of the 1950s O'Keeffe painted over 20 images featuring the trees of New Mexico, such as *Green Tree* (figure 5). In many cases she depicted them with gestural, expressive limbs waving in and out of the background. They portray the changing seasons, from a burst of autumn color to the dead gray of winter to emerging leaves in early spring. In *Piñons with Cedar* from 1956, a curving, twisting tree forms a pattern of tangled twigs against a soft shrub and a rosy hillside, and reaches into the bright desert atmosphere (page 169). Although O'Keeffe included the traditional landscape features of foreground, background, and sky in the composition, she eliminated any sense of depth by blending the form of the cedar into the background, joining the elements of the land in a unified whole. Both the piñon and cedar are evergreens, meaning that the bare, brown piñon in O'Keeffe's painting has reached the end of its life. But the emerging green cedar—like a phoenix rising from the ashes—promises renewal and a continuing natural cycle, giving hope that this harsh, beautiful, fragile place will endure. And so it has. Today, O'Keeffe's powerful landscapes encourage viewers to see the deserts of the American West through her eyes—with awe and wonder.

IN SEARCH OF THE PAST, IN STUDY AND SATIRE: JOHN CLYMER AND BILL SCHENCK

In 1964 John Clymer (1907–1989) was ready for a drastic change. The 57-year-old native of Ellensburg, Washington, had an immensely successful career as an illustrator on the East Coast. In three decades he had created over 80 cover illustrations for the *Saturday Evening Post*, more than any artist save Norman Rockwell (1894–1978).[24] But memories of his childhood in eastern Washington never left him. In 1964, he abandoned his work in commercial illustration to focus on painting the American West. John and his wife Doris left their Connecticut home in 1970 to relocate to the towering Teton Mountains in Wyoming. There, far away from the noise and crowds of the East Coast, the Clymers immersed themselves in stories of the past.

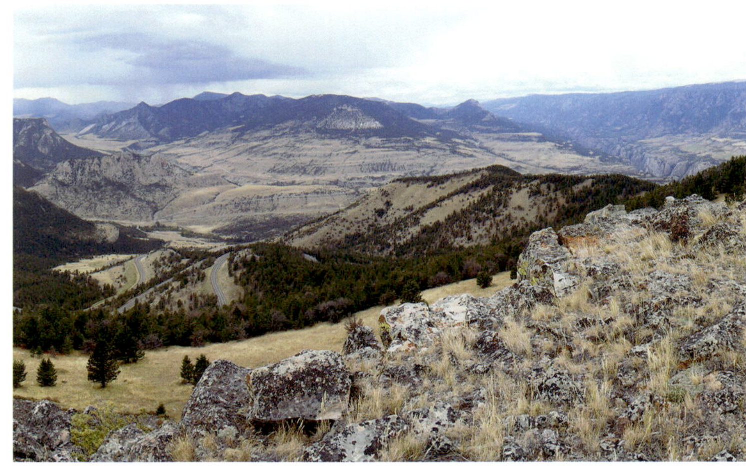

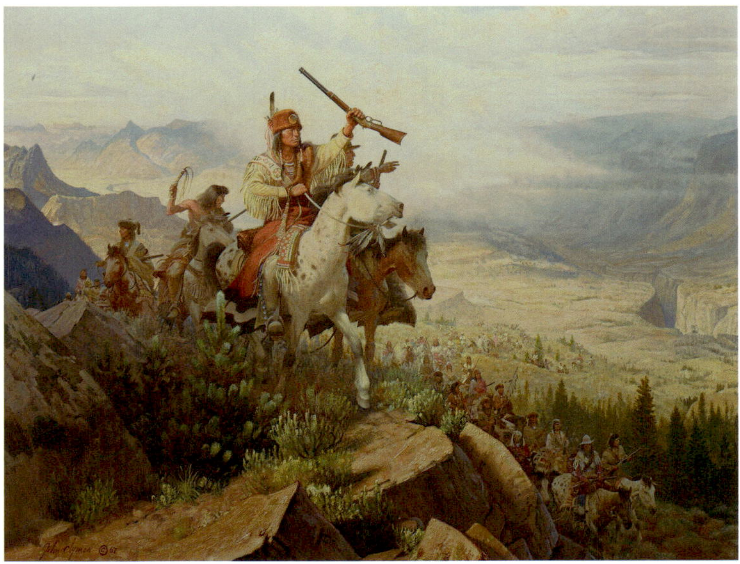

FIGURE 6 Photograph of Sunlight Basin from Dead Indian Pass. Courtesy of Mack Frost.

FIGURE 7 John Clymer, *Chief Joseph*, 1967. Oil on board, 30 × 40 inches. Tacoma Art Museum, Haub Family Collection, Promised gift of Erivan and Helga Haub.

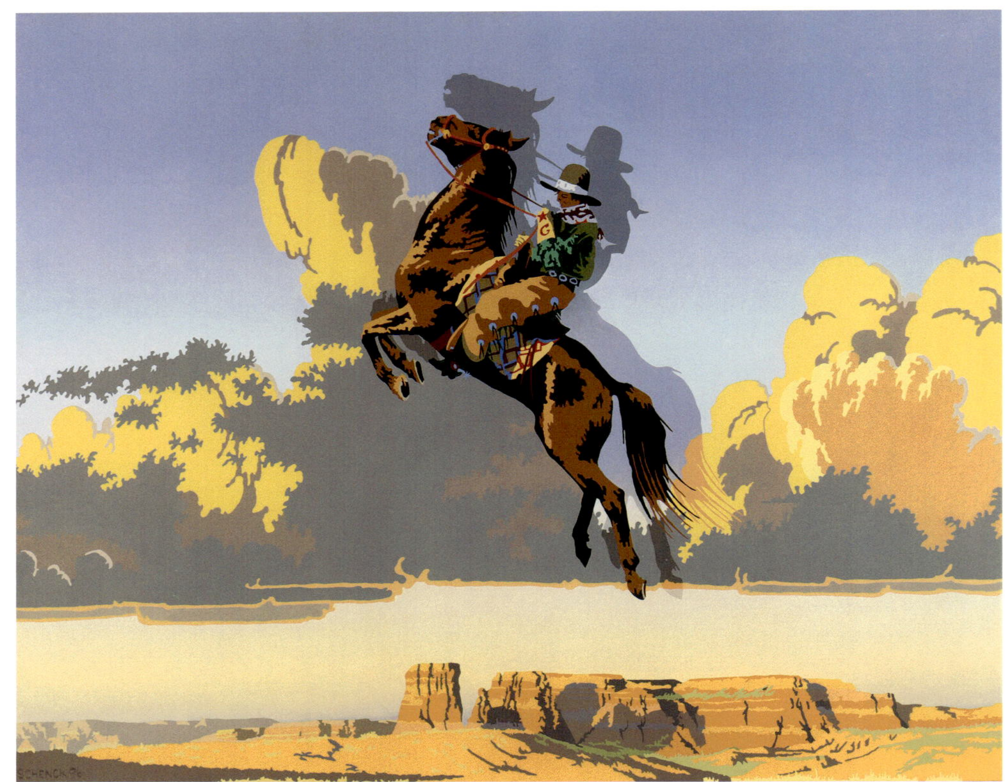

An enthusiastic historian, Doris researched the Frontier Era, and together the Clymers visited historic landmarks and retraced famous 19th-century expedition routes. "Going and seeing the actual places makes history come alive for me," Clymer remarked, "I think it is the accumulation of all these experiences, the research and the old stories, the trips on the old trails to actual places, that make it possible to do pictures that are real and believable."[25] His resulting artworks resemble western movie stills, carrying a narrative as clearly as a film or graphic novel.

Clymer's journey to retrace the footsteps of the Nez Perce people led him east of Yellowstone National Park to a high pass with breathtaking views of the dramatic mountain uplifts and deep canyons of Sunlight Basin in Wyoming (figure 6). The basin formed an ideal backdrop for his painting *Chief Joseph*, depicting the Nez Perce people who had traveled through the same spot in 1877 (figure 7). Clymer portrayed the chief like Napoleon crossing the Alps—sitting erect on his spotted Appaloosa horse, thrusting his rifle in the air and proudly leading his people forward. Clymer almost certainly read the 19th-century stories of the Nez Perce, when Chief Joseph was known worldwide as the "Indian Napoleon" for his skill in outmaneuvering the generals of the American cavalry.[26] Yet the actual flight of the Nez Perce in 1877 was anything but the triumphant march depicted in Clymer's painting. To escape confinement on a distant reservation, Chief Joseph fled his homeland in eastern Oregon with a band of over 700 men, women, and children, with the US Army in close pursuit. The journey was a heart-wrenching strain over a thousand miles long which ultimately resulted in defeat. If Clymer could visit Sunlight Basin today, he would now find a National Forest plaque marking the suffering of the Nez Perce: "This became a flight for their lives. By this time, all were exhausted and heartbroken."[27]

When Clymer painted *Chief Joseph* the hardships endured by the Nez Perce were no secret—the shameful treatment they had received was well documented in the early 20th century.[28] But rather than creating an image of a defeated "vanishing race," a frequent method of depicting Native Americans for much of the 19th century, Clymer chose to portray an unconquered leader. In his victorious image, Clymer revealed his respect and admiration for Chief Joseph, whom he considered a leading figure in American history. Today, Clymer's creative interpretations of historic events give us a glimpse into his own opinions about the past.

"Movies," explained Bill Schenck (born 1947), "were how I knew the most about the West."[29] When the artist was growing up in rural Ohio in the 1950s, he loved watching old westerns and visiting relatives in Wyoming for the summer. As an art student at the Columbus College of Art and Design in the 1960s, Schenck was drawn to the audacious pop art of Andy Warhol (1928–1987) and Roy Lichtenstein (1923–1997), who repurposed mass-produced imagery from America's consumer culture for their artwork.[30] But after Schenck first saw Sergio Leone's groundbreaking "spaghetti western" films in the late 1960s, with their extreme close-ups and distorted perspectives, he seized the idea of repurposing images from western cinema in his art. After early success in New York with large-scale canvases based on western film stills, Schenck relocated to the Southwest in 1975.[31] Taking a cue from pop art, he continued to find inspiration in a variety of appropriated imagery, including Maynard Dixon paintings, Edward Curtis photographs, western movie stills, and dime novel cover illustrations. In his finished paintings, Schenck reinterpreted historic images and myths of the West, satirically rendering traditional frontier characters in a brash, postmodern pop art style.

In the 1990s, Schenck's inventive paintings gained popularity in the midst of a changing approach toward western history. A 1991 *Los Angeles Times* review of his art remarked, "With 'Dances With Wolves' fresh in everyone's mind there's been a chic re-evaluation of the American West mythology. Cowboys and Indians—who's on the side of right?" In the midst of this shift, "Schenck appears as a lone gun encroaching on the romantic territory of Western art, adding satire and lust freely."[32] In Schenck's drive to call stereotypes into question through his artwork, he has continually portrayed the men, women, and landscapes of the West in a new light.

In particular, Schenck's paintings of powerful cowgirls counter the old-fashioned image of a "pioneer woman," often portrayed by early 19th-century artists as meek and wholly dependent on men for survival. In *Cowgirl Over*

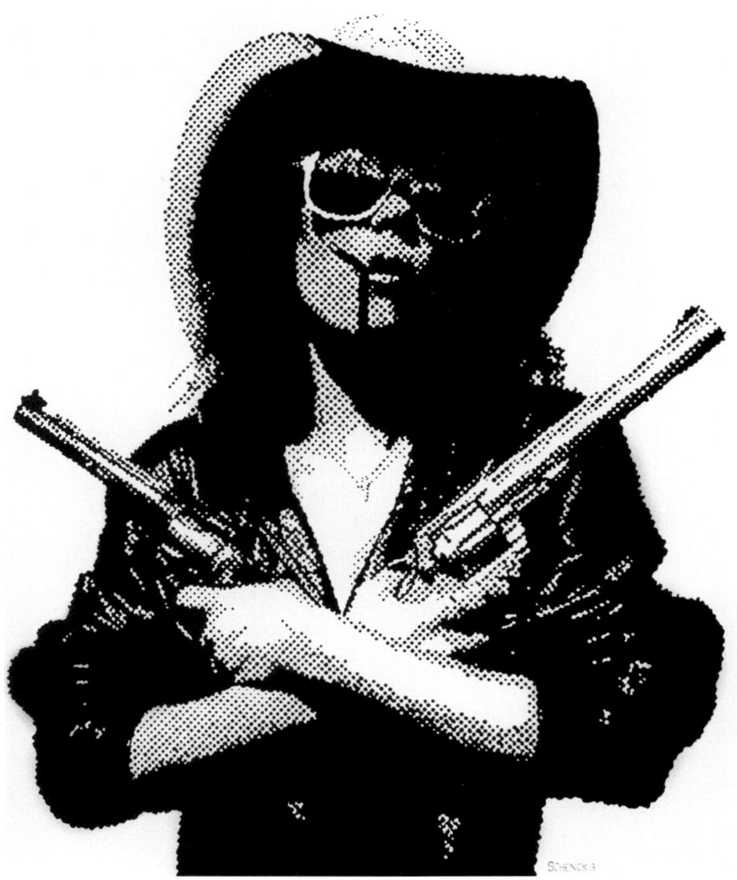

FIGURE 9 Bill Schenck, *True Romance State II*, 2013. Oil on canvas, 60 × 50 inches. Private collection. Image courtesy of Bill Schenck.

Kachina Mesa, Schenck depicts a cowgirl as a dominant icon of the American West (figure 8). Her shadow against the sky makes her appear to take flight before a flat stage backdrop of a classic Southwest landscape. The piece celebrates the beauty of the West and firmly places the independent cowgirl in the pantheon of mythic western characters. In his recent work, Schenck has reprised the self-empowered western woman as a dominant force not to be trifled with. In the 2013 painting *True Romance State II*, a defiant cowgirl crushes the traditional image of a male gunslinger found in film and fiction, completely reversing gender roles (figure 9). Throughout his career, Schenck's artwork has challenged viewers to question their perceptions of the West, reminding us that history—and myth—are constantly open to new interpretation.

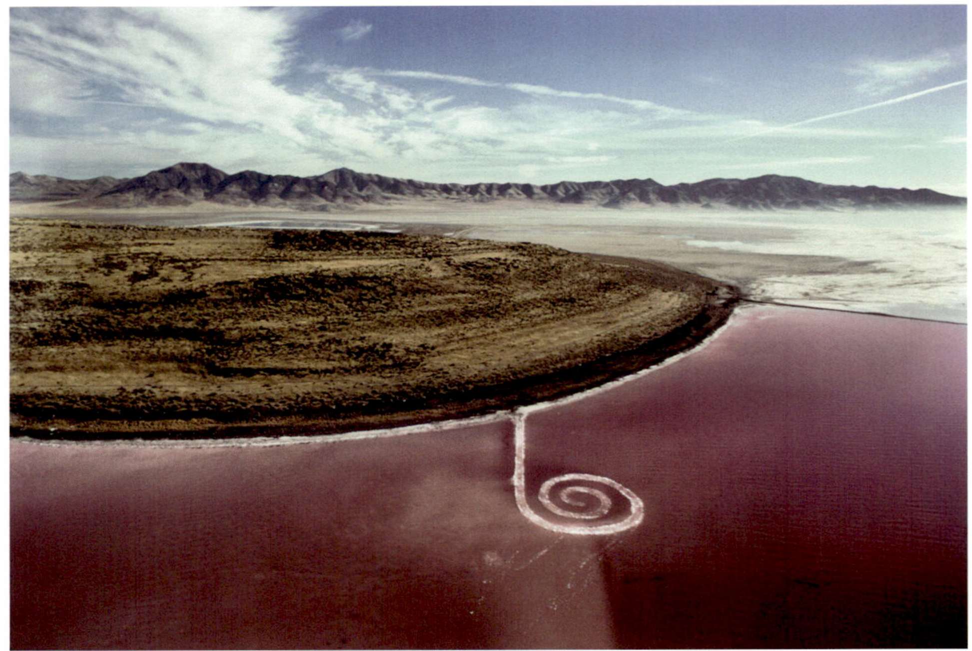

A small outpost of the National Park Service now marks the location where the celebratory Golden Spike completed the first transcontinental railroad in the United States. The desolate spot reminds us of the great changes caused by technological achievements—and also reminds us that the American West remains a stimulus for creative expression. Today, if you continue past the Golden Spike National Historic Site down a rough, unmarked dirt road cutting several miles through the sagebrush, you finally see the circular shape of Robert Smithson's *Spiral Jetty* extending from pale, shimmering shores into the Great Salt Lake (figure 10). The monumental 1970 sculpture, 1,500 feet long, uses the earth itself as an artistic medium and creates a new connection between art and the western landscape.

From 19th-century portraits, to 20th-century earthworks, to 21st-century pop art, the American West has provided inspiration to artists from all walks of life. As a whole, the careers of the eight artists presented here—Inman, Kane, Remington, Schreyvogel, Dixon, O'Keeffe, Clymer, and Schenck—span the entire United States. They studied art in Europe and at centers across America; some created their artwork in studios in the East, others in the West. But regardless of where they studied and worked, their images helped define this distinct region of the world. The art of the West calls viewers to examine ideas of Native American identity, to consider the effects of rapidly moving technologies, to celebrate our vibrant yet fragile natural resources, and to ponder how the past will be retold in the future as the 21st century continues to unfold.

1 Henry David Thoreau, *Walden; or, Life in the Woods* (Boston: Ticknor and Fields, 1854).

2 Herman J. Viola, *Indians of North America: Paintings by Henry Inman from the D. Harold Byrd, Jr. Collection* (Cody, WY: Buffalo Bill Historical Center, 1983), 10.

3 "The Winnebagoes," *Saturday Evening Post* 7, no. 378 (October 25, 1828), 2.

4 J. Russell Harper, ed., *Paul Kane's Frontier, Including Wanderings of an Artist among the Indians of North America by Paul Kane* (Austin: University of Texas Press, 1971), 13–14.

5 Kane painted two versions of Maungwudaus. One is in the Haub Family Collection, and the other is in the Royal Ontario Museum, 2009.11209.39. Donald B. Smith, *Mississauga Portraits: Ojibwe Voices from Nineteenth-Century Canada* (Toronto: University of Toronto Press, 2013), 154.

6 "Ojibway Indians," *Maine Farmer* 17, no. 52 (December 27, 1949), 2.

7 Kenneth R. Lister, *Paul Kane/The Artist/Wilderness to Studio* (Toronto: Royal Ontario Museum, 2010).

8 Peter H. Hassrick and Melissa J. Webster, *Frederic Remington: A Catalogue Raisonné of Paintings, Watercolors, and Drawings* (Cody, WY: Buffalo Bill Historical Center, 1996), 861.

9 "Needs of the Park," *Forest and Stream* 24 (May 7, 1885), 285.

10 C. A. Kenaston, "The Great Plains of Canada," *Century Magazine* (August 1892), 565–80.

11 James D. Horan, *The Life and Art of Charles Schreyvogel: Painter-Historian of the Indian-Fighting Army of the American West* (New York: Crown, 1969), 14, 17.

12 "Horse Gossip," *Michigan Farmer* 35, no. 21 (May 26, 1900), 404.

13 "Automobile News," *Scientific American* 89, no. 13 (September 26, 1903), 219.

14 Glenn E. Plumb and Rosemary Sucec, "A Bison Conservation History in the US National Parks," *Journal of the West* 45, no. 2 (Spring 2006), 23.

15 Maynard Dixon to Charles F. Lummis, May 26, 1900, quoted in Donald J. Hagerty, *The Life of Maynard Dixon* (Layton, Utah: Gibbs Smith, 2010), 49.

16 Charles Fletcher Lummis, *Some Strange Corners of Our Country: The Wonderland of the Southwest* (New York: Century, 1891), 37, 40.

17 Donald J. Hagerty, *The Life of Maynard Dixon* (Layton, Utah: Gibbs Smith, 2010), 133.

18 Eugen Neuhaus, *The Galleries of the Exposition: A Critical Review of the Paintings, Sculpture, Statuary and the Graphic Arts in the Palace of Fine Arts at the Panama-Pacific International Exposition* (San Francisco: Paul Elder, 1915), 22.

19 Maynard Dixon, "Toward American Art," *The Argus: A Journal of Art Criticism* 1, no. 3 (June 1927), 6.

20 Quoted in Marsden Hartley, *Adventures in the Arts: Informal Chapters on Painters, Vaudeville, and Poets* (New York: Boni and Liveright, 1921), 116.

21 Charles C. Eldredge, *Georgia O'Keeffe* (New York: Harry N. Abrams, 1991), 40–43.

22 Quoted in William H. Goetzmann and William N. Goetzmann, *The West of the Imagination* (New York: W. W. Norton, 1986), 424.

23 Georgia O'Keeffe, statement from *Georgia O'Keeffe Exhibition of Oils and Pastels*, exhibition brochure, An American Place (New York, January 22–March 17, 1939), reproduced in Barbara Buhler Lynes, *Georgia O'Keeffe Catalogue Raisonné,* vol. 2 (New Haven: Yale University Press, 1999), 1099.

24 Walt Reed, *John Clymer: An Artist's Rendezvous with the Frontier West*, 3rd ed. (United States: Walt Reed, 1995), 18.

25 Ibid, 32.

26 Timothy Egan, *Short Nights of the Shadow Catcher: The Epic Life and Immortal Photographs of Edward Curtis* (Boston: Houghton Mifflin Harcourt, 2012), 61.

27 Shoshone National Forest plaque, Dead Indian Pass, Wyoming State Highway 296.

28 In 1911 photographer Edward Curtis described the broken promises and harsh treatment the government dealt the Nez Perce. In the 1940s anthropologist L. V. McWhorter published multiple accounts of the War of 1877 from the perspective of the Nez Perce. See Edward S. Curtis, *The North American Indian*, vol. 8 (Seattle: E. S. Curtis, 1911) and Lucullus Virgil McWhorter, *Yellow Wolf: His Own Story* (Caldwell, ID: Caxton Printers, 1940).

29 Quoted in Norman Kolpas, "Billy Schenck: Pop Maverick," *Southwest Art* (August 2012), http://www.southwestart.com/featured/schenck-b-aug2012.

30 Amy Abrams, *Schenck in the 21st Century: The Myth of the Hero and the Truth of America* (Santa Fe: Western Skies, 2013), 18.

31 Norman Kolpas, "Billy Schenck: Pop Maverick." See note 29.

32 Josef Woodard, "Wild West Pop: Painter Bill Schenck takes alternately grave and whimsical views of cowboy and Indian mythology at Sacred Visions Gallery," *Los Angeles Times*, March 7, 1991.

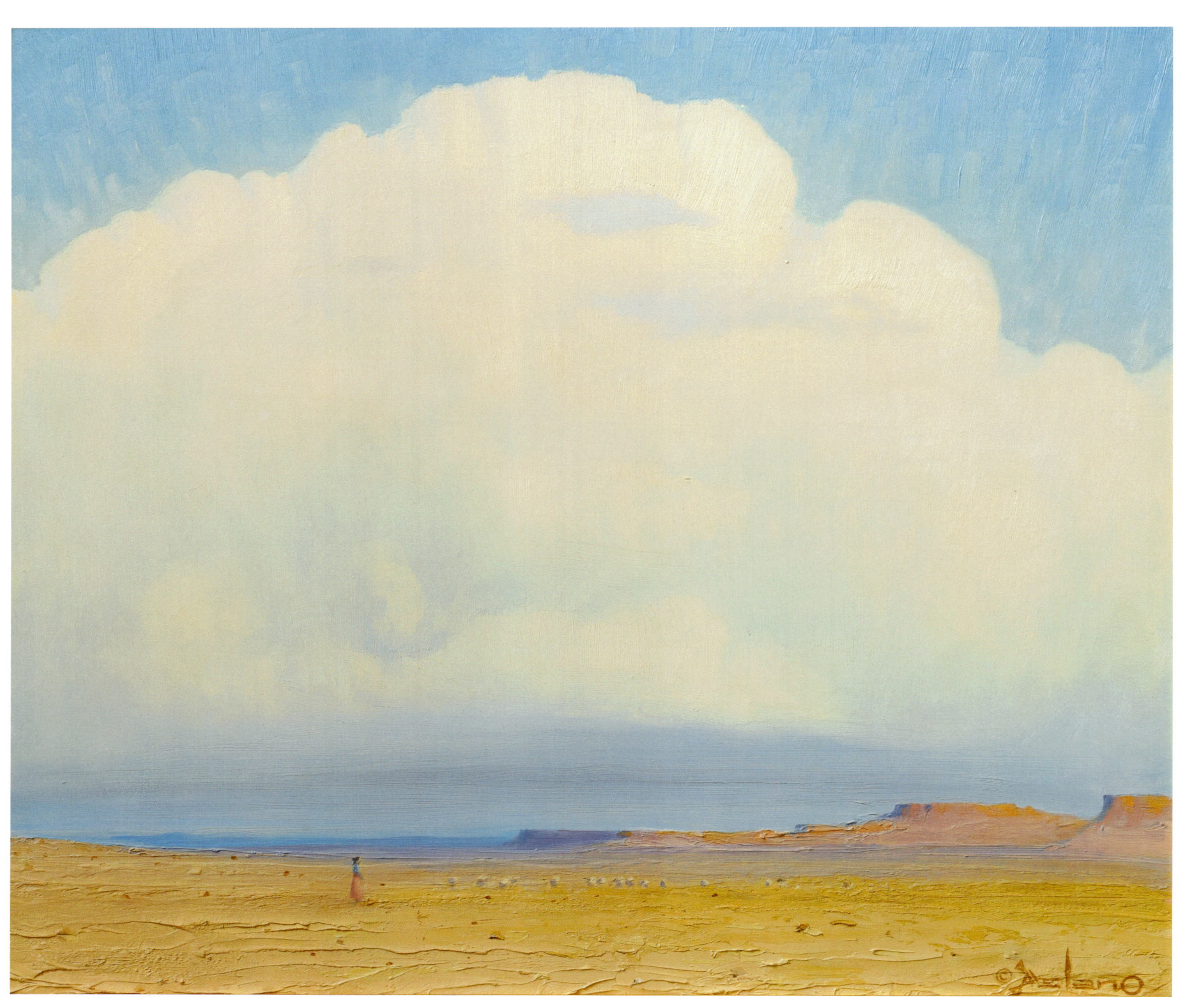

Desert Cloud

date unknown
Oil on board
20 × 24 inches

A dome of white soars against a brilliant blue, a stripe of rosy pink rests above a bar of golden tan. With bold brushstrokes, Gerard Curtis Delano captures the abstract forms of the Arizona landscape in *Desert Cloud*. The towering cloud completely dominates the composition, dwarfing tall red mesas and a broad plain. A Navajo woman and her flock of sheep are rendered as tiny specks of color in the foreground, further emphasizing the grand scale of the desert sky. After his first visit to Arizona and the Navajo Nation in 1943, Delano was captivated by the colorful landscapes and inspired by the local cultures. "There is a vastness, an immensity, and the peaceful hush of an enormous cathedral about Arizona's great canyons," he wrote.* Beyond beauty, Delano found a spiritual essence in the unique lands of the desert Southwest.

*Gerard Curtis Delano, quoted in Chase Reynolds Ewald, "Perspective: Gerard Curtis Delano (1890–1972)," *Western Art & Architecture* (Fall/Winter 2011), http://www.westernartandarchitecture.com/articles/western-art-and-architecture/fall-winter-2011/156/perspective-gerard-curtis-delano-1890-1972.html.

Taos Woman

circa 1924
Oil on canvas
32 × 24⅛ inches

Hands on hips, feet firmly planted at shoulder width, a woman of the Taos Pueblo projects a sense of determination in her strong stance. Using a modern style with bold blocks of color against the clean geometric shapes of a curved adobe wall and turquoise door, Kenneth M. Adams created a confident individual in command of her surroundings. Adams, a native of Topeka, Kansas, also possessed the determination to follow his own individual path in becoming an artist. He remembered, "When I started taking painting lessons, private painting lessons, I was looked upon as perhaps just a little odd."[*] Adams later studied under American modernist Andrew Dasburg and then moved to New Mexico in the 1920s, becoming the youngest member of the Taos Society of Artists. But he felt like something of an outsider until the 1930s, when he became involved with various federal art projects. "The WPA, during the depression, did much to eliminate the idea that the artist is an odd guy. He seemed to be accepted from that time forward as a part of the community," Adams recalled.[†] Becoming an art instructor at the University of New Mexico in the late 1930s, Adams forged ties between the arts community and society at large throughout the rest of his career.

[*]Oral history interview with Kenneth M. Adams, April 23, 1964, Archives of American Art, Smithsonian Institution.

[†]Ibid.

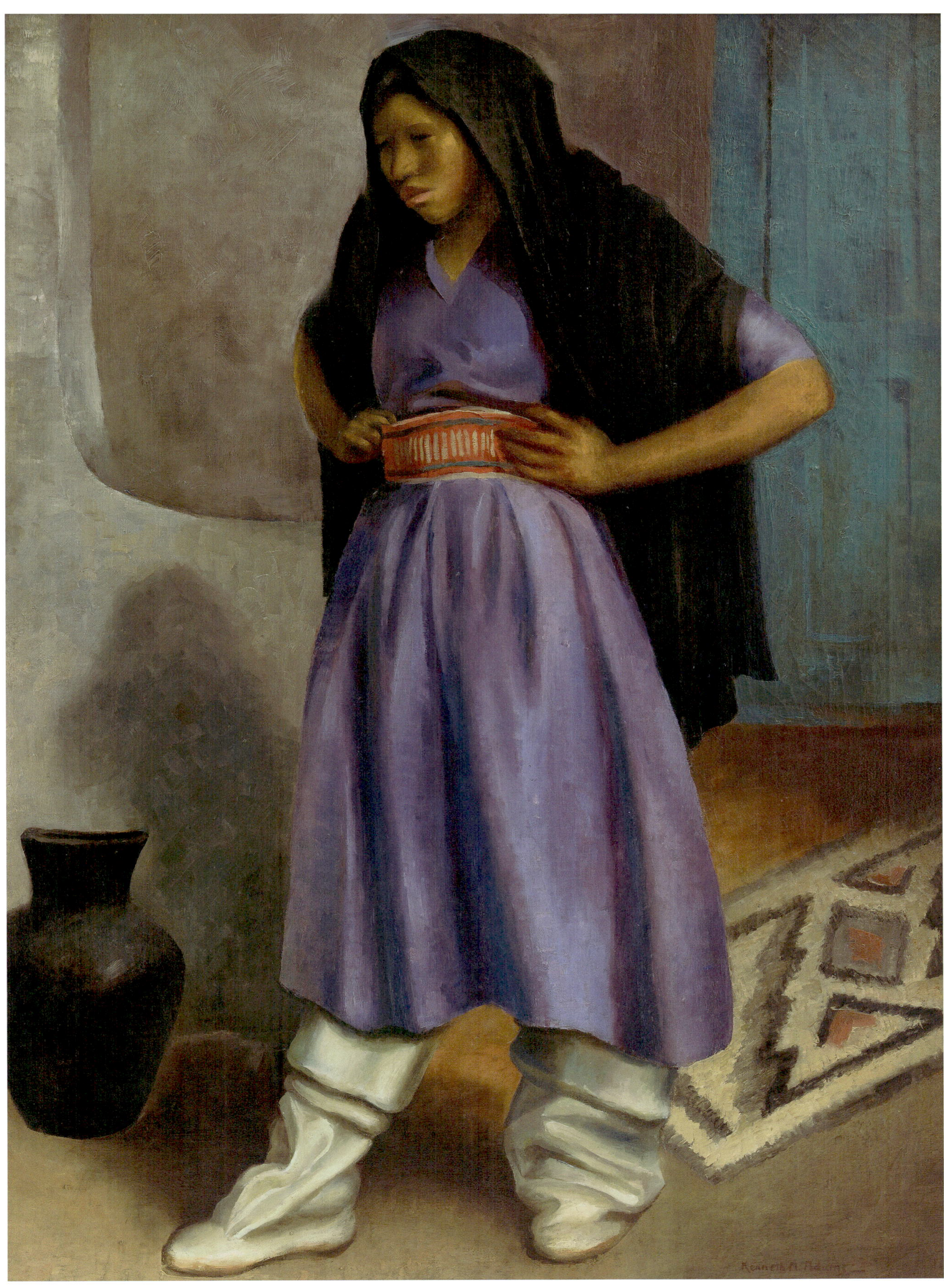

Parley on the Bozeman Trail

1964
Gouache on paper
20 × 30 inches

As a young boy growing up in southern Germany in the early 20th century, Nick Eggenhofer was enamored of stories of the American West. He read sensational dime novel accounts of the Frontier, watched the earliest western films, and eagerly listened to older relatives describe the thrilling performances of Buffalo Bill's Wild West. When he finally had his first chance to visit the western United States in 1925, the region did not disappoint. He became an illustrator specializing in western subjects, and began detailed research into the various transportation methods used in the West—constructing intricate scale models of 19th-century wagons and publishing the book *Wagons, Mules, and Men: How the Frontier Moved West* in 1961.

After Eggenhofer moved to Cody, Wyoming, the nearby windswept sagebrush plains became the backdrop for many of his paintings. In this work, he imagined a 19th-century scene of a meeting between Native Americans and a freight wagon team on the western prairie. Rather than portraying a modern 20th-century West, Eggenhofer preferred to depict scenes reminiscent of the dime novel stories and early western films he had loved as a boy.

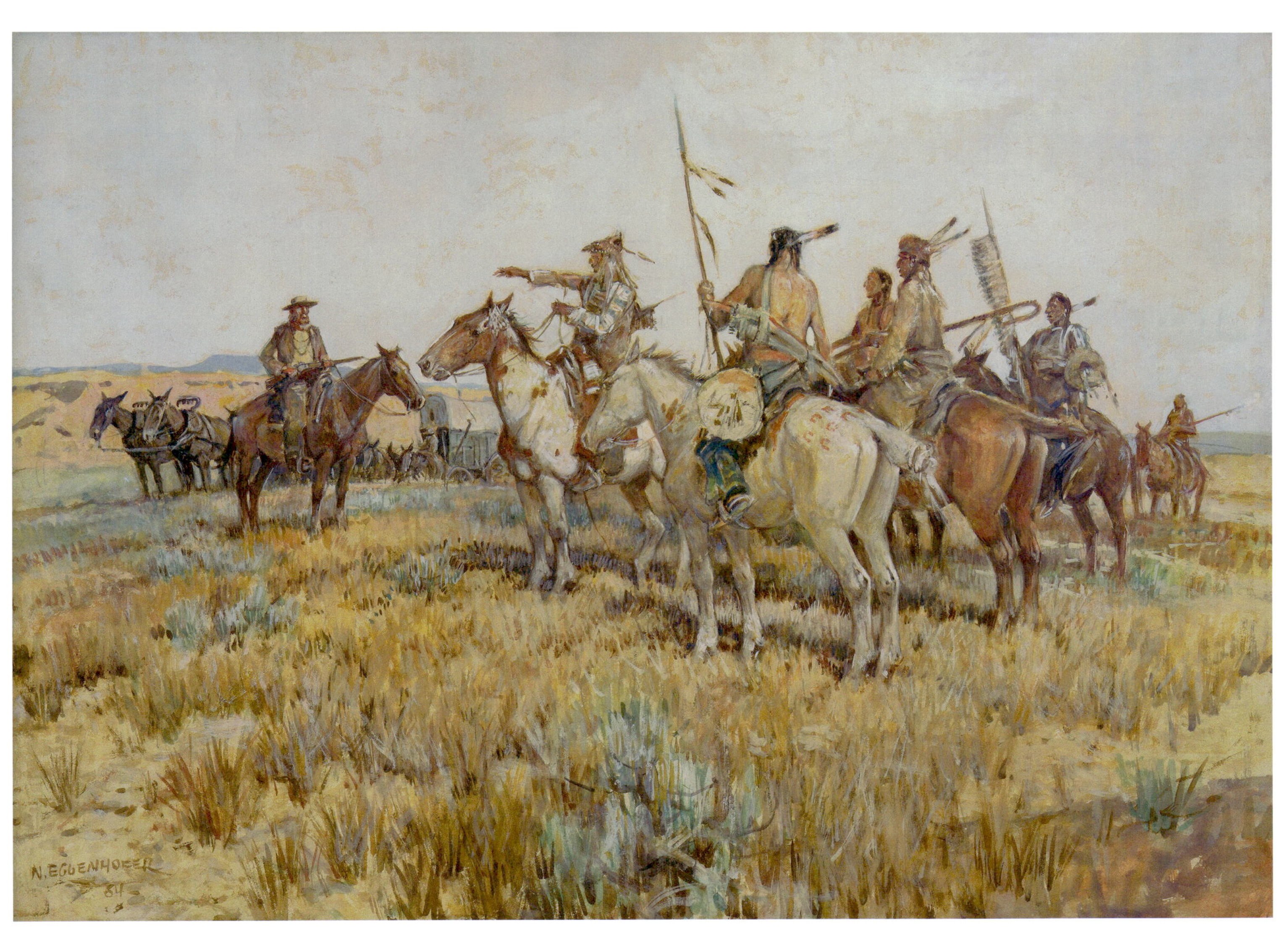
N. EGGENHOFER
84

River Bend Below Hondo

circa 1960
Watercolor on board
20 × 28¾ inches

Dark steel-gray clouds loom along the horizon as scattered sunlight pierces the overcast sky and washes the landscape in patches of gold. Rolling over the hills in a flash, a storm blows across a valley in south-central New Mexico, only to vanish within minutes. In warm yellows, greens, and blue-grays, Peter Hurd catches the crackle of stormy weather swiftly moving through his high desert home.

One of the first Anglo artists to be born in New Mexico, Hurd grew up in Roswell and later moved to Pennsylvania to study with renowned illustrator N. C. Wyeth—and eventually married Wyeth's daughter Henriette. The couple moved back to Hurd's childhood home and purchased a ranch in the Hondo Valley, west of Roswell. In addition to his work in illustration and portraiture, Hurd found inspiration in the rugged, arid land around him. In *River Bend Below Hondo*, Hurd erases any human imprint on the landscape, focusing simply on the beauty of the colors and light on a tumultuous, stormy day.

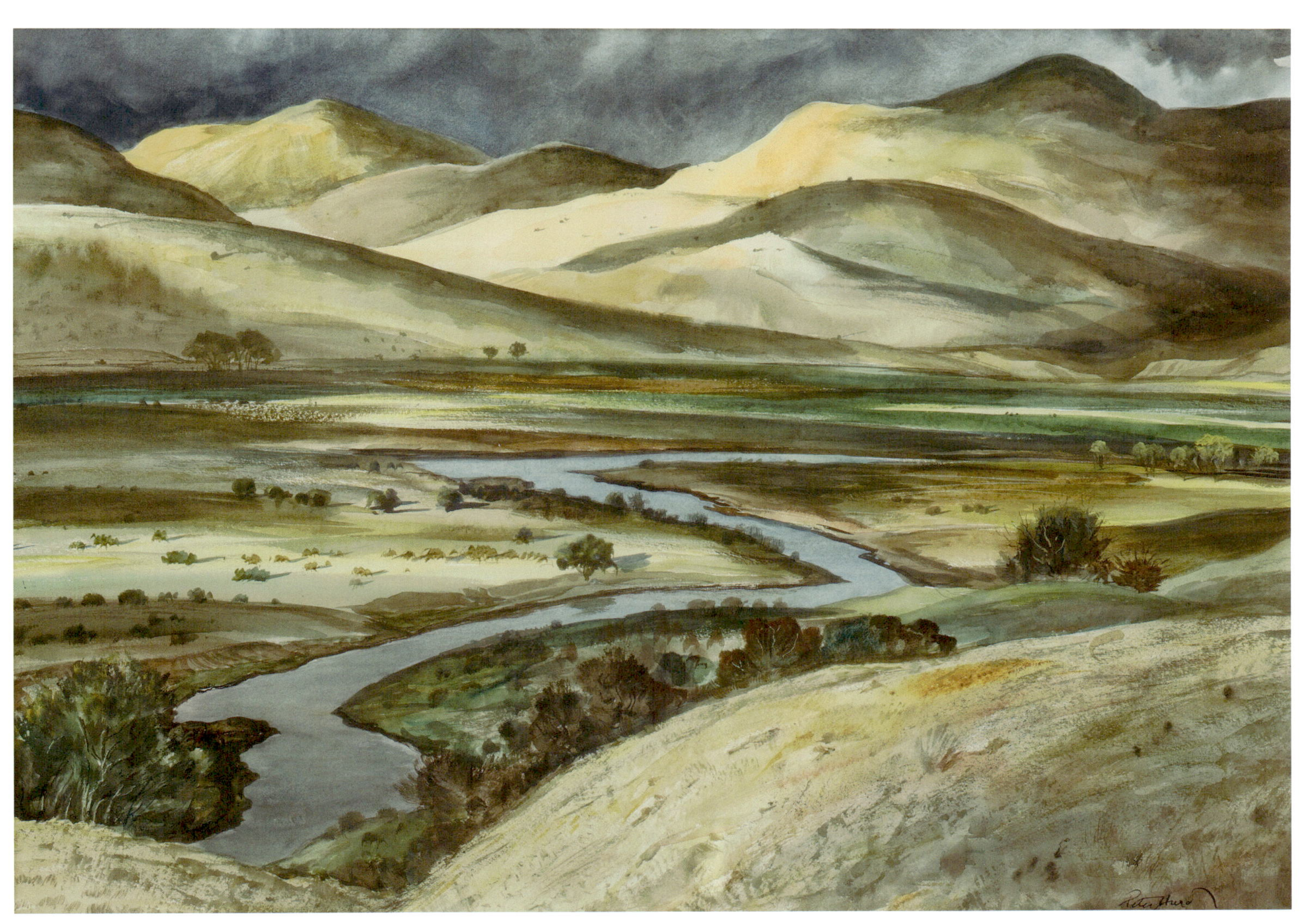

Trailing Them North

1963
Oil on canvas
24 × 48 inches

Four cowboys walked into a bar. On a June evening in 1965, Charlie Dye, Joe Beeler, John Hampton, and George Phippen donned their Stetsons and moseyed on down to a tavern in Sedona, Arizona—to talk about painting. They had the idea to form a new organization "to perpetuate the memory and culture of the Old West as typified by the late Frederic Remington, Charles Russell, and others."* Over a few rounds of beer, the Cowboy Artists of America was born—a group of rebels reacting against new movements and trends in modern art. Charlie Dye proudly described the CAA: "It's not like being a whore in black stockings like some of those big painters."† They considered their rejection from the mainstream art market to be a victory, and their work quickly gained a following of enthusiastic collectors.

Painted shortly before Dye helped form the CAA, *Trailing Them North* portrays a historic scene of two cowboys leading a vast herd of cattle. Rather than presenting the grueling hardships endured by working cowboys in the 19th century, Dye bathes the scene in a golden light, celebrating the cowboys as rugged American heroes. Today the CAA continues to be an active organization, with artists replicating older imagery and recording a halcyon, idealized image of the West—firmly cementing the cowboy myth in American culture.

*Objectives, *Cowboy Artists of America*, 2014, http://cowboyartistsofamerica.com/

†Quoted in William H. Goetzmann and William N. Goetzmann, *The West of the Imagination*, 2nd ed. (Norman, OK: University of Oklahoma Press, 2009), 368.

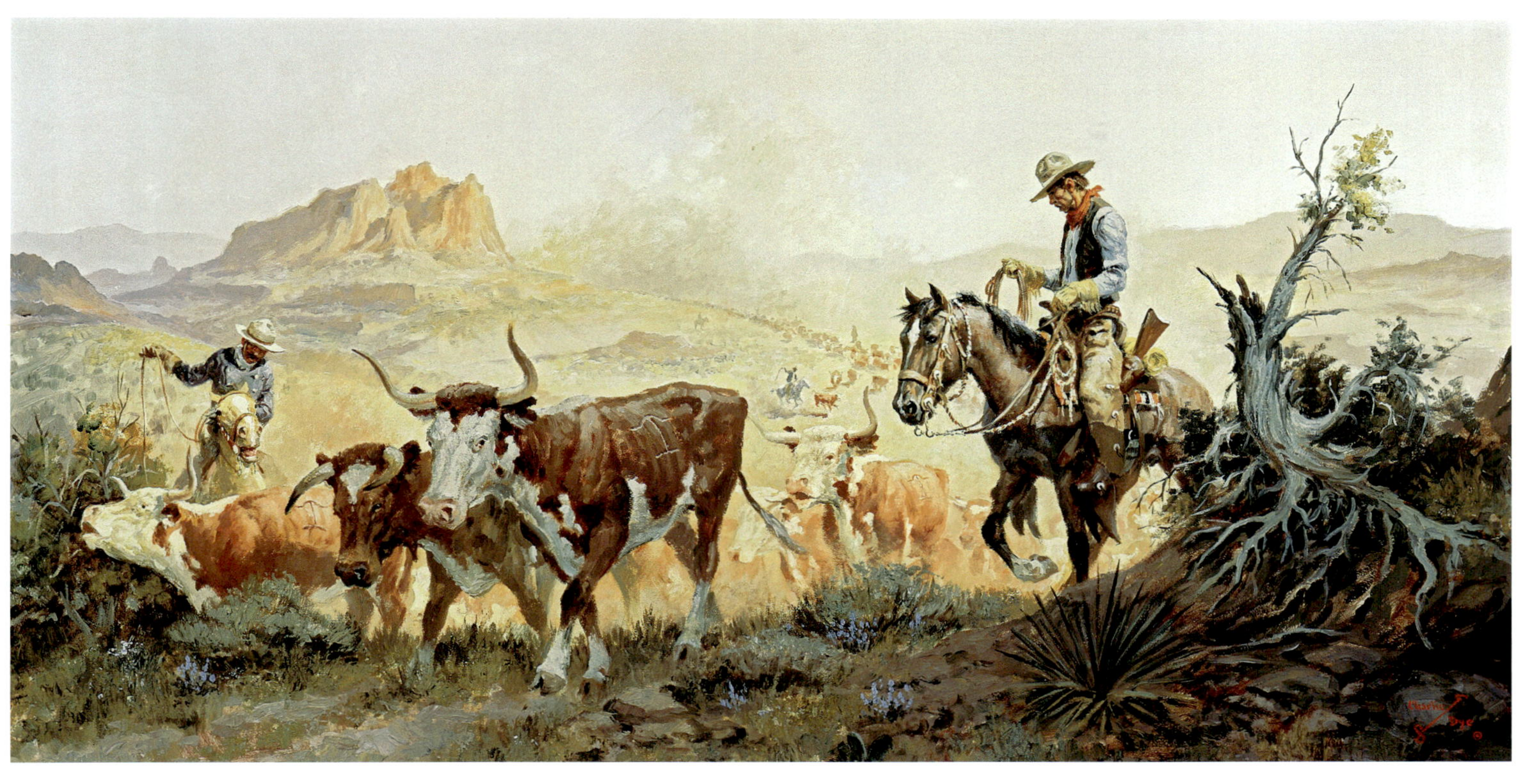

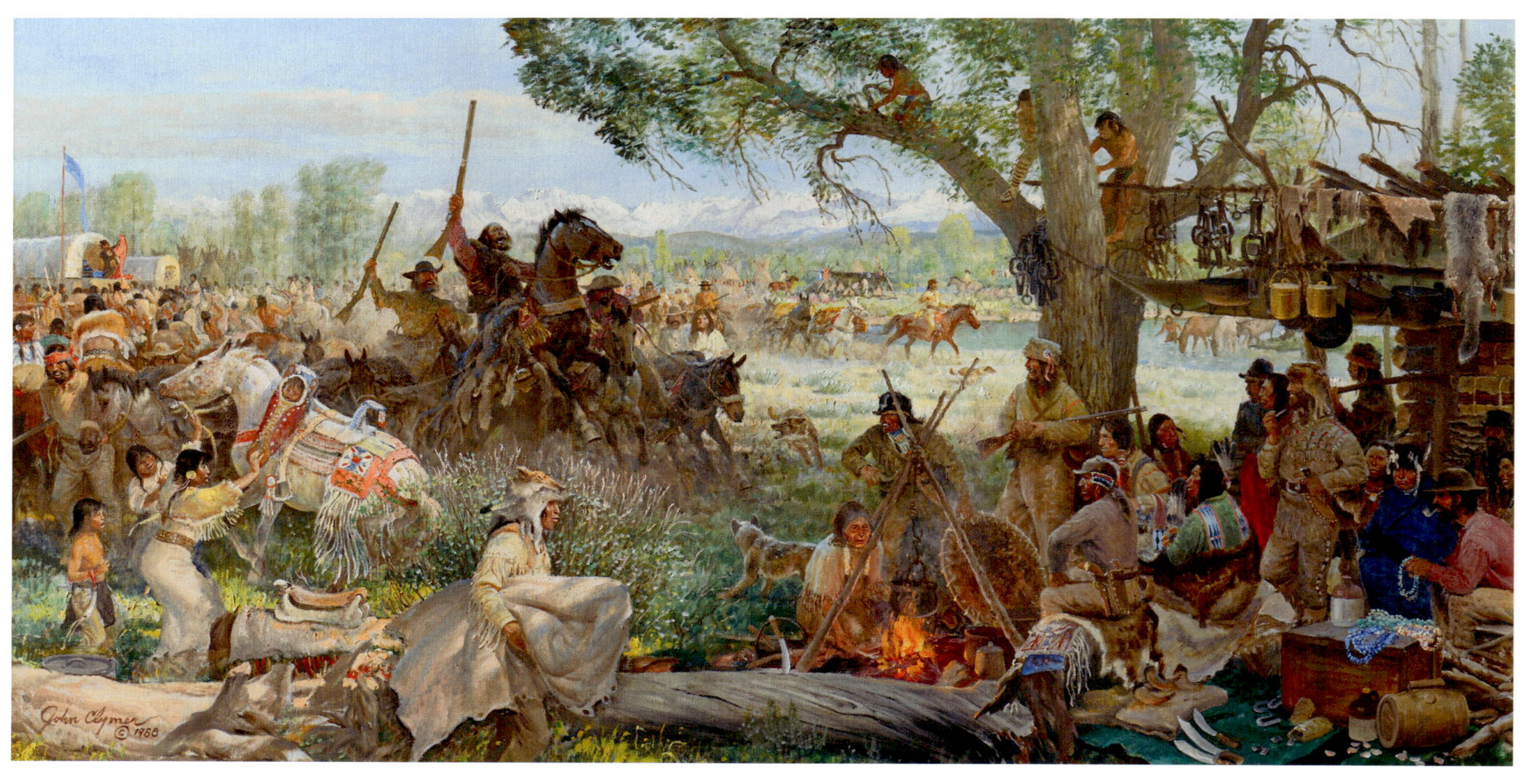

Late Arrivals—Green River Rendezvous

1988
Oil on canvas
24 × 48 inches

Since 1936, residents of western Wyoming have met in the shadow of the Wind River Mountains in July to reenact the famous rendezvous, a gathering of inhabitants, travelers, and traders that occurred on the same spot in the early 19th century. When John Clymer moved to Wyoming in 1970, he was drawn to the history of the mountain men who roamed through the region more than a century earlier. He visited the Green River Rendezvous site and researched the past with his wife, Doris, an enthusiastic historian. When Erivan and Helga Haub commissioned Clymer to paint a raucous rendezvous crowd assembled at Green River, the subject was a perfect fit for the artist. Like the reenactors who gathered every summer, Clymer carefully reconstructed a complex scene. Native Americans, French-Canadian trappers, British fur traders, and many more fill the canvas in a joyful cacophony with prancing horses and yipping dogs. Clymer imagined all the various residents and travelers in the West existing in harmony in the early 19th century, for a brief moment. *Late Arrivals—Green River Rendezvous* turned out to be Clymer's last finished painting. He passed away shortly after its completion.

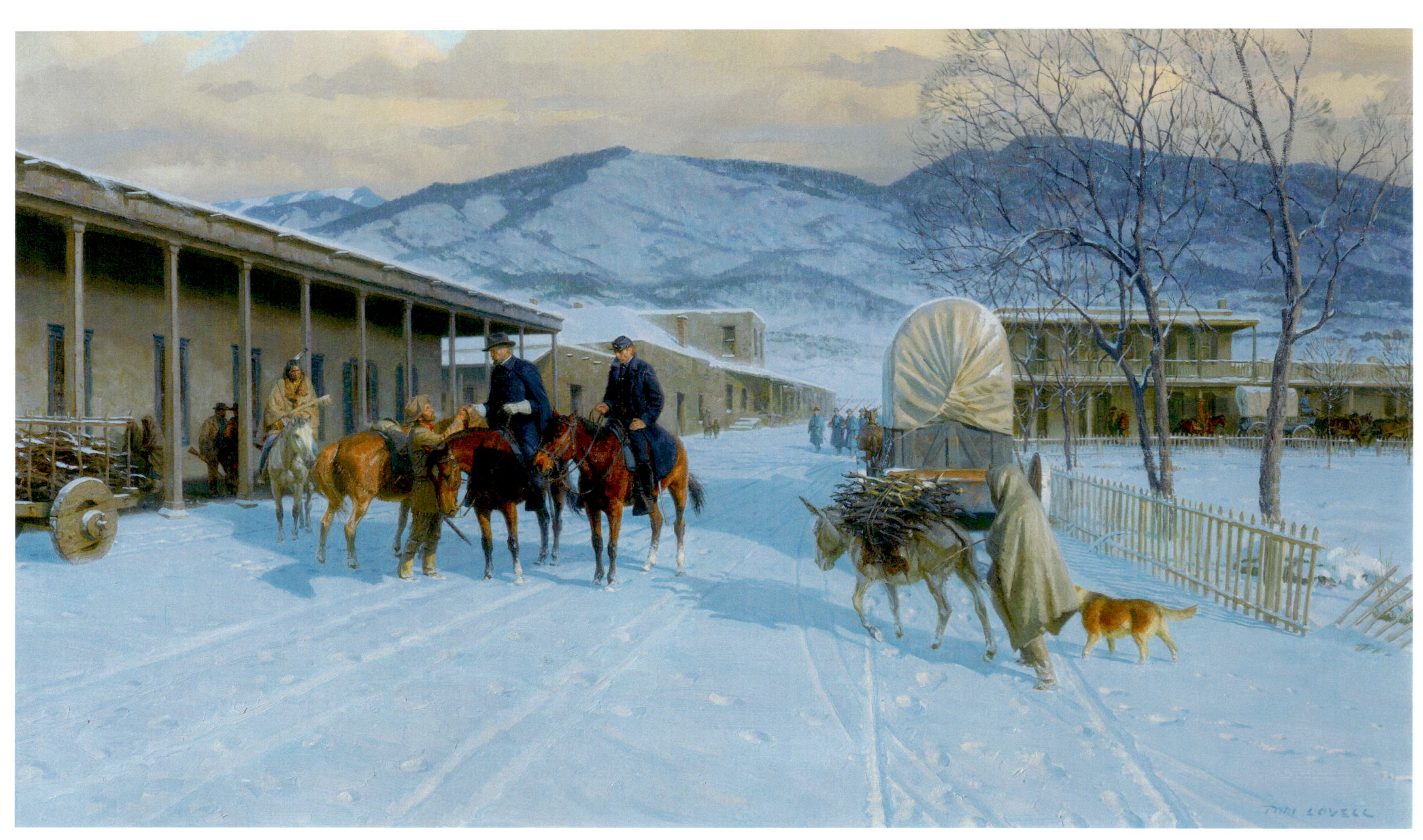

Old Santa Fe

circa 1990
Oil on board
23 × 40 inches

Tom Lovell worked as an artist in New York City for decades, creating magazine illustrations and military history paintings. But at age 66 he followed his childhood dream of heading west and relocated to Santa Fe, where he soon immersed himself in the history of the centuries-old community. Some 19th-century photographs of the Palace of the Governors inspired Lovell's painting *Old Santa Fe.* Built in 1610, the Palace is the oldest continually occupied public building in the United States. Before renovations in 1913, a tall balustrade covered the portal along the structure—as shown to the left in the painting. Alongside the historic architecture Lovell imagined a scene from the era of the Mexican-American War in the 1840s, when control of Santa Fe wavered between Mexico and the United States. In the painting, one of a pair of mounted cavalrymen hands over a saddlebag—perhaps containing mail—to a frontiersman in buckskin. A group of soldiers dressed in blue marches in the distance, rifles in hand. The flinty blue palette of the snow-covered scene conveys the sharp bite of cold air, helping viewers imagine the ancient place on a wintry day, long before Santa Fe became a bustling arts hub and tourist destination in the 20th century.

ROBERT LOUGHEED (1910–1982)

Alberta Morning

date unknown
Oil on Masonite
10 × 20 inches

In dashes of gold and green, Robert Lougheed captures the glorious colors of the brief summer in Alberta, Canada—one of his favorite locations to paint. With quick brushstrokes he creates lush textures in the shrubs, tall trees, and vertical mountain peaks, rendering a vivid landscape that nearly dwarfs the rider and packhorses ambling through thick grasses in the foreground.

Lougheed developed his loose, painterly style while studying under American impressionist Frank Vincent DuMond at the Art Students League of New York in the 1930s. To capture the vibrant, vast western landscape, Lougheed turned to DuMond's teachings on color and *plein air* painting and used wide, long-format surfaces. "The West is too big to be confined within the boundaries of the canvas. It is necessary to create the impression of a landscape that moves into the painting from one side and continues on out the other," Lougheed explained. "I started to paint the long proportion—twice the length of its depth."*

*Quoted in Don Hedgpeth, *Follow the Sun: Robert Lougheed* (Vail, CO: Diamond Trail Press, 2010), 238.

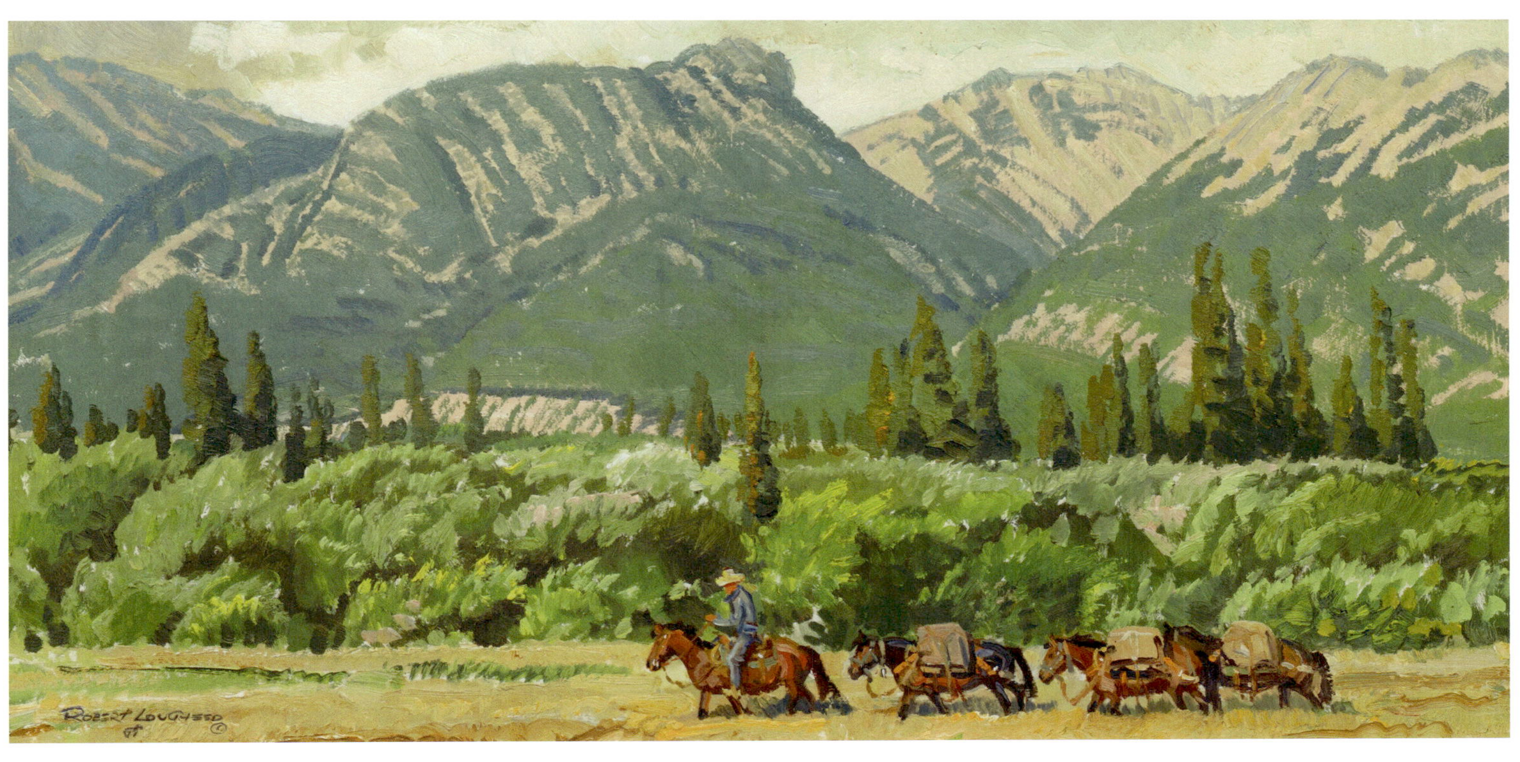

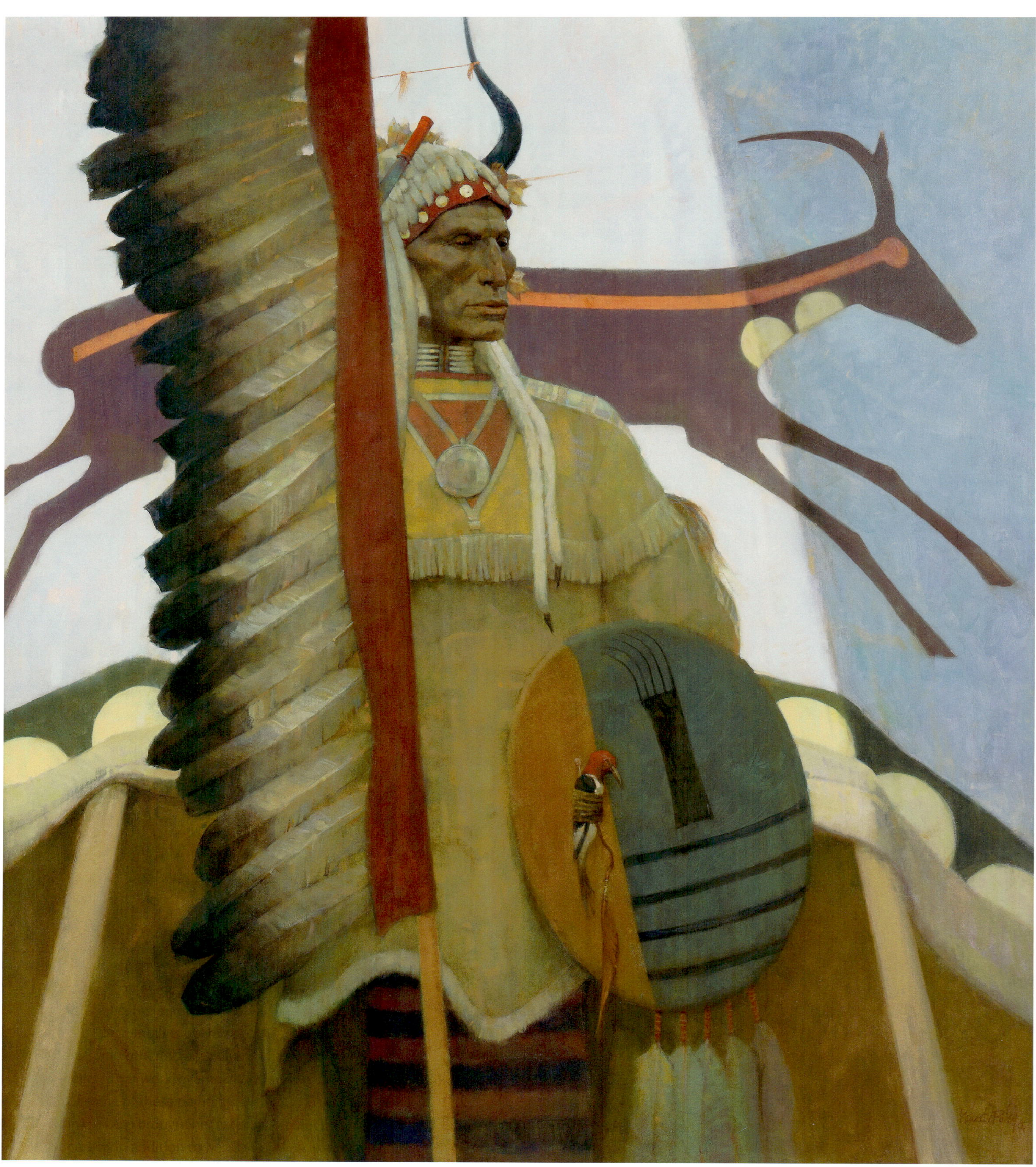

Plains Motif

1995
Oil on canvas
48 × 44 inches

Working for decades as an illustrator on the East Coast gave Kenneth Riley a keen eye for color and composition. Twenty years into a successful career, a commission from the National Park Service sent him to Yellowstone and the Grand Tetons in the late 1960s. Riley was hooked. "Those trips," he recalled, "convinced me that the West was where I wanted to live and work."* In 1973 he moved to Tucson, Arizona, and found inspiration in his desert surroundings and in historic written accounts of the West. In *Plains Motif*, Riley flattens the sense of depth with close cropping and large fields of color, emphasizing the individual forms of a vertical red stripe, round shield, and leaping pronghorn antelope. Rather than representing a specific moment from history, *Plains Motif* is a collage of imagery from the Great Plains: a tipi design and elaborate regalia arranged into a dynamic composition.

*Quoted in Michael Duty, *Cowboy Artists of America* (Shelton, CT: The Greenwich Workshop, 2002), 110.

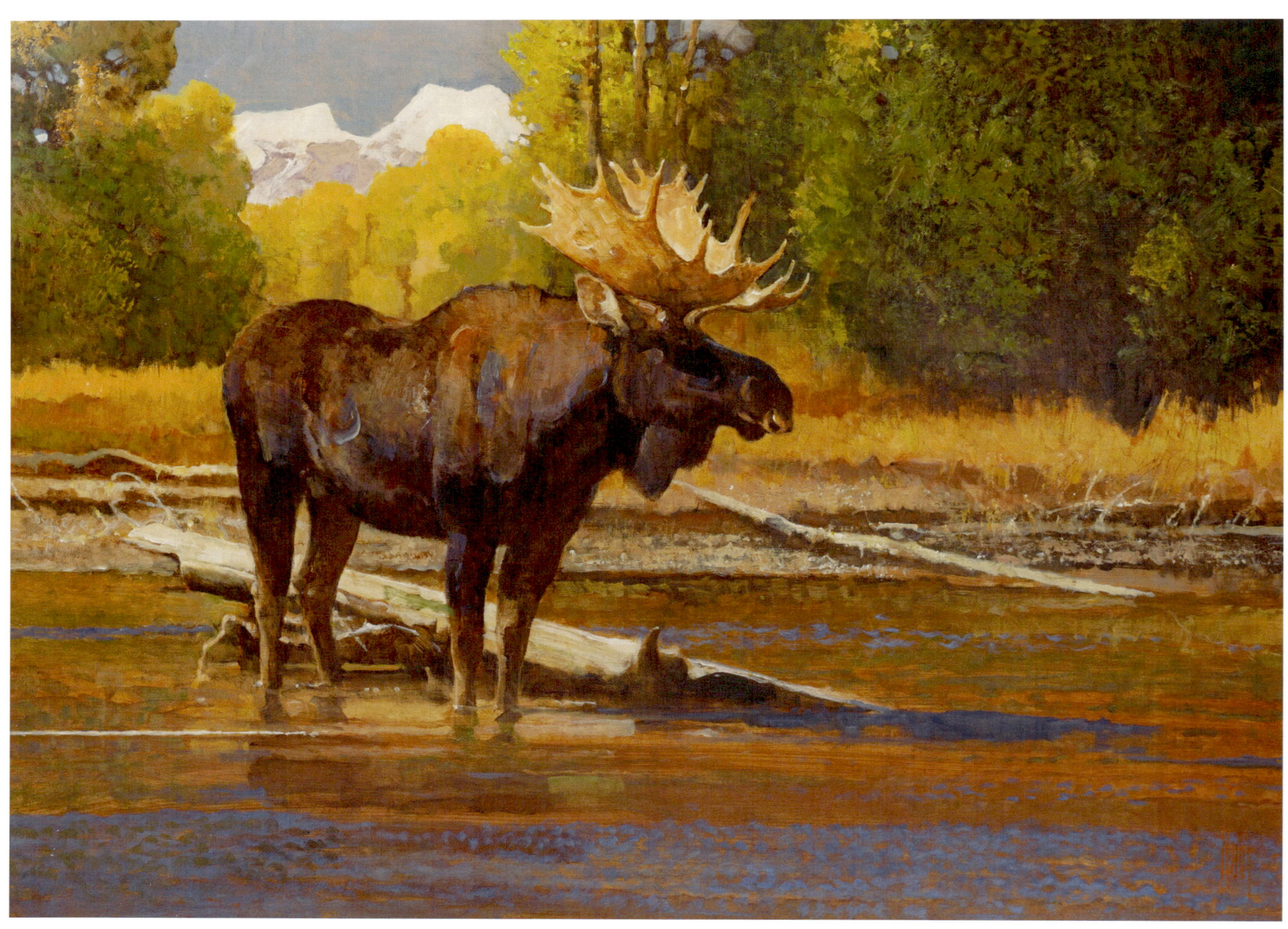

Along the Gros Ventre

circa 1995
Acrylic on board
24 × 34 inches

"When pursuing the elusive essence of an animal's character," explained Bob Kuhn, "it is imperative that one sees his subject in a wild state."* Kuhn began specializing in depictions of wildlife early in his career, as an illustrator for outdoor magazines in the 1940s. He traveled extensively to observe animals in their natural habitats, crossing through the western United States, Alaska, Canada, and Africa. As he turned to easel painting, Kuhn used brilliant colors and expressive brushstrokes—citing both Mark Rothko's abstract color field paintings and Carl Rungius's images of wildlife as influences. Accustomed to working quickly from his time as an illustrator, he began using quick-drying acrylic paint to build his images. *Along the Gros Ventre* portrays a stately bull moose standing in the Gros Ventre River in western Wyoming. In dabs of overlapping colors Kuhn captures the rainbow hues of autumn in the Tetons, a fitting setting for this proud animal of the West.

*Quoted in Donald J. Hagerty, *Leading the West: One Hundred Contemporary Painters and Sculptors* (Flagstaff, AZ: Northland, 1997), 66.

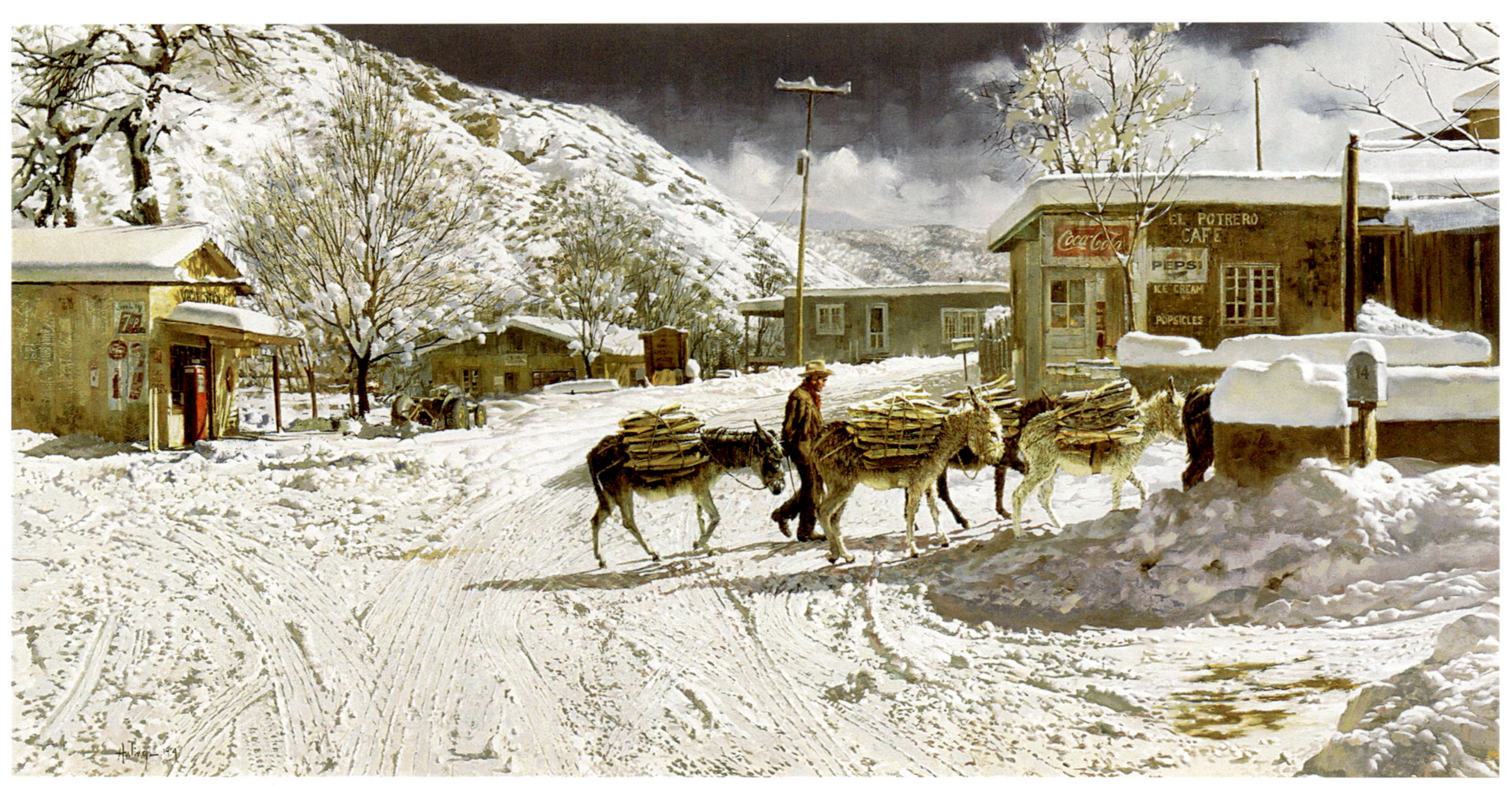

Coca-Cola
EL POTRERO CAFE
PEPSI
ICE CREAM
POPSICLES
7up

Woodbearers of Chimayo

1954
Oil on canvas
30 × 60 inches

Clark Hulings did not set out to become an artist. After earning a degree in physics in 1944 he traveled to Los Alamos, New Mexico, to work on the Manhattan Project. But after a brief time on the job, a bout of tuberculosis forced him to leave the position and slowly recover in Santa Fe—where he turned to painting. After working for a time in illustration, Hulings made realist easel paintings his primary focus beginning in the 1960s. He traveled across Europe and North America for inspiration, finding subjects to paint in unremarkable places. "Beauty," he wrote, "can be found even in a garbage cart."* In *Woodbearers of Chimayo* the composition focuses on a small New Mexico town dotted with soft drink ads, telephone poles, and a gas pump. While the laborer and his string of burros seem to be part of the historic West, frozen in time, the advertisements and telephone wires show that the modern, industrialized world is already part of this town. The humble burros and rusty signs present an image of the West far removed from romantic scenes of golden cowboys and spirited horses. But by catching the crystal light of a snowy day in a sleepy town, Hulings finds splendor in an unexpected place.

*Quoted in Susan Hallsten McGarry, "Clark Hulings: Timeless Beauty," *Southwest Art* (May 2007), http://www.southwestart.com /articles-interviews/featured-artists/timeless_beauty.

Washakie

1978
Bronze
36 × 29 × 14 inches

In hard bronze, the folds, scores, and ridges reveal a history of an artist's hand forming and scraping a soft wax surface. When creating the wax model for this bronze sculpture, Harry Jackson deliberately left the marks from his fingers and tools, creating a lively surface. The texture roughs over small details, simplifying the sculpture to basic forms: the wedge of the horse's head, the round arc of the feather headdress. The bold shapes lend the man a sense of dignity—fitting for a portrayal of Chief Washakie, a respected 19th-century Shoshone leader who advocated for peace and became an important ally of the US Army.

As a rebellious young painter, Jackson moved to New York City in the late 1940s and joined the abstract expressionist movement, becoming close friends with Jackson Pollock. But after early success with abstract painting he shocked the New York art world by returning to realism, inspired by seeing historic masterworks in Europe and visiting rough, untamed locations in the American West. Jackson's strong command of form and composition—honed by his years as an abstract painter—continued to influence his artwork for the remainder of his career.

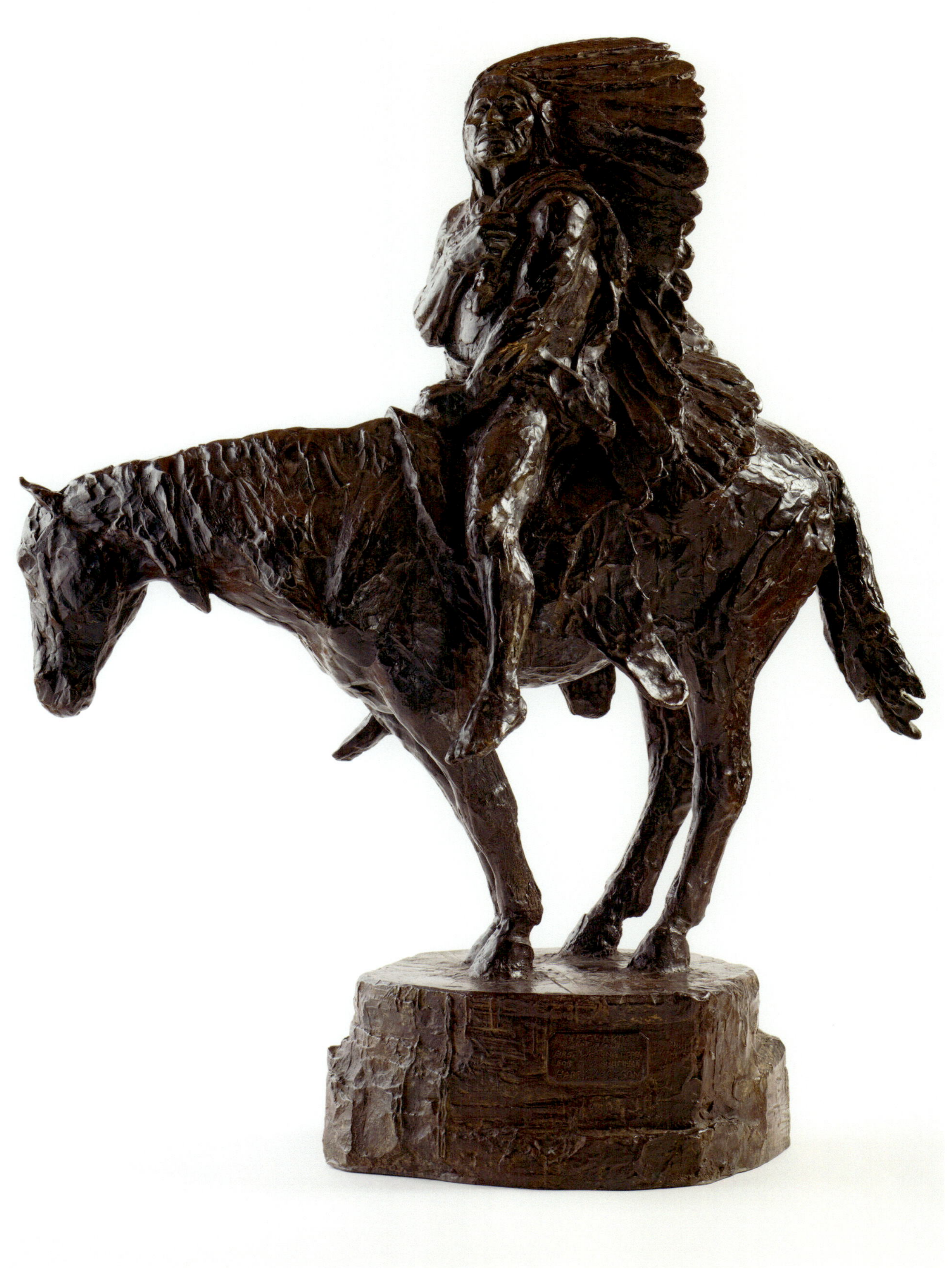

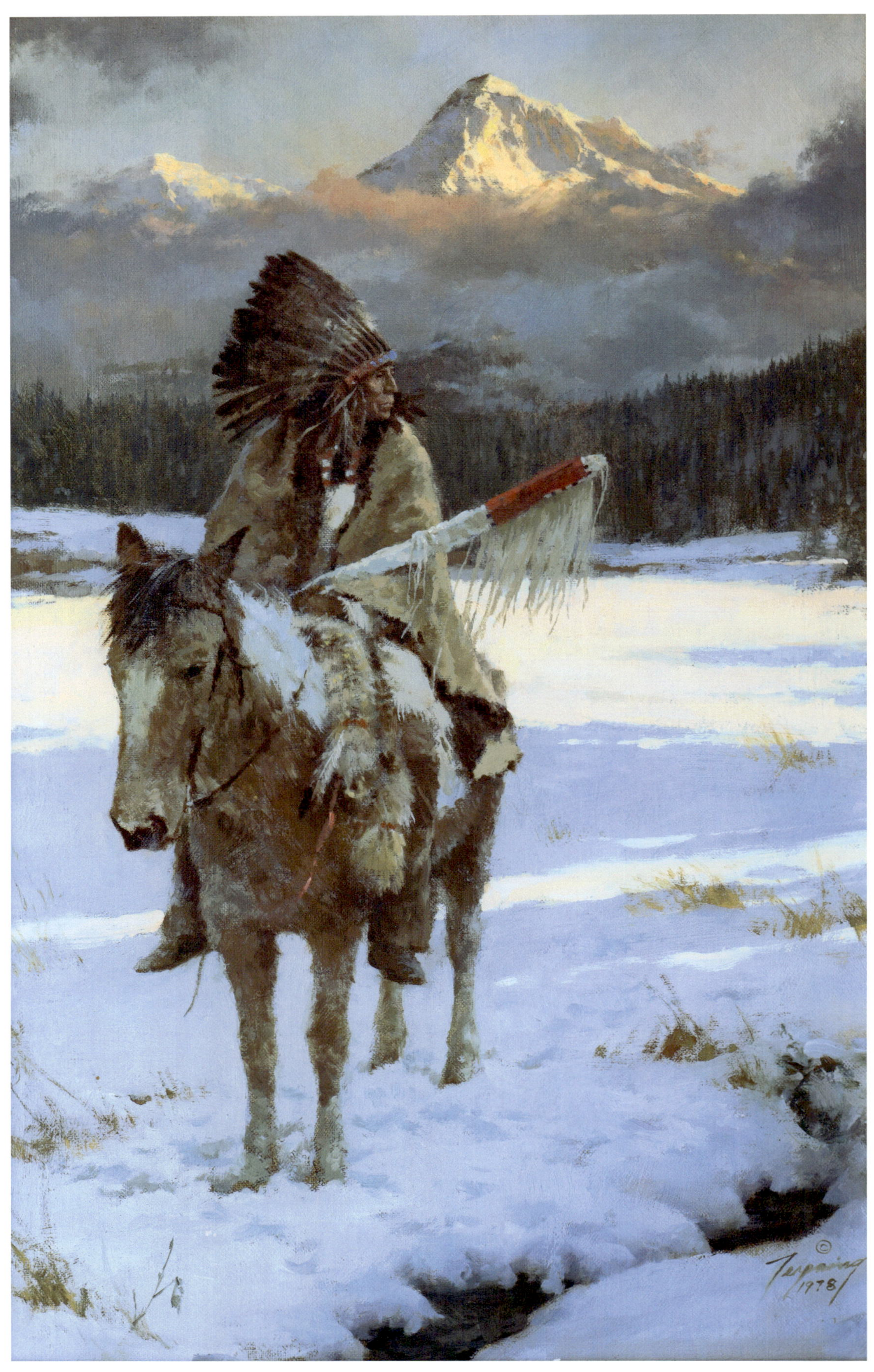

Winter Solitude

1978
Oil on canvas
18 × 12 inches

A veteran who served as a marine in World War II and as a combat artist in Vietnam, Howard Terpning was no stranger to the sufferings of a conflict zone. His varied career as an illustrator included commissions to paint scenes of the Vietnam War. Abandoning illustration in the 1970s to focus on painting the American West, he moved from Connecticut to Tucson, Arizona. Many of his paintings portray moments of introspection, like the calm figure contemplating a snowy scene in *Winter Solitude*. But Terpning also depicts the injustices dealt to Native Americans and their desperate fight to keep their land—recalling the emotions of his own experiences with combat. "I started getting feedback from native people, and they were such favorable impressions," Terpning explains. "They are the people I'm honoring."* Over the years Terpning's work has invited controversy—some admire his vivid colors and historical details while others see his paintings as overly sentimental interpretations of the past. Yet however his work is viewed, there is no denying he genuinely admires the people he paints.

*Quoted in Mike Boehm, "Howard Terpning's Paintings Keep Old West Alive," *Los Angeles Times*, May 17, 2012.

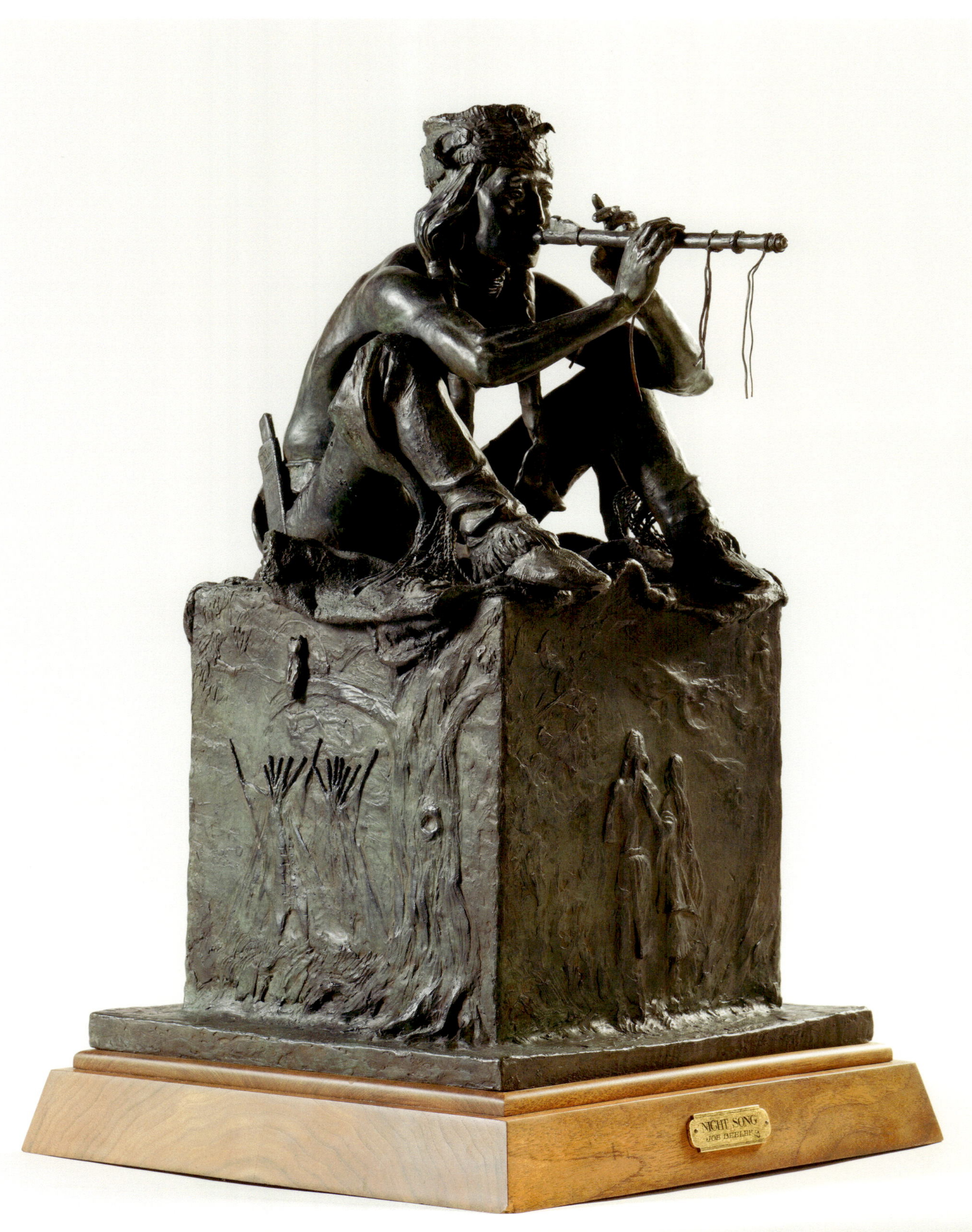
NIGHT SONG
JOE BEELER

Night Song

1984
Bronze
20 × 12 × 12 inches

As a boy growing up in the hills of southwestern Missouri, Joe Beeler dreamed of becoming a cowboy. After visiting the Gilcrease Museum on his honeymoon many years later, he resolved to become an artist of the American West. In the early 1960s he and his wife moved to Sedona, Arizona, where he sought new subjects to paint. In 1965 he helped found the Cowboy Artists of America, actively participating in the organization for the rest of his life.

After establishing himself as a painter Beeler also began working in bronze—much like the artists Frederic Remington and Charles Russell, whose work he enthusiastically emulated. His sculpture *Night Song* depicts an imagined scene of a seated Native American man playing a song on his flute to court a future bride. Two relief scenes on the square plinth hint at the larger narrative. On one face, two tipis stand side by side in the shelter of a tall tree. On another side, a man and woman walk together, her arm resting on his shoulder—a happy ending to the flute player's song.

FRAN JENKINS (BORN 1933)

Cougar

circa 2010
Serpentine stone
26 × 40 × 26 inches

Despite the fluid grace and smooth polish of her finished sculptures, Fran Jenkins's artistic process is not for the faint of heart. An active prospector in British Columbia, she searches the Canadian wilderness to find stone for her sculpture. After locating a source of serpentine near her mountain home, she selects individual stones to be hand-quarried from the site. A greenish rock riddled with mineral infusions, serpentine lends itself to a vibrant, tactile surface. Once the stone is transported to Jenkins's studio, she dons a dust mask and eye protection and works the hard rock with diamond blades, hammers, chisels, rasps, and files to slowly reveal a form. She finds inspiration in the wildlife of British Columbia, particularly the graceful, powerful large predators. In *Cougar*, the sinuous lines of the polished serpentine perfectly complement the muscle-bound form of the mountain lion, crouched and seemingly ready to spring from the rough base. From the source of the material to the local wildlife subject, *Cougar* embodies a sense of place in the Canadian mountains.

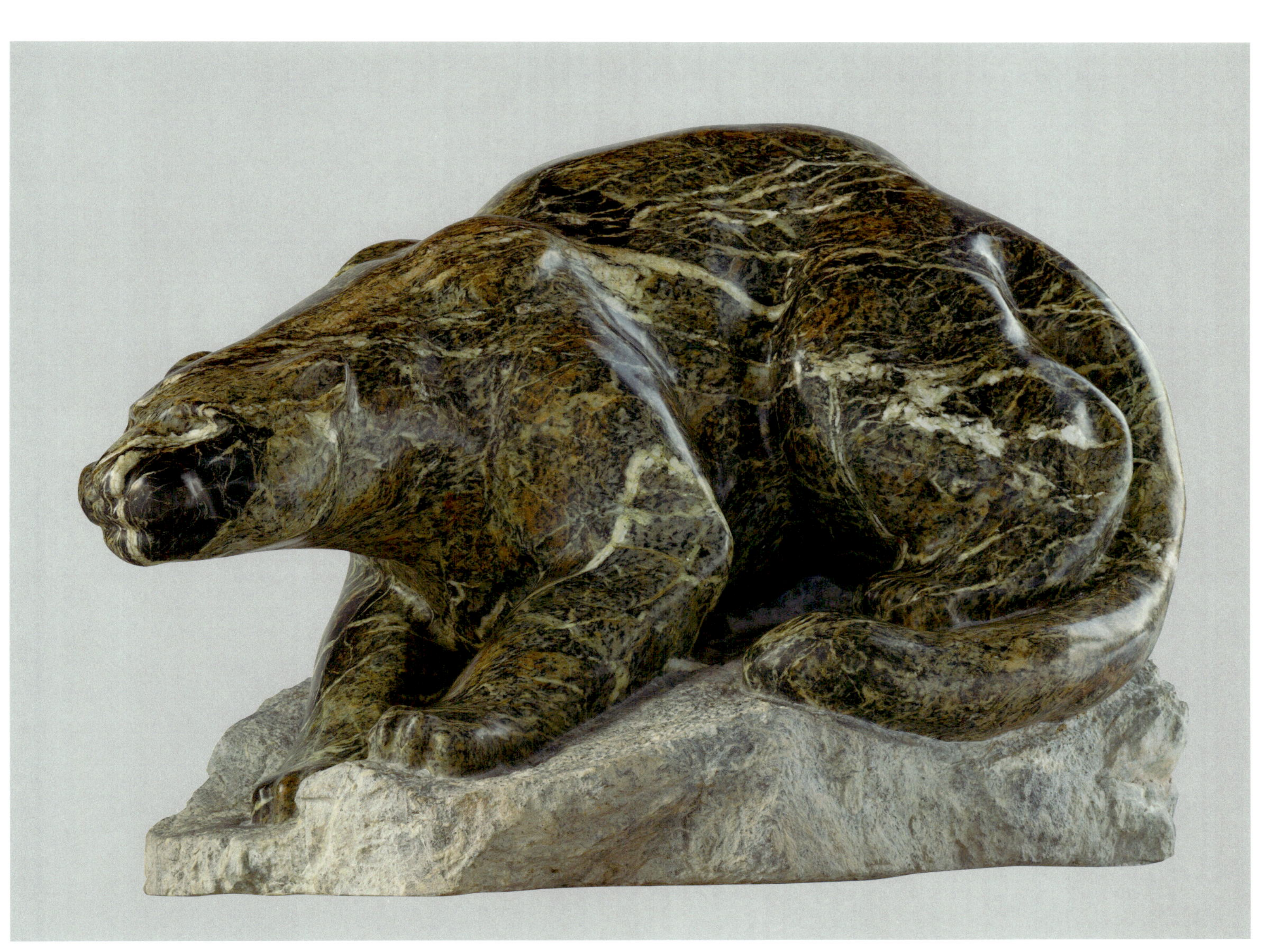

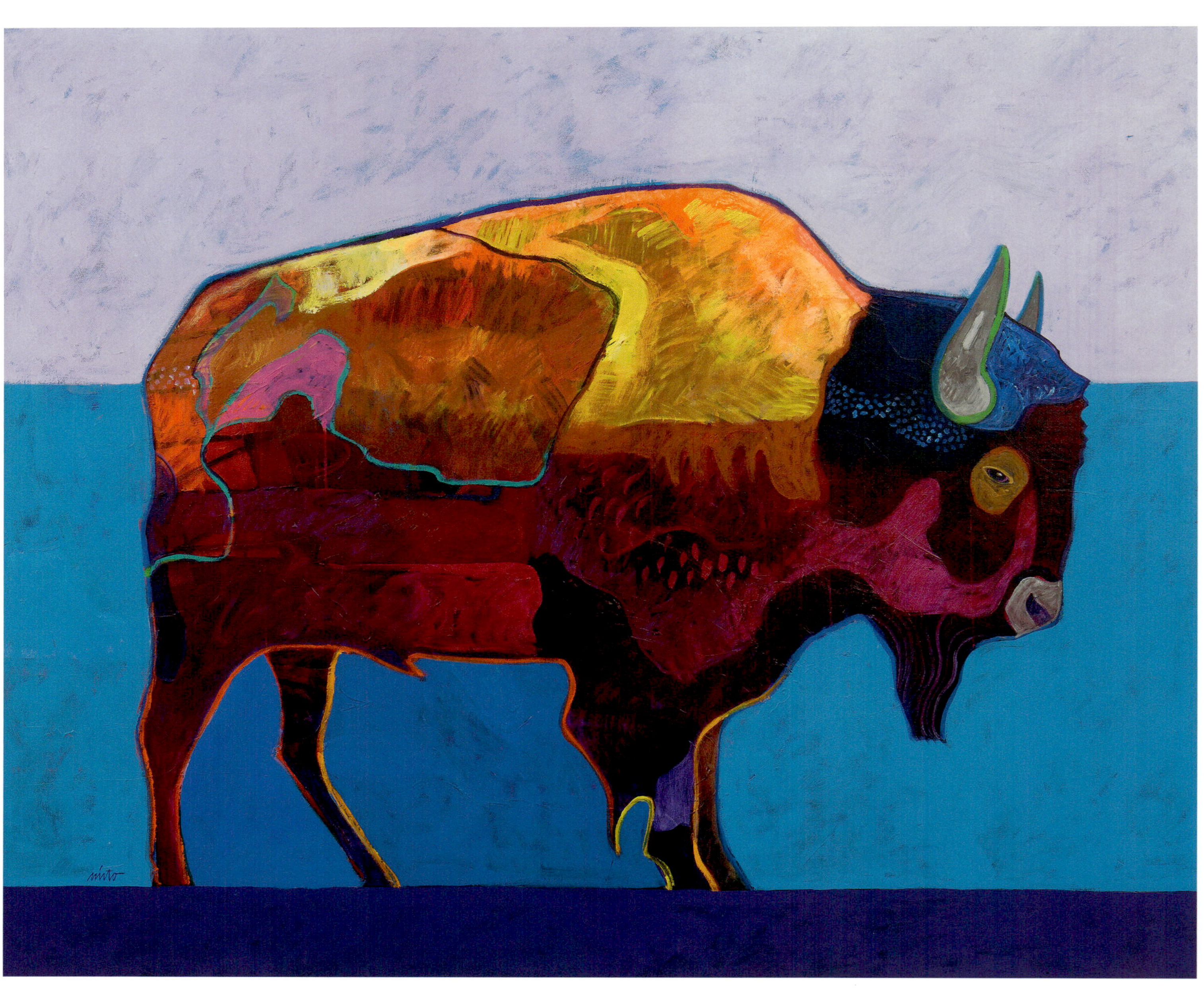

Buffalo at Sunset

1996
Acrylic on canvas
48 × 60 inches

The "wild beasts" of Paris stopped John Nieto in his tracks. On his first visit to France in the mid-1960s he was entranced by the brash colors in early 20th-century paintings by Henri Matisse and his fellow artists (called the fauves, French for "wild beasts"). Soon, Nieto blended the free colors of the fauvists with subjects inspired by his New Mexico home, connecting the modernist style to his centuries-old Spanish and Native American mestizo heritage. With his bold, fresh approach, Nieto challenges the notion that Native Americans existed only in the past. "People look back at the Native American era as a movie, a black and white movie," he remarked, "and I try with my color to bring it to life."* In *Buffalo at Sunset* Nieto depicts a proud bison bull in wild, electric colors—making one of the most universally recognized symbols of the Old West into a powerful icon for the future.

*"Nieto Fine Art," Executive Producer: Marybeth LaMotte,
YouTube video, 3:58, posted by Marybeth LaMotte, July 31, 2011,
http://www.youtube.com/watch?v=xlCKHcbdnsQ.

Bison of the CL Bar Ranch

2008
Oil on board
30 × 40 inches

When the bison hit their lowest numbers on the Great Plains of North America in the late 19th century, small captive herds preserved by ranchers helped save the species from annihilation. Today, bison can be found in all 50 states, in public herds and on private ranches and farms—an astonishing comeback from near extinction. When artist Ken Carlson visited the CL Bar Ranch in Wyoming, he found the distant Wind River Mountains formed an ideal backdrop for the herd of shaggy, semi-wild animals. In this painting, Carlson sought to portray the distinct personality of the lead bull in the center of the composition. Staring boldly at the viewer, feet firmly planted, this bison is a force to be reckoned with. We are still here, he seems to say, and we will endure.

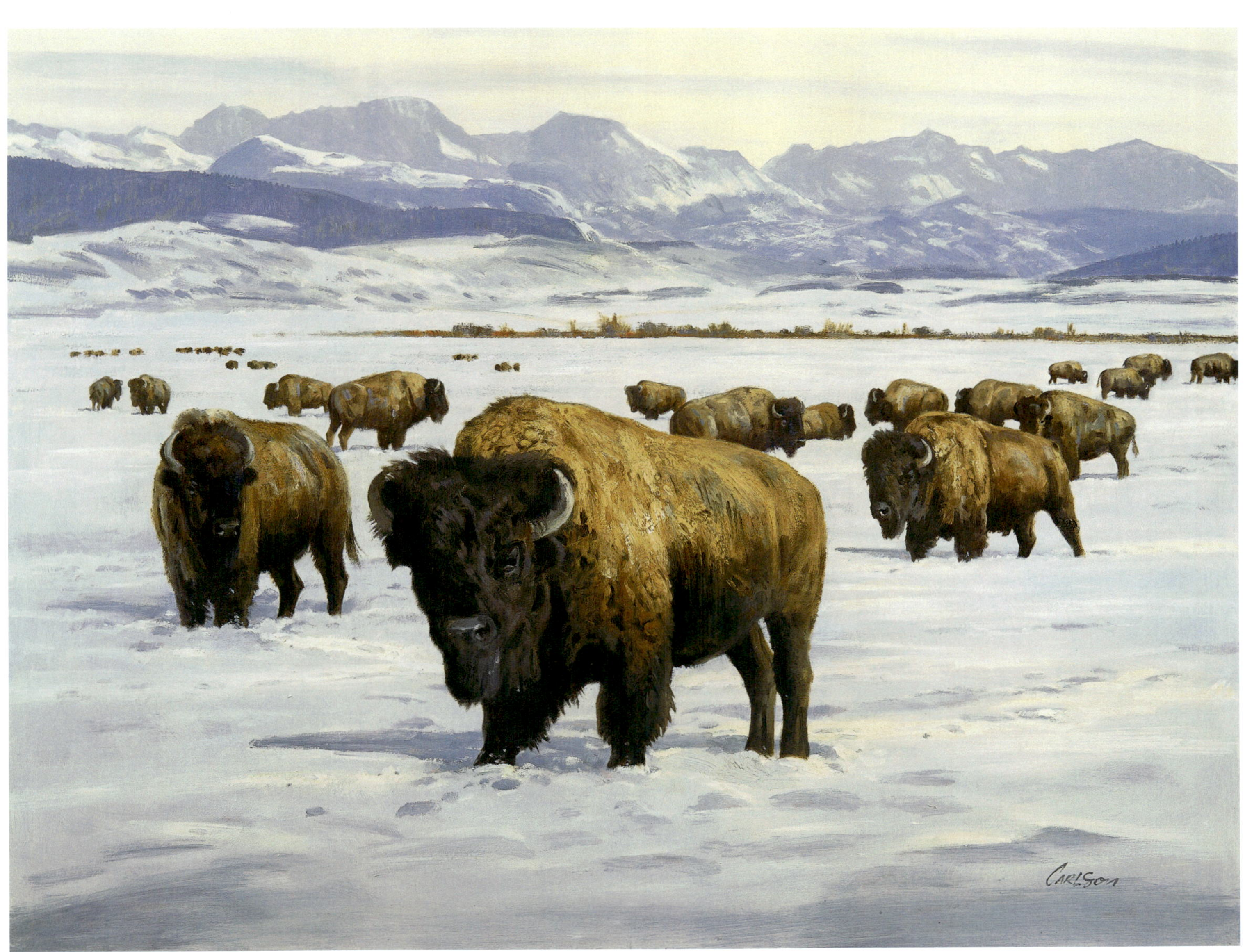
Carlson

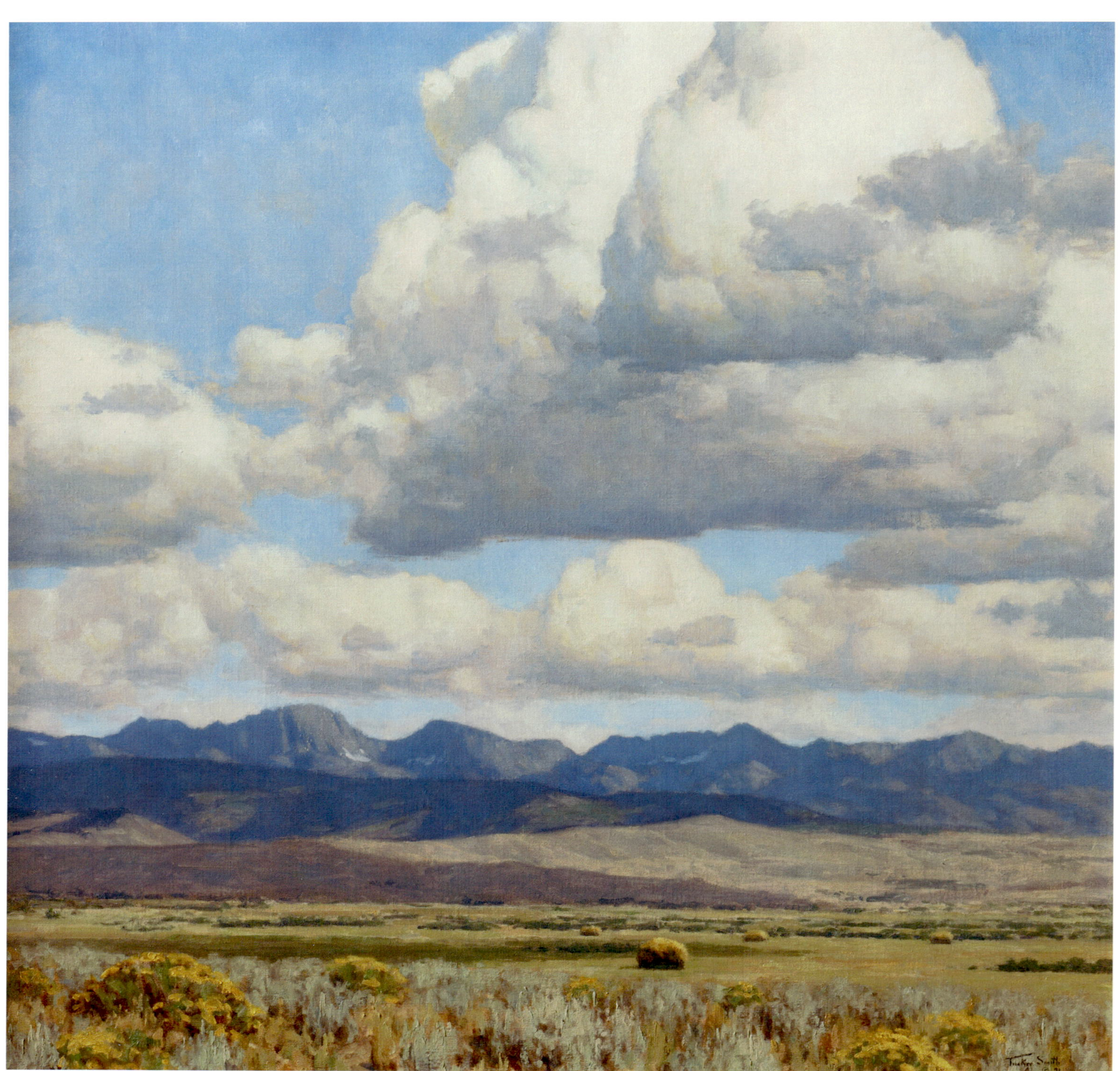

New Fork Valley

1991
Oil on canvas
32 × 30 inches

Tucker Smith was raised in the remote town of Pinedale, Wyoming, a community in the shadow of the Wind River Range where the pronghorn antelope outnumber the people and temperatures dip below freezing almost every month of the year. The winding dirt roads heading into nearby mountains lead to astonishing vistas of alpine lakes and jagged pinnacles. Below, the ever-changing high desert sky sweeps over gray-green sagebrush plains and rolling hills. In this painting Smith portrays the vastness of the landscape near his home—leaving out the distant fences and celebrating a land that still appears largely open. "The New Fork Valley of Wyoming lies at the foot of the Wind River Mountains. I grew up in this valley and it and the surrounding area remain my favorite," Smith remarks. "This world is changing so fast that I wonder how long we will have scenes like this."*

*Quoted in Christine Mollring, *Erivan and Helga Haub Family Collection of Western Art*, vol. 2 (Jackson, WY: Mollring Enterprises, 2005), 92.

Along the Rio Grande Valley

circa 1995
Oil on canvas
34 × 32 inches

Viewing the scene from above, Walt Gonske could see the Rio Grande Valley in northern New Mexico spread out before him like a tapestry. With a bird's-eye view, he portrays the distinct patterns of the landscape, exploring the juxtaposition between the smooth dirt road and the wild, tangled brush. The triangular roofs and rectangular sides of the buildings contrast with the freeform shapes of the trees and sloping hills, rendered in energetic, broad brushstrokes. Much like the Taos Society of Artists in the early 20th century, the remarkable landscapes and light of the Southwest inspired Gonske to leave his home on the East Coast and settle in New Mexico. In the 1970s he cofounded the Taos Six, a group of artists inspired by the original Taos Society who painted outdoors in northern New Mexico, critiquing each other's work and organizing group exhibitions. Today, using a modified RV—his "Paintmobile"—as a movable studio, Gonske paints on location and finds endless inspiration in the colors and forms of the Southwest.

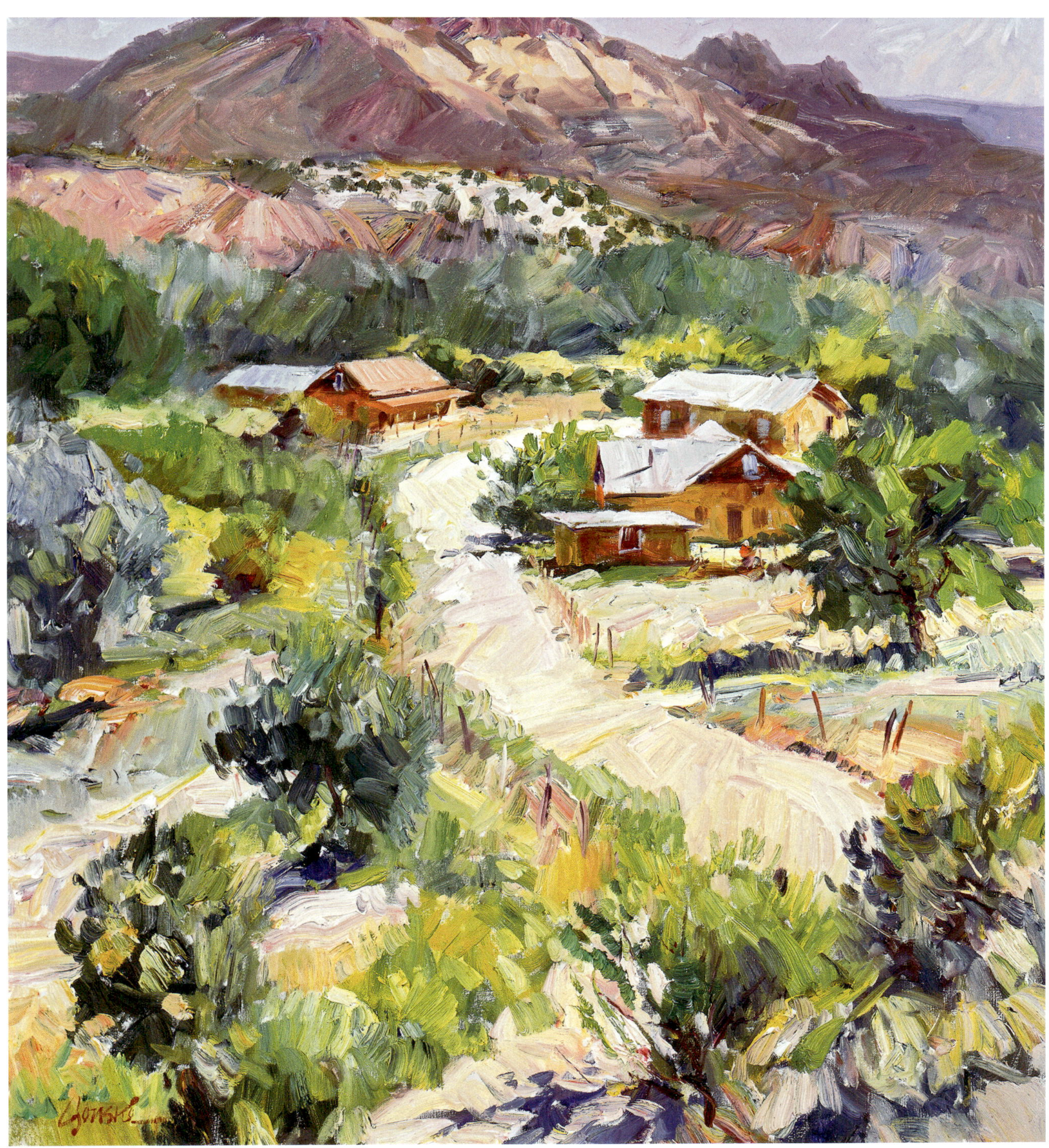

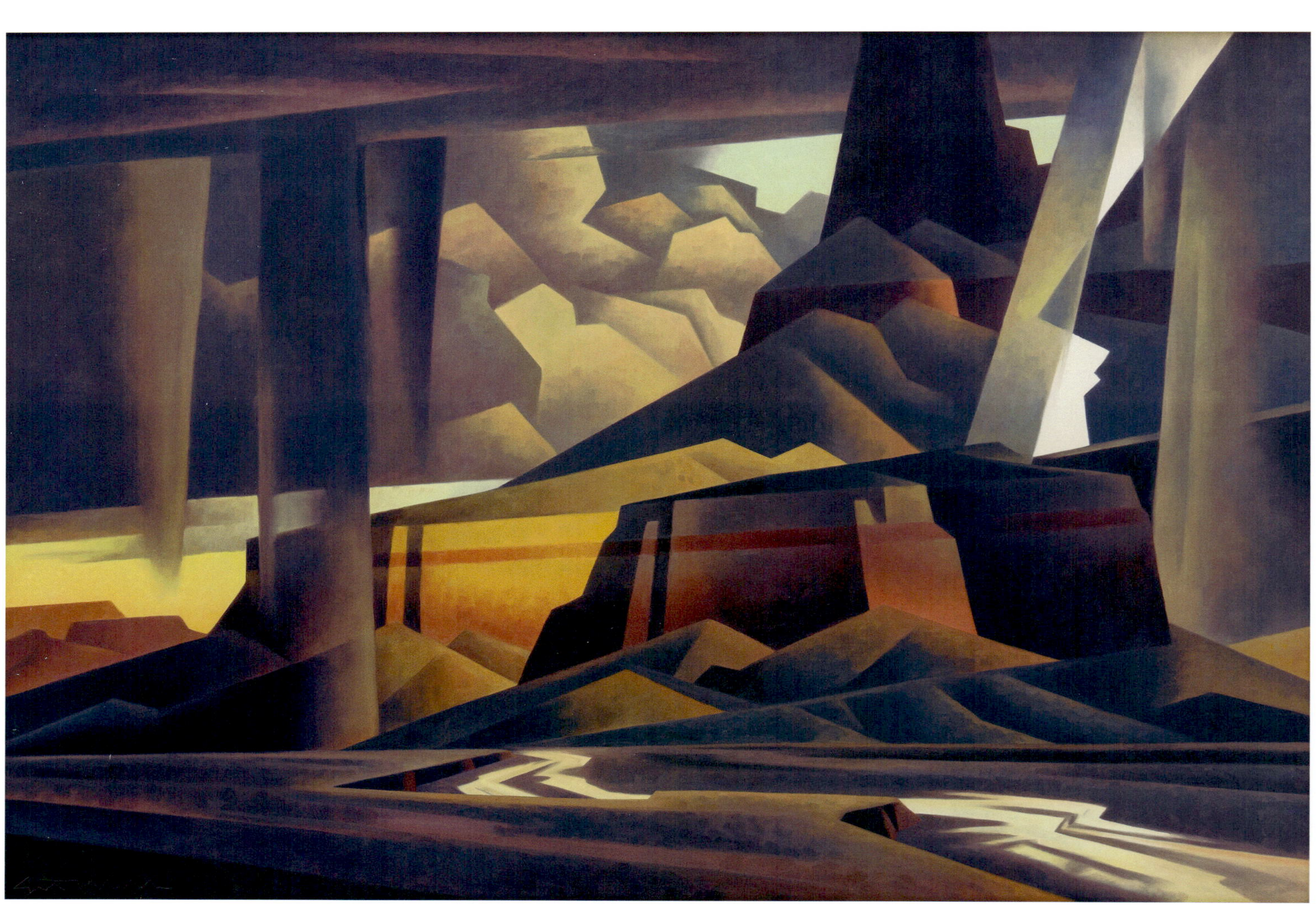

Rain and Runoff

2003
Oil on linen
36 × 54 inches

When Ed Mell became friends with a helicopter pilot, his perceptions of the landscape were transformed. Soaring above the tall mesas and deep canyons of Arizona, seeing the features of the land reduced to creases and ridges bound by a wide-angle horizon, Mell found a perfect subject for his abstracted, geometric painting style. Describing the views from a helicopter, he explained, "You get to go places that no artist or photographer hardly ever has the opportunity to. That creates an adrenal connection to the work—you just get excited."* In *Rain and Runoff,* towering clouds and columns of rain roll across rock spires and mesas, leaving a silver trail of water running along the desert floor. The red rocks are rendered deep purple in the changing light of the passing storm. In hard lines and bold shapes, Mell captures the excitement of the Southwest desert landscape.

*"InsideArt: Ed Mell," Produced and directed by John Carver, Wolf Creek Productions, 2004, YouTube video, 5:22, posted by Wolf Creek Productions, December 3, 2009, http://www.youtube.com/watch?v=ElHVmYo2b64.

Crow

circa 1980
Acrylic on canvas
32 × 28 inches

"Being a Crow Indian, I want to carry that tradition . . . but not in such a realistic way," says artist Kevin Red Star. "So I was able to come up with this particular style."* One of the first students to attend the Institute of American Indian Arts in Santa Fe, Red Star combined his interest in contemporary art with the visual culture of the Crow Nation. With *Crow*, he depicts a ceremonial rawhide shield decorated with a bison skull motif and eagle feathers. A traditional form, shields could be adorned with feathers or symbolic images in bright pigments. Although the shield is an object rooted in history, Red Star renders it in bold, flat colors with quick gestural brushstrokes—creating a modern image. His contemporary style of painting sends the message that Crow traditions are still very much alive and continuing to evolve.

*"Montana Stories: Kevin Red Star," Distill Productions, Vimeo video, 3:13, posted by Montana Office of Tourism, 2011, https://vimeo.com /30509876.

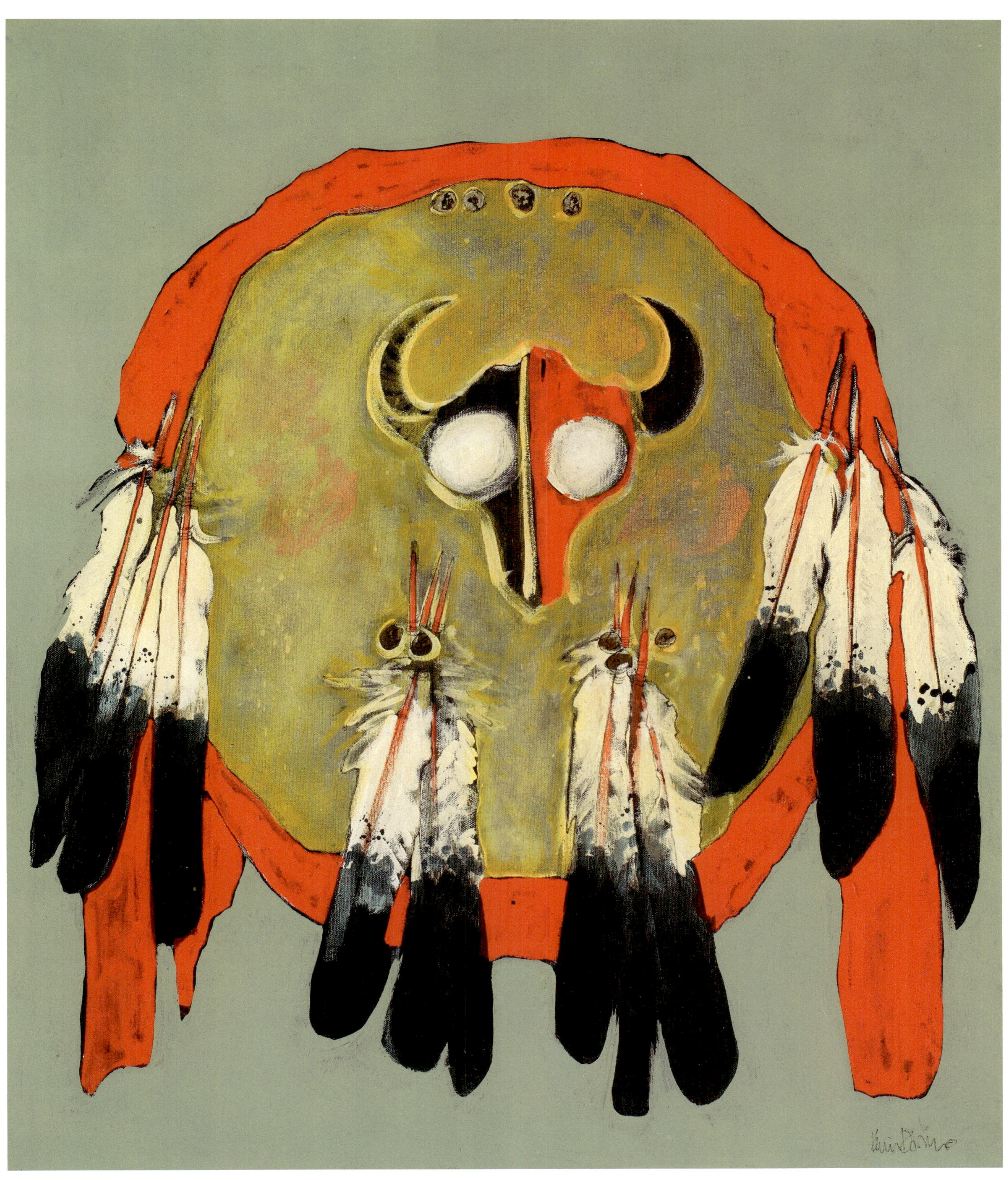

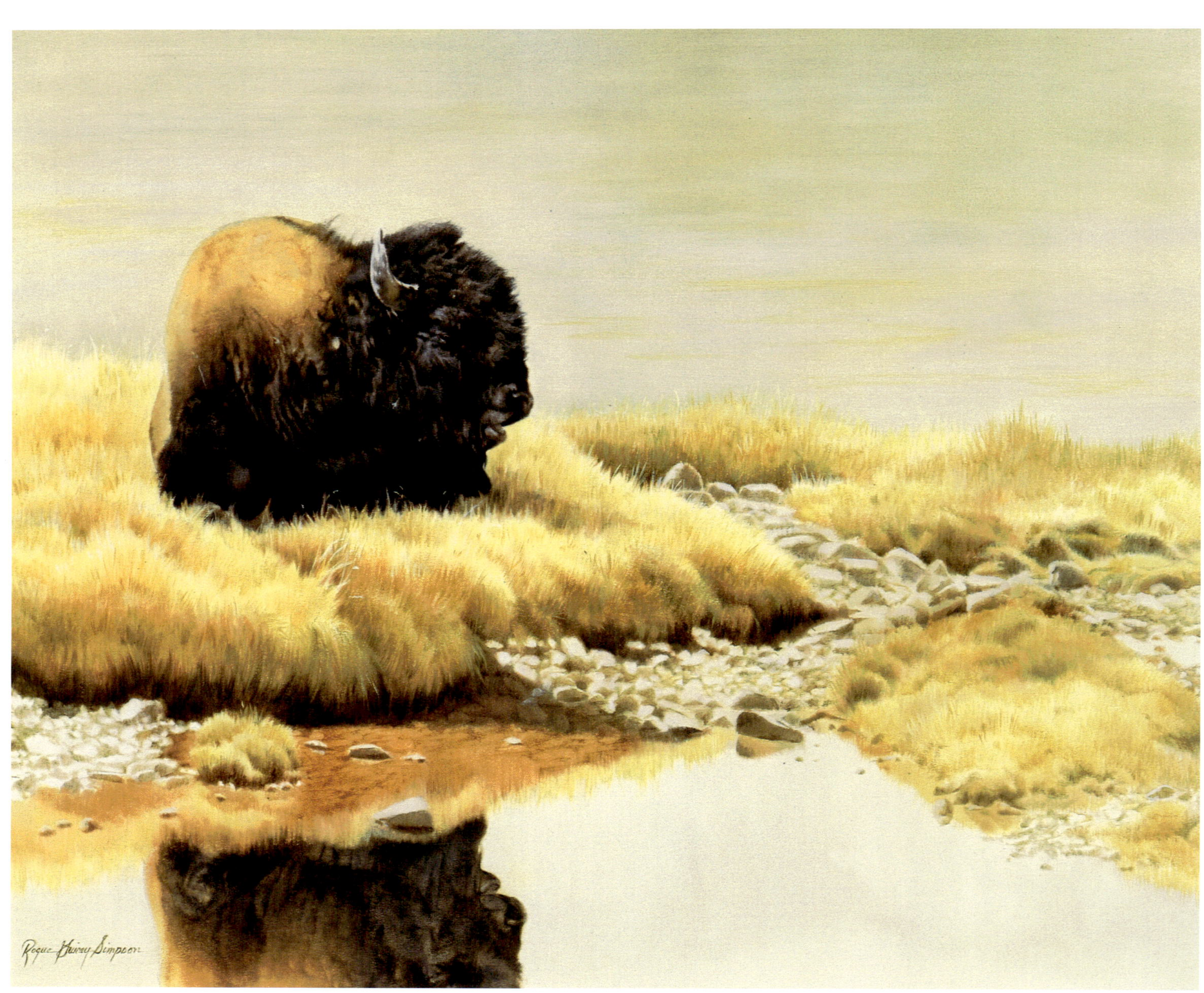

A Place in the Sun

circa 1995
Oil on board
16 × 20 inches

Gazing across the broad Hayden Valley in Yellowstone National Park, artist Rogue Guirey Simpson was inspired by one of the park's famous residents. She recalled, "This big bull was enjoying the chance to doze in the late September sun along the Yellowstone River. The pale sky and the still water provided a beautiful reflection and a great compositional element."* In *A Place in the Sun,* Simpson ignores the vast landscape of mountains and rolling hills, narrowing her focus to a single bison and a slim section of riverbank. In nearly monochromatic browns and yellows, the painting depicts various textures of thick furry hide, soft grasses, round river stones, and smooth waters. The solid, boulder-like bull exudes a sense of calm that belies his strength and ferocity. Reflected in a still pool, one animal and a few tufts of grass form an image of harmony in nature.

*Quoted in Christine Mollring, *Erivan and Helga Haub Family Collection of Western Art*, vol. 2 (Jackson, WY: Mollring Enterprises, 2005), 215.

Passing Showers—Yellowstone

1991
Gouache on paper
13½ × 10 inches

The bears of Yellowstone—fierce yet endearing—became one of the most popular tourist attractions in the national park soon after it was founded in 1872. Today, Yellowstone remains one of the few areas in the continental United States where you can catch a glimpse of these large, daunting predators. But if the humans in the park are scanning the horizon for bears, what are the bears watching?

In his detailed images of Yellowstone, Michael Coleman often features both the wildlife and the famous geysers of the park. *Passing Showers—Yellowstone* shows near-boiling water and steam shooting from a series of geyser cones. Influenced by Thomas Moran's vivid 19th-century watercolors of the region, Coleman catches the brilliant rainbow colors of the flowing hot springs with gouache, an opaque water-based paint. Recalling early 20th-century postcards and advertisements featuring Yellowstone's bears, Coleman places a black bear and her two cubs in the foreground, observing nature's splendor—and reminding us that Yellowstone, for all its tourists, remains a wild place.

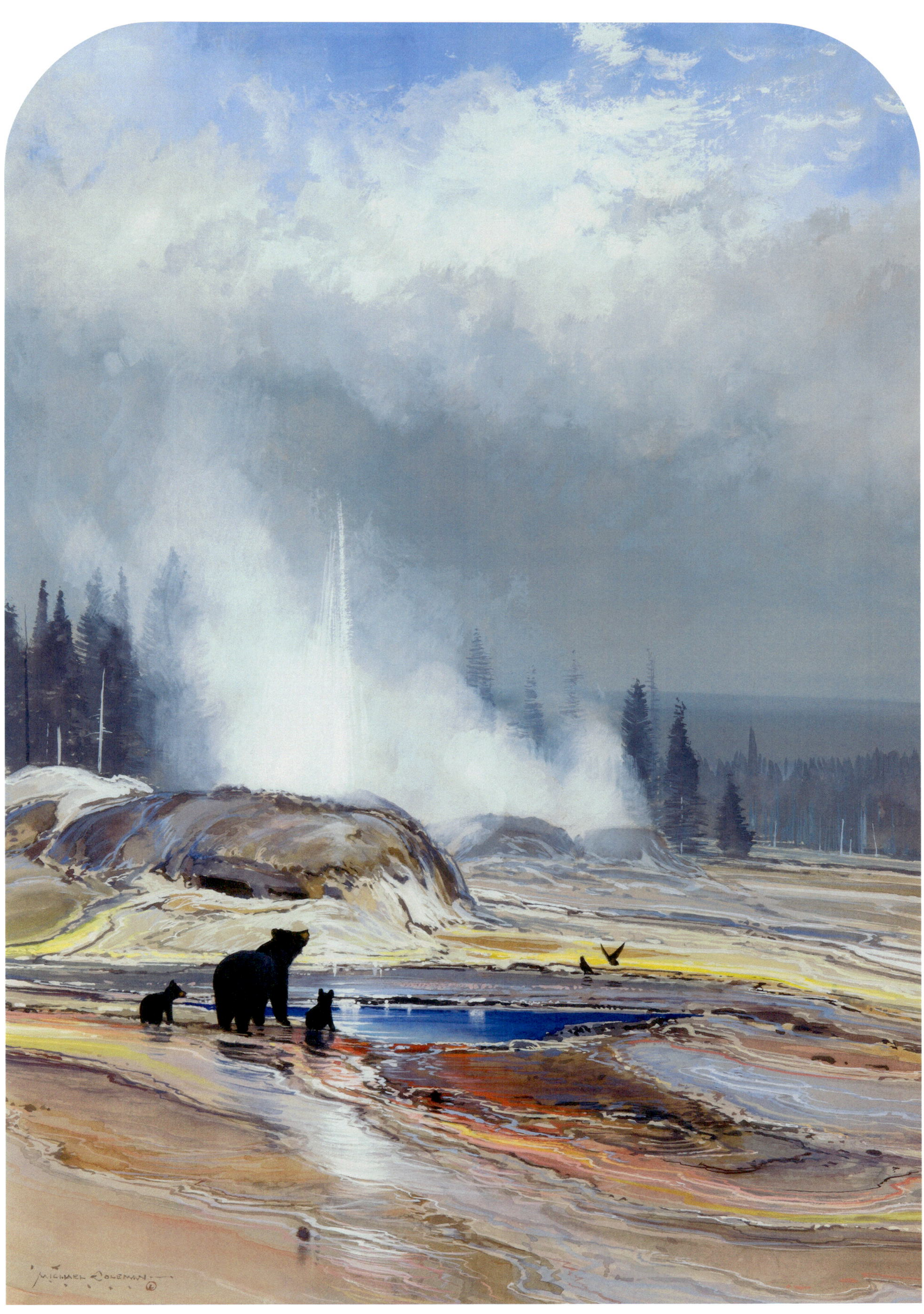

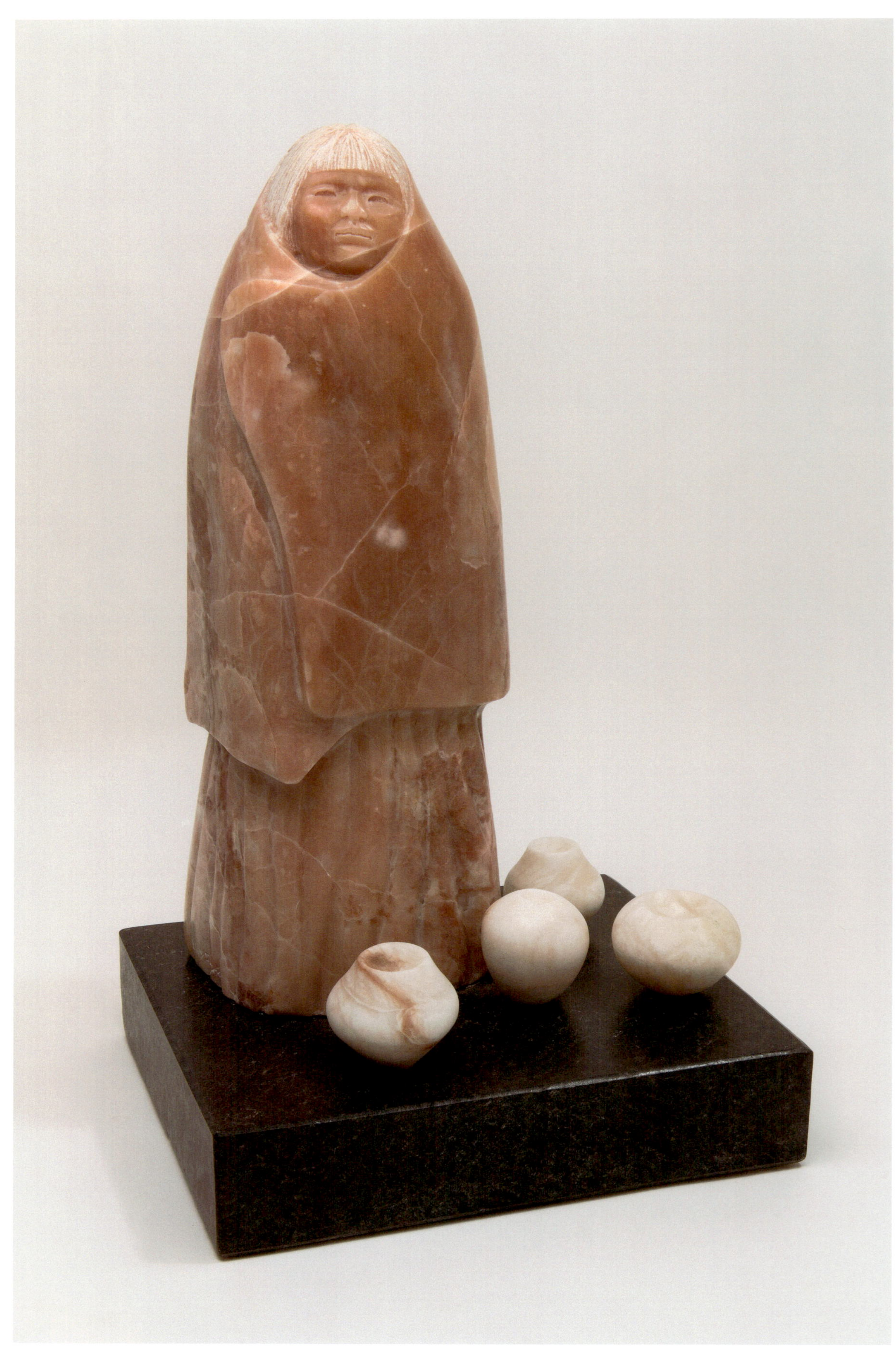

Santa Fe Indian Market

date unknown
Alabaster
20½ × 12 × 10¼ inches

In rosy alabaster, clean rounded shapes form the figure of a Native American woman. The natural variations in the stone create expressive patterns in the smooth surface of the woman's blanket, drawn over her head and around her shoulders. The curves of the figure are echoed in the round vessels at her feet. With minimal lines, sculptor Doug Hyde tells the story of a woman bringing her pottery to sell at the Indian Market in Santa Fe—an artist portraying another artist at work. Of Nez Perce, Assiniboine, and Chippewa heritage, Hyde first became interested in sculpture at the Institute of American Indian Arts under Apache artist Allan Houser. Today he handpicks stones to carve from quarries in Colorado and Utah and allows the material to guide his sculpture. "I never know if it's going to be a person or a bird or a fish or a combination of things," Hyde explains. "It's so exciting to carve into a stone and see the directions it will pull you."*

*Quoted in Norman Kolpas, "Doug Hyde: Spirits in the Stone," *Southwest Art* (July 2013), http://www.southwestart.com/featured/hyde-d-jul2013.

NANCY GLAZIER (BORN 1947)

Birds of a Feather

circa 1983
Oil on canvas
24 × 32 inches

Rendered in precise detail, a massive bison bull stands firm with his head raised to survey his surroundings, a quiet but formidable force. A thundercloud rising into the atmosphere above him echoes the strong curves of his form. But the small birds landing on his broad back, hitching a ride, show that even this proud monarch is an integral part of Yellowstone's symbiotic relationships and natural cycles. In *Birds of a Feather*, artist Nancy Glazier uses painstaking detail to portray a bison bull with a distinct sense of pride and power—a symbol of the American West itself. Like the photorealist painters of the 1970s, she is inspired by the precision of photography. It is no wonder that Erivan Haub found himself captivated by this painting. It was with the purchase of *Birds of a Feather* some 30 years ago that the Haubs began their collection of western American art.

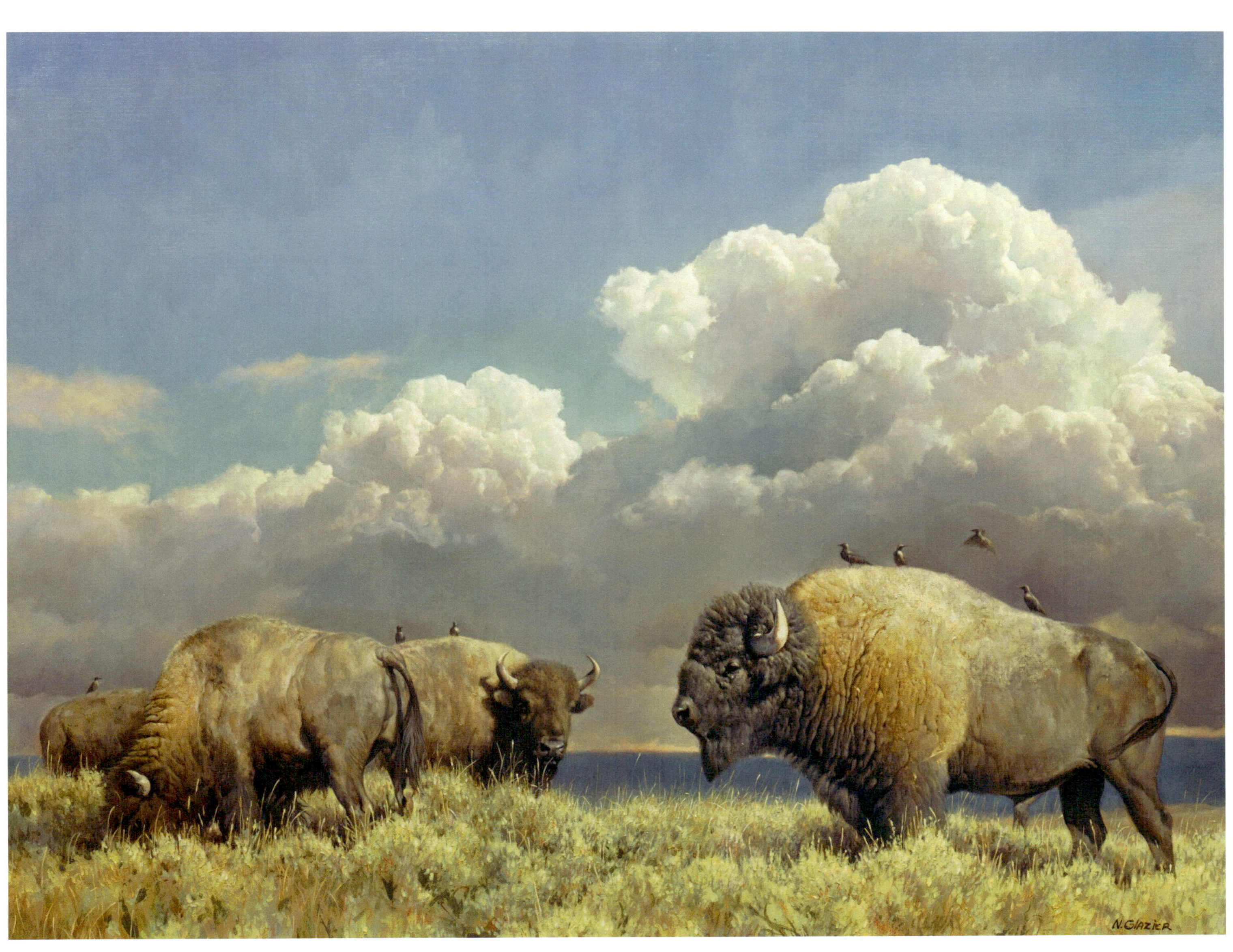

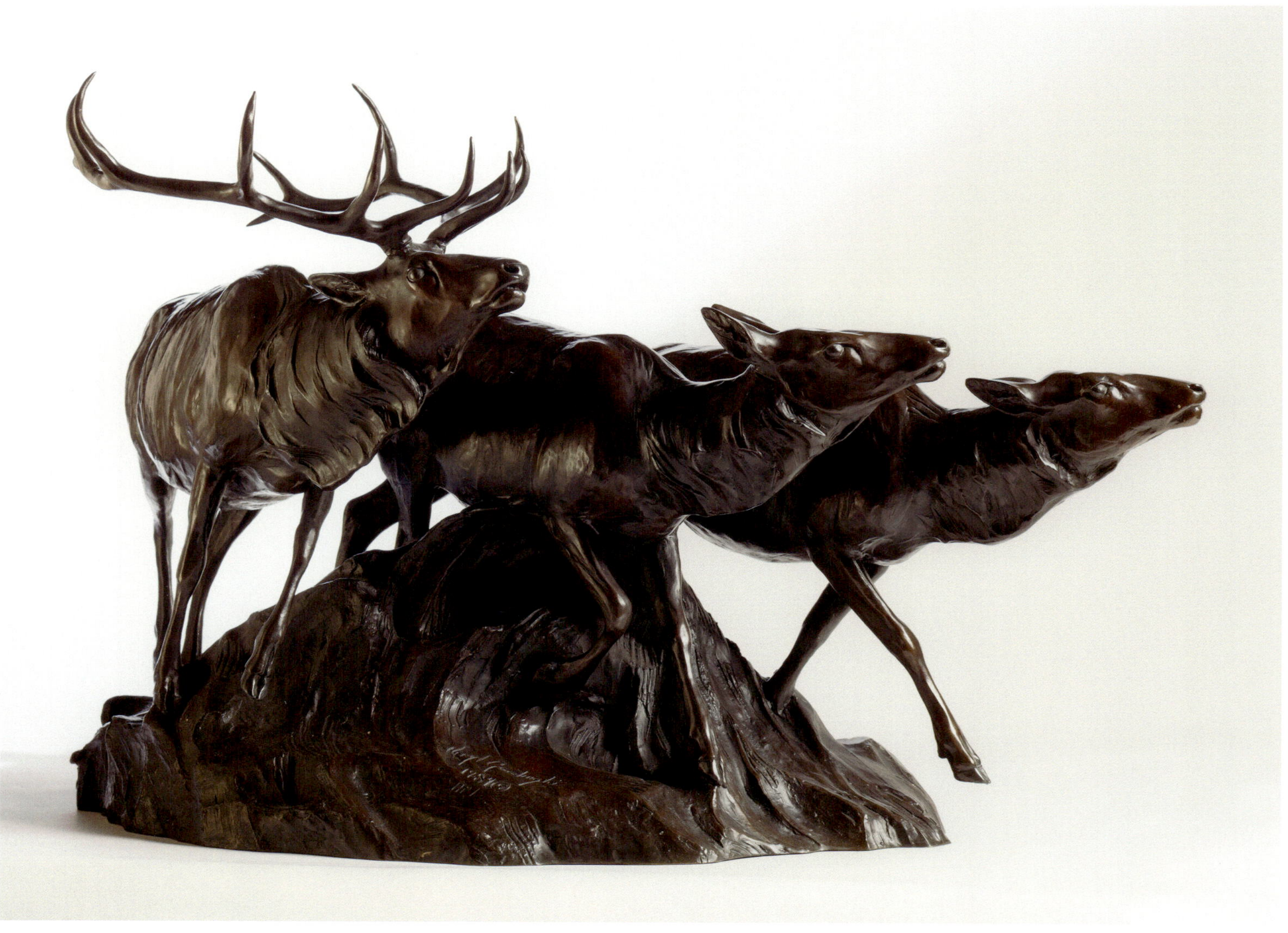

Spirit of Autumn

1984
Bronze
16 × 24 × 12 inches

A deep interest in conservation runs in Veryl Goodnight's family. The artist is descended from the famous Texas cattleman Charles Goodnight and his wife Mary Ann, who were instrumental in preserving a captive herd of bison in the late 19th century, helping to save the species. Today, Goodnight celebrates the wildlife of the American West with her sculpture. *Spirit of Autumn* portrays the elk's annual fall mating season, when males fight to herd together harems of females as the elk migrate to lower elevations. "Every fall finds me watching the bulls as they gather their harems," says Goodnight. "The ritual lasts only a few short weeks and is filled with a sense of urgency."* In fluid lines, Goodnight portrays a bull elk hurrying along two females, conveying the chaotic, heightened pace of elk country in autumn.

*Quoted in Christine Mollring, *Erivan and Helga Haub Family Collection of Western Art*, vol. 2 (Jackson, WY: Mollring Enterprises, 2005), 164.

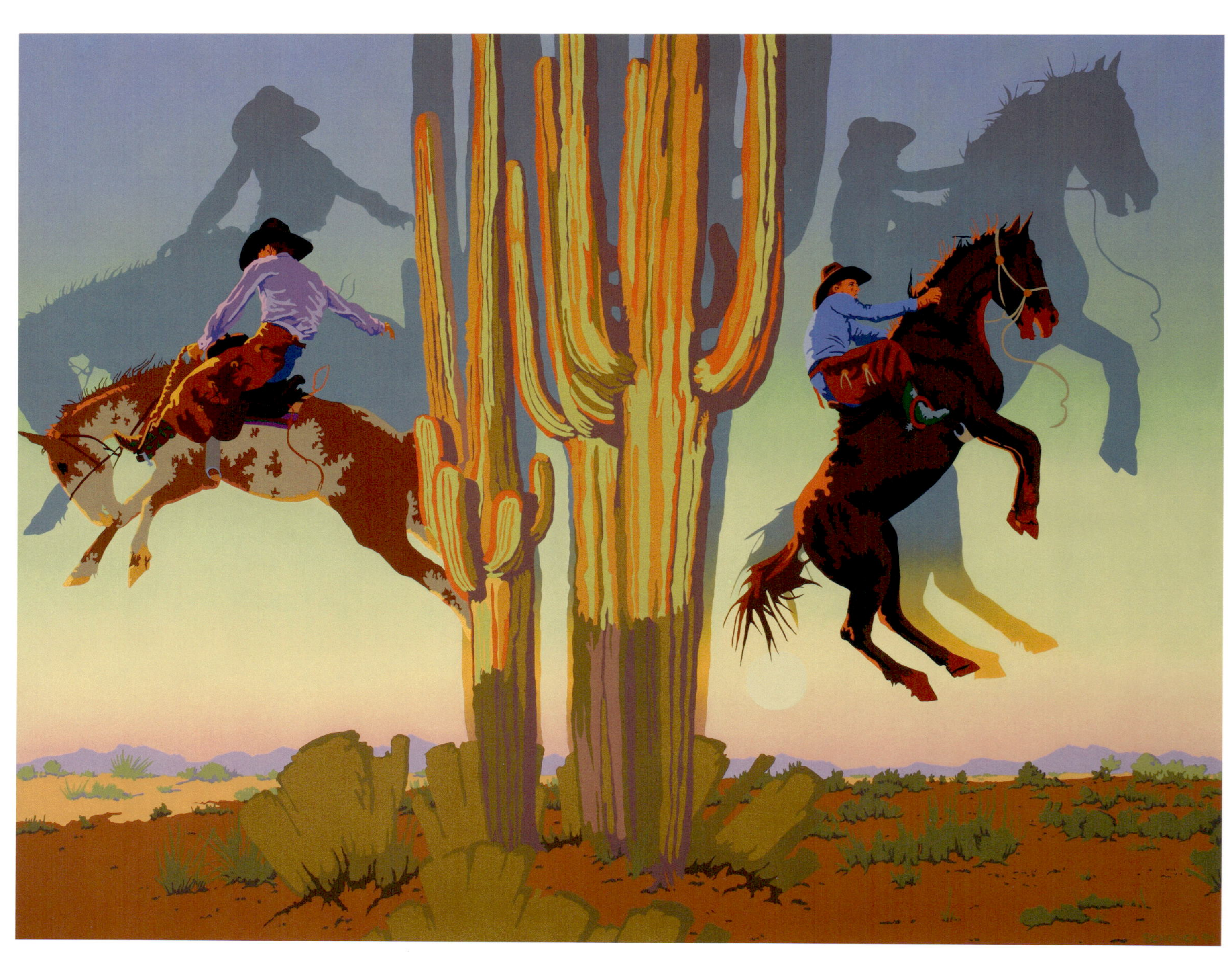

Snakes in the Grass

1996
Oil on canvas
45½ × 60½ inches

"Some people become born-again Christians," remarks Bill Schenck. "Well, I found Sergio Leone."* As an art student in the 1960s, Schenck had no intention of focusing on subjects from the American West—until Leone's innovative, jarring "spaghetti western" films led to his conversion. Influenced by the appropriated imagery of pop art, Schenck began using western film stills and a wide variety of popular culture sources as inspiration for his paintings. "I have the old pulp western magazines, I've got the old Zane Grey novels, I've got all the old movies," Schenck describes, "but I can't help just throwing a hand grenade into it."† Scrambling images from disparate sources, Schenck constructs a unique vision of the West. With bold colors, *Snakes in the Grass* portrays two rodeo cowboys on bucking broncos soaring above an iconic western desert landscape. Their sharp shadows against the sky create the illusion of a flat stage backdrop. With this surreal, exaggerated image, Schenck satirizes the highly romanticized, immortal status assigned to the mythic American cowboy.

*"Billy Schenck: Fine Artist," cdsavoia artist video, 4:54, posted January 6, 2014, http://www.cdsavoia.com/#!/artists/billy-schenck.

†Ibid.

STEVE KESTREL (BORN 1948)

Rattle Me Naught

2008
Bronze
6 × 9 × 6 inches

Raised in Alamogordo, New Mexico, in a region of sculpted hills and windswept sand dunes, the first artworks Steve Kestrel ever recalls seeing were WPA murals by Peter Hurd adorning the walls of the local post office. Inspired by the wildlife of the desert Southwest, he initially studied to become a veterinarian before switching majors to fine art. Working in stone and bronze, Kestrel's sculptures reflect his interests in the geologic formations, paleontology, and animals of the American West.

Wound into a tight, defensive ball, this bronze sculpture of a rattlesnake resembles a round, rough-textured river stone. All energy and muscle, the snake is coiled like a spring—both graceful and ominous. By revealing the curvilinear beauty of one of the most feared animals in the American West, Kestrel challenges viewers to reconsider the rattlesnake with a sympathetic eye. While they can indeed present a danger to humans, rattlesnakes also form a critical link in the ecosystem by limiting the size of rodent populations and serving as an important food source for birds of prey. In his work, Kestrel explains, he attempts to "take the emphasis off human-centered thinking—to have people understand the natural world."*

*Quoted in Mark Mussari, "Steve Kestrel: Letting Nature Lead," *Southwest Art* (January 2011), http://www.southwestart.com/featured /steve-kestrel-letting-nature-lead.

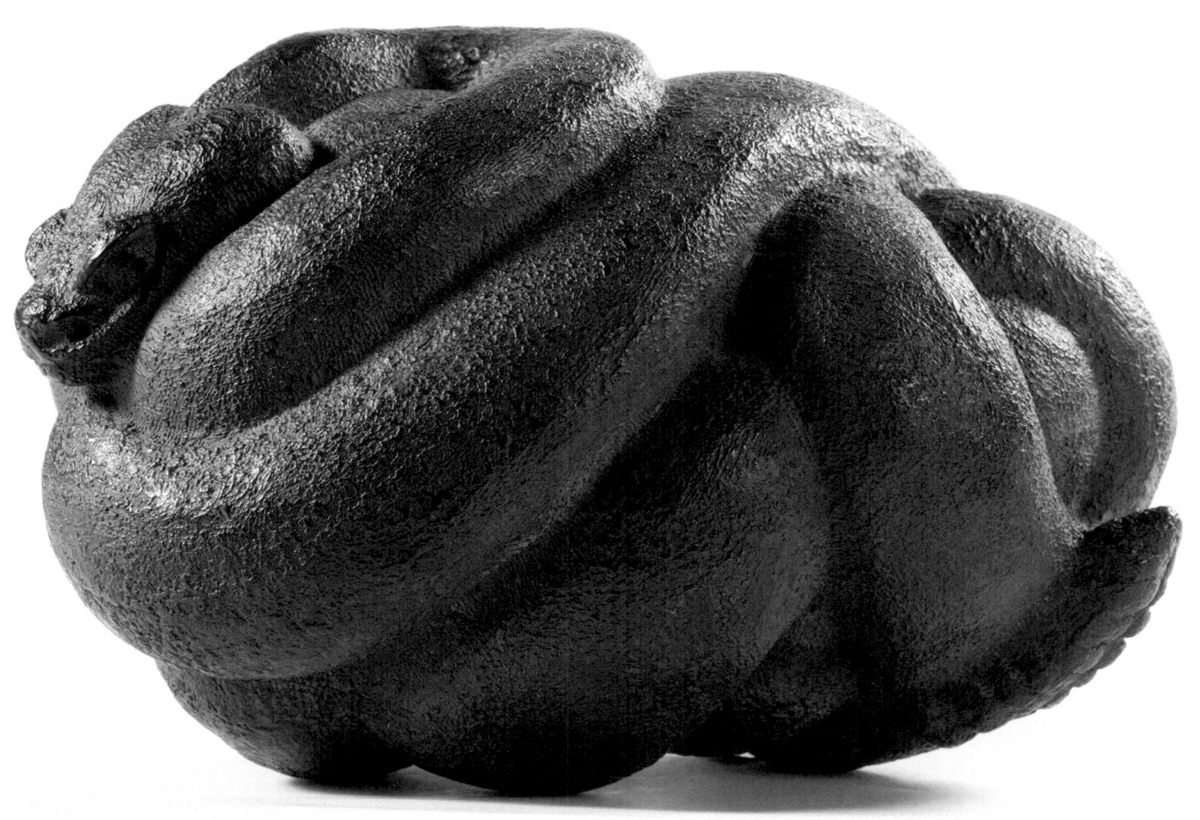

Chinle Wash

1986
Oil on board
30 × 40 inches

From the time she was born in Bridgewater, Connecticut, Lanford Monroe was immersed in art. "It never occurred to me that there was anything special about being an artist since everyone around me painted," she recalled. "I always assumed that I would be one too—it just seemed as natural as breathing."* Her mother, Betty, was a painter, and her father, C. E. Monroe, was a noted magazine illustrator. Artists John Clymer and Bob Kuhn were neighbors—and as a child Lanford occasionally posed for Clymer's illustrations. Her art training came primarily from her own parents, and she found inspiration in a wide variety of landscapes scattered across the United States. *Chinle Wash* depicts a valley in northeastern Arizona near Canyon de Chelly. In the autumn glow, Monroe shows the contrast of gold and blue in the dwindling sunlight and slow-moving stream. A single horse and rider follow a narrow path meandering alongside sculpted rock formations and cliffs. In soft, diffused light, she captures the beauty of a lonely, wild place in the desert Southwest.

*Quoted in R. E. C. Thompson, *Homefields: The Art of Lanford Monroe* (n.p.: Sporting Classics, Islet Bay Press, 2007), 19.

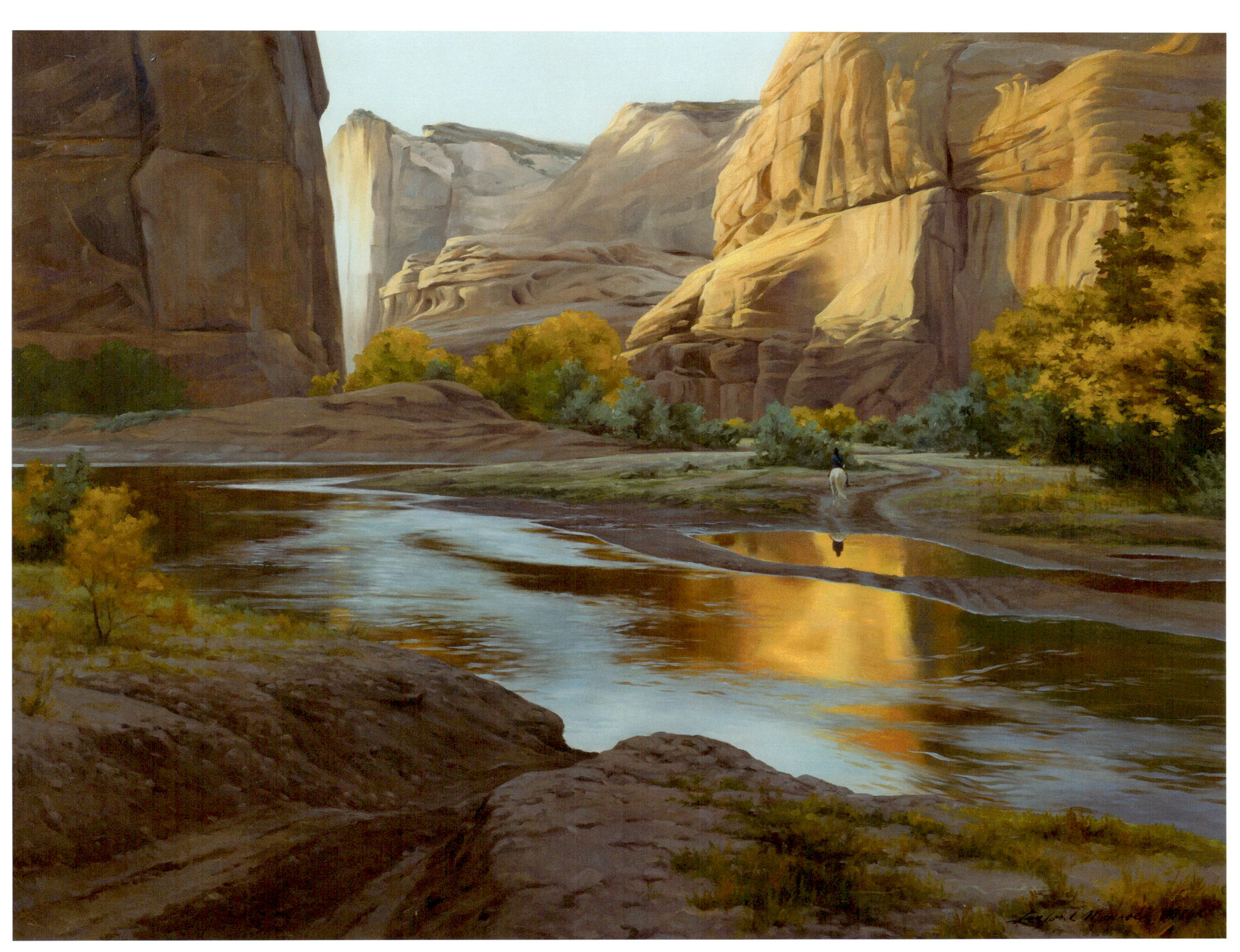

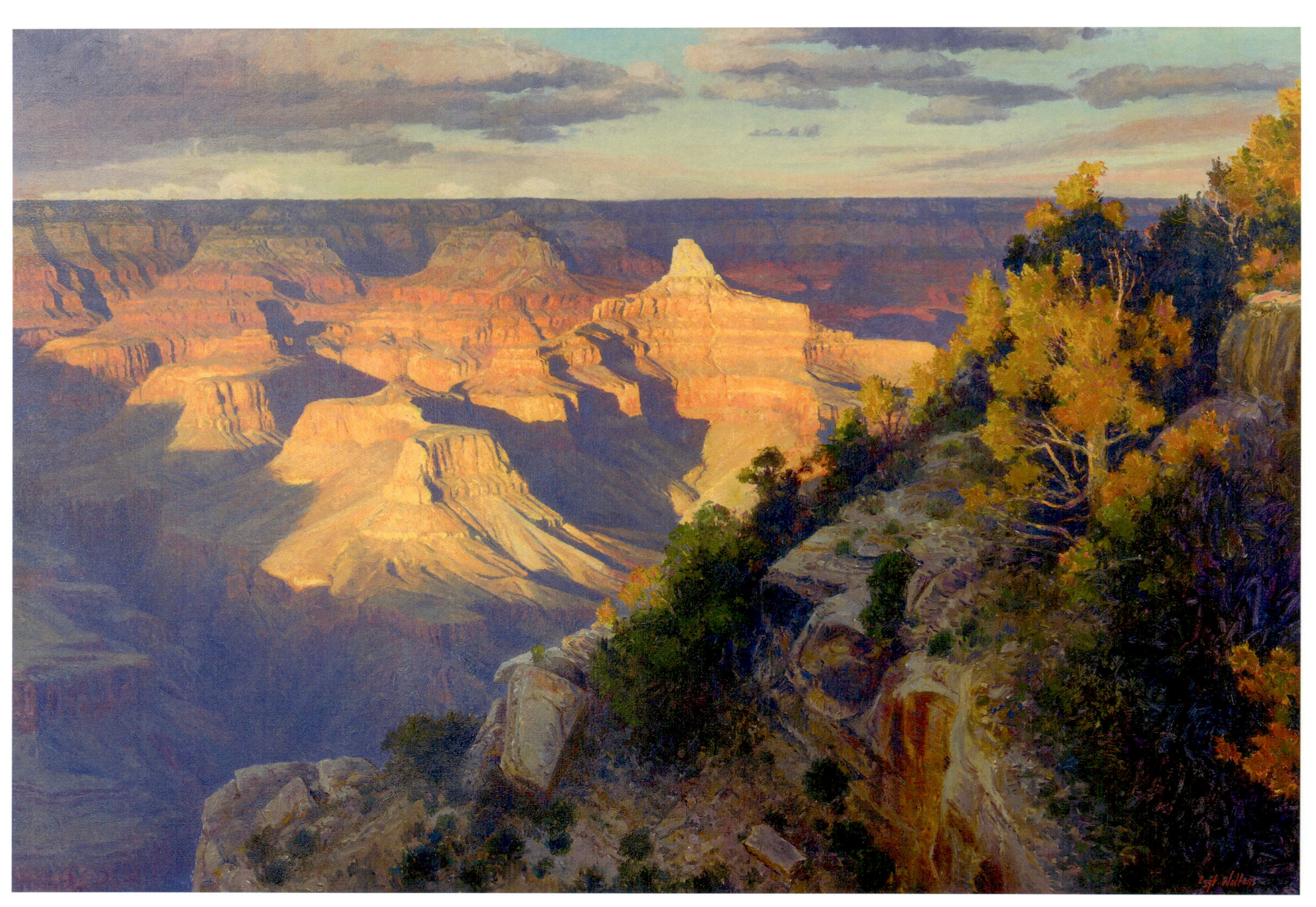

Supreme Moment of Evening

1993
Oil on canvas
40 × 60 inches

Perched precariously on the rim of the Grand Canyon, Curt Walters paints on site, securing his large canvases with bungee cords to protect against a sudden gust of wind. "I truly am renewed every time I see the Grand Canyon and its beauty," Walters says. "The Grand Canyon is simply the most sublime place on earth."* Although he paints a wide range of locations, Walters is best known for his renderings of the Grand Canyon, finding an endless variety of colors, forms, and perspectives in the vast chasm. Beyond painting, his admiration for the canyon has spurred him to actively support the Grand Canyon Trust's efforts toward restoring and preserving the air quality and ecosystem of the Colorado plateau.

In *Supreme Moment of Evening,* Walters conveys the splendor of the canyon at sunset in brilliant colors of orange, vermilion, and deep purple. But the sharp diagonal of its rim in the foreground gives viewers the sense of standing on a perilous slope—with little protection from the unfathomable drop into the canyon's depths. With strong lines and vivid colors, Walters captures the tension between the beauty and the danger ever-present in this place.

*Quoted in Allison Malafronte, "En Plein Air: A Conversation With Curt Walters," *Artist Daily: Plein Air Blog,* Oct. 15, 2008, http://www .artistdaily.com/blogs/pleinair/archive/2008/10/15/en-plein-air-a -conversation-with-curt-walters.aspx.

CLYDE ASPEVIG (BORN 1951)

White Cliffs of the Missouri

2009
Oil on canvas
40 × 60 inches

In the remote reaches of central Montana, far from the nearest town, the Upper Missouri River winds past sculpted rock formations, volcanic intrusions, and sheer white sandstone cliffs rising from the river's edge. In 1805, Meriwether Lewis and William Clark led the Corps of Discovery through this channel, marveling at the rock buttresses lining the water. In 1833, artist Karl Bodmer traveled upriver past the cliffs, making numerous sketches of the "white castles" along the river. For generations the white cliffs of the Missouri have been revered both for their rugged beauty and for their historic significance.

Today, the Upper Missouri River Breaks National Monument protects the towering rock uplifts and cliff formations that Lewis and Clark described over 200 years ago. In 2009, Erivan and Helga Haub traveled along the Upper Missouri past the cliffs with a group that included artist Clyde Aspevig. Captivated by the sites along the river, the Haubs commissioned him to paint *White Cliffs of the Missouri*. For Aspevig, a landscape painter and Montana native, the cliffs represented an ideal subject—a place worthy of preservation.

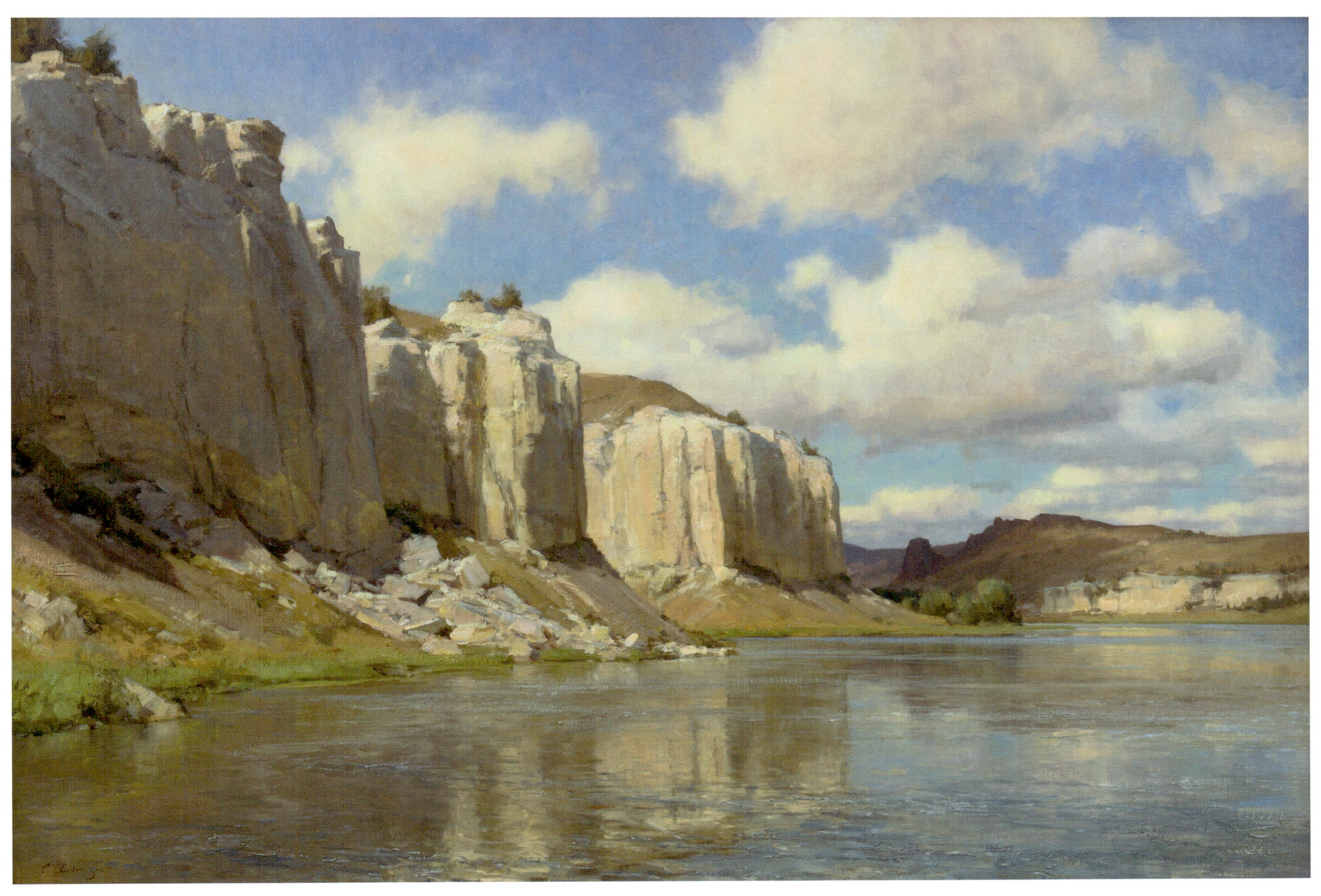

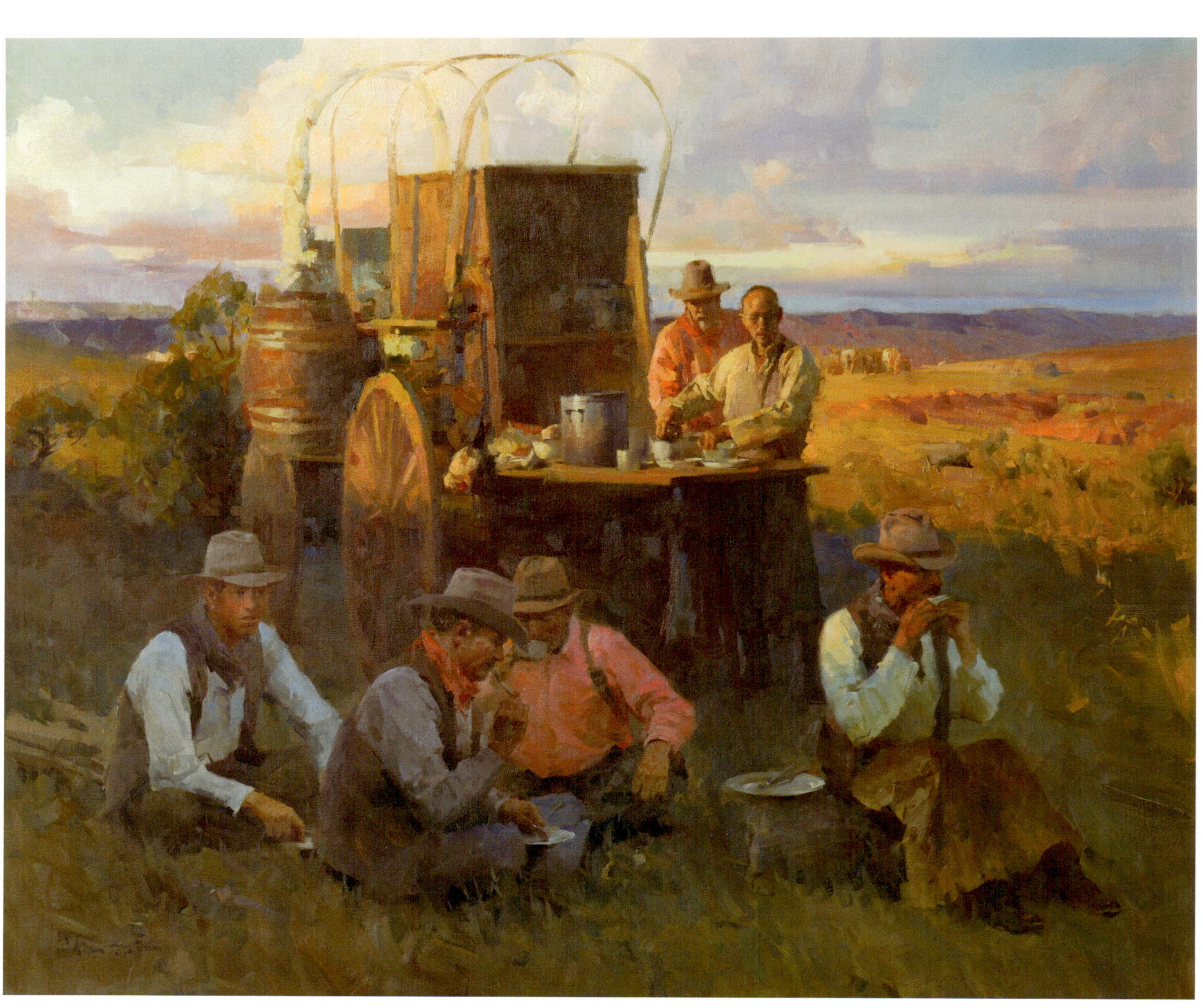

Beef, Beans and Biscuits

2004
Oil on canvas
32 × 40 inches

Many histories of the American West begin in the eastern United States and gradually move westward. By contrast, Mian Situ looks in the other direction, portraying stories that begin on the West Coast and move east. Born in Guangdong, China, and now living in California, Situ studies the history of Chinese immigration to the United States and paints scenes of Chinese experiences in the American West.

Starting in the mid-19th century, waves of Chinese immigrants began moving east toward the Rocky Mountains, working as railroad laborers, miners, and in a variety of other jobs. While they made significant contributions to developing the West, Chinese were often viewed as second-class citizens and subjected to intense racial prejudice, and they rarely appeared in historic images—something Situ seeks to change. In this painting, old-time cowboys in broad-brimmed hats gather around a chuck wagon for a meal. Their cook—presiding over an orderly spread and playing a vital role in the success of the cattle drive—is a Chinese immigrant. Using his art, Situ aims to shed light on this little-known chapter of American history and bridge cultural divides. "Art," declares Situ, "is the easiest way to communicate between different cultures, different races, and different backgrounds."*

*"Mian Situ: Fine Artist," cdsavoia artist video, 3:54, posted November 1, 2012, http://www.cdsavoia.com/#!/artists/mian-situ.

Fort Bent Dancers

2001
Oil on canvas
36 × 24 inches

Martin Grelle was thrilled to join the Cowboy Artists of America (CAA) in 1995. As a teenager he had a chance to meet CAA members James Boren and Melvin Warren when they moved to his hometown of Clifton, Texas. The two established painters encouraged Grelle to pursue a career in the arts and inspired him to study subjects from the American West. Today, he paints both romantic, imagined scenes of the past and images of contemporary western life. While many of his depictions of Native Americans portray an invented, halcyon historical era, in *Fort Bent Dancers* he presents a vibrant group of people in the present day. Wearing beautifully adorned regalia in vivid colors, these contemporary powwow dancers demonstrate how traditions from the past have evolved into the present. Grelle's quick, loose brushstrokes lend a sense of energy to the scene, conveying the motion of the dancers. With this painting, he shows that Native Americans remain an integral part of the modern American West.

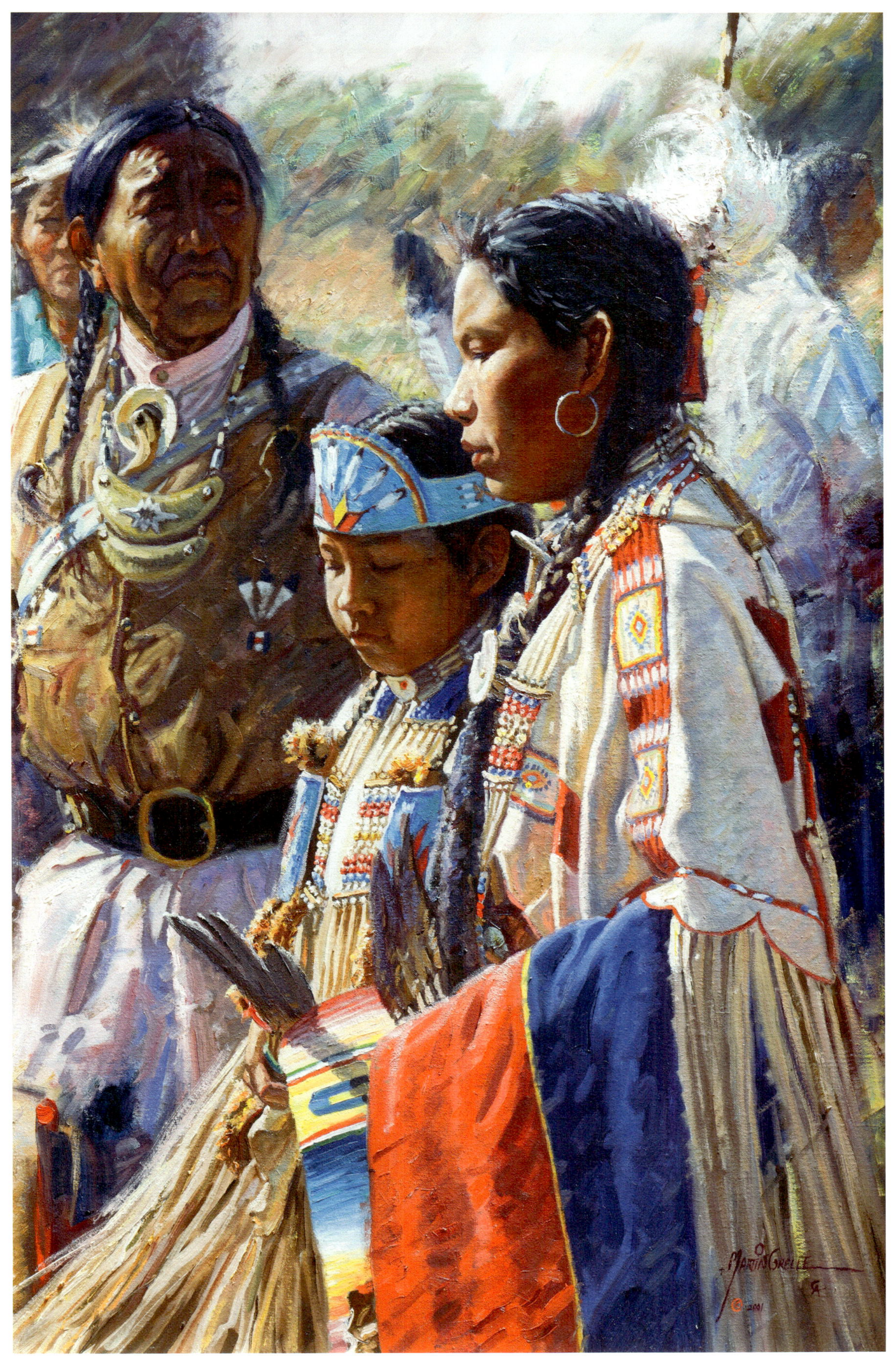

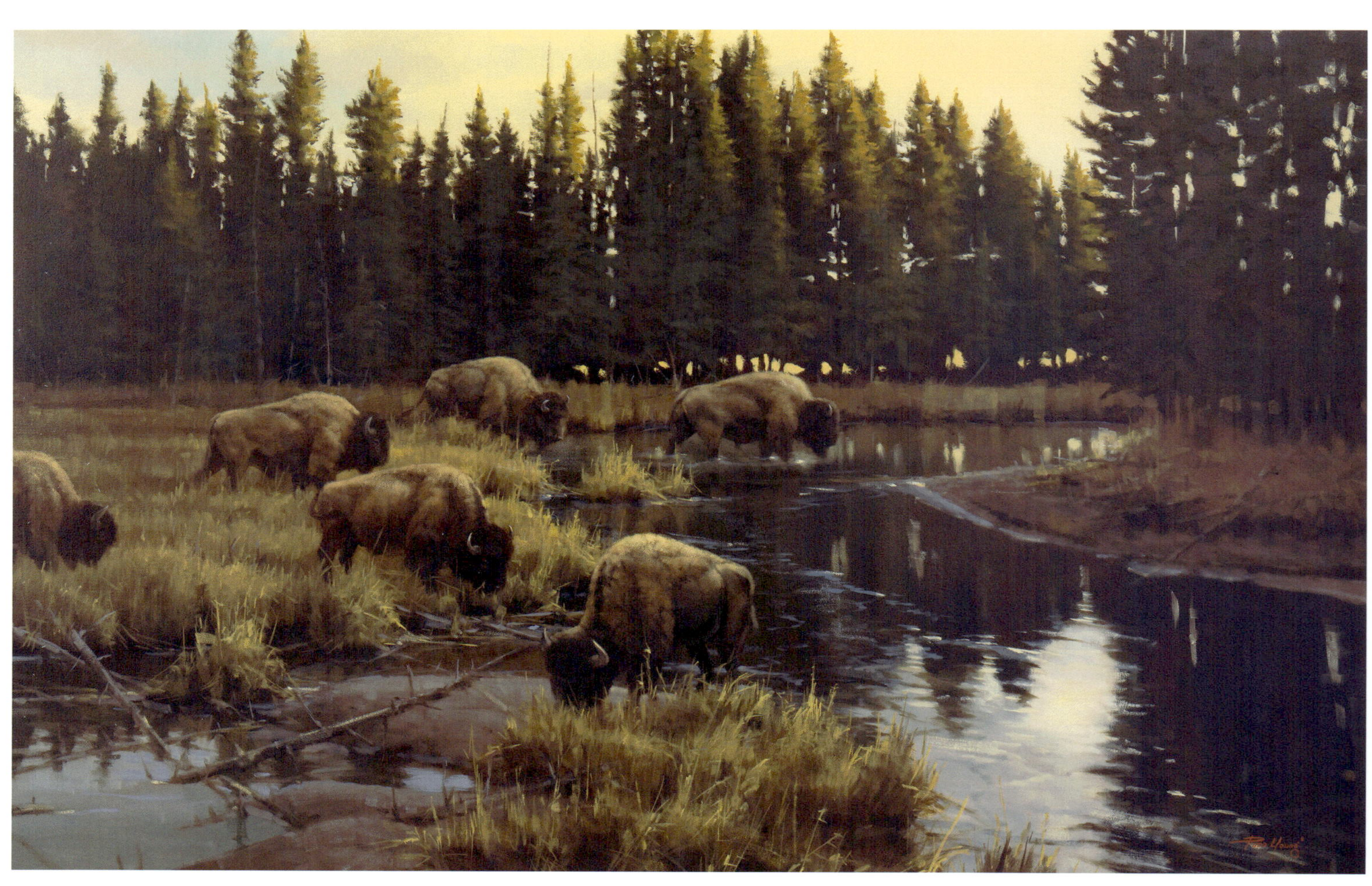

Yellowstone Crossing

circa 2000
Oil on canvas
30 × 48 inches

In the rustic splendor of the Old Faithful Inn inside Yellowstone National Park, a large painting of an erupting geyser can be found in the grand dining room, hanging above a massive stone fireplace built from volcanic rocks quarried from the park itself. In the historic 1904 hotel visited by travelers from across the globe, Paco Young's painting *Old Faithful* connects the log and stone interior to the explosive energy of the geysers immediately outside. His work *Yellowstone Crossing*, also portraying the first national park, shows a quieter image of bison at dusk, foraging along a slow-moving river—a scene resembling a peaceful "American Serengeti" in colors of deep green and dark gold.

After moving to Montana in 1994, Young found inspiration in painting the landscapes and wildlife of Yellowstone, Grand Teton, and Glacier national parks. His interest in the environment extended beyond his artwork, and by publishing prints of his work he assisted with fundraising efforts for various conservation groups. In paintings like *Yellowstone Crossing*, Young reveals the lumbering grace of Yellowstone's bison, encouraging viewers to respect these animals and their environment—and to protect these areas for future generations.

ARTISTS' BIOGRAPHIES

KIMBERLY DISNEY

MARGARET E. BULLOCK

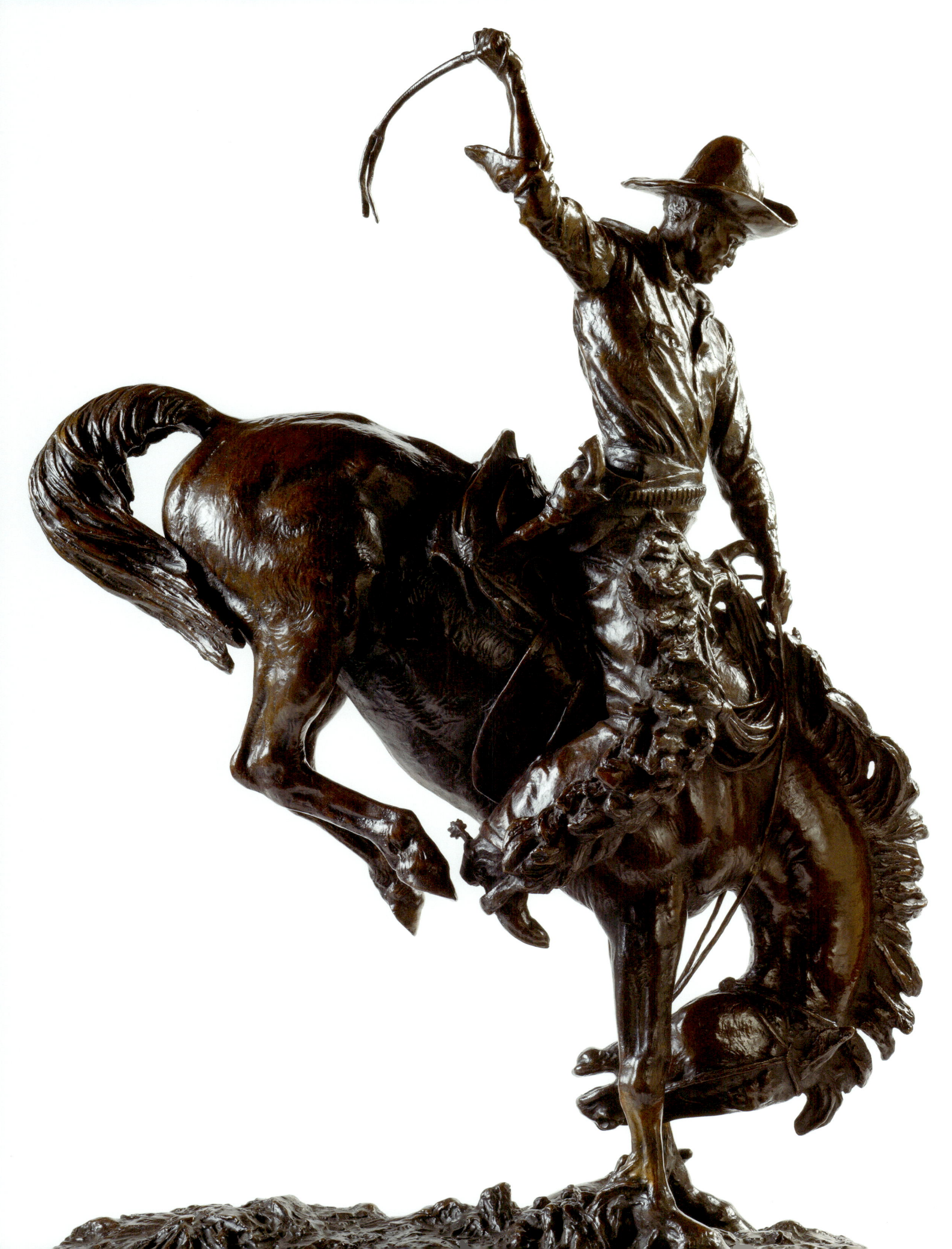

KENNETH M. ADAMS (1897–1966)

A native of Topeka, Kansas, Kenneth Adams received formal training at the Art Institute of Chicago and the Art Students League in New York, but the course of his career was not defined until he attended the Art Students League's summer session in Woodstock, New York, in 1919. There he studied under Andrew Dasburg, who became a major influence on Adams's career, advising him first to travel and study in Europe and then inviting him to New Mexico in 1924. He established a studio in Taos and began producing abstracted images of northern New Mexico in a style reminiscent of post-impressionism. In 1926 he became the last member elected to the Taos Society of Artists before it was disbanded in 1927. In the 1930s Adams completed several large murals throughout the Southwest before becoming an art instructor at the University of New Mexico in Albuquerque in 1937. He went on to teach at the university until he retired in 1963, producing work that most often depicted life in New Mexico.

CLYDE ASPEVIG (BORN 1951)

Born in northern Montana and raised in a farming community, Clyde Aspevig pursued painting from a young age. He attended Eastern Montana College in the early 1970s and graduated with a bachelor of fine arts in 1976. Aspevig briefly worked as a school teacher in Oregon but soon decided to pursue painting full time instead. He began painting western landscapes, and in 1982 became the first Montana resident since Charles Russell to exhibit at the Grand Central Galleries in New York City. He currently resides in Montana, usually working outdoors making oil studies that he turns into larger compositions in his studio. Aspevig describes himself as a composer, incorporating music and rhythm in his paintings to create a cohesive and harmonious composition. He also strongly believes in conservation and works to communicate a respect for the land in his paintings.

JOE BEELER (1931–2006)

A native of Missouri, Joe Beeler was born in the town of Joplin. He received a bachelor of fine arts from Kansas State Teachers College and then went on to study at Art Center School in Los Angeles. Moving to Oklahoma, he worked as an illustrator and also began painting cowboys and Native Americans, and exhibited his first one-man show at the Gilcrease Museum in Tulsa in 1960. Beeler's work was strongly influenced by Frederic Remington and Charles Russell, and in 1965 he began working in bronze. That same year he cofounded the Cowboy Artists of America with fellow western artists Charlie Dye, John Hampton, and George Phippen. Beeler lived the rest of his life in Arizona and won numerous awards for his western American artworks.

THOMAS HART BENTON (1889–1975)

American regionalist painter Thomas Hart Benton was born in Neosho, Missouri, and studied at the Art Institute of Chicago before traveling to Paris to study at the Académie Julian. He moved to New York in 1912 and served as a draftsman and illustrator for the US Navy in Norfolk, Virginia, during World War I. He began painting murals in the 1920s, and his large-scale works depicting regional scenes of everyday American life would make him famous. He taught for a time at the Art Students League in New York starting in 1926, but moved to Kansas City in 1935 to be an instructor at the Kansas City Art Institute. Benton became acquainted with fellow Midwest artists John Steuart Curry and Grant Wood, and together the three became the best-known proponents of regionalism, believing that art should communicate the spirit of a place. Benton lived in Kansas City for the remainder of his career and continued to take commissions for murals until his death in 1975.

OSCAR E. BERNINGHAUS (1874–1952)

Primarily self-taught as an artist, Oscar Berninghaus became one of the most successful painters among the Taos Society of Artists. He began sketching and painting at a young age, studying the lithographs his father sold and the work of other artists. He eventually took a few evening art classes in St. Louis at the School of Fine Arts, Washington University, his only formal training. He became a talented professional lithographer and engraver in St. Louis. In 1899 he went on a sketching trip to the Southwest sponsored by the Denver and Rio Grande Western Railroad, and the train's brakeman encouraged him to visit Taos. He spent a week there, met the artist Bert Phillips, and was encouraged to return. He began visiting Taos in the summers and was a founding member of the Taos Society of Artists in 1915. He eventually relocated there permanently in 1925, and focused on the everyday life of the Pueblo Indians around Taos and on the surrounding landscape.

ALBERT BIERSTADT (1830–1902)

Albert Bierstadt was born in Solingen, Germany, in 1830 but was brought to New Bedford, Massachusetts, in 1832. He was largely self-taught until he moved to Düsseldorf in 1853, where he studied under Emanuel Leutze and learned to paint in the German romantic style, producing large-scale idealized, detailed landscapes. He returned to America in 1857 and joined Frederick W. Lander's survey of an overland passage to California in 1859. He took along a stereoscopic camera and made many partial oil studies that he later used to create large-scale oils in his East Coast studio. He went west again in 1863 along with writer Fitz Hugh Ludlow, the pair visiting the Colorado Rockies, Yosemite Valley, Oregon, and the Columbia River Valley. Bierstadt became known for his sublime depictions of the American West. In 1871 he moved to San Francisco to be closer to the Yosemite Valley, where he worked with the photographer Eadweard Muybridge. He left California in 1873 and traveled widely through the American West, Canada, and Alaska in the late 19th century. His style of painting began to fall from favor later in his career and his market had dwindled by the time of his death in 1902—only to significantly recover in recent years.

FREDERICK BILLING (1835–1914)

German-born Frederick Billing had always been interested in art but his father forbade him to paint. Billing instead became a businessman in his hometown of Eschwege before he moved to Brooklyn around 1856. He enlisted in the Union Army in 1861 and served in the Civil War with his brother. He also began to paint landscapes. Billing was never formally trained and worked as an amateur throughout his career. He moved to Salt Lake City in the late 1870s for his health and went into the mining business. He also began to paint scenes of Utah, Wyoming, Colorado, and Idaho. He was a friend of Thomas Moran and his brother Peter and would accompany them on painting expeditions. The three collaborated on the painting *Falls of the Grand Canyon of the Yellowstone River*. Billing often worked from photographs and based at least one of his works on an etching by Thomas Moran. He moved to California in 1885, where he painted scenes of the Yosemite Valley and the Santa Cruz Mountains. He eventually settled in Santa Cruz, on the Wilhelmina Ranch, where he lived the rest of his life.

GEORGE CALEB BINGHAM (1811–1879)

Although he was born in Augusta County, Virginia, George Caleb Bingham eventually became famous for his idyllic scenes depicting everyday life in Missouri. Bingham's family moved to the Missouri area around 1818 and by 1835 the artist had made a name for himself as a self-taught portrait painter. His success afforded him the opportunity to travel east to study in Philadelphia and New York in 1838. In 1845 he began producing a series of paintings featuring life on the Missouri River, often depicting boatmen. That same year the artist sent two of his western paintings to the American Art-Union Exhibition in New York. Bingham was a member of the Whig party and became involved in local Missouri politics beginning in the 1840s. He was inspired to create another series of paintings, this time dealing with frontier political life. Bingham traveled farther west later in his life, visiting Colorado in 1872, just a few years before his death in 1879.

ERNEST L. BLUMENSCHEIN (1874–1960)

Ernest Blumenschein was born into a family of German immigrants and raised in Dayton, Ohio. His father was a professional musician and Blumenschein originally trained as a violinist but decided to pursue the visual arts in his late teens. He studied at the Art Academy of Cincinnati, then in 1892 transferred to the Art Students League in New York, supporting himself as a musician. He later spent a year at the Académie Julian in Paris. He returned to New York in 1896 and began a career as an illustrator and instructor at the Art Students League. In 1898, on the recommendation of the artist Joseph Henry Sharp, whom he had met in Paris, he traveled to New Mexico with painter Bert Phillips. Blumenschein made a number of subsequent trips to Taos, moving there permanently in 1919. A founding member of the Taos Society of Artists, he brought a modernist style to the group with his palette and techniques.

KARL BODMER (1809–1893)

Karl Bodmer was born in Zurich, Switzerland, and lived in Europe except for one expedition to America to accompany Prince Alexander Philipp Maximilian of Wied-Neuwied and record his journey up the Missouri River from 1832 to 1834. The party left from St. Louis in the spring of 1833 and eventually made it as far as Fort McKenzie in present-day Montana. On the journey Bodmer produced many portraits of Native Americans and notably sketched scenes of an Assiniboine attack on a camp of Blackfeet people living at Fort McKenzie as well as the scalp dance of the Minatarres (Hidatsa). When the Prince's party spent the winter of 1833–34 at Fort Clark he also became the last artist to paint the Mandans before a devastating smallpox epidemic. Bodmer is known for his exceptional draftsmanship and was able to depict his native subjects with striking exactitude. In the 1840s, his work appeared as 81 aquatints in Prince Maximilian's published account of his journey into the American Frontier. After returning to Europe, Bodmer settled permanently in Barbizon near Paris.

ROSA BONHEUR (1822–1899)

Rosa Bonheur was born in Bordeaux, France, in 1822 and was taught by her father, Raymond Bonheur, who was also a painter. She began exhibiting paintings at the Paris Salon in 1841 and continued to do so through 1853. Bonheur's work featured animals, which she always sketched from life. Her 16-foot-long painting *The Horse Fair*, now in the collection of the Metropolitan Museum of Art, earned her international acclaim in 1853. Bonheur saw George Catlin's Indian Gallery and his Native American performers when they came to Paris in 1845 and soon developed an interest in the American West. When William F. "Buffalo Bill" Cody came to Paris in 1889 for the Exposition Universelle he invited her to come to the grounds of Buffalo Bill's Wild West. Bonheur in turn invited him to her home Chateâu de By, where she made a full-length painting of him that he later reproduced in posters advertising Buffalo Bill's Wild West.

EDWARD BOREIN (1872–1945)

Edward Borein sketched his first cowboys and cattle drives at the age of five in his hometown of San Leandro, California. As a teenager he worked as a cowboy in Oakland, and then in 1891 he enrolled briefly at the California School of Design (now the San Francisco Art Institute). Finding school too structured, he quit after one month and headed to southern California and Mexico to work as a vaquero, sketching as he went. Returning to Oakland in 1904, he began working as an illustrator, building a successful career. In 1907 he moved to New York, where he opened a studio that became a gathering place for westerners, including such famous figures as Charles Russell and Will Rogers. Borein became lifelong friends with Russell and often visited him in Montana. While in New York, Borein learned etching at the Art Students League and became a master printmaker. He was equally adept at ink drawing and watercolor painting. He moved to Santa Barbara in 1921 and taught at the Santa Barbara School of the Arts until his death. He was a prolific artist renowned for his detailed images of cowboys, California ranch life, and Native Americans.

ALBERTUS DEL ORIENT BROWERE (1814–1887)

Born in Tarrytown, New York, Albertus del Orient Browere was the son of sculptor John Henri Isaac Browere and received his first training from his father. He moved to Catskill, New York, upon his father's death in 1834 and had to work as an apothecary for a time to support himself. Despite this he continued to paint, depicting scenes from the writings of James Fenimore Cooper and Washington Irving. Browere exhibited sporadically in New York through the 1840s and studied at the National Academy of Design. He was eventually drawn west to San Francisco by the excitement of the gold rush and made his first trip there in 1852. He returned briefly to Catskill in 1856 but left again for California in 1858, where he stayed until 1861, when he moved back to Catskill for good. While Browere never made his fortune in gold, he used his experience to produce a series of scenes depicting the life of a miner.

ELBRIDGE AYER BURBANK (1858–1949)

Harvard, Illinois, native Elbridge Ayer Burbank studied at the Chicago Academy of Design (later the Art Institute of Chicago) and began his career by illustrating landscapes along the Northern Pacific Railway for *Northwest Illustrated Monthly*. The job took him from Montana to Idaho and Washington, and instilled in him a love of the West. Burbank then continued his studies in Munich before returning to Chicago in 1892. He began his major body of work in 1897 when his uncle Edward E. Ayer, the first director of the Field Museum of Natural History in Chicago, commissioned him to paint a series of portraits of Native American leaders. Burbank famously painted Apache Chief Geronimo from life, the only artist known to have done so. Burbank went on to paint the leaders of tribes from the Great Plains, Southwest, and Pacific Coast, including Chief Joseph of the Nez Perce and Lakota Chief Red Cloud. He is best-known for his collection of Native American portraits, and many of his images are the only visual record ever made of his subjects.

THOMAS MICKELL BURNHAM (1818–1866)

Thomas Mickell Burnham was born in Boston, Massachusetts. He moved to Detroit in 1836 and began working as a sign painter. He established his own studio in 1838, specializing in portraits, genre scenes, and satirical paintings. After traveling briefly to Scotland in 1839 he moved back to Boston in 1840, where he lived and worked for the rest of his life. During his career Burnham exhibited at the National Academy and the Apollo Association in New York and the Athenaeum in Boston. In 1852 he went to the studio of Truman C. Bartholomew in Melrose, Massachusetts, to contribute to John Wesley Jones's *Great Pantoscope of California, the Rocky Mountains, Salt Lake City, Nebraska and Kansas.* The large-scale panorama was based on over a thousand daguerreotypes and sketches that Jones and his assistants had made on their 1851 journey from California to St. Louis.

KEN CARLSON (BORN 1937)

Born and raised in rural Morton, Minnesota, Ken Carlson taught himself to draw as a child and won a scholarship to the Art Instruction Schools in Minneapolis where he studied with wildlife illustrator Walter Wilwerding. He went on to study at the Minneapolis School of Art before becoming a commercial illustrator. Wildlife artists Carl Rungius and Bob Kuhn have been major influences on Carlson's work and he shares their belief that observation from life is the best way to create a successful likeness of an animal. The artist currently lives and works in the Hill Country of central Texas and travels widely in order to sketch his animal subjects. Once back in his studio, he turns his sketches and photos into large-scale, highly detailed, individual portraits. Carlson has received numerous awards throughout his career, including the first Bob Kuhn Wildlife Award at the Autry National Center's annual exhibition and sale in 2008.

GERALD CASSIDY (1869–1934)

Gerald Cassidy was born in Covington, Kentucky, in 1869 and was raised in Cincinnati, where he studied under Frank Duveneck at the Art Academy of Cincinnati. He was working as an art director at a lithography firm in New York City when, in 1899, he was diagnosed with tuberculosis and moved to a sanatorium in Albuquerque. After regaining his health he worked as a commercial artist in Denver, returning briefly to New York before moving permanently to Santa Fe in 1912. Cassidy became one of the first artists to establish a colony there and was known for his paintings of the regional cultures and the southwestern landscape. He gained recognition for his murals after winning the grand prize for his work *The Cliff Dwellers of the Southwest* in the hall of southwestern archaeology at the 1915 Panama-California International Exposition in San Diego. Cassidy died in 1934 from carbon monoxide poisoning while working on a commissioned mural in the Federal Building in Santa Fe.

GEORGE CATLIN (1796–1872)

George Catlin was born in Wilkes-Barre, Pennsylvania, and studied law and practiced from 1820 to 1823. He was first inspired to paint the Native American people of the West after seeing a delegation of Plains Indians pass though Philadelphia, where he was living in 1826. After his encounter with the Plains delegation, he began traveling up the Missouri River in 1832, painting as he went. His travels influenced him to be one of the first voices for conservation in the West, advocating for a type of national park or preserve in the Great Plains. By 1840 Catlin had visited 48 tribes and painted some 475 images. He published many of them in his book *Letters and Notes on the Manners, Customs, and Condition of the North American Indians* in 1841. He also used the collection of portraits and artifacts that he had amassed to create Catlin's Indian Gallery. He took this show to Europe in the 1840s, performing in London, Brussels, and Paris. Sadly, he had to sell the entire collection owing to financial difficulties that began in the early 1850s. By his own account, Catlin spent much of his later life traveling and painting in the Western Hemisphere, from South America to Siberian Alaska. He died in his sister's home in Jersey City, New Jersey, in 1872.

FREDERIC EDWIN CHURCH (1826–1900)

Born into a wealthy Hartford, Connecticut, family in 1826, Frederic Edwin Church had a father with the connections to secure his son a place as Thomas Cole's pupil in 1844. He studied with the famous Hudson River school painter for two years in Catskill, New York, before moving to New York City to start his career. Church found success easily and was known for his large-scale and highly detailed works. He traveled to South America in 1853 and again in 1857. Following this second trip, he produced one of the most famous paintings of the Civil War era, *The Heart of the Andes*. In 1859 Church sailed to the North Atlantic to sketch and paint icebergs and then changed subjects again when he traveled to Jamaica in 1865. After his time in the tropics Church made his way to the Old World in 1867, finding new inspiration in Jerusalem, Palestine, Athens, and Rome. He built his family a Persian-inspired castle he named Olana in Hudson, New York, in 1870 and lived there for the remainder of his life. Toward the end of his life, the exacting detail of Church's work began to fall out of style and he became relatively obscure by the time of his death in 1900. Today, however, Church is recognized as one of the most significant American artists of the 19th century.

JOHN CLYMER (1907–1989)

A Northwest native, John Clymer was born in Ellensburg, Washington, and moved to Canada after graduating from high school to work as an illustrator while taking night classes at the Vancouver School of Art. In the 1930s he traveled repeatedly to the East Coast and studied under illustrators N. C. Wyeth and Harvey Dunn. In 1937 he moved to Westport, Connecticut, which was known as an artist's colony. Soon Clymer's illustrations were appearing in national magazines such as *Cosmopolitan* and *Good Housekeeping,* and he illustrated more than 80 covers for the *Saturday Evening Post* during his long career. By 1964 Clymer had decided to devote himself to painting full time and embarked on a mission to create images of the American West that were as detailed and accurate as possible. With his wife, Doris, an amateur historian, Clymer developed a process that involved in-depth historical research and traveling to the site of the proposed image to create highly detailed compositions. The artist depicted diverse themes—fur traders, frontier mountain men, and wildlife of North America—but he had a special interest in depicting the Native peoples and scenery of the Pacific Northwest. He was elected to the Cowboy Artists of America in 1969 and moved to Teton Village, Wyoming, in 1970.

MICHAEL COLEMAN (BORN 1946)

A native of Provo, Utah, Michael Coleman still lives and works in his hometown. After spending his childhood in the outdoors, he studied art at Brigham Young University. His tendency toward traditional representation drew criticism from his instructors at a time when abstract expressionism was at its height. Undaunted, Coleman drew inspiration from the Hudson River school and from painters like Henry Farny, Thomas Moran, and George Inness. He had his first solo exhibition at the Buffalo Bill Historical Center (now the Buffalo Bill Center of the West) in Cody, Wyoming, when he was just 32. Coleman works mainly in oil and gouache, creating compositions that depict people in harmony with nature in the West. Fall and winter scenes are a particular favorite as Coleman enjoys using a dusky color palette. In addition to painting, the artist also works in bronze and won the 1999 Prix de West Award at the National Cowboy & Western Heritage Museum.

SAMUEL COLMAN (1832–1920)

Born in Portland, Maine, Samuel Colman grew up in New York City and was exposed to artists through his father's profession as a publisher. He may have studied with Asher B. Durand and is considered a second-generation Hudson River school painter. Colman traveled to France, Spain, Morocco, and Italy from 1860 to 1862. He was struck by Moorish design and traveled to North Africa again from 1871 to 1875. He worked in oils and watercolor, and began experimenting with etching in 1863. He would use that technique increasingly as his career progressed. Colman had established himself as a painter of European landscapes before his first trip to the American West around 1870. His first western subjects were the Yosemite Valley and the Green River in Wyoming. He began exhibiting Mexican scenes in 1895 and returned to the Pacific Coast in 1899. He turned to theory late in his career, publishing *Nature's Harmonic Unity* in 1912 and *Proportional Form* shortly before his death in 1920.

E. IRVING COUSE (1866–1936)

Eanger Irving Couse was born in Saginaw, Michigan, and early on became interested in Native Americans, sketching members of the Chippewa tribe who lived near his childhood home. He studied briefly at the Art Institute of Chicago in 1883 and then at the National Academy of Design in New York City. In 1886 he traveled to Paris and enrolled at the Académie Julian. Couse married in the late 1880s and his wife, Virginia Walker, soon convinced him to visit her family's ranch in southern Washington State so that he could spend time studying and painting the Native American tribes in the region; they returned for a longer visit in 1896. Couse first visited Taos, New Mexico, in 1902. Enamored of the area and fascinated by Pueblo Indian culture, he began spending summers there, eventually helping to found the Taos Society of Artists. He moved there permanently in the late 1920s. His images of Native Americans became widely known through calendars distributed by the Atchison, Topeka, and Santa Fe Railway Company.

CATHARINE CRITCHER (1868–1964)

Catharine Critcher began studying art in her early 20s at the Cooper Union School of Design in New York City and then at the Corcoran School of Art in Washington, DC. She established a successful portrait studio in the DC area, working there for over a decade before traveling to Paris in 1904 and studying at the Académie Julian. In 1905 she founded her own art school in Paris, the Cours Critcher, which she maintained until 1909. Returning to the United States, she became an instructor at the Corcoran School of Art. In 1919 she founded the Critcher School of Painting and Applied Arts in Washington, DC. Critcher first visited the West when she traveled to Taos, New Mexico, in the early 1920s. She returned there every summer for many years, doing a series of portraits, mostly of Native American subjects. In 1924 she was voted in as the only female member of the Taos Society of Artists. Later in her career she traveled to Arizona to sketch and paint on the Hopi Indian Reservation and also visited Mexico, Canada, and Nova Scotia.

CYRUS E. DALLIN (1861–1944)

The son of Mormon pioneers, Cyrus Dallin was born in the settlement of Springville, Utah, and exhibited a talent for sculpting from a young age. He was sent to Boston in the 1880s to study with Truman Bartlett and then went on to the Académie Julian in Paris. While in Paris, Dallin saw Buffalo Bill's Wild West and became interested in western American subjects. He used one of the Lakota performers as a model for *Signal of Peace,* the first in his series of four Native American equestrian statues. He completed and exhibited the other three in the series after his return to America in 1891. His work is noted for its detail and naturalistic modeling. In addition to his Native American works Dallin sculpted other American figures, including an equestrian statue of Paul Revere that stands near Boston's Old North Church, and the Angel Moroni for the apex of the Salt Lake Temple of the Church of Jesus Christ of Latter-day Saints.

CHARLES DEAS (1818–1867)

Charles Deas was born in Philadelphia in 1818 and received early training from artist John Sanderson. After failing to obtain an appointment to West Point, Deas moved to New York in order to study at the National Academy of Design. He was living in the city when George Catlin exhibited his Indian Gallery there in the 1830s. After seeing Catlin's work Deas was inspired to paint the West himself, leaving for Fort Crawford in 1840. In his early trips west to Fort Winnebago and Fort Snelling, in present-day Wisconsin and Minnesota, Deas painted portraits of Native Americans. He then set up a studio in St. Louis in 1841. By the time he accompanied Major Clifton Wharton and Lieutenant J. Henry Carleton to the Pawnee villages on the Platte River in present-day Nebraska, Deas had begun dressing like a fur trapper, earning him the nickname "Rocky Mountains." During this time the fur trappers also became a major subject in his work and his 1844 painting *Long Jakes, the Rocky Mountain Man* earned him national acclaim. His work became increasingly melodramatic as time went on and he completed his last major painting in 1847. In 1848 he was committed to the Bloomingdale Insane Asylum in New York, where he was confined for the remainder of his life.

GERARD CURTIS DELANO (1890–1972)

Born in Marion, Massachusetts, Gerard Curtis Delano trained at the Art Students League and the Grand Central School of Art in New York City before beginning his career as an illustrator. He traveled to Colorado in 1919 to work as a cowboy and gain firsthand experience to use in his artwork. He established a homestead near the Arapaho National Forest in 1920 but continued to work in New York, where his western illustrations appeared regularly in national magazines like *Cosmopolitan* and *Collier's*. Delano remained in New York until the Great Depression forced him to move back to Colorado. Fortunately, in 1936 he signed a two-year contract to provide weekly illustrations for *The Story of the West,* a series that chronicled the history of the West in *Western Story* magazine. Soon after, he gave up illustration and turned to painting full time. Visiting the Navajo Reservation in

Arizona for the first time in 1943, he was immediately struck by the beauty of the landscape and the people. The Navajo culture became a major focus in his work for the rest of his career.

MAYNARD DIXON (1875–1946)

After a successful career as an illustrator, Maynard Dixon built a reputation by creating work that blended modern art influences with scenes from the West. A native of Fresno, California, Dixon had little formal training aside from a few months of art classes at the Mark Hopkins Institute of Art in San Francisco; he learned primarily through sketching and his commission work for newspapers, books, and magazines such as *Sunset* and *Harper's Weekly*. He traveled throughout the western states and Southwest acquiring material for his works. During the 1910s, he turned from illustration work to pursue a painting career. At his San Francisco studio he worked in oil, watercolor, and gouache. By 1940 he was dividing his time between Utah and Tucson, Arizona. Dixon was interested in contemporary ideas about art, particularly post-impressionism and cubism, and adapted these elements into his own work. He became celebrated for his modernist landscapes of the West.

W. HERBERT DUNTON (1878–1936)

William Herbert "Buck" Dunton was an avid outdoorsman who grew up in Maine hunting and fishing. At the age of 18 he headed west to Montana to work as a cowboy and assistant to a bear hunter. To pursue a career as an illustrator he moved to Boston in 1897 and attended Cowles Art School, then to New York in 1903. He published his first illustration at the age of 21 and went on to have work appear in numerous popular magazines including *Harper's Weekly*, *Scribner's*, and the *Saturday Evening Post* as well as in a number of western novels. Dunton studied under Ernest Blumenschein at the Art Students League of New York, and on Blumenschein's invitation he first visited Taos, New Mexico, in 1912. Dunton became the youngest founding member of the Taos Society of Artists in 1915. In Taos he gave up illustration work and focused on painting, forging a successful national career. His most prominent patrons were Nelda and H. J. Lutcher Stark, who bought hundreds of his works. Their collection later became the foundation of the Stark Museum in Orange, Texas.

CHARLIE DYE (1906–1972)

Charlie Dye was exposed to the life of a cowboy from an early age in his hometown of Cañon City, Colorado. He began working as a cowboy in his teens and continued to do so until he left at 21 to study in Chicago at the Art Institute and then the American Academy of Art. From there he went to New York in 1936 and began a successful career as an illustrator. He was a highly skilled draftsman who paid great attention to detail. Dye did not make a foray into western American art until the 1950s, when he gave up illustration and moved back to Colorado. With his firsthand experience of the subject matter, he quickly found success as a painter and the working cowboy was one of his favorite subjects. Dye made Sedona, Arizona, his permanent home in 1962 and cofounded the Cowboy Artists of America with Joe Beeler, John Hampton, and George Phippen in 1965.

SETH EASTMAN (1808–1875)

Born in Brunswick, Maine, Seth Eastman studied drawing under Thomas Gimbrede when he attended West Point from 1824 to 1829. When he was stationed at Fort Snelling in Minnesota in 1830 he began to apply his artistic talents to Native American subjects, undertaking a serious study of the peoples of the Upper Mississippi River. Eastman returned to West Point from 1833 to 1840 to teach drawing, but by 1841 he was back at Fort Snelling making sketches that documented the everyday life and folklore of the Native cultures in the region. He is probably most noted for recording everyday, domestic scenes of his subjects. Beginning in 1851, he contributed over 275 pages of illustrations to Henry Rowe Schoolcraft's six-volume work, *Information Respecting the History, Conditions, and Prospects of the Indian Tribes of the United States*. In addition to his artistic pursuits Eastman served in the Civil War, retiring as a brigadier general in 1863.

NICK EGGENHOFER (1897–1985)

Born in the small Bavarian town of Gauting, Nick Eggenhofer spent his childhood fascinated by images he saw of the American West in German pulp magazines and in accounts of Buffalo Bill's Wild West touring Germany in the early 20th century. He immigrated to Union City, New Jersey, in 1913 and began taking night classes in drawing at Cooper Union in New York City. A few years later, while working as an apprentice at the American Lithographic Company, Eggenhofer submitted three watercolors to Street & Smith, publishers of the pulp magazine *Western Story*. This marked the beginning of his career as a western illustrator; he went on to create countless covers for *Western Story* and illustrated more than 50 books. The artist did not actually visit the West until 1925, when he drove to Santa Fe in a Model T Ford. Instead, he used scale models that he constructed in his West Milford, New Jersey, studio to prepare his illustrations. In 1961 Eggenhofer moved to Cody, Wyoming, fulfilling a lifelong dream of living in the West.

SALLY JAMES FARNHAM (1869–1943)

Artist Sally Farnham rose quickly to prominence as a sculptor of large-scale monuments, one of the few women to achieve success in this kind of work in the early 20th century. She first became interested in sculpture while traveling with her father through Europe, but it was not until she was bedridden for a time in the late 1890s that she tried her own hand at sculpting. Her husband, George Paulding Farnham, a painter and designer for Tiffany & Co., gave her some modeling materials to work with and she began experimenting. She was further encouraged by artist Frederic Remington, who was both a friend and mentor from her hometown of Ogdensburg, New York. Farnham had a lifelong love of horses, and trips to the Farnham family ranch in British Columbia inspired her to create western subjects, many featuring the horses she knew and loved so well. Farnham opened a studio and steadily began to acquire commissions—first for portraits, then for war memorials and other monuments. Her most significant public work was an equestrian sculpture of Simon Bolivar that was placed in New York's Central Park in 1921, a gift to the city from the Venezuelan government.

HENRY FARNY (1847–1916)

Henry Farny was born in Ribeauvillé, France, and immigrated to the United States with his family as a young child. They lived briefly in western Pennsylvania before settling in Cincinnati in 1859. Farny's first training came in the form of an apprenticeship to a lithographer and by the age of 18 his work was featured in *Harper's Weekly*. He studied in Italy, Germany, and Austria from 1867 to 1870 and then returned to Cincinnati to continue his commercial work. Farny made several major trips west from 1881 to 1894 and developed a strong affinity for the Native cultures of the Great Plains region. By 1890 he left his illustration work behind and, working from his field sketches in his Cincinnati studio, began producing detailed works depicting the Plains Indian way of life before the reservation period. The Plains peoples were the major focus of Farny's artwork for the next 20 years, becoming the signature work of his career.

NICOLAI FECHIN (1881–1955)

Nicolai Fechin was born in Kazan, Russia, in 1881 and showed an aptitude for art at a young age. He began his studies at the Kazan School of Art, then went on to the Imperial Academy of Art to study under Ilya Repin in 1900. Fechin focused mainly on portraiture but was also interested in painting scenes of everyday life and landscapes around his hometown. He stayed in Russia through World War I, but after the political upheaval caused by the Russian Revolution he and his family immigrated to New York in 1923 with the help of a friend, art collector W. S. Stimmel. Though he found success easily in New York, Fechin contracted tuberculosis and decided to move to the drier climate of Taos in 1927. He found that the Native people and landscapes around Taos reminded him of Kazan, and he became known for his bold and gestural works that depicted everyday life in New Mexico. He left in 1933 and eventually settled in California, but his Taos home—an adobe structure with wooden architectural details hand-carved by the artist—is now the Taos Art Museum and Fechin House.

JAMES EARLE FRASER (1876–1953)

The son of a railroad contractor, James Earle Fraser was born in Winona, Minnesota, but was soon taken to Mitchell, South Dakota, where he spent his childhood. As a teenager he began his formal training at the Art Institute of Chicago before going to Paris in 1896 to enroll at the École des Beaux-Arts. In 1898 an early model of what is now his most famous work, *End of the Trail,* was awarded a prize at

the American Art Association exhibition in Paris. Fraser had begun work on the piece while still a student in Chicago and had brought it with him to Paris. After winning the prize, Fraser began working for the American sculptor Augustus Saint-Gaudens, assisting him for two years in Paris before returning to New York with Saint-Gaudens and working for him for another two years. He taught sculpture at the Art Students League from 1907 to 1911 and then set up a permanent studio in Westport, Connecticut, in 1913. Fraser had a long career creating public sculpture throughout the country, taking commissions up until his death. He is best remembered for his 1913 design for the famous Buffalo Nickel and his monumental stucco version of *End of the Trail* that was displayed at the 1915 Panama-Pacific International Exposition in San Francisco, and is now installed at the National Cowboy & Western Heritage Museum in Oklahoma City.

NANCY GLAZIER (BORN 1947)

A native of Salt Lake City, Nancy Glazier received her first set of oil paints at the age of eight. When she was 16, her family relocated to Cody, Wyoming, where Glazier was able to study under the German muralist Adolph Spohr, who taught her the basics of painting. She soon took an interest in wildlife art. Glazier prefers to paint her subjects from life and travels around the United States visiting national parks and game preserves in search of wildlife. In 2000, the naturally right-handed artist decided to challenge herself and embarked on a series of still lifes, portraits, and seascapes that she executes with her left hand. While her wildlife paintings are characteristically done in tight focus, her left-handed work has a looser, more painterly quality that represents a new phase in her career.

WILLIAM GOLLINGS (1878–1932)

A native of Idaho, Elling William "Bill" Gollings grew up on farms in Idaho, Michigan, and New York. As a teenager he left home to travel through South Dakota and Nebraska, working as a cowboy and sheepherder. Fascinated by the work of artists who illustrated the West, particularly the illustrations of Frederic Remington, he purchased an oil painting kit from a catalogue and began learning how to paint. He eventually was able to sell enough paintings and obtain a scholarship to finance studies at the Chicago Academy of Fine Arts. He also met and studied with a number of other artists during his career, including Joseph Henry Sharp, Edward Borein, and Charles Russell. He later opened a studio in Sheridan, Wyoming, painting images of frontier life and Native American groups. He also became a talented etcher whose work was popular as illustrations and on Christmas cards.

WALT GONSKE (BORN 1942)

Born in Newark, New Jersey, Walt Gonske grew up in nearby Irvington and attended the Newark School of Fine and Industrial Arts before studying at the Frank Reilly School of Art. Reilly introduced Gonske to the work of Nicolai Fechin, who would become a major influence on his work. Gonske began a successful career in advertising in 1967 but decided to move to Taos and work as a landscape painter in 1972. He built his own studio in 1979, where he still lives and works today, and considers the move the best decision he ever made. He painted outdoors *en plein air* until he developed his "Paintmobile," a modified RV that provides shelter from the elements and allows him greater freedom and privacy while working. Gonske's landscapes capture the unique light of New Mexico and the influence of Fechin with their boldly applied paint.

VERYL GOODNIGHT (BORN 1947)

A descendant of the famous 19th-century Texas cattle rancher Charles Goodnight and his conservationist wife Mary Ann, Veryl Goodnight was raised near Denver, Colorado. She is a largely self-taught sculptor of animals who lives and works on a ranch overlooking Mesa Verde National Park. The rugged terrain provides Goodnight with many of her subjects, and she has always believed in working from live models, aiming to capture each animal's individuality in her sculptures. The conservation work of her forebears Charles and Mary Ann inspired her to create works that reference their efforts to save the buffalo from extinction. In addition she has produced many public works, the most famous being *The Day the Wall Came Down,* created to commemorate the fall of the Berlin Wall. It is permanently displayed at the George Bush Presidential Library and Museum, with a sister casting at the Allied Museum in Berlin, Germany.

MARTIN GRELLE (BORN 1954)

Martin Grelle was born and still lives in Clifton, Texas, and showed a talent for art at an early age. He was largely self-taught, but his talents were encouraged by his neighbors James Boren and Melvin Warren, members of the Cowboy Artists of America (CAA). Grelle had his first one man show in 1973 shortly after graduating from high school. He joined the ranks of his mentors when he was elected to the CAA in 1995. Like many of his fellow CAA members, Grelle places a strong emphasis on research and accuracy in his work regardless of whether his subjects are historical or contemporary. Living and working on his ranch just outside his hometown, Grelle's paintings usually depict the people and landscapes of the Southwest.

HERMAN W. HANSEN (1854–1924)

Herman Wendelborg Hansen spent his youth in his hometown of Dithmarschen, Germany, reading James Fenimore Cooper's tales of adventure in the American Frontier. At 16 he was sent to Hamburg to study painting by his father, who worked as a draftsman. Hansen went on to study in London before immigrating to America in 1877, where he found work as a commercial artist in New York and Chicago. An 1879 commission from the Chicago and North Western Railway sent Hansen west for the first time, to the Dakotas. After his return he studied at the Art Institute of Chicago from 1879 to 1882 and then settled permanently in San Francisco. He used his California base to travel throughout the Southwest and Mexico, collecting sketches to be turned into meticulously detailed paintings in his studio. His body of work deals mostly with Native American warriors, cavalrymen, and cowboys working out on the plains. He found particular success among German collectors. Much of Hansen's work was destroyed in his studio during the San Francisco Earthquake of 1906, but thanks to his popularity overseas a portion of his work has survived.

E. MARTIN HENNINGS (1886–1956)

A native of Penns Grove, New Jersey, Ernest Martin Hennings decided on a career in art after visiting the Art Institute of Chicago in 1899. He attended the Art Institute, graduating in 1904, and opted to continue his studies at the Royal Academy in Munich. While in Germany he studied under Walter Thor and Franz von Stuck, and became acquainted with fellow American artists Walter Ufer and Victor Higgins. Hennings returned to Chicago in 1914 after the outbreak of World War I and worked as a commercial artist and muralist. He traveled to Taos in 1917 under the patronage of former Chicago Mayor Carter H. Harrison and, like his contemporaries, was immediately inspired by the unique qualities of northern New Mexico. He began producing bold and colorful works that often featured the people of Taos. Hennings made Taos his permanent home in 1921 and was elected to the Taos Society of Artists in 1924. He was a part of the Society until it disbanded in 1927 and continued to live and work in Taos for the remainder of his life.

ROBERT HENRI (1865–1929)

Robert Henri was born Robert Henry Cozad in Cincinnati, Ohio, in 1865. When he was still a child, his father was accused of murder over a land dispute in the Nebraska town he founded, so his family fled and changed their names. Henri began his formal studies in 1886 at the Pennsylvania Academy of Fine Arts, then enrolled at the Académie Julian, Paris. Over the next 12 years he moved between Europe and the United States, teaching first at the Philadelphia School of Design, then establishing an art school in Paris, and by the early 1900s landing in New York. During this time he also exhibited widely, gaining an international reputation. In New York Henri's studio became a gathering place for artists, including the men who later became known as The Eight. The independent and outspoken Henri became the leader of the Ashcan School, a new movement that championed painting as a personal interpretation of an artist's experiences. Henri first visited the West when he traveled to Santa Fe, New Mexico, in 1916. There he painted a series of direct, expressive portraits of Native American sitters from the surrounding pueblos. He returned to Santa Fe over several subsequent summers.

VICTOR HIGGINS (1884–1949)

Born in rural Shelbyville, Indiana, in 1884, Victor Higgins left home at 15 to study at the Art Institute of Chicago. A friendship with Chicago Mayor Carter H. Harrison allowed him to travel to Europe and continue his studies. In the two and a half years he spent overseas, he became friends with fellow American artist Walter Ufer. A year after Higgins returned to the States, Harrison sponsored a painting trip to Taos in 1914. Ufer joined Higgins and both were struck by the quality of light and the unique landscape of the region. Higgins became a member of the Taos Society of Artists in 1917, and spent the next few years dividing his time between Taos and Chicago before making New Mexico his home in 1920. Although the Taos Society disbanded in 1927, Higgins continued to paint boldly colored images of the Southwest with a goal of producing a uniquely American art form distinct from European influence. The artist saw Taos as the perfect backdrop for this endeavor and remained there for the rest of his life.

JOHN D. HOWLAND (1843–1914)

John Dare Howland set out west from his hometown of Zanesville, Ohio, when he was just 14 years old. He eventually made it to St. Louis, where he found steamboat passage up the Missouri River. He worked as a trader with the American Fur Company on the Upper Missouri, hunting buffalo and trading with the Sioux peoples in the area. In 1858 he went to Colorado to mine gold near Pikes Peak. During the Civil War he served in the First Regimental Cavalry of Colorado Volunteers. Turning to illustration, Howland earned enough money from contributing work to *Harper's Weekly* to afford two years of study in Paris. After returning to America, he served as secretary on the Indian Peace Commission in Washington, DC from 1867 to 1869. He traveled to Paris again and then returned to the Americas to explore the Southwest and Mexico. He finally settled in Denver, where he founded the Denver Arts Club in 1886 and became best known for his paintings of bison.

GRACE HUDSON (1865–1937)

Born Grace Carpenter, the artist began her formal artistic training at the California School of Design (now San Francisco Art Institute) around the age of 15. After a brief failed marriage she returned home to Ukiah, California, opening a studio, teaching art, and assisting her father with his photography business. In 1890 she married John Hudson, a doctor for the San Francisco and North Pacific Railroad who later became an ethnographer. They shared a passionate interest in the Pomo Indians of Northern California, collecting a number of baskets and other objects. Grace Hudson began focusing on Pomo subjects in her work, eventually painting over 650 images. The exhibition of some of these paintings at the 1893 World's Columbian Exposition in Chicago brought her extensive attention and launched her national career. In addition to her California subjects, she also painted briefly in Hawaii and made sketches of Pawnee tribal members in Oklahoma Territory around 1903. Further, Hudson created illustrations for national magazines, including *Sunset* and *Cosmopolitan*.

CLARK HULINGS (1922–2011)

Born in Florida but raised in Spain and New Jersey, Clark Hulings studied at the Art Students League with Frank Reilly before attending Haverford College to earn a degree in physics. He had his first one-man show at the New Mexico Museum of Art in 1945, when he was living in Santa Fe recovering from tuberculosis. He attempted a brief career as a portrait painter in Louisiana before working as a freelance illustrator in New York in the 1950s. Hulings decided to move to Santa Fe in 1972 and devoted himself to easel painting. He created scenes from his travels all over the world but had an affinity for depicting the simplicity and dignity of a working life. Hulings became a charter member of the National Academy of Western Art in 1973 and won its first Prix de West award.

PETER HURD (1904–1984)

Peter Hurd was born and grew up in Roswell, New Mexico. He attended the US Military Academy at West Point, but resigned in 1923 and briefly attended Haverford College before traveling to Chadds Ford, Pennsylvania, hoping to study under N. C. Wyeth. Hurd studied with the famed illustrator for the next several years, marrying his eldest daughter, Henriette, in 1929 and moving back to New Mexico with her in 1931. After settling on a ranch near San Patricio, just outside Roswell, Hurd began painting colorful landscapes of the area surrounding his home, most often using watercolor and egg tempera. He also began taking commissions for murals and commercial work that included a series of military illustrations for *Life* magazine in the 1940s. Hurd was famously commissioned to paint Lyndon Johnson's official portrait in 1967, only to have it rejected by the President as "the ugliest thing" he'd ever seen. Nonetheless, Hurd lived out the rest of his life in New Mexico producing work with the region's land and people at its core.

DOUG HYDE (BORN 1946)

Doug Hyde is a sculptor of Nez Perce, Assiniboine, and Chippewa descent who was born in Hermiston, Oregon. He grew up on the Nez Perce Reservation outside Lapwai, Idaho, and attended the Institute of American Indian Arts from 1963 to 1966, where he studied under the Apache sculptor Allan Houser. He briefly attended art school in Los Angeles before enlisting in the army and serving two tours of duty in Vietnam. Hyde was injured and discharged in 1969 and returned to the Nez Perce Reservation, where he worked briefly as a tombstone cutter. He moved back to Santa Fe in 1972 and was a graduate student and instructor at the Institute of American Indian Arts until he opened his own studio in 1974. Hyde works in stone and uses a direct carving method, working without any preplanning and letting the natural features of the stone dictate the final form of the piece. His work deals with Native American stories, myths, and traditions, many of which were passed down to him by his grandfather. Hyde currently lives and works in Prescott, Arizona.

Henry Inman started his artistic career at a young age when he moved from his birthplace in Utica, New York, to New York City in 1812. There he began a seven-year-long apprenticeship with the portrait painter John Wesley Jarvis. Inman began working as a portrait painter on his own in 1822 and was immediately successful. He was a founding member of the National Academy of Design in 1826, where he served as vice president twice and exhibited every year until his death. In the early 1830s Thomas McKenney commissioned him to copy portraits of Native Americans made by Charles Bird King and James Otto Lewis. The approximately 100 copies that he completed were subsequently used to create lithographs for Thomas McKenney and James Hall's three-volume *History of the Indian Tribes of North America* (1836–44). Inman spent the remainder of his life in New York, with the exception of a brief trip to England in 1844.

HARRY JACKSON (1924–2011)

Harry Jackson spent his childhood in Chicago watching the cattlemen at the stockyards and visiting the Harding Museum to marvel at Frederic Remington's bronzes. At age 14 he ran away to work as a cowboy in Cody, Wyoming, but made return visits to Chicago to study at the Chicago Academy of Fine Arts, the Art Institute of Chicago, and the Frederick Mizen Academy. Jackson served in the Marine Corps during World War II in the Pacific Theater. After being wounded in action, he was named an official Marine Corps Combat Artist at age 20, the youngest combat artist to date. In 1944 he saw the abstract work of Jackson Pollock and was inspired to move to New York, where he befriended Pollock and showed promise as an abstract expressionist painter. His career took another turn when he traveled to Europe in the 1950s and decided to return to realism. Shortly after, he received a commission to create two mural-sized western paintings for the Buffalo Bill Historical Center (now the Buffalo Bill Center of the West) in Cody. From then on Jackson focused largely on western American sculpture and painting for the rest of his career, working from his home in Wyoming.

FRAN JENKINS (BORN 1933)

Born in British Columbia, Fran Jenkins is a sculptor of animals. She has been working with her primary medium of stone for the last 40 years, and has become adept at balancing fluidity and strength in her forms. In addition to being an artist Jenkins is also a prospector and in 2002 she located the quarry near her home in Langley, British Columbia, from which she currently mines her serpentine stone. Her work as a prospector gives her an ever greater understanding of the stone she uses in her sculptures. Jenkins has also begun creating works in clay to be cast in bronze.

FRANK TENNEY JOHNSON (1874–1939)

Frank Tenney Johnson grew up watching wagon trains head west from his home near the Overland Trail in Iowa. At the age of 14 he apprenticed with F. W. Heine, a panorama painter in Milwaukee who specialized in painting horses. In 1895 an inheritance enabled him to study at the Art Students League in New York for a brief period before returning to Milwaukee to work as a commercial artist. He later returned to New York to study at the Art Students League under Robert Henri, William Merritt Chase, and John Henry Twachtman. Johnson made his first trip to Colorado and New Mexico on a commission from *Field and Stream* in 1904, an experience that confirmed his decision to focus on western subjects. He purchased a home in Alhambra, California, in 1920 and traveled throughout the West in the 1920s and 1930s, eventually also acquiring property near Cody, Wyoming. Johnson was a highly successful illustrator of books and of magazines such as *Harper's* and *Cosmopolitan* as well as a fine artist. He was particularly known for his nocturnes—or nighttime images—of the West.

PAUL KANE (1810–1871)

Born in County Cork, Ireland, Paul Kane immigrated to Toronto, Canada, in about 1819. He was mostly self-taught and spent the early part of his career painting portraits in cities in the central United States and Canada, raising money to travel abroad and further his artistic studies. Kane left for Europe in 1841 and eventually made it to London, where he met George Catlin and saw his famous Indian Gallery for the first time. Catlin's work inspired Kane to create his own Indian Gallery for the Canadian Northwest. He returned to North America and set out on his first expedition in 1845, joining a Hudson's Bay Company expedition after being introduced to Superintendent Sir George Simpson. By 1848 Kane had traveled from Toronto to the Pacific Coast and back and had made portraits of a diverse range of Native Americans from the Great Lakes region to the territories that would become Washington and Oregon. A two-week exhibition of Kane's sketches was held at the Toronto City Hall upon his return in 1848. The artist traveled west once more to the Red River Colony in 1849, and finally published the journals of his travels as *Wanderings of an Artist Among the Indians of North America* ten years later. Kane died in his hometown of Toronto in 1871.

STEVE KESTREL (BORN 1948)

Sculptor Steve Kestrel was born in Alamogordo, New Mexico, and grew up in the southern New Mexican desert. He attended Eastern New Mexico University to study natural science and Colorado State University to study veterinary medicine. He eventually switched his major to studio art but, dissatisfied with the art instruction, he never finished his degree. Instead, he was mentored by New Mexico sculptor Boris Gilbertson. Kestrel learned the method of direct carving while working as an apprentice to Gilbertson and still uses the tools he inherited from his teacher. Today, Kestrel lives and works on his ranch in Redstone Canyon, Colorado, and many of his animal sculptures are made from rocks that he scavenges from the property. Kestrel's sculptures are distinctive because of their organic and natural forms, as he allows the final product to be informed by the characteristics of the stone. The artist also works occasionally in bronze.

CHARLES BIRD KING (1785–1862)

Charles Bird King was born in Newport, Rhode Island, in 1785 and moved to New York in 1800 to begin his formal training with the artist Edward Savage. Five years later he traveled to London to study with the American expatriate Benjamin West, returning to America in 1812. The artist eventually settled in Washington, DC in 1819, where he lived until his death. King is best known for his portraits of the Native American delegations that frequently visited Washington. He received his first commission from the Bureau of Indian Affairs in 1821–22 and continued to produce portraits for the government agency until 1842. The approximately 90 original paintings were installed in the War Department until they were moved to the newly constructed Smithsonian Institution in 1858—and were subsequently destroyed in the Smithsonian fire of 1865. His work survives, however, in the copies made by the artist Henry Inman and in King's personal copies and charcoal studies. Inman's copies of King's paintings were famously featured as lithographs in Thomas McKenney and James Hall's *History of the Indian Tribes of North America* (1836–44).

BOB KUHN (1920–2007)

Wildlife painter Bob Kuhn got his first experience drawing animals at the zoo in his hometown of Buffalo, New York. He went on to study anatomy, life drawing, and design at the Pratt Institute in Brooklyn, New York, and became a successful illustrator. Kuhn decided to devote himself to easel painting in 1970 and began traveling extensively through North America, Canada, Alaska, and even Africa to observe his animal subjects. Noted for his ability to capture both the animal and the landscape's character and individuality, Kuhn believed that painting from life was the best way to achieve a successful image. He was a member of the Society of Animal Artists and the National Academy of Western Art.

SYDNEY LAURENCE (1865–1940)

Born in Brooklyn, Sydney Laurence appears to have studied with the painter Edward Moran and was enrolled at the Art Students League in New York from 1888 to 1889. He exhibited frequently in New York and in the Paris Salons in the late 1890s and won a number of awards. From 1890 to 1904 he lived and worked in the artist colony in St. Ives, Cornwall, England, and exhibited at the Royal Society of British Arts in London among other international venues. In 1904 Laurence left his family in England and went to Alaska as a gold prospector. He began making images upon his arrival, but it was not until 1915 that he moved to Anchorage and once again established a studio. A prolific painter,

Laurence is known for his images of Alaska's frontier figures and its magnificent landscape, particularly of Mt. McKinley (now also known by its Native American name, Denali), which he painted many times.

WILLIAM R. LEIGH (1866–1955)

William Robinson Leigh was born into a West Virginia family impoverished by the Civil War. At the age of 14 he went to live with his aunt and uncle in Baltimore and studied art at the Maryland Institute. Relatives also supported his trip to Germany in 1883, where he enrolled in the Royal Academy, Munich. Leigh studied there for 12 years, returning to New York in 1896 to work as an illustrator for magazines such as *Scribner's* and *Collier's*. Though he loved western subjects he did not make his first trip west until he was 40 years old. Bartering a painting for a ticket on the Santa Fe Railroad, he made his way to the Grand Canyon. Enraptured, he shifted his focus to paintings of life in the West. He spent the remainder of his career making regular trips to the West, particularly to the Hopi and Navajo nations in Arizona.

ROBERT LOUGHEED (1910–1982)

Born on a farm in Massey, Ontario, Canada, Robert Lougheed landed his first illustration job with the *Toronto Star* when he was 19 and taking art classes at night. He moved to New York in 1935 to attend the Art Students League and studied the principles of *plein air* painting with Frank Vincent DuMond. The tenets Lougheed learned from DuMond would stay with him throughout his career, as he was always a strong believer in painting from life rather than from memory or a photograph. Lougheed found commercial success in the 1940s and 1950s creating logos like the famous red Pegasus for Mobil Oil and illustrating stories in magazines such as *National Geographic* and *Reader's Digest*. His success allowed him to spend half of each year traveling and painting. He settled in New Mexico in 1970 and produced landscapes of the Southwest and his native Canada. He was elected to the Cowboy Artists of America in 1967 and played an important role in the founding of the National Academy of Western Art in 1972.

TOM LOVELL (1909–1997)

Born in New York City, Tom Lovell began his career in illustration by making drawings for pulp magazines while attending the College of Fine Arts at Syracuse University. He earned his bachelor of arts in 1931 and by 1937 his work was appearing regularly in respected national magazines like *National Geographic, Time,* and *Life.* Lovell worked as an illustrator for four decades until 1969, when he received a commission from the Abell-Hanger Foundation to paint a series focusing on early oil extraction in West Texas. After that Lovell turned to painting western scenes full time. Like his contemporary John Clymer, Lovell placed a strong emphasis on historical accuracy and detail and employed a painstaking process of multiple rounds of research, preparatory sketches, and oil studies before beginning a final composition. He moved to Santa Fe with his family in 1975 and was elected to the Cowboy Artists of America in the same year. Lovell was also a founding member of the National Academy of Western Art and won their lifetime achievement award in 1992.

The majority of the sculptures and medals created by the artist Hermon Atkins MacNeil depict Native American figures. Trained at the Massachusetts Normal Art School in Boston and the École des Beaux-Arts and Académie Julian in Paris, MacNeil became an important sculptor as well as a teacher, instructing students in drawing and sculpture at the Art Institute of Chicago. During his work as an assistant on the architectural sculpture for the 1893 World's Columbian Exposition in Chicago, MacNeil saw Buffalo Bill's Wild West performing alongside the fair and became fascinated by the Native Americans who were part of the show. He made many sketches of the performers that became references for his later works. He subsequently made several trips to the Four Corners area of the southwestern United States, studying particularly the traditions and ceremonies of the Hopi (then called Moqui) and Zuni tribes. For much of his career MacNeil focused on Native American subjects in both small and large-scale sculptures, though a number of his late monument commissions celebrate historic Anglo-American figures.

PAUL MANSHIP (1885–1966)

A native of St. Paul, Minnesota, Paul Manship was born in 1885 and received his first artistic training in sculpture at the St. Paul School of Art and the Pennsylvania Academy of Fine Arts before winning a scholarship to study at the American Academy in Rome in 1909. While living in Europe, Manship traveled widely through Italy and Greece, and the exposure to classical Greek and Roman sculpture was a major influence on his work. After returning to America in 1912, he began producing classically influenced but simplified works that rejected the naturalism of the popular Beaux-Arts style. Manship received many public commissions in the 1930s, the most famous being his sculpture *Prometheus* at Rockefeller Center in New York City. He is probably best known for his neoclassical works but is also noted for his art deco sculptures of animals.

ED MELL (BORN 1942)

Phoenix native Ed Mell studied at Art Center College of Design in Pasadena, California, before moving to New York in 1967. There he worked as a junior art director at an ad agency for about a year before opening his own firm, Sagebrush Studios, with a friend. Mell continued to work as an illustrator in New York until he decided to move back to Phoenix in 1973 after teaching summer art classes on the Hopi Reservation in Hotevilla, Arizona. After his return to the Southwest the artist began painting landscapes and by 1979 had given up illustration completely to pursue painting full time. He began approaching the Southwest landscape in a geometric abstract style, stripping the

mesas and storm clouds he painted down to their raw angles. Mell added floral subjects to his repertoire in the 1990s and also works in bronze. He still lives and works in Phoenix, sometimes employing helicopter flights in his search for new landscapes.

ALFRED JACOB MILLER (1810–1874)

Baltimore-born Alfred Jacob Miller trained with artist Thomas Sully in Philadelphia from 1831 to 1832 before traveling to Paris to study at the École des Beaux-Arts and then on to the English Life School in Rome. After opening his studio in New Orleans in 1837, Miller was hired by Scottish Captain William Drummond Stewart to record his adventures. The artist traveled with Stewart's party along what would become the Oregon Trail to the mountain man rendezvous at the base of the Wind River Mountains in present-day Wyoming. Along the journey Miller sketched idyllic scenes of fur trappers living in harmony with both nature and Native Americans. These images would later help create a romanticized conception of the mountain man as living closely with nature. Miller returned from the rendezvous in 1838 and eventually joined Stewart at his home in Scotland, soon completing 18 large-scale oil paintings and some 200 smaller watercolors from his sketches. He spent the rest of his life creating works based on his only trip into the West, and died in Baltimore in 1874.

LANFORD MONROE (1950–2000)

Born in Bridgewater, Connecticut, in 1950, Lanford Monroe was the daughter of illustrator C. E. Monroe Jr. and his portraitist wife Betty. Monroe showed an early talent for art and spent her childhood years in the same neighborhood as western artists John Clymer and Bob Kuhn. She attended the Ringling School of Fine Art in Sarasota, Florida, after winning a Hallmark Scholarship. Monroe began her career working in watercolor but soon made the transition to oils and became known for her dramatic landscapes featuring North American wildlife. Monroe lived in many parts of the United States during the course of her career; at the time of her death she was working in a studio in Taos, New Mexico.

PETER MORAN (1841–1914)

Born in Bolton, England, Peter was the youngest of the four Moran brothers and was only three years old when his family moved to Philadelphia in 1844. He was apprenticed to the lithographers Herline and Hersel before leaving to study with his artist brothers Thomas and Edward. He then traveled to England and briefly studied with animal painter Edwin Landseer, but left because he was disappointed in Landseer's work. In 1864, seven years before his more famous brother Thomas's first trip to Yellowstone, Peter traveled to New Mexico. He visited again when he joined Captain Bourke on his ethnographic trip to the Pueblo Indians of the Southwest in 1881. In addition, he was a government agent and illustrated the census report *Indians Taxed and Indians Not Taxed* concerning the Shoshone Agency in Wyoming in

1890. Peter painted in watercolor and oil and made etchings, preferring animal subjects to landscapes. French painter Rosa Bonheur was a strong influence on his work.

THOMAS MORAN (1837–1926)

A native of Bolton, England, Thomas Moran moved to Philadelphia with his family in 1844 where he received his first training as an apprentice to a wood engraver. In 1871 he joined Ferdinand V. Hayden's government survey expedition to the Yellowstone region and traveled west for the first time. On the trip he became a close friend of photographer William H. Jackson and the two worked together to produce some of the first images of Yellowstone. Moran's detailed sketches were the first color images of the region and along with Jackson's photographs were instrumental in preserving Yellowstone as the country's first national park in 1872. After returning east, Moran completed his first major western painting, *Grand Canyon of the Yellowstone*, which was purchased by Congress in 1872. He went west again in 1873, this time accompanying Major John Wesley Powell to explore the Colorado River. He would become known for his immense, highly detailed canvases, many created in his Long Island studio. Moran made several other journeys west throughout his career and continued to paint well into his 80s.

JOHN NIETO (BORN 1936)

John Nieto was born in Denver but grew up outside Roswell, New Mexico, near the Apache Reservation. He studied fine art at Southern Methodist University in Dallas and earned a degree in 1959. After graduating he traveled to Paris where he was particularly struck by the boldly colored works of fauve painters like Henri Matisse and André Derain. Nieto's encounter with the fauves would prove to have a lifelong effect on his work and when he returned to the States he resolved to paint his native Southwest culture using a vibrant palette and modern forms. Nieto still produces works depicting Native American figures and southwestern themes. He has exhibited work both in the United States and internationally and his canvases are immediately recognizable for their large size, striking use of color, and graphic compositions.

GEORGIA O'KEEFFE (1887–1986)

One of the most celebrated modernists of the last century, Georgia O'Keeffe was born in Sun Prairie, Wisconsin, and studied at the Art Institute of Chicago and the Art Students League in New York. In 1916 her work was seen by photographer and gallerist Alfred Stieglitz, who encouraged her to pursue painting and introduced her to his circle of New York modernists, which included painters such as Marsden Hartley and Charles Demuth. Stieglitz gave O'Keeffe her first one-person show at his gallery in 1917, and the pair married in 1924. O'Keeffe became famous for the boldly colored, simplified abstractions of landscape and floral subjects that she often produced in series. Her career took a major turn during her first extended visit to New Mexico in 1929, when she found new inspiration in the arid landscape bathed in a rich light and scattered with scrubby vegetation and animal bones. After that 1929 trip she visited New Mexico almost yearly. After Stieglitz died in 1946 and she had settled his estate, she made it her permanent home in 1949. O'Keeffe's career spanned seven decades and she produced some 900 paintings. She lived near Santa Fe until her death in 1986.

EDGAR S. PAXSON (1852–1919)

Born in East Hamburg, New York, in 1852, Edgar S. Paxson never received formal artistic training. Instead, he attended the Friend's Institute School before going to work as a carriage and sign painter for his father, who was a carriage builder. Paxson set out west in 1875 and arrived in Deer Lodge, Montana, one year after the Battle of Little Big Horn in 1877. There he worked as a sign and scenery painter until moving to Butte in 1881. In Butte he continued his commercial work but also set up a studio and began painting Native American portraits and historical subjects. He completed his best known painting, *Custer's Last Stand*, in 1899. Paxson had spent years gathering information for the colossal work, interviewing Native Americans and US soldiers who had been near the battle. He moved to Missoula in 1906, where he lived until his death in 1919. He was commissioned to paint six historical scenes for the Montana State Capitol in 1911 and eight more history paintings for the Missoula County Courthouse in 1912.

BERT GEER PHILLIPS (1868–1956)

A native of Hudson, New York, Bert Phillips was fascinated by stories of the West from childhood. In his mid-teens he began his art training in New York at the Art Students League and the National Academy of Design. For several years he had a studio in New York before traveling to England and then to France to enroll at the Académie Julian in Paris. There the artist Joseph Henry Sharp told him about New Mexico, and in 1898 he made his first trip there with the painter Ernest Blumenschein. Phillips was immediately enchanted and permanently relocated to Taos, becoming the first of the Taos Society artists to settle there. Phillips was later instrumental in the formation of the Taos Society of Artists in 1915 and became well known for his idyllic images of Native American life. He also enjoyed success as a western illustrator and throughout his career painted a number of murals in New Mexico, Iowa, Arizona, and Missouri.

ALEXANDER PHIMISTER PROCTOR (1860–1950)

The sculptor Alexander Phimister Proctor was born in Bosanquet, Ontario, Canada, but grew up in Denver. He spent much of his youth exploring and hunting in the wilderness of the Rocky Mountains. He began his artistic training in earnest when he moved to New York in 1885 and studied at the National Academy of Design and the Art Students League. Proctor's work first gained national recognition when he was commissioned to sculpt life-size animals and equestrian monuments to decorate the grounds of the 1893 World's Columbian Exposition in Chicago. That same year he traveled to France and met the sculptor Augustus Saint-Gaudens. He would later work as an assistant on Saint-Gaudens's equestrian Civil War memorials in Chicago and New York. Proctor continued to work well into his 80s and completed numerous monumental and small-scale commissions depicting western and animal subjects.

WILLIAM RANNEY (1813–1857)

William Tylee Ranney was born in Middletown, Connecticut, and moved to Brooklyn in 1834 to study art. He stayed there until 1836, when he traveled to Texas to fight in the Texas War of Independence. Ranney arrived just days after the Texian Army's decisive victory over Mexican forces at the Battle of San Jacinto. He enlisted anyway, but served for less than a year. While in Texas he made sketches of people and scenery that he would use in his paintings upon returning to the East. In the mid 1840s Ranney began producing scenes of frontiersmen and later became known for his images of trappers and use of narrative. In 1853 the artist constructed a frontier-style home and studio in West Hoboken, New Jersey, complete with a stable to house the horses that he used as models in his western paintings. Ranney remained there until his death from tuberculosis in 1857.

KEVIN RED STAR (BORN 1943)

Kevin Red Star was born into an artistic family in Lodge Grass, on the Crow Nation in Montana. His father was a musician and federal police officer and his mother practiced traditional Crow beadwork. In 1962 Red Star was recruited to be a part of the inaugural class at the Institute of American Indian Arts in Santa Fe. He studied under James McGrath for three years and then earned a scholarship to the Art Institute in San Francisco, where he was exposed to the West Coast art scene. Red Star began compiling an archive of photos and a written history of the Crow people to use in portraits that explore the Crow collective heritage and identity. His artwork is frequently inspired by historic images of the Crow people, and his images are immediately recognizable for their bright colors and strong forms. Red Star works in many mediums including oil, acrylic, ink, and collage.

FREDERIC REMINGTON (1861–1909)

An East Coast native, Frederic Remington was born in Canton, New York, in 1861 and studied art at Yale University from 1878 to 1879. He traveled west to Montana Territory in 1881, and tried his hand at sheep ranching in Kansas in 1883. Although he failed at sheep ranching, his sketches of the West soon began appearing regularly in national magazines such as *Harper's Weekly* and *Scribner's.* In addition to being a prolific painter and sculptor, the artist was also a writer. By the time of his death in 1909 at age 48 he had written two novels, several short stories, and hundreds of magazine articles. While he began in illustration, Remington made a concerted effort to be recognized as a well-rounded artist, exhibiting paintings with the National Academy of Design, and casting sculptures in bronze starting in 1895. Although he made his permanent home in the East, Remington traveled to the West regularly to make new sketches for his work. His images of the western United States played a major role in shaping perceptions of the myth of the West in the American imagination.

KENNETH RILEY (BORN 1919)

Kenneth Riley was born in Waverly, Missouri, and began his studies at the Kansas City Art Institute under Thomas Hart Benton. He continued on to New York City, where he took classes at the Art Students League during the day and the Grand Central School of Art at night. After serving as a combat artist during World War II, Riley enjoyed a successful career as an illustrator for 25 years with his work appearing in *National Geographic, Life,* and the *Saturday Evening Post.* He was commissioned by the National Park Service to paint Yellowstone and Grand Teton National Parks in the late 1960s and from that point on devoted himself solely to paintings of the American West. He began with a broad focus on western history, and soon developed a particular interest in depicting Plains Indian cultures, using bold compositions and bright colors in his work. He moved to Tucson in 1973.

PETER RINDISBACHER (1806–1834)

Swiss immigrant Peter Rindisbacher was one of the earliest artists of European descent to record life on the American and Canadian frontiers. He was mostly self-taught with the exception of a brief stint with Swiss painter Jacob Weibel during his childhood in the Canton of Berne, Switzerland. Rindisbacher and his family immigrated to the Red River Colony in present-day Manitoba in 1821. The young artist recorded the entire journey through sketches, including the Inuit people who came to greet them at Resolution Island. The family remained at the Red River Colony until a flood drove them south to Wisconsin in 1826. Rindisbacher continued painting life on the Frontier, moving to St. Louis in 1829, where he produced drawings for the *American Turf Register and Sporting Magazine.* He died in St. Louis at the age of 28. At least two of his works were featured as lithographs in McKenney and Hall's *History of the Indian Tribes of North America* (1836–44).

JULIUS ROLSHOVEN (1858–1930)

Julius Rolshoven was born in Detroit, Michigan, and went to New York in 1876 to study at Cooper Union. He soon left New York for Germany and studied at the Düsseldorf Academy and the Royal Academy in Munich, then studied in Germany and Italy under American painter Frank Duveneck. Rolshoven remained in Europe traveling and exhibiting work until the start of World War I. He returned to the States, coming to northern New Mexico in 1916, where he began painting Native American portraits and scenes of the region. Many of

Rolshoven's works were staged inside a tent that he erected outside his studio because he found the southwestern light too harsh, preferring the soft, filtered light the tent provided. He remained in New Mexico until around 1920, splitting his time between Taos and Santa Fe. He was elected as an associate member of the Taos Society of Artists in 1917 and an active member in 1918.

CARL RUNGIUS (1869–1959)

Born into a German family of taxidermists and hunters, Carl Rungius grew up with an early interest in wildlife imagery. He studied art in Berlin between 1888 and 1890. An uncle invited him on a moose hunting trip to Maine in 1894 and from there Rungius traveled to Wyoming, where he was captivated by the grandeur and wildlife of the West. He decided to settle in the United States, basing himself in New York City as a magazine illustrator and making regular trips west during the summers. He gradually shifted his focus to fine art, specializing in images of the big game animals and landscapes of the West and making regular visits to Montana, Wyoming, and the Yukon to paint and hunt. His favorite spot became the Canadian Rockies, where he had a summer studio near Banff, Alberta. Rungius became involved in the early American conservation movement, joining the Boone and Crockett Club in the 1920s.

CHARLES M. RUSSELL (1864–1926)

Born in St. Louis in 1864, Charles Marion Russell was just 16 when he moved to Montana Territory, where he found work as a night wrangler for various Montana cattle outfits. In the late 1880s he began working as an illustrator, publishing images in magazines including *Harper's* and *Frank Leslie's Illustrated Newspaper*. He began painting full time in 1893, establishing a studio in Great Falls, Montana. Russell's first-hand experiences with both the cowboys and the Native Americans of the region became the core of his work. In 1904 he lived in New York City for several months, spending time in the studios of fellow artists and receiving advice from art editors at leading periodicals. This informal training in New York transformed his career and greatly refined his painting techniques. Throughout his life, much of Russell's commercial success can be attributed to his wife Nancy Cooper Russell, who became his business manager. After 1919, the couple spent their winters in Pasadena, California, befriending western film stars and art enthusiasts in Hollywood. After Russell's death in Great Falls in 1926, Nancy continued to promote his artwork and legacy for the rest of her life.

BIRGER SANDZÉN (1871–1954)

Sven Birger Sandzén was born in Bildsberg, Sweden. He graduated from the College of Skara in 1890, then studied further at the University of Lund, the Stockholm Artist's League, and later in Paris. A well-rounded scholar with an interest not only in art but also art history, aesthetics, and French, in 1894 he was hired as a professor at Bethany College in Lindsborg, Kansas, where he taught for 50 years. Sandzén made his first trip to Colorado in 1908, later visiting the area around Colorado Springs and returning there almost every subsequent summer. He also visited Santa Fe and Taos, becoming an associate member of the Taos Society of Artists in 1922. Sandzén was a prolific painter who also worked with printmaking, creating block prints, lithographs, and dry points. During the 1930s and early 1940s he also painted several post office murals under the Federal Art Project. Sandzén's favorite subjects were western landscapes.

BILL SCHENCK (BORN 1947)

Bill Schenck was born near Columbus, Ohio, and attended the Columbus College of Art and Design from 1965 to 1967. He came into contact with pop art when he took a spring break trip to New York in 1966 and met Andy Warhol's Factory crowd. After his return to Columbus, Schenck transferred to the Kansas City Art Institute in 1967, finding it a better fit for his unconventional style. He moved to the Soho area in New York City after earning a bachelor of fine arts in 1969 and began making photorealist works with a pop aesthetic using film stills from western b-movies. Schenck gained recognition in the New York art scene with these works, which connect the world of pop art with the myth of the West. After his success in New York, Schenck moved to Arizona and Wyoming, collecting a wide variety of imagery to use in his work. He spearheaded a "pop western" subgenre and strives to continually challenge myths and preconceptions about the American West in his work. Schenck lives and works at his home—the Double Standard Ranch—outside Santa Fe, and when he is not painting he competes as a rodeo rider in ranch sorting events under the name Billy Famous.

CHARLES SCHREYVOGEL (1861–1912)

Born in New York City to German immigrants, Charles Schreyvogel spent his early years working as an apprentice in lithography and attending classes at the Newark Art League. In 1886 he traveled to Munich to continue his studies, staying for three years. Upon his return to New York, Schreyvogel met and befriended William F. "Buffalo Bill" Cody and began sketching the cowboys, cavalry, and Native Americans who performed in Buffalo Bill's Wild West. The artist traveled west for the first time in 1893, visiting Arizona and the Ute reservation in Colorado. It was there he developed an interest in cavalry subjects, particularly past skirmishes on the Great Plains. Schreyvogel traveled west repeatedly in the 1890s and began producing highly detailed images of western battles. He first gained national recognition in 1900, when his painting *My Bunkie* was included in the National Academy of Design's annual exhibition. He continued to paint western subjects and experimented with sculpture in his Hoboken, New Jersey, studio until his death in 1912.

Olaf Seltzer was born in Copenhagen, Denmark. His drawing ability was noted by his instructors and he enrolled at the age of 12 in a preparatory art school for the Danish Royal Academy. In the early 1890s he immigrated to the United States with his mother, settling in Great Falls, Montana, where he first found work breaking horses and then became a machinist for the Great Northern Railway, sketching and painting in his free time. Seltzer became friends with painter Charles Russell, who also lived in Great Falls, and was mentored and influenced by the older artist. By the early 1900s Seltzer began working in oil, painting images of wildlife and imagined scenes of cowboy life. He later completed a group of Russell's paintings left incomplete upon Russell's death. Seltzer's most notable commission was a group of 100 miniature watercolors of Montana history for a New York collector. A highly prolific artist, Seltzer created over 2,500 works during his lifetime.

JOSEPH HENRY SHARP (1859–1953)

Born and raised in Ohio, Joseph Henry Sharp studied art in Cincinnati under Henry Farny and Frank Duveneck, and continued his education in Antwerp, Munich, and Paris in the 1880s and 1890s. On Farny's recommendation he visited the Southwest in 1883 and again in 1893, painting the Pueblo cultures of the region. While studying at the Académie Julian in Paris in 1895, he convinced fellow American painters Ernest Blumenschein and Bert Phillips to visit New Mexico for inspiration. Sharp made a permanent move to the West in 1902, to Crow Agency, Montana. There he hand-built a log cabin home, which was published as an example of ideal American design in the *Craftsman* magazine in 1906. He initially divided his time between Montana and Taos, New Mexico, alternately painting the Native peoples of the northern plains and the Taos Pueblo. After 1910, he made Taos his permanent residence, and in 1915 he helped found the Taos Society of Artists together with Blumenschein and Phillips. As one of the oldest members of the society and the first of the group to visit the area, today Sharp is recognized for his role in helping establish Taos as an important arts center in the Southwest.

HENRY MERWIN SHRADY (1871–1922)

Born in New York City and trained as a lawyer, Henry Shrady began drawing during his convalescence from typhoid. He started by sketching his pets and horses, then turned to animals in the Bronx Zoo, and later to specimens in the American Museum of Natural History. He then tried watercolor painting and had several works accepted and sold from exhibitions at the National Academy of Design. Ultimately, however, it was sculpture that caught his attention. A jeweler and producer of small bronzes saw one of Shrady's designs and offered to cast it. Shrady's earliest sculptures, cast in 1900, became the first in an extensive series and were among the first American bronzes to be created by the lost-wax process. In 1901, the sculptor Karl Bitter asked Shrady to create some of the large-scale plaster sculptures for the Pan-American Exposition in Buffalo, New York, the start of a series of commissions for monuments commemorating important American historical figures. That same year he won his largest commission, which extended over 20 years—the memorial to General Ulysses S. Grant on the edge of the Capitol Basin on the National Mall in Washington, DC.

ROGUE GUIREY SIMPSON (1943–2005)

Named for her grandmother's nickname, Rogue Guirey Simpson was born in Arizona and studied art at the University of Arizona in Tucson. She worked briefly as a commercial artist in San Francisco before moving to Vail, Colorado. Known for her sensitive wildlife paintings, Simpson preferred to observe her subjects in their natural habitat, collecting sketches and photos for use when painting in her studio. She made annual trips to Yellowstone and Grand Teton national parks, backpacking or traveling on horseback into the backcountry where she could observe wildlife in the wilderness firsthand. Simpson was a founding member of American Women Artists, an organization dedicated to the inspiration and encouragement of women in the visual arts.

MIAN SITU (BORN 1953)

Mian Situ was born in Canton, China, now known as Guangdong Province. He received his artistic training there, earning a bachelor and a master of fine arts from the Guangzhou Academy of Fine Arts. He went on to teach at the Academy for six years. Situ's style mixes realism and traditional European painting techniques. He lived in Canada for 10 years before moving to the United States in 1998. He is best known for his depictions of life in rural China, having spent much of his career traveling around rural villages in an effort to depict and preserve their fast-fading traditional ways of life and dress. In recent years the focus of his work has shifted to California landscapes and images of the Chinese immigrant experience in the historic American West. Situ uses the same attention to historical detail in these newer works and has gained much recognition for his western American paintings.

TUCKER SMITH (BORN 1940)

Tucker Smith lived on a farm outside his birthplace of St. Paul, Minnesota, until his family moved to Pinedale, Wyoming, when he was 12. He began drawing as a child and minored in art when he attended the University of Wyoming. At the time he did not see art as a realistic career choice and graduated with a bachelor of science in math in 1963. He worked as a computer programmer and systems analyst for the state until 1971, when he realized that his passion was art and decided to pursue painting full time. Smith is known for his wildlife paintings but also produces landscapes. He often combs the backcountry near his home in western Wyoming looking for new subjects, believing it is important to depict animals in their natural habitat.

Smith's work places a strong emphasis on the quality of light and he carefully depicts subtle differences caused by the seasons and time of day.

JOHN MIX STANLEY (1814–1872)

John Mix Stanley was born in Canandaigua, New York. He moved to Detroit in 1834 and began studying art under James Bowman, with whom he eventually partnered in a portrait-painting venture. On a visit to Baltimore around 1837 he saw George Catlin's Indian Gallery, and was inspired to create his own gallery of Native American portraits. Stanley made trips west to Oklahoma in 1842 and Texas in 1843. He was appointed draftsman to Colonel Stephen Watts Kearny's Army of the West in 1846 and traveled with them from Santa Fe to San Diego. Stanley worked in California, Oregon, and Washington in 1847 and 1848 and then sailed to Hawaii. Stanley is most famous for his group of over 150 Native American portraits, which he first exhibited as Stanley's Indian Gallery in New York in 1850. Three years later, he served as chief artist for the Pacific Railroad Survey led by Isaac Stevens, illustrating the route that later became the Northern Pacific Railway. The artist's collection of Native American portraits was on loan to the Smithsonian when it caught fire in 1865 and much of his work was destroyed. More of his collection was destroyed in a subsequent fire at P. T. Barnum's American Museum in New York. By the time of his death in 1872, fewer than 300 of his artworks are known to have survived.

JUNIUS BRUTUS STEARNS (1810–1885)

Junius Brutus Stearns was born in Arlington, Vermont, and later moved to New York. Initially he worked as a portrait painter, but as the demand for portraits took a downturn owing to the invention of the daguerreotype, Stearns began to take a stronger interest in history painting. He lived his whole life in the East except for a three-year stint in Europe starting in 1847, when he traveled to London, Paris, and Rome to study the work of the Old Masters. Stearns is probably best known for his five-part series depicting the life of George Washington, which he began in the late 1840s. He was also very active in the National Academy of Design in New York City, gaining admittance in 1849 and later serving as recording secretary. Stearns focused on scenes of daily life later in his career until his death from injuries suffered in a carriage accident near his home in Brooklyn in 1885.

GILBERT STUART (1755–1828)

Born in what is today Saunderstown, Rhode Island, Gilbert Stuart spent much of his early career in Europe. He studied with the American portrait painter Benjamin West in London from 1777 to 1782 and then moved to Dublin in 1787. There he painted the wealthy Protestant minority before returning to America in 1793, hoping to paint George Washington. He obtained his first sitting with the President after moving to Philadelphia in 1795, followed by additional sittings in 1796. Stuart based all of his subsequent images of Washington on these sessions. The artist lived briefly in Washington, DC starting in 1803, continuing to paint portraits of politically prominent individuals before moving to Boston in 1805, where he lived the rest of his life. Although he created over a thousand portraits during his career and painted well-known Americans such as James Madison and Thomas Jefferson, Stuart is best remembered for his images of Washington.

HOWARD TERPNING (BORN 1927)

Howard Terpning was born in Oak Park, Illinois. He postponed his higher education to serve in the Marine Corps from 1945 through 1946. Following his military service, he studied figure painting at the American Academy of Art in Chicago and then spent the next 25 years working as a successful commercial artist in Chicago and New York. He gave up commercial work in the 1970s and moved to Tucson, where he began producing historic images of Plains Indian cultures. Terpning was elected to the Cowboy Artists of America and the National Academy of Western Art in 1979. He lives and works north of Tucson, and the people of the Great Plains are still the main focus of his paintings.

WALTER UFER (1876–1936)

Walter Ufer showed an early talent for art and with his family's encouragement became an apprentice at a lithography firm in his hometown of Louisville, Kentucky. In the 1890s he went to Germany to study in Hamburg and Dresden, returning briefly to Chicago, then resuming his studies in Munich. From Germany he traveled to France, Italy, and North Africa, eventually returning to the United States and settling in Chicago, where he worked as an illustrator and portrait painter. In 1914 a group of patrons including Chicago Mayor Carter Harrison, Jr., sponsored Ufer's travel to the Southwest and covered his expenses for several subsequent trips. In 1917 he became a member of the Taos Society of Artists and made Taos, New Mexico, his permanent home. Like the other Society artists he focused on scenes in and around Taos, particularly the day-to-day life of the Taos Pueblo Indians. Ufer was an active Socialist and supporter of Leon Trotsky, and his images of Native Americans often subtly reference his view of their oppression by Anglo society.

CURT WALTERS (BORN 1950)

Curt Walters grew up in New Mexico and is a modern *plein air* impressionist painter. Though he has traveled extensively and painted landscapes both in the United States and internationally, Walters is best known for his images of the Grand Canyon. He first visited the canyon when he was 19 and it has since become the major focus of his career. Returning to the canyon year after year, Walters was surprised to see that his paintings recorded increasing air pollution over a period of several years. He subsequently became a conservation activist, fighting to reduce pollution and protect the areas around the canyon.

Walters began working with the Grand Canyon Trust in the 1990s, helping them to raise funds by donating artwork. Walters lives and works in Sedona, Arizona, where he uses field studies to create large-scale, strikingly detailed landscapes.

CARL FERDINAND WIMAR (1828–1862)

Carl Ferdinand Wimar was born in Siegburg, Germany, in 1828 and moved to St. Louis with his mother in 1844. He studied under French artist Leon Pomarede and opened his own studio in St. Louis around 1850. Wimar left St. Louis for Düsseldorf in 1852, where he studied with the painter Emanuel Leutze alongside other American artists such as Albert Bierstadt. The work Wimar produced in Germany combined traditional European history painting with subjects from the American West, and he often chose to depict sensational, imagined scenes of confrontations between Native Americans and Anglo settlers. He returned to St. Louis in 1856 and journeyed west for the first time, traveling up the Missouri River in 1858 and 1859, collecting sketches and photographs of Native Americans. After Wimar actually came into contact with Native Americans his subjects became less romanticized and he focused more on the changing landscape and the effects that European colonization had on Native cultures.

N. C. WYETH (1882–1945)

Newell Convers Wyeth was born in Needham, Massachusetts, in 1882 and first studied art at the Eric Pape School of Art in Boston. He then went on to the Howard Pyle School of Art, where Pyle became a major influence on Wyeth's painting. After his first *Saturday Evening Post* cover in 1903, Wyeth traveled west in 1904 to gain firsthand experience to use in his illustrations, a tenet Pyle had instilled in him. On his first trip to Arizona and Colorado, he visited Native American reservations and participated in cowboy roundups. He returned in 1906 to sketch mining operations in Colorado. His images of the West appeared regularly in national magazines like *Harper's Monthly* and *Ladies' Home Journal,* and he also illustrated a series of famous novels for *Scribner's.* He gained financial security through his success in illustration and was able to devote more time to painting at his studio in Chadds Ford, Pennsylvania.

PACO YOUNG (1958–2005)

Paco Young was born in Biloxi, Mississippi, in 1958 and spent his formative years in Nashville, Tennessee. He studied at the Memphis College of Art and earned a bachelor of fine arts in 1981. Young was mainly a wildlife painter and spent the years after graduation traveling around the United States painting with his wife. In 1994 they settled in Bozeman, Montana, where Young continued to paint the regional wildlife. Many of his works were reproduced as prints and are used by organizations like the Rocky Mountain Elk Foundation and the National Rifle Association to raise money for wildlife conservation. In 2001 Young was commissioned by the National Park Service to paint

Yellowstone's most famous geyser, and his work *Old Faithful* is now a permanent installation in the historic Old Faithful Inn inside Yellowstone National Park. Young passed away in Bozeman in 2005.

EUSTACE PAUL ZIEGLER (1881–1969)

Eustace Paul Ziegler was the son of an Episcopal priest and harbored a desire to be an artist. He received formal training in his hometown at the Detroit Museum of Art before he traveled to Alaska in 1909 to work at the Episcopal Mission in Cordova. Though his main purpose in the territory was to serve as missionary, he also continued painting, starting with religious scenes but soon moving to images of the landscape and of Native Alaskans, fishermen, miners, and construction workers. Affectionately known as "Zieg," he became known for his depictions of life on the Alaskan frontier. He moved to New Haven briefly in 1920 and studied with William Sergeant Kendall at Yale before returning to Cordova. Ziegler and his family moved to Seattle in 1924 after he accepted a commission to paint murals in the offices of the Alaska Steamship Company. He remained in Seattle for the rest of his life and helped found the Puget Sound Group of Northwest Painters.

ADDITIONAL WORKS FROM THE COLLECTION

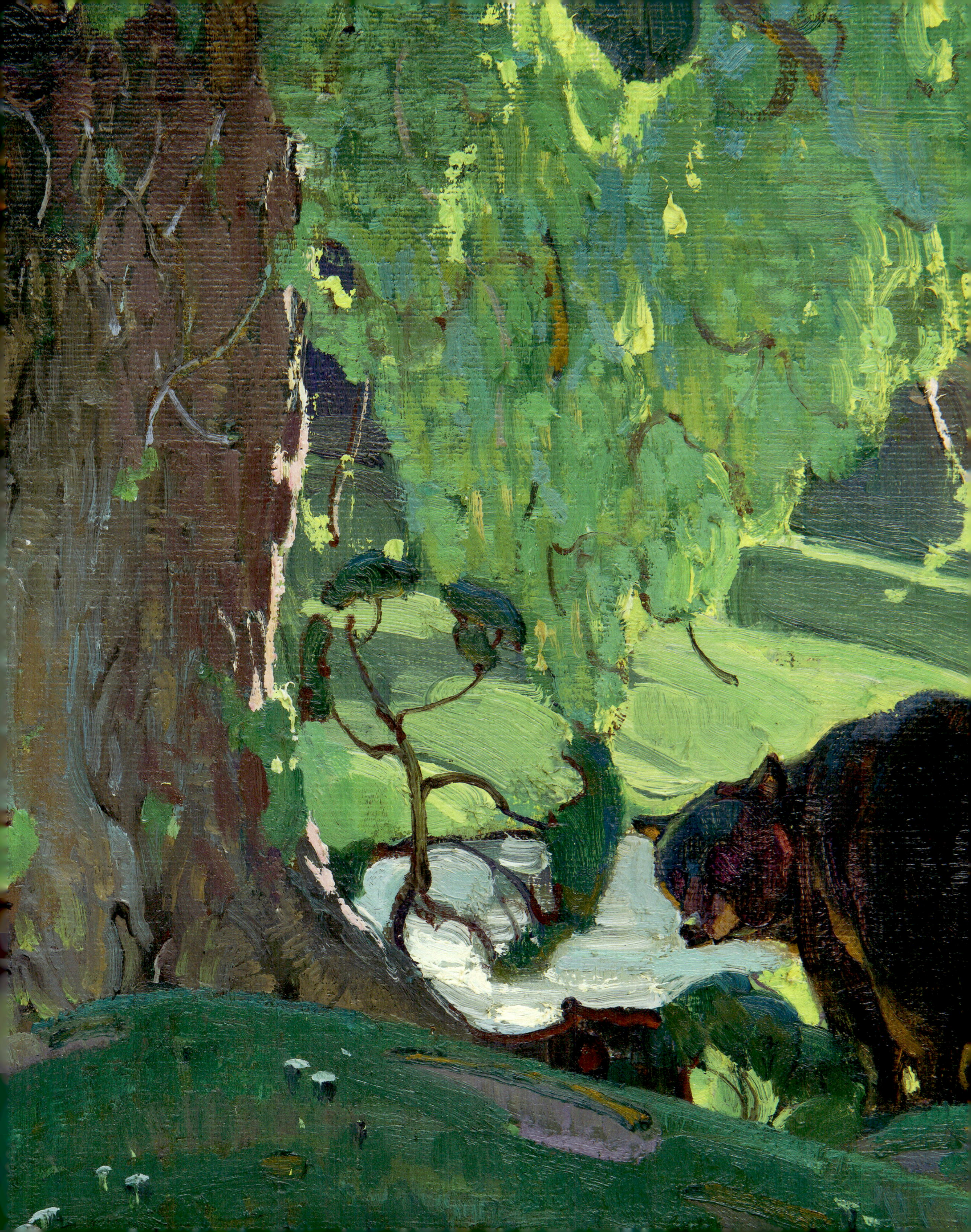

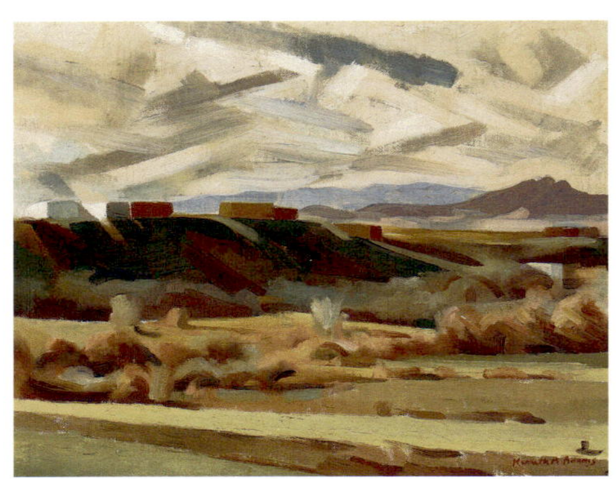

KENNETH M. ADAMS (1897–1966)
Ranchos de Taos, circa 1925
Oil on board
12½ × 16¼ inches

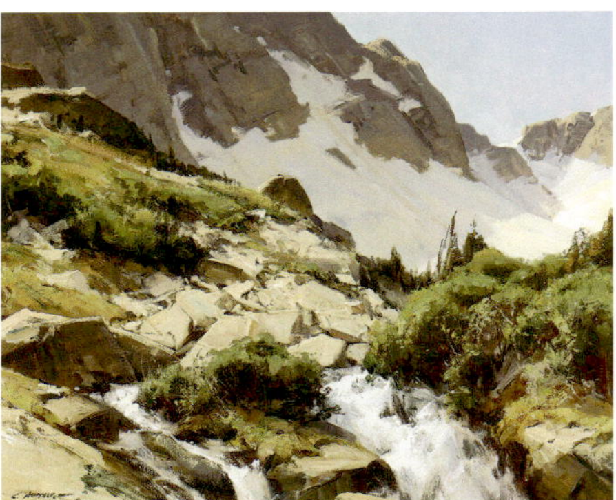

CLYDE ASPEVIG (BORN 1951)
Glacier Fed, 1995
Oil on canvas
24 × 30 inches

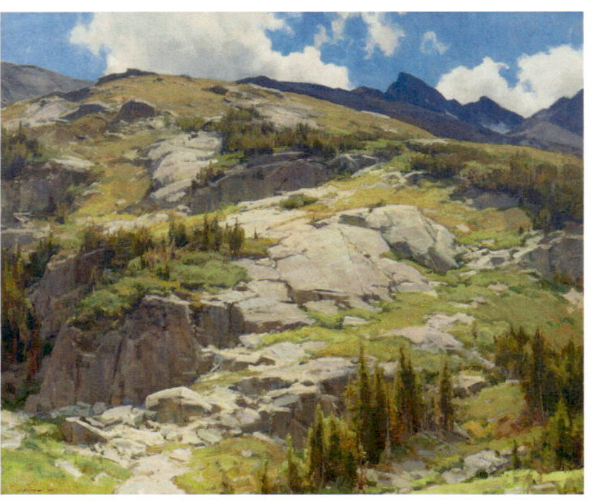

CLYDE ASPEVIG (BORN 1951)
On the Way to Heaven, 1995
Oil on canvas
50 × 60 inches

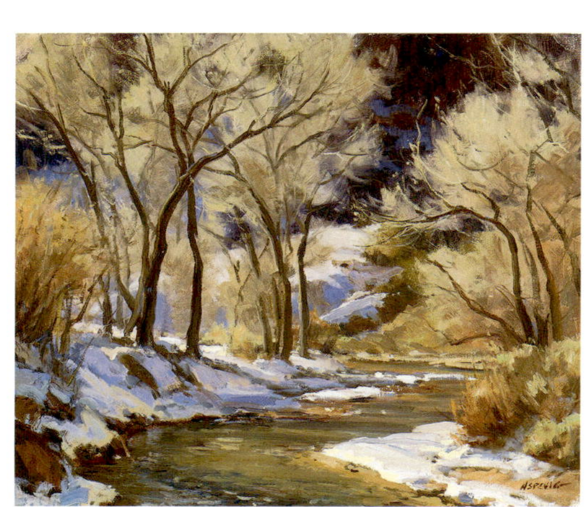

CLYDE ASPEVIG (BORN 1951)
Virgin River, circa 1995
Oil on canvas
20 × 24 inches

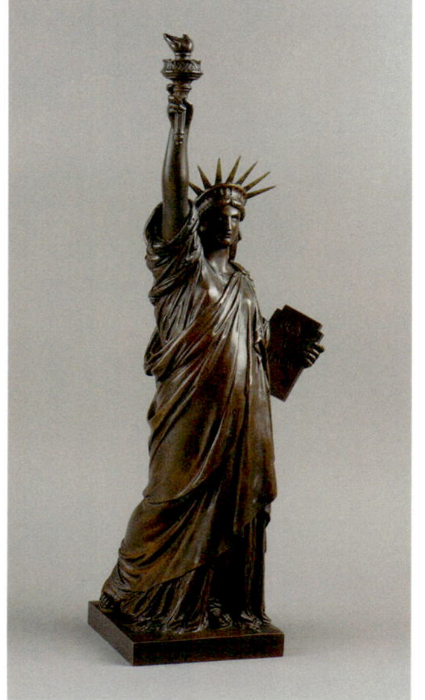

FRÉDÉRIC AUGUSTE BARTHOLDI
(1834–1904)
Liberty Enlightening the World,
modeled 1884; cast 1906–20
Bronze
20⅞ × 8½ × 6½ inches

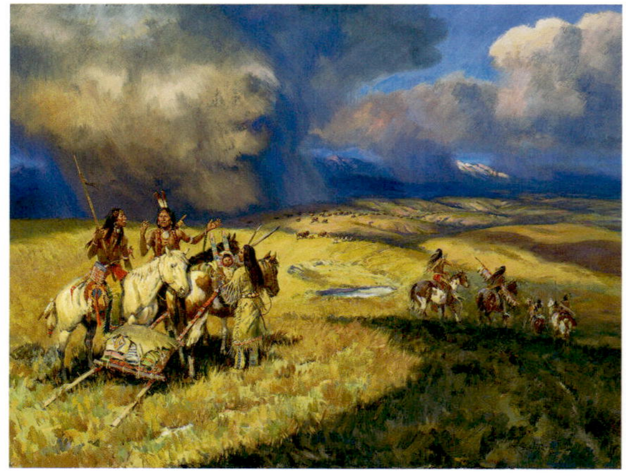

JOE BEELER (1931–2006)
In the Land of Plenty, 1993
Oil on canvas
30 × 40 inches

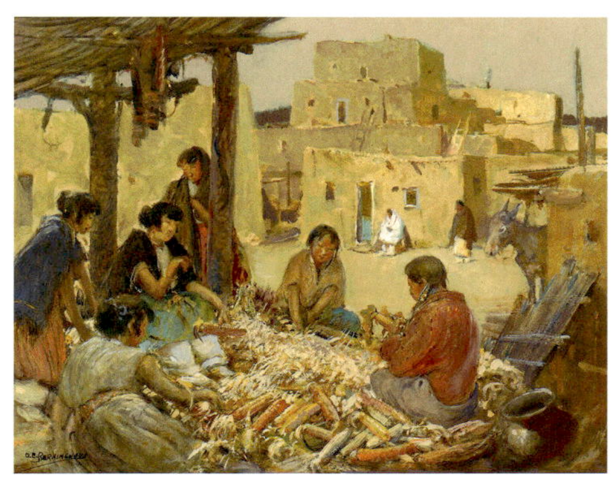

OSCAR E. BERNINGHAUS (1874–1952)
Autumn Bounty, circa 1945
Oil on board
12⅛ × 16 inches

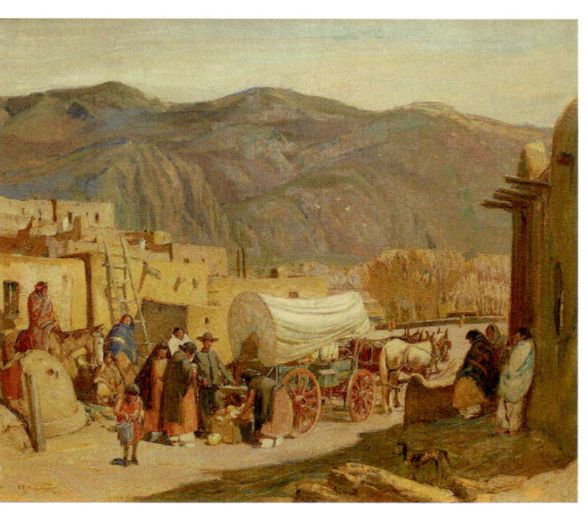

OSCAR E. BERNINGHAUS (1874–1952)
Market Place in Taos, circa 1945
Oil on canvas
25 × 30 inches

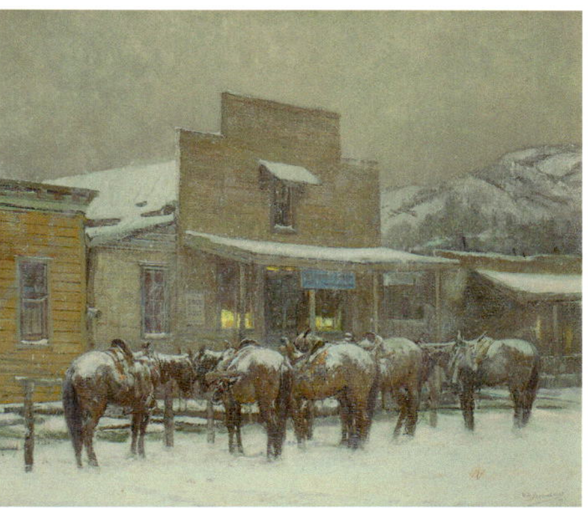

OSCAR E. BERNINGHAUS (1874–1952)
Horses at Hitching Post, 1948
Oil on canvas
20 × 24⅛ inches

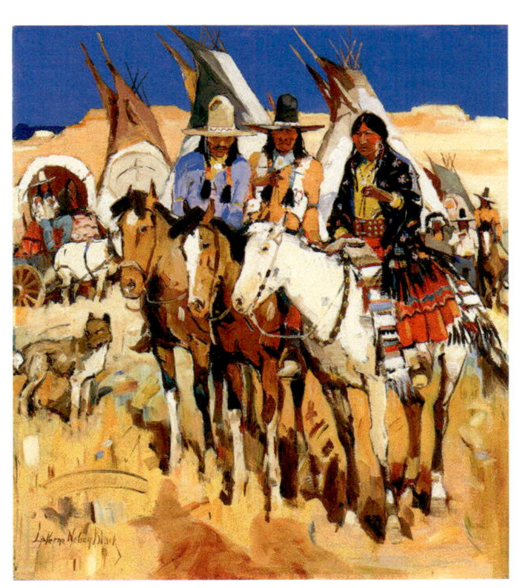

LAVERNE NELSON BLACK (1887–1938)
Apache Indian Encampment, circa 1930
Oil on canvas
22 × 20 inches

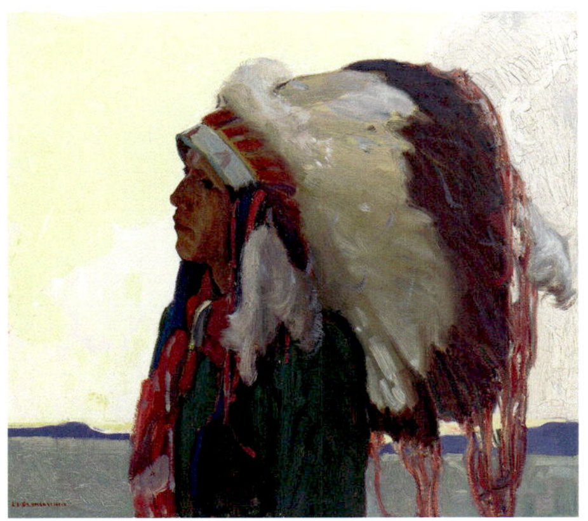

ERNEST L. BLUMENSCHEIN (1874–1960)
Taos Indian Chief, circa 1915
Oil on canvas
14½ × 16½ inches

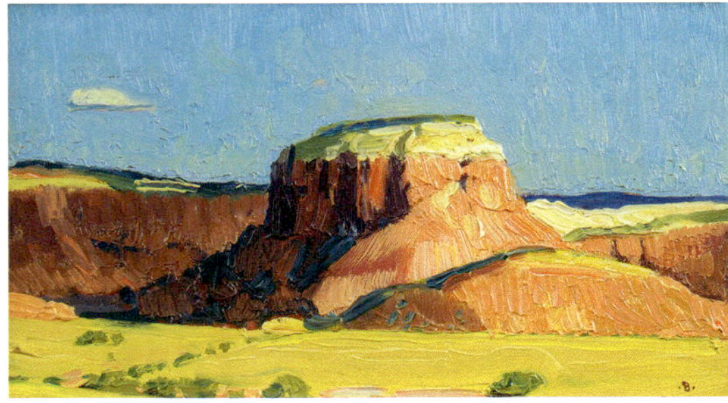

ERNEST L. BLUMENSCHEIN (1874–1960)
Mesa Near Abiquiu, New Mexico, circa 1920
Oil on panel
3¼ × 6 inches

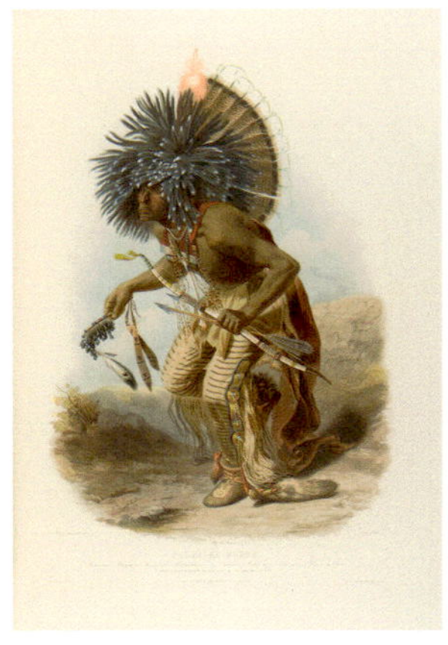

HELEN G. BLUMENSCHEIN (1909–1989)
Deer Dance, Taos Pueblo, date unknown
Oil on canvas
25 × 39¾ inches

At the request of Taos Pueblo, this image is not reproduced.

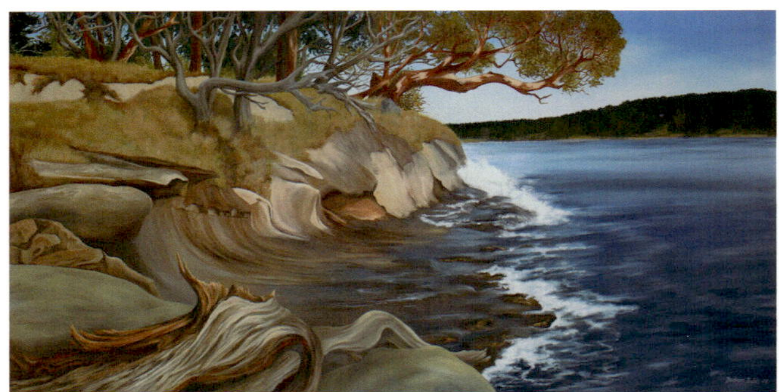

KARL BODMER (1809–1893)
Maximilian Prince of Wied's Travels in the Interior of North America, London: Ackermann, 1840–43
5 bound volumes with 20 colored aquatint engravings
24¾ × 18 inches
(largest volume)

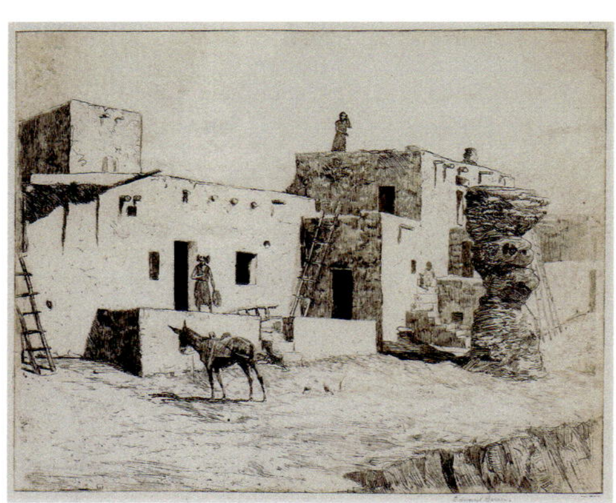

BARBARA BOLDT (BORN 1930)
Galiano Island, 2009
Oil on canvas
36 × 72 inches

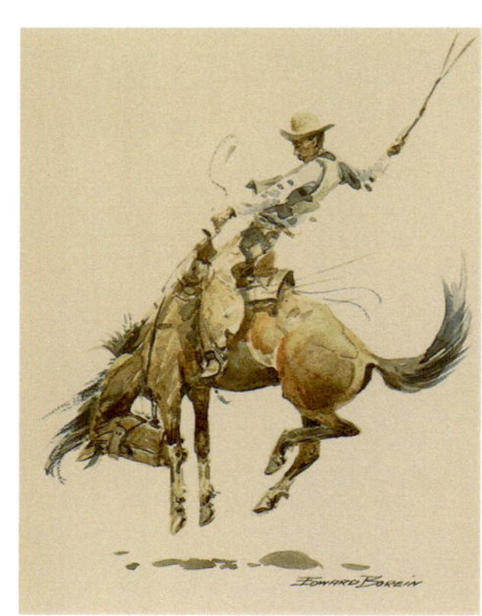

EDWARD BOREIN (1872–1945)
Dance Plaza, Walpi, 1915
Etching on paper
9 × 12 inches

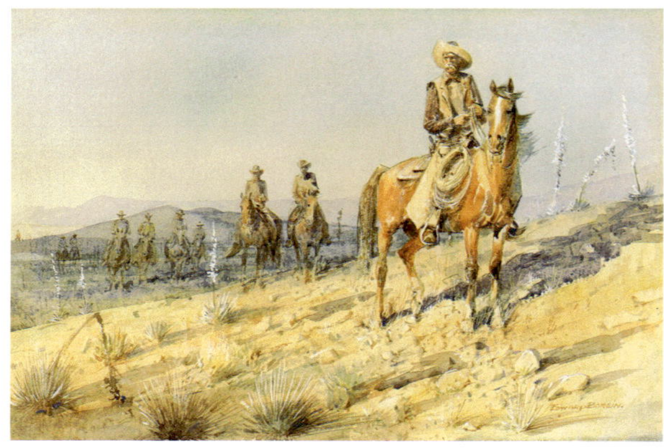

EDWARD BOREIN (1872–1945)
Bucking Bronc, date unknown
Watercolor on paper
7½ × 6¼ inches

EDWARD BOREIN (1872–1945)
The Texans, date unknown
Watercolor on paper
9½ × 14¾ inches

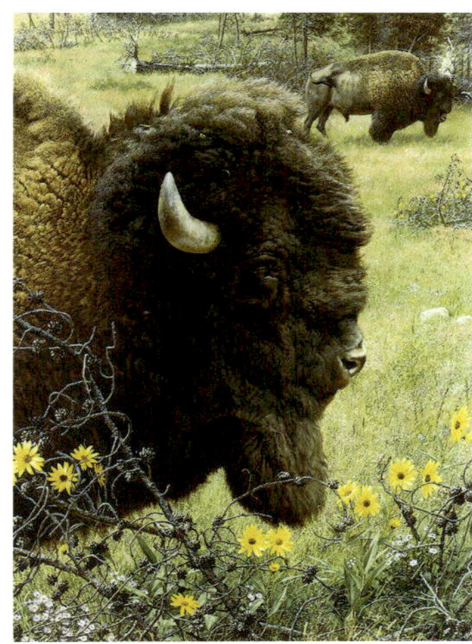

CARL BRENDERS (BORN 1937)
Witness of a Past—Bison, 1988
Gouache on paper
31½ × 23⅝ inches

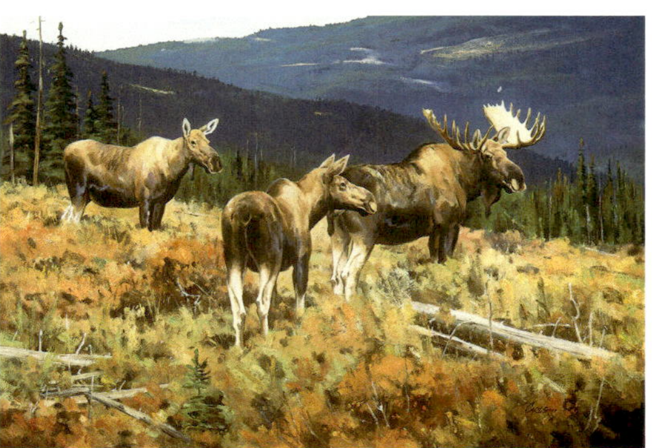

KEN CARLSON (BORN 1937)
Back Country, 1993
Oil on canvas
24 × 36 inches

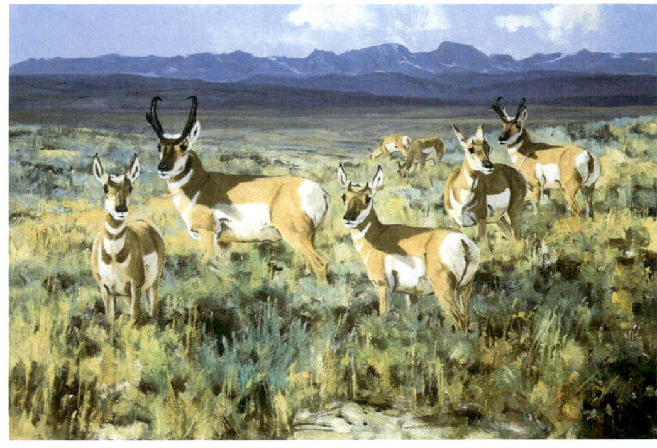

KEN CARLSON (BORN 1937)
Wind River Summer, 1994
Oil on canvas
24 × 36 inches

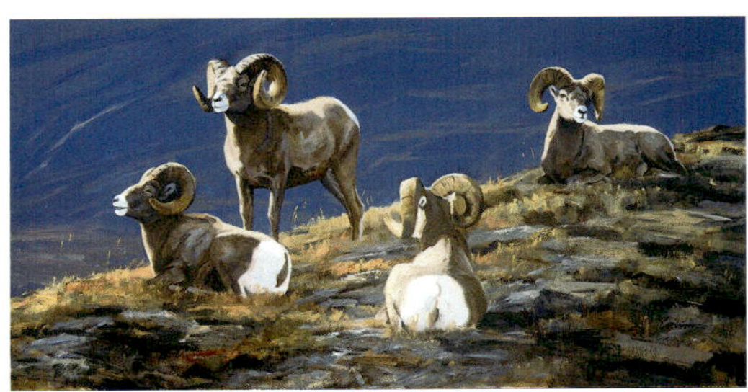

KEN CARLSON (BORN 1937)
A Quiet Time, 1995
Oil on canvas
18 × 36 inches

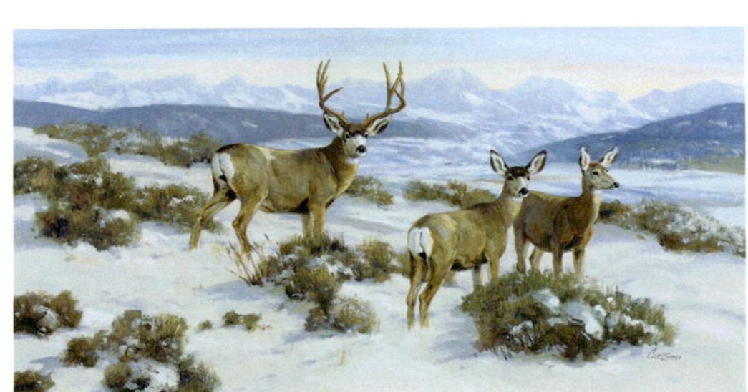

KEN CARLSON (BORN 1937)
Mule Deer of the CL Bar Ranch, 2008
Oil on board
18 × 36 inches

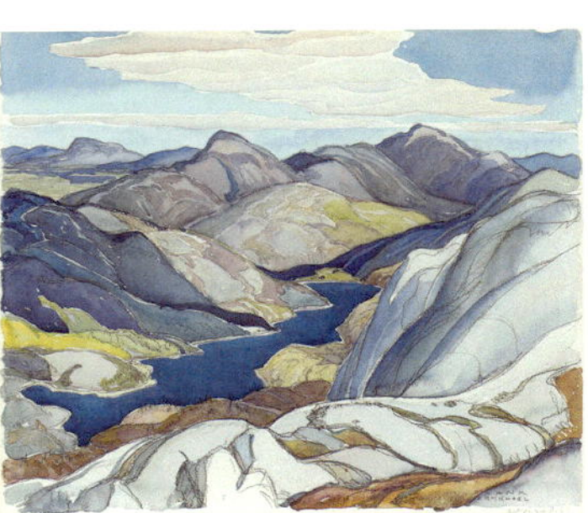

FRANKLIN CARMICHAEL (1890–1945)
Cranberry Lake, 1929
Watercolor on paper
10½ × 14 inches

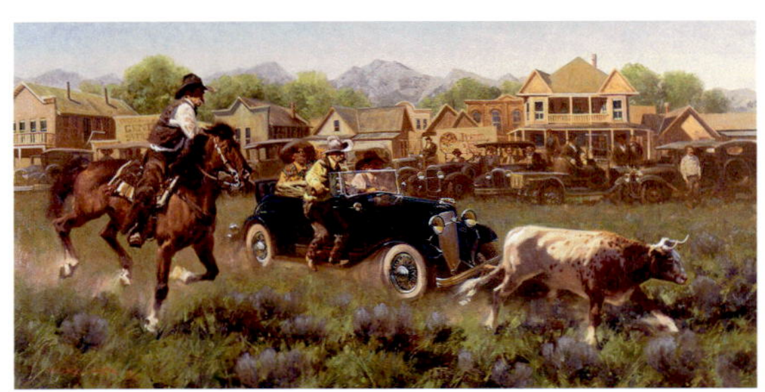

GARY CARTER (BORN 1939)
The Windshield Cowboys, 1993
Oil on canvas
20 × 40 inches

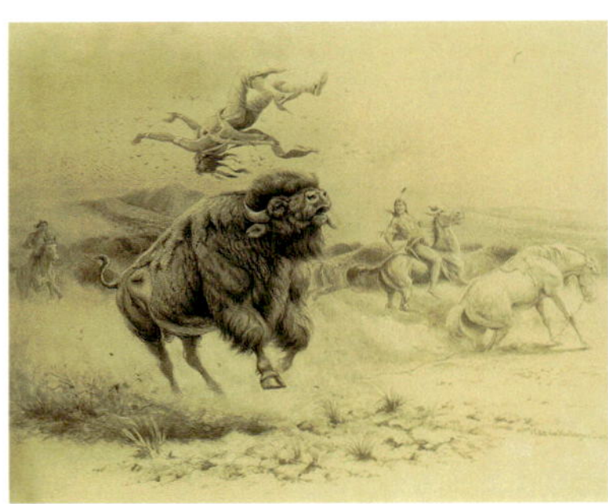

WILLIAM DE LA MONTAGNE CARY
(1840–1922)
The High Toss, circa 1870
Pen and ink wash on paper
15½ × 19½ inches

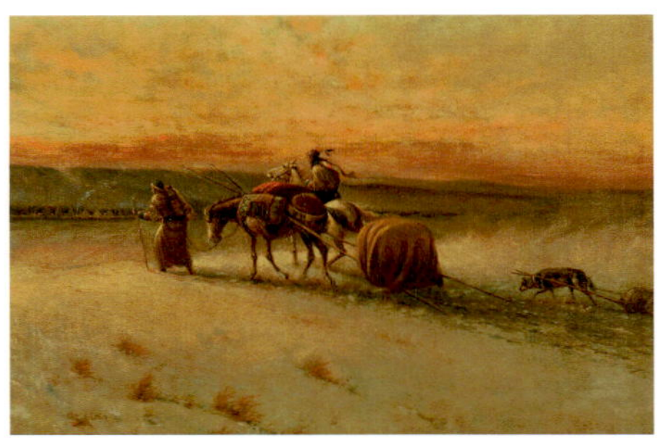

WILLIAM DE LA MONTAGNE CARY (1840–1922)
Returning to Camp, circa 1880
Oil on canvas
19½ × 30⅛ inches

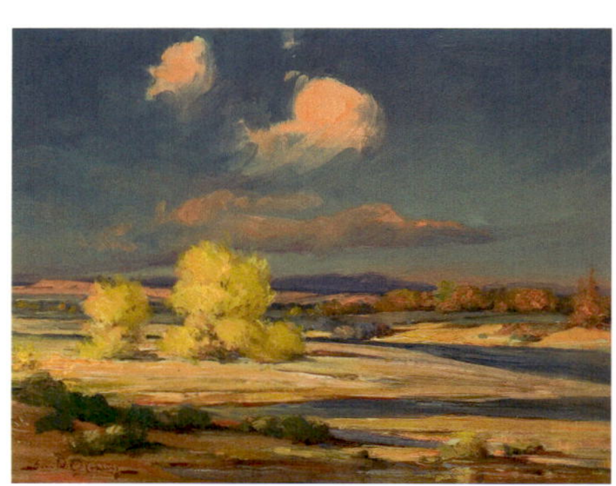

GERALD CASSIDY (1869–1934)
On the Rio Grande River, date unknown
Oil on board
12 × 16 inches

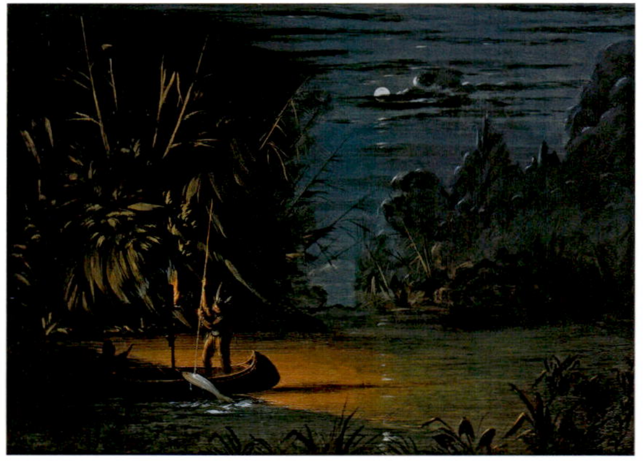

GEORGE CATLIN (1796–1872)
Ojibwa Spearfishing Salmon by Torchlight,
1855–65
Oil on canvas
18½ × 26 inches

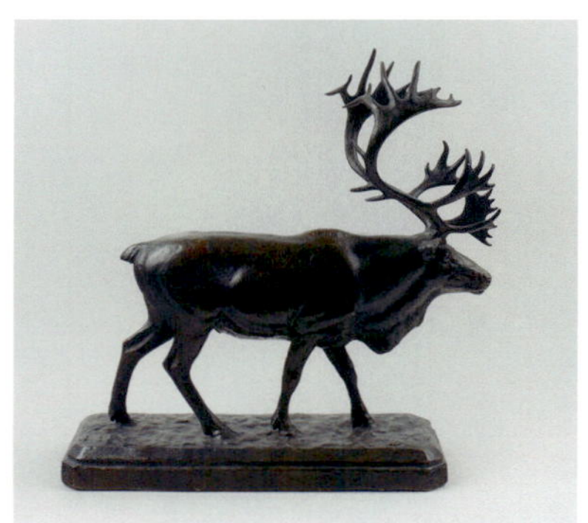

JAMES LIPPITT CLARK (1883–1969)
Caribou, 1925
Bronze
13¼ × 13½ × 4¾ inches

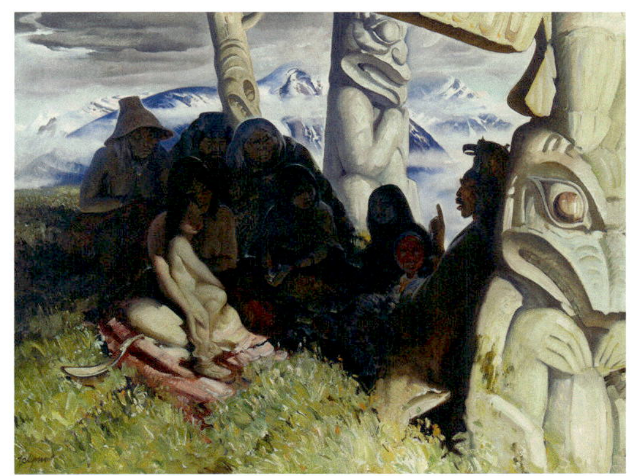

JOHN CLYMER (1907–1989)
The Storyteller, circa 1935
Oil on canvas
36 × 48 inches

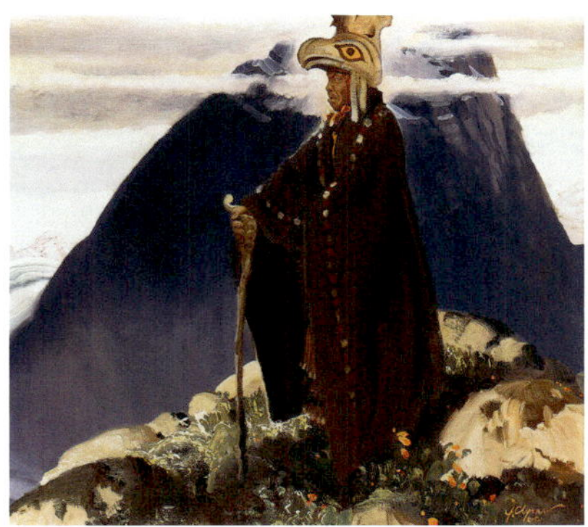

JOHN CLYMER (1907–1989)
Thunder Mountain, circa 1935
Oil on canvas
18 × 20 inches

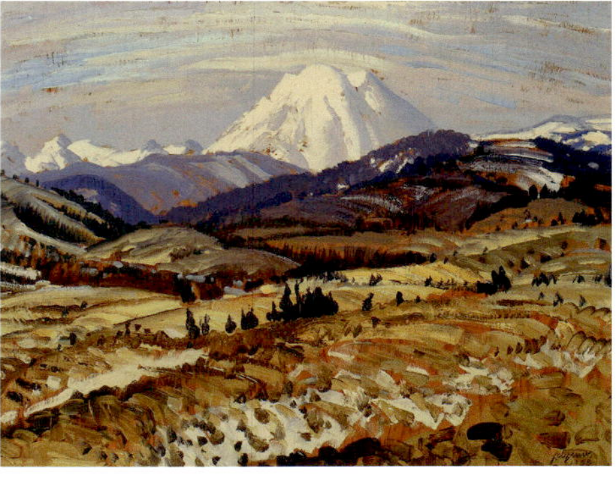

JOHN CLYMER (1907–1989)
Mt. Rainier from Umtanum Ridge, 1938
Oil on board
12 × 16 inches

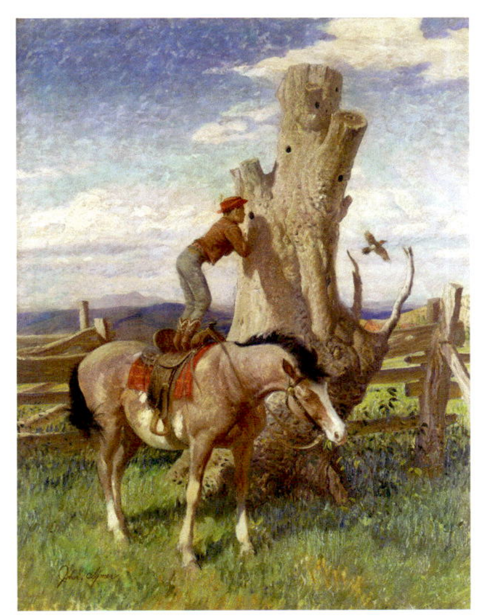

JOHN CLYMER (1907–1989)
Boy on Horse, 1949
Oil on canvas
31⅞ × 25⅛ inches

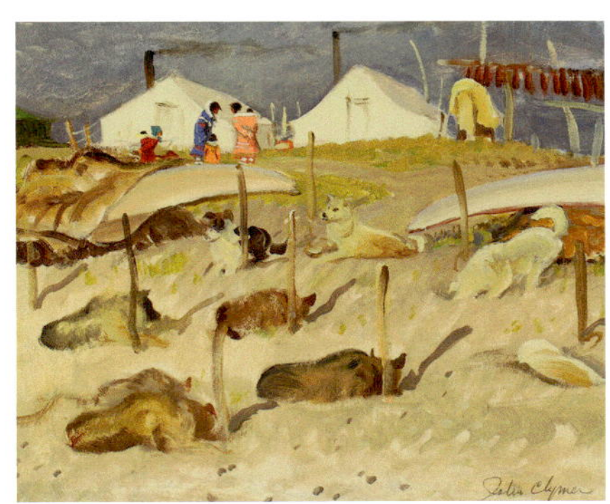

JOHN CLYMER (1907–1989)
Dogs at Kotzebue, Alaska, 1954
Oil on board
8 × 10 inches

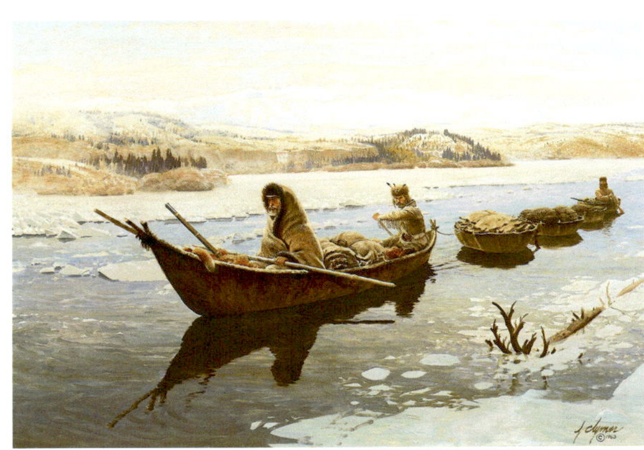

JOHN CLYMER (1907–1989)
Bullboats Down the Yellowstone, 1963
Oil on canvas
24 × 36 inches

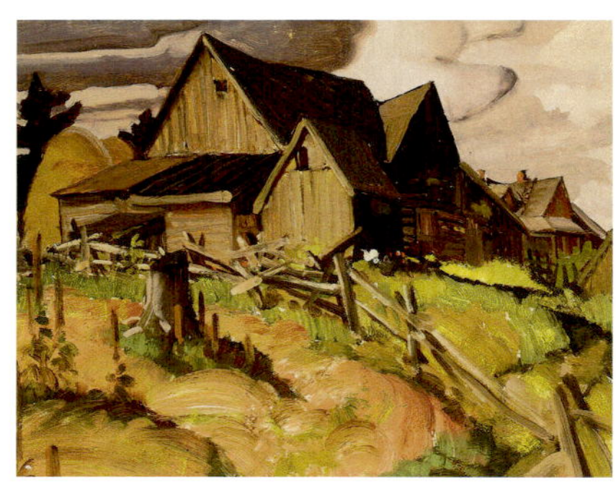

JOHN CLYMER (1907–1989)
Ontario Farm, 1963
Oil on canvas
12 × 16 inches

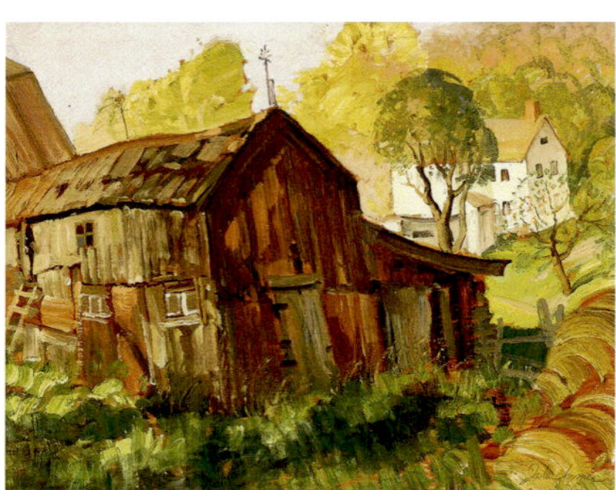

JOHN CLYMER (1907–1989)
New England Barn, circa 1963
Oil on canvas
12 × 16 inches

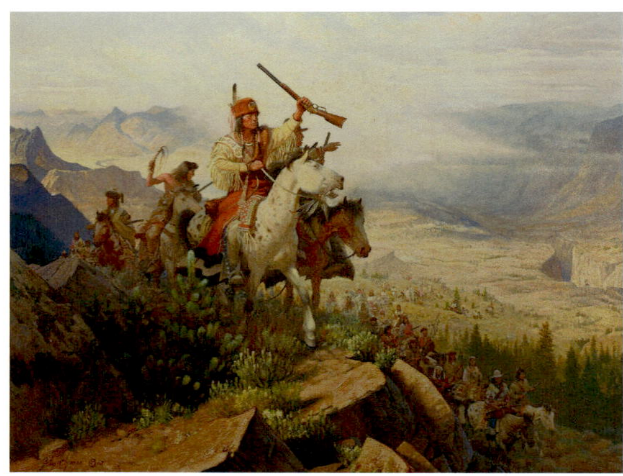

JOHN CLYMER (1907–1989)
Chief Joseph, 1967
Oil on board
30 × 40 inches

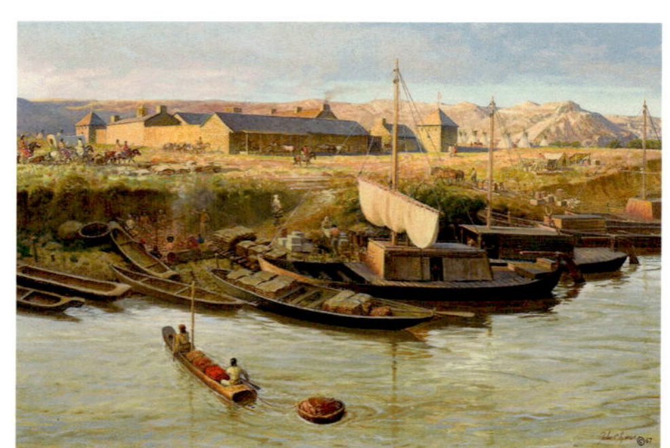

JOHN CLYMER (1907–1989)
Old Fort Benton, 1967
Oil on board
24 × 36 inches

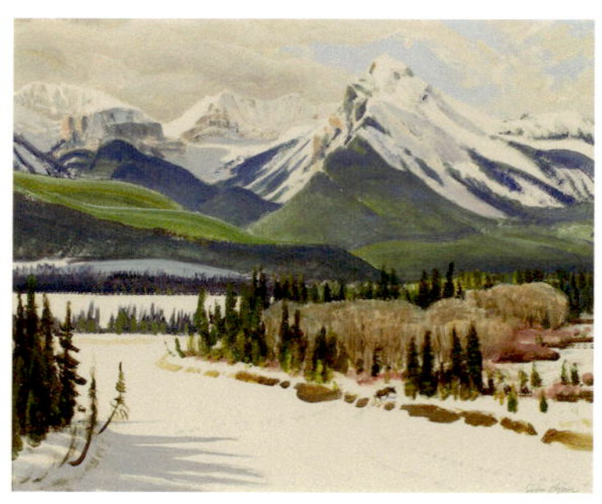

JOHN CLYMER (1907–1989)
Winter on the Bow River, 1967
Oil on board
8 × 10 inches

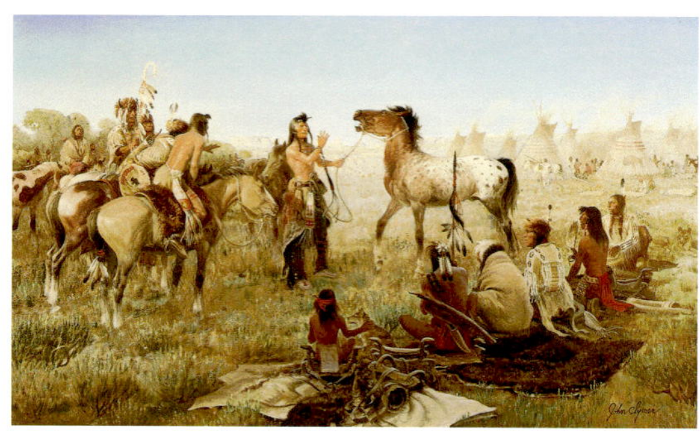

JOHN CLYMER (1907–1989)
The Horse Trader, 1969
Oil on canvas
24 × 40 inches

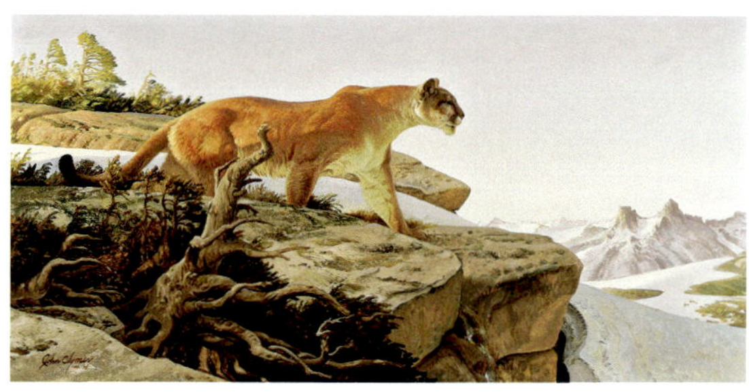

JOHN CLYMER (1907–1989)
Mountain Lion, 1975
Oil on canvas
24 × 48 inches

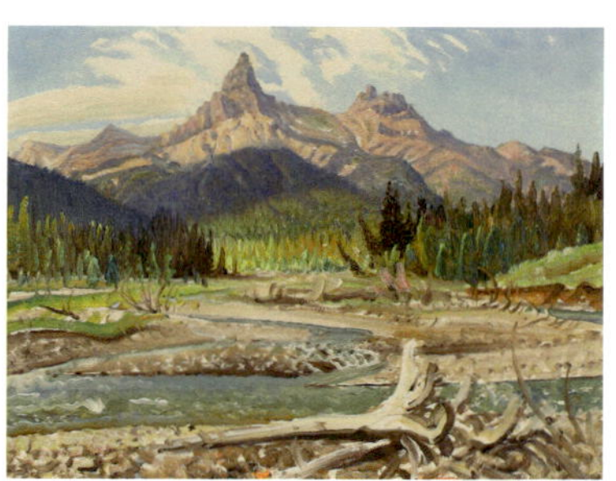

JOHN CLYMER (1907–1989)
Pilot and Index Peaks, 1975
Oil on board
12 × 16 inches

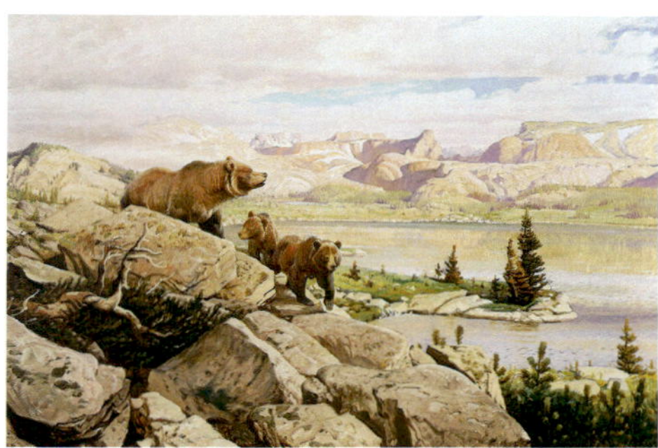

JOHN CLYMER (1907–1989)
The Twins, circa 1975
Oil on board
23⅜ × 35⅜ inches

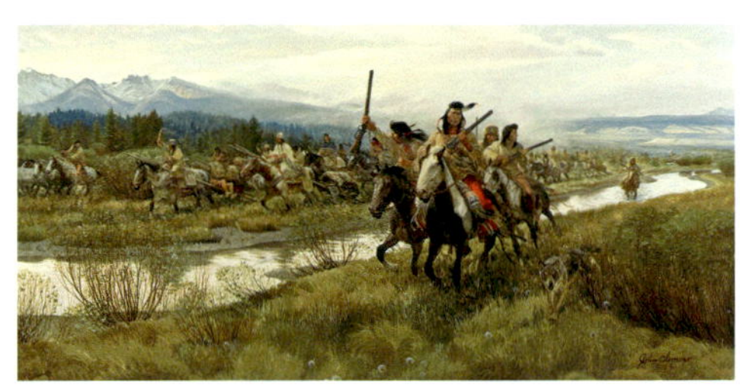

JOHN CLYMER (1907–1989)
Nez Perce 1877—Escape from the Big Hole, 1976
Oil on canvas
24 × 48 inches

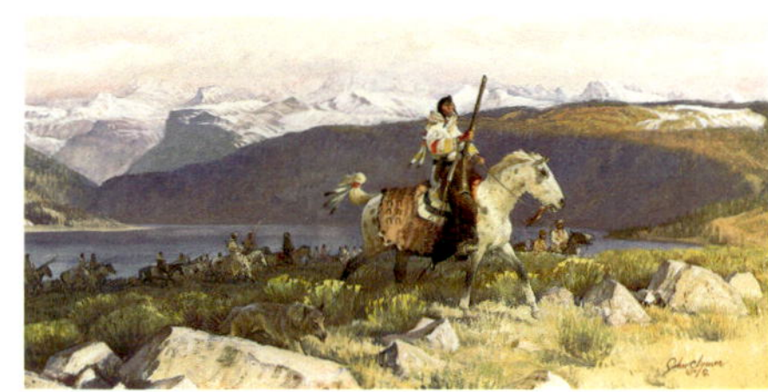

JOHN CLYMER (1907–1989)
Roving Band, 1976
Oil on canvas
15 × 30 inches

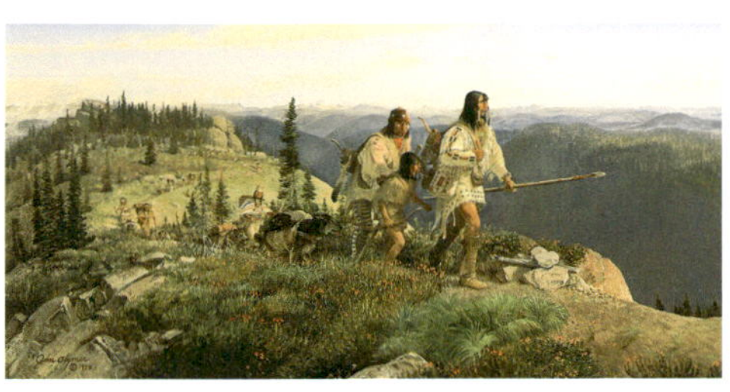

JOHN CLYMER (1907–1989)
Old Nez Perce Trail, 1978
Oil on canvas
24 × 48 inches

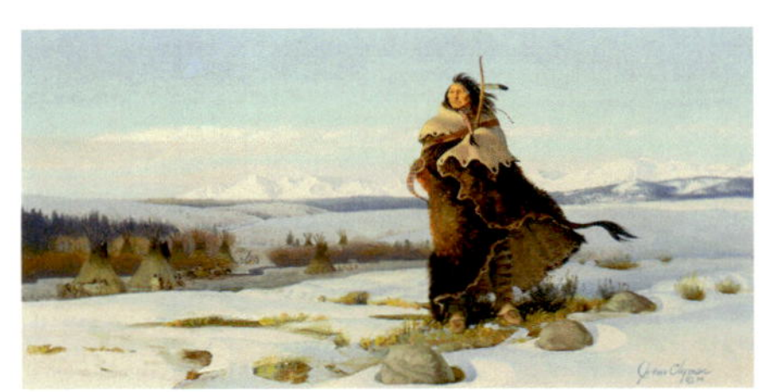

JOHN CLYMER (1907–1989)
The North Wind, 1978
Oil on board
10 × 20 inches

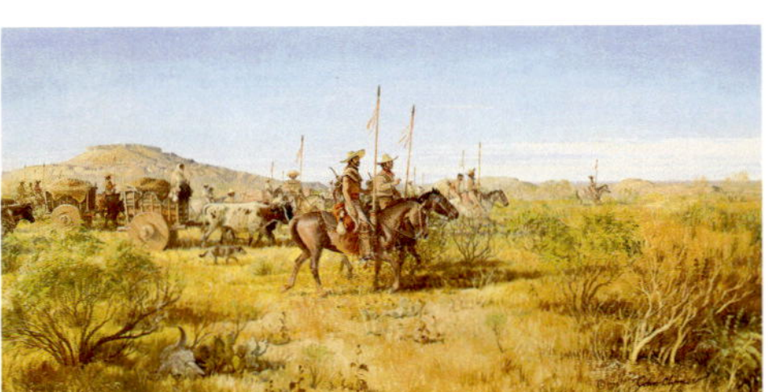

JOHN CLYMER (1907–1989)
Ciboleros, 1979
Oil on canvas
24 × 48 inches

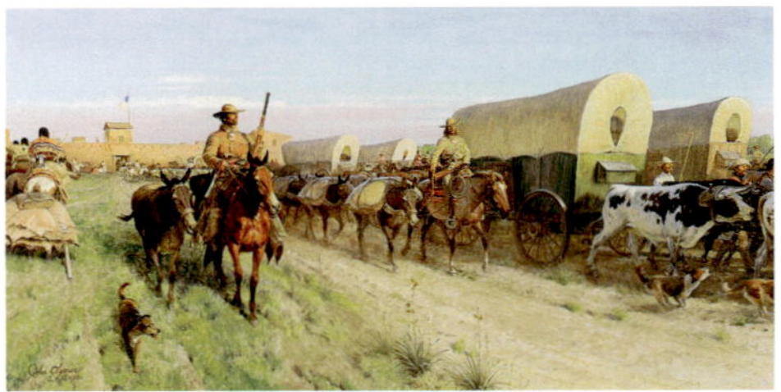

JOHN CLYMER (1907–1989)
William Bent—Caravan to St. Louis, 1980
Oil on canvas
24 × 48 inches

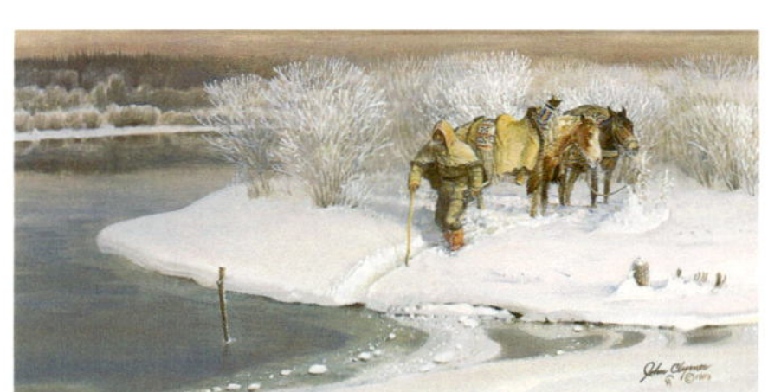

JOHN CLYMER (1907–1989)
Frost on the Willows, 1983
Oil on canvas
15 × 30 inches

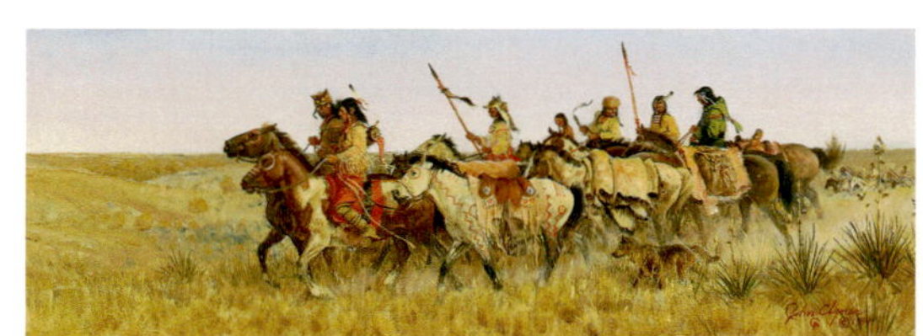

JOHN CLYMER (1907–1989)
Prairie Hunters, 1984
Oil on canvas
8 × 22 inches

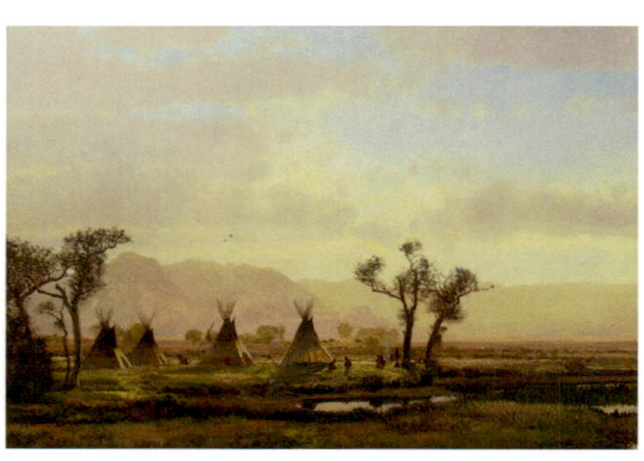

MICHAEL COLEMAN (BORN 1946)
Evening on the Snake, circa 2000
Oil on panel
20 × 30 inches

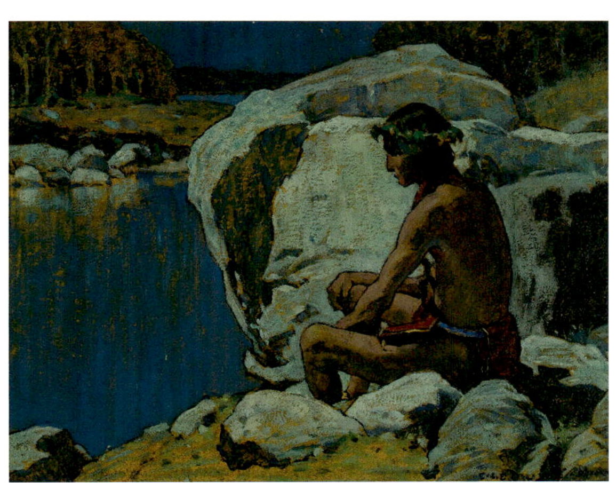

E. IRVING COUSE (1866–1936)
Moonlight, 1930
Oil on board
9 × 12 inches

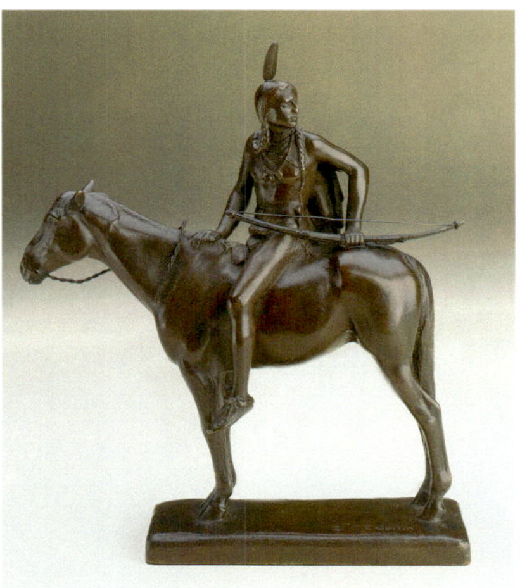

CYRUS E. DALLIN (1861–1944)
On the Warpath, 1917
Bronze
9 × 8½ × 2¼ inches

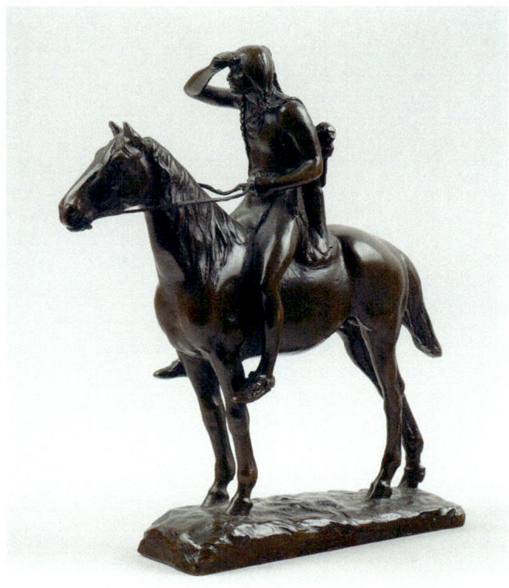

CYRUS E. DALLIN (1861–1944)
The Scout, 1918
Bronze
8⅛ × 8 × 3 inches

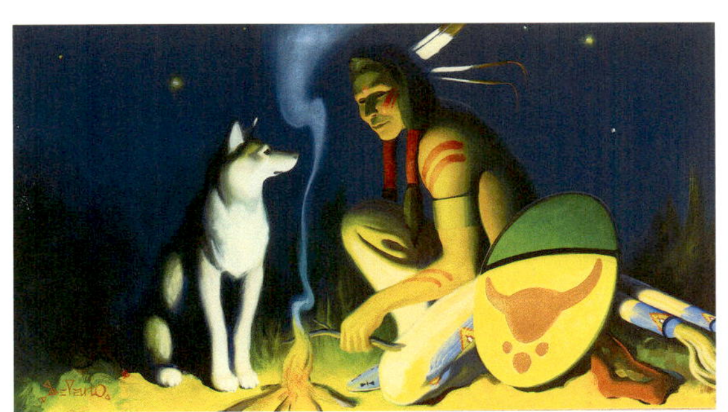

GERARD CURTIS DELANO (1890–1972)
By the Campfire, circa 1930
Oil on canvas
22 × 40 inches

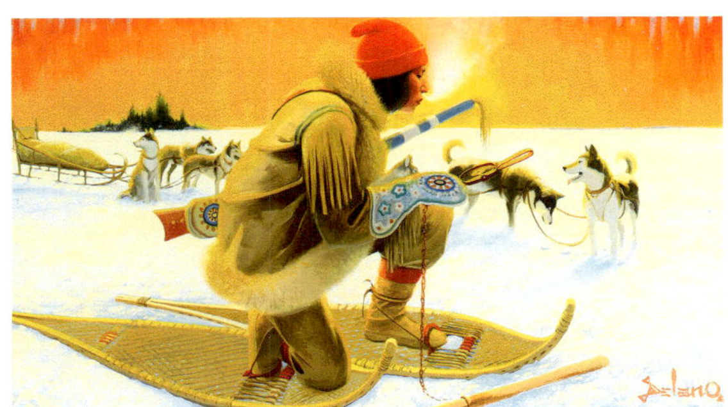

GERARD CURTIS DELANO (1890–1972)
On the Trapline, circa 1930
Oil on canvas
22 × 40 inches

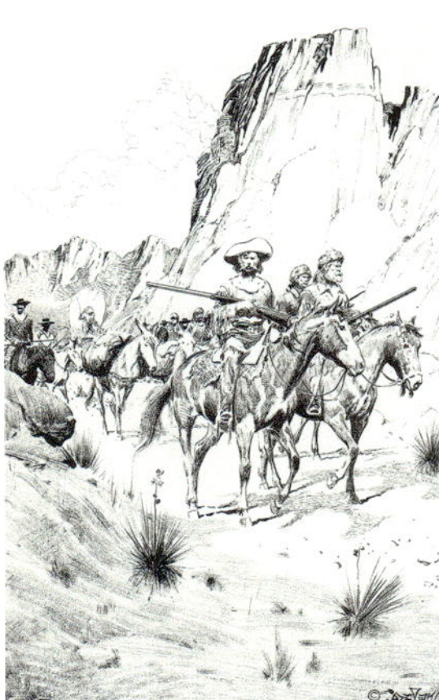

GERARD CURTIS DELANO
(1890–1972)
Fremont Expeditions, 1843–1848,
circa 1936
Ink on paper
19 × 12½ inches

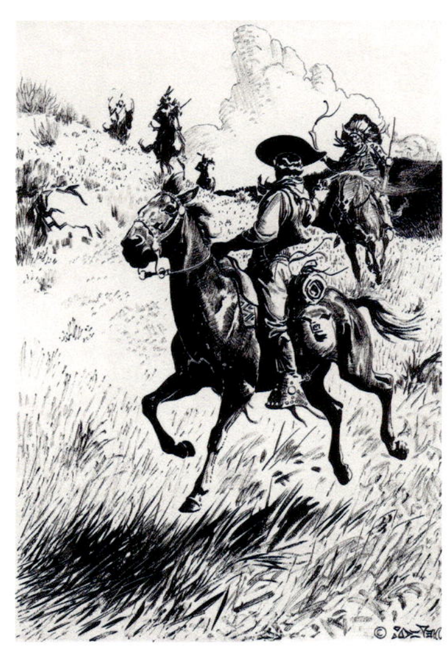

GERARD CURTIS DELANO
(1890–1972)
The Pony Express, 1860, circa 1936
Ink on paper
19 × 12½ inches

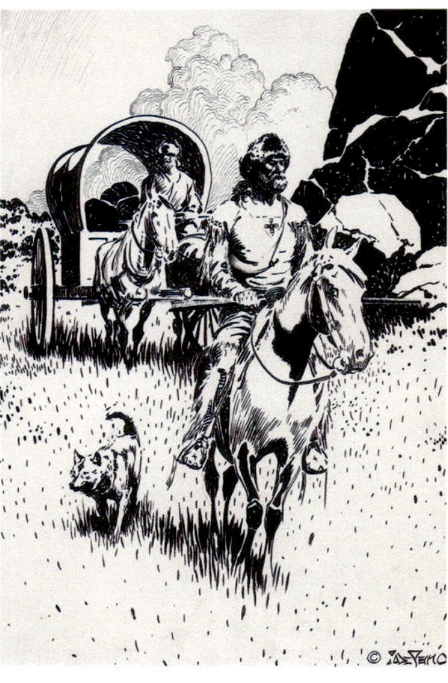

GERARD CURTIS DELANO
(1890–1972)
Trappers with Red River Wagon,
circa 1936
Ink on paper
19 × 12½ inches

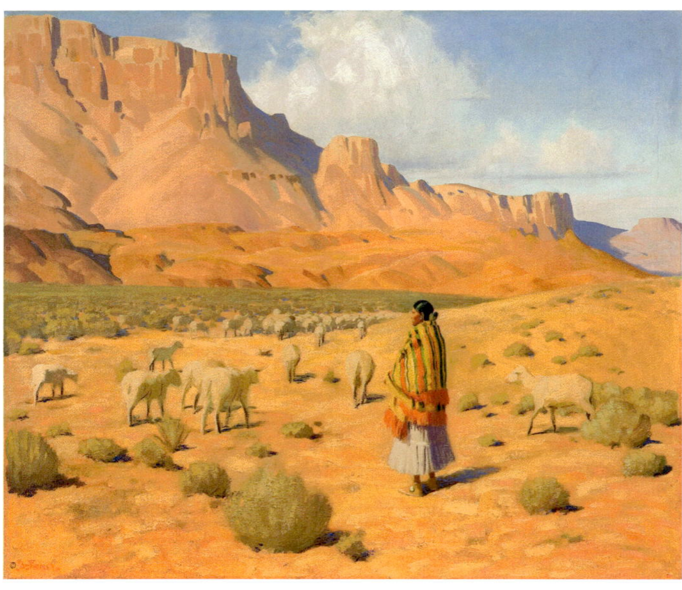

GERARD CURTIS DELANO (1890–1972)
In the Navajo Country, 1943
Oil on canvas
30¼ × 36 inches

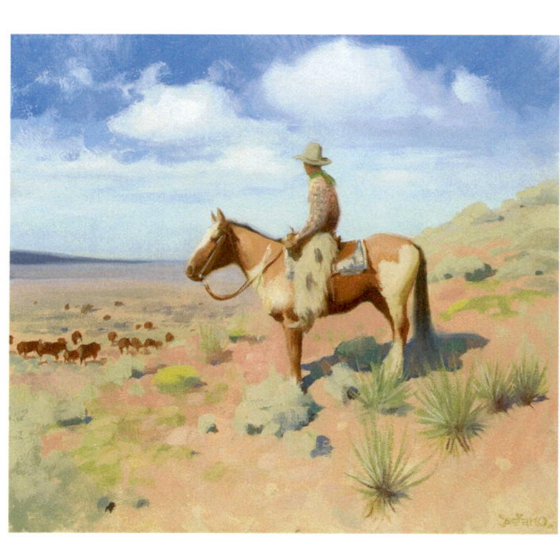

GERARD CURTIS DELANO (1890–1972)
The Cowboy, date unknown
Oil on canvas
16 × 18 inches

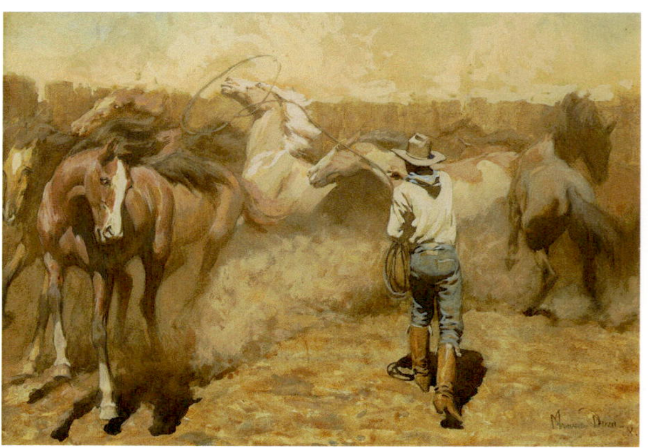

MAYNARD DIXON (1875–1946)
Roping a Palomino, 1908
Watercolor on paper
14 × 21 inches

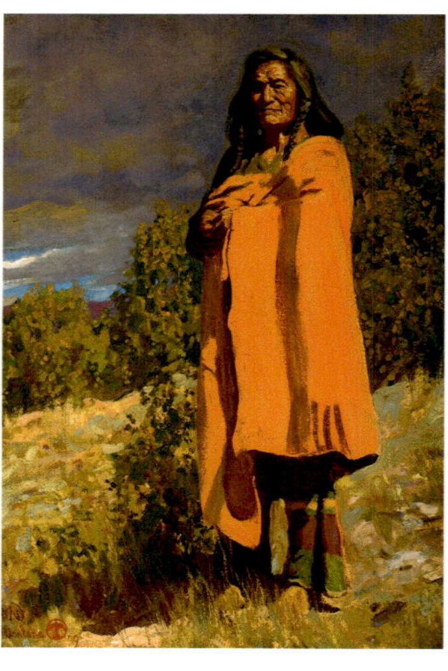

MAYNARD DIXON (1875–1946)
Old Flathead, 1909
Oil on canvas on board
20½ × 14½ inches

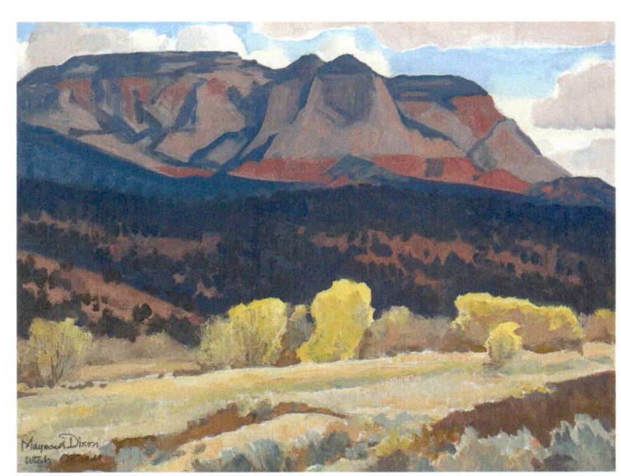

MAYNARD DIXON (1875–1946)
Sungleam and Shadow, 1941
Oil on canvas
12 × 16 inches

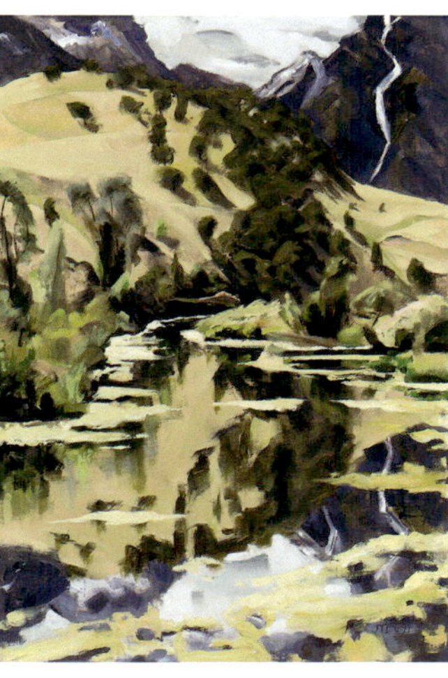

JOELLYN DUESBERRY (BORN 1944)
Approaching Storm, Spring Creek, MT,
1994
Oil on linen
28 × 20 inches

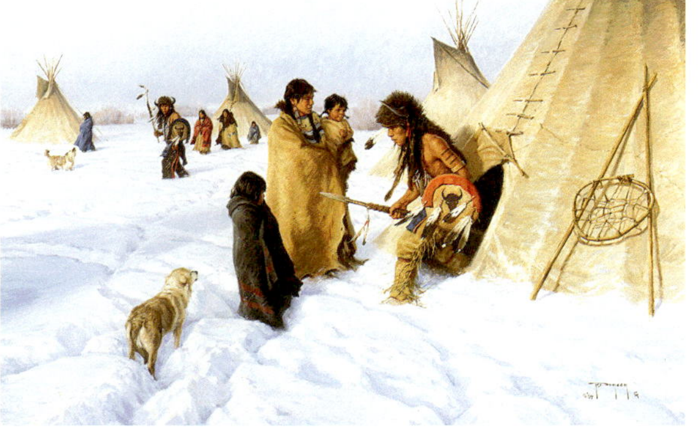

ROBERT DUNCAN (BORN 1952)
Going to Call the Buffalo, 1984
Oil on canvas
30 × 48 inches

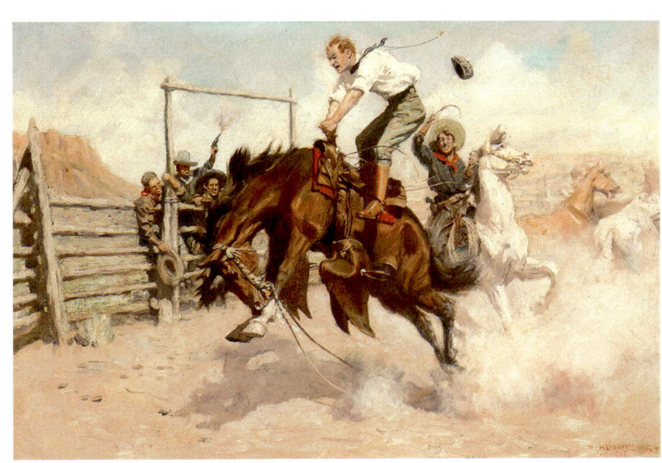

W. HERBERT DUNTON (1878–1936)
The Tenderfoot, 1907
Oil on canvas
21 × 30 inches

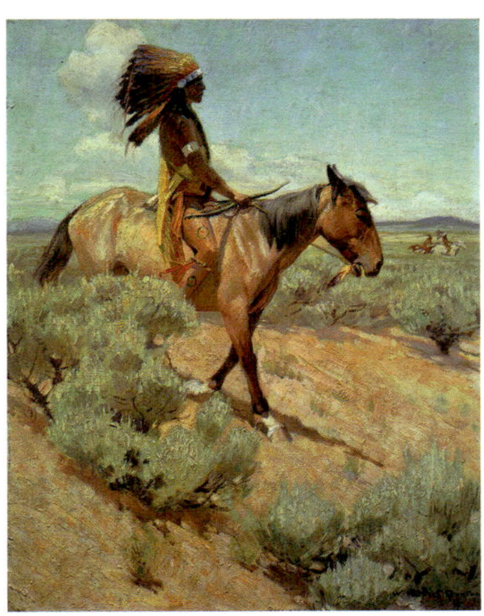

W. HERBERT DUNTON (1878–1936)
The Chief, 1913
Oil on canvas
20 × 16 inches

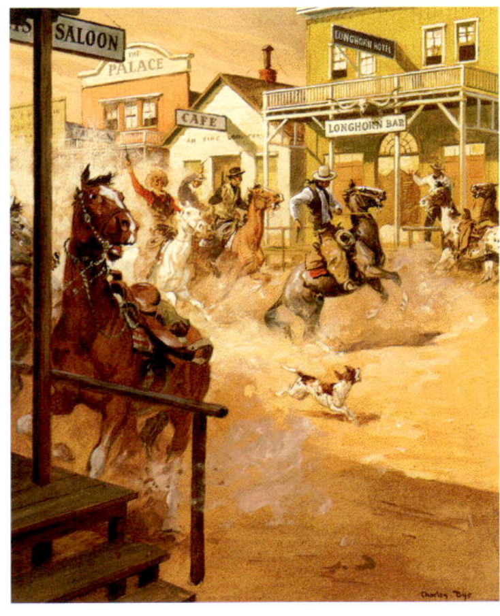

CHARLIE DYE (1906–1972)
Bustin' into Town, circa 1965
Oil on board
15 × 13½ inches

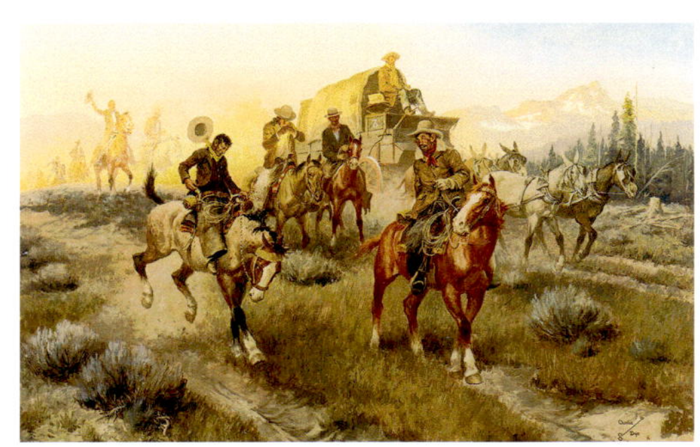

CHARLIE DYE (1906–1972)
A Rawhide Outfit, 1971
Oil on canvas
30 × 48 inches

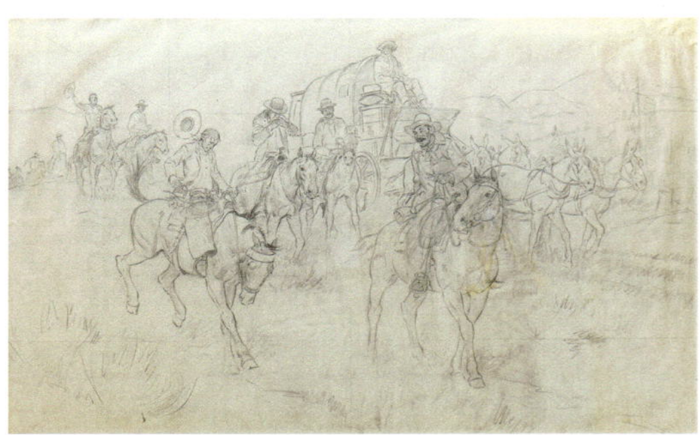

CHARLIE DYE (1906–1972)
Study for A Rawhide Outfit, circa 1971
Graphite on paper
30 × 48 inches

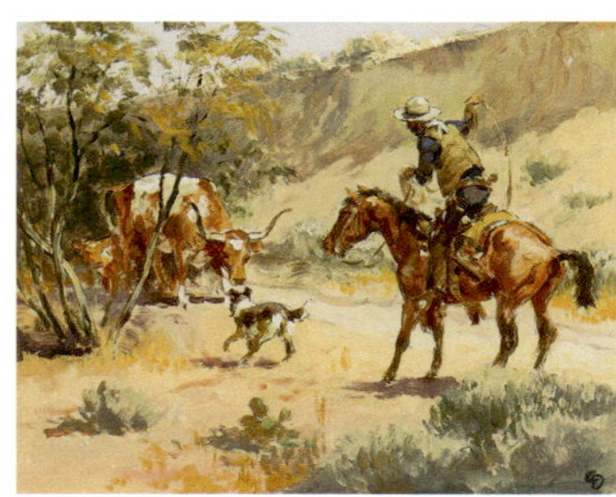

CHARLIE DYE (1906–1972)
Morning Round Up, 1971
Oil on board
7 × 9 inches

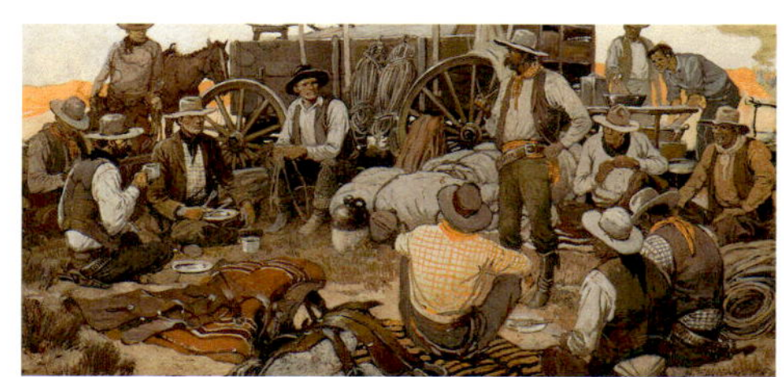

NICK EGGENHOFER (1897–1985)
A Well Deserved Dinner, date unknown
Gouache on paper
8 × 17½ inches

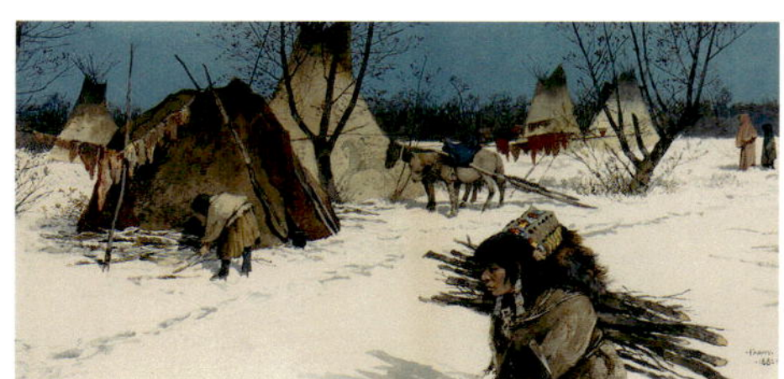

HENRY FARNY (1847–1916)
Winter Encampment of the Crow Indians, 1882
Watercolor and gouache on paper
12⅞ × 27⅜ inches

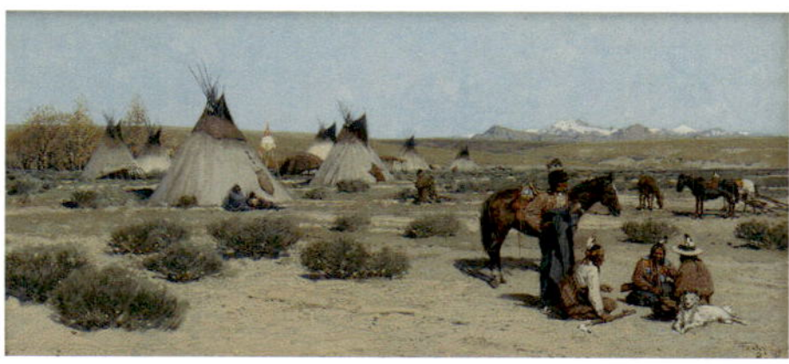

HENRY FARNY (1847–1916)
Indian Encampment, 1893
Gouache on paper
7½ × 16⅜ inches

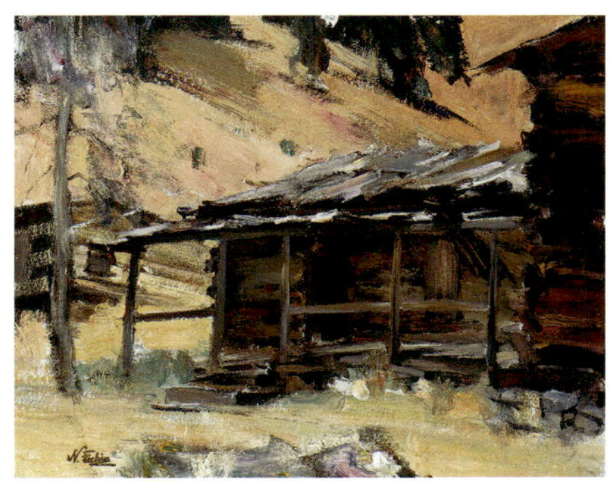

NICOLAI FECHIN (1881–1955)
Log Cabin with Porch, circa 1930
Oil on canvas
16⅜ × 20⅝ inches

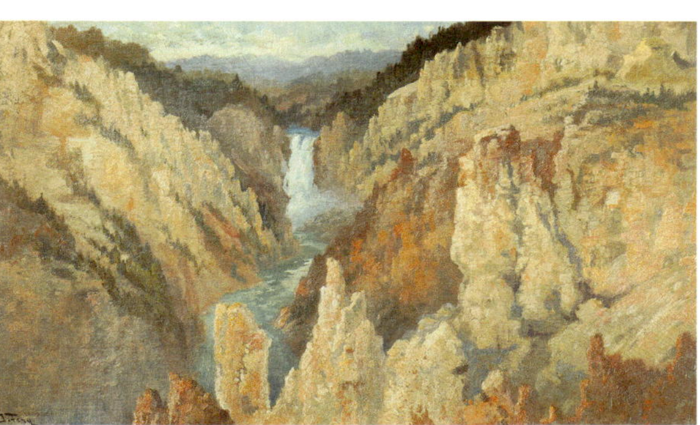

JOHN FERY (1859–1934)
Lower Yellowstone Falls, 1914
Oil on canvas on board
14 × 24 inches

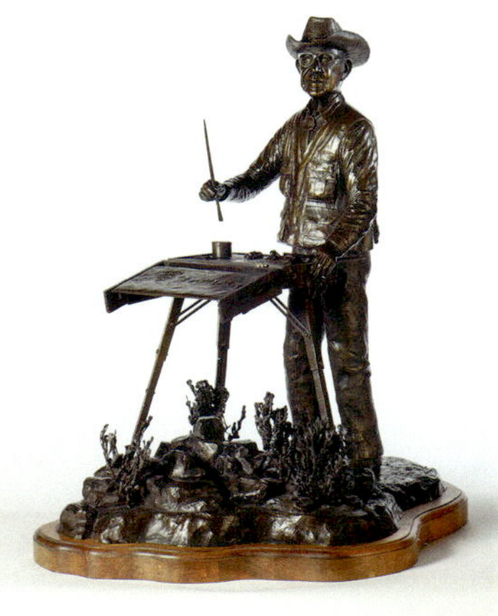

MIKE FLANAGAN (BORN 1941)
John Clymer en Plein Air, circa 1980
Bronze
30 × 20 × 26 inches

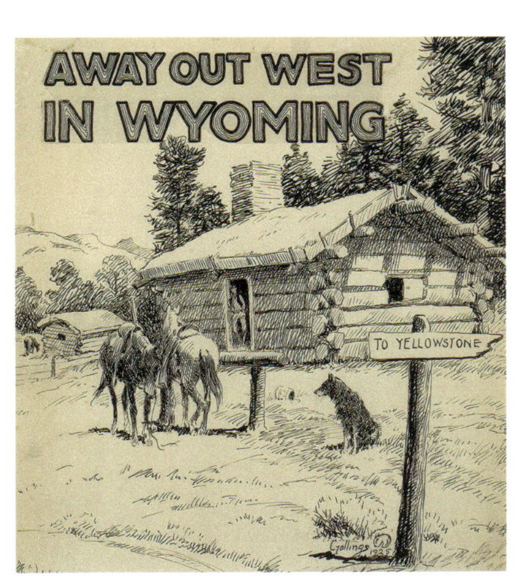

WILLIAM GOLLINGS (1878–1932)
Away Out West in Wyoming, 1925
Pen and ink on paper
12¼ × 11½ inches

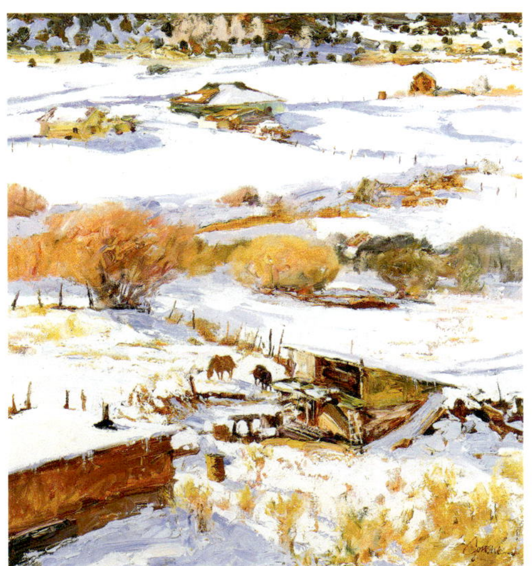

WALT GONSKE (BORN 1942)
Rodarte Winter, circa 1995
Oil on canvas
34 × 32 inches

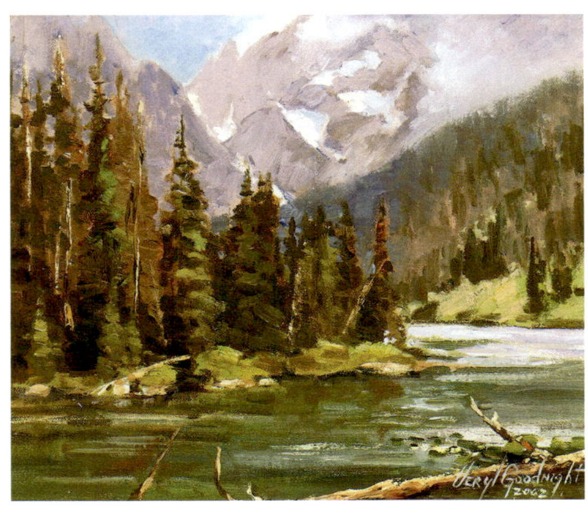

VERYL GOODNIGHT (BORN 1947)
Storm over String Lake, Tetons, 2002
Oil on board
10 × 12 inches

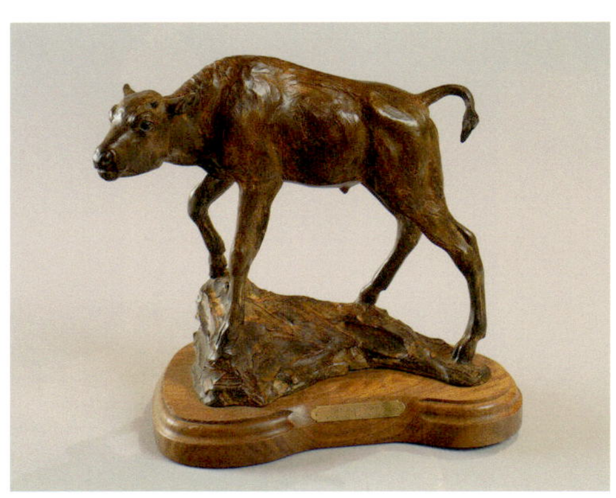

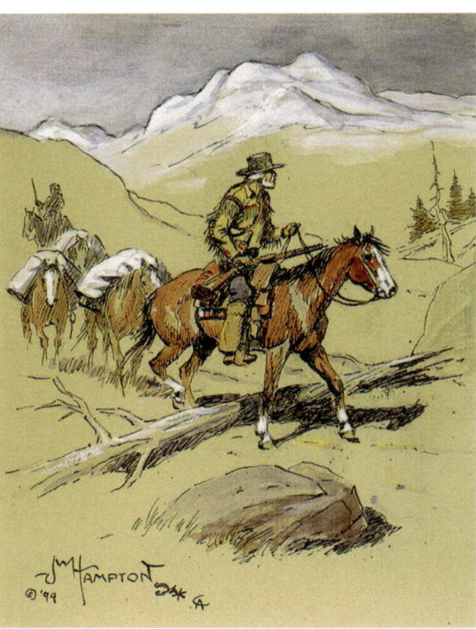

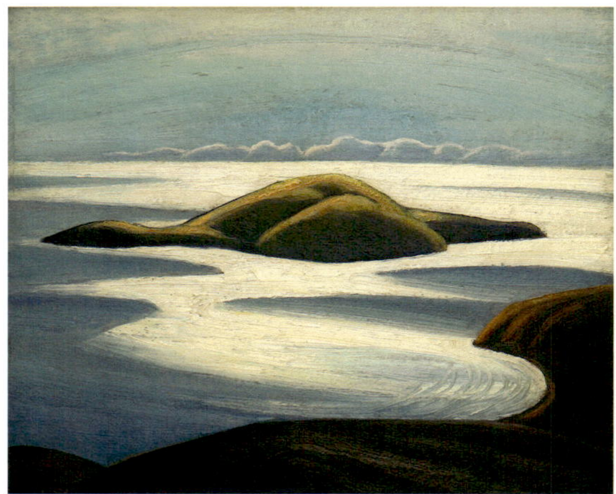

VERYL GOODNIGHT (BORN 1947)
Survivor, 2003
Bronze
12 × 14 × 7 inches

JOHN W. HAMPTON (1918–1999)
Packing Out, 1999
Pen and watercolor on paper
10 × 8 inches

LAWREN STEWART HARRIS (1885–1970)
Lake Superior Sketch Pic Island, circa 1924
Oil on board
12 × 15 inches

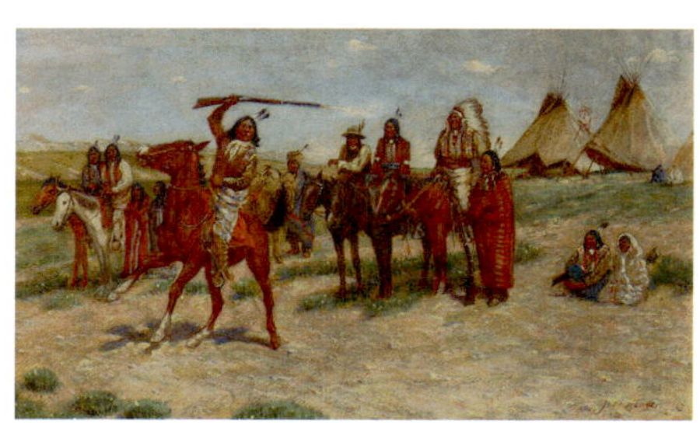

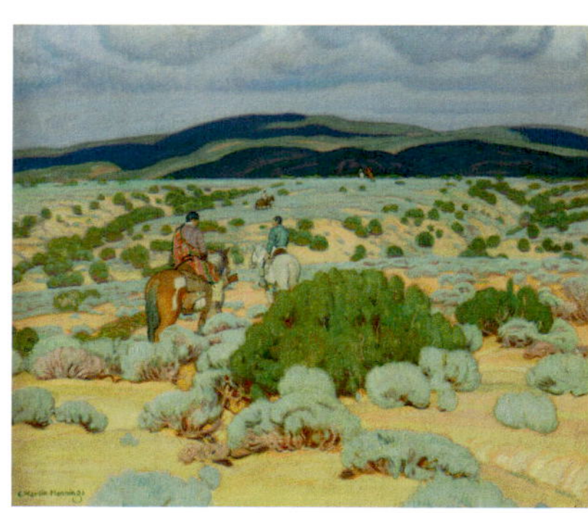

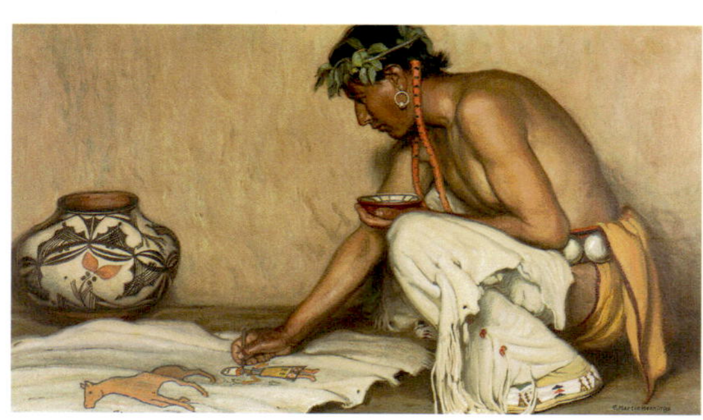

JOHN HAUSER (1859–1913)
Starting the Race, 1903
Gouache on board
11¾ × 20½ inches

E. MARTIN HENNINGS (1886–1956)
Rabbit Hunt, Taos, circa 1930
Oil on canvas
25 × 30 inches

E. MARTIN HENNINGS (1886–1956)
Indian Painter, circa 1936
Oil on canvas
20 × 36 inches

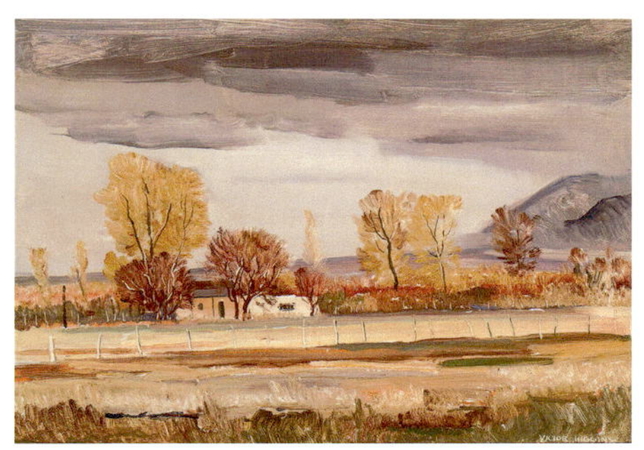

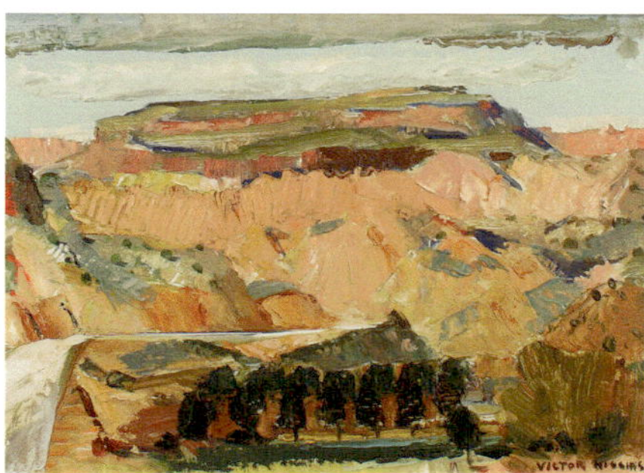

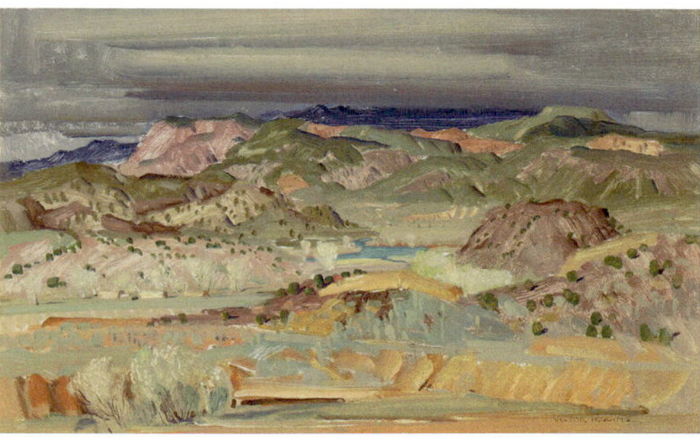

VICTOR HIGGINS (1884–1949)
Grey Skies, circa 1945
Oil on Masonite
12 × 17 inches

VICTOR HIGGINS (1884–1949)
Mesa, circa 1945
Oil on board
10 × 14 inches

VICTOR HIGGINS (1884–1949)
Rio Grande, circa 1945
Oil on board
11 × 18 inches

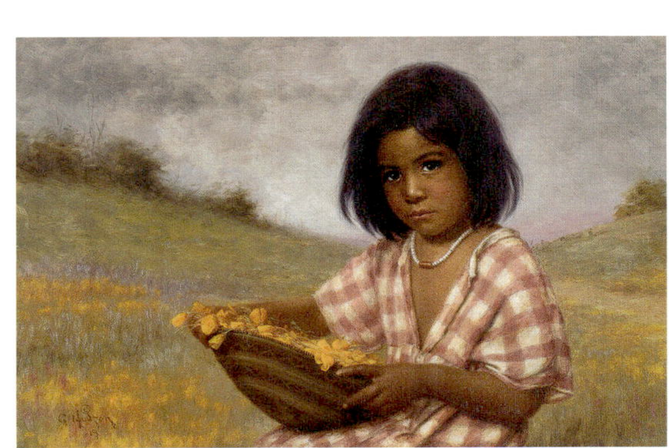

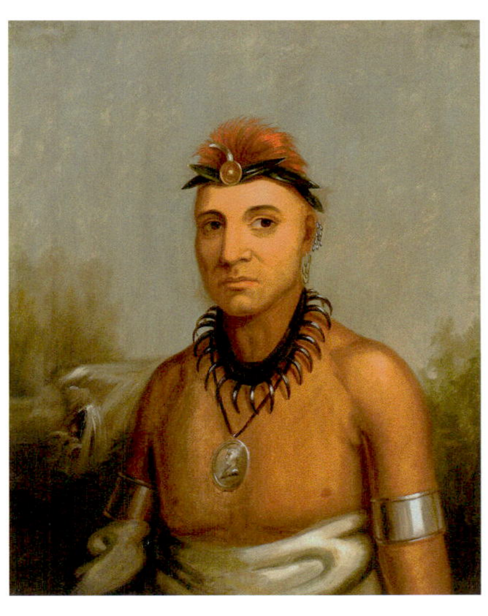

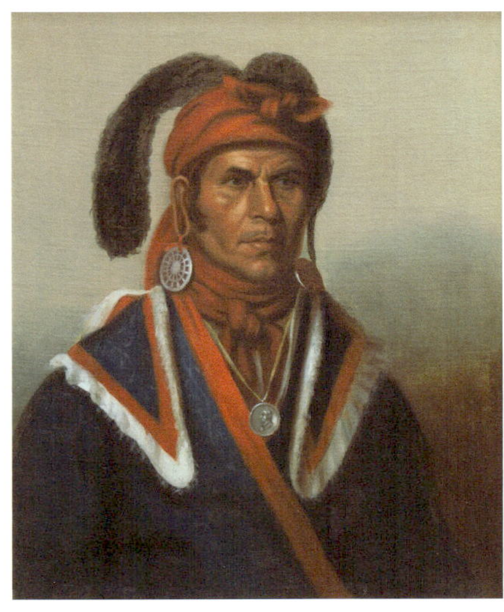

GRACE HUDSON (1865–1937)
Off the Highway, 1919
Oil on canvas
10 × 16¼ inches

HENRY INMAN (1801–1846)
Chief of the Foxes, circa 1832
Oil on canvas
30 × 25 inches

HENRY INMAN (1801–1846)
Holato Mico (Blue King), circa 1832
Oil on canvas
30¼ × 25 inches

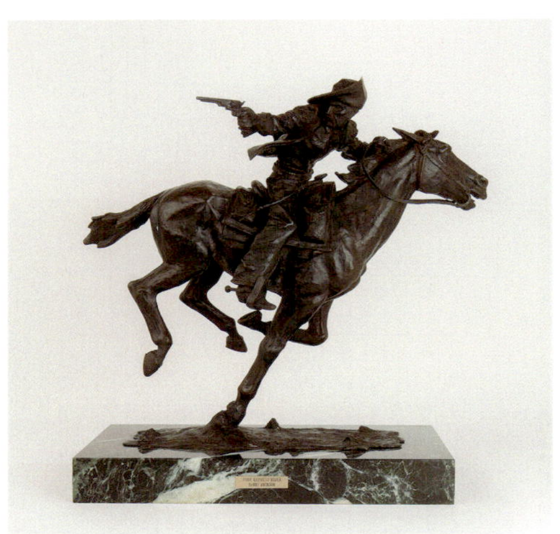

HARRY JACKSON (1924–2011)
Pony Express, 1967
Bronze
21 × 18½ × 14 inches

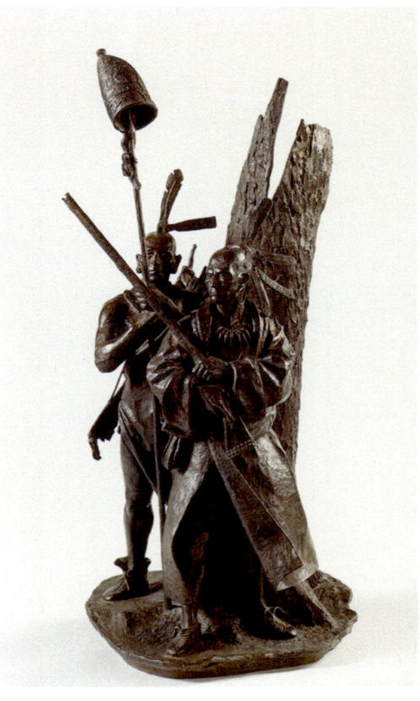

HARRY JACKSON (1924–2011)
Algonquin Chief and Warrior, 1971
Bronze
32 × 15 × 14 inches

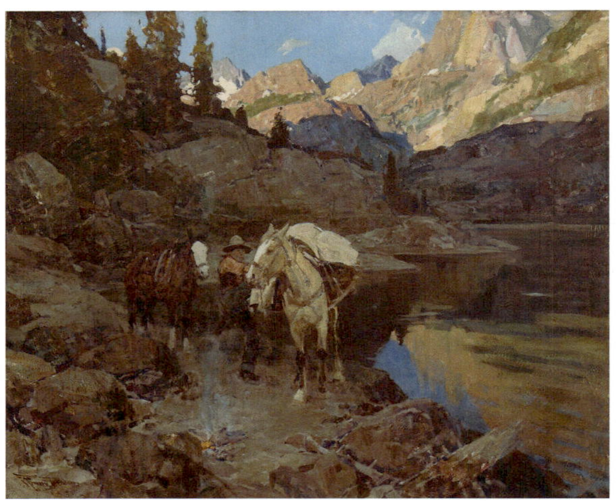

FRANK TENNEY JOHNSON (1874–1939)
Sunrise at Lake Sabrina, 1931
Oil on canvas
32 × 40 inches

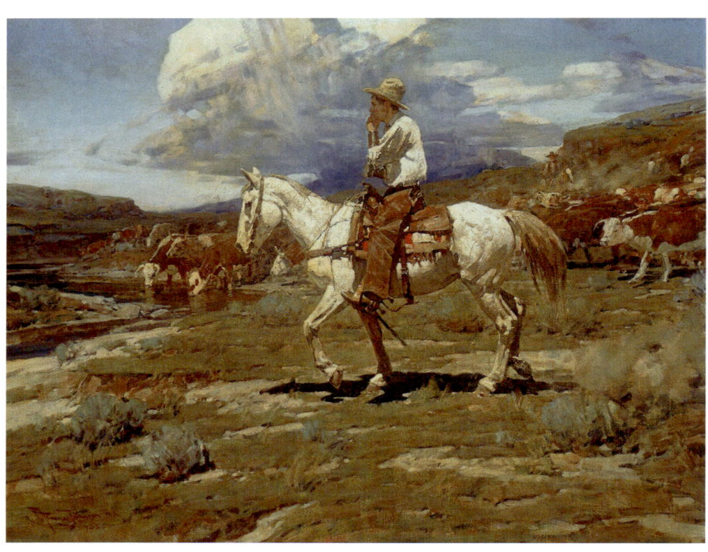

FRANK TENNEY JOHNSON (1874–1939)
On the Drive, 1938
Oil on canvas
30 × 40 inches

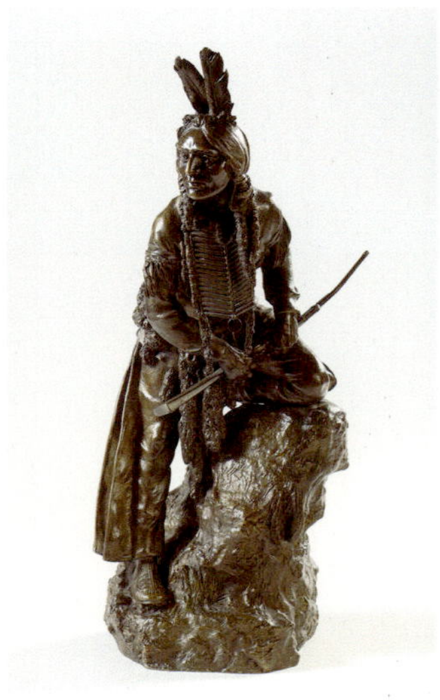

CARL KAUBA (1865–1922)
The Indian Scout, circa 1905
Bronze
17⅞ × 8 × 7 inches

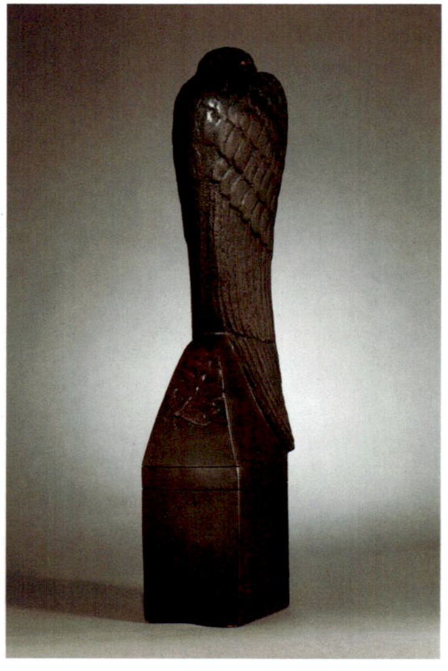

STEVE KESTREL (BORN 1948)
Trickster, 1985
Bronze
27 × 5 × 6 inches

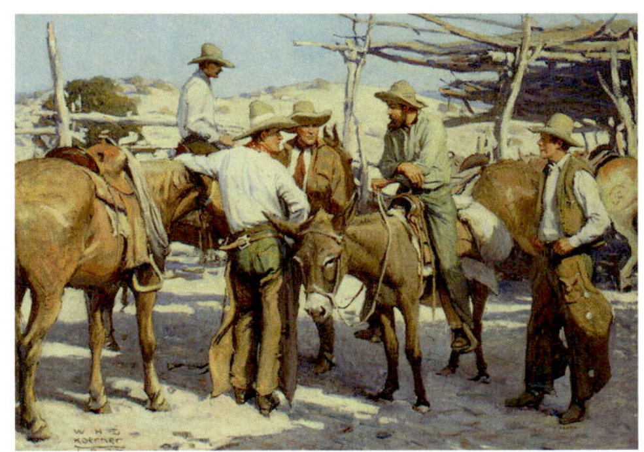

W. H. D. KOERNER (1878–1938)
Not Much of a Hand, 1927
Oil on canvas
28 × 40 inches

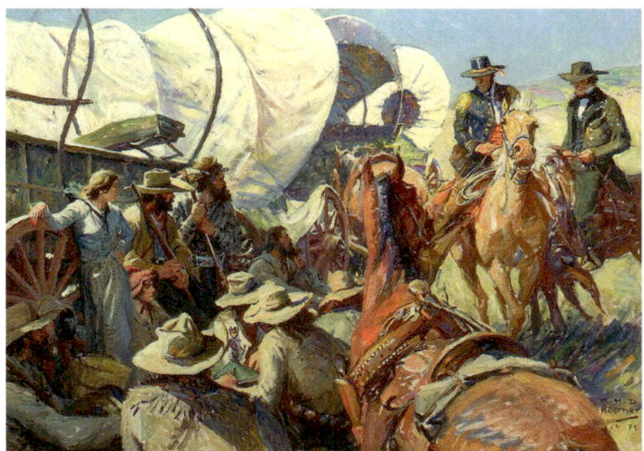

W. H. D. KOERNER (1878–1938)
Rights to the Land, 1935
Oil on canvas
28 × 40 inches

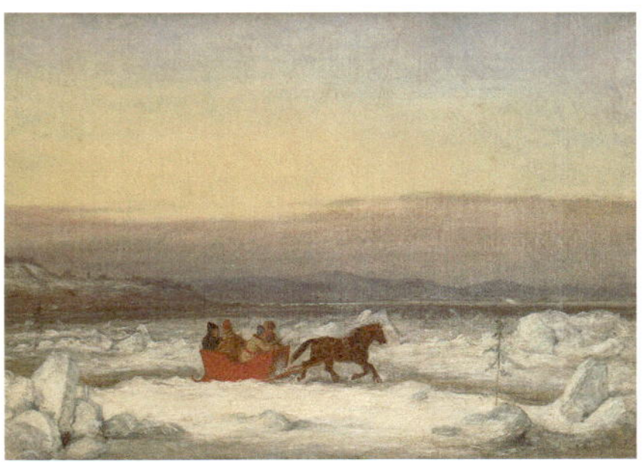

CORNELIUS KRIEGHOFF (1815–1872)
*French Canadians Crossing the Frozen St. Lawrence,
A View of the Citadel in the Distance,* 1855
Oil on canvas
10 × 14 inches

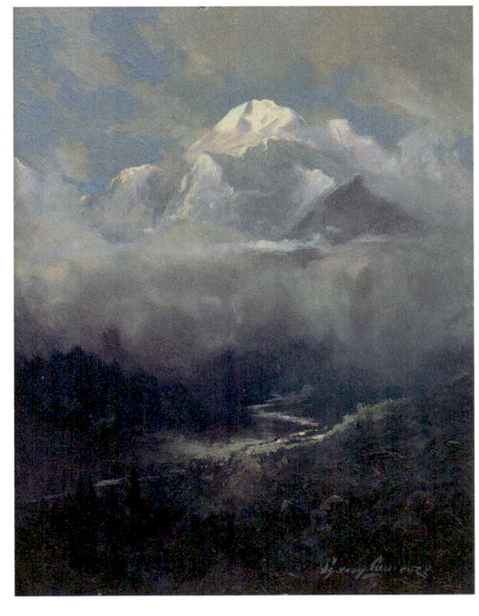

SYDNEY LAURENCE (1865–1940)
Mount McKinley, circa 1925
Oil on board
10 × 8 inches

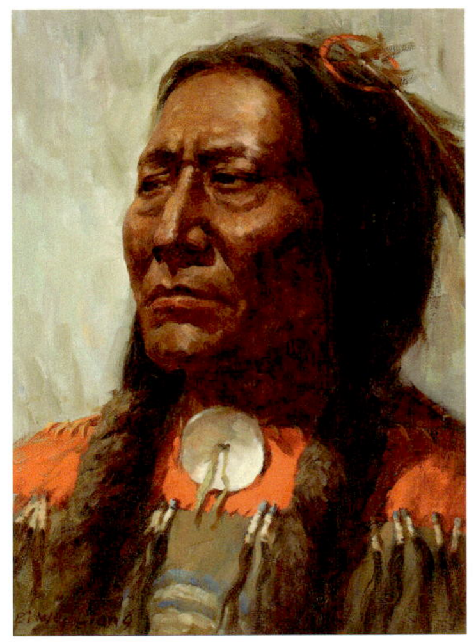

BI WEI LIANG (BORN 1957)
Mad Wolf, Blackfeet, circa 2011
Oil on linen
16 × 12 inches

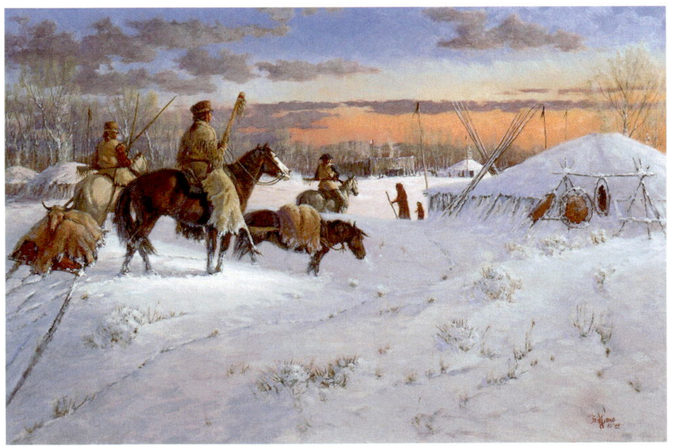

TED LONG (1932–2007)
Winter at Fort Mandan, Lewis and Clark 1804–05, date unknown
Oil on canvas
20 × 30 inches

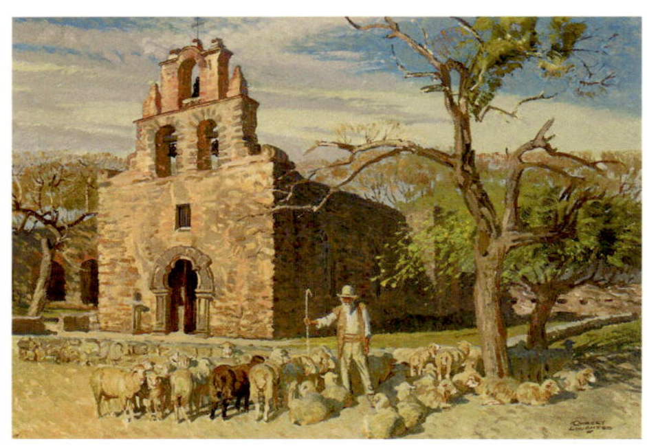

ROBERT LOUGHEED (1910–1982)
Old Mission of San Antonio, 1980
Oil on board
20 × 30 inches

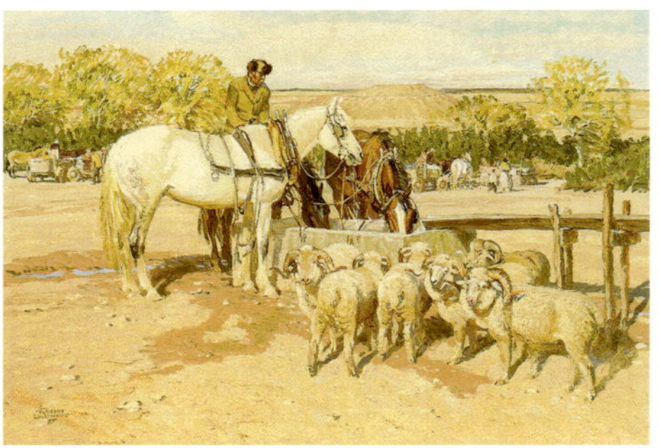

ROBERT LOUGHEED (1910–1982)
Navajo Drinking Trough, date unknown
Oil on board
20 × 30 inches

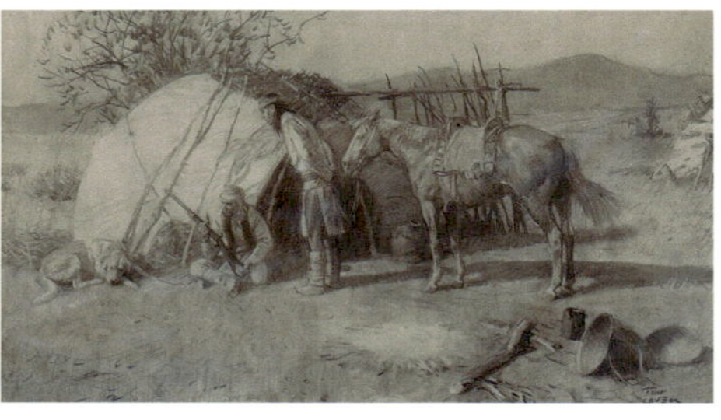

TOM LOVELL (1909–1997)
Study for The Gun Doctor, circa 1985
Charcoal on paper
13½ × 24½ inches

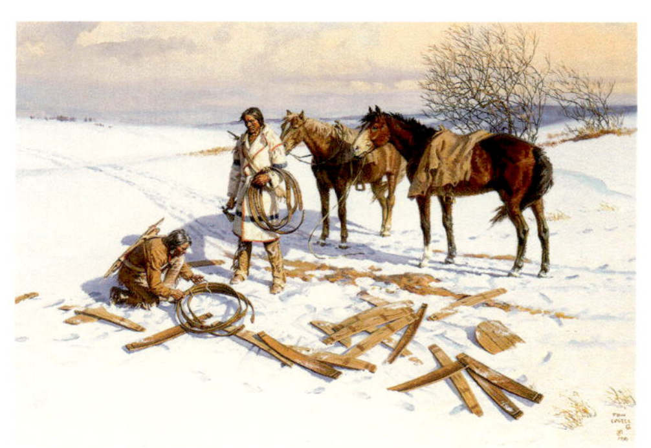

TOM LOVELL (1909–1997)
Barrel Hoops for Arrowheads, 1991
Oil on canvas
24 × 34 inches

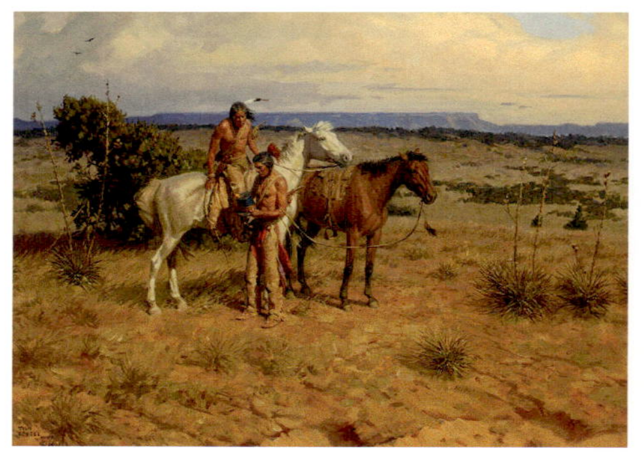

TOM LOVELL (1909–1997)
The Dragoon's Hat, 1991
Oil on canvas
20 × 28 inches

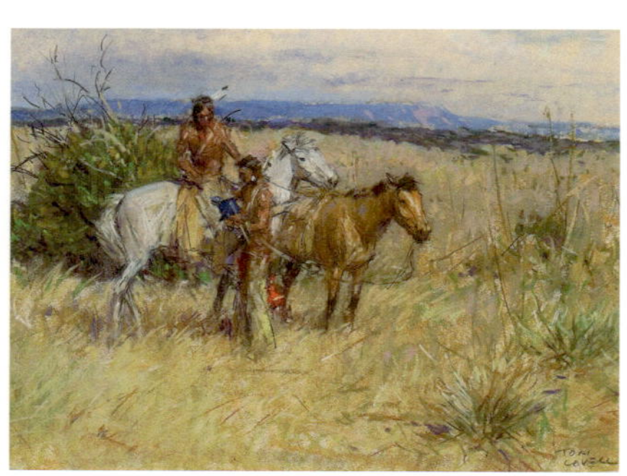

TOM LOVELL (1909–1997)
Study for The Dragoon's Hat, circa 1991
Pastel on paper
7½ × 11 inches

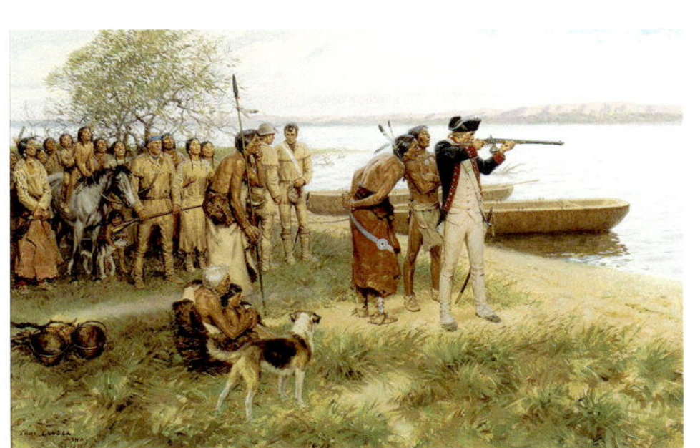

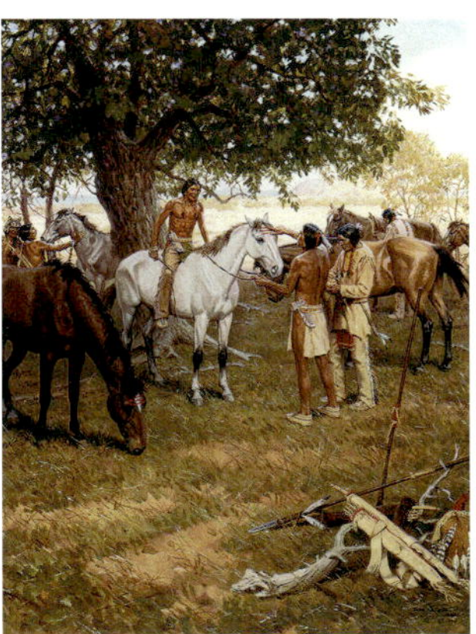

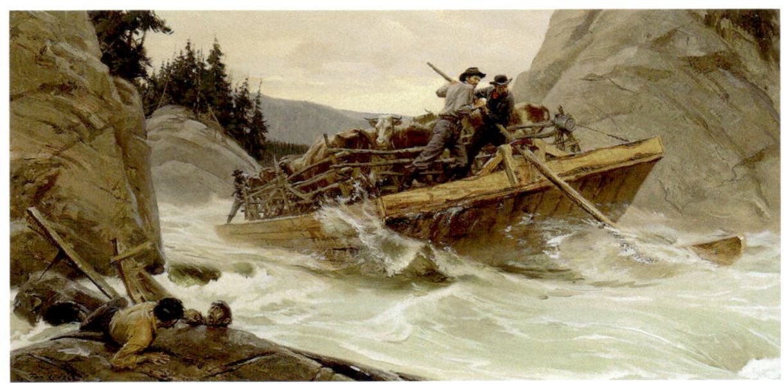

TOM LOVELL (1909–1997)
Captain Clark and the Air Gun, 1991
Oil on canvas
24 × 38 inches

TOM LOVELL (1909–1997)
Painting the Stolen Horses, 1994
Oil on canvas
36 × 28 inches

TOM LOVELL (1909–1997)
Cattle Drive—Five Fingers Rapids, Yukon, date unknown
Oil on canvas
17 × 34 inches

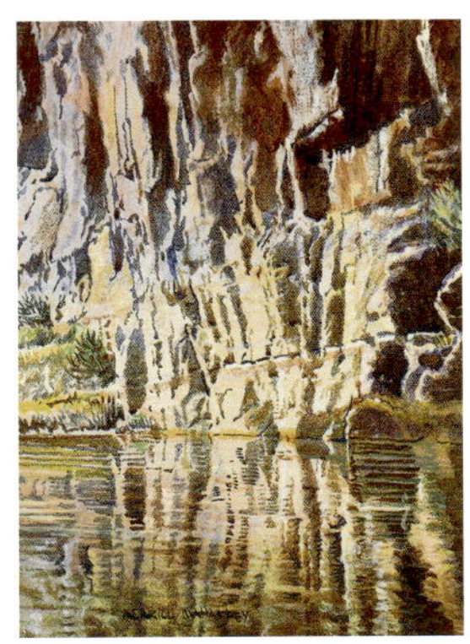

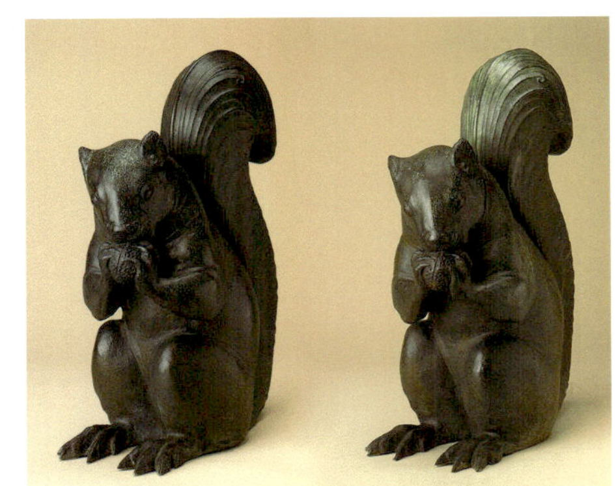

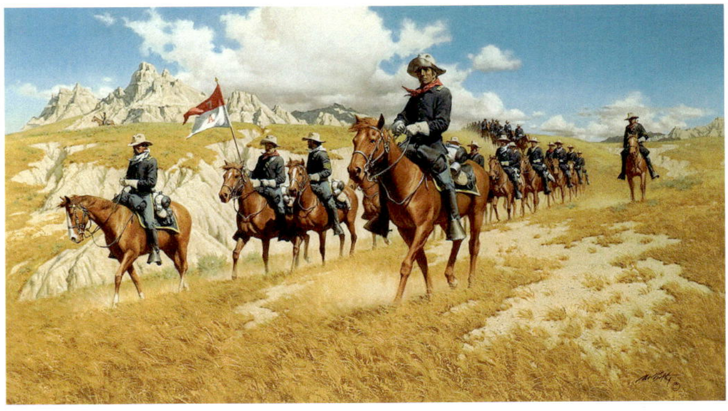

MERRILL MAHAFFEY
(BORN 1937)
Green River Reflections, 1997
Acrylic on board
11 × 8½ inches

PAUL MANSHIP (1885–1966)
Pair of Squirrels, circa 1930
Bronze
16 × 6½ × 12 inches, each

FRANK MCCARTHY (1924–2002)
In the Badlands, circa 1985
Oil on canvas
22 × 40 inches

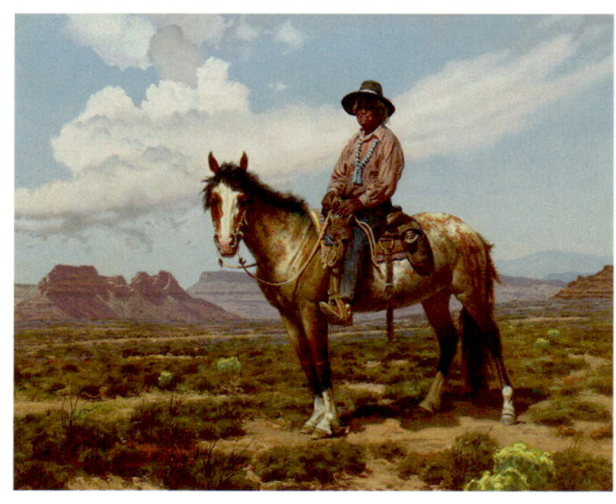

R. BROWNELL MCGREW (1916–1994)
Charlie Salt, Mounted, 1983
Oil on board
24 × 30 inches

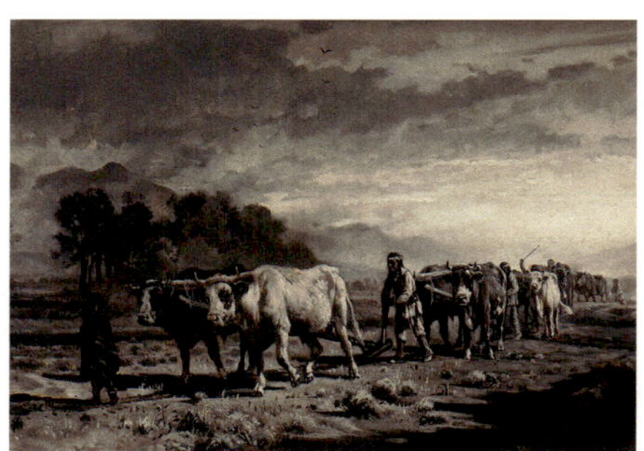

PETER MORAN (1841–1914)
The Taos Harvest—A Straight Furrow, circa 1882
Oil on board
11 × 16 inches

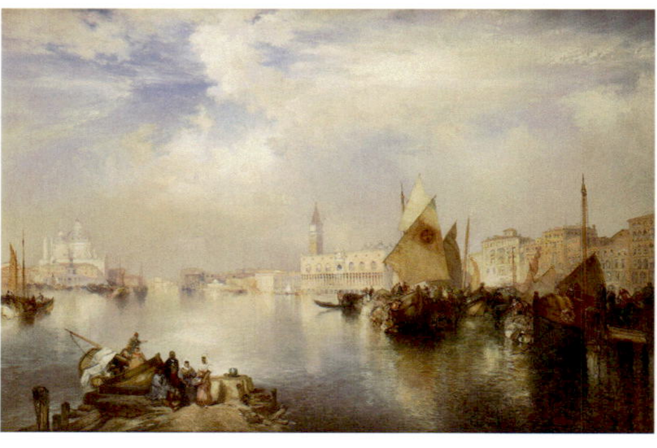

THOMAS MORAN (1837–1926)
Grand Canal, Venice, 1904
Oil on canvas
20⅛ × 30⅛ inches

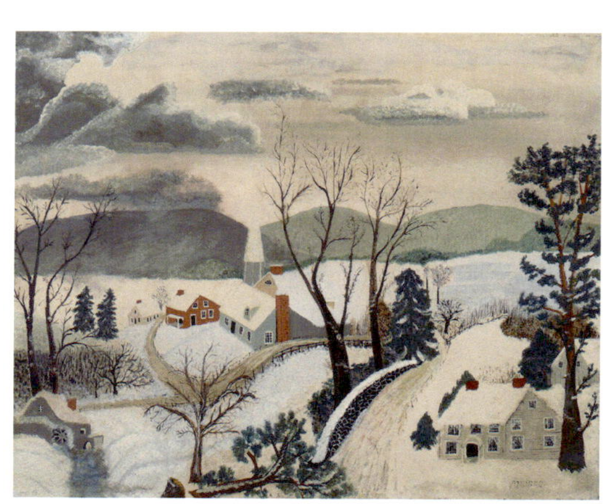

ANNA MARY ROBERTSON (GRANDMA) MOSES
(1860–1961)
In Days Gone By, 1942
Oil on board
16 × 20 inches

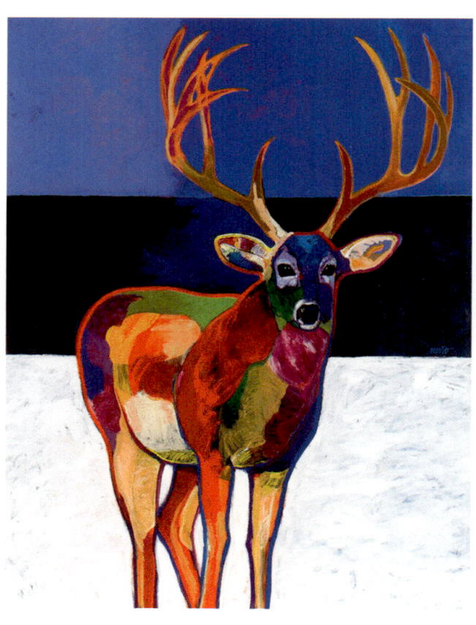

JOHN NIETO (BORN 1936)
White-Tailed Buck, 1999
Acrylic on canvas
60 × 48 inches

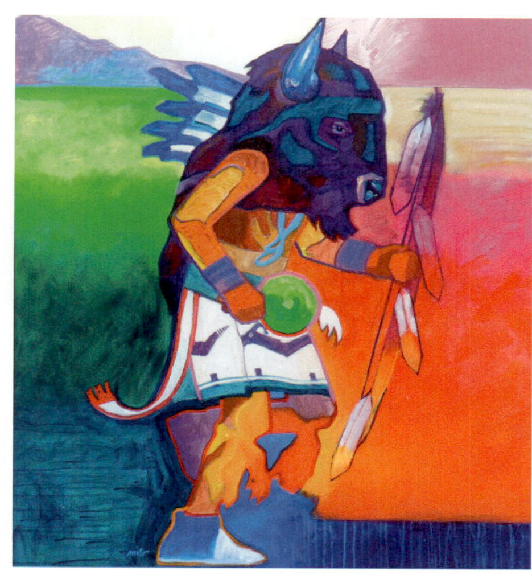

JOHN NIETO (BORN 1936)
Buffalo Dance, 2007
Acrylic on canvas
44 × 40 inches

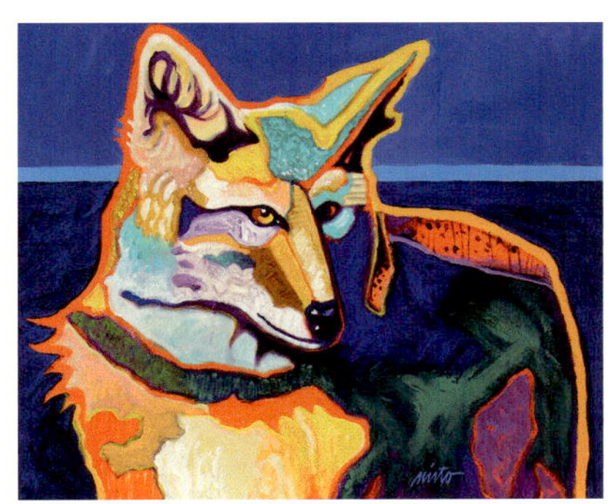

JOHN NIETO (BORN 1936)
Coyote, 2008
Oil on canvas
16 × 20 inches

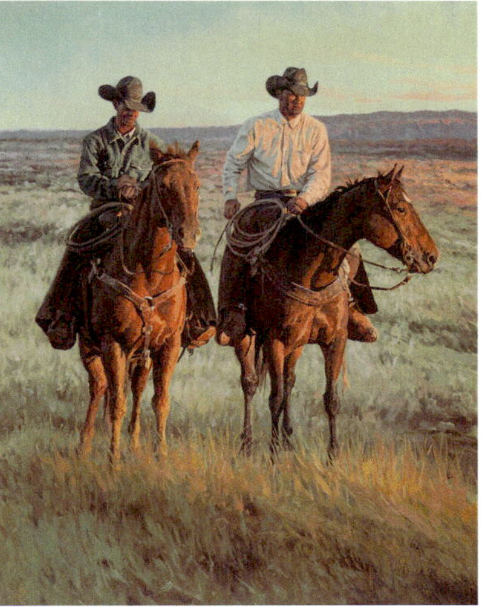

BILL OWEN (1942–2013)
Cowboys of the CO Bar, circa 2005
Oil on canvas
30 × 24 inches

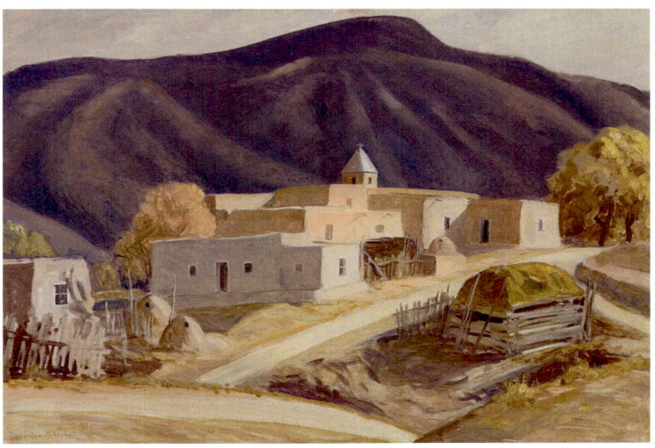

SHELDON PARSONS (1866–1943)
Chimayo, date unknown
Oil on board
24 × 36 inches

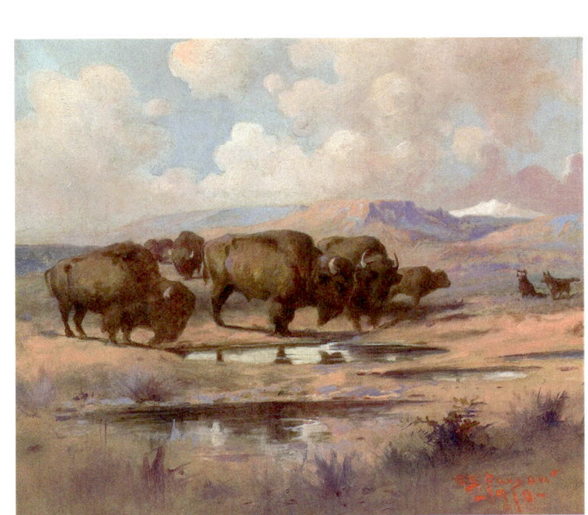

EDGAR S. PAXSON (1852–1919)
Buffalo Watch, 1910
Oil on canvas
10 × 12 inches

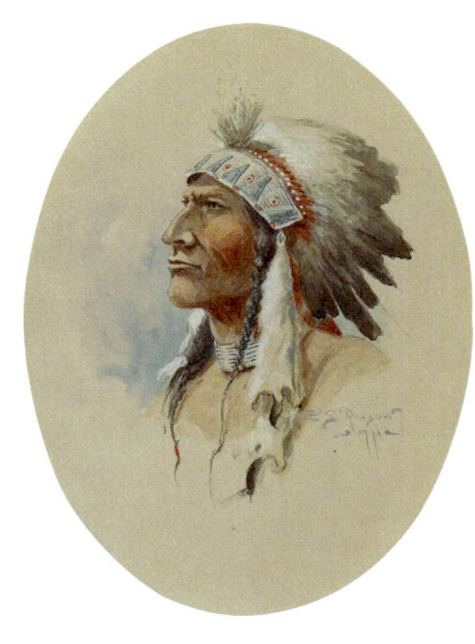

EDGAR S. PAXSON (1852–1919)
Sioux Chief, 1911
Watercolor on paper
12½ × 9½ inches

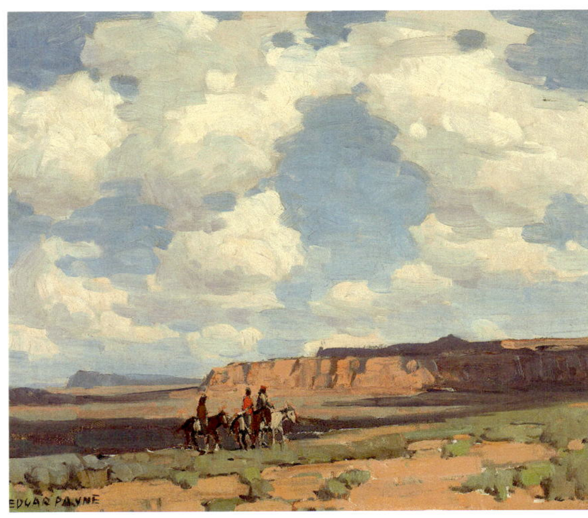

EDGAR PAYNE (1883–1947)
Desert Clouds, circa 1930
Oil on canvas
20 × 24 inches

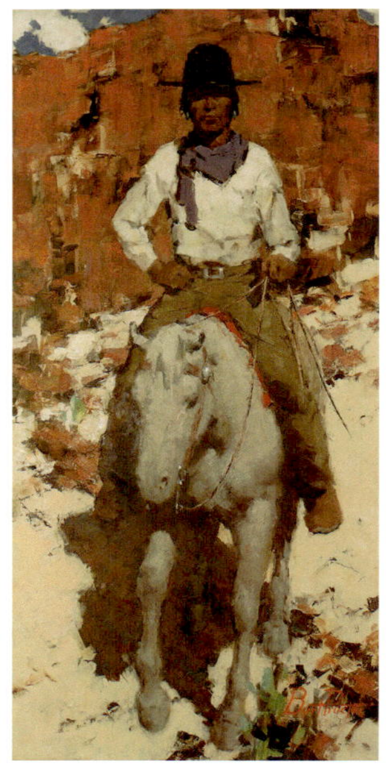

BURT PROCTER (1901–1980)
Navajo Rider, date unknown
Oil on canvas
36 × 18 inches

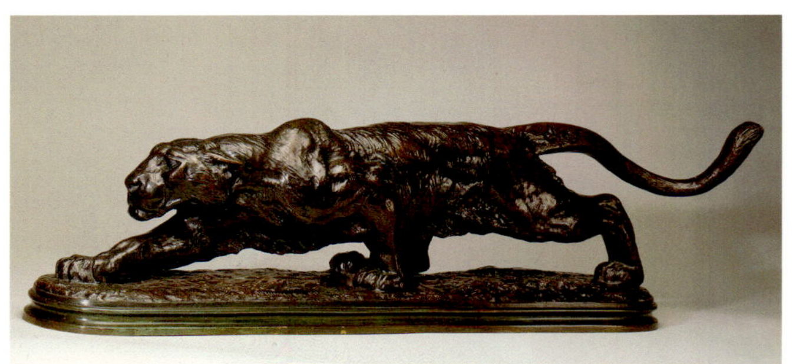

ALEXANDER PHIMISTER PROCTOR (1860–1950)
Panther, 1891–92
Bronze
9¾ × 37 × 6½ inches

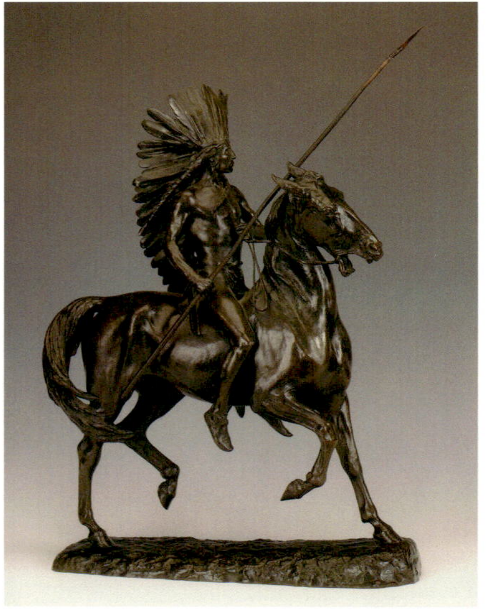

ALEXANDER PHIMISTER PROCTOR (1860–1950)
Indian Warrior, 1898
Bronze
21¾ × 17 × 5 inches

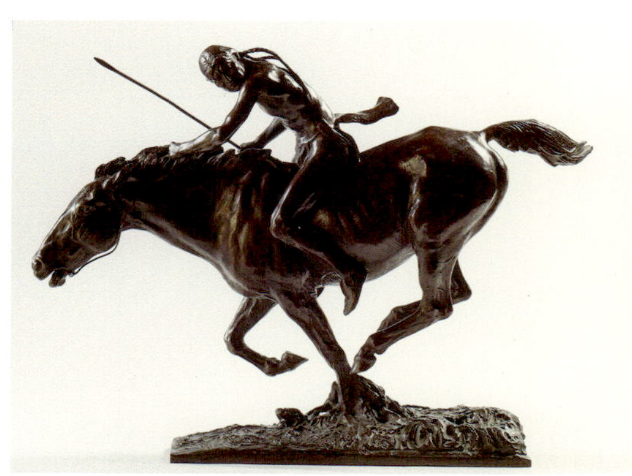

ALEXANDER PHIMISTER PROCTOR (1860–1950)
Pursued, 1914
Bronze
16½ × 23 × 6 inches

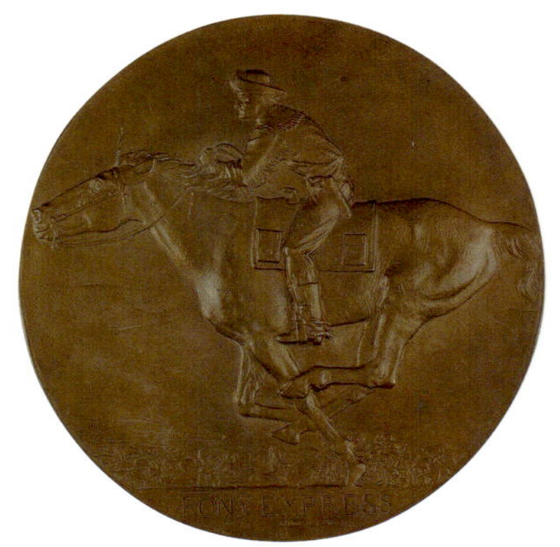

ALEXANDER PHIMISTER PROCTOR
(1860–1950)
Pony Express, 1931
Bronze relief
Diameter: 17 inches

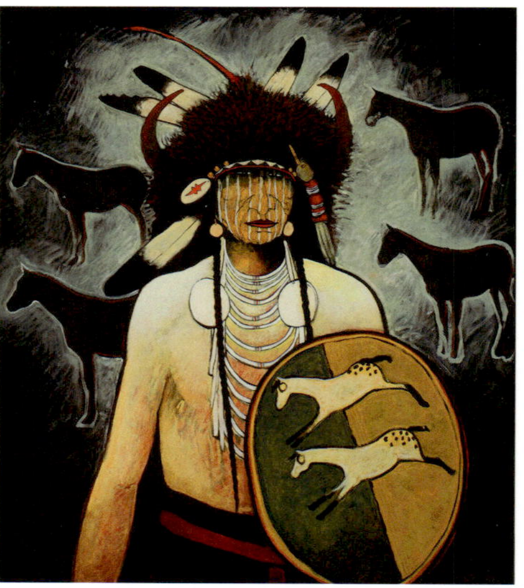

KEVIN RED STAR (BORN 1943)
Buffalo Horse Medicine, circa 2007
Mixed media
44 × 40 inches

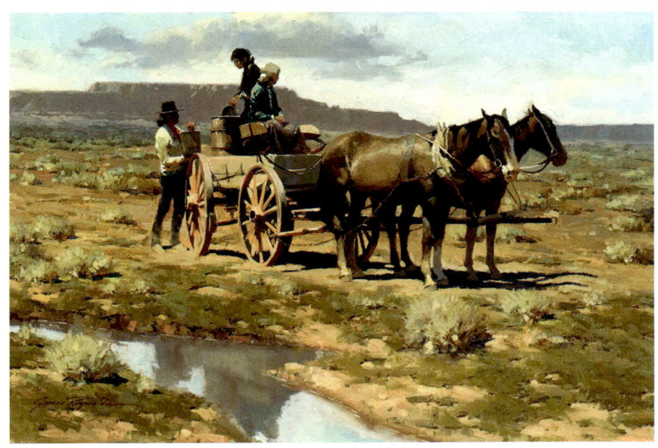

JAMES REYNOLDS (1926–2010)
The Water Hole, date unknown
Oil on board
24 × 36 inches

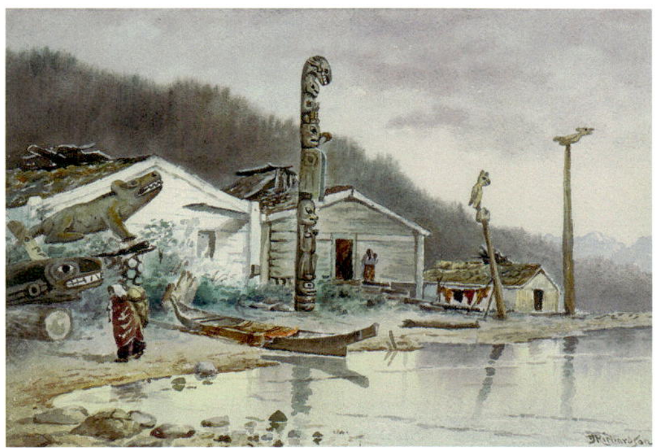

THEODORE J. RICHARDSON (1855–1914)
Wrangell, Alaska, circa 1890
Watercolor on paper
10 × 14½ inches

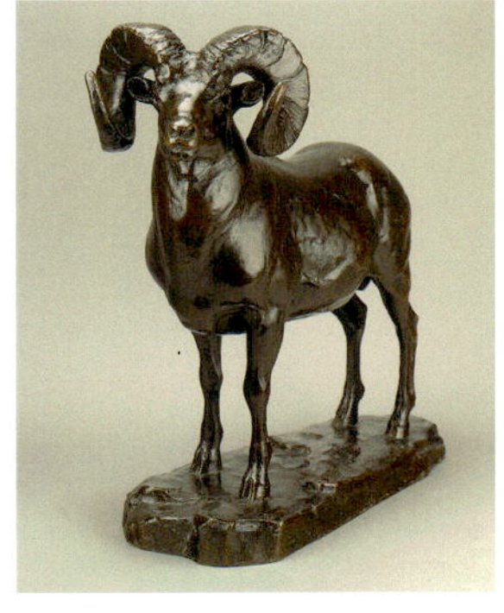

CARL RUNGIUS (1869–1959)
Bighorn Sheep, 1916
Bronze
17 × 17 × 7 inches

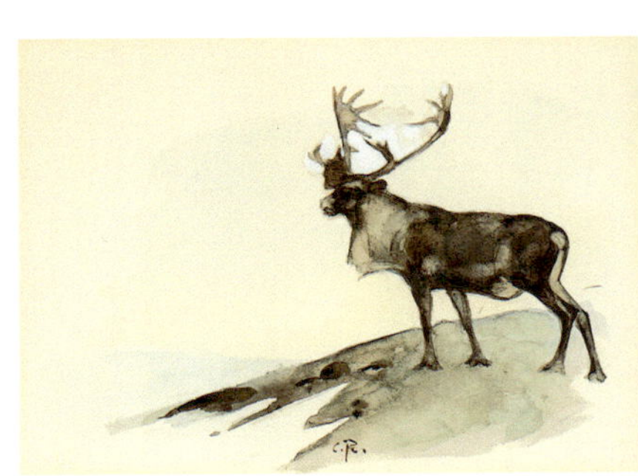

CARL RUNGIUS (1869–1959)
Caribou, circa 1906
Gouache on paper
5 × 7 inches

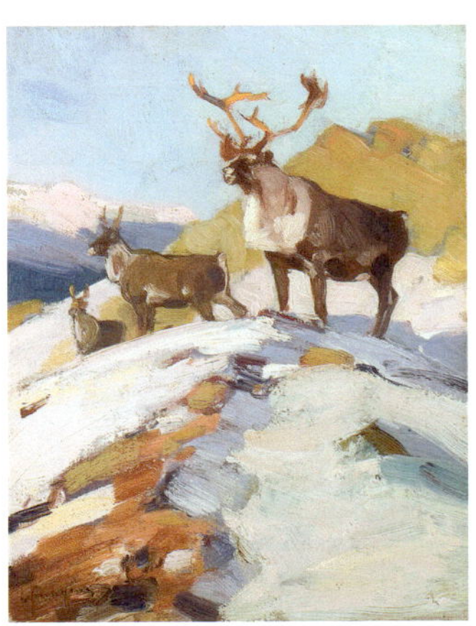

CARL RUNGIUS (1869–1959)
Caribou, circa 1915
Oil on board
10 × 8 inches

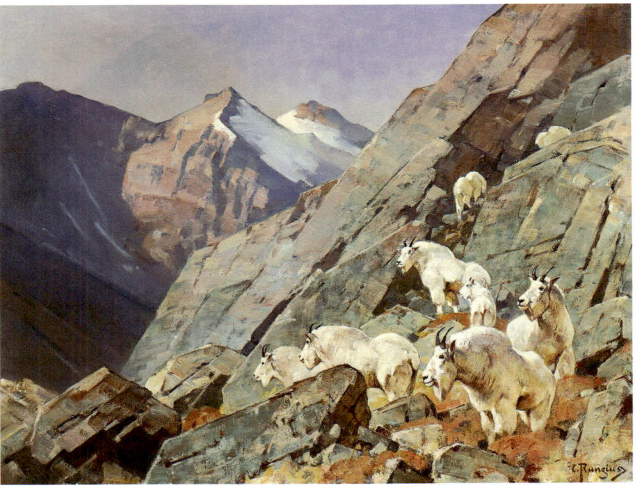

CARL RUNGIUS (1869–1959)
Mountain Goats, circa 1955
Oil on canvas
30 × 40 inches

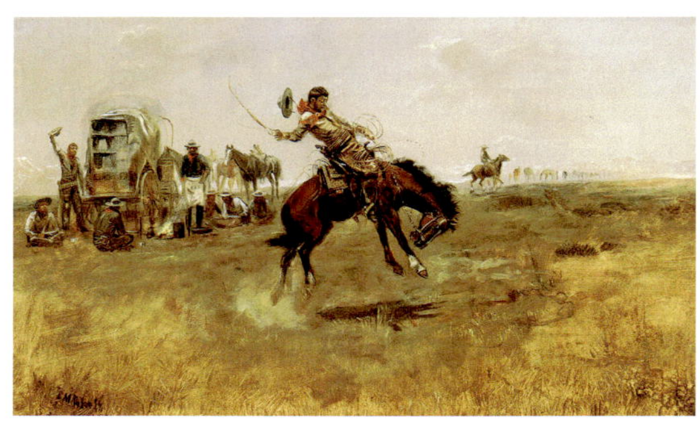

CHARLES M. RUSSELL (1864–1926)
Rider of the Rough String, 1890
Oil on canvas
14 × 24 inches

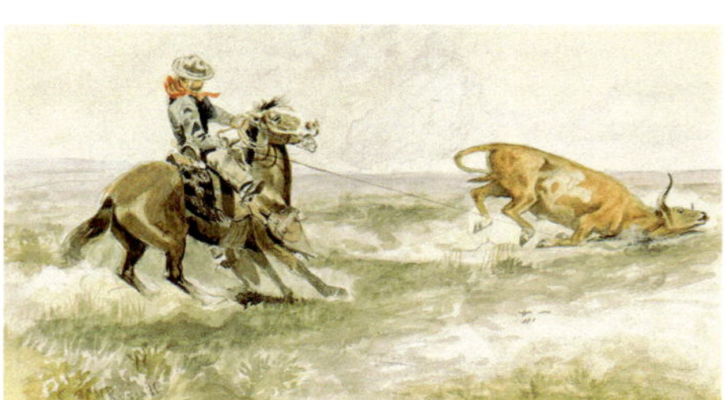

CHARLES M. RUSSELL (1864–1926)
Cowboy Lassoing a Steer, circa 1892
Watercolor on paper
6¼ × 11¾ inches

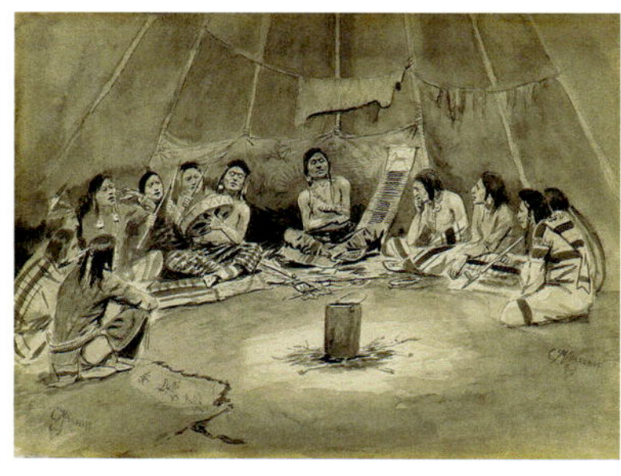

CHARLES M. RUSSELL (1864–1926)
The Bone Game, circa 1894
Watercolor on paper
11 × 15¼ inches

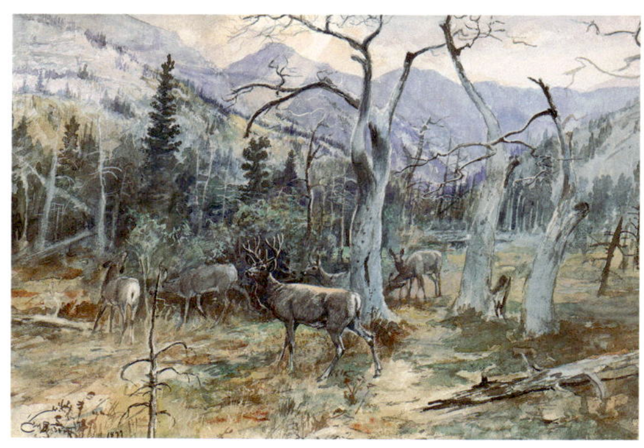

CHARLES M. RUSSELL (1864–1926)
Nature's Monarchs, 1899
Watercolor on paper
14½ × 20¼ inches

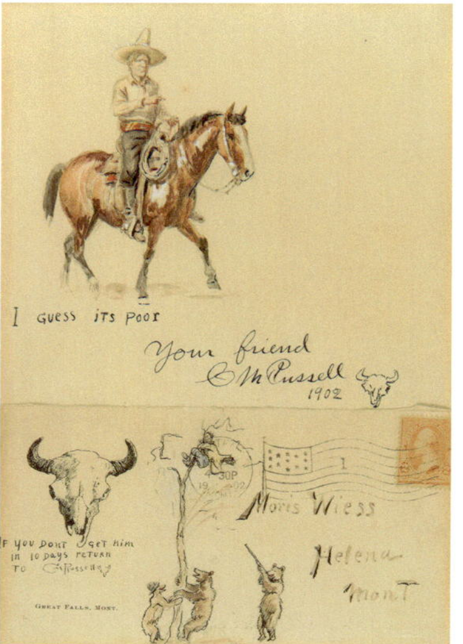

CHARLES M. RUSSELL (1864–1926)
Illustrated letter and envelope to Moris Wiess
[Maurice S. Weiss], 1902
Ink and watercolor on paper
9 × 6 inches

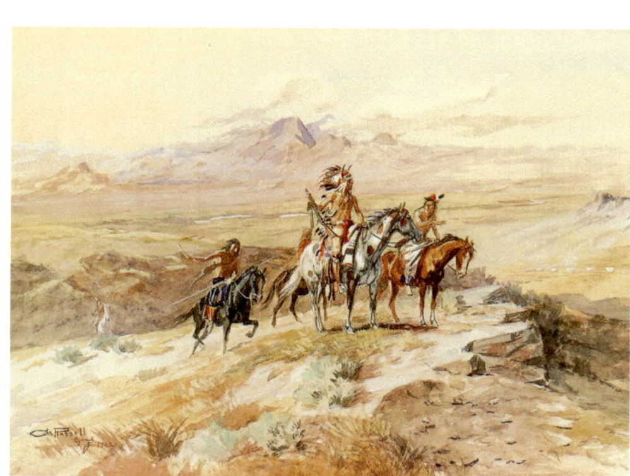

CHARLES M. RUSSELL (1864–1926)
Indians Scouting a Wagon Train, 1902
Watercolor on paper
14½ × 21⅜ inches

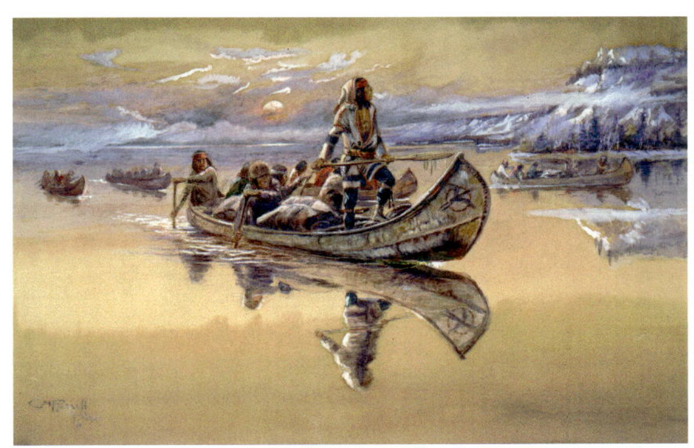

CHARLES M. RUSSELL (1864–1926)
Indian Canoe Party, 1906
Watercolor on paper
13¾ × 21⅝ inches

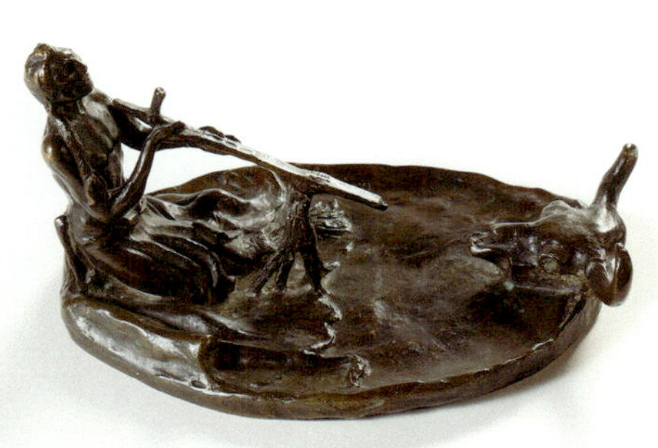

CHARLES M. RUSSELL (1864–1926)
Smoking with the Spirit of the Buffalo, circa 1914
Bronze
5 × 9 × 5½ inches

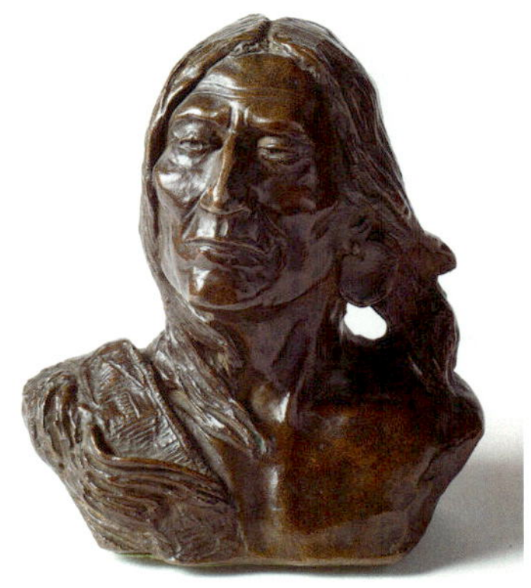

CHARLES M. RUSSELL (1864–1926)
Sleeping Thunder, modeled 1901;
cast 1927–29
Bronze
7 × 6⅝ × 4½ inches

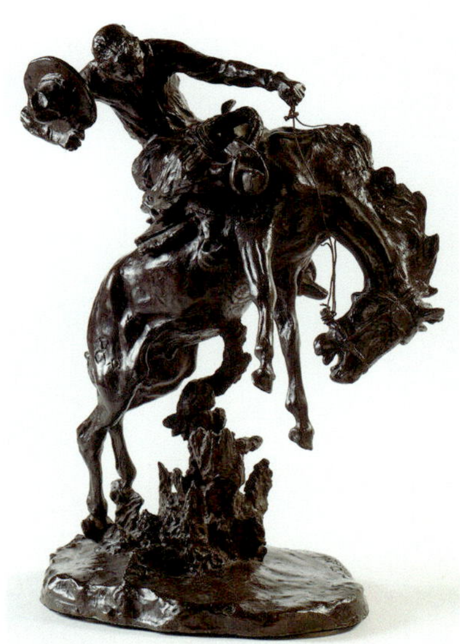

CHARLES M. RUSSELL (1864–1926)
A Bronc Twister, modeled 1911;
cast circa 1929–33
Bronze
18 × 14½ × 9½ inches

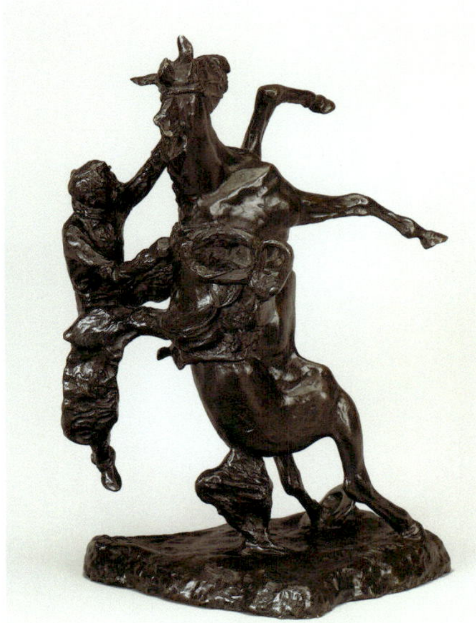

CHARLES M. RUSSELL (1864–1926)
Where the Best Riders Quit, modeled 1921–22;
cast circa 1929–34
Bronze
14½ × 7¾ × 8½ inches

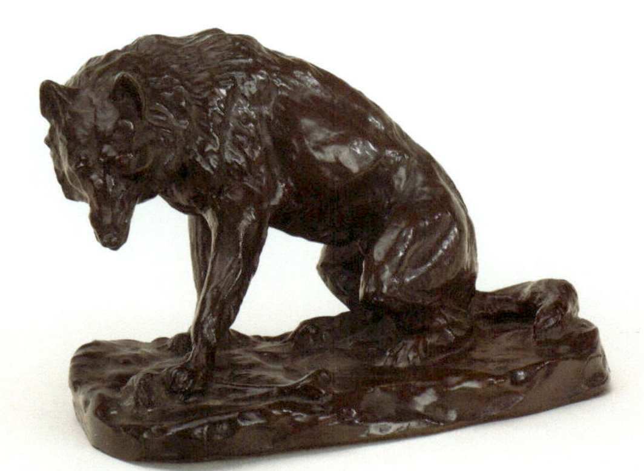

CHARLES M. RUSSELL (1864–1926)
Wolf with Bone, modeled circa 1901; cast circa 1941–42
Bronze
7 × 6⅝ × 4½ inches

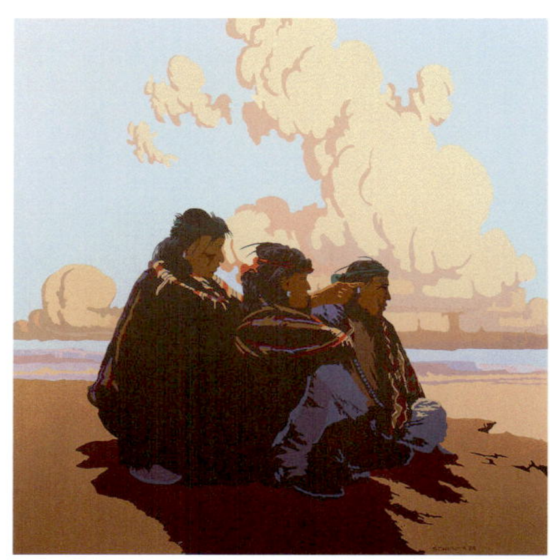

BILL SCHENCK (BORN 1947)
Three Zunis, 1989
Oil on canvas
51 × 51 inches

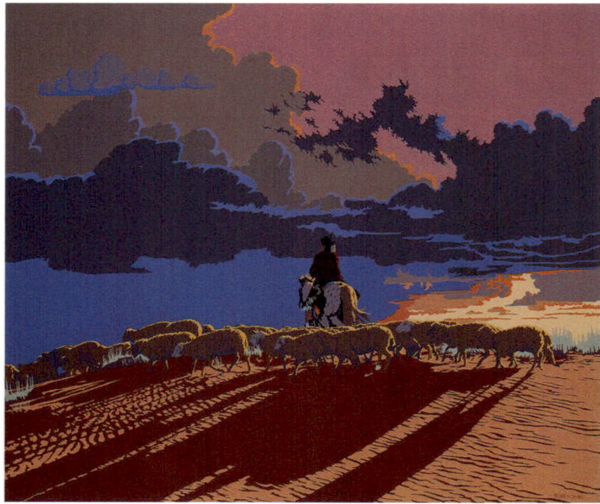

BILL SCHENCK (BORN 1947)
Along the High Sands, 1990
Oil on canvas
50 × 60 inches

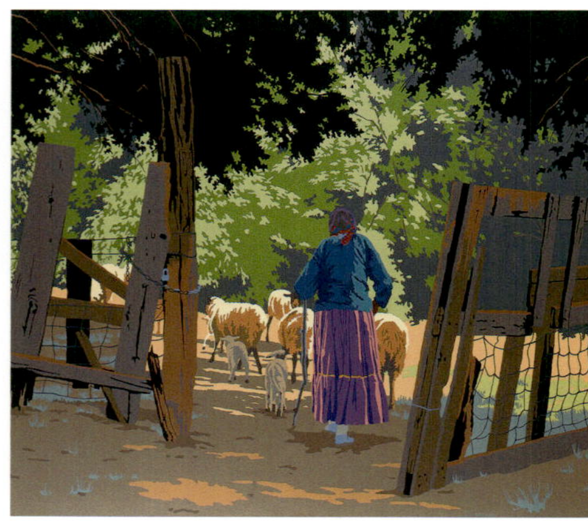

BILL SCHENCK (BORN 1947)
A Walk to Water, 1992
Oil on canvas
48 × 56 inches

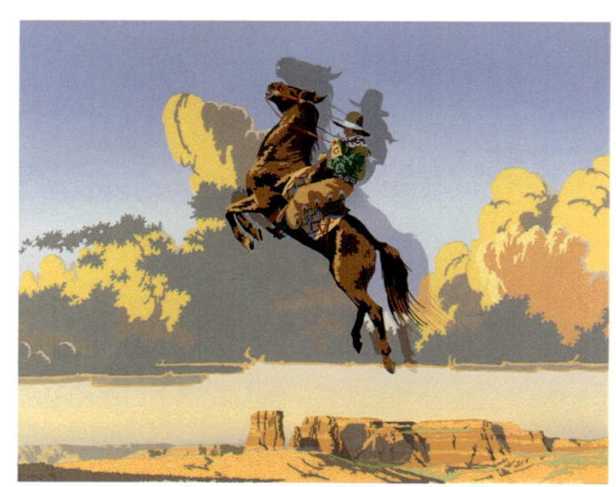

BILL SCHENCK (BORN 1947)
Cowgirl Over Kachina Mesa, 1996
Oil on canvas
35 × 45 inches

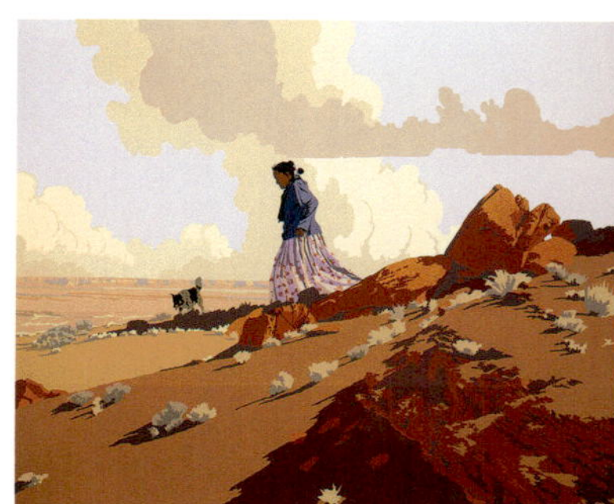

BILL SCHENCK (BORN 1947)
An Ancient Place, 1999
Oil on canvas
40 × 50 inches

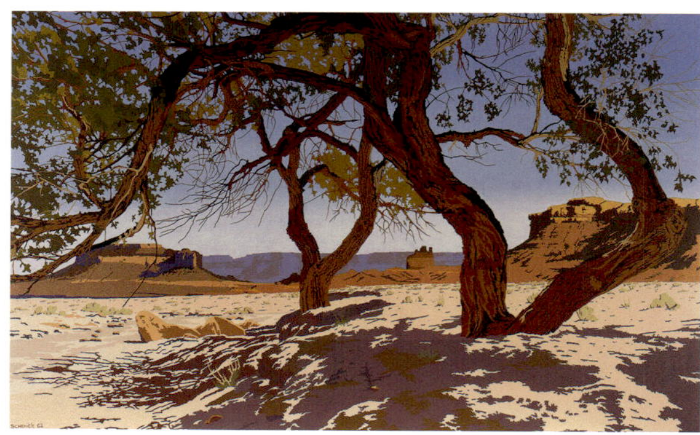

BILL SCHENCK (BORN 1947)
South of the San Juan River, 2002
Oil on canvas
48 × 80 inches

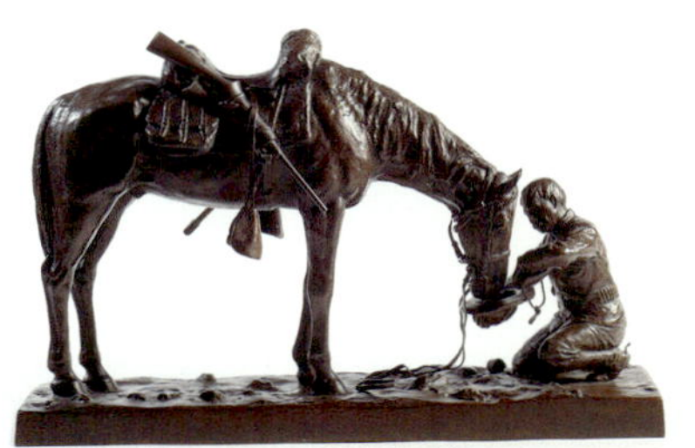

CHARLES SCHREYVOGEL (1861–1912)
The Last Drop, 1903
Bronze
11⅝ × 18¾ × 5¼ inches

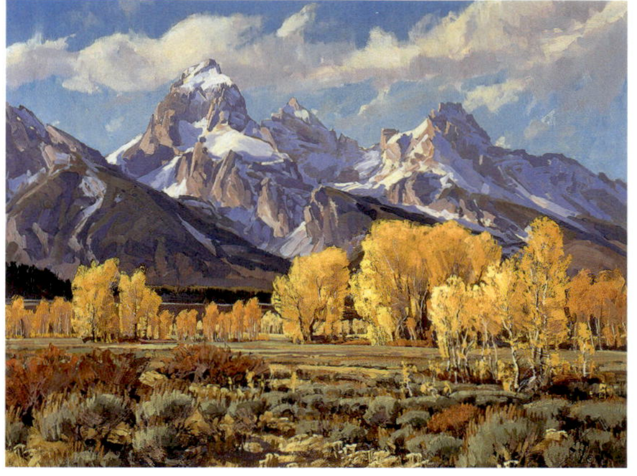

CONRAD SCHWIERING (1916–1986)
Golden Time, 1979
Oil on canvas
30 × 40 inches

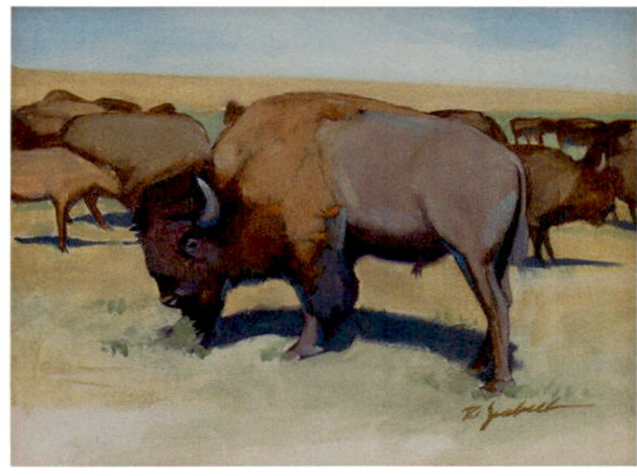

ROBERT SEABECK (BORN 1945)
Buffalo, circa 1998
Oil on panel
9 × 12 inches

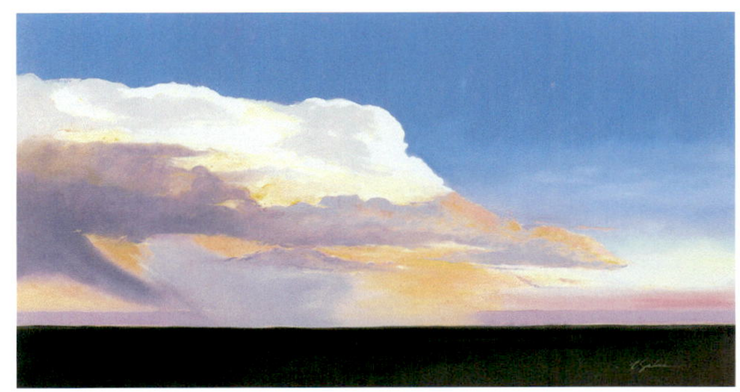

ROBERT SEABECK (BORN 1945)
Clouds, circa 1998
Oil on Masonite
25 × 48 inches

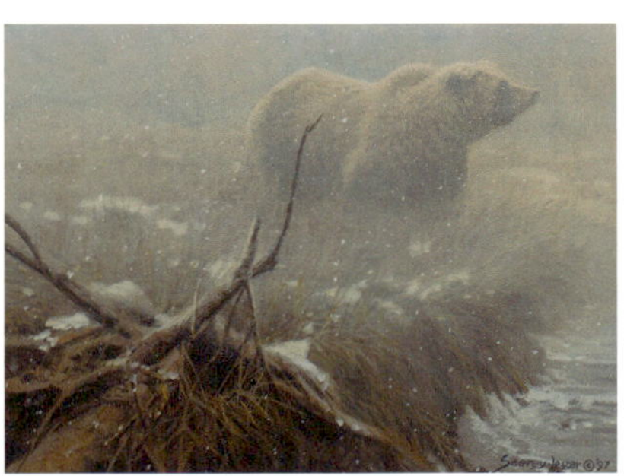

JOHN SEEREY-LESTER (BORN 1945)
Autumn Flurry, 1997
Acrylic on board
9 × 12 inches

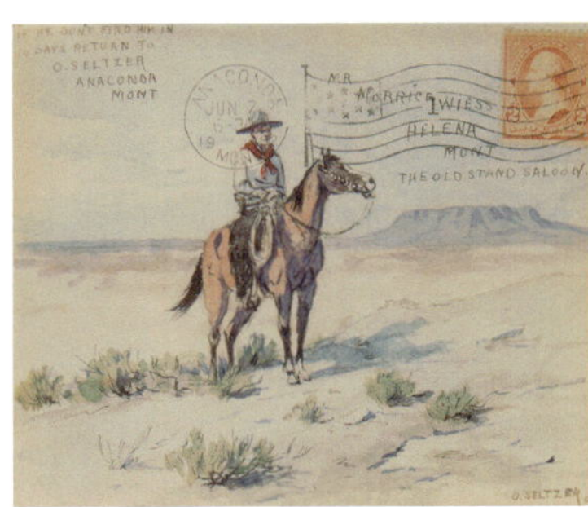

OLAF C. SELTZER (1877–1957)
*Cowboy on Horse—Illustrated Envelope
to Mr. Morrice Wiess* [Maurice S. Weiss],
1902
Mixed media on paper
4 × 5 inches

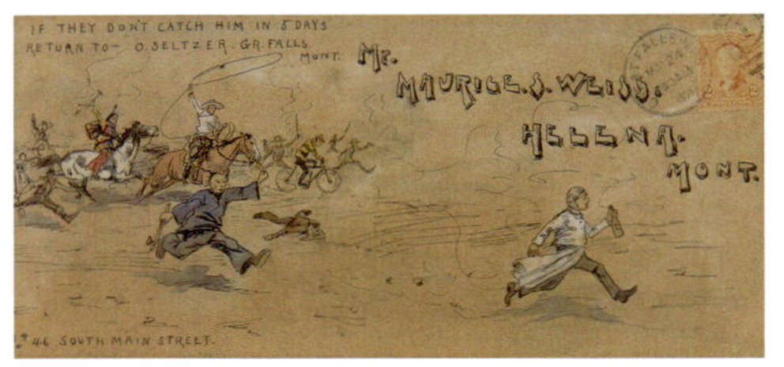

OLAF C. SELTZER (1877–1957)
The Race—Illustrated Envelope to Mr. Maurice S. Weiss, 1903
Mixed media on paper
4 × 8½ inches

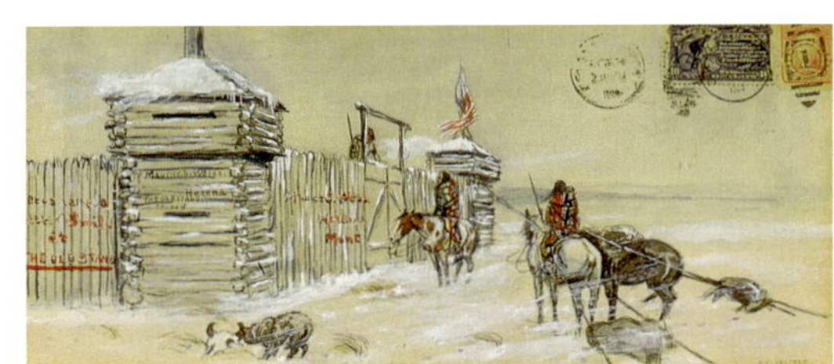

OLAF C. SELTZER (1877–1957)
The Fort—Illustrated Envelope to Maurice S. Weiss, 1904
Mixed media on paper
4½ × 10½ inches

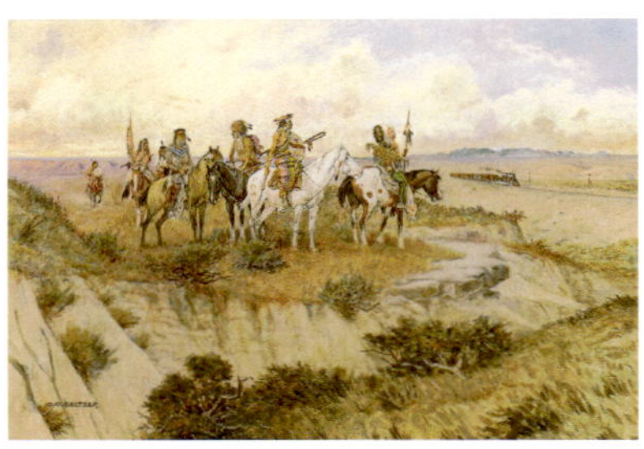

OLAF C. SELTZER (1877–1957)
Trail of the Iron Horse, circa 1930
Oil on canvas
20 × 30 inches

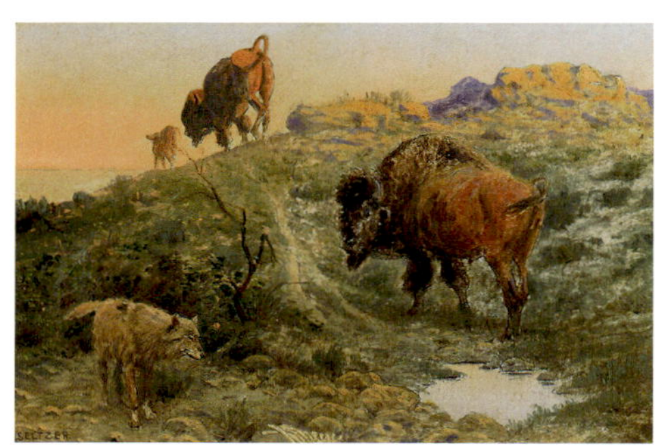

OLAF C. SELTZER (1877–1957)
Buffalo Family, date unknown
Oil on board
6⅝ × 10¼ inches

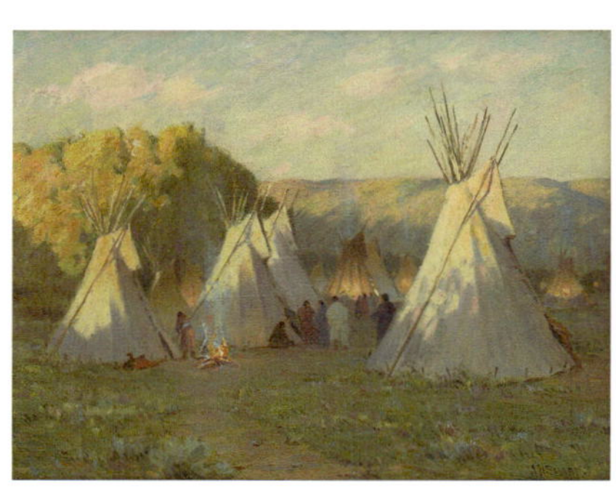

JOSEPH HENRY SHARP (1859–1953)
An Indian Encampment at Sunset, circa 1908
Oil on canvas
12 × 16 inches

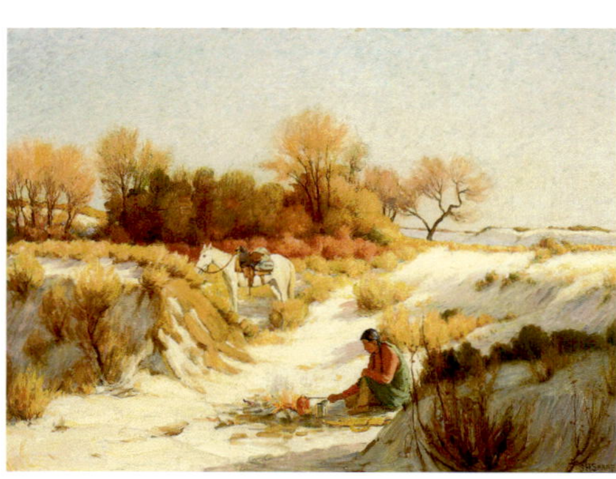

JOSEPH HENRY SHARP (1859–1953)
The Scout, circa 1910
Oil on canvas
26 × 36 inches

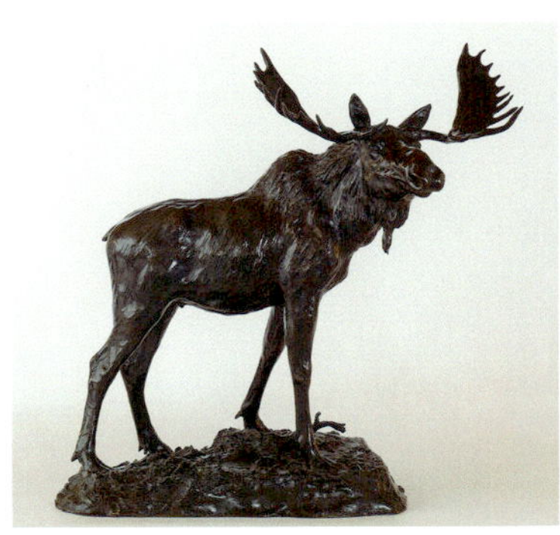

HENRY MERWIN SHRADY (1871–1922)
Bull Moose, 1900
Bronze
20 × 19 × 10 inches

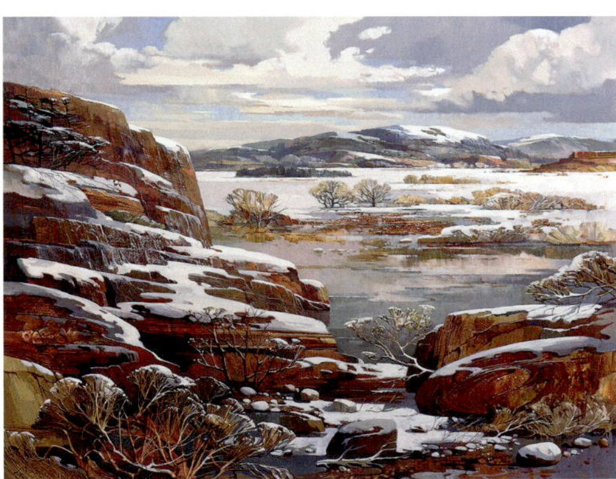

LAURENCE SISSON (BORN 1928)
Canyon and Snow Harmonies, date unknown
Oil on panel
37½ × 47½ inches

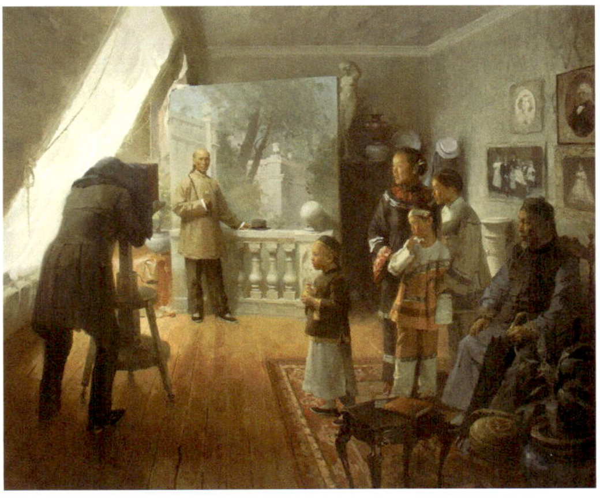

MIAN SITU (BORN 1953)
The Entrepreneur—San Francisco, 2006
Oil on canvas
44 × 54 inches

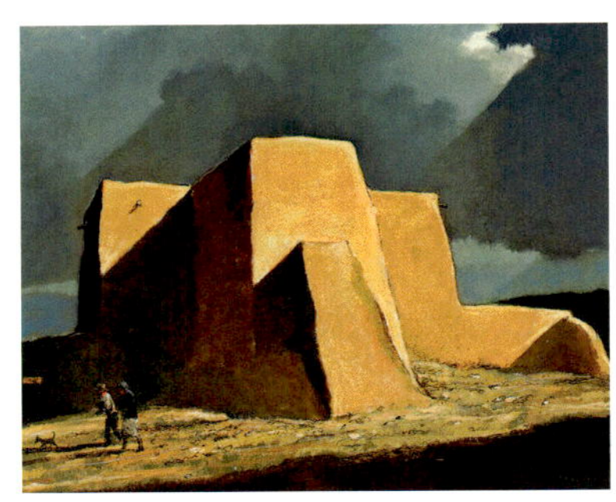

ERIC SLOANE (1905–1985)
Sunshine and Adobe—Ranchos de Taos Mission, 1946
Oil on board
17 × 22 inches

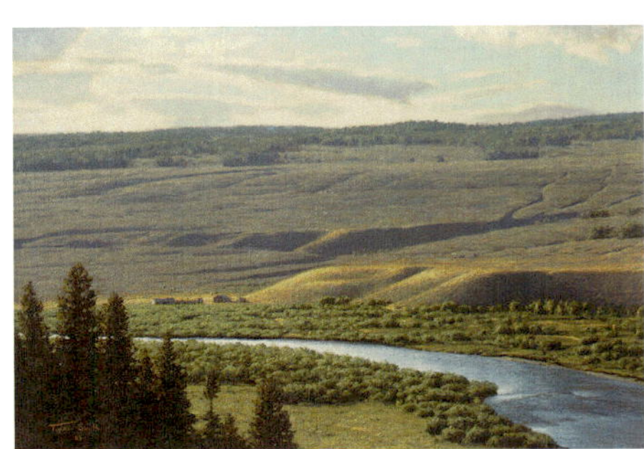

TUCKER SMITH (BORN 1940)
Big Bend of the Green River, 1983
Oil on canvas
16 × 24 inches

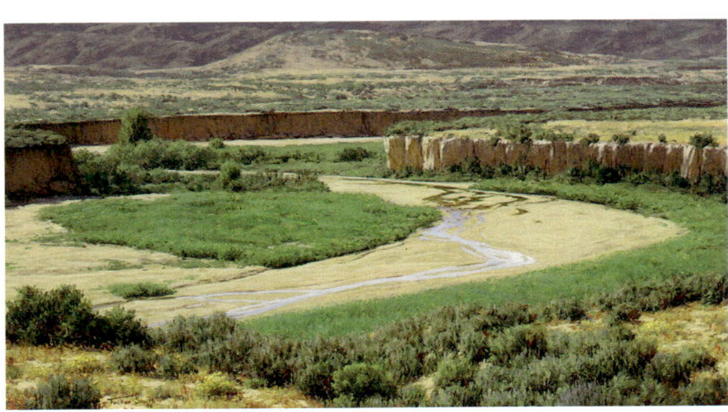

TUCKER SMITH (BORN 1940)
Wyoming Wash, 1985
Oil on canvas
16 × 30 inches

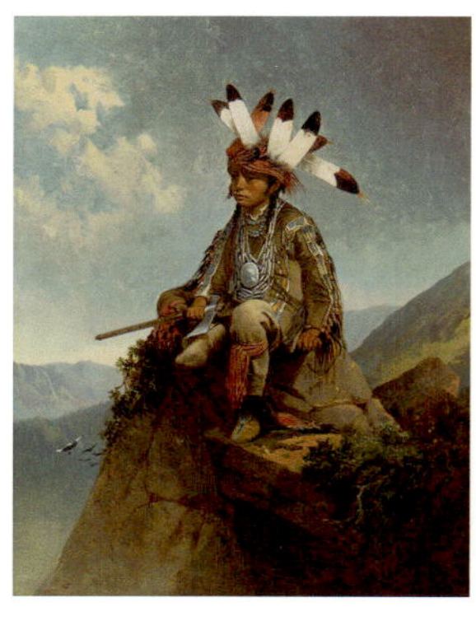

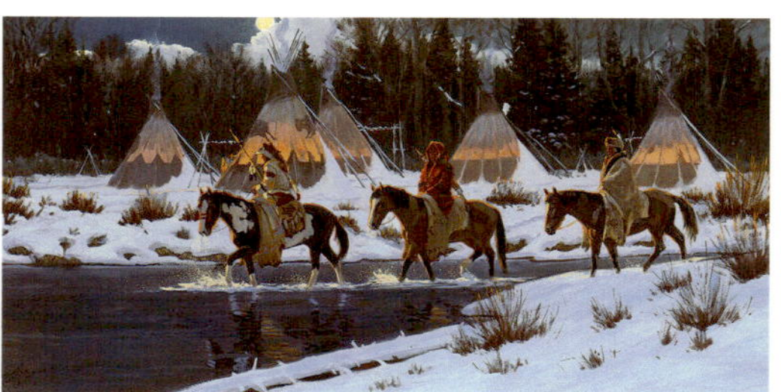

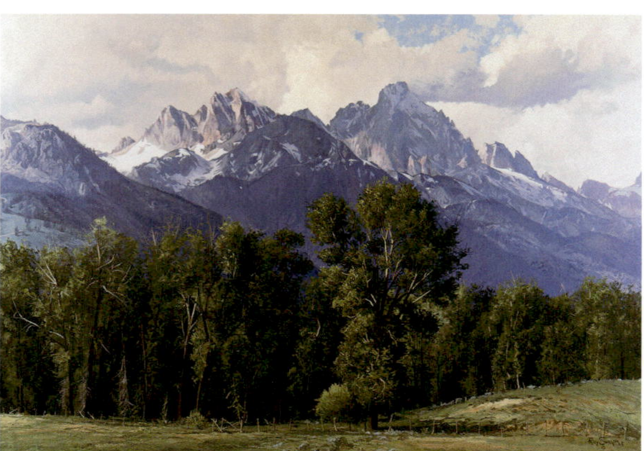

JOHN MIX STANLEY
(1814–1872)
Young Chief, 1868
Oil on canvas
20 × 16 inches

RON STEWART (BORN 1941)
Warm Homecoming, 1998
Oil on canvas
15 × 30 inches

RAY SWANSON (1937–2004)
Teton Spring, date unknown
Oil on canvas
40 × 60 inches

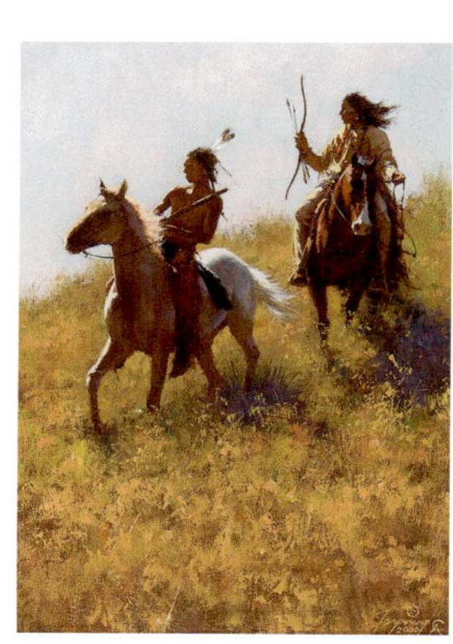

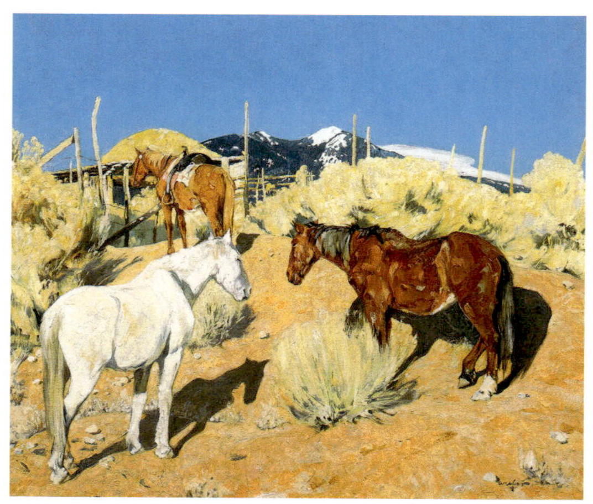

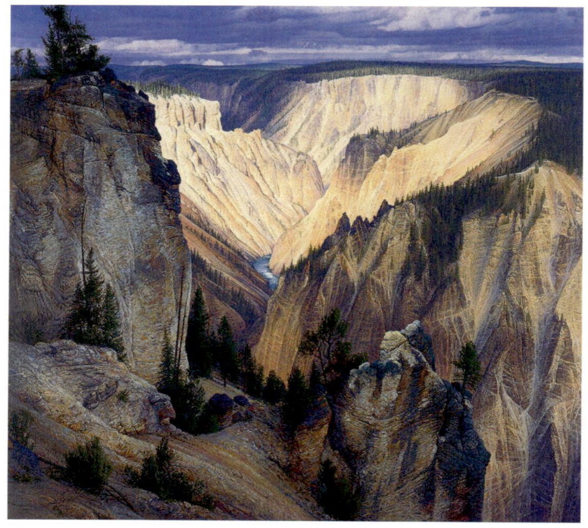

HOWARD TERPNING (BORN 1927)
Flanking the Enemy, 2000
Oil on board
12 × 9 inches

WALTER UFER (1876–1936)
Waiting for the Gate to Open, circa 1935
Oil on canvas
25 × 30 inches

CURT WALTERS (BORN 1950)
Grand Canyon of the Yellowstone, 1984
Oil on canvas
48 × 54 inches

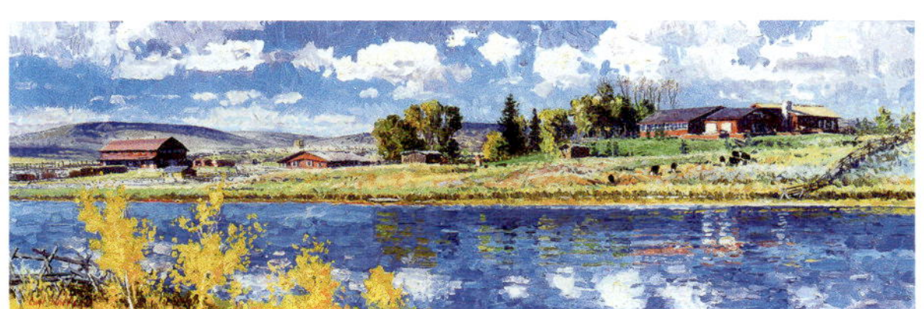

CURT WALTERS (BORN 1950)
CL Bar Ranch Fall, 1990
Oil on canvas
10 × 30 inches

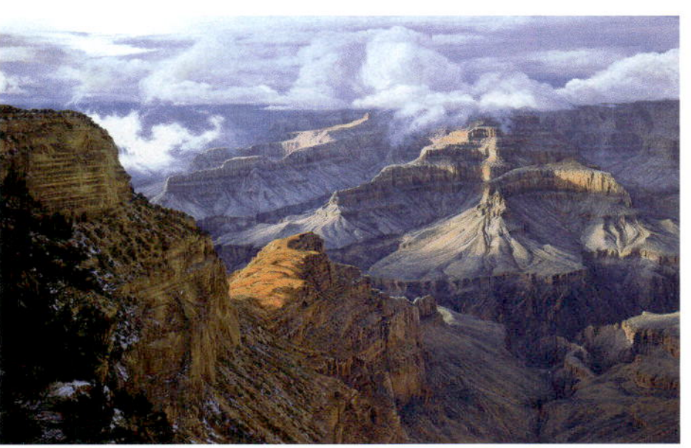

CURT WALTERS (BORN 1950)
The Cathedral Staircase, 2002
Oil on canvas
60 × 96 inches

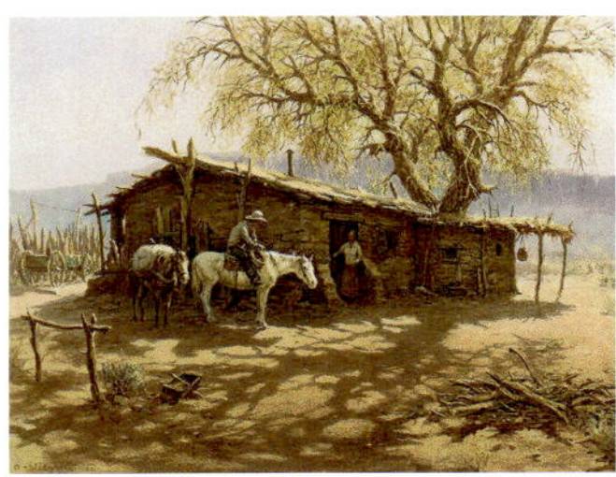

OLAF WIEGHORST (1899–1988)
The Stranger, date unknown
Oil on canvas
28 × 38 inches

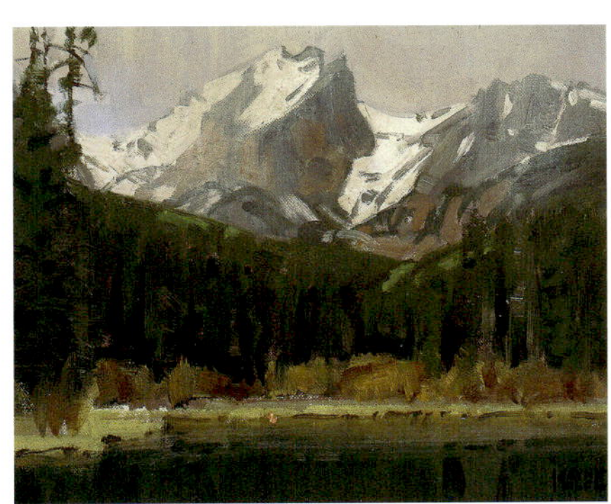

WAYNE WOLFE (BORN 1944)
Mountain Showers, circa 1990
Oil on board
8 × 10 inches

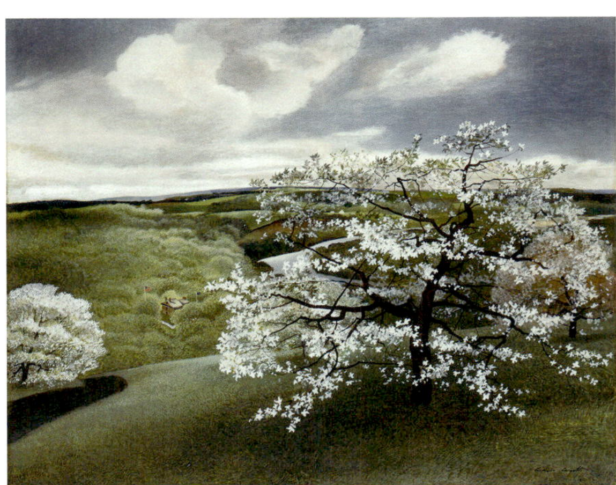

ANDREW WYETH (1917–2009)
Dogwood at Valley Forge, 1941
Tempera on Masonite
22½ × 29¼ inches

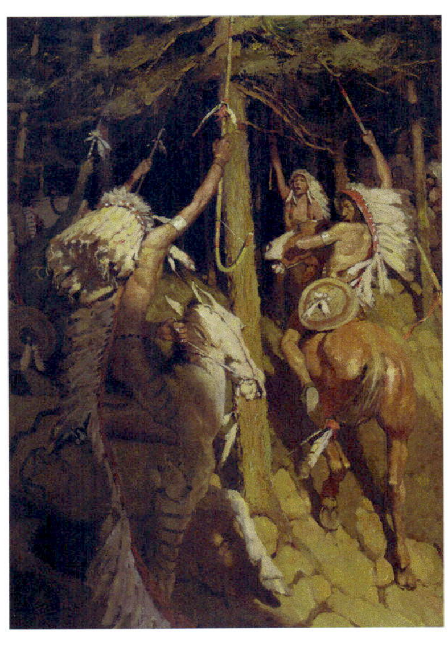

N. C. WYETH (1882–1945)
The Mystery Tree, 1908
Oil on canvas
36 × 26 inches

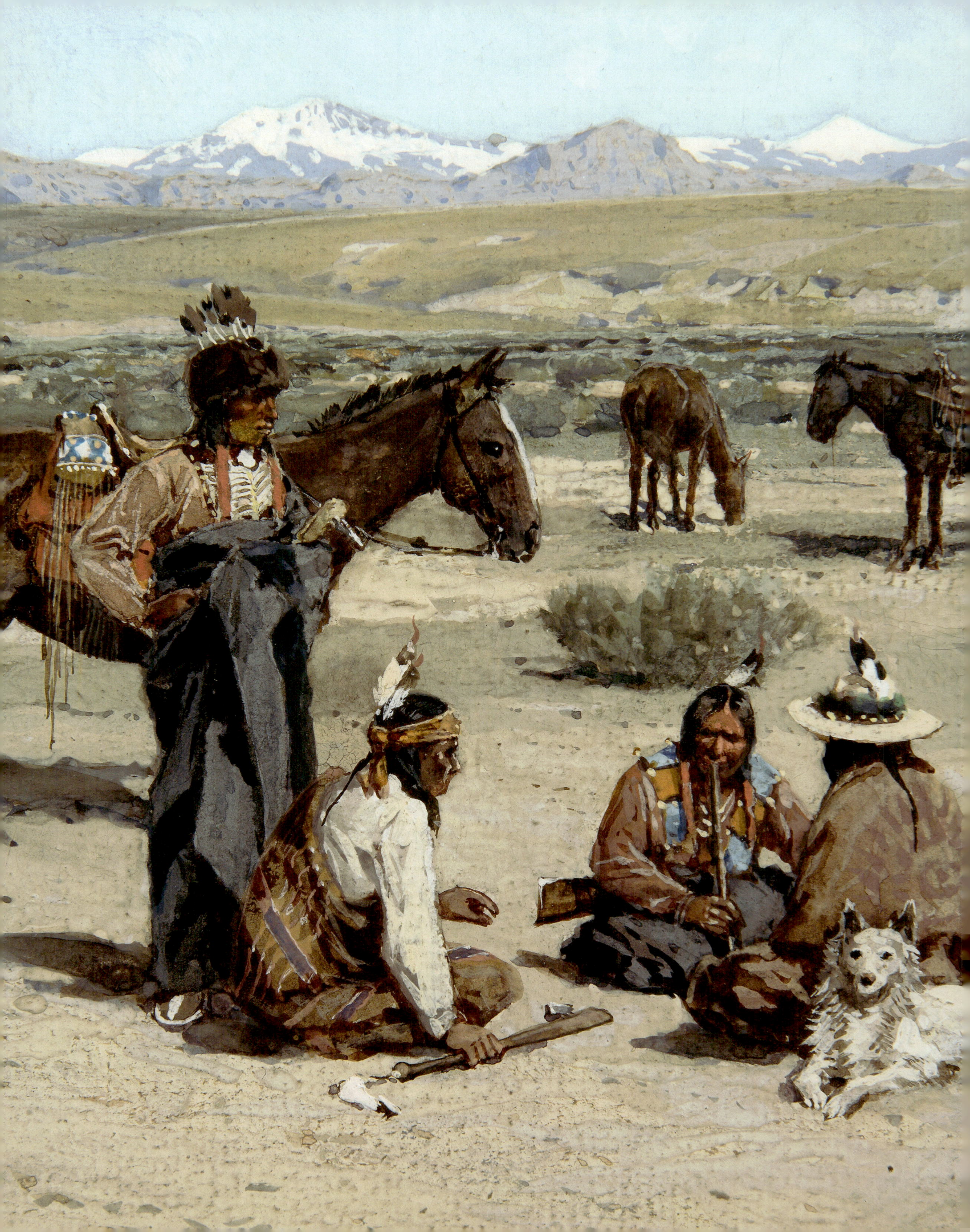

LAURA F. FRY

CURATOR'S ACKNOWLEDGMENTS

What a marvelous adventure the past two years has been. Little did I know what a wild ride would be in store for me when I first heard the announcement of Erivan and Helga Haub's transformational gift of western American art to the people of Tacoma. In relocating to Tacoma I have continued my own journey ever westward, from the green hills of the Ohio River Valley to the shores of Puget Sound. The Tacoma Art Museum now has the unique opportunity to examine anew: How do we consider the American West?

For this opportunity, I extend my deepest gratitude to Erivan and Helga Haub for their generosity in donating their unparalleled collection of western American art to Tacoma—and indeed to the United States. This art collection, together with funds for a building expansion and endowment, makes a new contribution to American art as a whole. I also extend my heartfelt thanks to Christian and Liliane Haub for their gracious assistance with the planning for the new gift, the building expansion, and this collection catalogue.

Going forward, it is our goal at the Tacoma Art Museum to provide for new research through the Haub Family Collection. My thanks to Peter H. Hassrick and Scott Manning Stevens for contributing fantastic essays and presenting new scholarship for this first publication of the Haub Family Collection. Thanks also to Kimberly Disney, the first Haub Fellow, and to Margaret Bullock, Curator of Collections and Special Exhibitions at Tacoma Art Museum, for their research and contributions of the selected artist biographies.

Thanks to our editor, Margaret L. Kaplan, for her wonderful work on this publication. Thanks also to Ed Marquand, Jeff Wincapaw, Susan E. Kelly, Adrian Lucia, and all the staff at Marquand Books, for creating this elegant book, and to Patricia Fidler at Yale University Press for working with Tacoma Art Museum on this publication.

A special thanks to Zoe Donnell, the Exhibitions and Publications Manager at Tacoma Art Museum, and Alison Maurer, Curatorial Fellow. Without their incredible organizational and editing skills, this catalogue would not have been possible. Thanks to Stephanie Stebich, Director, and Rock Hushka, Director of Curatorial Administration and Curator of Contemporary and Northwest Art, for their guidance and support throughout this project. Thanks to my colleagues in the Curatorial Department for their herculean efforts in this year of transition: Ellen Ito, Ben Wildenhaus, and Jessica Wilks.

I wish to thank photographers Richard Nicol, Arnica Spring, David Swift, and Horst Ziegenfusz for their beautiful photography work in this publication. As we traveled the world to photograph artwork, thanks to Dagmar Henkel, Harvey Norris, and Jason Black for their thoughtful assistance on site.

Finally, thanks to my family. It was my incredible father, Alan J. Fry, who first inspired my interest in the art of the West from our Cincinnati living room, and I hope to honor his memory with my work today. Thanks to my mom, Patricia, and my brother Bill, one of my best editors to date. And to my wonderful husband, Jason B. Jones, thank you for your unfailing support through this adventure—I could not have done it without you.

With the efforts of many, it is my hope that this first publication of the Haub Family Collection at Tacoma Art Museum will present a new perspective on the art of the American West, resonating for years to come.

Detail of Henry Farny, *Indian Encampment*, 1893 (page 286).

This publication is supported in part by an award from the National Endowment for the Arts, Art Works.

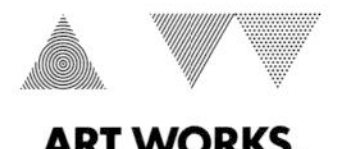

Seasonal support provided by ArtsFund.

All works, unless otherwise noted, are Tacoma Art Museum, Haub Family Collection, Promised gift of Erivan and Helga Haub. Ron Stewart's *Warm Homecoming* (reproduced on p. 304) is Tacoma Art Museum, Haub Family Collection, Promised gift of George Haub.

Tacoma Art Museum
1701 Pacific Avenue
Tacoma, WA 98402
tacomaartmuseum.org

Published in association with Yale University Press
302 Temple Street
P.O. Box 209040
New Haven, CT 06520-9040
yalebooks.com/art

Library of Congress Cataloging-in-Publication Data
Tacoma Art Museum.
    Art of the American West : the Haub family collection at Tacoma Art Museum / Laura F. Fry, Peter H. Hassrick, Scott Manning Stevens.
       pages cm
    Includes bibliographical references.
    ISBN 978-0-300-20760-6 (hardback)
    1. Art, American—West (U.S.)—Catalogs. 2. West (U.S.)—In art—Catalogs. 3. Haub, Erivan, 1932– —Art collections—Catalogs. 4. Haub, Helga—Art collections—Catalogs. 5. Art—Private collections—Washington (State)—Tacoma—Catalogs. 6. Tacoma Art Museum—Catalogs. I. Fry, Laura F. II. Hassrick, Peter H. III. Stevens, Scott Manning. IV. Title.
    N6525.T33 2014
    709.78'074797788—dc23   2014020864

Produced by Marquand Books, Inc., Seattle
marquand.com

Designers: Susan E. Kelly and Jeff Wincapaw
Typeset by Maggie Lee in Ideal Sans and Knockout
Editor: Margaret L. Kaplan
Project Manager: Zoe Donnell
Proofreader: Carrie Wicks
Indexer: Beth Chapple
Color management by iocolor, Seattle
Printed and bound in China by Artron Color Printing Co., Ltd.

IMAGE CAPTIONS
Dimensions for all works in this publication are provided as height by width by depth unless otherwise noted.

Endsheets: Karl Bodmer, *Winter Village of the Minatarres*. Aquatint engraving, published in *Maximilian, Prince of Wied's Travels in the Interior of North America*, London: Ackermann, 1840–43; pp. 2–3: Thomas Moran, *Green River, Wyoming* (detail), 1907 (also p. 72); p. 4: Clyde Aspevig, *White Cliffs of the Missouri* (detail), 2009 (also p. 245); p. 15: E. Martin Hennings, *Towering Aspens* (detail), circa 1940 (also p. 166); p. 253: Alexander Phimister Proctor, *Buckaroo* (detail), 1915 (also p. 88); p. 273: W. Herbert Dunton, *Summer Silhouette* (detail), circa 1930 (also p. 155).

COPYRIGHT PERMISSIONS
All reproductions of artwork held in copyright appear courtesy of the artists or the following representatives:

Back cover and pp. 169, 178, Georgia O'Keeffe: © 2014 Georgia O'Keeffe Museum / Artists Rights Society (ARS), New York; p. 294, Anna Mary Robertson (Grandma) Moses: Copyright © 1961 (Renewed 1989) Grandma Moses Properties Co., New York; p. 305, Andrew Wyeth: © Andrew Wyeth.

Every effort has been made to identify and acknowledge copyright holders for the works reproduced in this publication. Tacoma Art Museum would be grateful for further information concerning any artist for whom we have been unable to locate a rightsholder. Any errors or omissions will be corrected in subsequent editions.

PHOTOGRAPHIC CREDITS
Tacoma Art Museum acknowledges and appreciates the work of the photographers and lenders whose images of artwork are reproduced in this publication:

p. 8: photo © Tacoma Art Museum, photo by Arnica Spring; pp. 10, 96 (figs. 1, 2), 102, 104, 105, 123, 225, 236: photo © Tacoma Art Museum, photo by Richard Nicol; pp. 18, 174: photo courtesy of the Library of Congress; p. 19: photo courtesy of the Oregon Historical Society; pp. 20, 22 (fig. 4), 100 (fig. 7), 101: photo courtesy of the Buffalo Bill Center of the West; pp. 22 (fig. 5), 25, 79, 103, 118, 130, 152, 156, 161, 180, 193, 204, 217, 221, 226: photo courtesy of Laura McCurdy; pp. 23 (figs. 6, 7), 47, 60, 128, 138: photo courtesy of Gerald Peters; pp. 24, 26, 28, 35, 49, 50, 53, 56, 59, 67, 68, 75, 76, 85, 88, 91, 92, 98, 106, 109, 110, 113, 116, 121, 134, 137, 141, 145, 146, 148, 151, 162, 164, 166, 170, 177, 179 (fig. 7), 184, 191, 194, 196, 199, 202, 207, 208, 210, 213, 218, 233, 234, 239, 241, 246, 249: photo © Tacoma Art Museum, photo by David J Swift; pp. 31, 32, 36, 38, 40, 43, 44, 55, 63, 64, 71, 72, 81, 82, 87, 100 (fig. 6), 114, 124, 127, 133, 143, 155, 158, 169, 187, 189, 200, 214, 222, 229, 230, 242, 245, 250: photo © Tacoma Art Museum, photo by Horst Ziegenfusz; p. 97: photo courtesy of the Seattle Seahawks; p. 99: photo courtesy of the Wisconsin Historical Society; p. 175: photo courtesy of the Nelson-Atkins Museum of Art, © Nelson Gallery Foundation, photo by Thomas Palmer; p. 176: photo courtesy of the Detroit Public Library; p. 178: photo courtesy of the Georgia O'Keeffe Museum, Santa Fe / Art Resource, NY; p. 179 (fig. 6): photo courtesy of Mack Frost; p. 181: photo courtesy of Bill Schenck; p. 182: photo courtesy of Dia Art Foundation, New York, photo by Nancy Holt, 1995.

For pp. 274–305, all photography is courtesy of Laura McCurdy with the exception of the following: photo courtesy of Gerald Peters: Bartholdi, p. 274; Cary, *Returning to Camp* (p. 278); Clymer, *Boy on Horse* (p. 279); Dallin, *On the Warpath* (p. 283); Proctor, *Panther, Indian Warrior, Pony Express* (p. 296); Russell, *Indian Canoe Party, Where the Best Riders Quit, Wolf with Bone* (p. 299); Wyeth, *Dogwood at Valley Forge* (p. 305); photo © Tacoma Art Museum, photo by Richard Nicol: Berninghaus, *Horses at Hitching Post* (p. 275); Clymer, *Mt. Rainier from Umtanum Ridge, Dogs at Kotzebue, Alaska* (p. 279); Clymer, *Winter on the Bow River* (p. 280); Clymer, *Pilot and Index Peaks* (p. 281); Goodnight, p. 288; Koerner, *Not Much of a Hand* (p. 291); Liang, p. 291; Nieto, p. 295; Red Star, p. 296; photo © Tacoma Art Museum, photo by David J Swift: Clymer, *Chief Joseph* (p. 280); Dixon, *Roping a Palomino* (p. 284); Dye, *Study for A Rawhide Outfit* (p. 286); Fery, p. 287; Flanagan, p. 287; Hauser, p. 288; Hennings, *Rabbit Hunt, Taos* (p. 288); Inman, *Holato Mico (Blue King)* (p. 289); Jackson, *Algonquin Chief and Warrior* (p. 290); Kauba, p. 290; Lovell, *Study for The Gun Doctor* (p. 292); McGrew, p. 294; Paxson, *Sioux Chief* (p. 295); Proctor, *Pursued* (p. 296); Russell, *Smoking with the Spirit of the Buffalo, Sleeping Thunder, A Bronc Twister* (p. 299); Schreyvogel, p. 301; Seerey-Lester, p. 301; Shrady, p. 303; Smith, *Big Bend of the Green River* (p. 303); photo © Tacoma Art Museum, photo by Horst Ziegenfusz: Aspevig, *On the Way to Heaven* (p. 274); Bodmer, p. 276; Clymer, *The Storyteller* (p. 279); Coleman, p. 282; Farny, *Indian Encampment* (p. 286); Jackson, *Pony Express* (p. 290); Johnson, *Sunrise at Lake Sabrina* (p. 290); Laurence, p. 291; Russell, *Illustrated letter and envelope* (p. 298); Seabeck, *Buffalo* (p. 301); Seltzer, p. 301; Seltzer, *The Race* (p. 302); Sharp, *An Indian Encampment at Sunset* (p. 302); Stanley, p. 304; Wyeth, *The Mystery Tree* (p. 305).

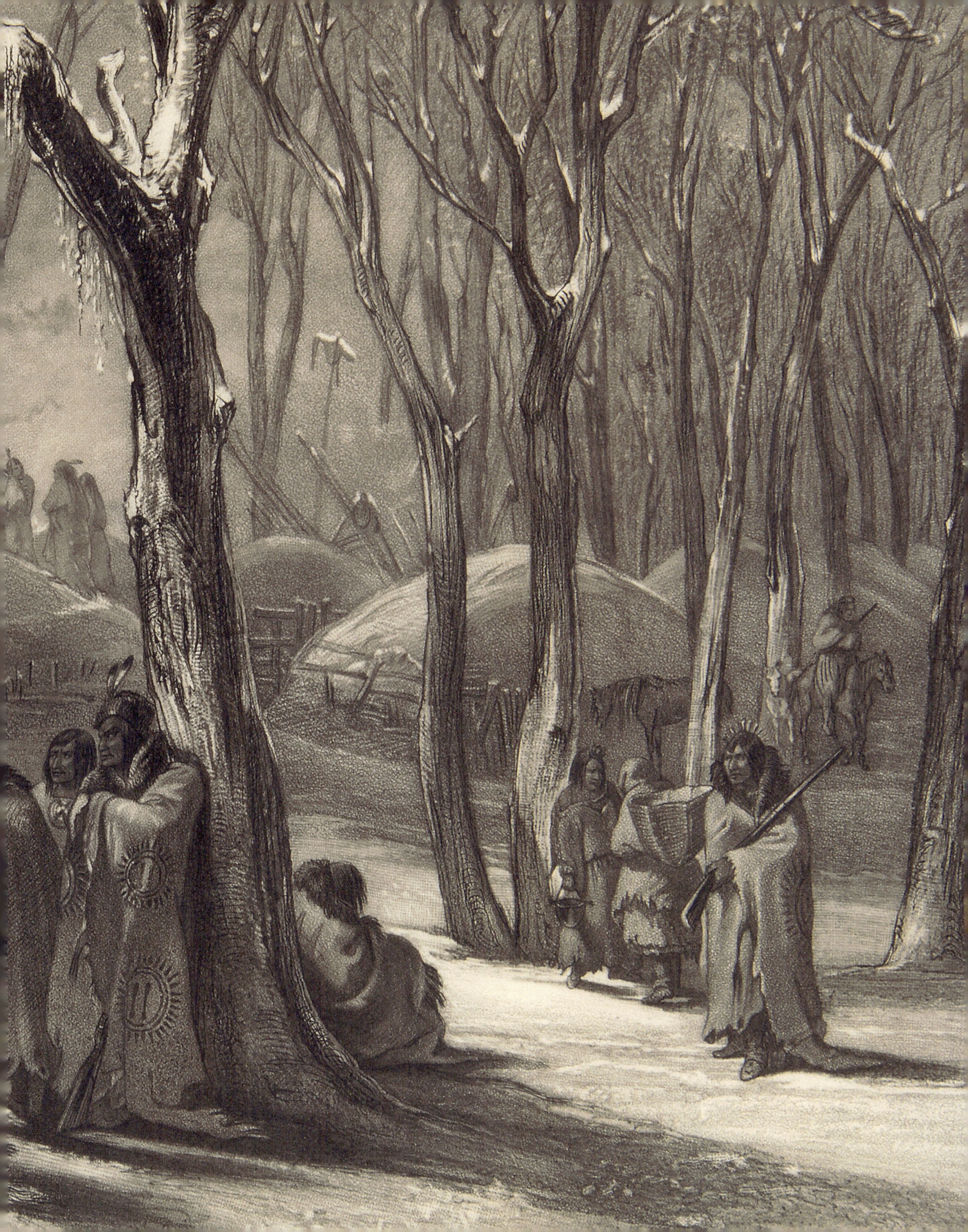

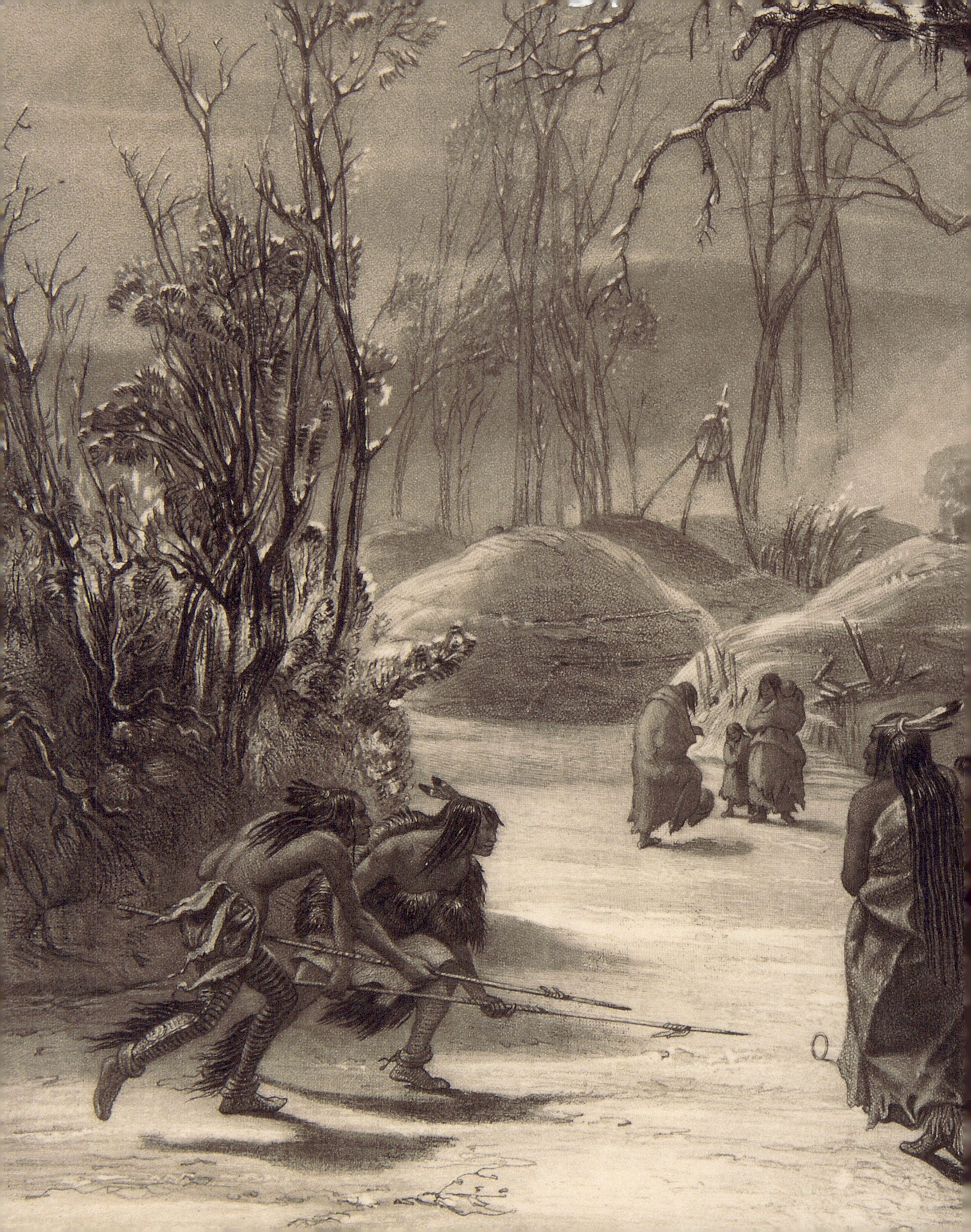